WORLD DEVELOPMENT REPORT 2002

Building Institutions for Markets

Published for the World Bank
Oxford University Press

Oxford University Press

OXFORD   NEW YORK   ATHENS   AUCKLAND   BANGKOK   BOGOTÁ
BUENOS AIRES   CALCUTTA   CAPE TOWN   CHENNAI   DAR ES SALAAM
DELHI   FLORENCE   HONG KONG   ISTANBUL   KARACHI
KUALA LUMPUR   MADRID   MELBOURNE   MEXICO CITY   MUMBAI
NAIROBI   PARIS   SÃO PAULO   SINGAPORE   TAIPEI   TOKYO
TORONTO   WARSAW

and associated companies in

BERLIN   IBADAN

© 2002 The International Bank for Reconstruction and
Development / The World Bank
1818 H Street, N.W., Washington, D.C. 20433, U.S.A.

Published by Oxford University Press, Inc.
200 Madison Avenue, New York, N.Y. 10016

Cover design by Debra Naylor, Naylor Design, Inc.
Cover photographs: top, © 2001 Stephen Simpson/FPG; middle,
© 2001 Stone/Paul Chesley; bottom, Yosef Hadar, World Bank.
Inside design and typesetting by
Barton Matheson Willse & Worthington, Baltimore.

Manufactured in the United States of America
First printing September 2001

ISBN 0-19-521607-5 clothbound
ISBN 0-19-521606-7 paperback
ISSN 0163-5085

Text printed on recycled paper.

Foreword

This *World Development Report* is about building market institutions that promote growth and reduce poverty, addressing how institutions support markets, what makes institutions work, and how to build them.

This theme is a natural continuation of last year's Report, which demonstrated that markets are central to the lives of poor people, that institutions play an important role in how markets affect people's standards of living and help protect their rights. This Report identifies how institutions can promote inclusive and integrated markets, and ensure stable growth and thus dramatically improve people's incomes and reduce poverty. It is about equal opportunity and empowerment for people, especially the poor.

Some countries have successfully harnessed market-oriented reforms to improve the welfare of all their people. But in other countries, markets have not given people as much incentive to engage in wider trade, the ability to use fully their skills and resources, and opportunities to increase their income.

Effective institutions can make the difference in the success of market reforms. Without land-titling institutions that ensure property rights, poor people are unable to use valuable assets for investment and income growth. Without strong judicial institutions that enforce contracts, entrepreneurs find many business activities too risky. Without effective corporate governance institutions that check managers' behavior, firms waste the resources of stakeholders. And weak institutions hurt the poor especially. For example, estimates show that corruption can cost the poor three times as much as it does the wealthy.

Addressing the challenge of building effective institutions is critical to the Bank's mission of fighting poverty.

We recognize the central importance of institutions in the development process through the Comprehensive Development Framework, which stresses the interdependence of institutions with the human, physical, and macroeconomic sides of development.

The Report emphasizes the importance of historical context: where countries are today affects where they can go. It also takes a pragmatic approach to institution building, focusing on what can be done practically rather than on what should be done in an ideal world. Social and political factors affect the pace of change, and sweeping reforms are not always possible. It is important to work on the areas where opportunities present themselves; each step can take countries forward—if correctly designed. And smaller reforms can build constituencies for larger ones.

This Report recognizes that one size does not fit all in institution building and provides policy guidance on how to develop appropriate institutions. Building on the successes of countries, and learning from the failures, the Report provides a deeper understanding of market-supporting institutions and a better appreciation of how people may build such institutions. In identifying how to promote institutional change, it looks at the roles of private and public, and national, local, and international, actors. It draws on a wealth of research and practical experience from inside and outside the Bank, as well as on insights from many disciplines, presenting new research and data on institutions.

From these diverse sources, the Report distills four lessons on building effective institutions:

- Design them to **complement** what exists—in terms of other supporting institutions, human capabilities, and available technologies. The availability and costs of supporting institutions and capacity determine the impact of any particular institution. By understanding how institutions interact, we can identify priorities.

- **Innovate** to identify institutions that work—and those that do not. Sometimes this requires experimentation. Even in countries with similar incomes and capacities, innovation can create stronger institutions because of differences in local conditions, differences that range from social norms to geography. Countries can gain from expanding successful public innovations and adopting private innovations. But they must also have the courage to drop failing experiments.

- **Connect** communities of market players through open information flows and open trade. Exchanging information changes behavior. It creates demand for institutional change by holding people to account and by supplying ideas for change from outside the community. Linking communities of people in networks of information and trade is thus a priority for those building market-supporting institutions.

- Promote **competition** among jurisdictions, firms, and individuals. Developing country market actors often face too little competition, and changing this will significantly improve institutional quality. Greater competition modifies the effectiveness of existing institutions, creates demand for new ones, and increases choice for consumers. Competition among jurisdictions highlights successful institutions and promotes demand for them. Competition among firms and individuals does the same.

These broad lessons, as well as the detailed analysis and many examples throughout this Report, will help us and policymakers build institutions that ensure stable and inclusive growth and thus improve people's incomes and reduce poverty.

James D. Wolfensohn

This Report has been prepared by a team led by Roumeen Islam and comprising Arup Banerji, Robert Cull, Asli Demirgüç-Kunt, Simeon Djankov, Alexander Dyck, Aart Kraay, Caralee McLiesh, Russell Pittman; and Helena Tang, Nazmul Chaudhury, Jeffrey Hammer, Richard Messick, and Tatiana Nenova made additional contributions. The team was assisted by Theodora Galabova, Paramjit Gill, Yifan Hu, Olga Ioffe, Claudio Montenegro, Stefka Slavova, Mahesh Surendran, and LiHong Wang. Andrei Shleifer and Joseph E. Stiglitz provided valuable suggestions during the writing of the Report. Bruce Ross-Larson is the editor of the overview, chapter 1, and chapter 10. Andrew Balls provided editorial assistance. The work was carried out under the general direction of Nicholas Stern.

The team was advised by a panel of experts comprising Carl Anduri, Abhijit Banerjee, Kaushik Basu, Timothy Besley, François Bourguignon, Antonio Estache, Cheryl Gray, Avner Greif, Nurul Islam, Emmanuel Jimenez, Daniel Kaufmann, Michael Klein, Yingyi Qian, and Kenneth Sokoloff.

Many others inside and outside the World Bank provided helpful comments and wrote background papers and other contributions, and their names are listed in the bibliographical note. Much of the background research was supported by a generous grant from the Dutch government. Research was also supported by the Swiss Trust Fund. The World Bank Development Data Group contributed to the data appendix and was responsible for the Selected World Development Indicators.

The team undertook a wide range of consultations for this Report, from the initial outline to the final draft. During the Report's planning stage in 2000, a February workshop in Berlin and a July workshop in Washington, D.C. provided an exchange of ideas among academics and policymakers from around the world. During the drafting stage in 2001, a consultative meeting on the media was held in April, and a consultative meeting on judicial systems was held in May. In addition, the authors held consultations with a wider community that included nongovernmental organizations, holding meetings in Paris (with representatives from the French Conseil d' État, the Organisation for Economic Co-operation and Development, the French Development Agency, and the Competition Council); in London (Department for International Development, Overseas Development Institute, and nongovernmental organizations); and in Amsterdam (Amsterdam Institute for International Development). The team also conducted a series of videoconferences with audiences in Bangladesh, Brazil, Egypt, Japan, Mexico, Morocco, South Africa, and Thailand. A consultation with the International Confederation of Free Trade Unions was also held.

Rebecca Sugui served as executive assistant to the team; Leila Search as program assistant and technical support; and Shannon Hendrickson, Joanna Kata-Blackman, Mei-Ling Lavecchia, and Rudeewan Laohakittikul as team assistants. Maria Ameal and later Eva Santo Domingo served as resource management assistant.

Book design, editing, and production were coordinated by the Production Services Unit of the World Bank's Office of the Publisher.

Contents

PART III   GOVERNMENT

PART IV   SOCIETY

Boxes

Figures

Tables

Definitions and data notes

The countries included in regional and income groupings in this report are listed in the Classification of Economies table at the end of the Selected World Development Indicators. Income classifications are based on GNP per capita; thresholds for income classifications in this edition may be found in the Introduction to Selected World Development Indicators. Group averages reported in the figures and tables are unweighted averages of the countries in the group unless noted to the contrary.

The use of the word *countries* to refer to economies implies no judgment by the World Bank about the legal or other status of a territory. The term *developing countries* includes low- and middle-income economies and thus may include economies in trasition from central planning, as a matter of convenience. The term *developed* or *industrial countries* may be used as matter of convenience to denote the high-income economies.

Dollar figures are current U.S. dollars, unless otherwise specified. *Billion* means 1,000 million; *trillion* means 1,000 billion.

The following abbreviations are used:

EU	European Union
FDI	Foreign direct investment
GATT	General Agreement on Tariffs and Trade
GDP	Gross domestic product
GNP	Gross national product
HIV/AIDS	Human immunodeficiency virus/ acquired immune deficiency syndrome
IPR	Intellectual property rights
NGO	Nongovernmental organization
OECD	Organisation for Economic Co-operation and Development
PPP	Purchasing power parity
R&D	Research and development
SMEs	Small and medium-size enterprises
TRIPS	Trade-Related Aspects of Intellectual Property Rights
WTO	World Trade Organization

PART I

Introduction

CHAPTER 1

Building Institutions: Complement, Innovate, Connect, and Compete

How do we account for the persistence of poverty in the midst of plenty? If we knew the sources of plenty, why don't poor countries simply adopt policies that make for plenty? . . . We must create incentives for people to invest in more efficient technology, increase their skills, and organize efficient markets. Such incentives are embodied in institutions.

—Douglass C. North, 2000

In the 11th century the Maghribi traders of North Africa wanted to expand business across borders, all around the Mediterranean. Trade in each center was free of formal regulations and restrictions, and competitive, with many buyers and sellers negotiating prices through brokers, open-bid auctions, and direct dealings. Cross-border trade also was generally free of formal regulations and restrictions. But it was fraught with uncertainty about selling prices, the quality on arrival, and the possibility of theft. Only if merchants traveled with their goods to distant markets could they ensure the safe arrival and sale of their merchandise. Such risks and costs naturally limited trade.

So in all major trading centers around the Mediterranean, the Maghribis set up overseas agents to represent their interests and exchange information about markets. Being from the same community, these agents were seen as trustworthy. And with fewer contractual problems, Maghribi merchants no longer needed to travel to ensure that they would not be cheated. Information flowed freely in this network bound by social ties. And the rules of the organization, although not written, were self-enforcing. Remaining in the coalition of traders best served each member's interests. Social ties cemented mutually beneficial business relationships, and cross-border trade flourished.

Today, a millennium later, people everywhere face similar problems in striving to improve their well-being through market activity. African entrepreneurs lack information about potential business partners. Poor farmers in Latin America lacking formal title to their land cannot use it as collateral to secure access to credit. Budding entrepreneurs in Central Asia, trying to start new businesses, run into political obstacles from established firms and the state.

Despite the problems, many people in rich countries and poor are engaged in productive—and rewarding—market activity. As *World Development Report 2000/2001* argued, income from participating in the market is the key to boosting economic growth for nations and to reducing poverty for individuals. This Report is about enhancing opportunities for poor people in markets, and about empowering them. What makes market activity rewarding and possible for some, and not others? Why are some market systems inclusive and integrated, allowing benefits to flow to the poor as well as the rich, the rural people as well as the urban? And why are other markets localized and segmented?

The Maghribi example illustrates some of the reasons. Markets allow people to use their skills and resources and to engage in higher-productivity activities if there are institutions to support those markets. What are these institutions? Rules, enforcement mechanisms, and organizations supporting market transactions. Extremely diverse across rich and poor communities and nations, they help transmit information, enforce property rights and contracts, and manage competition in markets. All market-supporting institutions do one or more of these things. And in so doing, they give people opportunity and incentives to engage in fruitful market activity.

This Report is about people building institutions that support the development of markets. The 2000/2001 Report underscores the importance of institutions in affecting poor people's participation in markets. This Report discusses both institutions that support growth and those that directly affect access of people left out of many market activities. It considers those institutions that provide opportunities for people and that empower them. It goes beyond the 2000/2001 Report by analyzing what institutions *do* to promote growth and facilitate access and by suggesting *how* to build effective institutions. And it emphasizes how institutions can help people make better use of the assets they own and how to accumulate more. In focusing on institution building, it does not devalue the importance of policy. But good policies are not enough. The details of institution building matter for growth and poverty reduction.

The Report contributes to existing work on institutions and markets in several novel ways. It provides a diagnostic framework for understanding how institutions support market activity. Bridging the gap between theory and evidence across disciplines, it also builds on existing evidence on the role of institutions and institutional change. It extends previous empirical work on institutional change to developing countries and presents a framework for institutional change. It confirms that one size does not fit all in considering institutional design. But it does more than that. It illustrates *how* to proceed in building more effective institutions. It provides policy guidance by taking a pragmatic approach. The aim is not to define what should be done in an ideal world, but what can be done in today's world.

In understanding what drives institutional change, the Report emphasizes the importance of history. Many developing countries have been nation-states for a short time compared with industrial countries. The evolution of nations teaches that building institutions takes time and that the process within each country may stall or reverse because of political conflicts or economic and social conditions. It offers lessons about the process of change and the importance of norms and culture in

particular countries. Institution building is generally a cumulative process, with several changes in different areas building up to complement and support each other. This Report identifies elements of such a strategy. Even small changes can build momentum for future changes. The whole is greater than the parts, and even moderate progress in the parts can contribute to a better system to promote growth and reduce poverty.

Four main lessons emerge for institution building. The first two are about supplying effective market-supporting institutions. But supplying institutions is not enough. People must want to use them too. Thus, the second two lessons are also about creating the demand for such institutions, and about the forces for change within countries.

To ensure effective institutions:

- *Design them to complement what exists—in terms of other supporting institutions, human capabilities, and available technologies.* The reason? The availability and cost of supporting institutions, existing levels of corruption, human capacity and technology determine the impact of a particular institution. That is why institutions that achieve their goals in industrial countries may not do so in developing ones. Much of the important work in building institutions lies in modifying those that already exist to complement better other institutions and in recognizing what not to build in a particular context, as much as what to build. "Best practice" in institutional design is a flawed concept.
- *Innovate to design institutions that work—and drop those initiatives that do not.* Even in countries with similar incomes and capacities, innovation can create stronger institutions because of differences in local conditions—differences ranging from social norms to geography. Experimentation, which has some costs that must be recognized, can nevertheless help identify new and more effective structures. Countries can gain from expanding successful public innovations and adopting private innovations. But they must also have the courage to drop failing experiments.
- *Connect communities of market players through open information flows and open trade.* Exchanging goods and services outside existing networks and communities creates demand for market-supporting institutions. Exchanging information through open debate creates demand for institutional change by holding people to account, by changing behavior, and by supplying ideas for change from outside the community. Linking communities of people in networks of infor-

mation and trade is thus a priority for policymakers building market-supporting institutions.

■ *Promote competition among jurisdictions, firms, and individuals.* Greater competition modifies the effectiveness of existing institutions, changes people's incentives and behavior, and creates demand for new institutions. Developing country actors may face too little competition, often because of current institutional structures. Changing this will improve the quality of other institutions. Competition among jurisdictions—for example, among different states within a country or between countries—highlights successful institutions and promotes demand for them. Competition among firms and individuals does the same.

This chapter first provides a framework for evaluating the role of institutions in supporting market transactions, growth, and poverty reduction. It then focuses on the four main lessons on institution building, followed by a discussion of the impact of political and social forces on institutional evolution.

How do institutions support markets?

Small vendors engage in simple spot-market transactions, with buyers and sellers dealing face to face in fairly standard products whose quality is easy to verify. A rural vegetable market in a poor country is such a market. Large multinational firms exchange more differentiated products, facing greater difficulties in verifying quality and bigger separations in time and space between the *quid* and the *quo*. International exchange of food products is an example of such a market. Most economies have both types of markets—the first more common in developing countries, the second in industrial economies.

Developed markets, more global, inclusive, and integrated, offer more opportunity choice. Underdeveloped markets, more likely in poor countries, are more likely to be local and segmented. So, compared with farmers in Canada, poor farmers in Bangladesh have fewer opportunities—and far fewer formal institutions (such as banks and formal courts) to reduce their risks and increase their opportunities.

What limits market opportunities? Transaction costs from inadequate information, incomplete definition and enforcement of property rights, and barriers to entry for new participants.[1] What increases them? Institutions that help manage risks from market exchange, increase efficiency, and raise returns (boxes 1.1, 1.2, and 1.3).

Box 1.1
A poem on the problems of trade

If I knew you and you knew me
'Tis seldom we would disagree;
But never having yet clasped hands
Both often fail to understand
That each intends to do what's right
And treat each other "honor bright"
How little to complain there'd be

If I knew you and you knew me.
When'er we ship you by mistake ,
Or in your bill some error make
From irritation you'd be free
If I knew you and you knew me.
Or when the checks don't come on time
And customers send nary a line,
We'd wait without anxiety,

If I knew you and you knew me.

Source: Who's Who in the Grain Trade 35 (June 20, 1922–23); cited in Bernstein 2001, *World Development Report 2002* background paper.

Yet not all institutions promote inclusive markets. The Maghribis lowered transaction costs among themselves, but in so doing excluded other communities. Institutional designs that evolve through either historical circumstances or directed action by policymakers are not necessarily the best institutions for all society—or for economic growth and poverty reduction. Moreover, institutions that once supported market transactions can outlive their usefulness—for example, privatization agencies and bank restructuring agencies. The challenge for policymakers is to shape policies and institutional development in ways that enhance economic development. The Maghribis operated under a policy of free trade that enhanced their opportunities. It was to take advantage of these opportunities that they developed their institutions.

Clearly there is no unique institutional structure guaranteed to lead to economic growth and poverty reduction. Large firms in the United States and the United Kingdom are often publicly held, with dispersed ownership, and are widely traded. But that is not the case in other high-income countries such as France or Canada, where ownership structures are highly concentrated (figure 1.1). And to promote competition, policymakers can use quite different guidelines. In East Asia competition authorities consider a market share of 50 to 75 percent to be evidence of possible monopoly

Box 1.2
What are institutions?

Institutions are *rules, enforcement mechanisms, and organizations.* This Report considers those institutions that support market transactions.[2] Distinct from policies, which are the goals and desired outcomes, institutions are the rules, including behavioral norms, by which agents interact—and the organizations that implement rules and codes of conduct to achieve desired outcomes. Policies affect which institutions evolve—but institutions too affect which policies are adopted. Institutional structure affects behavior. But behavior may also change within existing institutional structures.

Institution builders can be diverse—such as policymakers, businesspeople, or community members. Corporate, collateral, and bankruptcy laws are *public institutions*, as are the judiciary, tax collection agencies, and regulatory agencies. Banks, reciprocity between community members, and land inheritance norms are *private institutions*. Many private institutions exist under the aegis of public institutions. Private banks, for example, operate within the framework of public law. Social norms exist within (or without) formal laws.

The enforcement of rules can be internal, implemented by the parties affected by the rules, or external, implemented by a third party. Informal institutions and private formal mechanisms generally rely on their own members for enforcement. Individual agents organize themselves into informal groups, such as business associations (chapter 3) or mutual insurance systems (chapter 9) when the cost of collective action is low and the rules can be easily monitored. In these groups, expulsion from the community is a form of punishment.

External enforcement mechanisms, such as judicial systems or third-party arbitration, are critical mechanisms for the development of integrated markets. They allow access to market opportunities for a broader group of market participants. For external enforcement mechanisms to be effective, the legitimacy of the enforcer is vital. When the state acts as an agent that shares the objectives and beliefs of its citizens—and implements rules consistent with them—it is more likely to build effective formal institutions to support market development.[3]

Effective institutions are those that are *incentive-compatible.* Institutions with internal enforcement mechanisms are effective because there is a mutually recognized system of rewards and penalties. An important issue in the design of public institutions is ensuring that the incentives that are created actually lead to desired behavior. Take the example of deposit insurance, which is designed to protect depositors from the risks inherent in financial institutions (chapter 3). Experience has shown that deposit insurance can weaken the incentives of financial managers to lend depositors' funds prudently and can lead to excessive risk-taking. In circumstances like this, complementary regulations are required to realign incentives, such as regulations to ensure that bank managers have a significant financial stake in bank performance.

Informal and formal institutions
Formal institutions include rules written into the law by government, rules codified and adopted by private institutions, and public and private organizations operating under public law. For example, organizations include firms operating under corporate law. Informal institutions, often operating outside the formal legal system, reflect unwritten codes of social conduct. Examples include land inheritance norms and moneylenders using social networks to determine creditworthiness based on the reputation of the agents involved.

People in both rich and poor countries rely on informal institutions to facilitate transactions, but these institutions are relatively more important in poor countries where formal institutions are less developed. Moreover, poor people in poor countries are often ill served by the limited formal institutions available. In poor countries, and poor regions in particular, informal institutions substitute for formal institutions (box figure). Countries and communities can go a long way toward resolving information and enforcement problems without using their formal public legal systems.

Informal rural credit in selected developing countries, 1980s and 1990s

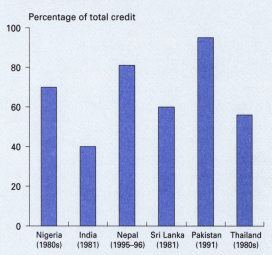

Percentage of total credit

Source: Kochar 1997; Besley and others 2001; Ijere 1986, cited in Adegbite 1997; Mansuri 1998; Desai and Mellor 1993.

Networks, such as those of the Maghribis, that are based on common ethnic, religious, and other common ties, are closed groups; that is, entry into the group is limited. In such groups, costs of information processing and definition and enforcement of property rights are lowered by mutual ties or trust. Although these transaction costs are lower in closed groups, the informal and norm-based institutions that such groups rely on tend to support a less diverse set of activities than do formal legal institutions. As countries develop, the number and range of partners that market participants deal with increases and market transactions become more complicated, demanding more formal institutions. Conversely, public or private agents may build formal institutions to enable a more diverse set of activities.

Box 1.2 *(continued)*

Legislators may purposefully base formal law and judicial practice on social norms. In some cases this may consist of simply codifying and modifying existing practices and writing them into law (Bernstein 1999). But this is not simple, particularly in heterogeneous societies. Choosing how to weigh each group's norms and standards is critical in determining not just the efficiency impacts, but also legitimacy and distributional implications.[4] For example, in multiethnic Uganda, English was adopted as a neutral common language for the formal functions of the state. Such concerns extend to standards or rules in international markets as well.

Ideally, informal and formal institutions should complement each other. Together, they can reduce transaction costs more than either can alone. Formal courts, for example, deter litigation and facilitate informal settlement simply by providing the threat of enforcement (chapter 6). Far more disputes arise in business transactions than go through a formal dispute resolution process (Bernstein 1999).

Public versus private roles
Governments have an important role in providing public goods, such as laws that delineate property rights and the judicial institutions that enforce these rights and establish the rule of law. But governments have been known to impede the development of markets through arbitrary exercise of state power, overtaxation, corruption, short time horizons, cronyism, and the inability to uphold public order. For example, governments may establish restrictive trading rules in response to lobbying by business monopolies intent on safeguarding their monopoly interests. The balance between markets and state power, and between business and social interests, is a delicate one in the course of institutional development. Historically, the government's role in the protection of property rights and the provision of other public goods has been closely linked to its role in ensuring peace or law and order. Conflicts over property between private agents, and between the state and private agents, are some of the most important issues that governments have had to deal with, because they often lead to a breakdown of law and order.

Market development and private business flourish when the behavior of those who govern is not arbitrary (see box 1.3). For example, detailed analyses of the evolution of corporate law in several countries show that in the early stages of development, private business was typically subject to the arbitrary whims of those in power. The state, with primary control rights, granted the permission to incorporate case by case (Pistor and others 2000). At later stages, the right to incorporate was no longer a personal favor but was granted to any entrepreneur that met a set of predetermined conditions.

Box 1.3
Institutional evolution and economic development: private traders and public rulers

In medieval Europe, the political power of local rulers was extensive. Local rulers could confiscate the property of individual traders from other regions without incurring penalties. In response, private mercantile guilds evolved to promote trade and to guard against the arbitrary action of local rulers. These guilds established agreements with merchants in foreign cities and with local authorities themselves. Arbitrary confiscation was punished by the withdrawal of large amounts of business by the guild, and so local rulers were forced to respect the rights of its members. This change in the balance of power helped to promote the security of foreign traders.

In the 12th century, traders in Europe established community-based mechanisms to facilitate the exchange of credit and trade across borders. These mechanisms were based on the community accepting responsibility for the performance of its members vis-à-vis other communities. For example, when a Genoese merchant defaulted on a loan from a merchant in London, community leaders in Genoa were responsible for enforcing the contract by imposing sanctions on the defaulter. Community origin was easily established, meaning that reputation within the community was important, and agents could be trusted not to renege on their contracts.

As cities grew in size and number, so did the communities of merchants and traders, making collective action more difficult. Unrestricted entry into trading led to more competition among traders, and increased problems of information and enforcement. Growth meant trading with members from other social and ethnic backgrounds, which meant that social connections could not easily be used as a basis for information or enforcement.

Members no longer wanted to be collectively responsible for individual breaches of contract. So leaders pushed for an enforcement and sanctioning system based on individual responsibility rather than community responsibility. To the extent that community growth implied more intracommunity social and economic diversity, it also reduced the political viability of the community. But the extent to which communities could abolish community-based mechanisms depended on a reliable third party to enforce contracts. In England, the monarch performed this role, and in 1275 King Edward I issued a statute outlawing community responsibility for debts.

The example illustrates a general principle: as economies grow and develop, different types of institutions are needed to facilitate transactions. Many different actors can push for new institutions. But the role that the state plays depends on its capacity and political viability: a strong state that respects the law itself and refrains from arbitrary action is a critical factor.

Source: Greif 1997a.

Figure 1.1
The concentration of ownership varies tremendously across countries

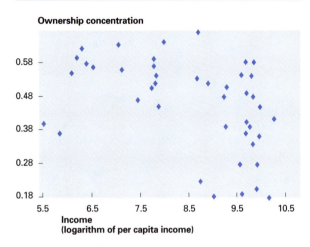

Ownership concentration

Income
(logarithm of per capita income)

Note: Ownership concentration is measured by the combined stakes of the three largest shareholders in the 10 largest privately controlled firms.
Source: La Porta, Lopez-de-Silanes, and Shleifer 1999.

power, whereas in Africa the range is 20 to 45 percent. Within South Asia some farmers rely on cooperatives to market their goods; others use informal contracts with private traders.

This Report provides a framework that applies across the range of market-supporting institutions. It cuts through the complexity and diversity of institutional structures by focusing on what institutions do. Understanding what they do is the first step in building effective institutions. Institutions do three main things:[5]

■ *They channel information about market conditions, goods, and participants.* Good information flows help businesses identify partners and high-return activities—and assess their creditworthiness. Information about businesses helps governments regulate effectively. Institutions can affect the production, collection, analysis, verification, and dissemination—or the withholding—of information and knowledge. They do this for participants in, and between, communities and markets. Examples include accounting firms and credit registries, which facilitate information processing, or government regulations on the media, which restrict the dissemination of information.[6]

■ *They define and enforce property rights and contracts, determining who gets what and when.* Knowing one's rights to assets and income and being able to protect those rights are critical for market development. These include the rights of the private sector in relation to the state. Institutions can reduce the potential for disputes and help enforce contracts. Examples include a country's constitution, its judicial system, and the full array of social networks.

■ *They increase competition in markets—or decrease it.* Competition gives people incentives to do better and promotes equal opportunity. In competitive markets resources are more likely to follow the merits of a project than the social or political connections of an entrepreneur. The degree of competition also affects innovation and economic growth (chapters 2 and 7). But while some institutions facilitate competition, others impede it. For example, by overregulating the entry of new business, governments can constrain competition. And by organizing market activities around a closed group of participants—recall the Maghribis—outsiders will find it harder to compete even while opportunities for those in the group may increase (chapters 3 and 9).

The transaction costs of acquiring information, enforcing property rights, and restraining competition can prevent the emergence of inclusive markets. But effective institutions can reduce those costs. Consider the following example. If the quality and value of the grain that traders buy from a farmer cannot be easily determined, and if traders have little information about a farmer, they have to inspect each bag of grain to assess quality. Traders also provide credit to farmers. But if traders have little information on the ability of farmers to repay the debt—or if farmers cannot use the assets they own as security—providing credit is risky. These problems are magnified for smaller and poorer farmers. The trader may impose higher interest rates on poorer farmers, and the farmers may be more likely to default than if they were exposed to competition.[7]

Through these three functions, all institutional structures affect the *distribution* of assets, incomes, and costs as well as the incentives of market participants and the efficiency of market transactions. By distributing rights to the most efficient agent, institutions can enhance productivity and growth. By affecting the incentives to invest—for example, through strengthening property rights—they can affect investment levels and adoption of new technology. By delineating market rights, such

Box 1.4
Courts and the expansion of trade

Studies of manufacturing firms in eight African countries demonstrate the supporting role institutions play in market development. These country studies show that the absence of effective public dispute resolution mechanisms in cases of breach of contract has limited the expansion of trade and market development. Courts tend to be slow and inefficient. The absence of formal contract enforcement mechanisms has limited the growth of firms and the development of financial institutions. The small scale of the formal productive sector has, in turn, prevented the development of complementary institutions.

Another study analyzing six countries in Africa (Burundi, Cameroon, Côte d'Ivoire, Kenya, Zambia, and Zimbabwe) shows that among these countries, the presence of a more developed legal system encouraged firms to undertake riskier activities because well-functioning legal systems helped to adjudicate and settle disputes that arose from such market activities.

Source: Bigsten and others 2000; Collier and Gunning 1999.

Box 1.5
Weak institutions hurt poor people

Mounting evidence shows that the poor bear the greatest burden of institutional failure. Take corruption, a highly regressive tax. Demands for bribes and unofficial fees for services hit poor people hardest. In far too many cases legal systems and the judiciary fail to serve poor people. Their illiteracy and inability to pay for legal representation put formal legal institutions beyond reach. The failure of the state to protect property also hurts the poorest disproportionately, because they cannot afford to protect themselves from crime. And badly designed regulatory institutions reduce the provision of infrastructure to the poorest in society.

World Development Report 2000/2001 stressed that poor people are often more vulnerable than others to macroeconomic crises and natural disasters. Market institutions that support growth of overall incomes can reduce their vulnerabilities to shocks and help them insure against bad times. Some of the institutions discussed in this Report have an important and direct role in this. For example, financial institutions help mitigate their risks, allowing individuals to diversify their savings and risks and allowing them to smooth their consumption over good times and bad.

Source: World Bank 2000d.

as through competition law, they limit producer rents and protect consumers from high prices. And by clarifying rights for the disadvantaged in markets, institutions can directly affect the lives of poor people. For example, giving formal titles to poor people whose occupancy rights were not recognized by lenders allows them to borrow and invest.

How do institutions support growth and poverty reduction?

Institutions that support market transactions can thus affect poor farmers in Latin America as much as they affect wealthy businessmen in Canada. Country case studies, as well as cross-country empirical work, provide important insights into institutional development and market development (box 1.4). They confirm how market-supporting institutions affect people's lives by influencing growth, determining people's access to markets, and enabling poor and rich people to make the best use of their assets. Moreover, weak market-supporting institutions can hurt the poor disproportionately (box 1.5).

A growing body of research links institutional success (and failure) to economic growth and market development over time and across countries. A wide range of indicators captures the performance of different, often overlapping sets of institutions. For example, the success of the state in providing laws and the performance of the judiciary and police reflect whether citizens and investors perceive the state as respecting property rights. Access to financial services and the sophistication of financial markets reflect how successfully institutions protect the property rights of borrowers and lenders. High levels of public corruption reflect how the behavior of public agents in state institutions responds to the types of incentives that exist for politicians and civil servants to pursue the public good over their self-interest.

Positive relationships between economic development and these indicators of institutional success have been widely documented. But most studies do not establish links between *specific* institutions and specific outcomes. Instead, they highlight the wide variety of institutions that support markets. For example, income and the rule of law—encompassing the collective importance of property rights, respect for legal institutions, and the judiciary—are highly correlated. For another example, the development of financial institutions predicts growth (figure 1.2).

On institutional development and economic growth, important differences have been found between coun-

Figure 1.2
Financial depth generates growth

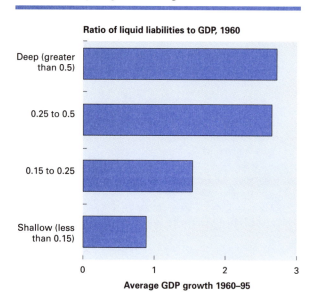

Ratio of liquid liabilities to GDP, 1960

Deep (greater than 0.5)

0.25 to 0.5

0.15 to 0.25

Shallow (less than 0.15)

0   1   2   3

Average GDP growth 1960–95

Note: Figure based on partial scatter from the instrumented cross-sectional regressions in Beck, Levine and Loayza 2000.

tries that once were colonies and are now industrialized and former colonies that are still developing. Both groups trace key features of their institutions to former settlers. A big part of the difference in later institutional development—and its impact on growth—is the effort of settlers in establishing well-functioning legal institutions.[8]

In the United States and New Zealand, colonizers settled in large numbers and transplanted institutions common to, and understood by, the general populace, mostly new immigrants. In such countries the transplanted legal institutions were widely used, adapted to local circumstances, and changed with economic development. Developing countries on every continent also received formal legal systems, transplanted by colonizers. But their indigenous populations had little access to or understanding of these legal systems. So the institutions were not adapted to local circumstances. Cross-country evidence suggests that the quality of institutions that support growth and poverty reduction through market development is lower in these countries than in the former group and has therefore not supported economic growth and poverty reduction to the same extent.

Institutions also affect how countries deal with conflict. A recent study found that growth and poverty outcomes in Asia, Latin America, and Sub-Saharan Africa since the mid-1970s have depended on the quality of institutions for conflict management.[9] In divided societies, such as those with ethnic fragmentation or high inequality, low-quality institutions for managing conflict—including low-quality government institutions and inadequate social safety nets—magnify external shocks, triggering distributional conflicts and delaying policy responses. Prolonged uncertainty in the economic environment and delayed policy adjustments curtail subsequent economic growth.

How do you build effective institutions?

Recalling the framework of information, enforcement, and competition, policymakers building institutions first need to assess what is inhibiting market development or leading to certain market outcomes (box 1.6). Rather than focusing first on specific structures, they need to focus on the functions that are missing and determine why. Policymakers need to ask:

- *Who needs information on what?* For example, do bankers lack information on the creditworthiness of potential borrowers?
- *Are everybody's property rights and contracts clearly defined and enforced?* For example, do farmers have enforceable rights to land they use?
- *Is there too little competition—or too much?* For example, is an infrastructure monopoly inhibiting entry or are firms not undertaking high-return research because they lack safeguards on intellectual property?

Once the institutional gap is identified, the next step is to design the appropriate institution. Both supply and demand factors are important. Moreover, as countries change and develop, so will the appropriate institution. To be effective, such an institution must be designed so that the incentives of market actors are aligned to achieve the desired outcome. Four key approaches toward institution building hold across all sectors and countries: complement what exists, innovate to identify institutions that work, connect communities through information flows and trade, and promote competition.

Complement what exists
Developed market economies have institutional structures that depend heavily on a capable state—a provider of public goods, a regulator, and an adjudicator. But the involvement of the state in markets must be consistent with its capacity. *World Development Report 1997* emphasized matching the capability of the state with the tasks that government organizations take on.

Box 1.6
Who builds institutions?

Institutional reform is not just the preserve of national governments. Individuals and communities, local entrepreneurs, multinational companies, and multilateral organizations can build institutions, often in partnership with each other. National governments may initiate reform or may simply respond to pressures from the private sector or from external actors.

In some cases of systemic institution building, governments have been effective in successfully transplanting laws, organizations, and agencies. In other cases systemic reforms did not have the desired outcomes. The contrast between Poland and Russia is instructive in this regard. Poland had a more recent history of a market system, and Polish policymakers and business people had a better understanding of the requisite institutional framework. Polish reforms focused on clarifying property rights between the state and private actors—for example, by imposing hard budget constraints on public firms. Russia did not have a recent history of market development, and reforms did not initially have the desired effects, partly because there was no clear delineation between private and public institutions. Firms were not immediately exposed to hard budget constraints, as shown by widespread arrears in taxes and other payments (Recanatini and Ryterman 2000).

Institution building at the sectoral level has also met with varying success. In Tanzania and Zambia the public sector intervened in agricultural marketing with the stated aim of stabilizing farmer incomes. In most cases these reforms failed—leading to lower marketable output and often corruption. Worse, the experiences affected perceptions of the overall integrity of public institutions. Successes include the reform of business registration in Bulgaria, now conducted online and taking around two days, not three weeks as in the past.

Local business interests, the foreign business community, nonprofit organizations, the media, and international organizations have all been involved in direct institution-building efforts in developing countries. For example, membership in the North American Free Trade Association has hastened the pace of domestic reform in Mexico. Some countries in Eastern Europe are implementing wide-ranging institutional reforms as they strive to become members of the European Union.

Recent developments surrounding the AIDS crisis illustrate how different groups may affect the process of institutional change.

Many agents of change: health crises and patents
More than 95 percent of HIV/AIDS cases are in developing countries. But the average cost of the antiretroviral treatments, which have reduced AIDS mortality by 70 percent in industrial countries, is still more than $10,000 a year, far beyond the reach of most people in poor countries.

Some developing countries—Brazil, India, South Africa, and Thailand—have taken steps to reduce the cost of AIDS treatment through the design and application of their intellectual property rights laws—an international institution—to allow compulsory licenses permitting the production of generic drugs and the import of cheaper generic drugs. In Thailand generic drugs became available at just 10 percent of the price of the patented product.

These measures led to threats of trade sanctions and law suits from the drug manufacturers. But collective action, initiated by international agencies and NGOs, helped increase access to AIDS drugs by enforcing existing public health safeguards, permitted under the Trade-Related Aspects of Intellectual Property Rights agreement but not previously implemented. The news media were instrumental in publicizing the disparities in the availability of AIDS treatment and promoting public debate on the issue. As a result, the U.S. government retracted its trade sanction threats. And pharmaceutical companies agreed to reduce prices—and more recently to drop a lawsuit on intellectual property rights against the South African government.

Source: Perez-Casas and others 2000.

This Report builds on that analysis by examining how existing information, enforcement costs, and the cost of building and maintaining institutions affect the way governments support private transactions in markets. It also examines how market development is affected by the extent to which government actors themselves respond to the institutions they build. As countries develop, the types of institutions they need and demand also change.

One of this Report's messages is that institutions that work in industrial countries may not produce similar results in poorer countries because of differences in:

- Complementary institutions, such as those promoting transparency and the enforcement of laws
- Existing levels and perceptions of corruption

- Costs, relative to per capita income, of establishing and maintaining institutions
- Administrative capacity, including human capabilities
- Technology.

Both existing and newly transplanted institutions can be more effective in poor countries if they are systematically modified to take these differences into account.[10] This may sometimes mean changing priorities in terms of which types of institutions to build first, and whether to build at all at a given time.

Complementary institutions. Government interventions can reduce many market failures, but governments may also fail in trying to support market transactions. For example, governments may impose regulations to try to compensate for market failures or as a way of re-

stricting private activity. Choosing between market failures and potential government failures is not easy, but
measures can be taken to limit both. However, the limited capacity of developing country governments to implement regulations means that many activities in
poorer countries are overregulated.

For regulatory systems in developing countries to
have a realistic chance of success, they need to be simpler, often less information-intensive, and less burdensome on the courts. Many developing countries, however, despite their weaker judicial systems, tend to have
very complex debt collection procedures (figure 1.3).

Regulations in industrial countries can also be very
complex, but they do not impose as many additional
costs as they do in poorer countries—for several reasons.
Enforcement capacity in richer countries is stronger, and
judges may face other incentives that affect their performance and judicial efficiency (chapter 6). Regulators are
more accountable, and complementary institutions (such
as those affecting judges' wages or careers, or those which
promote transparency) provide checks and balances to
protect market participants. In developing countries,
where there are fewer supporting institutions (for example, where courts are weak or lack credibility), one solution is to write simple rules and have fewer of them.

Where informal institutions operate effectively, and
when formal institutions require supporting institutions, building new formal institutions may not be a
priority for policymakers.

- Studies of land titling in various countries show that
  formal titles may not have the desired effects when
  input, output, and credit markets and institutions
  are underdeveloped and the demand for agricultural
  goods is low (chapter 2). In such cases traditional
  community-based mechanisms are more effective in
  delineating property rights.
- Corporate governance is difficult in poorer countries
  because of weak legal systems and the lack of private
  information intermediaries. In this situation concentrated ownership structures—and business groups
  and associations—may provide more effective corporate oversight than dispersed ownership structures.

Costs, capacity, and corruption. The cost of government regulation, whether in financial or other terms,
needs to be consistent with a country's per capita income to be effective. For example, a recent study covering 85 countries found that in many developing

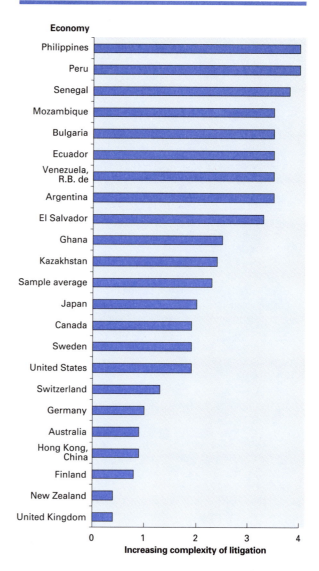

Figure 1.3
Complexity of procedures in debt collection

Economy

Increasing complexity of litigation

Note: For the definition of complexity see chapter 6. The sample
average is based on 96 countries.
Source: Survey done for *World Development Report 2002* in
conjunction with Lex Mundi, an international association of law firms.

countries, the financial cost of complying with regulations for registering a business is very high relative to
per capita gross national product (GNP) (figure 1.4a)
and higher than industrial country averages.[11] Surprisingly, developing countries that have less administrative capacity also require more procedures to register a
business (figure 1.4b). The high cost, whether in complexity or resources, deters entry into the formal sector,
potentially reducing competition and incurring ad-

Figure 1.4a
Cost of business registration (as percentage of GNP per capita) is higher for lower-income countries

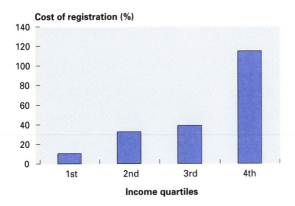

Cost of registration (%)

Income quartiles

Figure 1.4b
Lower-income countries have more procedures

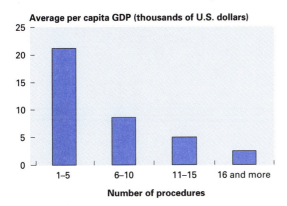

Average per capita GDP (thousands of U.S. dollars)

Number of procedures

Figure 1.4c
More procedures are associated with higher corruption

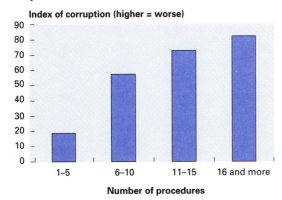

Index of corruption (higher = worse)

Number of procedures

Note: Costs are defined as official fees as a percentage of 1999 GNP per capita.
Source: Djankov and others 2001, *World Development Report 2002* background paper.

Box 1.7
Human capital and institutional design

Human capital affects the quality of the rules that govern market transactions and the enforcement of these rules. Literacy levels and technical skills vary greatly across and within countries. The poorest economies of the former Soviet Union have income levels lower than many countries in Asia and Africa but nearly universal primary education. So literacy is less of a barrier for Armenians using formal institutions than it may be for some Angolans—and it is less of a problem for today's Malaysians than it was for those of a generation ago. The rules and organizations that govern markets have to allow relevant market actors to use them easily. This argument holds within countries as well—for example, across poorer rural and richer urban areas.

The usefulness of institutions also depends on the capability of their administrators. Judges untrained in corporate law and accountancy, for instance, may not be the best arbiters of bankruptcy cases. Successful institution builders have had either to tailor institutions to prevailing administrative capacity (using, for example, simpler bankruptcy rules) or to complement institution building with a strong focus on concurrently developing technical expertise for administrators (from accountancy skills to regulatory economics).

ditional costs in the form of increasing corruption (figure 1.4c).[12] A World Bank study also finds that in many African countries, restrictive regulations and practices are often aimed at generating rents for officials and favored private agents or groups, constraining business activity in both agriculture and industry.[13]

Since building institutions is costly, requiring a minimum threshold demand before they can operate efficiently, small countries can face problems. Small countries and those countries wishing to expedite access to institutions may wish to rely on foreign institutions—such as foreign banks or foreign stock market listings—rather than build supervisory and regulatory capacity at home (chapter 4). Hungary and Estonia, for example, encouraged the entry of foreign banks, supervised and regulated in their country of domicile.

Human capability. More human capital may be needed to use some market institutions—such as formal judicial methods to resolve disputes—and to administer regulations or develop standards (box 1.7). For example, competition authorities need people who understand the complex details of competition cases. As countries build human capabilities, they need to consider where to focus their attention. Human capital and the array of market institutions in an economy have a dynamic relationship. Agents need human capital to benefit from certain institutions. And over time, as agents learn, institutions need to be adapted. As can be seen from the experience of East Asia, actively promoting literacy and primary education can have a big payoff in the eventual quality and success of formal institutions, as both users and administrators are more able to work with market institutions.

Technology. Infrastructure regulation shows that technical standards used in industrial countries may be inappropriate for developing countries (chapter 8). In poor countries service providers using low-cost technology often operate in the informal sector for parts of society not reached by formal operators. Regulators are typically hostile to informal providers. But some developing countries recognize the benefits of allowing those providers to operate. In Paraguay about 400 private water suppliers operate their own wells and provide piped water to households unserved by the public sector. Imposing strict standards on providers using simple technology would immediately drive these private suppliers out of business. A more gradual evolution in regulation is needed.[14]

Countries do not have to go through a long learning-by-doing process in all aspects of institutional development. They can transplant and modify some institutional forms from other countries and shorten the development process by learning from other countries. They can also use Internet technology to reduce institutional constraints and improve the effectiveness of institutions. In many developing countries the Internet is already providing the means for accelerated learning, improved information flows, reduced enforcement costs, and enhanced competition in markets (box 1.8). But to leapfrog stages in development through technology, policymakers need to increase access to technology for market agents. Market rules affect access.

International rules and standards. Standardizing laws and regulations generally reduces the information and enforcement costs of transactions across borders and can enhance trade efficiency. International standards also have the potential to provide benefits much larger than those under bilaterally agreed standards between countries for both poor and rich countries. But depending on which standards are chosen, international standards can also be costly for poor countries and can have significant distributional consequences *between* countries.

International trading rules and principles, enshrined in the World Trade Organization (WTO), promote trade (chapters 5 and 7). But some standards, through their

Box 1.8
Computerization and land registration in Andhra Pradesh, India

Buying property in Andhra Pradesh used to be complex and take a long time. After the purchase the buyer visited the local office of the Sub-Registrar of Assurances in person, had the property valued and stamp duty calculated, purchased stamp paper, and had a writer draft the deed in the requisite legal language. The purchaser also had to provide additional documents related to income and other properties owned. All these documents were then scrutinized by the registrar, and recorded, before an exact copy of the final deed was copied by hand and certified.

In Andhra Pradesh, 387 subregistrar offices registered about 1.2 million documents a year, 60 percent of them for agricultural land. A yearly manual update of property information was carried out, since hundreds of thousands of property files were updated with the new sales from the year.

Land registration offices throughout the state are now equipped with computerized counters under the Computer-aided Administration of Registration Department (CARD) project, initiated and financed by the state government to improve efficiency and increase duty collections. Starting with a pilot project in 214 locations over 15 months, the entire database was transferred to computers, the copying and filing system was replaced with imaging, and all back-office functions were automated. Standardization and greater transparency in property valuation procedures boosted stamp duty revenues. Registration processing time was cut from 10 days to 1 hour.

Source: Case study by Dr. Subhash Chandra Bhatnagar, University of Delhi. World Bank 2000, as part of the E-Government Focus Group, available at http://www1.worldbank.org/publicsector/egov.

distributional effects, can discriminate systematically against poor countries. For example, the Trade-Related Aspects of Intellectual Property Rights Agreement (TRIPS) can impose significant costs on poor countries, because strong patent protection is not as appropriate for them as it is for rich countries. Many industrial countries themselves only recently adopted laws safeguarding intellectual property, and the nature of these laws has evolved over time in response to changing domestic economic and political factors. Developing countries also lack the supporting institutions to implement TRIPS effectively—these will take time and resources to build.

Another example is the adoption of international accounting rules by companies in many developing countries. This has enhanced their access to credit in international markets. Voluntary adoption of standards by firms wanting to obtain credit in international markets is likely to be beneficial. But these standards are not appropriate for smaller firms (chapter 3). And forcing small firms in developing countries to adopt them would raise their costs and possibly push them into the informal sector.

For international standards to truly benefit all countries by facilitating trade—and to avoid systematic biases against developing countries—the standards need to reflect realities in developing countries. These include the costs of adhering to standards as well as the benefits, and particularly important are the costs imposed on the poor. Important questions are: Whose standards should be adopted and why, and what is the process under which these standards are negotiated? The process of reforming international rules needs to be transparent, and developing countries need to be active participants to influence outcomes in their favor. But human capital constraints may prevent developing countries from representing their interests. In such circumstances international donors could help enhance their representation, or developing countries could pool their scarce technical skills and have common representation at international negotiations or hire private specialists to represent them.

Variation within countries. Some variation in institutions may be desirable for both efficiency and distributional reasons, even between regions within countries. Even industrial countries do not standardize all laws and regulations within the country. For example, Australia and Canada have different laws in different states for secured transactions. Different states in the United States have different corporate laws. The differences exist because of variations in economic and social structures—variations that can be particularly instructive for large countries such as Brazil, China, India, and the Russian Federation. Of course the costs of standardization versus diversity will vary depending on the institution and the relative distribution of gains and losses. Where spillover effects across jurisdictions are large and not sustainable at the macroeconomic level, variation may be less desirable.

Innovate to identify institutions that work

Even at similar levels of development, countries differ in many ways—in their norms, geography, and endowments. Innovation, often through experimentation, can help accommodate those differences and produce more effective institutions. Experimentation also has costs,

---

Box 1.9
Private innovation supported by formal institutional change

In Bangladesh an economics professor had an idea—to help poor people help themselves by giving them small loans to start businesses despite their lack of collateral or credit histories. He started the Grameen Bank in 1976 using his social connections in government to manage a village branch of a government bank. The success of this endeavor, followed by expansion to other bank branches, led the government to eventually change the laws governing the Grameen Bank. It was established first as an independent entity with government control, then as an effectively private bank run by a public official, and finally as an effectively private bank run by a private individual and an independent board of directors. Today, Grameen Bank has branches in more than half the villages in Bangladesh and more than 2 million borrowers.

In Peru another innovative individual began with an experiment. He found that in Lima it took 728 bureaucratic steps for a person with an informal right to housing to get legal title. He followed up with a 10-year public information campaign, proving to politicians that there was a "hidden consensus for reform" for simplifying the procedures for formalization. Faced with overwhelming public support for simplification, the Peruvian congress unanimously passed legislation to formalize titles. Today, a simple legal procedure for establishing land titles for poorer people works in parallel with the formal system.

These two stories show how the state can work with private actors to promote institutional innovation by directly supporting experiments—or at least by allowing them to proceed and be tested and then, if they are successful, by encouraging their growth. The stories also show the importance of other factors in promoting innovation. Social connections and networks can reduce barriers to experimentation. Openness in information sharing provides the impetus to adopt and expand successful experiments.

Source: De Soto 2000; Yunus 1997.

---

however, and these need to be balanced against potential benefits.

Policymakers can replicate successful local innovations. But they also need to be flexible enough to drop unsuccessful experiments. Because innovation can come from many sources, collaboration by the different actors in society is vital, as shown by the development of microfinance institutions in Bangladesh, where the government adapted its formal legal structure to accommodate private innovation, and the process of land titling followed in Peru (box 1.9).

In some cases, greater local autonomy and participation may foster institutional experiments that lead to innovation. For example, Aguas Argentina, a privatized monopoly that provides water and sanitation services in Buenos Aires, worked under a novel institutional arrangement to design new ways to organize service delivery. The monopoly worked with local government, a low-income community, and a nongovernmental organization (NGO) to create a new organizational form to improve service delivery. The community was experimenting with two systems: a low-cost sewerage system and a double water system (with one connection to the network for small volumes of potable water and another drawing on groundwater sources too salty for drinking but good for washing and bathing). The double water system was dropped at the experimental stage because it was too expensive to develop, while the sewerage system was maintained. To expand its water network, Aguas Argentinas took over those systems built at lower cost by the community, giving customers a discount on the price in exchange. In effect, it had contracted out construction to the community.[15]

Innovation through experimentation can happen at different levels. Experimentation and innovation occur on at least three levels: national public policymaking, private commercial practices, and local action by communities and civil society leaders (see box 1.16). Local experimentation has the advantage of allowing many innovations to be tried simultaneously—with the successful ones replicated and the failures contained. But not all innovations can be left to local or decentralized communities—since local actions may have consequences across communities and too much experimentation can lead to each community having different rules. Local innovation can also open institutions to capture by local elites, inviting corruption. When effective innovations are identified, policymakers can help expand such institutions by replicating them in other areas (for example, through adopting a law) or by sharing information on the innovation.

Who innovates determines institutional evolution. Depending on who innovates, institutions can evolve in quite different ways (and with quite different distributional consequences), as shown by the evolution of bankruptcy law in the United Kingdom and the United States (box 1.10). As history shows, during the development process the institutions adopted favor those who control the process.

Debates among people who formulate policy, those who implement it, and those outside government can help in disseminating information on institutional in-

Box 1.10
Distributional effects of innovation depend on who innovates: bankruptcy law in two countries

The United Kingdom created its bankruptcy regime through explicit legislation that recognized the importance of decentralized contracting: legislation stated that corporations were free to make the rules under which they would transact. Lenders and borrowers in the United Kingdom had the power to innovate through contracts, and over time commercial practice was incorporated into law. In the United States judges and legislators held that power.

The U.K. system, designed by private agents engaged in borrowing and lending, is today characterized by a great concentration of rights in favor of the principal lender. The principal claimant appoints a receiver who uses his powers for the sole purpose of repaying this principal's debt. The court's role is much less significant than it is in the United States, and the judgment is not subject to court review.

In the United States, Chapter 11 bankruptcy law is characterized by a partial dispersion of rights away from secured claims (priority lenders). U.S. legislation was amended several times at moments of economic crisis at the instigation of the judiciary. At these times preservation of companies rather than their dissolution was uppermost in the minds of legislators and judges—leading to a debtor-friendly bankruptcy law. Upon default a company in the United States may seek protection from its creditors, usually retaining control over the business.

Source: Franks and Sussman 2000.

novation.[16] The tension between experimenting and standardizing public institutions within countries will be settled in favor of the latter when effective institutional forms are found. Policymakers have to ensure that successful local innovations can be scaled up. They must also be willing to drop outdated institutional forms. Hungary, in the early years of its transition, for example, experimented with a particular form of bankruptcy law, which was later dropped when conditions changed and a more effective alternative emerged (box 1.11).

Connect communities through information flows and trade

Open information exchange and open trade promote institution building by creating demand for market-supporting institutions.

Open trade. Going beyond allocative efficiency, open trade does more.

■ It exposes market participants to a larger, more diverse, group of trading partners, increasing the de-

Box 1.11
Experimentation and adaptation: bankruptcy institutions in Hungary

In 1992 the Hungarian government adopted a bankruptcy code giving creditors very strong rights to file for bankruptcy. The intention was to impose a hard budget constraint on firms, particularly on large enterprises. The law therefore stated that the creditor could file for bankruptcy if a company was three months or more overdue on any debt (known as an automatic trigger). Since accounting systems were underdeveloped, information on the true performance of firms was not readily available, and the available information was not always reliable. The solvency or insolvency of a firm was therefore hard to measure.

The short time frame and the establishment of such a strong trigger for bankruptcy proceedings led more than 5,000 firms to file for bankruptcy. The government had not expected such a large number of bankruptcies, particularly of small firms. The automatic trigger allowed the government to assess quickly the true condition of firms. But because the courts dealt with so many cases, they quickly developed experience in handling bankruptcies. The result: the authorities abolished the trigger in 1998. Not only were courts better able to adjudicate bankruptcies, but better information systems had developed to allow creditors to monitor companies. Market dynamics and supporting institutions had evolved enough so that the law was no longer needed.

Source: Gray and others 1996.

Box 1.12
Trade and institutional change in Thailand

In the early 19th century, with labor scarce and land abundant, land had little value in Thailand. Slaves rather than land were taken as collateral in financial markets. Correspondingly, land markets were underdeveloped. There was little demand or need for the development of formal institutions. But there was a well-developed legal system to govern transactions in labor commitments. In theory, all land belonged to the king. In practice, individuals could use and sell the land, as long as they paid taxes and did not let it lie fallow for more than three consecutive years.

In the latter part of the century, international trade opened up, and transport costs declined. A rice export boom led to a rapid expansion of production and use of land. Land became more valuable, land disputes more common. The demand for formal institutions, such as registries, to convey information and enforce property rights increased.

The government responded by implementing a series of procedural and administrative changes, beginning in 1892. The first initiative, to document land rights, was modified and improved several times; the final legislation was passed in 1954. The current legislation is a compromise between traditional practice, which allowed citizens to bring unoccupied forestland under cultivation as private property, and the more formal requirement of land titling based on detailed land surveys.

Such institutional evolution is not unique to Thailand, for industrial countries have also shown that trade, by changing the terms of trade, gives rise to the demand for clear property rights and a need for the state to define them.

Source: Siamwalla and others 1993; Stifel 1976.

mand for formal institutions to provide information and enforce contracts.[17]

- It helps firms learn about technology and about organizational and managerial forms.
- It exposes markets to greater competition and changes in relative returns, which induce institutional change (see below).
- It exposes countries to a different set of risks, possibly supporting the creation of additional institutions to manage the new risks.
- It brings new market participants from other countries or regions who also demand more effective institutions to support market transactions.

The case of Thailand illustrates how liberalization of trading rules led to a shift in agricultural returns—and to institutional change in the market for land (box 1.12).[18] Similar patterns are observed in other countries and sectors. The development of standards for rice within Japan was spurred after markets within Japan were connected (box 1.13). The demand for formal

land titles in many countries (chapter 2) developed once markets for goods produced on the land were accessible or when new members entered the community.

Empirical work spanning over 110 countries shows that measures of institutional effectiveness (such as the quality of institutions for public service delivery, or perceptions of the rule of law) are significantly related to openness in international trade. This is so even after accounting for differences in size, per capita income, legal heritage, years the country has been independent, and other factors (figure 1.5).[19]

Greater openness in trade and capital markets has been associated with the development of financial systems, as historical and cross-country analyses clearly show. Large incumbent firms that have access to finance—through either retained earnings or established links with financial institutions—do not always have an

Box 1.13
Institutional evolution of rice markets and standardization in Japan, 1600–1920s

In Japan's Tokugawa period (1600–1868), local private traders collected and marketed the rice shares of both the *daimyo* (feudal lord) and the peasant. The traders had to be big, since poor inland transport meant that rice was shipped in large sailing vessels and later steamships—a costly and risky venture. When the network of railroads was extended to local areas, locally segmented markets began to form a nationwide market. And with the economies of scale in transport and related risks, small traders could market their rice, using small shipments from many local centers.

The competition among small traders from different rice-producing regions increased the pressure to standardize rice grades. Better and more stable quality and standards ensured higher prices in urban markets. Groups of farmers and traders began taking the initiative by labeling the quality of rice in various regions. By 1900 these voluntary efforts were transformed into official regulations by local government agencies, which began to set standards for the packaging of rice shipped to other regions. By 1910 there were 33 rice-grading warehouses (*beiken soko*), managed by private companies or cooperatives, serving several purposes—inspecting, grading, repackaging, and storing.

Innovations in finance followed. As farmers and traders brought ungraded rice to the warehouse, it issued a "rice exchange note." The precursor to today's inventory credit, these notes were also used as collateral for loans from banks and pawnshops, easing capital constraints for farmers and traders.

More trade among different communities led to the developments of standards, first adopted by private traders and later by government. These early institutional changes promoted new institutions to support market exchange.

Source: Kawagoe 1998.

Figure 1.5
Greater openness and quality of institutions

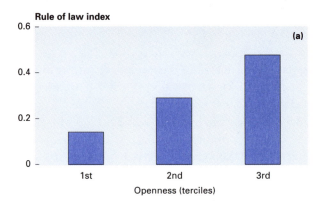

Rule of law index

Openness (terciles)

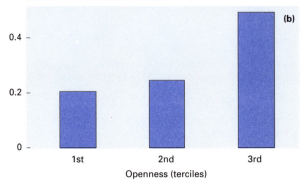

Government effectiveness index

Openness (terciles)

Note: The figures show the partial relationship (after accounting for the effect of differences in the legal systems, ethnic diversity, GNP per capita, years that the country in question has been independent, country size, and inequality of income) between an indicator of rule of law/ government effectiveness and openness for over 100 countries in 1997–98. The countries have been divided into three groups of equal size.
Source: Islam and Montenegro forthcoming, *World Development Report 2002* background paper.

incentive to promote financial systems that would facilitate new entry into their markets. Opening the economy to trade and financial flows can automatically reduce rents that incumbents receive from preferential access to financial institutions. And over time the lower rents can reduce opposition to financial sector reform.[20]

Rather than improve their own systems, policymakers in open economies can import whole aspects of the institutional system: laws, regulations, and enforcement systems. Because of the political problems and costs of importing foreign agencies, including foreign human capital, there are not many examples. Many countries have allowed foreign banks to operate in the domestic financial sector, helping financial services grow even

with underdeveloped supervisory and regulatory systems. To get around weak judicial systems, poor countries can export the enforcement of contracts. For infrastructure deals in which private investors from rich countries invest in poor countries, for example, international arbitration clauses can be used in cases of dispute.

Open information flows. Open information exchange, a driver of institutional development, can both improve the quality of other existing institutions and create a demand for new ones. Better information makes monitoring peoples' behavior easier. This ability to monitor behavior changes behavior and institutional quality even when institutional structure does not change. Better information can also change social norms and so change people's incentives to participate in different institutions. And it can inform policymakers and other market participants about the benefits of institutional reform and about the constraints on institutional reform.

Information from the media and low-cost information on the Internet can enhance the functioning of public institutions. Evidence indicates that corruption, for example, is lower in countries with a free press (box 1.14). There is also evidence that free media, by providing a check on political actions, can raise policymakers' awareness of the social effects of policies, improving the provision of social services. A study in India found that the media affected how the government responded to floods and famines: the distribution of relief was greater in states with higher newspaper circulations. The more information the local media provided, the more effectively citizens could develop a collective voice and put pressure on the government.[21]

Recent research for this Report shows that competition in the provision of information can significantly increase the impact of the media on the quality of institutions. For example, where the state does not control information through monopoly or concentrated ownership of the media industry, the media can do much in checking corruption (figure 1.6). The effect of private monopolies on information flow can be expected to be similar.

Information about the potential benefits and costs of particular institutional arrangements can change the incentives for those who engage in market transactions and the demand for institutions. In Nepal the publication of simple facts about the costs of business licens-

ing—both in time spent and in bribes paid—led the government to undertake reforms that reduced licensing time from years to days.[22] With poor information flow in an economy, regulatory rules and policies are unclear. So regulated firms and customers do not know, or cannot find out, what regulations apply to them or how to comply with them.[23]

Promote competition—among jurisdictions, firms, and individuals

Competition among jurisdictions, among firms in product markets, and among individuals does much for institutional change.[24] Often, current institutional

Figure 1.6
Diversity of information providers and quality of institutions

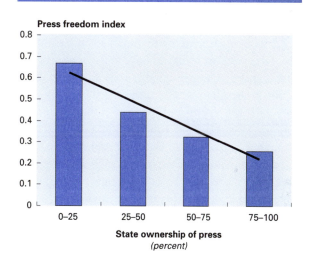

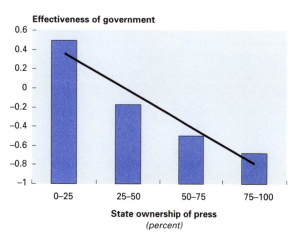

Source: Djankov and others 2001, *World Development Report 2002* background paper.

structures may inhibit competition. Competition makes institutions more or less effective by affecting relative returns and changing the incentives of agents. For example, as competition in markets increases, traditional norm-based institutions may become inadequate or obsolete.[25] Competition can reduce the effectiveness of closed groups, such as guilds or business networks, whose existence and effectiveness depend on superior access to such inputs as information. This can create the demand for new institutions or improve the quality of existing institutions by changing behavior. In places as varied as Thailand and Uganda, greater competition for land increased land disputes and created the demand for more formal procedures for recording transactions. Competition in product markets has led to institutional change in labor markets (chapter 7). And there is some evidence that competition between firms can be a partial substitute for strong shareholder rights in inducing managers to act in the interest of owners.

Firms competing in product markets, forced to increase efficiency, have the incentive to lobby policymakers to implement institutional changes that lower their costs. Competition also affects the distribution of gains among market players, and so increases the demand for institutional change among those who want to maintain their gains in the light of changing economic factors. But sometimes institutions, such as rules governing intellectual property, may be needed to limit the degree of competition in markets and to foster innovation.

For firms in international capital markets, competition can produce demand for better institutions, such as accounting standards (chapter 5). In turn, domestic banks, to compete with foreign banks outside their home markets, may pressure their regulators to improve prudential regulations. This happened in Mexico after it signed the North American Free Trade Agreement. A World Bank study looking at institutional performance cites competition as a key factor affecting institutional performance, since it changes the incentives for individuals to succeed.[26]

Jurisdictional competition also fosters institutional evolution. A study of corporate law evolution shows that competition between countries—and between foreign firms operating in a country—has created pressure for change in corporate laws (box 1.15). In the United States competition between states to attract business has led to institutional evolution of different forms in the various states. For example, personal bankruptcy

Box 1.15
Competition and the evolution of corporate law

A study investigating legal change in 10 jurisdictions, including both industrial and developing countries over more than 100 years, found competition among firms operating within countries and across borders to be important in promoting changes in the corporate law. The changes were often enacted in response to crises, owing to competitive pressures, or as a conscious effort to standardize corporate law across countries.

Studies of Europe in the late 19th century highlight jurisdictional competition in the development of corporate law. There was a shift from concession systems, in which rulers granted the right to incorporate case by case and often as a special favor, to a system of registration in which any company meeting certain minimum requirements could incorporate. For example, in France in 1867, the shift was induced by the expansion of English companies on the continent. Once France allowed companies incorporated in England to operate as a corporation in France, without special approval by parliament, it faced pressure from domestic companies to drop the concession requirement at home.

Israel in 1999, Japan in the 1990s, Chile in 1981, and Delaware in the United States (where there have been continuous changes) provide examples of jurisdictions that changed their corporate laws in response to competitive pressures in the 20th century.

Source: Pistor and others 2000, *World Development Report 2002* background paper.

and corporate laws vary across the states. Education systems vary across districts.

Markets with more competition may require fewer formal institutions, since competition can substitute for regulation. Take infrastructure: greater competition, possible with technological changes, has allowed regulators to lower the frequency of price reviews (chapter 8). Sectors previously considered natural monopolies became potentially competitive, so governments now rely more on competition to deliver desired outcomes, such as affordable prices for consumers.

But the competition from new infrastructure providers can also complicate regulation. Before the privatization of state monopolies in many countries, state infrastructure monopolies cross-subsidized some customers—in many cases lowering costs for poorer households by charging higher prices to business users. After privatization, governments aiming to protect poorer customers have found it difficult to regulate the privatized firms in a way that provided adequate profits for firms while providing adequate services to the poor (chapter 8).

There are times when institutions restricting competition are desirable. Some market rents may need to be tolerated to fund the adoption of new technology, and institutions restricting competition may be needed to promote market development. And regulating the degree of competition among banks can enhance financial stability by reducing the incentives for risk taking.

How do political forces, social pressures, and shocks affect the pace of change?

Political forces and social pressures can either accelerate or retard the development of new institutions. Shifting social, political, and economic balances are in turn affected by a government's institutional reform efforts. In industrial markets, however, the state is constrained from arbitrarily changing rules and laws, and there tend to be more checks and balances on various actors, public and private.

Political forces. An institution exists in part because some constituencies gain from its existence and so have the incentives and influence to support it. This distributional aspect is particularly important when institutions benefit a small group or minority in society for whom the costs of collective action are low and benefits are large. Checks and balances on political power, from firms and interest groups, can support the interests of the majority. But minority interests may in some cases oppose the modification of institutions.

So policymakers wishing to embark on reforms may have to create new institutions rather than modify existing ones. According to some, this was important in the recent establishment of a regulatory authority for telecommunications in Morocco. But even though building new institutions may be desirable, the costs of collective action—including those of information collection, enforcement, and competition—may be so great relative to perceived benefits that they would frustrate the formation of a new political coalition that would push for institutional change.

Institutions often change when the power of those who directly benefit from the existing structures is undermined or when they no longer reap any benefits so that they no longer have the incentive to oppose change. One way to accelerate institutional change is to co-opt the opponents of reform. In China after 1978, local governments were encouraged to collect federal taxes since they could keep any collections above a certain level. Local governments were also able to raise additional taxes, not shared with the national government.

But all reforms are not equally difficult politically. Some ineffective institutions may exist in part because there are no interest groups pressing for change—not because some interest groups oppose change. Or it may be that those who would oppose change do not have much political sway. Whatever the reason, reforms in these areas could be accelerated. And as these reforms breed new constituencies and forces, they can lead to a demand for greater change. The key is to find the opportunities and to work in these areas.

Although indigenous institutional development responds to changing economic and social conditions, a central issue for transplants is managing distributional conflicts. Institutional change creates winners and losers. For example, bankruptcy law designates the rights to income and assets for creditors. Corporate law distributes rights among owners, managers, and the government. Regulation covering service provision to the poor transfers economic gains from producers to poor consumers and between levels of government (chapter 8).

The distribution of power among different levels of government largely determines the type of regulatory structure likely to be effective. A study of the evolution of regulation in infrastructure conducted for this Report argues that the allocation of regulatory authority in the now industrial countries closely followed the political structures of those countries.[27] The degree of political and administrative centralization in a country significantly affects the intervention by the upper level of government in regulation. In the United States—where the states are large and there is a great deal of autonomy—local regulation of concessions for water and electricity was gradually overtaken by state-level regulation. The greater centralization was hastened by corrupt municipalities or complex regulatory issues between local jurisdictions. Traditionally, regulation of natural monopoly infrastructure firms evolved in response to political pressure from firms or communities. In response to high prices and high profits, the public demanded government intervention. By contrast, France has a very centralized political system and has generally adopted a much more centralized regulatory structure.

When transplanting regulatory agencies from industrial countries, the domestic political structure and balance of power must be considered along with the qual-

Box 1.16
The interplay of social, political, and economic forces in the reform of land institutions in China

Before the 1960s rural land in China was the responsibility of communes. In the early 1960s farmers in Anhui Province began calling for a restructuring of communes, so that earnings could be linked to work. Local leaders began experimenting, allowing some households to contract for individual plots. The demonstration led others to push for plots, and the resulting productivity increases led to formal sanctioning by local leaders of this system. At that time the central government was not involved. Later, the system was partially reversed because of central government disapproval. Then in 1978 a severe drought in Anhui led to a food crisis, and provincial leaders allowed households to cultivate any land the collective farms were unable to work. Nearby villages emulated the practice.

The central government began accepting local institutional innovation after almost 20 years, when faced with an economic crisis. Central government officials formally adopted the Household Responsibility System, under which households could contract with local leaders to produce on their "own" land. Initial distributions, although different from village to village, were essentially the same within the village. In other words, both social and productivity considerations determined land allocations in the transition to individual and more formal rights. But the contracts with households did not assure them of very stable land use rights. Although such rights were supposed to be allocated for a period of years, most villages in China adopted the practice of periodically readjusting landholdings in accord with changes in household makeup. Chinese farmers and officials have not been of one mind regarding social versus efficiency considerations. Surveys of farmers in the 1990s indicated that they wanted more secure land rights, but many also favored readjustments. Chinese farmers indicated that they would overwhelmingly support a no-readjustment policy if their welfare concerns could be addressed by other means (such as preferential allocation of wasteland or taxes). Lack of consensus on the institutional structures to protect farmer welfare probably slowed the effective implementation of land contracts.

In some cases land readjustments also reflected the desire of local cadres to maintain influence. Control over land remains one of the main sources of economic and political power for local officials. Perhaps as a result, land system rules regarding tenure—both formal and informal—and practices have varied widely around the country. Although the central government approved 15- and then 30-year tenures, this was not implemented. Field research indicates that *county-* and *provincial-*level officials from jurisdictions that rely heavily on agriculture are more likely to have interests that are similar to those of farmers than local officials.

China's story reveals some important lessons for institutional reform.

- Experimentation has been key for institutional reform, in this case at local levels. The central government was important in validating a successful experiment and thus in accelerating its acceptance around the country.
- Institutional reform takes time. Chinese land policies will continue to be modified as several important issues are resolved and as other supporting institutions evolve.
- At different stages in the process of institutional reform, the role of local versus other leaders varied significantly.
- When changing established norms, governments need to be aware of dual role played by institutions—in this case formal, but in many others informal—in affecting both efficiency and equity. Social concerns affect the pace of reform. Explicit considerations of these issues can help policymakers undertake institutional reform.

Source: Prosterman, Schwarzwalder, and Hanstad 2001; *World Development Report 2002* background paper.

---

ity of information that is available to different levels of government. Such issues are particularly important in large countries such as Brazil, India, and Russia. Information problems at the national level tend to be more severe, but so could be the risk of regulatory capture at local levels. While economic analysis may argue for a certain design, for effective institution building, political and social realities and their dynamics will need to be considered.

History shows that politics influence the development of financial systems.[28] Financial institutions, particularly banks, provide an easy way for governments to channel the economy's resources in directions they deem politically desirable.[29] The effective functioning of government agencies, such as tax collection agencies and financial supervisory authorities, depend critically on politics and checks and balances on political power.

Many developing countries have recently tried to establish autonomous revenue agencies to free tax collection from political influence. What determines the success of these reforms? The authority granted to these institutions, and the political commitment to support their greater autonomy (chapter 5).

Political instability also affects investment within countries, as cross-country empirical studies show. In countries more polarized and less politically stable, policymakers are less committed to strengthening the legal system and protecting private property rights.[30] Weak property rights in politically unstable countries lead to lower investment.

Social pressures. Social structures such as inequalities in income distribution and in the influence of different ethnic groups also affect the demand for institutional reforms and their sustainability (box 1.16).

More inequality sometimes means lower institutional quality. Empirical work across countries—using indicators of institutional development that measure the rule of law, corruption, enforcement of property rights, and an overall index of these indicators—suggests that there is some association between the distribution of income and institutional quality, with very unequal distributions of income being associated with a lower quality of institutional development.

Why might this be? Perhaps more unequal societies are more polarized or less likely to engage in social or economic transactions with each other. More polarized societies also may be less likely to agree on institutional reform, much as they may find it more difficult to agree on policy reforms.[31] Or perhaps when a few players, such as large business groups, dominate economic transactions, they have little incentive to support formal institutions that would enhance competition in their activities. Those players, often part of well-knit networks, can conduct most of their business through reputational mechanisms.

The differences in the development paths of North and South America are often cited as examples of how social factors—such as equality in the distribution of human capital and other resources, differences in ethnic diversity, and the economic power of the dominant group in these economies—can affect institutional development and growth.[32] Countries in both regions imported institutions from Europe. A more equal initial distribution of income and a less polarized society in the United States is cited as an important factor promoting institutional reform. There was more participation by broad segments of the population in a competitive market economy. More egalitarian societies may also be less polarized. This factor is probably more important for ethnically diverse countries, particularly during economic downturns when conflicts tend to be magnified.

Other forces may be at work. True, the history of the industrial countries is full of examples of periods and countries of high inequality. Consider the prevalence of sweatshops, unhealthy working conditions, and extensive child labor in much of the United Kingdom during industrialization. But this inequality did not keep the United Kingdom from the forefront of industrial development. So it is not clear that initially high income inequalities will always prevent later broad-based market development. There may be countervailing forces at work, such as the open exchange of information, open trade and competition, and innovation, all promoting institutional development.

The recent experience of the East Asian economies suggests that policies to promote equality, through investments in education, can yield high returns. People who are literate and educated are more likely to participate in and demand formal market-supporting institutions. This Report provides some guidance for institution building in the social sectors (box 1.17). Promoting opportunity in this way can promote social cohesion, important for consensus-building on reforms.

Large initial inequalities in wealth in closed markets can also engender situations where strong economic interests may "capture" the state, leading to regulatory structures that favor their narrow interests and prevent broad-based markets. Market participants can have a key role in the design of institutions that affect their transactions. Creating inclusive institutions with more social legitimacy—systems in which business interests and government can work together in an open and transparent fashion in establishing institutions—can lead to faster progress than in closed systems.

Shocks. Large shocks to economic and political systems change the balance of economic, social, and political power—and thus the effectiveness of institutions. Sometimes shocks forestall reform and at other times they can accelerate it. During economic depressions, for example, business and financial groups often come under greater scrutiny. It is claimed that periods of economic depression in Europe reduced political and social support for financial development, particularly for the development of equity markets.[33] But country experience also shows that since market-supporting institutions need some stability to be effective, large economic or political shocks may be needed for all but gradual change. And sometimes several large shocks are needed.[34] For policymakers and politicians, periods of crisis can sometimes provide opportunities, at least in some sectors, to undertake bolder institutional reforms—and these are opportunities to be seized.

A detailed analysis of the evolution of corporate law in industrial and developing countries shows that economic crises create demand for reform. For example, the recent financial crises affected reform in Malaysia (box 1.18).[35]

Shocks in technology also create demand for new institutions. Regulators need to develop new institutions to deal with such technological breakthroughs as the Internet. For example, the spread of e-banking and the provision of financial and other information over the Internet offers lower transaction costs—and new opportunities for fraud.

Box 1.17
Applying the lessons to the social sectors

Some of the key problems institutions face in the delivery of social services are information, enforcement, and competition.

Limited *information* about the beneficiary is available to the provider of services, complicating the targeting of income transfers to those truly in need. In Moldova, for example, before recent changes in transfer systems, a 1997 survey found that the richest 10 percent of the population enjoyed almost a fifth of all social assistance payments, while 38 percent of poor households got no form of social assistance at all.

Enforcement by public officials of good quality is difficult. In relatively poor areas of most countries, there are difficulties in maintaining staff and providing services, especially for public providers. Evidence from Canada (Anderson and Rosenberg 1990) to Indonesia (World Bank 1994b), and from India (The Probe Team 1999, p. 44) to Zambia (World Bank 2001f) shows substantial differences in vacancy rates in health posts between urban and rural areas.

Then there are the issues of *competition*. For example, competition by the government in providing social transfers may drive out private institutional arrangements—such as family networks, which can be targeted more effectively to the poor than more arm's length (public) social assistance.[36] A study from the Philippines, simulating the results of introducing an unemployment insurance scheme, found that net private transfers to the unemployed would fall by 92 pesos for every 100 given by the government (Cox and Jiminez 1995).

Complementing what exists. The demand for modern *public* institutions to deliver universal social services and widespread social assistance is fairly recent. In health the large national systems of the United Kingdom and Canada date from 1948 and the 1970s, respectively. and in education, the achievement of universal primary education, requiring public funding, occurred late in the 19th century. The origins of national social assistance schemes are also fairly recent.

In each case, extensive reliance on the private sector preceded the participation of governments. In fact, as today's richer countries grew more advanced, they could provide more *formal* social services at a price-quality mix demanded by the population. They could ensure adequate training of public providers. And they had the complementary institutions (such as more reliable income and asset ownership records) to better target social assistance to the neediest and that were free from corruption.

For developing countries, public involvement in these areas has accelerated. With poor complementary institutions—inadequate monitoring capacity, poor communication networks—providing universal coverage immediately may be too ambitious. Public financial constraints, including low fiscal resources, may also worsen quality of services. So recognizing the need to be flexible in price-quality goals is important.

Innovating to identify what works. Despite the lack of complementary institutions, developing countries can use innovative methods to ease many of the information and enforcement problems in these areas. The use of providers closer to the community—such as NGOs, whose motivations are different from both private sectors and civil servants—can be a solution for both service delivery and the provision of social assistance. What many NGOs bring to the table is a credible promise not to exploit weaknesses in the monitoring systems of government.

In many sparsely populated and poor areas, such as one might find in rural Africa, it is unusual to find private, modern medical facilities unless provided by NGOs, particularly faith-based NGOs. In delivering social assistance, NGOs based in the community may be better able than formal agencies to discover who is most in need of aid and may be organizationally more flexible in delivering appropriate assistance to the neediest. The community may also serve as the arbiter of who has the most needs—as in the *mahalla* system in Uzbekistan.

For many of the poorest countries, the best option for targeting social transfers effectively may be to experiment with different self-targeting mechanisms to find the system that best ensures that few other than the poor use the transfers. Innovative approaches using less desirable consumption goods for the poorest (as in Bangladesh in the 1970s and Tunisia in the early 1990s) have proved useful (for Tunisia, see Tuck and Lindert 1996). Well-designed public works programs that pay below-market wages are also a good self-targeting way to ensure that resources get to those who need them.

Connecting communities. Promoting open information exchange has been very important in building successful service delivery institutions. In the state of Ceara in Brazil, one factor in the dramatic improvement of health service delivery was an innovative monitoring approach. But also critical was a substantial public relations campaign that preceded the program, increasing its visibility, enthusiasm, and prestige. In this way, the program recruited a cadre of interested local monitors (Tendler and Freedheim 1994).

Sometimes, simply providing information to local communities is enough to stimulate improvements in quality in service delivery. Recent technological advances, including the Internet, allow government and private agents to provide information cheaply. The rate of sharing information is dramatically enhanced. Take Uganda. In 1995 a study to track expenditure from the central government to individual schools found that as little as 30 percent of nonsalary recurrent budget allocations meant to reach schools actually did. The results of this study were publicized in newspapers and posted at local facilities. A follow-up survey in 1999 showed an increase in actual disbursements, averaging very close to 100 percent (Ablo and Reinikka 1998). Another variation that does not depend on technological improvements is sharing information through the use of traveling teachers.

Promoting competition. Competition between public and private providers improves institutional quality. In Malaysia a reliable system of public clinics has maintained pressure on the private sector to keep prices reasonable (van de Walle and Nead 1995; World Bank 1992). But competition is possible only in areas densely populated enough to support multiple providers. This leaves unaddressed the problem of remote areas with many poor people. In the United States, for example, voucher systems are almost always advocated only for urban areas.

Box 1.18
Crises and institutional change in Malaysia

Malaysia had one of the most developed capital markets in East Asia in the early 1970s. At first, securities market regulation followed mostly the English system of market self-regulation. Although a comprehensive securities act was enacted in 1973, jurisdiction over market supervision was divided among several state agencies—including the ministry of finance, the registrar of the companies, and the capital issues committee.

In 1993, after a decade of rapid market development, controls were unified in a new securities commission. Before the financial crisis in 1997, the commission had determined to replace the detailed merit regulations system with a liberalized system based primarily on disclosure. But in the wake of the

crisis and with the aim of reducing capital outflows, policymakers adopted selective capital controls.

After an evaluation of the crisis, a series of more substantial institutional changes were introduced in preparation for continued liberalization. Focused on transparency and governance, these changes included new accounting standards, merger and acquisition rules, capital adequacy rules for stock brokering companies, and broker commission liberalization.

The implication for policymakers is clear: if crises expose real vulnerabilities in markets, policymakers should take advantage of these times to fix the vulnerabilities.

Source: World Bank staff.

Organization and scope of the Report

The second part of this year's Report concentrates on firms. It addresses institutional issues that affect productivity and risk management in agriculture: the rights to land, the credit in rural areas, and the institutions that support innovation and dissemination of ideas in agriculture. It also concentrates on the problems of governance for firms, looking at institutions, internal and external to the firm, that enhance investment in firms and ensure good management—especially the interaction between ownership structures and legal frameworks and between private institutions (such as business associations) and public ones. And it explores the critical role of financial institutions, the necessary supporting institutions for their development, and the role of the supervisory and regulatory system in ensuring a healthy financial system. It draws on new research done for the Report on the role of politics in financial development, institutions to secure access for new borrowers, and the effects of foreign bank entry and privatization.

Part III of the Report concentrates on government. It examines how political institutions support good governance, focusing on the policymaking process, the incentives for corruption, and the institutions of taxation. It next explores issues of judicial efficiency, and the experience with reforms aimed at improving efficiency, and examines the causes and consequences of cross-country differences in judicial procedures from a new survey covering over 100 countries. It then discusses the main impediments to competition in markets, gathering new data on business entry regulations

around the world and on competition authorities and legislation. Last, it assesses the regulation of monopolies in developing countries and the consequences for service delivery to poor people.

Part IV of the Report concentrates on society. It discusses how norms and codes of conduct in societies influence markets and public institutions and in turn are influenced by market developments. It also explores the role of the media in expressing and disseminating the concerns and values of society—and the effects such information flows have on institutional quality and thus on economic and social outcomes. It draws on a new study of media ownership around the world written for the Report.

Market-supporting institutions are a big topic, for these institutions are everywhere and varied. So much remains to be learned about them. This Report offers policymakers some guidance that has been distilled both from the history of institutional evolution and from the lessons of recent experience—the varied experiences of the transition economies in the 1990s, the continuing struggles in many poor countries around the world, and the successes of some of the emerging economies in the past decades.

At the same time, the Report does not address all possible institutional problems in all possible fields. Rather, it focuses on a subset of these institutions from many fields to illustrate that the framework (inform, enforce, compete) and messages (complement, innovate, connect, and—again—compete) can be applied regardless of the specific sector studied. It does not cover in detail institutions that previous *World Devel-*

opment Reports have covered. This Report, one in a series looking at critical development issues, is a natural continuation of *World Development Report 2000/2001,* which discusses the central role of markets in the lives of poor people. It leaves some important issues for *World Development Report 2003,* which will focus on issues related to the environment as well as on social cohesion and stability.

Conclusions

Development experience shows that markets can provide the means to attain sustained increases in living standards for people around the world. *World Development Report 2000/2001* argued that markets are central to the lives of poor people. By providing opportunities to engage in productive activities, and by empowering citizens, they can promote growth and reduce poverty. But for markets to provide widespread benefits, they need to be inclusive and integrated. Policies that promote growth and reduce poverty are important, but the details of institutional design matter as well.

Improvements in living standards, and overall improvements in the lives of poor people, depend on institutions that support growth as well as those that directly enhance the access of poor people to markets. That is, poor people are affected by what other market actors do.

Building effective institutions is a complex task. Experience indicates that one size does not fit all. But notwithstanding the uniqueness of countries, analysis of country experience does hold important lessons for institutional development.

This Report provides a framework for institutional development. It builds on the work of several disciplines, combining theory and evidence. It extends empirical evidence on the details of institutional design across a wide range of countries, and within countries over time, to understand the process of institutional change. And it provides guidance on how to build new institutions, modify existing ones, and create the forces for change.

Most times institutional change is a step-by-step process. The Report acknowledges as well that many reforms are difficult because there are constituencies which benefit from existing institutions and often interest groups which would promote change do not do so. But it is also true that some institutions continue to exist not because there is concerted support for them, but because forces that would press for change

are not adequately organized to do so. Reforms to such institutions are not as difficult to implement politically and, once implemented, could not only improve the way markets work but can help build momentum for further change. Both the supply of institutions and the demand for them matter. Development experience does not provide a universal guide as to which particular institutions should always be created first. However, within each sector, the Report does identify areas where the introduction of a particular institutional structure may need to wait for the development of other supporting or complementary institutions or conditions. In other words, some priorities can be identified.

This Report also considers the interaction between informal or norm-based institutions and formal institutions. Many poor people, particularly those in poor countries, do not have access to formal institutions. Innovative designs may help bridge the gap between informal and formal institutions and gradually increase the access of those left out. Simplifying formal institutions, providing more information about them to users, strengthening human capital, and accepting informal institutions when formal institutions would not have their desired impact are some of the ways in which institutional designs can be modified to suit the needs of poorer countries and of poor people.

Local, national, and international actors, public or private, affect how institutions evolve over time. The balance of power between private and public actors, and the state's recognition of both its strengths and limitations, is an important factor in market development. A strong and capable state is necessary to support markets, and an arbitrary and corrupt state can impede their development. But it is not only the balance between private and public actors that matters. The design of institutions and the pace of reform are affected by how local and national leaders and national and international leaders interact. All of these interactions are affected by the nature of information flows and the capabilities of the various parties.

The four main lessons of this chapter are that for effective institution building policymakers need to complement what exists, innovate to suit local conditions, foster open trade and open information exchange, and foster competition among regions, firms, and individuals. The incentives provided to people depend on the whole set of institutions and affect their performance. So when building an institution or modifying one, the key thing to consider is whether supporting institutions—without which the institution would not be effective—exist. If not, perhaps it would be better to work on the supporting institutions first or to modify design so that the planned institution can work without the supporting institution. Also important are the levels of human capital needed, the extent of corruption, and costs relative to per capita income. With scarce human capital, complex regulations cannot be enforced as they are in countries with highly skilled personnel. These factors argue for simplification of institutional design. Higher costs relative to per capita income of accessing formal institutions will mean that the disadvantaged and poorer members of society will be unable to access these institutions. Corruption is facili-

tated by complexity of regulation in nontransparent markets and where other incentives for bureaucratic efficiency (such as wages or promotion) are weak. In these countries, to complement existing conditions, regulation needs to be streamlined. Technological differences are also relevant. To accommodate country-specific differences in culture and endowments, innovation should be encouraged and accepted. Finally, providing opportunities for trade will develop markets and the demand for institutions that support transactions in markets. Open information sharing will do the same. Competition among regions and among firms, often limited by current institutional structures, will help identify new institutional forms and create the demand for new institutions.

PART II

Firms

FIRMS ARE KEY BUILDING BLOCKS OF MARKETS, PRODUCING GOODS and providing services that form the basis of market exchange. This part of the Report considers institutional issues for three groups of firms. *Farmers* are the focus of chapter 2, which looks at ways for agricultural producers in developing countries to increase their productivity and reduce their risks through improving the institutions that govern the markets for land, credit, technology, and agricultural output. For firms, a key institutional question is how to enhance investment and ensure good management; chapter 3 covers the problems of *Governance of Firms* (focusing on those outside the financial sector), through an examination of interactions between ownership structures and legal frameworks, and public and private institutional players. In chapter 4, *Financial Systems,* which perform critical functions for market systems, are considered; the chapter discusses the necessary institutional conditions for their development and the role of the supervisory and regulatory system in ensuring a healthy financial system.

CHAPTER 2

Farmers

Most of the world's poor people earn their living from agriculture, so if we knew the economics of agriculture we would know much of the economics of being poor.

—Theodore W. Schultz, 1980

Farmers operate in the market, like other entrepreneurs. But markets in rural areas, and particularly agricultural markets, suffer especially from problems of information, inadequate competition, and weak enforcement of contracts. Building institutions that reduce transaction costs for farmers, therefore, can greatly improve the way agricultural markets operate. This is especially important for poverty reduction, because poor people are more likely to live in rural areas and make their living from agriculture-related activities (figure 2.1). Well-functioning agricultural markets also have important benefits for the rest of the economy. As agricultural productivity improves, farmers leave agriculture for more productive employment in industry and services, promoting overall growth.[1]

Three particular challenges face policymakers building institutions for agricultural markets. First, agricultural activity is usually *geographically dispersed* and distant from major urban centers. A problem in providing rural credit, for example, is that formal providers of credit, such as banks, may find it costly to obtain information on geographically scattered small farmers. So interest rates on formal loans to small farmers, if loans are available at all, tend to be prohibitively high. Similarly, costs for judicial services and the marketing of produce can be high because of the distance between farms and major towns.[2] In all such cases, informal institutions serve as substitutes for formal institutions—

effectively in some environments, but as incomplete surrogates in others.

Second, farming in many countries has historically suffered from *urban bias* in public policy. For example, state marketing boards in several African countries resembled the systems used by the colonists to gather food during the Second World War.[3] Both these systems subsidized urban consumers of food by requiring farmers to sell their output at less than the market price. Other examples of urban bias include overvalued exchange rates to make imports cheaper for urban consumers, excessive agricultural export taxes, and high effective rates of protection for domestic industries that provide agricultural inputs.

Public investment in infrastructure, education, and other services in rural areas also tends to be lower than in urban areas. Lower investment increases transaction costs in marketing, which can be a major institutional constraint to developing agricultural productivity. Public or private efforts to build specific institutions that ease information costs, such as grades and standards or market information systems, can help to boost agricultural development (box 2.1). Beyond physical access to markets, large segments of the rural population, and the rural poor in particular, often face considerable obstacles in accessing agricultural markets. This is because their relative lack of education can make some useful formal institutions, such as institutions for disseminating technological information, harder to access.

Third, agriculture is heavily dependent on *the vagaries of climate*. Poor farmers often rely on their own savings and the help of family and friends when floods or droughts strike. But these insurance mechanisms are

Figure 2.1
Poverty head counts, urban versus rural, selected countries, 1990s

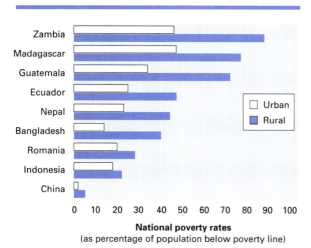

National poverty rates
(as percentage of population below poverty line)

Note: National poverty lines are used, so results are not comparable across countries.
Source: World Bank data.

of little use when savings are meager or when the entire circle of family and friends suffers from the same disaster. Wealthier farmers and those in richer countries can purchase forms of disaster insurance and benefit from public subsidies when struck by adversities. These subsidies are costly for poorer economies, and markets for disaster insurance require an array of complementary institutions unavailable in most developing countries.

How can governments or communities build effective institutions to raise farmers' returns and lower their risk?[4] This chapter addresses this question by drawing on evidence from successes and failures of institutional arrangements across countries. The interlinked institutions governing farmers' physical and financial assets—those for *land* and for *finance*—are particularly important. Secure and transferable rights to land stimulate income-generating investment and reduce uncertainties about future incomes. So do well-functioning rural financial institutions, which provide credit for both income-enhancing and risk-reducing investments and insurance. Institutions for generating and disseminating *agricultural technology* directly affect the yields and risk inherent in agricultural production.

In many countries, marketing problems are the biggest institutional constraints to increasing agricultural productivity. Connecting small, isolated communities into larger markets, and particularly into global markets, stimulates demand for farmers' output. This,

in turn, generates demand for inputs. The more open the market, the greater is the demand for effective formal institutions for farmers—from documented property rights in land to better access to credit.

Informal institutions and simplified procedures may be appropriate in situations where complementary formal institutions are absent or where the overall demand for agricultural output is low. In such cases the costs of complex formal institutions may be high compared with their benefits. For example, in areas where there is little competitive pressure on land, communal rights to land can be sufficient for tenure security. Formal titles may be more appropriate in situations where high demand for land gives rise to disputes over land and informal institutions can no longer resolve these disputes satisfactorily.

Innovation, often through experimentation, can identify techniques that overcome the inherent high transaction costs in rural areas. These can range from simple databases that permit technological information sharing among small farmers to improved enforcement mechanisms inherent in group-based lending.

This chapter concentrates on specific agricultural institutions, including land rights, rural financial institutions, and institutions that create and deliver agricultural technology. Many other critical issues that relate to agriculture are dealt with in other chapters of the Report—for example, openness to international trade in chapter 7 and water and electricity pricing in chapter 8—and in other Bank reports.[5]

Building more secure and transferable rural land institutions

Historically land was abundant and was held communally or could be obtained by any who laid first claim to it. But as population grew, land in many parts of the world—specifically, agricultural land—became more scarce, until its relative scarcity raised its value. As land became more important as a productive asset, it moved into individual or family ownership. With private property came the need to prove ownership. Even in ancient Egypt and Mesopotamia, titles for land were important for land transactions (box 2.2).

Today the nature of property rights in agricultural land varies widely across countries. Both governments and communities have built institutions to define these rights. In some countries, such as Uzbekistan, the state owns all land. In China private ownership of land is also prohibited; government regulations allow private citizens to lease land legally for 15 years, although prac-

Box 2.1
Agricultural marketing institutions

When complex agricultural marketing arrangements in developing countries fail, it is usually because of the lack of effective supporting institutions. The state has a role to play in building better marketing institutions, but not through s*tate marketing bodies,* which have clearly been unable to balance conflicting state objectives, including credit provision, tax collection, and food security and price stability for urban consumers. Instead, the state can facilitate private marketing institutions, such as contract farming and cooperatives.

Contract farming arrangements, or "out-grower schemes," are attractive for farmers in developing countries because they help small farmers access modern inputs, such as credit and seeds, and market their produce to domestic and international markets. These schemes range from agreements between individual traders and farmers, as in many Asian countries, to more formal systems in countries of Latin America, Central Europe, and East Asia. Even though the institution is private, governments can help build it in two ways: as information facilitator, helping to match small farmers with domestic traders and agrobusiness firms; and through complementary institutions, especially contract enforcement mechanisms (such as courts to resolve contractual disputes, or grades and standards).

Farmer cooperatives are more common in industrial countries than in the developing world, dominating the dairy sector in Finland, wheat in Canada, rice in Japan, and grain in Argentina. By tackling the problems caused by the relative smallness of individual farmers, cooperatives can be very successful in dealing with both information asymmetries and competitive power versus purchasers. They do this through collective action, pooling resources and lowering the unit costs of transactions. For marketing cooperatives in developing countries, the record has a clear lesson: governments should stop trying to impose "top-down" cooperative structures on farmers. Cooperatives such as Anand in Gujarat, India, or UGC in Mozambique have seen success because they are voluntary in nature, which helps mitigate some collective action problems, such as low effort by participants (a problem that has plagued state-led agricultural cooperatives). Also, they have experimented with context-specific institutional design, which has improved trust, transparency, and innovation.

Whatever the organization of marketing, purchasers can still incur high costs to verify the quality of goods they buy. Two institutions have evolved to meet these needs: grades and standards provide a greater level of certainty about the quality of produce, and market information systems provide information to farmers.

Because agricultural products have a vast array of characteristics, *grades* (classifications based upon quantifiable attributes) and *standards* (rules of measurement) are used to separate similar products into categories and describe them with consistent terminology. This evaluation system can significantly reduce information costs by allowing traders to contract "remotely" through commodity specification rather than through on-site visual inspection. But the benefits go beyond this. Because grades and standards can be independently certified, they facilitate access to credit, through the use of warehouse receipt schemes, inventory credit, and commodity exchanges. They can also expand the market by allowing price and quantity comparisons, and thus trade, across markets with common standards.

In the rice market in Japan, standards and grades were created when the spread of railroads began to link once-isolated mar-

kets. Throughout the world the expansion of trade between communities has created a similar demand for such standards and grades. Private merchants usually initiate standards. But as the volume of exchange increases, the importance of public intervention to promote the use and adaptation of standards increases.

International standards are often sponsored by larger farmers and firms in developing countries. These standards may promote overall exports. Yet smaller farmers who are currently involved in export markets may be left out of the process. The setting of high-level standards may raise their costs. These farmers have two options. First, they may reap part of the benefits of standardization, such as lower information costs, through the use of informal institutions that have evolved to mitigate informational problems (as with informal brokering arrangements in Ethiopia). Second, policymakers can reach out to enroll poor farmers in certification programs to integrate them into the wider agricultural markets, as is being done by Mayacert, a nongovernmental organization (NGO) operating in Guatemala.

Market information systems (MIS) generically describe dissemination networks of *public* data that provide information on agricultural markets. For farmers, knowledge of market information (such as the prevailing price of a commodity in key wholesale markets) can help them to plan their production, harvesting, and sales according to market demand. For traders, better information improves their ability to decide whether to hold products in storage or ship them to the most lucrative markets. In both cases MIS are of special use to smaller farmers or traders, who lack the scale economies to gather such information on their own account.

In most industrial countries, private agencies provide agricultural market information for a fee, while public agencies collect market data and make the information available free of charge. Given the high cost of collecting and disseminating such information in areas lacking standardization of quality and weights and adequate communication infrastructure, any user fees charged by private agencies are likely to be high. So the public sector has an important role in poorer countries.

Public sector MIS systems are not widespread—a survey of 120 developing countries identified only 53 such systems (Shepherd 1997). But they are usually barely functional. This is due to inadequate financing, inability of bureaucrats to collect reliable market information, and reluctance of traders to divulge information for fear of being taxed.

Nevertheless, several innovative strategies for effective dissemination of market information are being explored. For example, the government of Andhra Pradesh, India, makes prices of produce in different regional markets available on a website that is updated daily. Again, a major role for the public sector may be to help market participants improve their *own* information flows by expanding the availability of low-cost communication technology. For example, the exchange of market information in Ghana, the Philippines, and Bangladesh was boosted when governments made rural access a condition for granting licenses to mobile telephone companies. Consequently, market traders increasingly gather and convey information among themselves through the use of their own cellular telephones.

Source: Chaudhury and Banerji 2001, *World Development Report 2002* background paper.

Box 2.2
Early institutions of land ownership in Mesopotamia and Egypt

From the dawn of agriculture around 10,000 years ago until a couple of centuries ago, land has been abundant relative to population in much of the world. Land in early times was usually owned, if at all, by the king or the temple. In Egypt the Pharaoh Menes (c. 3100 B.C.) carried around deeds certifying his ownership of all land, granted to him by the king of the gods. But private land ownership and land sales were also recorded. In Uruk (in southern Mesopotamia, c. 3000 B.C.), there are records of individuals who "owned" land, although titles did not exist—and tablets give information on the sale of this land.

Some of the earliest existing physical records of private landholdings date from the reign of Hammurabi (16th century B.C.), whose famous code also laid down specific circumstances under which the king would step in to resolve land disputes. In Hammurabi's time, land assignments were delineated by pegs around the boundary, and a record of all landholdings was kept in the palace. By the third century B.C., it had become common for Egyptian landholders to keep a document of possession with themselves. By the time of the Sassanian era (A.D. 224 to 651), property ownership in Mesopotamia required a written deed, witnessed and then registered with the state.

Source: Powelson 1998.

Box 2.3
***Quilombos* in Brazil: infrastructure, social change, and a new demand for land registration**

Until recently settlements known as *quilombos* have been hidden away in Brazil. Tucked away in geographically remote settings, these communities are inhabited by the descendants of runaway slaves. Their remoteness was originally an effort to avoid discovery and scrutiny by slave owners. Today the settlements are connected to the rest of Brazil and the world by new and improved road, river, and rail links. As a result the value of this land has grown for ranchers, mining companies, and land speculators, who have been attempting to take over some of the *quilombo* lands for development. Initially these efforts were relatively successful because *quilombo* inhabitants did not have formal titles. Since their ancestors had been illiterate, no documents testified to the existence of their communities, and all official records of slavery were officially destroyed in 1890.

Yet a government-sponsored effort is now under way to give *quilombo* dwellers legal title to ancestral lands This process was eased by the adoption of a new constitution in Brazil in 1988, 100 years after slavery ended, which finally recognized the rights and status of descendants of runaway slaves. By 2000, 743 *quilombo*s, some dating back to the 17th century, had been identified across Brazil and were seeking formal recognition of their status. There have been some attempts to expedite the titling process, such as accepting the oral testimony of the oldest residents as proof of settlement claims. Still, the process of regularization has not gone as fast as could be hoped, and the government is trying to accelerate it.

Source: Rohter 2001; Fundação Palmares 2000.

tices differ across different localities. Similarly, although private ownership is forbidden in most Central Asian countries, some governments have developed well-defined and often-codified use rights to state property and have built organizations to administer them.[6] Privately determined and ill-defined "squatters' rights" constitute ownership and transferability of cultivated land for many small farmers in Latin America. Communities and tribes in many African countries have informal, individual use rights to communally owned property.[7] Land tenure is transferable in most of South Asia, but uncertain institutional arrangements have resulted in clashes about ownership and the potential for government seizure of land, leading to insecurity in some areas.

Secure and transferable land rights can be provided by both informal and formal institutions. Such systems must provide information on who owns the land, who has a secured interest in the land, where land transactions are registered, and how to access this information. The community-defined ownership or use rights in parts of Africa, for example, perform these functions.

In many cases establishing formal titling is an unnecessary cost in the medium term. But formal property rights systems enforced by the state are needed to reduce land disputes where population growth or demand for agricultural produce leads to competitive pressures on land or where transactions with those outside the community are common. For example, the demand for formal individual property rights was stimulated in England by the demand for wool and thus for sheep. In Kenya the demand for formal land rights was triggered by the emerging global market for plantation crops, while in Thailand the cause was the internationalization of its market for rice following the 1826 Bowering Treaty. Better infrastructural services that connect remote lands to the market can also stimulate the demand for formal institutions to delineate and enforce property rights, as has been the case in Brazil (box 2.3).

Improving agricultural productivity through better land rights

Improved security of tenure can raise the expected returns from investment and ease credit constraints. This in turn can raise investment levels and productivity. Secure tenure to land helps assure investors that the returns to their investment will not be expropriated by government or private agents. Better land tenure also increases access to credit, since land can be used as collateral (discussed in chapter 4).

If land tenure is secure, a functioning land market that allows transfer of property from one owner (or a possessor of user rights) to another can help raise productivity by transferring land from less efficient cultivators to more efficient ones. This overall productivity gain, of course, is greater if there are functioning credit markets—otherwise the more efficient farmers would not be able to raise the capital needed for the purchase. Productivity increases also depend on sellers being able to engage in other income-generating activity. Several studies of China, one of the few countries that has experimented with allowing different systems of transfer rights across different provinces, have confirmed that higher levels of transferability were positively correlated with higher levels of farm investment.[8]

In many developing countries extensive regulation of land market transactions has meant that land markets seldom operate freely. Since transparency tends to be low and administrative capacity limited, these regulations also encourage corruption. Lowering these costs of land transactions may be of particular importance in parts of Asia, especially South Asia, where a flourishing land market could improve productivity by avoiding excessive fragmentation and subdivision of landholdings (box 2.4).

When are formal titling institutions needed?

Formal land titles can increase access to credit and raise investment in land. But these functions greatly depend on the broader institutional environment. Governments should embark on large-scale titling programs only where competitive pressures and potential disputes mean that community land tenure arrangements are ineffective.

Efforts to issue documented and registered land titles have gained prominence in recent years. In many cases, titles have formalized undocumented tenancy rights, which can range from long-established community- or tribe-based systems, as in the Brazilian *quilombos* exam-

Box 2.4
Examples of policy barriers to the operation of land markets

Even when land transfer is allowed by law, extensive regulation of transactions can frustrate the operation of the land market. The following barriers can be reduced by government actions.

Restrictions on land sales. Some countries prohibit land sales outright. In many transition countries land privatization has been accompanied by ceilings on sale prices and moratoriums on resales. Governments have indirectly restricted land sales by mandating that any land transaction has to be approved by a higher authority.

High sales costs. High transaction taxes or high fees can discourage land sales or drive them into the informal sector. In the Philippines and Vietnam the tax on land transactions is almost 20 percent of land value. Costs can also be high when lack of competition results in high fees for services associated with land sales.

Restrictions on land subdivision. Such restrictions have been established in former colonial environments to prevent the disintegration of large farms often formerly owned by colonialists, without any economic justification. For example, Zimbabwe continues to have these restrictions, while South Africa has just recently begun the process of repealing its regulation.

Restrictions on the use of land for collateral. Examples include Vietnam, where the value of land as collateral is limited by law and where foreign banks are not allowed to take land as security for credit. Also, creditors cannot own or exchange land use rights, and any land that is repossessed is auctioned off by the state. In Mexico banks can obtain the use right but not the ownership of land.

Lengthy land registration processes. In Mozambique there is a backlog of about 10,000 applications for land rights, which means long delays between receipt of an investment plan and eventual granting of the land right. In Cameroon the minimum amount of time it takes to register a plot is 15 months, and registration commonly takes between 2 and 7 years. In Peru the official adjudication process takes 43 months and 207 steps in 48 offices, although an expedited process is now being implemented in selected areas.

Source: Deininger 2001, *World Development Report 2002* background paper; de Soto 2000.

ple in box 2.3, to occupancy rights by squatters on land.[9] Formal land titles have also been established during land privatization processes (as in the transition countries). As discussed in *World Development Report 2000/2001*, clearly defining land rights during land reforms is key to improving the lives of poor people—farmers and nonfarmers alike.[10]

But the financial and administrative costs of a formal land titling program are high. This raises the question of what types of institutions are needed, and when.

Formal land titles create secure and transferable property rights by providing better information. Informal land right systems are based on the knowledge of community members and neighbors. These individuals may know the quality of a piece of land, who truly owns it, and its precise physical demarcation. But outsiders to the community who want to buy land have little access to this information, and no way to ensure the reliability of the information they obtain. Formal land titles can help to remove this source of uncertainty. At the same time, by resolving ownership disputes, they can thwart arbitrary seizure. They also ensure that the price of the land more closely reflects its value rather than the added costs associated with verifying its ownership status and physical location.

Property owners may clearly demand the establishment of formal titling systems when informal systems become less effective. This usually occurs when land becomes relatively scarce and in dispute. Increased openness to other communities and competition in product markets—reflecting strong market demand for agricultural output—has often increased the demand for formal titles. In areas of new settlement or frontiers (as in Brazil), formal titles can enhance the security of agricultural ownership.[11] For 35,000 squatter families living on encroached forest reserve land in Thailand, a land reform project in the 1980s provided occupancy certificates that could be upgraded to full land titles. Since the 1980s the World Bank has been supporting land titling projects in Thailand. Studies have found that these efforts have encouraged significant productivity-increasing investments and greater access to credit. The Bank is continuing to work with the Thai government on a 20-year program to improve the land titling and administration system.[12]

In other situations community-based approaches offer a cheaper and effective alternative to formal institutions.[13] The first situation occurs where buyers and sellers know each other at the local level and where there is strong peer pressure to avoid socially disruptive property disputes. In these cases the main source of demand for land is often from within the community; the community is strong and close-knit; there is consistency and continuity of community leadership; and any certificates of ownership issued by those in the community are accepted by others in the community. The second situation occurs where community arrangements are also legally valid and enforceable. Under Nigerian law, for instance, "customary tenure" is defined as those

systems administered by communities or their leaders. The great majority of these holdings are held under rights of inheritance derived ultimately from community membership—rights that are defensible in the local courts.[14]

The third situation arises where administrative and institutional shortcomings mean that formal titling does not result in more secure tenure than informal alternatives. The effectiveness of formal titles depends on the quality of the title—such as clarity—and respect for the law. National legislation for tenure reform has limited capacity to change behavior when indigenous arrangements on land persist.[15]

The fourth situation occurs where the benefit of formal titles is low because of failures in other agricultural institutions. That has been the case in Kenya, for example.[16] If complementary markets for credit and for marketing of inputs do not work, then the first policy responses, given limited institutional or organizational resources, should be in those areas.

Available empirical evidence from studies on Asia and Latin America suggests a positive relationship between tenure security and investment. For example, studies for the Brazilian frontier found formal titles increased productivity by providing clear information about ownership rights in undeveloped areas.[17]

Land titles can also improve access to credit. But titles alone are not sufficient—cross-country experience suggests that the difference has been the existence of complementary institutions. In Thailand the existence of formal land titles has facilitated the flow of both formal and informal credit (box 2.5). Moreover, increased investments in titled land raised its value and improved access to credit.[18]

At the same time, studies have generally found that formal titles have little effect on access to and use of credit in very poor regions in Africa, India, and some parts of Latin America (box 2.6). Two related factors explain this finding. First, complementary formal credit institutions may not be widely available. A study of two villages in southern India found that transferable land rights had little effect on credit, probably for this reason.[19] Land titles alone may not lower the high costs of enforcement and of managing very small loans that formal lenders deal with in lending to small farmers. For instance, a study for Paraguay found that the effect of formal titles on credit varied strongly with size. Smaller producers holding fewer than 20 hectares were excluded from the credit market.[20] Second, the lack of

Box 2.5
Informal collateral transactions using land titles in Thailand

While formal title documents for rural land can facilitate credit transactions, the costs of registering liens can be high, and the process can be time-consuming. Therefore, lien registration may not be compatible with loan transactions of relatively smaller amounts or short duration. Alternative arrangements have emerged, however, that take advantage of the value-enhancing effects of titles on collateral while avoiding the high transaction costs of formal lien registration. In Thailand in the 1980s a study found that borrowers sign a power-of-attorney authorization to a lawyer representing the lender (typically a trust of local businessmen) and leave the title document with the attorney. The cost of foreclosure in such a case is low, and the risk to the lender is reduced considerably. This procedure screens out borrowers with overly risky projects at a very low transaction cost compared with a formal registration of lien. While these arrangements have been documented for Thailand, they are likely to exist in many other regions of the world where the transaction costs of registering formal liens are high.

Source: Siamwalla and others 1990.

Box 2.6
Do indigenous land rights constrain agricultural investment and productivity in Africa?

Most African farmers still hold their land under indigenous, customary, or communal land tenure systems. In the traditional African society, the household, the village, and the kin group provided insurance against risks, access to informal credit, and security. Lineage rules of inheritance helped to enforce intergenerational transfers. The threat of sanctions, which included exclusion from the social structure and its benefits, was the major instrument of enforcement of the rules. Even where households have become geographically dispersed, the common inheritance of land in the village and the social support system of the traditional society continue to bind them together.

In the past such land tenure systems were thought to provide insufficient tenure security to induce farmers to make necessary investments in land (World Bank 1974; Harrison 1987). But research has shown that such systems can be effective. The evidence from rain-fed cropping areas suggests that indigenous tenure systems have been flexible and responsive to changing economic circumstances (Place and Hazell 1993; Bruce and Migot-Adholla 1994). Harrison (1990) found that smallholders in Zimbabwe, despite not having private title to their land, have achieved rapidly increasing maize yields and that their productive performance is not inferior to that of the biggest commercial farmers in the country. Mighot-Adholla and others (1994a) found similar results for Ghana.

Source: Bruce and Mighot-Adholla 1994; Collier and Gunning 1999; Soludo 2001, *World Development Report 2002* background paper.

other complementary formal institutions, specifically enforcement mechanisms, makes a difference. In Kenya, for instance, where banks were prevented from foreclosing on property used as collateral, a study found that banks did not make loans to farmers despite the existence of formal titles.[21]

Building effective institutions for the land market
Formal land market institutions include land registries, titling services, and land mapping. In building these institutions, three characteristics should be kept in mind: clear definition and sound administration of property rights; simple mechanisms for identifying and transferring property rights; and thorough compilation of land titles and free access to this information.[22] Although this discussion focuses on rural land markets, most of the lessons hold for urban markets as well.[23]

Clear definition and sound administration. A land registry, where titling information is filed, helps to solve the central problem of information on property rights. Many of the functions of a land registry can be performed by the private sector. But the government has a role in ensuring that the registry provides comprehensive ownership evidence to the public at low cost. For this, it has to enact land registration laws that define

rules for original adjudication of registered title, establish if and how provisional rights can be registered, and stipulate how these rights subsequently mature. The government also needs to establish an authority (which can be public or private) to ensure the impartial maintenance of land registers, to determine the nature of these registries, and to delineate the method by which a register for the whole jurisdiction is to be compiled and subsequent transactions are to be recorded.

Clearly defined land parcels need to be based on credible land surveys. Otherwise, increasing land disputes—the resolution of which, given the overworked judicial systems in many developing countries, usually takes a long time—can undermine the fundamental aim of land registries. In Indonesia, for example, land disputes account for 65 percent of all court matters.

Administration of the surveys has to address two concerns. First, survey standards should be commensurate with the country's (and region's) level of economic development. In Zambia, for instance, standards require the same degree of survey precision for office blocks in the capital as for 5,000-hectare farms in sparsely populated areas.[24] In poorer countries, more comprehensive survey coverage of land boundaries at a lower level of precision and cost (using neighboring parcels and landmarks) may be preferable to a low level of coverage at a high level of precision (say, satellite-aided mapping). Second, there needs to be an adequate supply of survey professionals, so that the land registration process is not unnecessarily lengthy. In Zambia, for instance, supply restrictions by the tightly knit association of surveyors meant that there were only seven qualified surveyors in the entire country in 1994. Indonesia, Malaysia, and the Philippines have also reported similar restrictions and lack of surveying capacity.[25] Pressure by media groups, civil society, and government to ease such anticompetitive behavior could yield results.

Simplicity of identification and transfer. In practice, establishing formal land rights can be a lengthy and cumbersome process. There are simple ways to ease this. One is to convert occupancy rights into full title. In Mozambique, for instance, land rights are granted to cultivators based on actual occupation for the last 10 years. Oral testimony is sufficient to support land ownership claims, and communities can request formal titles at any point. Similarly, oral testimony is being accepted in many cases of formalizing the *quilombos* in Brazil (see box 2.3). Suffering from a backlog of land disputes in the regular court system, Mexico established specialized agrarian courts (box 2.7). The admission of oral evidence and a degree of decentralization have made such courts accessible to the poor at reasonable cost.

Computerization can also simplify the identification and transfer process (as in the example of Andhra Pradesh, India, given in box 1.8). Although the initial investments in technology can be large, they can have high payoffs in speeding up land transactions in densely populated areas. Tax payments can also be used as a proof of possession that can eventually be converted into ownership. This mechanism also provides an incentive for landowners to pay taxes. Finally, transferability of land rights can be eased by reducing regulation-induced costs of transactions (see box 2.4).

Thorough compilation and free access to titling information. Incomplete land registries, where certain land plots are not part of the information base, are a common feature of developing countries. A combination of

---

Box 2.7
A transparent and accessible institutional framework for granting land rights in Mexico

Mexico established a special institutional infrastructure for granting land rights, which has three elements: (a) an ombudsman's office to supervise the regularization of land ownership; (b) a system of special courts to attend to the large number of existing land conflicts (and provide an opportunity for quick appeal of any irregularities occurring during the regularization process); and (c) a modern registry to record land rights that had been established to ensure that they could be used in commercial transactions.

Beneficiaries agree that the program has increased tenure security, and evaluations have demonstrated the positive impact it has had on the functioning of land markets. This transparent and accessible institutional framework has also improved governance in areas that were hitherto dominated by local cliques and party bosses.

Source: Deininger 2001, *World Development Report 2002* background paper.

---

technical, administrative, and legal impediments may cause this problem. For example, in Indonesia and Madagascar a lack of coordination between the legal and the fiscal cadastre, or official register of land ownership, prevents the government from knowing how much land it owns.

Land registries that are not publicly accessible raise the cost of transactions. In Tajikistan and several other countries of the former Soviet Union bureaucratic intermediaries are needed because the land registries are closed to the public. In other countries, such as Indonesia, there is separate title recording, which requires extensive cross-referencing between the legal and fiscal systems. This separation affects not only the speed of access (which can be eased by computerization), but also the integrity of the system.

Experimentation through pilot projects helps identify institutions effective for a given context. An example comes from Côte d'Ivoire, where the World Bank is working with the authorities on the Plan Foncier Rural. A pilot project helped to develop the methodology for the systematic clarification and certification of rural land tenure. Mapping and documentation of land rights is carried out by the professional team, accompanied by the land user or owner, neighbors, and village chiefs, moving from field to field within a village area. Any disputes that arise are settled by the entire entourage on the spot. When mapping and documentation of ownership and user rights are completed, the information is made publicly available so that claimants can openly register disagreements. If no conflicting claims to a parcel have been made within three months, the tenure status is considered satisfied.[26]

Building effective and accessible rural financial institutions

One study of the rural environment states that

> *Few banks would even consider making agricultural loans, and those who did charged extremely high interest rates. Rural credit was fertile ground for the loan sharks, and year after year, farmers turned over their crops to help pay exorbitant interest charges on loans made to keep their farms operating. Should a crop fail, the chances of a farmer extricating himself and his family from a loan shark's clutches were virtually non-existent.*[27]

This study was depicting the situation in rural North Carolina in the United States in the early 20th century. The description could apply just as accurately to many developing countries today, where formal institutions such as commercial banks have relatively little incentive to offer services to rural clienteles.

Over time, formal credit provision has increased in rural areas of industrial and some developing countries (figure 2.2 shows the evolution for some Asian countries). Increasing prosperity among farmers; better rural infrastructure; integration of the urban and rural financial systems; and the development of complementary institutions such as formal credit histories or collateral systems for rural borrowers, which lower the costs of lending, have all contributed to this increased access to formal credit (chapter 4).[28] In some countries, specific rural credit institutions such as cooperative banks and credit unions have also been successfully developed. But the provision of crop insurance for farmers has had mixed results even in industrial countries. [29]

In industrial countries today, specialized commercial institutions for offering credit, such as microcredit organizations and agricultural development banks, are relatively rare. As markets became more integrated, nonspecialized commercial banks began to supply credit to agriculture, supplanting both informal credit institutions and specialized agricultural banks. The financial viability of many of the formal specialized agricultural banks, such as France's Credit Agricole and

Figure 2.2
Evolution of formal institutional borrowing of farm households, selected Asian countries

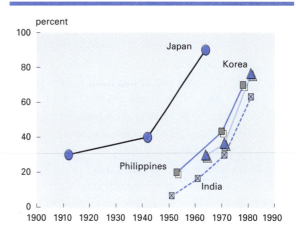

Source: Desai and Mellor 1993.

Indonesia's Bank Rakyat Indonesia, was improved by pooling agricultural risks with nonagricultural ones. The broader development of financial markets (chapter 4) and the development of complementary institutions such as those for enforcing contracts are also important for this process.

But in many developing countries, effective and accessible formal rural financial institutions are still rare—largely because of the lack of complementary institutions. Accessing finance is particularly difficult for poor farmers. To address this problem, policymakers initially created financial institutions that were specific to the agricultural sector, without much success.

Developing countries have often relied on transplants of rural and agricultural credit institutions that have been successful in the United States, Western Europe, and Japan. Among them are various forms of cooperatives (often adapted from the German *Raiffeisen* model), post office deposit schemes, and state marketing agencies that provided credit. French colonies in Africa built specialized agricultural banks based on the original design of the Credit Agricole. Latin American countries have often used lessons from the historical experience of the United States to set up public and cooperative farm credit systems.[30]

By the late 1980s, most of these institutions had clearly failed. Part of the problem was specific—transplants were not suited to country circumstances. But other issues also contributed. Urban bias policies, repressive financial policies, and loan targeting to narrow interest groups reduced the financial viability of banks lending to rural sectors. Debt relief programs also raised effective costs for lenders.

As a result, informal financial institutions still dominate in most poorer countries and for poorer farmers. In the mid-1990s, 81 percent of rural borrowing in Nepal was from informal sources, while farmers in Nigeria received 30 percent of their loans from informal moneylenders and 40 percent from *esusu* clubs (cooperative credit arrangements).[31]

Within countries, informal sources of credit are disproportionately used by poorer farmers. Data from Nepal in the 1990s show that 97.5 percent of those with per capita consumption below 2,000 rupees (the very poorest rural group) borrowed from informal sources. No rural borrowers with per capita consumption above 50,000 rupees borrowed informally.[32] Surveys from India and Pakistan show similar results.[33] In Thailand a study found that nonborrowers and those who borrowed exclusively from the informal sector tended to have fewer assets as well as lower incomes. Only the largest farmers borrowed from commercial banks as well as some farmers associations, and informal loans were also smaller in size.[34]

But the mix between different types of informal lenders has changed with the increased commercialization of agriculture.[35] In India, Pakistan, and the Philippines studies report that crop loans from moneylenders and landlords have been replaced by loans from "commission agents," or traders, who advance credit to buy inputs against a promise that the farmer will sell the produce through them at harvest.[36] These arrangements are usually better for the poorer farmers because they provide access to otherwise unavailable input and marketing arrangements (see box 2.1).

Improving rural lending institutions

Information and enforcement issues are fundamental problems faced by both informal and formal lenders in agriculture. Lenders overcome these problems through a range of institutional mechanisms, which can be "secured" or "unsecured" (table 2.1).

Secured loans, offered in exchange for some collateral, are the preferred option for most formal lenders in rural areas because such loans automatically lower information and enforcement costs.[37] Assessing the value of collateral and selling the collateral in case of default can be costly. But in environments with overall

Table 2.1
Types of rural lending institutions

Type of loan	Informal institutions	Formal institutions
Secured	Pawnbrokers Moneylenders who take possession of land titles Labor-pawning institutions	Commercial banks Rural development banks Government credit programs Mortgaged credit from traders (sellers of inputs)
Unsecured	Moneylenders Credit from traders (purchasers of output) Credit from traders (sellers of inputs) Friends and family Savings groups (including ROSCAs, ASCRAs, and chit funds) Labor-bonding institutions	Some credit unions Credit cooperatives Farmers' associations Nonbank financial institutions (e.g., insurance companies) Microcredit groups

Note: ROSCAs are rotating savings and credit associations; ASCRAs are accumulated savings and credit associations. Labor pawning, a historical artifact, involved offering a family member's labor as security. Labor pawning was prevalent in precolonial West Africa (Austin and Sugihara 1993).

weak formal institutions, these costs are still cheaper than the costs of gathering credit information about many small and scattered borrowers or of attempting to enforce a contract through an inadequate legal system.

Building effective systems for secured transactions can promote the development of formal rural financial institutions (chapter 4). In some developing countries, the use of formally collateralized loans is quite limited. Land cannot be used as collateral if legal claims, such as laws limiting "ownership" of seized land to use rights only, are not clear. In some developing countries many assets, such as warehouse receipts or inventory credit, are still not recognized as collateral. Indian law explicitly recognizes warehouse receipts as title documents, but there is no such recognition in Ghanaian law. One way around this enforcement problem is to use movable property as collateral—it can be given to the creditor to hold.

Collateralized loans tend to be given mostly to larger farmers in developing countries. For the lender, such farmers usually have two advantages over poorer and smaller counterparts. First, collateral is easily available—their property rights over land are more likely to be formally registered, and they are more likely to have movable property of high value. Second, because loan amounts are larger, the lender's unit cost of processing the loan or using the formal judicial system for enforcement are lower.

Poorer farmers often rely on *unsecured loans* from both formal and informal sources. Rural credit institutions in developing countries, whether formal or informal, gather information about the borrower's reputation by word of mouth. These institutions are usually localized and have easy access to information. A study for Thailand, for example, found that informal lenders are often the shopkeepers in the village because the store acts as a center for village gossip and thus information.[38] Some formal institutions, such as credit unions and cooperatives, also tend to be localized and can use past credit history with the institution itself as the main guide for future lending.

Formal and informal lenders, and large and small rural borrowers, interact in complex ways in financial markets in developing countries. Formal lenders such as commercial banks lend directly to the larger farmers and traders for their personal use. But they may also make wholesale loans to traders, who then act as informal lenders, making retail loans in smaller amounts to small farmers and middlemen (box 2.8).

How can rural lending institutions be improved? Experimenting with context-specific institutional design and using new technology to reduce costs are two promising avenues.

The design of new rural lending institutions can be improved by incorporating innovations based on the successful elements of informal institutions and formal interventions. Social and peer pressures, which are particularly effective enforcement mechanisms in informal lending, can contribute to the success of formal rural credit programs in weak institutional environments.[39] Newer microcredit institutions, including those backed by the World Bank and other donors, have adapted many of the same mechanisms for inducing repayment.[40] Some nongovernmental organizations (NGOs) are also trying to emulate informal lenders by serving as a bridge between banks and poor borrowing groups. MYRADA in southern India acts as such an intermediary, aiming to help borrowing groups deal directly with the banks after a few loan cycles.

Successful rural finance institutions cannot always be transplanted from one socioeconomic environment

Box 2.8
The intersection of formal and informal lending: marketing agents in the Philippines

Rice marketers in the Philippines—paddy traders, rice millers, wholesalers, and retailers—act as moneylenders primarily to establish a claim over the farmers' produce and to ensure that they are part of the trading chain. A key to their success as credit intermediaries is that in the absence of sufficient resources of their own, the rice marketers borrow much of their lendable capital (80 percent in one survey) from formal financial institutions. The traders' intimate knowledge of and close contact with the farmers and subsidiary traders ensure that information and enforcement costs are low and that repayment rates are high. Moreover, the rice marketers are a good risk for formal institutions because they have a good history of repayment and the size of their loans is relatively large. These informal rural lenders may also use banks as places to keep their savings.

Source: Floro and Ray 1997.

to another. Experimentation around a basic institutional form has been a good way to identify successful institutions. So thriving microfinance institutions around the world differ in operational details. Innovations on different aspects, such as the targeted group and the repayment periods, have been altered to suit the characteristics of different countries.

Giving incentives to loan officers, and rebating a small part of the loan for early repayment, the Unit Desas, part of Bank Rakyat Indonesia (BRI-UD), improved the repayment rate (to 92.5 percent in 1995).[41] Successfully experimenting with its institutional form, such as the size and composition of its "solidarity groups" of borrowers, BancoSol in Bolivia has grown from a subsidized lending program operated by an NGO to a self-sustaining commercial bank. Learning from successive experiments about how to adapt credit delivery to the local context and farmer needs, an Albanian rural credit program funded by the World Bank grew from offering small-scale credit in seven village credit funds in 1992 to a full-scale rural development project supporting hundreds of village credit funds by 1995 and a follow-up microcredit project since 1999.[42]

Experimentation helps to understand the impact of a rural finance institution. For example, an element of the Grameen Bank's programs is the requirement that borrowers repay their loans in small installments according to a rigid (weekly) schedule.[43] Imposing a regular repayment schedule can be costly, however. It reduces the attractiveness of long-gestation projects, such as those in agriculture, and helps to explain why informal lenders appear to thrive even in villages where microfinance programs are active.[44]

Technological innovations can also help credit provision. First, the continuing extension of credit-rating services to rural areas brings the promise of eventual integration of urban and rural banking, as has occurred in industrial countries. So far, such information intermediaries are developing mostly in middle-income countries, such as Argentina.[45] "Meta-information intermediaries" are also being developed. These rate financial intermediaries themselves rather than their clients, the first step in the development of credit reference bureaus. Further, they offer financial information in a standardized format. The Micro-Banking Standards Project, funded by the Consultative Group to Assist the Poorest, has recently collected, analyzed, and published data on the financial status of participating microfinance organizations.[46] Micro-Rate, a private credit-rating agency that specializes in evaluating microlenders, offers a similar service.[47]

Second, information technology can reduce transaction costs for both state and private actors. For example, Compartamos, a Mexican NGO, has started giving its field staff inexpensive handheld computers to record data, thereby reducing paperwork and speeding synchronization of data. This has allowed field staff to access and update records far more easily.[48]

Some institutional designs tailored to poor rural areas have been successful. Small minimum balance requirements and liquid savings products are attractive to rural borrowers. In such schemes offered by some rural banks in Asia and Latin America, lenders offset high unit costs by having interest rates increase with the account balance. Administrative costs can also be lowered by maintaining lean field offices and offering efficiency bonuses to motivate staff to be more productive.[49]

Many of the elements explaining the successes of institutions such as the BRI-UD in Indonesia and the Bank for Agriculture and Agricultural Cooperatives in Thailand can be found in any successful institution.[50] These include simplicity in financial contracts, transparency in operations, and integration across markets. Operational autonomy and freedom from political interference are critical for providing the institutions with the freedom to experiment with the terms and types of financial products offered.[51] Moreover, successful rural financial institutions tend to be large, usually serving millions of households. This allows them to reduce

transaction costs and risks by realizing economies of scale and diversifying their portfolios.[52]

The most successful institutions began by financing mainly nonfarm activities and started making agricultural loans only after they had grown into mature institutions. A striking aspect of successful rural financial institutions is that they all operate in relatively densely populated rural areas.[53] Geographic density reduces costs of transactions and makes it feasible, for example, for SafeSave in Bangladesh to send out staff to collect savings from its members on a daily basis.[54] Thus there is a question whether these designs can exist in sparsely populated countries.

Developing rural savings institutions

Besides access to credit, safe and liquid *savings* instruments are vital for farmers' well-being. In the absence of loans, savings are the only resource for investments. They also provide "self-insurance" against the periodic shocks to income common to agriculture, as farmers add to savings in good times and draw on their savings when times are difficult. Market women in rural parts of western Africa often save their daily earnings by giving them to *susu* men (itinerant savings collectors). The fact that the depositors are willing to pay the deposit taker a fee suggests that there is a demand for safekeeping institutions.

Savings institutions in rural societies are still informal, and savings are often not in financial assets. Rural households in developing countries save in physical assets such as livestock and jewelry. This does not always provide security because these assets may not hold their value in bad times. The success of such a strategy also depends on the level of development of the market for that asset (box 2.9).

The development of formal rural savings institutions, as with rural credit institutions, is inhibited by high costs of operation. Governments have attempted to provide savings facilities in rural areas. But these efforts, on average, have failed to cover their administrative costs. Even some of the fast-growing microfinance programs have relied on external agencies or governments for their sources of funds. The only major exception has been BRI-UD in Indonesia, but here the flow of savings has been from the rural sector to the urban sector.[55]

Insuring against risk in agriculture

Agricultural risk is considerable and covariant—usually all borrowers in an area are affected similarly. These problems are compounded by information problems, which are especially large in developing countries. For crop insurers, specific events such as floods or a locust attack are verifiable, and thus these risks are insurable. But when the yield on an insured crop is reported to be lower than expected, the reasons can be many and are difficult to untangle, and the true value of output is hard to verify. Insurance also provides incentives for fraud or "moral hazard" (low effort or investment by the farmer).

As a result, formal insurance mechanisms for agricultural households are difficult to implement even in richer countries. Unsuccessful attempts to offer generalized crop insurance in developing countries have contributed to the decline of agricultural banks.[56]

In both industrial and developing countries, premiums collected in general agricultural insurance schemes have never been enough to offset the indemnities paid out to farmers (figure 2.3). The situation is clearly worse when high administrative costs are added to the costs related to monitoring the insured. These schemes have historically needed significant government subsidies to stay operational.

Narrowly focused "named-peril" schemes are the only agricultural insurance mechanisms that have functioned without large government subsidies; they have succeeded precisely because they minimize the potential for deception by farmers and do not depend on the farmers' actions or investment. In industrial countries today, agricultural insurance is offered only as event insurance, for example against hail or floods—risks whose occurrence is relatively easy to monitor. In the United States, named-peril plans are the only mechanisms offered by private insurers without government subsidies.[57]

If general crop yield insurance is to be provided in developing countries, it is likely to require subsidies, even if administrative costs are kept at a minimum. A 1995 study of a general crop insurance scheme in India confirmed that it offered considerable subsidies.[58]

Given the limited availability of formal insurance for farmers in developing countries, most insurance arrangements are informal.[59] A study of northern Nigerian villages found that credit contracts were dependent on the nature and amount of shocks affecting borrowers, with lenders bundling credit and insurance.[60]

"Social insurance" agreements between members of a village stipulate that those who are better off once crops are harvested and sold are required to make transfers to the needy. Sometimes, as when individuals have an incentive to leave the community, enforcing this agreement so that these transfers actually occur can be

Box 2.9
Livestock as savings: contrasting evidence from India and Burkina Faso

Faced with risky environments, rural households often rely on the sale of assets to smooth consumption in the face of income shocks. The main assets that farm households possess are productive assets, in the form of land or livestock. Unlike land, livestock is portable and may offer a useful way for households to buffer against production shocks. In an influential article, Rosenzweig and Wolpin (1993) presented evidence that the sale of livestock, notably bullocks, is used as a consumption-smoothing device by rural households in India. The market for bullock sales and purchases is well integrated regionally, with 60 percent of bullock sales in the sample villages taking place with buyers outside the village. As a consequence, bullock prices do not seem to vary with village-specific production shocks, an important consideration for choosing an asset that one might have to sell in bad times.

An interesting contrast is provided by Fafchamps, Udry, and Czukas (1998), who examined livestock sales and purchases in Burkina Faso and found very little evidence of a similar phenomenon. What explains the difference in these two sets of findings? Livestock markets in rural Burkina Faso, which is much less densely populated than India, are less integrated. Furthermore, the more widespread the agricultural shock (in the case of Burkina Faso, the study period included a drought that affected large parts of the country), the more contemporaneous are household decisions to sell livestock, and the lower the efficacy of sales in smoothing consumption.

difficult (chapter 9). Village-based mutual insurance is also limited because the main sources of risk affect the entire community. Informal insurance arrangements thus face a difficult tradeoff. The very factors that make these informal risk-sharing mechanisms work—geographic proximity and social ties—also limit participants' ability to diversify as a way to lower risk.[61]

Building effective institutions for agricultural technology and innovation

Two centuries ago, Thomas Malthus argued that the world would exhaust its food supplies because population grew geometrically but agricultural production grew arithmetically. Technological change has proved Malthus wrong. Agricultural innovations—such as high-yielding seeds, herbicides, fertilizers, agricultural machinery, and resource management techniques—allowed food production growth to outpace population growth. One of the fastest ways to increase agricultural productivity rapidly is the adoption of new agricultural technologies. Rapid productivity growth boosts farmer incomes and helps farmers manage risk.

Figure 2.3
Financial performance of generalized agricultural insurance programs

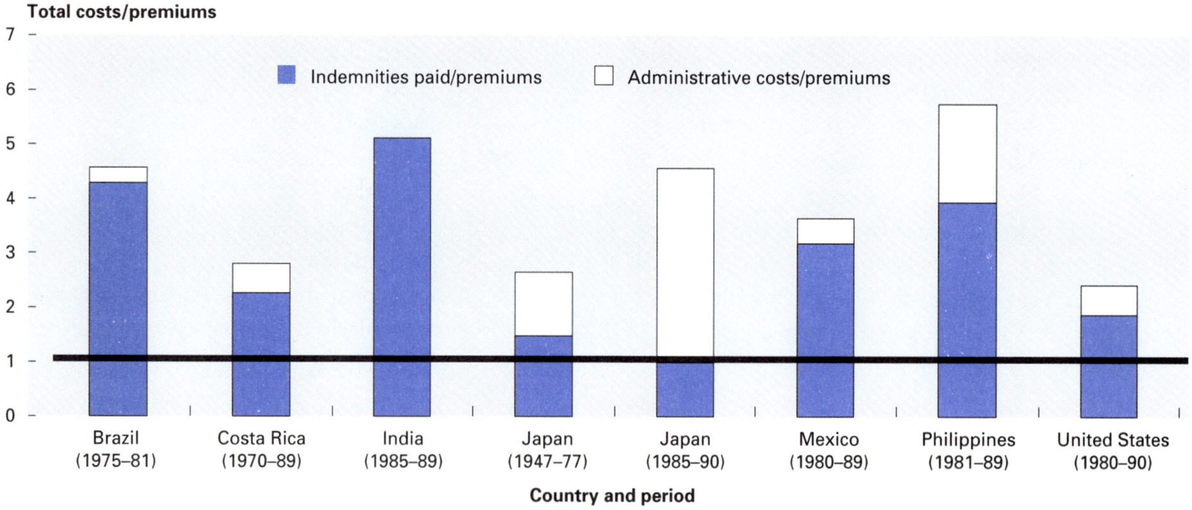

Note: The height of the bars indicates the sum of indemnities and administrative costs as a ratio to premiums collected. For premiums to fully cover costs, this ratio should not exceed one. The figure for India does not include the 1989 rabi season, and data for administrative costs are not available. For Japan data are for paddy only, and administration cost data are based on 1989 only. For Mexico figures are for crop insurance only.
Source: Hazell 1992.

The Green Revolution in South Asia during the 1960s and 1970s illustrates the benefits of agricultural technology. During the Green Revolution small farmers dramatically increased their productivity by adopting high-yielding rice and wheat varieties and using complementary inputs of irrigation and fertilizer. The Green Revolution also generated secondary income effects for landless households.[62] More generally, new technologies have more than doubled global crop yields over the last four decades.[63] Between 1965 and 2000 productivity gains in output per hectare of cereal crops averaged 71 percent globally.[64]

Research to develop agricultural technologies, as well as extension services to deliver them, generate high social rates of return across regions—usually more than 30 percent (figure 2.4).[65] Newer irrigation management techniques, as well as seeds resistant to drought and to pests, have helped to reduce risk. Finally, as discussed in *World Development Report 2000/2001,* numerous studies show that the poor benefit from advances in agricultural technologies, not only through reduced risk, but also through increased demand for their labor and lower food prices.

Many agricultural technologies have characteristics of public goods. That is, they may be at least partially nonrival (one person's use does not lower another person's benefit from it) and nonexcludable—a person who does not pay for the product can still receive it (table 2.2). Private firms will not supply goods and services based on these technologies because they cannot restrict the benefits from the technologies to only those who paid for them. Farmers may not pay for marketing information, for example, if they are able to receive it free from friends and peers. One study in the United States estimated that between 1975 and 1990 private returns to seed companies were only 10 percent of social returns for nonhybrid seeds.[66]

These problems are compounded by the large externalities associated with new agricultural technologies. For example, a farmer may impose a negative externality on his neighbors by failing to vaccinate his livestock against a disease that then spreads to their herds. Conversely, natural resource management techniques produce positive externalities by protecting the quality of resources for future generations. As the Green Revolution showed, adopting new agricultural technology has significant positive externalities for the rural poor. Finally, the lengthy time needed to develop new technologies and the uncertain payoffs can lead to less private research than would be socially desirable.

Figure 2.4
Median rates of return on agriculture research and extension by region

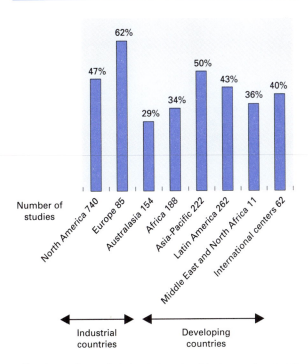

Note: Rates of return include private and social returns on investment for both extension and research programs between 1953 and 1998. *Source:* Alston and others 2000.

Taken together, these characteristics of agricultural technology suggest a need for at least some public involvement in the development and delivery of agricultural technologies. The question is, to what extent and in what form?

Public institutions that have provided agricultural technology are under pressure to reform. Fiscal pressures and criticism for inefficiencies have slowed financial support for public institutions in many countries. Moreover, technological shocks, such as the advent of new biotechnologies, and global movements to strengthen intellectual property rights have focused attention on the role of the private sector in developing agricultural technologies. Liberalization of entry into agricultural research and extension services, as well as increased competition, have strengthened existing institutions and led to innovative institutional designs. Better information sharing between providers and users of technology—often through decentralization and through international arrangements among technology providers—has also improved institutional quality.

International experience has shown that for private goods technologies such as machinery and biotechnology for commercial farms, research and extension services can be left to the private sector. Public involvement is required only for public goods, such as knowledge-based technologies, and where there are strong market failures and externality effects (such as the secondary effects of technology for poor households). Yet even in these cases, public involvement does not necessarily translate into public provision or monopoly. Moreover, in research there are potentially large payoffs from regional collaborations among several countries—particularly for smaller and poorer countries, where research capacity is low and markets are small.

Delivering existing agricultural technologies to farmers

One of the primary barriers to the adoption of new agricultural technology is lack of knowledge.[67] Extension services are an institution aimed at filling this gap. Another major barrier is overregulation of agricultural technology transfer. This section discusses these two factors.

Extension services. The main functions of extension services are twofold: to inform farmers of new products and techniques, and to gather and transfer information from farmers to other participants. This includes collecting feedback on farmer needs as input for research priorities, and learning techniques from one farmer and sharing them with others, for example, irrigation techniques.

In the 1950s and 1960s large-scale extension systems emerged when governments throughout the world invested heavily in services for delivering new agricultural technologies.[68] Estimates show that public sources provide 81 percent of total extension services, with universities, parastatals, and NGOs accounting for 12 percent, and the private sector accounting for only 5 percent. Most of the private sector extension services are provided in industrial countries.[69]

The benefits of extension services are enormous—more than 80 empirical studies have demonstrated that extension services generate rates of return averaging more than 60 percent.[70] Numerous other studies show that extension services substantially improve technology adoption rates, awareness, and productivity.[71] These returns are not only for dissemination of sophisticated technologies. Information sharing on rural technology,

Table 2.2

Where will the private sector invest in agricultural technologies?

Type of good	Public good	Common pool	Toll	Private
Features	Nonexcludable and nonrival	Rival but not excludable	Excludable but nonrival	Excludable and rival
Examples	■ Weather forecasts ■ Market information ■ Livestock management techniques ■ Fertilizer application schedules ■ Natural resource management techniques	■ Self-pollinated seed varieties ■ Shared fishery, common pasture management techniques	■ Soil analysis ■ Farm management computer programs ■ Training courses and private consultation in farm management and production practices	■ Hybrid seeds ■ Biotechnology products (for example, inputs and seeds) ■ Fertilizers, chemicals ■ Agricultural machinery ■ Veterinary supplies
Likelihood of private provision	Very low	Low	Higher	High

Source: Umali-Deininger 1997; World Bank 2000a.

including simple innovations for the poor and illiterate, can have a substantial impact on productivity (box 2.10).

Despite these successes public extension services have been criticized for being inefficient, ineffective, and poorly targeted. In Kenya, for example, an evaluation in 2000 found that government extension services supported by the World Bank did not meet farmer needs and were targeted toward groups that had a low marginal impact on overall productivity.[72] A 1997 World Bank review of 31 extension projects revealed pervasive problems of inadequate client orientation, weak human resource capacity, and low levels of government commitment.[73]

Some of the problems in public extension services originate from external factors, such as lack of political commitment and dependence on complementary policies. Another problem is that public extension providers are not always made accountable for their actions, and the capacity to manage large and complex extension schemes is limited.[74] Three main types of institutional reform for improving extension services are discussed here—*decentralization, privatization*, and *separation of funding from execution*. Each reform consists of a different combination of public and private involvement. Other important techniques include more participatory approaches and increased use of the media (chapter 10).[75]

While keeping both service delivery and funding within the public ambit, several countries have *decen-*

tralized public extension institutions. This strategy involves transferring responsibility for administrative, fiscal, and political decisions from central to local or regional authorities—usually to government agents but potentially to community groups. By bringing decision-making closer to clients, decentralization can increase information flows, build local capacity, and improve accountability. This in turn can improve efficiency, service quality, and access. After the decentralization of extension in Colombia, costs per farmer fell 10 percent, the area covered by extension services tripled, and the number of beneficiaries more than doubled.[76]

Despite its potential, decentralization of extension services presents three major challenges. A national framework is required to avoid confusion of responsibilities between administrative levels and wide variations in quality. Also, decentralization should not apply uniformly to all extension functions. Some activities, such as policy development, highly specialized technical support, and market information services (in which there are more significant economies of scale), can be conducted more efficiently by centralized authorities. Finally, local governments may lack capacity to implement these new institutional responsibilities. (For example, in the Philippines inadequate linkages between research and extension services were exacerbated by decentralization.)[77]

A second strategy is the *privatization of public extension services.* The private sector is likely to invest in dis-

Box 2.10

Creating an information-sharing network for the poor: SRISTI in India

In Gujarat, India, a seven-year-old NGO, SRISTI, has pioneered a pathbreaking way for poor farmers to tap into the innovations of their compatriots in the 5,500 villages scattered across the state. Volunteer workers armed with laptop computers travel from village to village searching for low-cost innovations that can improve the earning power or quality of life for poor villagers. Innovations covered in the SRISTI database include an eminently affordable (less than $10) shoulder-carried pump that can be used to spray the small fields that most poor farmers cultivate and a small stopper that, when attached to rope-and-pulley systems in wells, allows women to rest during the fatiguing process of drawing water. These innovations are catalogued in a database and then circulated through a quarterly newsletter. Work is under way to disseminate the database on-line, with villagers retrieving information through kiosks. To improve access for the illiterate, the kiosks can provide data through a voice interface. By directly addressing the informational constraint faced by dispersed rural communities, SRISTI has a tangible impact on easing the burden of poverty for its constituents.

Source: Slater 2000.

Box 2.11

Private sector extension services in Argentina

During the 1970s the productivity of Argentine dairy farming was seriously hampered by poor cattle nutrition and poor farm hygiene. Faced with unstable supply and quality problems, the two largest dairy processors—Santa Fe–Cordoba United Cooperatives (SANCOR) and La Serenisima—established extension services for their suppliers. SANCOR's program included financing for agronomist technical assistance, farm visits, artificial insemination services, and accelerated heifer-rearing programs. By 1990, 120 farmers' groups were participating in the program, and each group had assumed responsibility for the cost of technical assistance. La Serenisima created 25 extension branch offices, each of which provided technical assistance to groups of up to 25 medium-to-large-scale farmers. La Serenisima's program also made extensive use of press and broadcasting media to inform farmers of livestock management techniques.

The results of these private extension efforts were extremely positive. Although the number of dairy farms supplying SANCOR decreased by 24 percent, milk production increased by 15 percent between 1976 and 1985. Milk production for La Serenisima jumped by almost 50 percent despite a 6 percent decrease in dairy farm areas of suppliers.

Source: Umali-Deininger 1997; World Bank 1989a.

semination of goods where knowledge is embodied in the technology itself—for example, in hybrid seeds. The private sector is also better able to extract a return from extension services in commercial farming, even for technologies with public goods characteristics. As illustrated in Argentine dairy farming, private agroprocessing and marketing firms that contract with farmers may provide extension services for knowledge-based technologies as well as for private goods (box 2.11).

Privatization of extension services has enhanced competition and helped develop more effective institutions. For example, partial privatization in the Netherlands reduced overhead expenditure by 50 percent and increased farmer satisfaction ratings by 40 percent.[78] Commercial providers are not the only solution. Institutions for collective action such as farmers' associations have played a central role in delivering extension services—as in the Central African Republic in the early 1970s.[79] Complete privatization, however, can lead to underprovision of public goods or make extension services unaffordable for small and subsistence farmers, as was the case in Chile in the 1970s.[80]

Separating *public provision of extension with private funding* usually involves charging farmers a fee to cover a portion of the cost of the extension service and has the obvious benefit of cost recovery. This type of institutional design may also increase competition by encouraging alternative providers to enter the extension market. Moreover, the fee payment increases the accountability of service providers to farmers. An innovative approach in Nicaragua that introduced paid extension services significantly improved cost-effectiveness and led to a more responsive service. Even poor farmers purchased extension services.[81]

The separation of funding from execution can also take the form of *private provision with public funding*. The main advantage of this separation is to stimulate competition among private sector providers to improve efficiency and service quality. Contracting private providers in specific functions of extension has proved a successful reform strategy in countries ranging from Estonia to Madagascar. In Nicaragua the government has financed extension services by issuing to farmers vouchers for extension services that could be redeemed with either private or publicly provided extension.[82]

Deregulation of input markets. Institutional obstacles often restrict the delivery of new technology. Although most industrial countries have liberalized agricultural technology markets, governments in developing countries tend to overregulate the transfer of agricultural technologies. This is particularly the case in seed markets, but it also applies in markets for machinery, fertilizers, low-risk pesticides, and feed mix.[83] Overregulation is of special concern in developing countries, since it creates opportunities for corruption in less transparent environments and may hinder innovation.

Several types of barriers are applied. First, many developing countries restrict competition, by limiting channels for the introduction of inputs to parastatal monopolies or by controlling market entry. Second, governments have introduced complex systems for testing, approval, and release of new varieties. In particular, compulsory registration and certification of seed varieties, often designed on the basis of public seed-breeding programs, are unsuited to testing seeds from private plant-breeding programs.[84] Finally, key channels for technology transfer, such as trade, technology licensing, and foreign direct investment, are often restricted in developing countries.

Removal of various regulatory barriers and introduction of more flexible standards encourages greater private sector participation in both research and distribution. A powerful illustration of these effects took place in Turkey during the 1980s, when deregulation of the government seed production and sales monopoly (supported by the World Bank) significantly increased introduction of new seed technologies. As a result the returns to maize yields increased by 50 percent and income per hectare rose by $153—equivalent to an annual net economic gain of $79 million.[85] Similar examples exist in the deregulation of agricultural machinery markets in Bangladesh, seed markets in Peru, and agricultural input markets in Zimbabwe.[86]

Besides reducing import and entry barriers to agricultural technologies, competition and information flows are stimulated by (a) introducing voluntary seed certification systems, supported by incentives for certification and enforcing strict disclosure laws for information on seeds and other agricultural inputs; (b) introducing voluntary seed varietal registration or, as an interim measure, introducing automatic registration for seeds approved in selected other countries; and (c) maintaining only those regulations that address genuine public health and environmental externality concerns, but not on the grounds of protecting farmers from potential misinformation.

Developing new technologies for agriculture in developing countries

Research to develop agricultural products presents fundamental institutional challenges. First, it is often long-term and risky and can require significant human resource capacity. Also, agricultural technologies often have public goods characteristics and generate externalities. Third, there is a tension between economies of scale in research and development (R&D) and the need for location-specific technologies. The existence of economies of scale in R&D suggests that research activities should be concentrated. But many agricultural products must be tailored to local conditions, such as climatic and soil conditions—a fact that suggests a need for fragmentation in research. For example, frost-resistant wheat developed for Canadian farmers is of little value to farmers in Sudan. This effect is compounded by the information gaps between researchers and users, which suggests that research institutes need to have effective communication with end users, often through physical proximity.

In developing countries, the demand for location-specific technologies may be too small to attract private sector investment, as evidenced by the lower levels of such investment (both absolute and relative to gross domestic product) in developing countries (figure 2.5).[87] Similarly, patterns of research expenditure indicate that most private R&D on agricultural seed focuses on development products with longer shelf life, herbicide resistance, and greater suitability for mass production

Figure 2.5
Agricultural research intensity, public and private, 1993

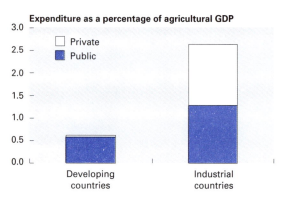

Source: Pardey and Beintema 2001.

techniques. In contrast, developing country priorities are often greater nutritional content and robustness.[88] With some exceptions, notably in research for export crops, the private sector invests little in adapting technologies to local conditions or refining agricultural resource management techniques in developing countries. These are areas of high social returns.[89]

Location-specific technologies for developing countries are more likely to require public intervention and local research or adaptation. Three main institutions affect innovation in agriculture: intellectual property rights, agricultural research institutions, and competitive grants and negotiated contracts.[90]

Intellectual property rights and private sector research. Intellectual property rights (IPRs) protect the rents from innovation by regulating replication. R&D costs of developing some agricultural technologies are high compared with technologies in some other industries. For example, it is estimated that new plant protection chemicals cost more than $150 million to develop.[91] Also, private firms are less able to appropriate the returns from agricultural technologies than from those in many other industries. In agriculture, products can be readily imitated through reverse engineering, or seeds can be bred and resold.

Yet much of the empirical evidence on the benefits of IPRs is inconclusive (see chapter 7 and *World Development Report 1998/1999*). Critics note that numerous agricultural inventions were made without the protection of IPRs, even for private goods. Also, the protection conferred by IPRs is highly limited for some technologies—it would be difficult for a technology producer to enforce IPRs against a heterogeneous group of small farmers who save and replant seeds for their own use. Because of this, private sector investment has concentrated more on seeds with built-in protection for intellectual property. Examples include genetically transformed seeds that will not germinate after the first crop and hybrid seed technology that increases yields and resistance by combining varieties so that the seeds do not breed true and subsequent crops do not perform as well.

The lack of empirical evidence on the benefits of IPRs and the problems with their enforcement raise questions about whether IPRs create value. A more serious concern is that IPRs may impose substantial costs on developing countries. IPRs balance the need to create incentives for innovation with the need to ensure fair access to new technologies. If IPRs are excessively strong, they can reduce access to agricultural inventions by increasing prices, as documented by various studies, and can potentially enable restrictive business practices.[92] In this scenario, poorer farmers in developing countries will not have access to wealth-enhancing opportunities because they will be unable to afford new technologies. Furthermore, technology development could be hindered when new products are dependent on many other IPRs, raising the costs of innovation. The genetically modified "golden rice," which has the potential to alleviate vitamin A deficiency, a major cause of blindness and immune dysfunction in poorer countries, is reported to be developed with technologies protected by up to 70 patents from 31 different organizations.

Two main strategies can help ensure that IPRs maintain incentives for innovation but do not restrict access to new agricultural technologies in developing countries. The first strategy concerns the type of IPR system that is implemented. Under the 1994 Trade-Related Aspects of Intellectual Property Rights Agreement (TRIPS), which sets minimum standards for IPRs in member countries of the World Trade Organization, two types of plant variety protection systems are permitted—patent protection, or a *sui generis* system (meaning a design unique to the context).[93]

The difference between these two options is vast. Under a *sui generis* system, farmers can replant seeds saved from a previous crop, but under a patent system they are generally prohibited from doing that. Similarly, a *sui generis* system allows breeders to use seeds freely as they research new plant varieties; a patent usually forbids such use. By choosing the option of a *sui generis* system over patents, therefore, countries can help to maximize farmer and breeder access to new plant varieties. Argentina, Chile, and Uruguay are examples of countries that have already successfully implemented *sui generis* systems with clauses to help protect farmers' access to plant varieties.

The second strategy being followed is to build the capacity to manage intellectual property. This approach is also relevant for public research institutes in industrial countries, where intellectual property has required these institutions to invest in resources, appropriate policies, and systems to manage it. In developing countries, managing intellectual property includes seeking partnerships and development assistance from private technology producers.

Some successful examples of capacity building exist. The Kenyan Agriculture Research Institute (KARI) and Monsanto established a partnership to develop virus-resistant sweet potatoes, with Monsanto providing royalty-free licensing of intellectual property, direct funding, basic research components, and technical assistance for KARI to develop and test the product in preparation for its release in 2002.[94] In Mexico a multinational corporation contracted to sell intellectual property to large-scale farmers in the lowlands but donated the technology to small, poor farmers in the highlands. In both cases, the private firms enhanced their public relations image at little opportunity cost, since neither Kenyan nor highland Mexican farmers would have purchased the technologies without the donation.

The potential of these arrangements is limited, however, because they apply almost exclusively to segments of markets, such as marginal farming areas or markets in small and poor countries, that would not support a private sector return. The arrangements also require significant negotiating power and are highly unlikely to be sustained if farmers develop the capacity to pay for technologies.

Public research institutions. Agricultural technology markets in developing countries often cannot support private sector returns, even with IPRs, and there are public goods and externality effects. So some level of public sector involvement is required. One such form of involvement is public agricultural research institutes. Currently, national agricultural research institutes (NARIs) account for a large share of agricultural research activity in almost every country and yield high returns on investment (see figure 2.5).

Despite this record, public research institutes are under pressure to reform. They have been criticized for stifling competition by crowding out efforts of the commercial sector. Furthermore, two types of information asymmetries—those among public research institutes themselves and between the institute and the farmer—have caused waste. One study revealed that 40 percent of African wheat-breeding programs would have generated higher returns by screening and adapting foreign wheat varieties rather than by locally breeding new varieties. Open information sharing could help build better institutions. Public research institutions have also faced widespread criticism for lacking information on farmer needs and the incentives to respond to those needs.[95]

These pressures for institutional reform are reinforced by a global slowdown in rates of public agricultural research investment over the last two decades.[96] Some NARIs have faced drastic cuts; in Russia, for example, funding for some agricultural research institutes plummeted by more than 50 percent during the 1990s.[97]

Two strategies have proved effective in addressing the competition and informational problems facing many public research institutions. These are to clarify the public research mandate, and to introduce mechanisms for information sharing among stakeholders in research.

Under the first strategy, specific priorities and responsibilities for the public sector, based upon public goods and externalities issues, are identified. Key areas for public sector research include plant breeding for crops and environments that are overlooked by the private sector but that will generate social returns, and public research where the primary products are information and advice, such as resource management techniques and prebreeding products.[98] Malaysia, Zimbabwe, and the Maghreb countries are all examples where NARIs are refocusing on smallholders rather than commercial market needs for these reasons.[99] By contrast, refocusing on commercial markets in China weakened public agricultural research output and productivity.[100]

The second strategy is to build more effective institutions through open information sharing. Several institutional changes can help address information gaps between technology developers and farmers. For example, farmer representation on governance committees can help to ensure that information on farmer needs is incorporated in research. Successful examples exist in Mali and Zimbabwe. Another approach involves farmers in testing and adapting new products. This helps to refine technologies that meet user needs and can also increase awareness and therefore dissemination of new technologies. For example, farmer testing was a factor in the rapid adoption of the West African Rice Development Association's drought-resistant rice varieties in Guinea.[101]

Strengthening the links between extension and research services is another way to improve information flows to researchers about farmers' needs and to farmers about new technologies (box 2.12). Research-extension links have, however, had a mixed record of success. In China a pilot scheme to establish research-

Box 2.12
Increasing information flows between farmers and researchers in Ghana

Historically, different government ministries in Ghana were responsible for agricultural research and extension services. In the late 1990s efforts began to strengthen these linkages. Liaison committees composed of research and extension workers were established in each major agroecological zone. Each committee was charged with producing joint plans for research and extension activities and for conducting joint training sessions, field visits, and on-farm trials. Already, evaluations show that these organizational links have led to more collaboration and information sharing between research and extension, although at a cost of time-consuming meetings and with problems of low monitoring capacity.

Source: World Bank 2000a.

Box 2.13
International spillovers and the CGIAR

The Consultative Group on International Agricultural Research (CGIAR) exemplifies an institutional mechanism for encouraging international spillovers. The system was established in 1971 under the leadership of the World Bank in response to widespread concern about food security. The 16 research centers of the CGIAR are trustees of more than 600,000 samples of genetic resources—the largest collection in the world. By enabling free public and private access to these resources, the CGIAR system helps ensure that the benefits from these genetic resources are shared across the world. More than 50 percent of wheat varieties and 30 percent of maize varieties released in developing countries are direct transfers from the CGIAR system—and these figures have doubled over the last 20 years as a result of CGIAR efforts. The influence of CGIAR is even greater when local adaptations of technologies originating from the CGIAR system are considered. Approximately 30 percent of new rice, wheat, and maize varieties released in developing countries are adapted to local conditions from CGIAR parent varieties. Partnerships with national agricultural research institutes are also proving fruitful: research collaboration between CIMMYT, a CGIAR center, and South Africa resulted in maize varieties for poor farmers with 30 to 50 percent higher yields.

Source: Byerlee and Traxler 2001; CGIAR 2001.

extension centers enhanced information sharing between researchers and farmers. By contrast, a 1997 evaluation of research-extension links in Bangladesh found no change in the responsiveness of researchers to user needs.[102] More successful ventures have provided research and extension staffs with incentives to work together to solve farmers' problems.[103]

User financing for public research can also help to improve information flows between farmers and researchers. User contributions reinforce the implicit contract between public researchers and users, which encourages greater participation in research by farmers, as well as a more client-oriented approach by researchers. This strategy also allows diversification of funding sources.

Another fundamental reform is to make NARIs more autonomous, removing them from direct government control and placing them under new autonomous legal frameworks, with an independent governance structure and more administrative flexibility. Creating autonomous agencies can help to improve information flows by facilitating greater stakeholder participation, both in management decisionmaking and in funding of agricultural research. Autonomous NARIs in some Latin American countries have evolved to resemble private corporations more than government agencies.[104] In practice, however, autonomy rarely achieves the flexibility and stakeholder representation it aims for, largely because of political pressure and flawed implementation (chapter 5). [105]

Finally, sharing information on existing technologies among NARIs generates ideas and improves institutional quality. Public research institutions should focus more on adapting existing foreign technologies to local conditions rather than duplicating existing technologies, as in the wheat-breeding example mentioned above.[106] Promising developments in this direction are the recent initiatives to establish consortiums and contracting arrangements between NARIs and international research agencies, such as the Consultative Group on International Agricultural Research (CGIAR) (box 2.13).

These cooperative arrangements are especially needed for technology development for countries without the human, physical, and financial capacity for research. Through information sharing, research capacity is leveraged rather than built. Spillovers from international research in those agricultural technologies that are global public goods have been shown to benefit both developing and industrial countries. One study estimated that returns from planting or adapting CGIAR wheat varieties are worth more than $3 billion for the United States alone.[107]

Competitive grant funds and contracting. Just as the separation of public funding from public provision offers benefits by enhancing competition in agricultural extension, so it does in agricultural research—competition helps build better institutions.[108] Competitive grant funds (CGFs) achieve this competition in research by separating the execution of technology development from the funding and determination of research priorities. Allocation of funds to research providers is made on a competitive basis by requesting and reviewing research proposals.

In most developing countries CGFs are relatively new, but they are becoming increasingly popular as a means of allocating public funds. This is particularly so in Latin America, where the availability of research suppliers has enabled substantial increases in funds channeled through competitive grant processes. In the United States, where CGFs have operated for decades, one-sixth of public funding for agricultural research is distributed through competitive grants.[109]

A central advantage of CGFs is that they stimulate competition in innovative activity. Competitive grants allow allocation of resources to the most efficient technology developers and encourage higher-quality research through competition within the private and public sectors. Furthermore, CGFs can be structured to foster open information sharing. For example, requiring joint proposals from providers encourages economies of scale and scope in innovative activity. Adopting demand-driven agendas that require beneficiaries to participate in the design of funded projects increases the relevance of research, as in the case of the Association for Strengthening Agricultural Research in East and Central Africa. Adoption of new technologies can be accelerated by financing joint research and extension projects, as has occurred in Latin America. Finally, CGFs may also encourage more stability in funding by pooling resources from different government departments or industry sources. That is the case in Australia, where multiple government departments and farmers' associations contribute to CGFs.

Experience has shown three main lessons regarding the use of CGFs. First, CGFs should complement, rather than replace, core funding through regular block grants. It is difficult to meet long-term core research needs of many agricultural technologies through CGFs, which, in order to promote competition, are short term in nature (usually three years).[110] Even for long-term core research needs, however, efficiency gains can be re-alized by shifting block grants away from government research institutes to negotiated long-term contracts between public funding institutions and private and public researchers. Although this strategy is still relatively uncommon in practice, Australia and Senegal are examples of countries that are experimenting with such negotiated contracts.[111]

Second, where there are relatively few research providers—as is often the case in small and poor countries—the potential benefits from introducing competition through CGFs are obviously limited. CGFs entail significant fixed administrative costs, reaching up to 20 percent of funds in smaller countries. Objective peer review of grant applications also becomes difficult in countries with small numbers of researchers. Approximately 40 developing countries employ fewer than 25 researchers, and 95 employ fewer than 200 researchers.[112] To overcome these challenges, some countries are beginning to experiment with regional CGFs, such as FONTAGRO in Latin America, which was established to encourage greater competition and more innovative and higher-quality research, facilitate open exchange of information and technology, and build research capacity in the region. A similar example exists in East and Central Africa, and there are plans to establish a CGF for West and Central Africa.

Finally, experience has shown that CGFs are better able to reduce information gaps between farmers and researchers and meet user needs if they have an independent governance body that is representative of stakeholders, including public sector, scientific, and farmers' representatives. Although direct representation of a heterogeneous group of smallholder farmers on CGF selection boards is difficult, intermediary organizations may help to substitute for farmer participation. For example, to promote demand-driven research, the agricultural research center VBKVK in Udaipur, India, requires NGOs that work closely with farmers to participate on the selection boards of CGFs.

Conclusions

Farmers in developing countries can benefit from institutional change that allows them to undertake high-return activities and investments. With the majority of the world's poor living in rural areas and directly or indirectly deriving their incomes from agriculture, such productivity increases can translate into a reduction in poverty for many. Agriculture is still an important economic sector in many of the world's poorest countries, and a more productive farming sector would also boost overall growth.

The sections in this chapter have outlined a range of institutional options to improve productivity—analyzing those reforms that do not work, as well as those that do. Access to markets, local or global, is an important factor affecting demand for market-supporting institutions and the forces for further change in domestic markets. The benefits from many institutional forms relative to the costs increase when demand for agricultural products rises. For example, the relative costs of collective action by private farmers should decline as the opportunities for gain increase. Marketing institutions such as agricultural cooperatives or standards arise in response to such potential gains. Policymakers have a role in connecting markets, but also in facilitating information sharing on initiatives in other countries. The need to replace existing informal agricultural institutions with more formal alternatives depends on the demand for them and on the existence of supporting institutions.

When building institutions, it is critical to keep in mind how institutions can complement each other. Formal land titles are more likely to yield benefits in terms of greater investment if there are also credit institutions, formal registries, and courts to enforce titles efficiently. But credit for poor farmers is affected by their ability to use their assets as collateral as well as by the overall growth of the financial sector. Demand for credit, demand for marketing institutions, and demand for formal titles are also linked to access to new technology and the opportunities it provides for income-increasing investments. A mix of public and private initiatives will be needed to meet the needs of developing countries in terms of diffusion of existing technologies and development of new ones. Taking advantage of the flexibility inherent in TRIPS is also important for developing countries.

Before concentrating efforts on a particular institution, policymakers need to think about the most important constraints for a given context. Often, initial efforts can lead to the buildup of pressures for further change—if the right constraints are identified. As countries and communities grow and change, the types of institutions that work change. Encouraging and being receptive to innovative designs, particularly in poor areas, is essential.

CHAPTER 3

Governance of Firms

Corporations exist to economize the costs of buying and selling everything under the sun.

—Ronald Coase, 1937

In firms, entrepreneurs match their ideas and ability with the resources provided by investors. Throughout history entrepreneurs have found that their ability to pursue investment projects has been hindered by the inevitable time gap between when they gather resources and when they can make payment. Investors—be they workers, suppliers, or financiers—are cautious about committing their resources to the control of an entrepreneur in exchange for a promise or contract.

For the investor, there are two distinct risks. One is the squandering of resources by the entrepreneur; the other is the confiscation of goods by a political power. This chapter focuses on the governance of firms, which is largely a matter of the allocation and exercise of control over resources within firms. A variety of private and public institutions make promises and contracts credible by improving information inflows, defining rights and enforcing them, and affecting competition. These institutions are essential for the mobilization and efficient allocation of resources through firms.

Corporate governance institutions are defined in this Report as the organizations and rules that affect expectations about the exercise of control of resources in firms. Well-functioning governance institutions allow entrepreneurs to invest resources and create value that is shared among the investors in a firm, the managers, and employees, as well as with the entrepreneur/manager. These institutions therefore determine the expected returns to committing resources in firms. Where governance institutions are weak, the emergence and growth of firms are discouraged. Governance institutions include traditional corporate governance mechanisms, such as the board of directors and corporate and bankruptcy laws (chapter 6); product market institutions such as regulators responsible for competition (chapter 7); labor market institutions (discussed in *World Development Report 1995: Workers in an Integrating World*); capital market institutions, such as financial intermediaries (chapter 4); and the judiciary (chapter 6).

Historically, two broad institutional approaches have been used to assure investors that their resources will be put to good use in firms: a *private* and sometimes *informal* approach, and a *legal governance approach*. Both approaches facilitate information flows and create incentives for investors to focus on firm efficiency and to monitor insiders. They aim to give resource providers the power to intervene without incurring heavy transaction costs when entrepreneurs and managers abuse their control.

For an example of the private and informal governance approach, consider the situation in the 12th century, when many governments were weak in much of the world. At the time one of the most promising investment opportunities involved expanding from trade *within* local communities to long-distance trade *across* communities. In the traditional approach entrepreneurs reduced trading risks by relying on self-finance and on family or community members. Private institutions relied on reputational penalties to enforce contracts (chapters 1 and 9). This approach facilitated market development by permitting entrepreneurs to move from a situation of very limited exchange to a situation of some (and occasionally considerable) trade.

The legal governance approach developed the typical firms that emerged from the Industrial Revolution. These firms in later history differed from their predecessors in scale and scope. The standard relationship among firms was hierarchical to ensure coordinated production and marketing. In the 19th and 20th centuries, more formal governance institutions, such as explicit contracts and laws to protect investors, allowed firms to exploit opportunities created by the Industrial Revolution. The development of constitutional and legal systems designed to check arbitrary behavior of public and private agents strengthened property rights. These institutions spurred market development, economic growth, and poverty reduction.

The advantage of the legal governance approach is that it can expand wealth-creating opportunities, making it possible to assemble the significant resources needed for large enterprises and facilitating entry into markets. Identification with a network is not required to pursue opportunities. New entrants do not need to have social connections or large amounts of initial wealth to start a business. This approach relies far more heavily on a state that imposes legal sanctions and enforces contracts. By enabling productivity-enhancing investments, these legal institutions can promote growth and poverty reduction.

A recent study that examined the efficiency of resource allocation by firms shows that not all firms have effective governance. For 65 nonsocialist countries between 1963 and 1996, and for large and small firms with both state and private ownership, the study estimated the average sensitivity of industry investment to industry value added in the manufacturing sector.[1] A high degree of sensitivity would reveal two forces at work. Firms and industries where investment projects yield strong returns as measured by value added would be able to attract added resources, and these industries would expand. By contrast, where past investment projects are now yielding declining returns, as measured by value added, investment would decline and industries would contract.

The findings indicate that in lower-income countries the degree of sensitivity is low, so that investment is much less likely to be affected by changes in value-added (figure 3.1). In Germany, Japan, and the United States the sensitivity of investment to value added is twice as great as in Mexico, three times that of Malaysia, and more than six times that of Bangladesh, India, and Kenya. This compounds the problem for

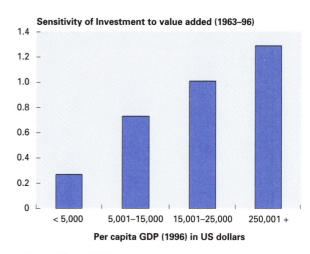

Figure 3.1

Flows of new investment are insensitive to value added in developing countries

Sensitivity of Investment to value added (1963–96)

Per capita GDP (1996) in US dollars

Source: Wurgler 2000.

poorer countries because such investments are critical for higher growth and poverty reduction. Resources are slow to flow to industries that experience increases in their ability to create value and remain for long periods of time in industries where there has been a reduction in the value created. They "underinvest" in growing industries and "overinvest" in declining industries.

Corporate governance institutions, including institutions that provide legal protection for investors, institutions that produce information for investors, and ownership structure of firms, are highly correlated with these measures of the efficiency of investment. After accounting for other factors, the same study finds that an increase in any of these variables increases the sensitivity of resource allocation to changes in value added. For example, better legal protections for investors are highly associated with a greater willingness to curtail new investment flows to industries that experience declines in value added. For a country like Bangladesh, this sensitivity would double for an increase of one standard deviation in any of the institutional variables. This suggests the importance of better firm governance for growth and poverty reduction.

A range of other factors plays a role in creating these differences in the efficiency of investment. The ability of firms to exploit opportunities in some growing industries is limited by differences in macroeconomic conditions, demand conditions, entry restrictions (see chapter 7), and the supply of critical inputs into productive industries. Without denying the importance of such factors, the focus here is on the role of governance institutions for firms.

Formal governance institutions offer long-term benefits. Such institutions increase opportunity for firms by promoting investment in high value added activities. By promoting the growth of firms and employment within firms, these institutions can increase economic growth and reduce poverty. Yet the development of laws, internal governance institutions, well-developed financial and information intermediaries, and effective regulators often faces large obstacles. The effectiveness of these governance institutions depends on the existence of complementary institutions and on capacity. Thus, in poor countries, where there are few limits on arbitrary state actions, weak enforcement of contracts, and poor provision of information, private institutions rather than legal governance institutions are likely to dominate.

Policies that help build political support for legal reforms and create demand for new institutions, such as openness in trade and open information sharing among the different parties affected by reforms, are as important as the specifics of individual reforms. Competition can also increase the efficiency of such private mechanisms and promote institution building. And developing country policymakers will need to be open to innovative approaches by private agents to ensure effective governance.

The chapter begins by looking at the types of firms that exist around the world. It then discusses the presence and effectiveness of private governance institutions, which include ownership concentration, business groups, and business associations, and goes on to identify corporate governance institutions based on formal legal systems, such as boards of directors and corporate and bankruptcy laws. The chapter does not discuss governance of state-owned firms, which was addressed in *World Development Report 1997: The State in a Changing World* and other recent World Bank publications. Issues concerning infrastructure firms are discussed in chapter 8.

What firms around the world look like

The vast majority of enterprises are small in most countries, regardless of their geography or level of development. The importance of small formal sector firms in selected countries is highlighted in table 3.1. Even in

Table 3.1

Share of small formal sector firms in selected economies, selected years

Economy	Year	Percentage		
		Number of firms	Employment	Total output
Australia*	1991	92.0	35.7	23.1
Austria	1990	75.5	20.2	14.6
Belgium	1991	97.2	38.4	50.3
Bulgaria	1997	97.5	18.9	21.8
China*	1991	58.9	6.0	5.2
Colombia*	1993	93.4	40.5	27.4
Croatia	1995	96.9	26.7	34.9
Denmark	1991	98.3	55.4	46.5
France	1990	98.6	46.7	39.0
Georgia	1997	82.0	26.0	42.0
Hong Kong, China	1993	97.8	58.4	53.8
Hungary	1996	98.8	53.1	46.5
India*	1992	76.2	17.3	13.4
Indonesia*	1995	98.7	73.2	28.4
Israel*	1992	93.9	39.4	—
Italy	1989	99.2	63.4	53.9
Japan	1991	98.1	66.5	—
Jordan	1991	93.7	21.5	—
Kazakhstan	1996	87.6	23.9	25.9
Korea, Rep.	1995	98.5	55.3	25.2
Latvia	1996	98.3	41.1	39.8
Lithuania	1996	98.0	43.1	41.8
Netherlands	1990	96.7	49.7	46.5
Norway	1990	81.5	54.8	50.5
Portugal	1991	99.0	48.7	43.7
Romania	1997	97.4	19.5	40.1
Spain	1991	99.4	67.5	—
Sweden	1991	97.6	39.5	41.4
Switzerland	1991	97.5	39.5	—
Turkey*	1992	86.7	28.3	25.7
United Kingdom	1991	98.5	42.1	19.5

*Refers to firms in manufacturing industries only.

— Not available.

Note: Small firms are defined as registered firms with fewer than 50 employees.

Source: World Bank Small and Medium Enterprise Database.

the transition countries, known for their large firms, most firms are small. If informal sector firms were included, the numbers would be even larger.

In small firms, particularly sole proprietorships that rely on internally supplied resources, governance issues are much simpler than in large firms. A study of 54 industrial and developing countries finds that in developing countries, the growth of small and medium-size enterprises is constrained by institutional factors.[2] For smaller firms which have the potential to grow, the willingness and ability to mobilize resources within firms is affected by the presence of an arbitrary or predatory state (for example, firms may start small and remain small to avoid taxation or harassment by the state). The institutions that can help provide checks on the authority of the state are discussed in chapter 5.

Resource mobilization is also affected by the absence of a strong legal system that supports markets, such as a court that ensures that debts are repaid (chapter 6). For smaller firms, private governance institutions play a more important role than formal corporate governance mechanisms in allocating control rights or claims *within* the firm. Other institutions that may facilitate entry and growth of firms relate to competition and regulation, discussed in chapters 6 and 7.

Despite the preponderance of small firms, large enterprises can account for significant fractions of employment and national output (see table 3.1). While the small firm sector includes a large number of firms with widespread entry and exit, large and established firms are more stable across economies. For instance, one study finds that growth in the size of firms accounts for over two-thirds of all industry growth.[3] Much of this chapter is concerned with large firms and those smaller firms that have the potential to grow. It is in these firms that concerns about diversion of resources by insiders and the state are most important.

The vast majority of enterprises are also not publicly traded. Publicly listed firms constitute 0.16 percent of all registered firms in developing countries and 0.55 percent in industrial countries, according to a sample of 37 countries around the world.[4] However, publicly traded firms are still important, as they may account for a significant share of the economy. For example, publicly listed firms account for around 40 percent of value added in the United Kingdom, and for 25 percent of value added in Japan. In developing countries such as Poland and Thailand, publicly traded firms account for 7 and 9 percent of value added, respectively. Although the number of these large firms and of publicly listed firms is small compared with the number of firms, the economic importance of these firms in the economy can be substantial. Because of their size, their performance can also have significant political and social consequences.

Many of the differences in the size of firms depend on the nature of demand and supply of goods and services, as well as differences in government policies such as taxation. Some of these differences, however, arise from differences in the effectiveness of private and formal governance institutions for firms.

Private governance institutions for firms

There are three main kinds of governance institutions that are not formal laws: ownership structures, business groups, and associations. These three institutions affect the amount of information available to all parties involved with a firm, contract enforcement, and accountability of entrepreneurs and managers to those who invest in the firms.

The amount of information available to all parties involved with a firm influences how investment projects are financed. In the absence of full information about the firms and those who control them, investors demand higher returns. Information problems mean it is relatively cheaper for firms to use internally generated capital first, then trade credit, then debt finance (where limited control is given up in exchange for finance), and, last, equity finance (where control rights over the firm are exchanged for finance). Two types of investors usually have an informational advantage compared with others. Investors who by the nature of their transactions with the firm have a better idea of the prospects of the firm, such as suppliers to and buyers from firms, can ensure that entrepreneurs or managers adhere to their commitments. Large investors also have advantages because their large stake in the company gives them voice so that they do not need to rely on elaborate legal protections.

In smaller firms, with concentrated (or sole) ownership, the principal governance issues concern the implicit or explicit contracts that the owners have with traders and suppliers, with employees with firm-specific skills, and with banks and other financial institutions. Suppliers and buyers extend credit to their business partners. The provision of trade credit embodies implicit contracts; purchasers expect the debtor firm to produce the goods at a certain price, quality, and quantity.[5] Evidence from a sample of 40 industrial and developing countries indicates that there is less reliance on trade credit and more reliance on other forms of credit when the country's legal system is well developed. This suggests that the comparative advantage of nonfinancial firms in providing credit is likely to be smaller when well-developed alternatives exist.[6]

As the size of firms increases, day-to-day control and overall management are delegated to nonowners. The division between owners and managers makes governance issues more complicated. Looking across time in individual countries, there is a correlation between the strength of institutions that support information flows and provide legal leverage to the nature of financiers, and ownership structures. The United States today has one of the strongest and most effective legal protections for equity investors. In the 19th century, before these institutions had developed, the financing and ownership of firms differed dramatically from current patterns. Before 1873, for example, the only investors that owned simple equity were founders and sponsoring banks. Bank representatives on corporate boards provided a low-cost monitoring system for the large equity investors. Individual investors, aware of these concerns, limited their involvement to holding corporate debt or preferred stock that had debt-like features.[7]

How ownership concentration affects governance

In lower-income countries, firm ownership tends to be highly concentrated. Large firms controlled by management and owned by a diverse group of small shareholders are the exception rather than the rule.[8] There is a relationship between ownership structure and the strength of legal institutions across countries, with concentrated ownership tending to substitute for weak legal protections.[9] Concentrated ownership gives investors information and control and so ensures that their resources are used in their interests. Concentrated owners have the ability to halt the diversion of resources without having to resort to courts. In high-income countries, with stronger legal protections, ownership is more dispersed. But this is not uniformly the case. Countries such as Germany and Sweden, which have strong legal protections, nonetheless have concentrated ownership structures, but there firms have more choice with respect to governance and dispute resolution mechanisms (chapter 6).

The primary advantage of more concentrated ownership is that it motivates the shareholders to monitor the managers of the firm *and* provides the owners with leverage over the managers. But with concentrated ownership, governance problems may arise between different categories of investors—such as minority and majority shareholders. Majority shareholders may act in ways that reduce the share of gains going to minority shareholders; they may pursue private benefits.

Evidence suggests that concentrated ownership delivers greater benefits when those owners in control have appropriate incentives and when owners outside the firm have more leverage. A study of firms in East Asian economies, for example, found that the market placed a higher value on those firms whose controlling

shareholder had a larger equity stake.[10] With larger equity stakes, the controlling shareholders' wealth is more directly linked to the performance of the firm. Cross-country work also provides evidence that investors are willing to pay more for assets when, besides a controlling shareholder, there are legal protections that grant shareholders, regardless of their size, rights over the allocation of resources and returns.[11] Legal protections complement concentrated ownership and enhance firms' access to external finance. They enhance the firms' ability to fund more promising investment projects. The potential negative effects of concentrated ownership can also be reduced by introducing competition in markets (chapter 7) and by ensuring the exit of underperforming firms (see the discussion below).

Ownership structures in privatization: lessons for corporate governance. The spread of privatization programs around the world has been propelled by the inefficiency of state-owned firms and the resulting search for significant improvements in performance. But there have been disappointments, particularly in the transition economies. Squandering and diversion of resources by political actors have often been replaced by squandering and diversion of resources by private actors. This has raised a new question about privatization: how to ensure that it produces benefits. It has become clear that competition and regulation are essential complements to successful privatization (chapters 7 and 8). This section focuses on how differences in corporate governance institutions also help to explain differences in privatization outcomes.

Ownership structures chosen at the time of privatization by political actors reflect economic and political concerns. The two predominant approaches to privatization are to use public share offerings, which are more likely to result in wide share ownership, or asset sales, which are usually associated with the sale of a majority stake to a single investor or to a consortium. Voucher privatization, used in some transition economies, like public share offerings, introduces more widely held firms than direct asset sales.

In most countries, the choice of privatization method has been linked to the strength of formal corporate governance protections. Both the strength of legal protections for minority investors and the extent of checks and balances on political actors—which enhances enforcement of legal protections—have a significant impact on the privatization route, according to a recent study of 49 industrial and developing countries.[12] Countries with weaker legal protections have been more likely to use asset sales. But even though the initial level of legal protections was low, several of the transition economies used voucher privatizations as their primary form of sale.

In countries where initial institutional quality was high, privatization has been associated with significant improvements in institutional quality. A study finds that privatization has had a significant impact on stock market development around the world.[13] The market capitalization of privatized enterprises now exceeds $2.5 trillion. Such enterprises are the largest companies in 17 of the 23 emerging markets in the study. These firms are of sufficiently high profile and political importance that they can lead the way in improving corporate governance structures. Evidence of actual or potential abuses of authority in such firms has been a driving force behind legal reforms.

The counterbalance to these positive developments is the indication that in countries with weak institutional quality at the initial stage, formal governance institutions have not developed and those that have developed have been difficult to sustain. For example, a World Bank study of stock market development in transition economies shows that privatization policies that relied on the development of formal corporate governance institutions for effectiveness, by compelling firms to list on stock exchanges as part of the privatization process, have not succeeded in developing markets.[14] In mass privatization countries—such as Bulgaria, Lithuania, and the Former Yugoslav Republic of Macedonia—many of the stocks were illiquid, and stock market regulators, to the extent they were available, could not monitor adherence to listing standards. These problems have resulted in significant delisting of shares, reports of abuses of minority shareholders, and a subsequent concentration of control. Following an initial increase in the number of listed firms, there has been a steady decline.

More promising, from the perspective of long-term trends in stock market development, have been initial public offerings (IPOs) in countries such as Croatia, Hungary, Poland, and Slovenia, which sold a smaller number of stocks. Some hybrid countries used both methods. A recent study finds that in transition economies the strongest performance improvements are associated with firms that have concentrated ownership structures, particularly when the concentrated owner is foreign.[15] The study estimates that the impact on performance is eight times greater for foreign ownership than for widely held firms.

Recent experience in Latin America illustrates the difficulty of relying on privatized firms to spur institutional development. Initial sales of shares in companies brought with them significant portfolio investments, diversified ownership structures, and increased stock market development. But the governance institutions have not been sufficiently strong to maintain these ownership structures, particularly in light of abuses by controlling shareholders. In recent years ownership structures have changed, with foreign companies assembling controlling majority stakes.

Business groups

Many business opportunities are exploited through firms affiliated with business groups, which are a group of companies that do business in different markets under a common administrative or central control.[16] Members of business groups may be small, medium-size, or large firms, although large firms usually dominate the groups. Equity holdings across companies and common directors provide a coordinating mechanism within groups, but ties among group members are also made through family and social relations.

Business groups exist across the world. The *keiretsu* in Japan, *chaebol* in the Republic of Korea, *grupos economicos* in Latin America, and business groups in China and India are examples of ways to organize and conduct business along different lines, outside and around the formal market mechanisms. A study of 14 developing countries provides some systematic evidence of the importance of group-affiliated firms.[17] The findings for publicly listed firms on which financial information is available is displayed in figure 3.2. The study finds that group-affiliated firms dominate the business landscape, controlling on average more than 52 percent of reported assets in 1990 and 59 percent in 1997 in these countries.

Business groups are central to the process of resource allocation within firms in developing countries. Despite advances in financial and trade liberalization, the dominance of group-based resource allocation has not diminished over time. World Bank research provides evidence of how economic power is concentrated in relatively few hands through business groups. In Japan the top 15 families control less than 3 percent of the GDP value of listed corporate assets. The contrast with lower-income countries in East Asia such as Indonesia, the Philippines, and Thailand is striking. Here the top 15 families account for more than 50 percent of listed cor-

Figure 3.2
Proportion of assets in publicly traded firms accounted for by group-affiliated firms

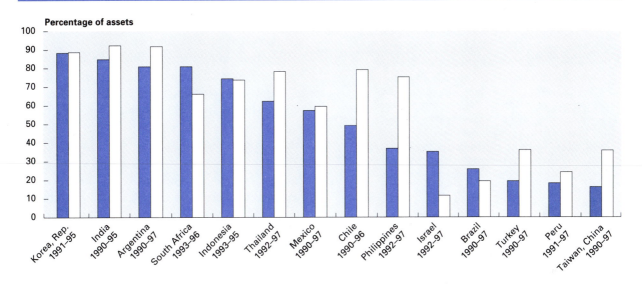

Source: Khanna and Rivkin 2001.
Note: This exhibit is derived from the data used and described in Khanna and Rivkin 2000. The authors used all available data in each reference year, but financial information was not available for some listed companies.

porate assets and more than 20 percent of GDP in each country.[18]

The creation of business groups can be viewed as a private response to institutional weaknesses in markets. For example, without strong financial and information intermediaries, capital markets work poorly at pricing risk and providing a source of capital for investment. Group-affiliated firms, in principle, can create an internal capital market, financing new firms and cushioning members during financial downturns. In the absence of functioning markets for corporate control, group affiliation can also coordinate the replacement of underperforming management teams. In countries where active executive labor markets do not exist, internal labor markets within groups can match management talent with assets.

On the negative side, where groups dominate business, there may be little competition among those who control resources, since information and control rest with a few centrally located actors. If these people are not skilled or well motivated, resource allocation will suffer and they might extract funds for personal gain from the firms they control. Group-affiliated firms are often affiliated with banks and may be able to attract a major share of enterprise financing to the exclusion of outside enterprises. The interests of groups may also

conflict with the interests of social welfare. The economic power of groups translates into political power, and that power can be used to extract preferential treatment from political agents or to block reforms.

There is evidence to support both views of business groups. If it is true that group affiliation is a response to weaknesses in markets, it should be possible for group firms to expand their scope of activity quite broadly through diversification. Evidence from Chilean and Indian firms suggests that diversified business groups can deliver superior performance compared with nonaffiliated businesses when the groups are large enough. For example, firms associated with the most diversified Indian business groups outperformed focused unaffiliated firms by 22 percent but outperformed firms in moderately diversified business groups by 43 percent.[19] Groups also appear to play an important role in exploiting new business opportunities in some settings. This is consistent with earlier evidence from Japan, which showed the ability of group-affiliated firms to operate internal capital markets. The Toyota automobile company started off as an offshoot of a business group that was focused on creating machinery for the textile industry. Recent studies of 14 countries with significant business groups examined whether such groups systematically filled in for gaps in capital markets

Box 3.1
Business groups and restrictions on competition in Kazakhstan

Over the latter part of the 1990s, many large and medium-size enterprises in Kazakhstan came under the control of five national-level business groups and multiple regional groups with political connections. The concentration of economic power in these business groups has created the incentives and the ability to lobby government agencies and public officials for preferential treatment, in such areas as trade restrictions, non-market-based financing, preferential public contracts, and protection from new entrants. Bank financing is often directed to these firms, but repayment is not enforced. As a result, state governments often pay indirectly for these loans.

Business interests with political clout have also used their power to harass competing firms. One illustrative case is described in a recent report commissioned by the U.S. Agency for International Development. A local entrepreneur had established a profitable small hotel. But a new hotel, whose owner had political influence, opened close to the existing one. Soon after, the local sanitary inspector closed the first hotel, claiming that the supply of running water on the premises was inadequate. The experience, however, ended on a positive note. After two years of court battles and the intervention of the regional governor, the first hotel was reopened.

Source: Djankov and Nenova forthcoming.

and delivered superior performance. There was significantly better financial performance in group-affiliated firms in six of the countries, significantly worse in three, and no significant effect in five countries.

There is also evidence that group affiliation can be associated with negative outcomes, particularly when groups are controlled by entrepreneurs with weak incentives or ability. In Russia and Kazakhstan a few groups have been able to dominate many industries and foreclose financing and business opportunities for other entrepreneurs (box 3.1). In East Asian economies the market has placed a lower value on firms where the controlling shareholder had control through group structure but lower equity stakes.[20] Lower market value in such group-affiliated firms implies higher cost of access to external finance from non–group members. But the continued existence of such structures implies that the benefits of group membership to firm owners must outweigh these costs.

The key policy question is how to increase the benefits that business groups bring while lowering the costs. Policies to open firms to domestic and interna-

tional competition are one obvious answer. Access to export markets provides a greater incentive for group-affiliated firms to focus on efficiency—which highlights the importance of institutions that improve product market competition (chapter 7).

Experience also suggests that capital market openness can reduce the potential costs imposed by business groups while allowing firms to capture benefits from membership. In India, for example, firms with foreign institutional investors performed better than those with domestic institutional investors. In Canada the capital and labor market liberalization following the passage of the North American Free Trade Agreement between the United States and Canada has attenuated some of the costs associated with firms run by family members and has also begun to reduce the dominance of these structures.[21]

Formal business associations and informal networks
Business associations—voluntary, long-term, renewable partnerships among firms—are another set of private institutions that can facilitate exchange and the expansion of business activity. They do this by improving information flows, enhancing reputational penalties, and lowering the costs of dispute resolution. Relative to alternative private approaches, such as business groups or ethnic-based trading associations (chapters 1 and 9), these organizations are more inclusive and adaptable to changes in the surrounding environment.

Business associations are widespread in many industrial and developing countries. In some cases governments have mandated membership.[22] In Brazil during the 1930s, for example, the government created compulsory associations for both labor and businesses. By the mid-1970s, the business sector had also created many voluntary associations, sometimes parallel to the government-created ones. By the mid-1980s most large and medium-size businesses in Brazil belonged to several associations.[23]

The characteristics of business associations vary greatly across countries. In some cases business associations are industry-focused, while in other cases as in the transition economies, they cut across industries. In some cases membership in associations may be mandatory. In general, however, the observed high levels of membership arise largely from voluntary integration of firms into business associations.

A handful of studies have attempted to explore whether business associations perform socially beneficial functions.[24] Cross-country comparisons indicate that business associations perform a variety of functions. These can be grouped into market-supporting and market-complementing and -substituting functions.[25]

■ *Market-supporting functions:* Business associations operate as a counterpart in dialogue with the government. They channel and coordinate an individual firm's efforts in lobbying for the improved provision of public goods, such as protection of property rights, better public administration, and infrastructure.

■ *Market-complementing and -substituting functions:* Business associations operate in parallel with existing institutions by providing alternative private solutions for market failures. For example, they lower the costs of acquiring information on potential trading partners and provide a means to coordinate and amplify penalties for breach of contract (box 3.2).[26]

Cross-country comparisons suggest that the role of business associations may change as markets develop. For example, in Russia basic trading information is a critical input for enterprises, and business associations have specialized in providing and diffusing information. In the more stable institutional environment of Bolivia, business associations have other functions. These include business counseling for new enterprises and, for older enterprises, matching prospective employees with employers. Bolivian associations facilitate the establishment of small start-ups: the average number of days necessary to open a new business is 41 for members, but almost 65 days for nonmembers. At the same time, associations reduce labor search costs for medium-size enterprises: the average number of days required to fill a vacancy is 36 for a member, compared with 51 for a nonmember.

Business associations are more effective when they provide well-defined benefits to members, have high membership density, and have an effective internal interest-mediation system.[27] These conditions, however, are not sufficient to guarantee effectiveness. Two external constraints—a competitive environment and appropriate discipline by the state in refraining from discriminatory behavior and corruption—promote effective associations.

When formal legal systems that support information flows and accountability are underdeveloped, a careful evaluation of corporate responses such as ownership concentration and business groups is needed. Concentrated ownership and business groups can substitute for

Box 3.2
Business associations and trade credit

Extending trade credit to a potential buyer involves risk. Membership in organizations that facilitate the sharing of information on potential buyers can help reduce this risk and promote a firm's growth.

A study of five transition economies—Poland, Romania, Russia, Slovakia, and Ukraine—using firm-level data suggests that membership translates into better trade credit terms, especially for business relationships older than two months. A study on Kenya and Zimbabwe shows a similar effect, with potential buyers identified through business networks more likely to receive trade credit than other customers. Firm-level data on Vietnam provides added evidence on the role of business networks as information-sharing mechanisms, with the relationships established through these networks facilitating better access to trade credit. Firm-level data suggest that business associations and arbitration courts are substitute mechanisms for resolving disputes between trading firms.

Source: Johnson and others 2000; Fafchamps 1999; McMillan and Woodruff 1999a; Hendley, Murrell, and Ryterman (2000).

formal institutions in providing the functions of governance. But competition in markets and the threat of bankruptcy are necessary complements, to provide checks and balances for those who control resource allocation within firms. Steps to eliminate these structures without addressing weaknesses in formal institutions are unlikely to succeed. Even if they were to succeed, it is not clear what the benefits would be in the absence of an alternative functioning governance framework. From this perspective, the goal of those aiming to improve corporate governance should be to address the underlying market failure, to facilitate conditions where networks are beneficial and to develop alternatives, to introduce competition into the economy, and to enhance openness in trade and information flows.

Laws and formal intermediaries

With formal corporate governance institutions, there can be specialization in delivering the functions of governance. Some institutions, such as disclosure laws, auditing firms, and financial and information intermediaries, focus on bridging information gaps. Other institutions, such as corporate and bankruptcy laws and their associated enforcement institutions, specialize in lowering the costs of dispute resolution. Yet other institutions, such as boards of directors, specialize in managing remaining incentive problems stemming from information gaps between entrepreneurs and managers.

For these formal governance institutions to operate effectively, several related conditions must be met. The information available to resource providers must be timely, accurate, and reliable, and in a form that regulators and investors alike can understand. The laws that limit the authority of entrepreneurs or managers must be enforced efficiently by competent and impartial judges (chapter 6). The demands on the state increase with greater reliance on formal institutions. Not only do state actors directly determine the costs of dispute resolution, but state actors are closely involved in bridging information gaps by setting specific standards and by affecting the incentives of private information intermediaries.

The most basic measure of legal protections is the degree to which courts can be expected to enforce contracts and refrain from confiscating assets (chapter 6). A recent study finds that expectations of basic contract enforcement affect firm size, after accounting for a variety of other contributing factors such as the state of demand, technology, and type of industry.[28] Although the study is restricted to the European countries, differences in legal protections probably help explain the significant differences in firm size between industrial and developing countries as well.

The absence of complementary formal institutions may make legal reforms difficult. One study found that statutory legal protections in Russia, which were much lower than the world average in 1992, were some of the world's highest by 1998.[29] But coincident with these improvements in measures of legal protections has been reportedly weak enforcement, which has driven down equity values. Anticipated benefits from the adoption of sophisticated legal protections is limited because developing countries have low levels of enforcement of basic legal protections. The priority is facilitating enforcement, through efforts to create an effective and constrained state (chapter 5) and to improve the efficiency of the judiciary (chapter 6), or to adopt legislation that does not strain the capacity of legislators and politicians.

A question is whether countries need to adopt sophisticated corporate and bankruptcy laws at all. Arguments in favor of mandated protections for outsiders— that is, financiers—are that there are advantages to having checks that protect unsophisticated investors

and to the standardization offered by national laws which lower enforcement costs. Arguments against such protections are that they can limit potential innovations by investors and entrepreneurs. In principle, some argue, all that is required is for the state to uphold contract law and for companies to devise efficient protections and write them into their articles of association

History, however, reveals the political necessity for more sophisticated laws, written and enforced by governments. All countries that have had corporate forms for a significant period have, through innovation and experimentation, produced specific laws that shift power away from entrepreneurs, such as corporate and bankruptcy laws. In other words, they have developed sophisticated legal protections beyond contract law (box 3.3).

The empirical question remains whether more detailed laws that allocate power to providers of resources— and influence the organization of firms—improve the way resources within firms are allocated. Recent efforts to quantify the extent of legal protections for equity and debt financiers provide some answers (box 3.4). This evidence suggests that there is a strong association between the presence of legal protections and indicators of current and future firm performance. It also suggests that increased legal protections create the possibility for more diversified ownership structures—moving away from concentrated structures dominated by the state, business groups, and foreign firms—because they allow the protection of minority shareholders. Figure 3.3 shows the relationship between shareholder rights and stock market development. In countries with weak protection of shareholders, dominant or controlling shareholders can expropriate benefits that would otherwise accrue to minority shareholders.

Parties controlling corporations may find such control valuable, since they are able to extract private benefits from the corporation, to the exclusion of other stakeholders. They can influence who is elected to the board of directors or the appointment of the chief executive officer, and they can transfer assets on nonmarket terms to related parties or consume resources at the expense of the firm.[30] A competitive market for corporate control can discipline firms that provide poor returns for investors. But in most countries, takeovers are rare. In practice, the effectiveness of the market for control as a corporate governance mechanism depends on having liquid stock markets, and the costs of mounting a takeover are high.[31] Moreover, incumbent controlling

Box 3.3
The need for formal laws: the development of corporate law

The United Kingdom, France, the United States, and Germany were the first countries to enact corporate statutes. They have spearheaded the development of corporate law. The United Kingdom had features of free incorporation as early as 1688; France proclaimed free incorporation in 1791; the state government of New York passed a corporate statute in 1811; and the German government passed a commercial code in 1861.

Laws of incorporation signaled a shift of authority over resources within firms from the state to private parties. They preceded sophisticated corporate laws, which allocated authority among the different private parties involved in firms. Economic crises following the passage of free incorporation laws, with booms in firm formation followed by busts, motivated the governments of all four countries to establish specific points of leverage and control for investors. For example, Germany's first national corporate law was replaced by a much more restrictive one in 1884, following a crisis. Innovation and experimentation led policymakers to identify decisions that could compromise the resources provided by investors—such as a change in the firm charter, the dissolution of the firm, or the volume or pricing of shares in the firm—and shifted power over these decisions away from insiders. Protections for labor were introduced primarily in bankruptcy rather than corporate laws, with employees given priority over unsecured claims and sometimes over secured claims.

Across industrial countries, governments introduced these protections, which suggests the political if not economic inability to sustain a system that relied solely on sophisticated investors and insiders devising their own mechanisms to deal with potential disputes.

Source: Pistor and others 2000, *World Development Report 2002* background paper.

Box 3.4
Measuring the strength of legal protections for shareholders

Quantitative measures of legal protections focus on the degree to which national laws shift power from management or controlling shareholders.[33]

Shareholders exercise their power by voting for directors and by voting on major corporate issues. Evaluation of the extent of shareholder protection focuses on voting procedures within firms. Investors are better protected when companies in a country are subject to one share–one vote rules. When votes are tied to dividends, insiders cannot have substantial control of the company without having substantial ownership of its cash flows, which moderates incentives to divert resources from the firm. Laws in different countries allow divergence from the one share–one vote principle. Companies can issue nonvoting shares, low and high voting shares, founders' shares with extremely high voting rights, or shares whose votes increase when they are held longer. Companies can also restrict the total number of votes that a given shareholder can exercise at a shareholders' meeting, regardless of how many shares the shareholder controls.

Corporate law specifies rules protecting the voting mechanism against interference by insiders. A recent study constructs a measure showing how strongly legal systems protect minority shareholders against managers or dominant shareholders in the corporate decisionmaking process. Six basic rights are identified.

First, must shareholders show up in person to vote, or may they send an authorized representative or mail their proxy vote? Second, are shareholders prevented from selling their shares several days before a shareholder meeting? Third, is cumulative voting for directors allowed? This gives more power to minority shareholders to put their representatives on boards of directors. Fourth, do minority shareholders have legal mechanisms to guard against perceived oppression by directors, besides outright fraud, such as the right to force the company to repurchase shares of minority shareholders who object to certain basic decisions of the management? Fifth, do shareholders have a preemptive right to buy new issues of stock, to protect shareholders from dilution? Sixth, what is the percentage of share capital needed to call an extraordinary shareholders' meeting? In Mexico, for example, it is 33 percent, which prevents minority shareholders from organizing a meeting to challenge or oust management.

Source: La Porta and others 1998.

parties and management have been vocal in lobbying governments to provide antitakeover protection.

A recent study measuring the private benefits of control in 18 countries with the largest stock markets (as of 1997) finds that these benefits are significantly different across countries and may amount to much of firm value.[32] The value of these benefits ranges from a quarter to a half of market capitalization in Chile, Korea, and Mexico. In contrast, private benefits are on average below 4 percent in Denmark, Hong Kong (China), Sweden, and the United States. Legal protections can play a large role in limiting expropriation of company value by those in control. The study shows that the weak legal rights that noncontrolling shareholders enjoy explain more than 70 percent of the systematic differ-

ences in private benefits, especially for the quality of general investor protection, minority rights in the transfer of control, and standards of law enforcement.

Despite the benefits from introducing formal institutions of corporate governance, shifting from a network-based system imposes costs on established

Figure 3.3
Shareholder rights and stock market development

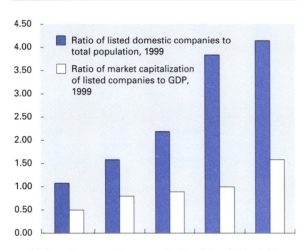

Ratio of listed domestic companies to total population, 1999

Ratio of market capitalization of listed companies to GDP, 1999

Higher values mean stronger protection of shareholder rights

Source: La Porta and others 1998.

members of a network. Established firms are able to accumulate surplus capital because of their reputation for repayment, their ability to provide collateral, or their ability to enforce repayment by others. The implied redistribution of benefits helps to explain the widespread resistance to many governance reforms by leading business groups around the world. Similarly, managers who have free rein are likely to oppose reforms that shift power to outside investors.

One potential force for change is openness to trade and financial flows, which changes the relative power of interest groups and their returns. Incumbents might favor openness because it increases export opportunities or the availability of low-cost capital for them. But openness is often reciprocal, and the result is the introduction of competing firms and foreign investors that have different corporate governance institutions. Foreign competitors in product markets might have lower costs of capital, leading to domestic pressure for legal reform and to lower costs associated with legal protections. Foreign investors need access to information through public channels to identify opportunities and because they are not part of established networks, and they need legal protection in case of abuse. Foreign firms and investors therefore enter to constitute new interest groups.

In some countries—for example in Latin America—the trend among domestic firms toward foreign stock market listings has also been a catalyst for change. The evidence points to rapid changes in regulations in response to financial flows in some areas, but slower movements on disclosure legislation and on corporate, bankruptcy, securities, and labor laws. Brazil is a case where there has been more rapid change on regulations affecting the securities market than in securities and corporate laws (box 3.5).

Resolution of insolvency

Bankruptcy law is an important governance institution that allocates decisionmaking power and claims to assets during times of financial distress. Efficient insolvency regimes, in terms of bankruptcy laws and enforcement mechanisms, make both debtors and creditors better off. Insolvency regimes balance the objective of protecting the rights of creditors—essential to the mobilization of capital for investment—and preventing the premature liquidation of viable enterprises. The evolution of most systems also shows the importance of balancing social and political pressures. The evolutionary paths of corporate insolvency procedures

Box 3.5
Legal and regulatory change in Brazil

The Brazilian stock market is the largest in Latin America and has traditionally been dominated by a few large companies. Firms are often controlled by families or by state-owned corporations, and boards of directors tend to be dominated by insiders. Multiple classes of shareholding facilitate the extraction of benefits by insiders. By one estimate, the private benefits that a controlling shareholder can extract from the value of the company is among the highest in the world—some 23 percent of firm market value in 1997. These features have limited market development and stimulated many proposals for reforms.

Meanwhile, parallel reforms have been undertaken by the securities market regulator to improve disclosure requirements and protect minority shareholders during changes in corporate control. A series of directives from the regulator requires disclosure of the terms and prices of block sales of shares and now requires a mandatory offer for minority shares when the threshold of 50 percent of votes is reached. These regulations have triggered a noticeable reduction in the private benefits that a controlling shareholder can extract from a company.

Source: Nenova 2001b.

have depended to a large extent on who initiates legal changes and on prevailing economic and social pressures (chapter 1). This section discusses some important elements of bankruptcy law.

The details of the law matter. Both the letter of the law and the structure of the insolvency system matter for economic outcomes. This is demonstrated, for example, by comparing the 1992 and 1998 Russian bankruptcy laws. The law of 1992 stipulated that the condition for initiation of bankruptcy was that the total amount of outstanding debts exceed the total value of company assets on the balance sheet. But this condition was not effective because it was relatively easy for a manager to manipulate the balance sheet value of the company's assets.[34] With low transparency and few legal safeguards, it was difficult to ascertain the true condition of firms or to act against poor performers. In contrast, the 1998 law was modified to make initiation of bankruptcy easy. A creditor holding even a small amount (less than $5,000) of debt overdue for three months could file for the bankruptcy of the firm. As a consequence, the number of initiated proceedings jumped from 4,320 in 1997 to 8,337 in 1998, and to over 13,000 in 1999.

The adoption or modification of bankruptcy laws has often occurred in periods of economic crisis, such as the recent East Asian financial crisis. During these times, when maintaining stability in output is a concern, bankruptcy laws have tended to become more debtor-friendly. This has been the case in Indonesia and Thailand, as well as in Argentina. Historical examples confirm the importance of financial crises in the design of bankruptcy systems. The United States, for example, initially had a very creditor-friendly law, which was subsequently revised to be more debtor-friendly during crises (chapter 1).

As a result of the East Asian financial crisis, all the affected countries passed new bankruptcy legislation. The key question is whether such legal changes merely redistributed pending claims or whether the value of claims—for both debtors and creditors—increased. A recent study shows that values for all parties—creditors and debtors—increased in reaction to anticipated reforms in the Thai bankruptcy system.[35] Following positive news about reforms, there was a large increase in the value of claims. Equity values of both corporate borrowers and creditor institutions increased more than 25 percent.

For small entrepreneurs, personal bankruptcy law is important. Most new firms begin as sole proprietorships. For these firms, personal bankruptcy rules have a significant effect on the risks they bear in setting up a business and on the decision to set up a business itself. For example, a study in the United States finds that potential entrepreneurs in states with unlimited homestead exemption in case of bankruptcy have 25 percent less chance of securing a loan. This is because creditors have less collateral to claim in case of default. But homeowners in these states are 40 percent more likely to start a business.[36]

Principles of insolvency regimes. Legal rights for creditors expand firms' access to credit, as well as the breadth and depth of debt markets. A simple way to protect creditors in insolvency is to respect the absolute priority of claims in bankruptcy or restructuring by paying senior creditors first, followed by junior creditors, and finally shareholders out of the residual value. But if shareholders receive nothing during bankruptcy, managers acting on behalf of shareholders will attempt to delay or avoid bankruptcy, for example, by undertaking high-risk projects when the corporation runs into financial distress. For this reason, the preservation of some part of firm value for shareholders during bankruptcy, even when absolute priority would not leave residual value for the owner, is usually recommended.[37]

An important consideration is whether the law provides for an automatic trigger that makes a firm file for bankruptcy—for example, nonpayment or delayed payment on debt, as was stipulated for Russia. Automatic triggers reduce the loss of value associated with managers or major shareholders delaying the bankruptcy decision. They also help to clarify the rights of different parties when complementary institutions are lacking (see the example from Hungary in chapter 1).

The presence of complementary institutions can be critical, so the trigger must be carefully designed. The Thai bankruptcy law of 1999 introduced a trigger stipulating that if the debtor owed a group of creditors more than one million baht, the main creditor had to petition for bankruptcy.[38] However, the trigger did not have the intended effect because complementary institutions were absent. Although the trigger itself was well defined, the next step in the bankruptcy procedure—the determination of insolvency—was not. In particular, nine conditions of insolvency were set forth in the Bankruptcy Act 2483. These were difficult to meet, resulting in few bankruptcy cases being initiated even after the revised law came into force. The accounting rules also did not specify in what currency the company's assets should be recorded, which made it easier for owners to manipulate the balance sheet and make the company appear solvent, preventing creditors from filing for bankruptcy.

Social and political considerations can dominate the ranking of creditor interests. Country experience indicates that social considerations are paramount in times of financial distress. Corporate bankruptcy law usually affects large firms whose financial difficulties may have significant regional or employment effects. Some countries have introduced creative variations on the normal liquidation procedure in an attempt to alleviate the negative impact on employees. For example, a procedure similar to a process under English insolvency law was recently introduced in Kazakhstan. The enterprise is sold as a unit to a new owner, and a contract is signed requiring the new owner to rehire all employees. Creditors, who often provide the acquisition financing, generally support this procedure. In 2000 nearly 38 percent of liquidations in Kazakhstan were conducted under this procedure. Variations of this procedure exist in many countries, such as Indonesia and Korea. A downside of this procedure is that potential new owners may be unwilling to rehire all the employees, and it may not be economically viable for the firm to keep all its workers.

Another important consideration in the design of bankruptcy laws is deciding who can file for reorganization or liquidation. Related concerns are the attention paid to the debtors' and the creditors' roles, the roles of the company's management and other stakeholders in preparing reorganization proposals, the ability of management to operate the company during the reorganization, and whether an automatic stay of assets exists. For example, studies show that the ability of managers to keep their positions adversely affects creditor rights and is associated with less access to external finance.[39]

The evidence from industrial and developing countries indicates that the success of structured or formal bargaining mechanisms in bankruptcy depends on the strength of the judicial system. The efficiency of the insolvency procedures in producing quick resolutions determines who files for formal bankruptcy. Several developing countries have established specialized judicial or quasi-judicial bodies to deal with insolvent companies, taking the proceedings out of the court system.

But not all these experiments have succeeded in improving outcomes. In India, for example, the Board for Industrial and Financial Reconstruction was established in 1987 to reorganize or liquidate insolvent large and medium-size companies. However, in its 13 years of existence the board took, on average, 1,664 days from the time of registration to decide on reorganization plans, and 1,468 days to decide on liquidation.[40] In addition, 35 percent of cases registered in 1996 were still undecided at the end of 2000, along with 63 percent of cases registered in 1997.

Alternative procedures for dealing with financial distress center on versions of asset sales or cash auctions. Cash auctions are easy to administer and do not rely on the judicial system.[41] Although attractive from a theoretical perspective, these proposals have not been widely used, other than in Sweden and Mexico. A problem with the auction mechanism is its reliance on liquid secondary markets. Simplified institutional designs—such as automatic triggers—that clearly state which actions should be taken and leave less room for discretion are more effective in developing countries with weak administrative capacity and limited information flows (chapter 1).

Boards of directors as a check on insider authority

The board of directors of a firm is in a position to play a pivotal role in defining its strategic direction. Moreover, the board's responsibility for executive recruitment and for setting compensation policy and rights over dismissal gives it leverage over managers.

The roles and duties of board members depend on national laws as well as on company statutes. The importance given to various stakeholders' property rights varies across countries. In the United States the board's duty is to shareholders, while in the Netherlands the objective is to achieve a satisfactory balance of influence of all stakeholders. In many countries, such as Germany, directors have a duty beyond that to shareholders and the law also mandates that larger firms include representatives of labor on the board.

The extent to which boards protect the interests of investors and other stakeholders and hold managers accountable depends on the incentives and powers of the board. Board members serve as a weak check on insider authority when insiders appoint and dismiss board members themselves. Voting rules, such as the absence of cumulative voting, ensure that whoever has the most shares can appoint all the board members. In such circumstances, board members will be more inclined to represent the interests of those who appointed them rather than the interests of a broader set of investors in the firm. Moreover, compensation for services has historically been only weakly related to firm performance, giving the board a poor incentive to focus on monitoring insiders.

In recent years a broad consensus has developed on the elements required to increase the incentives of board members to monitor managers and provide a check on abuses of authority. Private sector organizations in over 30 countries have issued codes of "best practice." Building on analysis of boards and performance in industrial countries, recommendations focus on increasing the percentage of board members not directly tied to management and ensuring that such outside nonexecutive board members chair subcommittees—including those on financial reporting and compensation—where there are bound to be conflicts of interest between management and investors.

The Organisation for Economic Co-operation and Development has recently promulgated international corporate governance standards. Active debates focus on whether it should be left to firms to adopt such practices on their own, whether this should be encouraged through required disclosure of actual practices, or whether the adoption of certain practices should be mandated. In Germany, for example, the corporate law specifies the composition and authority of the supervisory board.[42] The United Kingdom has set up a voluntary system of disclosure. Evidence indicates that this has led to large changes in board structures; elements of this standard-setting approach have been followed elsewhere.

But in most developing countries a lack of mechanisms to enforce adherence will limit the impact of such standards. In practice, even in industrial countries it is difficult to find systematic evidence linking the adoption and use of independent boards to improved firm performance.[43] If the board members are truly outsiders, they face difficulties in monitoring management, as they are often dependent on management for the provision of information. And even if they have the information, they may lack the expertise, the time, and the incentive to monitor management actions.

These problems are magnified in developing countries. The vast majority of large firms in developing countries have concentrated ownership structures with a controlling shareholder, often a member of a business group. The controlling shareholder can dominate the board selection process, particularly when there is no cumulative voting. This makes it unlikely that board members will be independent. Added to these problems, public information flows in developing countries are weak. An independent director relying on these information flows would have difficulty performing a monitoring role.

All this is not to detract from the potential value of independent boards. But as long as enforcement is weak and little public information is available, the traditional boards dominated by those with a relationship with the firm, such as buyers, suppliers, and stakeholders, may be in a better position to improve the functions of governance. Policymakers interested in improving governance have to do more than impose obligations on companies to produce board structures that comply with standards, such as independence. Where steps are taken to improve information and enforcement, board reforms will complement these changes.

Institutions that provide investors with information
In formal corporate governance systems, laws and boards create potential limits to the diversion of resources. But investors also require timely, accurate, and reliable information on which to base their decisions. Empirical evidence indicates that the quality of information available helps explain the wide cross-country differences in the sensitivity of investment to value added. Better-quality information is associated with firms making more investments in high value added activities.[44]

Firms in developing countries provide and have access to often limited information of relatively poor quality. An accounting benchmarking study has compared national statutory accounting standards with international accounting standards to provide one index of cross-country differences.[45] Although this is an imperfect measure that does not capture differences in lapses in enforcement, the results are nonetheless revealing (figure 3.4).

A study following the East Asian financial crisis provides evidence on the extent of information gaps. It found that more than two-thirds of the largest publicly traded banks and corporations produced financial statements with little relation to international accounting standards. Table 3.2 shows that weaknesses in accounting standards included lack of disclosure about transactions in which the manager or entrepreneur had

Figure 3.4
Accounting standards across countries

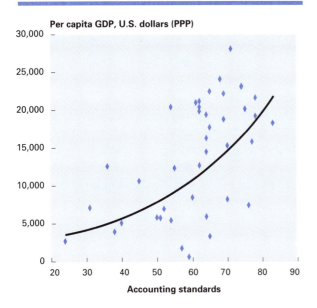

Per capita GDP, U.S. dollars (PPP)

Accounting standards

Note: The figure shows a scatter plot of the relationship between an indicator of accounting standards and GDP per capita.
Source: Center for International Financial Analysis and Research (CIFAR), cited in La Porta and others 1998.

Table 3.2
Financial statements do not disclose useful information for resource providers

International accounting standard category	Percentage of firms in compliance
Related party lending and borrowing	30
Foreign currency debt	37
Derivative financial instruments	24

Note: Sample includes 73 of the largest publicly traded banks and corporations in Indonesia, the Republic of Korea, Malaysia, the Philippines, and Thailand.
Source: Rahman 1998.

an identifiable conflict of interest, as well as widespread lack of disclosure of liabilities. One of the most surprising findings was that this lack of disclosure took place despite the involvement of auditing firms affiliated with the top international firms and in many cases was perfectly legal according to national standards. Although not the primary cause of the crisis, poor information was a contributing factor to the crisis. Investors who relied on publicly available information were in a weak position to identify bad practices and therefore to protect themselves or to distinguish between good and bad investments.

The ability of brokerage houses to estimate accurately the earnings of large publicly traded firms provides another indication of the information challenge. It also illustrates the extent of the difference between countries with strong regimes for producing information and those with weak regimes. A recent study measures the average forecast error between the earnings estimates of financial analysts and actual earnings as an indication of this challenge.[46] Countries with the lowest forecast error included the Netherlands and the United Kingdom, while countries with the highest

forecast error included China and Mexico. Institutional differences across countries, including the extent of accounting disclosure, help to account for these differences. Most firms are neither large nor publicly traded, particularly in developing countries. But where information flows are distorted for these firms, the challenge for those trying to evaluate smaller firms that are not publicly traded is significant.

In some countries, private actions to improve information quality developed before public steps, with private organizations stepping in to satisfy the growing demand for information. In other countries, governments have played a more prescriptive role (box 3.6). In the United States, for example, auditing and bond-rating firms developed because of rapid growth and rising need for external capital, starting with the railroad companies. Private and public actors played complementary roles.

Private initiatives provide only limited incentives to entrepreneurs to disclose information. They were also not standardized. Entrepreneurs have the incentive to reveal information about good projects but to hide information about projects with poor returns. In essence, the purchaser of the service (the company) is not always the party with the greatest interest in obtaining high-quality audit services. Measures such as audit committees and nonexecutive directors can be adopted to better align the interests of auditors and managers. But risks of incompetence and the possibility of collusion with management remain.

In countries where the setting of accounting standards was initiated by the private sector, the state has intervened. Standards and requirements issued by the

Box 3.6
Limitations to private governance in accounting

With the emergence of the joint stock company, financial reporting became an important instrument of corporate governance. Financial reporting made managers account for the use of the capital provided by owners. The audit also emerged as a tool so that an independent expert could provide assurance to the owners about the completeness and reliability of the information provided by the managers. Previously, when the number of parties involved in an enterprise was small, a contractual approach was adequate, and the need for external regulatory intervention was limited.

In the countries with a common law tradition such as the United Kingdom and the United States, a self-organizing profession of accountants emerged, starting in the mid-19th century. This gradually built up a body of commonly accepted practices for auditing and preparing accounts. These were accepted voluntarily by enterprises and did not initially require legal backing to enforce them. Over time—and often in response to corporate collapse or scandal—legislators intervened to address coordination problems. These problems arose from several factors: the presence of large bodies of shareholders who negotiated accounting and auditing arrangements on a contractual basis with management; the absence of legal authority on the part of the accountancy profession to oblige enterprises to follow their rules; and the losses caused to third parties—for example, to creditors in cases of insolvency—who were not privy to the contractual relationships among owners, managers, and auditors.

Initially, the elaboration of many of the detailed requirements (such as accounting standards) was left to the accountancy profession. Over time, legislators and regulators gradually took control over setting standards in the area of accounting, auditing, and ethics and exercised greater influence over the requirements for entry to the profession as well as members' accountability. This turned professional bodies from self-regulating organizations, exercising delegated regulatory authority over their members, to organizations exercising authority delegated from the state.

For countries with a Roman law tradition, the pattern of evolution has been different. In countries such as Germany and France, legislation establishing joint stock and limited liability companies was much more prescriptive in terms of detailed accounting and auditing requirements. In addition, many of the requirements were directly responsive to the needs of the state as user of financial information—for example, the influence of taxation rules on general purpose accounting requirements. Further legislation did not confer regulatory authority on preexisting, voluntary, self-regulating groups but instead established public law bodies to govern the profession. Access to the profession was controlled by state examination, judges were involved in disciplinary matters, and the activities of the bodies—for example, in representing the private interests of their members—were clearly circumscribed by law.

Despite their quite different origins and development processes, these two separate traditions for regulating accounting and auditing have converged to a significant extent. These two experiences also highlight different paths that developing countries today may take.

Source: Hegarty 2001, *World Development Report 2002* background paper.

---

profession were not perceived to be adequate to prevent failures or abuses, to ensure that its members properly complied with those requirements, or to guarantee that all interested parties had appropriate input to the development of those standards. But if standards are set by the state, there is a danger that the information sought by policymakers, with their interest in taxation, may be very different from the needs of investors. Private input into standard setting can help ensure that there is enough innovation to meet business needs.

Governments also need centralized and accessible share registries and property registries, which facilitate independent collection of information and verification of information produced by the company. Laws on disclosure increase information flows. An independent auditor's job is to offer judgment on whether the financial information made available to investors fairly represents the performance of the company according to the accounting standards. Since the users of the audit

report may include stakeholders that were not involved in the negotiation of the audit contract, all industrial economies have legislative or regulatory requirements for audit to protect stakeholders—although the scope of these requirements can vary in response to other public policy considerations. For example, it is common to exempt firms below a certain size from audit requirements because of the limited use made of their accounts.

As international transactions have grown in scope, there has been an increase in demand for the standardization of information across borders. In response, an International Accounting Standards Committee (IASC) was established in 1973 and produced International Accounting Standards (IAS). Large firms have voluntarily adopted these standards to gain access to international capital markets. For small and medium-size firms however, these standards may not be appropriate because they are explicitly shareholder-oriented and because the

Box 3.7
Evolution of international accounting standards

Since the early days of the International Accounting Standards Committee (IASC), certain small or developing countries have chosen to adopt International Accounting Standards (IAS) as their national standards rather than incur the expense of developing their own local standards. But it was soon accepted that the full benefits of IAS would accrue only if they were accepted for use by larger, internationally active companies, especially for purposes of raising capital across borders. IASC therefore began to focus on producing standards that would meet the information needs of investors in listed companies and on seeking recognition for those standards from the securities market regulators responsible for determining the conditions—including those on financial reporting—to be met by companies seeking to be traded on their markets. Steady progress has been made and, except in the United States and Canada, all the world's major securities markets accept—for regulatory purposes—financial statements from companies registered abroad that are prepared in accordance with IAS.

In May 2000 IOSCO, the international organization of securities market regulators, officially endorsed IAS subject to certain conditions. In June the European Commission announced its intention to propose legislation that would make it mandatory for listed companies to use IAS in their consolidated financial statements by 2005, at the latest. This legislation was published in February 2001. However, the remainder of the approximately 4 million enterprises subject to other EU accounting legislation is exempt.

Source: Hegarty 2001, *World Development Report 2002* background paper.

requirements of IAS are complex and would be too costly for small and medium-size firms to adopt (box 3.7).

For countries considering accounting reform, the first lesson is that one size does not fit all, and there can be a strong argument for having different financial reporting regimes for different categories of enterprises. Multiple regimes can impose costs, but these need to be weighed against the benefits. At least two distinct categories can be identified:

■ For companies seeking to raise capital on the market, and especially those seeking foreign investors, IAS are now recognized as the international accounting standards. It is essential that these companies be permitted to use "pure" IAS, since any modification to these standards means that the resultant standards cannot claim compliance with IAS. As the Asian crisis showed, involving local affiliates of international

auditing firms is not sufficient to enhance information quality because the affiliates tend to follow national standards.

■ For other companies, however, the use of IAS may be excessively burdensome or inappropriate in light of their stakeholder or user groups. Simplified accounting and reporting requirements, which respond to the information needs of the taxation authorities, may be more appropriate. But care should be taken not to allow the needs of one user group to distort the accounts, since they would cease to be relevant for other users, including management. Specific needs of individual users can be addressed through supplementary reports based on, and reconciled with, the general-purpose accounts.

The nature of the information provided and demanded is affected by the nature of the users and providers. Along with government, financial intermediaries—including pension, mutual, and hedge funds—create a demand for added information and analysis. Information intermediaries, such as bond-rating agencies and financial analysts in brokerage houses, combine the audited financial statements with other sources of information and offer judgments about a firm's prospects. The financial press is yet another institution that can collect and disseminate information (chapter 10).

Incentives for intermediaries

Mechanisms are needed to ensure that organizations involved in collecting and offering judgments on the quality of financial information are accountable both to the users and to the providers of information. There are many potential conflicts of interest. An auditor, for example, might own equity in or provide added services to the same firm for which it provides audit services. A brokerage house might provide investment banking services to a company covered by its financial analysts. Information intermediaries might have higher returns from engaging in insider trading or manipulating stocks than from providing quality information.

What produces incentives for intermediaries to provide timely, accurate, and reliable information? Among the forces providing pressures for efficiency are competition, reputational effects, and penalties imposed by a regulatory authority. Policies that influence the supply of firms seeking external capital and the extent of institutional investors increase the demand for information and are likely to sharpen the incentives provided by reputation and competition. Openness stimulates demand further, allowing domestic firms to list on foreign exchanges and reducing restrictions on investments by foreign institutional investors.

The experience of the industrial countries suggests that relying solely on private institutions is not a sustainable approach. Given the substantial fixed costs and time needed to develop publicly available information flows, developing countries need to consider alternatives. One approach, discussed in chapter 4, is to focus on banks and private information flows. Another alternative is to allow domestic companies to engage foreign information intermediaries by cross-listing shares on a foreign exchange, where disclosure requirements are stringent, or to participate in international bond issues. The experience of large Chinese state-owned companies, which have sold a minority of their shares to investors through offerings on the Hong Kong stock exchange and the New York stock exchange, shows both the potential and the limitations of such an approach. Beginning in the early 1990s, firms from emerging international markets have tapped this market, accounting for a majority of dollars raised in recent years (figure 3.5). Privatized companies account for more than one-third of this revenue.[47] But the significant costs associated with complying with listing requirements means that this option is available only to a few large firms. Moreover, the problem remains that investors must still seek redress in the firm's home country, which may lack laws to protect investors or enforcement mechanisms.

Conclusions

Institutions which affect the governance of firms are important for determining how resources are allocated, and who has rights over resources, both within countries and between countries. Therefore, they affect growth and poverty reduction. Governance institutions for small and large firms differ. Large firms are few in number relative to small ones. However, on average they account for a significant proportion of value added and employment. Moreover, weak governance in these firms has been associated with financial and economic crises, which can have severe consequences for poor people. But when these firms do well, they contribute significantly to growth and have a direct impact on the lives of people. Powerful incumbent firms also have an incentive to prevent changes in institutions that may reduce their gains and have often opposed policies that fa-

Figure 3.5

Capital raised through new depository receipt programs

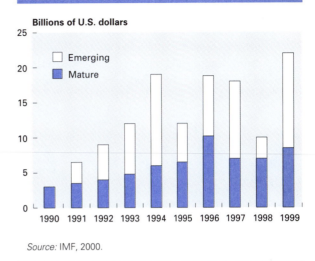

Source: IMF, 2000.

cilitate entry of new firms. Actions can be taken to limit these incentives. Such pressures have existed in the development experience of many nations, but successful development initiatives have sought to balance the gains that large firms provide with the negative effects on policies towards new entry and change.

But in most developing countries, another kind of problem is prevalent. And that regards the relation between the state and private business. In poor countries there are often few limits on state arbitrariness; that is, public officials themselves are not bound by the laws which they adopt, and do not keep their established "contracts" with private agents. Often, there is also weak contract enforcement between private agents and poor information provision. These problems hinder new entry into the formal sector. In these contexts, private institutional approaches will continue to dominate; they will substitute for the lack of effective formal publicly provided alternatives. In these circumstances policymakers will benefit from being open to innovative approaches by private agents.

Openness to trade in goods and services and to information sharing can increase the efficiency of such private mechanisms and can promote further institution building by creating forces for change. Formal governance institutions can offer long-term benefits to complement private initiatives. Such institutions increase opportunity for firms, and by promoting investment in high value added activities, they enable growth of firms and employment within firms. They support increased economic growth and poverty reduction. There are often large obstacles to the development of laws and internal governance institutions, and to regulatory agencies. New initiatives in institution building need to complement and build on existing institutions. For example, adopting laws which require regulators to have extensive information on firms may not be a priority without prior attention to building information flows, such as those which accounting systems provide. Policies that help to build political support for governance changes, such as openness in trade and in transparency or open information sharing among the different parties affected by reforms, are as important as the specifics of individual reforms.

CHAPTER 4

Financial Systems

The availability and access to finance can be a crucial influence on the economic entitlements that economic agents are practically able to secure. This applies all the way from large enterprises (in which hundreds of thousands of people may work) to tiny establishments that rely on microcredit.

—Amartya Sen, 1999

Economic history provides ample support for the idea that financial development makes fundamental contributions to economic growth. Financial development played a critical role in promoting industrialization in countries such as England by facilitating the mobilization of capital for large investments (box 4.1). Scholars have also argued that well-functioning banks spur technological innovation by identifying and funding those entrepreneurs with the best chances of successfully developing new products and implementing innovative production processes.[1]

A large body of evidence suggests that financial development contributes significantly to growth, even after accounting for other growth determinants.[2] Through its strong effect on overall economic growth, financial development is central to poverty reduction. Recent research also shows that financial development directly benefits the poorer segments of society and that it is associated with improvements in income distribution.[3] Preliminary evidence suggests that measures of financial development are positively and significantly correlated with the share of income of the bottom quintile of the income distribution.[4] Thus, arguments that the development of the formal financial system only benefits the rich do not appear to be supported by the empirical evidence.

The historical experience of industrial nations and the experience of developing countries today point to another important lesson. Sound public finances and a stable currency are key to the development of private financial institutions.[5] For example, the Dutch "financial revolution" started with the development of public debt in the form of negotiable securities, and England solved the liquidity and public debt problems by introducing long-term and perpetual annuities.[6] More recently, governments that have suppressed their financial systems in order to finance public spending have ended up with troubled and underdeveloped financial systems.

One of the important functions of financial systems is to shift risk to those who are willing to bear it. Financial contracts can help pool and diversify risk. Recent studies find that financial development also tends to reduce aggregate economic volatility.[7] This is an important insurance mechanism for the poor or near-poor, since negative economic shocks increase the numbers of the poor. However, although financial systems have risk-reduction capabilities, in the absence of supporting institutions that provide prudent risk-taking incentives, financial development can lead to the magnification of risk rather than its mitigation.[8]

Financial markets arise to reduce the information costs of borrowing and lending and of making transactions. In so doing, financial systems serve a number of functions that are essential in a modern economy.[9] They provide payment services that facilitate the exchange of goods and services, mobilize savings, allocate credit, and monitor borrowers. By evaluating alternative investments and monitoring the activities of borrowers, financial intermediaries overcome information problems and increase the efficiency of resource use.

Box 4.1
The financial revolution versus the industrial revolution

It is commonly believed that technological development in England during the late 18th century was the driving force behind the industrial revolution and modern economic growth. An alternative perspective gives more emphasis to the significance of institutional change and particularly to the role of financial institutions in the process. For example, some argue that capital market improvements, which mitigated liquidity risk, were the primary cause of the industrial revolution. Many of the inventions already existed but required large injections and long-term commitment of capital, which was not possible without further development of financial markets. The industrial revolution had to wait for the financial revolution.

As in England, a sophisticated financial system developed in the United States before its industrial revolution in the 19th century. The Dutch Republic, long before its remarkable growth in the 17th century, had a financial revolution that involved institutional innovations such as the adoption of negotiable international bills of exchange to finance the economy's external trade, negotiable securities to finance the public debt, a convenient payment system, a stable currency, a strong private banking system, and securities markets.

Source: Hicks 1969; Rousseau and Sylla 1999; Sylla 2000.

Financial systems limit, pool, and trade risks resulting from these activities.

Financial assets, with attractive yield, liquidity, and risk characteristics, encourage saving in financial form. A financial system's contribution to growth and poverty reduction depends upon the quantity and quality of its services, its efficiency, and its outreach.

Financial institutions include banks, insurance companies, provident and pension funds, investment and pooled investment schemes (mutual funds), compulsory saving schemes, savings banks, credit unions, and securities markets. In developing countries, particularly in poorer areas, highly personalized types of lending with enforcement mechanisms based on local reputation and group norms also play a very important role.

The challenge facing policymakers is to build robust financial systems that assist in risk mitigation in the event of shocks. This chapter provides lessons for policymakers to help them reach this goal, based on research and on country experiences, most of which have become available in recent years.

Policymakers should consider improving the legal and regulatory environment rather than building a par-

ticular financial structure. What is important is to have secure rights for outside investors and efficient contract enforcement mechanisms—central themes of this Report. Openness to trade and greater competition contribute to the development of financial institutions, regardless of the country's legal origin, colonial history, or political system.

Financial regulation becomes a far easier task when it makes use of the monitoring and disciplining ability of market participants. An essential element of improving the quality and effectiveness of market discipline for financial institutions is ensuring the accuracy and availability of information on the operations of these institutions. Developing countries with poor information and human resources and lacking the complementary institutions that would facilitate the monitoring and enforcement of capital standards may still benefit from additional buffers that are easier to observe and enforce. Examples are liquidity requirements and rules that require action by regulators under well-specified conditions.

Bank privatization affects the efficiency of financial services. Individual country experiences show that effective regulation and a clean balance sheet are critical for successful privatization. Competition improves efficiency, increases incentives for innovation, and promotes wider access. Recent evidence indicates that access to finance by smaller firms does not decrease with foreign entry. Country experiences demonstrate that an efficient banking system requires a contestable system—one that is open to entry and exit—but not necessarily one with many competing institutions.

Even in the most developed financial systems, information problems and the relatively high fixed costs of small-scale lending limit the access of small firms and microenterprises. A system of complementary institutions can help. Improving collateral laws and establishing collateral registries, improving information about small borrowers through credit registries, and reducing costs through the use of computerized credit-scoring models are ways of improving access for small borrowers.

This chapter discusses how financial structure varies across countries and the effect of financial structure on economic outcomes. It then considers regulation of banks, ownership, and competition in the banking sector and institutions to increase access to banking for those who are currently left out. Issues related to stock market development are also covered in chapter 3. Nonbank financial intermediaries are covered in a recent World Bank report and are not addressed here.[10]

Should policymakers promote bank-based or market-based financial systems?

As economies develop, the needs of the users and the providers of financial services change. Informal finance becomes less important, and self-financed capital investment gives way first to bank-intermediated debt finance and later to the emergence of capital markets, as additional instruments for raising external funds (figure 4.1).[11] Although banks dominate most formal financial systems, the relative importance of the stock market tends to increase with the level of development (box 4.2).[12] Far more finance is raised from bank loans, however, than from selling equity, even in industrial countries.[13]

Economists have debated the role of financial structure—the advantages and disadvantages of bank-based financial systems relative to market-based systems—for more than a century. At the end of the 19th century German economists argued that the German bank-based financial system had helped Germany overtake the United Kingdom as an industrial power. During the 20th century the debate expanded to the United States and Japan.[14] More recently, the question of the overall design of a financial system has demanded the attention of policymakers, with the urgent need to design financial systems in many transition economies.

Should policymakers concerned with promoting growth and poverty reduction focus on developing banks or developing stock markets? Some argue that banks have advantages over markets when complementary institutions are weak.[15] Even in countries with weak legal and accounting systems and poor contract enforcement, powerful banks can force firms to reveal information and pay their debts, thus facilitating industrial expansion.[16] Conversely, well-developed stock markets quickly reveal information, which reduces the incentives for individual investors to acquire information. This can reduce incentives for identifying innovative projects, hindering efficient resource allocation.[17] Furthermore, since investors can sell their shares inexpensively, their incentives to monitor managers rigorously are diminished, which hinders corporate control and national productivity.[18] But stock markets provide the ability to diversify risk and customize risk management devices.

The importance of financial structure for economic development has been extensively examined in recent research. Country-, industry-, and firm-level investigations all show that for a given level of development, distinguishing countries by financial structure does not help explain cross-country differences in long-run GDP growth, industrial performance, new firm formation, firm use of external funds, or firm growth.[19]

Figure 4.1
Financial system development across income groups

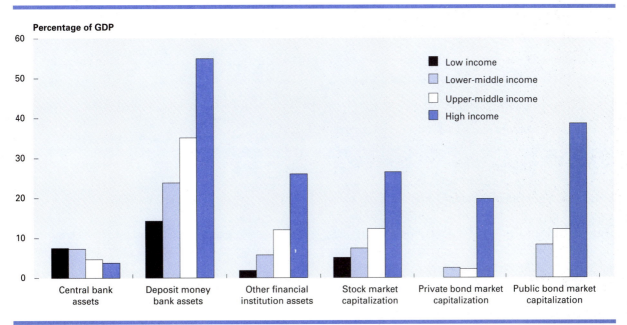

Box 4.2
Financial structure varies across countries: better information and legal systems that protect property rights play a role

A recent World Bank study built a database starting in the 1960s on financial markets and intermediaries for more than 100 countries. The study developed a number of indicators that measure the relative size, activity, and efficiency of financial intermediaries and markets. The indicators, on the whole, show a tendency for financial systems to become more market based as countries become richer. The table presents the relative activity measure of financial structure and shows that countries can be classified as market based either because they have very liquid markets (as is the case for the United States) or because they have poorly developed banking sectors (Mexico and Turkey). To the extent that a country's laws help potential shareholders feel confident about their property and voting rights without fear of corruption, and to the extent that comprehensive, high-quality information about firms is available to outside investors, financial systems tend to be more market based.

Financial structure across countries

Country	Value traded/ GDP (percent)	Bank credit/ GDP (percent)	Structure- activity
Germany	18.7	85.7	0.661
India	4.8	24.1	0.701
Japan	38.3	103.9	0.433
Mexico	6.3	14.8	0.371
Nigeria	0.03	12.5	2.619
Thailand	20.3	51.1	0.401
Turkey	6.2	12.9	0.318
United States	34.4	65.2	0.277

Note: Value traded/GDP = value of all shares traded on the exchange as share of GDP. Bank credit/GDP = claims by commercial banks on the private sector as share of GDP. Structure-activity = logarithm (bank credit/value traded).
Source: Beck, Demirgüç-Kunt, and Levine 2000a; Demirgüç-Kunt and Levine forthcoming.

Financial structure tends to change during the development process, however, because banks and markets have different requirements concerning information and contract enforcement in order to function effectively. For example, the information that a bank collects is private and is gathered from its relationship with individual clients. It does not necessarily depend on other complementary institutions, such as accounting standards. Once banks have invested in a firm, they use the threat of cutting off future credit for enforcement. By contrast, equity markets require strong protection of minority shareholder rights, good public in-

formation and accounting systems, and low levels of corruption to develop.

Financial structures generally do not change rapidly, but there are exceptions. For example, Indonesia and Turkey experienced changes in their financial structures, owing to rapid growth of their stock markets in the 1980s following financial liberalization. The Republic of Korea is another notable exception because of the rapid development of its nonbank financial sector, where strict government banking regulations did not apply. In Chile nonbank financial intermediaries and the stock market also experienced rapid development in the early 1980s, largely as a result of the privatization of the pension system.[20] Efforts to change financial structure overnight usually do not succeed. Attempts to build stock markets in several transition economies and African countries in recent times have not been very successful because the underlying legal, information, and enforcement mechanisms were underdeveloped (box 4.3).

Policies to promote financial development are likely to be more effective if efforts are directed at developing the legal and regulatory environment to support the natural evolution of financial structure. Financial system development depends critically on the protection of private property. Recent studies have shown that legal protection of minority shareholders and creditors is a sig-

Box 4.3
Promoting stock markets in developing countries

As countries become richer, wealthier households and corporations have more complicated financial needs, and financial markets emerge to meet this demand. But this is not the whole story. Why, for example, does India have a stock market while other low-income countries find it so difficult to develop one?

There are many examples of failed efforts to develop stock markets. In the early- to mid-1990s, attempts to develop stock markets in The Gambia and Zambia did not prove successful. These countries built stock exchanges and provided people to staff them. There were, however, so few listed companies and so little market exchange that these stock exchanges could not generate the fees to be self-sustaining.

Besides differences in income, some of the differences in experience can be explained by differences in legal systems, the availability and quality of information, and corruption. Low income, inadequate laws and regulations, information problems, corruption, and lack of enforcement all play a role in deterring stock market development.

nificant determinant of financial development across countries. A recent World Bank study confirms that legal traditions have played an important role in affecting financial development.[21] Building financial institutions requires policymakers to focus on the fundamentals: property rights and the enforcement of those rights. This is true whatever the level of income and regardless of the political and macroeconomic environment of the country. Countries can modify aspects of their legal systems and can adapt judicial systems to make contract enforcement more efficient and predictable (chapter 6).

Political differences associated with the relative power of the state and private property holders have influenced the formation of legal traditions. Decentralized political systems, for example, may work to offset the tendency of central governments to control markets and thwart competition. In Europe governments suppressed market forces in response to the Great Depression. Similar attempts in the United Kingdom and the United States were not successful. Another example is the militaristic Japanese government of the 1930s, which was able to suppress the bond and stock markets and force small banks to merge with large banks in an effort to direct credit to military-related industries. Sometimes severe economic crises can undermine the power of incumbent politicians and promote reforms, as, for example, the experience of Chile in the late 1970s demonstrates.

Countries face other influences that affect the development of their financial institutions. For example, countries more open to trade and capital flows may face higher levels of competition, which can foster improvements in institutions, regardless of their legal, political, or colonial origin. Case studies and cross-country experience support the view that trade openness has a positive effect on development of financial institutions, regardless of historical influences. More open economies, in terms of trade, capital markets, and information flows (chapters 1, 3, and 10), and more competitive markets (chapter 7) will see faster development of demand for institutions and will improve the functioning of existing institutions.

What form should financial regulation take?

As long as there have been banks, there have also been governments to set rules for them, maintain the purity of coinage, hold high reserves, restrict interest rates, and provide credit to the government or favored parties.

Traditionally, bank regulators in many developing countries have used financial regulation chiefly as a means to pursue specific development objectives. They have concentrated on regulations affecting credit allocation, while paying little attention to prudential aspects of monitoring. This has undermined the efficiency and stability of financial systems, leaving them vulnerable to economic shocks. Following the wave of financial crises that hit developing countries in the 1980s, there has been a shift in regulatory policy. Today, the goal of modern financial regulation is largely prudential regulation to promote an efficient, safe, and stable financial system.

Prudential regulation is expected to promote systemic stability. Official supervisors act as delegated monitors for depositors, working to overcome information problems that would be beyond the resources of individuals. Nevertheless, the recent spate of banking crises—whose severity was exacerbated by international financial linkages—has had severe consequences for growth and poverty reduction. These crises have renewed interest in improving financial regulation through the creation of international standards in bank regulation and supervision.

Limiting the fragility of financial systems

Financial systems are fragile because financial institutions and markets are in the business of pooling, pricing, and trading risk. Financial institutions add value in large part because they are better able to collect, evaluate, and monitor information than individuals. Such specialization comes at a cost, however. Financial institutions are vulnerable not only to the risks they actually take, but also to perceptions of those risks by individual market participants. Changes in perceptions can lead to large swings in asset prices. Banks are the most fragile part of the financial system, owing to the "demandable" nature of their liabilities, which makes them vulnerable to sudden withdrawals.

In many countries policymakers have designed safety net policies to deal with the fragility of financial systems—in particular, to prevent runs on banks, losses in bank capital, and bank failures. Prudential regulation is an important component of the safety net. Standards on capital adequacy, loan classification, provisioning and suspension of interest, and limits on connected lending are all critical elements of prudential regulation. Deposit insurance is another important component of the safety net.

Safety nets seek to lessen the likelihood of crises by reducing bankers' incentives to take risks and depositors' incentives to withdraw their funds—thereby insulating banks from runs. Unfortunately, making depositors less sensitive to bank risk also has unintended consequences. Because a bank's cost of attracting funds no longer depends on the riskiness of its asset portfolio, bankers face incentives to take excessive risks ("moral hazard"). These incentives for excessive risk-taking by banks are greatest during times of adverse economic shocks, when more loans become nonperforming. This means that bank capital is eroded and owners have increased incentives to take on more risk.

Ironically, in many countries the very safety nets that were meant to limit the vulnerability of the financial system have been identified as the greatest source of fragility (box 4.4).[22] Experience with deposit insurance underscores the importance of the complementary institutions that countries at lower income levels may not have, a theme emphasized throughout this Report. Some countries are not yet equipped for certain types of regulation because necessary complementary institutions such as effective bank regulation and supervision have not developed. In those instances the temptation to adopt regulations that exist in more industrialized countries should be resisted.

In trying to prevent individual bank failures, badly designed safety nets can severely undermine the incentives of financial institutions, their creditors, and even the regulators themselves. Prudential regulations are only effective if they are properly enforced. Enforcement is much easier if regulations are incentive-compatible, encouraging and making use of the monitoring and disciplining ability of market participants. Financial systems in which incentives encourage prudent risk-taking will be less crisis prone and better able to assist in risk mitigation in the event of shocks.

Financial institutions are prone to excessive risk-taking, owing to the limited liability of their shareholders and to their use of financial leverage.[23] One way of ensuring that owners retain prudent risk-taking incentives is to require them to have a significant amount of their own money at risk. This can take the form either of capital or of future expected profits. Capital adequacy requirements that set minimum capital requirements are imposed for this purpose. If the institution is expected to be sufficiently profitable in the future—if it has a high enough "franchise value"—this also acts as a deterrent, since the owners are also reluctant to risk their future profits. Thus, entry regulations that manage the amount of competition existing in the financial sector can also serve to align the incentives of the owners and regulators.

Outside monitors of financial institutions can complement supervision by regulators. Using the private sector to extend the reach of the regulator is possible when regulations and safety net policies do not undermine the monitoring incentives of private agents. Outside creditors of financial institutions have the incentive to monitor, gather, and use information on financial institutions when they have their own money at risk. These monitors include depositors (if deposit insurance coverage is kept relatively low); larger, more sophisticated creditors that do not expect compensation when things go wrong (box 4.5); or other financial institutions (for example, when interbank deposits are not insured, institutions are encouraged to monitor one another). Enforcing prompt disclosure of accurate information would greatly improve the monitoring ability of all private parties. Rating agencies and other professional analysts further facilitate the collection and analysis of such information and contribute to monitoring.

Preliminary research findings, using regulatory information for more than 100 countries, indicate that regulations that encourage and facilitate the private monitoring of banks tend to boost bank performance, reduce nonperforming loans, and enhance bank stability. These regulations include requiring that banks are audited by certified external auditors, improving banks' accounting statements and disclosure, and providing market participants with incentives to monitor by eliminating deposit insurance. This result is stronger for middle- and higher-income countries because effective private monitoring requires a sufficient number of relatively sophisticated private agents.[24]

Most countries rely on regulators and supervisors to do the bulk of their monitoring. As with bank owners and creditors, supervisors need the right incentives. In developing countries, economic environments are more volatile, there are fewer formal financial institutions, and those that exist tend to be controlled by a small number of powerful individuals. It is often difficult to discuss supervisory incentives independent of politics, since regulatory agencies are seldom very independent. Furthermore, even in middle-income countries such as Argentina, Brazil, and the Philippines, regulators can be sued and held personally liable for their actions. Adequate legal protection against personal lawsuits, especially those brought by aggravated owners of banks being regulated, is necessary for proper regulatory intervention.

Supervisors' incomes are low compared with those of private bank employees. Supervisors also tend to

Box 4.4
Designing a bank safety net: the role of deposit insurance

Bank safety nets are made up of various components, such as the existence of a lender of last resort, insolvency resolution, prudential regulation and supervision, and deposit insurance. A bank safety net is difficult to design and operate because it must balance the conflicting objectives of guarding against financial crises that can magnify economic shocks and avoiding moral hazard problems that give rise to imprudent banking practices. Finding the right balance between crisis prevention and market discipline is the most important challenge facing policymakers.

Deposit insurance that guarantees certain property rights for depositors is an important element of the safety net. Because governments find it hard to make a credible commitment that rules out ex post insurance after a bank failure, explicit or implicit deposit insurance schemes are an important part of every country's safety net. The number of countries adopting explicit deposit insurance schemes has been increasing in recent years.

Whether to adopt an explicit system and what kind of system to adopt are crucial questions in the design of safety nets. A recent World Bank project has begun to answer several key questions regarding the impact of deposit insurance on financial sector stability, or the ability of markets to exert discipline on banks, and on financial development, using a large database comprising deposit insurance schemes and design features around the world.

This research shows that explicit deposit insurance schemes can lead to excessive risk-taking, reduced market discipline, and increased financial fragility in countries with poor complementary institutions, including poor regulation and supervision, poor contract enforcement ability, and high levels of corruption. The research shows that unless the overall institutional environment is strong, the adoption of explicit deposit insurance does not lead to increased confidence in the financial system and to greater financial development.

Analysis of individual design features indicates that keeping coverage low and narrow in scope reduces moral hazard problems. For example, there might be benefits from keeping coverage limits below one or two times the level of GDP per capita. Introducing elements of co-insurance, such as subordinated debtholders without any insurance, having access to funds (but not necessarily accumulating large sums that can be abused), and involving banks in management and monitoring are elements that similarly can reduce moral hazard.

These results have important policy implications. Without adequate development of complementary institutions, there are real risks that deposit insurance can increase the probability of crises, leading to poorly functioning financial markets. Unfortunately, many of the recent adopters of such schemes have been those countries with poor complementary institutions.

Growth in explicit deposit insurance systems worldwide, 1934–99

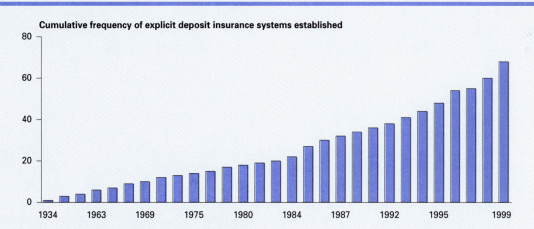

Source: Cull, Senbet, and Sorge 2000; Demirgüç-Kunt and Detragiache 2000; Demirgüç-Kunt and Huizinga 2000; Demirgüç-Kunt and Sobaci 2000; Kane 2000.

have inadequate resources at their disposal. Low pay makes it difficult to attract qualified personnel and upgrade skill levels. The prospect of high-paying private sector jobs at the end of regulatory careers creates incentives for corruption. Public/private pay differentials exist in rich countries as well as in developing countries, but a World Bank survey of bank supervisors around the world shows that developing countries have greater difficulty retaining their supervisors.[25]

These observations argue for increasing supervisors' salaries and restricting their employment in the banking sector after their service in the public sector. How-

Box 4.5
The role of subordinated debt in establishing credibility: the case of Argentina

Requiring banks to maintain minimum ratios of subordinated debt and regulating features such as maturity and maximum allowable yield impose market discipline on banks and limit banks' incentives to take on risk. Banks that take on excessive risk find it difficult to sell their subordinated debt and are forced to shrink their risky assets or to issue new capital to satisfy their private debt holders. Therefore, subordinated debt provides useful signals for bank supervisors.

For small banks, subordinated debt can take the form of uninsured deposits held by large domestic banks or by foreign banks. For large banks, subordinated debt includes notes issued in international capital markets or to foreign banks.

If subordinated debt has limited maturity, it forces banks to be regular issuers, which provides continuous market information for investors and regulators. Interest caps limit the risks banks can take, since they cannot pay higher interest rates, above the limit, to compensate for additional risk. If the subordinated debt instrument is relatively homogenous, the rates at which it is trading can be compared across banks, facilitating monitoring.

Subordinated debt regulation can be difficult to implement. Developing capital markets are shallow and illiquid. Most im-

portant, it may be difficult to ensure that borrowers and creditors are unrelated parties. Nevertheless, as part of regulatory reforms aimed at enhancing the safety and soundness of its banking industry in the wake of the 1994–95 financial turmoil following the devaluation of the Mexican peso, the Argentine Central Bank introduced a subordinated debt regulation in 1996 which became effective in 1998.

A recent study investigated how the subordinated debt regulation has been working in practice, analyzing the characteristics of banks according to how they have reacted to the regulation. The results show that the banks that were able to comply with the regulation are those that are relatively strong and less risky. Perhaps most important, the regulation makes it clear to all parties that supervisors are aware of the failure to comply with subordinated debt. This has the benefit of enhancing discipline over supervisors. While it is difficult to ensure proper implementation of subordinated debt, using it to enhance regulatory monitoring and incentives seems to hold promise, particularly in middle-income countries.

Source: Calomiris 1996; Calomiris and Powell 2000.

---

ever, unless limitations on future employment are accompanied by substantial pay increases, they make it even more difficult to attract qualified staff.

The organization of the supervisory authority also influences the incentives faced by the regulators and their ability to resist political pressures. Proper functioning of the supervisory authority requires insulation from political pressures. In most countries supervision of financial institutions is under the authority of the central bank, generally one of the more independent agencies in the system. According to a survey of 70 countries by the Institute of International Bankers, however, in about one-third of the countries, supervision of credit institutions is conducted in agencies separate from the central bank.[26]

Although much less common, the blurring of boundaries in financial services has led to a growing trend to consolidate supervision of all financial institutions under one supervisory agency. Potential drawbacks of a single agency include difficulties in maintaining independence and elimination of useful competition between regulators (box 4.6).

Another question concerns whether to include prudential supervision, as well as monetary policy, in the responsibilities of the central bank. The most common criticism of combining monetary policy and supervi-

sion is that it can create conflicts of interest. The central bank may be reluctant to raise interest rates to stem inflation for fear that this would hurt the banks. However, the information supervisors require can be used to improve forecasts of future financial problems and economic developments. Combining monetary policy and supervision also provides the potential for economizing on scarce human capital. In countries with poor market discipline, limited information flows, and low levels of human resources, retaining supervision in the central bank may be desirable. Regardless of the institutional arrangement, the independence of the supervisor in its regulatory functions and extensive information sharing between the monetary authority and the supervisory authority are vital for effective supervision.

Nevertheless, despite all efforts, it is generally difficult to provide regulators with proper incentives, since they tend to have multiple objectives. One possible solution is to reduce incentive problems by introducing rules to tie the hands of the supervisors and reduce their discretion through mandatory "prompt corrective actions" that must be followed in specific circumstances. For example, in dealing with weak banks, it has become increasingly common to recommend that countries adopt a prompt corrective action and structured early-intervention approach similar to that embodied in U.S.

Box 4.6
Institutional design for bank supervisors

While the number of single supervisory agencies (SSAs) is growing, such agencies are still the exception. As of June 1999, only eight countries—Austria, Denmark, Japan, the Republic of Korea, Malta, Norway, Sweden, and the United Kingdom—had SSAs, out of the 70 countries surveyed by the Institute of International Bankers. These SSAs typically cover prudential and market integrity functions and can also cover consumer and competitiveness oversight functions.

Most SSAs are too new to allow detailed analysis of costs and benefits. Focusing only on prudential oversight, however, it is possible to lay out the conceptual arguments. Among the arguments in favor of such agencies:

- The blurring of boundaries in financial services makes consolidated and integrated approaches to regulation and supervision more necessary.
- The associated emergence of financial conglomerates, spurred by economies of scale and scope, requires a similar regulatory approach.
- Economies of scale and scope in regulation and supervision are possible, as are lower costs of information sharing and coordination.
- Establishing an SSA can be a way to create an institutional setup that is more independent, professional, and insulated from political pressures than existing supervisors.
- One regulatory agency may also reduce regulatory costs for financial institutions, as they do not need to interact with several agencies.

SSAs also have some conceptual disadvantages.

- An SSA may be too difficult to manage and too vulnerable to political favoritism. In other contexts, specialization and competition between regulators has been advocated as a means to avoid regulatory capture and minimize unnecessary regulation.
- There remain many financial institutions that are specialized by function, such as insurance companies, and that need not be supervised by an all-embracing agency.
- An SSA might create the impression that a larger range of financial institutions has an impact on systemic risks than is actually the case.

Source: Claessens and Klingebiel 2000a; Taylor and Fleming 1999.

legislation. This approach requires structured, prespecified, publicly announced responses by regulators triggered by decreases in a bank's performance—such as capital ratios—below established numbers; mandatory resolution of a capital-depleted bank at a prespecified point when capital is still positive; and market value accounting and reporting of capital.

Opponents of this approach argue that with greater financial complexity, monitoring financial institutions' risk requires greater discretion. Inflexible rules can hamper the authorities' ability to conduct supervision. A further problem is that application of these rules in poor countries is complicated by the lack of appropriate information. For example, capital is difficult to evaluate (see the discussion below). In these cases, simpler indicators—such as inability to make payments—that are easier to monitor and that make noncompliance obvious may be needed. Such rules may bring greater transparency, may help supervisors resist political pressures, and may be particularly appropriate where supervisory quality is poor.

Regulatory incentive problems again underline the importance of using the private sector to extend the reach of the regulators. Informing public opinion by maintaining an open flow of reliable information is an essential element of making the public intolerant of poor banking and poor regulatory performance and creating demand for institutional reform. With greater public awareness, political pressures that inhibit banking enforcement also diminish.

International standards

The response to recent financial crises has included the creation of international standards in bank regulation and supervision. Standardization of regulation and supervision can certainly have benefits, to the extent that it reduces information problems and improves the access of developing country institutions to the international financial system. For example, at the time of the 1988 Basel Accord, which recommended a minimum risk-weighted capital adequacy ratio of 8 percent, there were developing countries that did not even have capital requirements. By 1999, along with increasing openness and links with international markets, only 7 of the 103 reporting countries had minimum capital ratios under 8 percent. More than 93 percent of the countries claim to adjust capital ratios for risk in line with Basel guidelines.

Developing countries tend to be considerably farther from full compliance than industrial countries, however. In developing countries regulations are adopted even though supervisors do not have the information flows to verify compliance, and incentive structures to help reveal such information are missing.[27] As is the case with international standards in other areas, financial standards also tend to reflect conditions in industrial countries. For example, it may be that in developing economies more prone to shocks, higher capital adequacy standards would be desirable. But given the difficulties with implementation, these would have even less chance of being enforced. It is relatively easy to adopt regulations such as capital adequacy ratios; it is much more difficult to implement the underlying procedures (such as measuring the value of capital) that give meaning to these rules. Book capital is not an adequate indicator of an institution's health. The true net worth of a bank depends on the market value of the loans in its portfolio, which are generally difficult to value, owing to their illiquid nature. In developing countries volatile prices and underdeveloped markets make this task even more difficult. Often, a bank is insolvent in market value terms long before its accounting capital is depleted.

Better accounting can help. Good accounting and provisioning practices are necessary to make book capital a meaningful measure. Bank supervisors are expected to classify bank loans into different categories, based on their quality, and to require loss provisions of different amounts based on this classification. However, because forward-looking classifications are generally difficult to justify and enforce, realistically this translates into requiring that provisions are made when a loan goes into arrears. For example, if interest on a loan is in arrears by more than 90 days, accounting standards in many countries will forbid the bank from showing that interest as already having accrued in its income statement. Interest accrual on nonperforming loans was allowed for up to 360 days in Thailand in 1997 and is allowed for loans overdue up to 180 days in many African countries. In most countries it is even more difficult to prevent banks from making new loans to cover interest payments and conceal nonperforming loans, a practice known as evergreening.[28]

Therefore, standards that focus on supervised capital adequacy may be inadequate in developing countries. For example, the ending of liquidity requirements—holdings of central bank, reserves, cash, and government paper—in developing countries came about in emulation of the emerging consensus among OECD members. Lower liquidity requirements did somewhat reduce financial sector taxation. Although liquidity ratios are not needed for prudential purposes in high-income countries, developing countries have not been able to upgrade bank supervision and regulation sufficiently to offset the loss of this buffer.[29] In environments where human capital and supporting institutions are scarce, simpler rules like liquidity requirements can offer advantages over more complex ones.

Free trade in financial services increases the intensity of cross-national regulatory competition. Unfair and inefficient regulatory strategies become harder to enforce because firms and citizens of individual countries observe more favorable regulations elsewhere. Viewed from this perspective, the globalization of financial markets is a process in which increasing international competition can exert market discipline on government regulators and restrict the freedom of politicians and regulatory bodies to use financial institutions as a conduit for delivering political favors. Globalization of financial services could also benefit the poor directly if sufficient attention were paid to improving their literacy and Internet access.

Another benefit of allowing different regulatory strategies across nations is the scope these differences offer for experimentation with different ways of responding to innovative behavior by regulated parties. Just as the institutions seeking to minimize their regulatory burdens may be quite creative in evading prudential regulations such as connected lending limits or restrictions on foreign exchange exposures, so regulators might benefit from being equally creative in re-regulating, without being restrained by international regulatory standards.

Enhancing efficiency in the financial sector: the role of ownership and competition

Developing countries often have concentrated banking sectors with high levels of state ownership. Figure 4.2 shows that outside North America and Europe there are very few countries where state banks comprise less than one-quarter of banking sector assets. The data underlying figure 4.2 imply a strong negative correlation between the share of sector assets in state banks and a country's per capita income level.[30]

In explaining why public ownership of banks is so widespread, proponents of state control argue that governments can better allocate capital to highly productive investments. A second argument in favor of state control is that with private ownership, excessive concentration in banking may lead to limited access to credit by many parts of society, negatively affecting development. A third popular argument is that privately owned banks are more crisis prone and that public ownership has a stabilizing effect on the financial system. However,

Figure 4.2
State ownership in banking, 1998–99

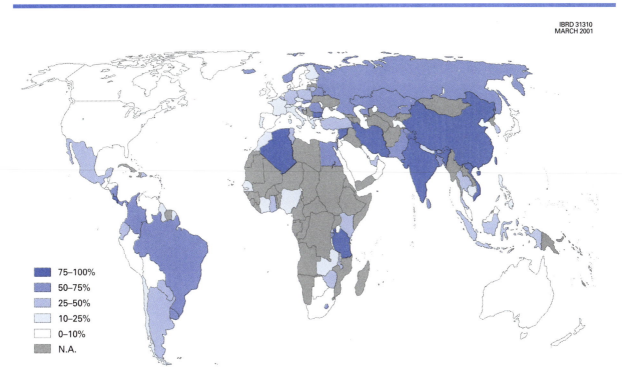

IBRD 31310
MARCH 2001

- 75–100%
- 50–75%
- 25–50%
- 10–25%
- 0–10%
- N.A.

Note: The figures shows the percentage of assets in state-owned banks, with most of the observations from 1998–99 (World Bank Survey of Prudential Regulation and Supervision) and, where those data were not available, La Porta, Lopes de Silanes, and Shleifer (2000). Thus, some very recent ownership changes, notably in Latin America, are not taken into account.
Source: World Bank 2001a.

recent evidence indicates that greater state ownership of banks tends to be associated with lower bank efficiency, less saving and borrowing, lower productivity, and slower growth.[31] There is no evidence that state ownership lowers the probability of banking crises.[32]

Moreover, the negative effects of state ownership appear to be more severe in developing countries than in industrial economies. Industrial country markets provide greater checks and balances on public owners. Some of the poor performance of state banks stems from weak internal incentives. A larger part probably arises from intervention by policymakers because state ownership enables officials to use banks as a source of patronage jobs or to direct credit to supporters.[33] The evidence is clear that state bankers face political conflicts that generally result in poor performance.

Although the potential benefits of shifting to private ownership appear to be large for developing countries, those countries are also the least institutionally capable of achieving successful privatization. Bank privatization

can bring about increased competition as credit is increasingly allocated to productive endeavors rather than politically advantageous ones. As in other sectors, it is important to encourage competition in the financial system to reduce costs and encourage innovation. Unlike the case in most other sectors, however, excessive competition in banking can erode franchise values and create an unstable environment. Therefore, increased competition requires a strong regulatory environment.

Bank privatization
In a sound regulatory and supervisory environment with good transaction design, privatizing banks leads to improved performance. For example, data from the privatization of 18 provincial banks in Argentina since 1992 show that the balance sheets and income statements of the newly privatized banks began to resemble more closely those of other private banks. There were fewer nonperforming loans, administrative costs fell relative to their revenues, and less credit was extended

to public enterprises.[34] These changes support cross-country findings that enhanced productivity follows privatization.[35]

Successful bank privatization requires an appropriate transaction design. New owners must know that some of their own capital is at risk and that the supervisory authorities will take action in the event that the privatized bank becomes insolvent. This means that a clean break between the government and the new owners is necessary for successful privatization.

New owners must start off with a viable entity. This means that serious adjustments to state bank balance sheets must take place before the banks are sold. This step is especially important, as the public banks that governments are willing to sell have almost always incurred losses over time and are often insolvent. If the new owner acquires a failing bank, the regulator is far more likely to show regulatory forbearance. Chile, for example, lacked the fiscal resources to clean up the banks' balance sheets before its large-scale bank privatization in 1975. Subsequent problems were partly attributable to low supervisory capability. But the 1982 crisis also occurred because the new owners and the government both recognized that the new owners had assumed insolvent institutions—and both parties to these transactions therefore expected some regulatory forbearance.

Balance sheet adjustments can be accomplished by replacing nonperforming assets with performing assets, typically government bonds. Or policymakers can create a residual entity to house nonperforming assets and liabilities not assumed by the purchaser (the so-called good bank/bad bank solution). Although no strong evidence exists on the superiority of one method over another, the link between the government and the new owners cannot be credibly severed unless the new owner truly begins with a solvent institution. Recognizing and resolving the losses of the state bank will likely involve substantial fiscal costs. Fiscal planning must therefore play a part in a successful bank privatization process.

In many instances the key stumbling blocks to successful privatization have been reluctance to cede majority control of banks to private agents and reluctance to permit foreigners to bid for banks. Developing countries can reap benefits from foreign entrants in terms of sector efficiency and stability.

Among the transition economies Hungary was the most willing to cede majority control of its banks to foreign interests. Hungary has also enjoyed higher eco-

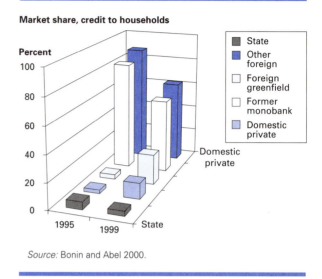

Figure 4.3
Evolution of the Hungarian banking sector

Market share, credit to households

Source: Bonin and Abel 2000.

nomic growth rates than its neighbors; some of this better performance can be attributed to better-functioning banks (figure 4.3). Poland was initially reluctant to sell to foreign interests, and the Czech Republic was slow to sell controlling shares to any owner, foreign or domestic. Changes in these attitudes help to explain part of the subsequent improvement in economic growth.[36]

Dynamics of institutional change: privatization

In environments where regulation and supervision are weak—a situation that characterizes many developing economies—it is probably unrealistic to hope that large shifts in ownership, carried out over a short period of time, will ultimately prove successful. This does not mean that developing countries should abandon privatization. Rather, countries should pursue privatization bank by bank as governments continue working to improve supervisory capability.

Private ownership of banks can also catalyze other institutional changes. There appear to be important relationships between private ownership and demand for better financial information, much of which is provided by supervisory authorities. Markets also monitor banks better when there is greater private ownership.[37]

Mexico provides an example. All the banks in Mexico were nationalized in the early 1980s. Pronationalization forces stressed the abuses of concentrated ownership, which were thought to have contributed to the 1982 crisis by facilitating the outflow of private sector savings. It was hoped, therefore, that state ownership, coupled with strong capital market and exchange controls and credit subsidies for public investment and social programs, would reduce volatility in the banking sector.[38] However, public banks increasingly became a source of financing for the public deficit. The banks also progressively lost both their risk-assessment skills and a large number of their most qualified personnel.[39] Beginning in 1988 with the removal of some interest and exchange rate controls, the Mexican government started to liberalize the banking sector, culminating with the reprivatization of all banks in 1992.

To ensure the success of such a large-scale privatization effort, the authorities would have had to be either very confident in their regulatory and supervisory capabilities or willing to sell to reputable foreign banks. Neither of those conditions held in the Mexican case. After widespread failures, beginning with the "Tequila Crisis" of 1994, the Mexican authorities intervened in many banks and eventually had to undergo a second round of privatization in which foreign ownership was allowed. In 1999 the World Bank extended a Bank Restructuring Facility Loan to Mexico to support pending bank resolution transactions. The loan helped underwrite the cleanup, restructuring, and reprivatization of Banco Serfin, which was purchased by the Spanish bank Santander, and also helped facilitate a handful of mergers.

Research results from Argentina indicate that privatization is more likely to occur when the direct benefits to politicians from banks, such as patronage and subsidized credit to supporters, are low and when financial constraints on politicians tighten (box 4.7). The episode illustrates that governments often become locked into undesirable institutions due to vested interests. In the case of Argentina's provincial banks, it took a crisis and financial assistance from the international financial institutions to compel provincial policymakers to change their course. Some provinces still chose not to privatize.

Market structure

Independence from political decisionmaking can improve governance in the banking sector. Privatization may be the only way to ensure this effectively. There remain questions, however, about the appropriate structure of the private banking sector. Excessive competition may create an unstable banking environment, while insufficient competition may breed inefficiency or reduced credit access for borrowers. For lack of a bet-

---

Box 4.7
The political economy of banking reform

There is little systematic evidence as to what factors lead politicians to relinquish state control of banks. The best of the limited evidence that is available comes from Argentina, where 18 state-owned provincial banks were privatized between 1992 and 1999. Because policymakers in different provinces were making the similar decision of whether to privatize their bank, within a relatively short time period and within the same broad institutional environment, Argentina provides a testing ground for the forces that drive bank privatization.

The main insights are that provincial policymakers were more likely to privatize after there was a hardening of their budget constraints and when funds were available, as part of the privatization, to clean up the balance sheets of their failing banks. The hardening of budget constraints was the result of the adoption of the Convertibility Plan and associated revisions to the charter of the central bank. Under the plan, the central bank's main role was to protect the value of the currency. This meant it could no longer rediscount loans from provincial banks to the provincial governments. In addition, the central bank's lender of last resort capabilities were severely restricted, which meant that the provincial banks would have to maintain depositor confidence largely on their own (for a more detailed discussion, see Dillinger and Webb 1999).

During the "Tequila Crisis," which began in late 1994 and continued through early 1995, the weaker banks in Argentina—including many public provincial banks—experienced dramatic deposit outflow. To handle this liquidity crunch, these banks received short-term loans from other public banks (mainly Banco de la Nación). After the crisis, however, most of the provincial banks were not in a position to pay off these loans, and some were insolvent. The federal government, with assistance from the Inter-American Development Bank and the World Bank, created the Fondo Fiduciario, a trust fund that offered long-term loans to provinces that agreed to privatize their banks. The loan proceeds were used to retire the short-term obligations incurred during the crisis. In this way, provincial bank balance sheets were cleaned up before privatization (Clarke and Cull 1999a, 1999b).

These were not the only factors that drove privatization decisions. Privatization occurred earlier, for example, where overstaffing was less severe and where a bank's performance was worse (see econometric evidence in Clarke and Cull forthcoming). But incentive changes associated with the Convertibility Plan and revisions to the central bank charter, together with the Tequila Crisis and the creation of the Fondo Fiduciario, contributed to the shift in ownership structure in Argentine banking. Periods of crisis may offer similar opportunities in other countries with high shares of state ownership in banking.

ter measure, bank concentration is often used as a proxy for the level of competition in the sector. Empirical evidence on the impact of concentration is slowly emerging, but most of it still comes from industrial countries, especially the United States.[40]

It is difficult to generalize about the effects of concentration. Conceptually, concentration may intensify market power and reduce competition and efficiency. If economies of scale drive bank mergers and acquisitions, increased concentration should imply efficiency improvements. In addition, larger banks may hold a more diversified portfolio of assets, which may enhance sector stability. Large banks, however, may be "too big to fail" or even too big to be disciplined by bank supervisors. This means that they may become more leveraged and hold riskier assets than smaller banks, since they can rely on policymakers to assist them when adverse shocks hurt their solvency and profitability.

Concentration need not reduce competition. In Canada, for example, where the five largest banks account for more than 80 percent of all banking assets, researchers have found no evidence of monopolistic behavior.[41] Concentrated systems can be competitive if they are contestable, with the potential for entry and exit providing market discipline. Recent cross-country evidence also indicates that greater concentration is not closely associated with banking sector efficiency, financial development, or industrial competition.[42] Similarly, analysis of bank-level data from 80 countries shows that concentration has little effect on bank profitability or margins.[43]

What does the evidence imply for developing countries, where banking sectors tend to be highly concentrated, not very competitive, and in many cases prone to crisis? Because concentration alone may not be a good proxy for assessing competition and contestability, it is important to complement concentration measures with measures of entry and exit restrictions themselves. The evidence indicates that tighter restrictions on entry into banking are associated with higher average interest rate margins and overhead expenditures.[44] Additional restrictions on foreign entrants are associated with lower sector portfolio quality and greater likelihood of a banking crisis.[45] Evidence on entry restrictions suggests that it is the contestability of the market that is positively linked with bank efficiency and stability, rather than the actual level of concentration.

Developing countries appear to suffer from all the anticompetitive disadvantages of concentration while reaping few of the benefits of greater stability. The balance therefore tips in favor of permitting more entry. If there are viable local private banks, new entry should probably be gradual, so that the franchise value of local banks does not quickly erode, since this could increase instability. At the least, where high concentration coincides with substantial state ownership and thus poor performance, governments should consider privatization as a means of making the local market more contestable.

Governments have often created restrictive entry policies to achieve a balance between competition and stability. Such policies should not, of course, be a means of protecting entrenched interests from competition. Since the competition from other financial institutions and through other forms of financial intermediation is stronger in industrial country markets, some have argued for less restrictive entry rules in developing countries.[46] Moreover, since the evidence indicates that banking sectors in developing countries tend toward concentration and a lack of competition, liberalizing entry policies appears to offer potential benefits. All countries must maintain some limits on entry for prudential reasons. Restrictions should not be lifted so rapidly that existing banks' franchise values are suddenly wiped out. The entry process must therefore be managed over time and be transparent. Some countries might benefit from establishing a firm timetable for liberalization, made binding through domestic laws and regulations and possibly backed up by international agreements.[47] Similarly, because some failures are inevitable, governments need to establish transparent rules for bank exit—that is, for intervention and resolution (box 4.8).

How foreign entry and e-finance can change the nature of financial markets

Financial globalization has its benefits, but it also increases risks. Many of these were discussed in *World Development Report 1999/2000: Entering the 21st Century*. Most developing countries are too small to be able to afford to do without the benefits of access to global finance, including the use of the financial services of foreign financial firms. This section focuses on the impact of foreign bank entry and the implications of new developments in technology and communications.

Foreign bank entry

In a number of developing countries, there has recently been a big increase in the share of banking assets controlled by foreign companies (figure 4.4). Most of this

Box 4.8
Strengthening bank exit mechanisms: lessons from Latin America

Strong capital and adequate monitoring alone can fail to curb moral hazard problems sufficiently if exit mechanisms do not work properly. Bank exit is the strongest disciplining device. Detailed studies of Latin American countries provide some general lessons regarding reform of bank failure resolution frameworks.

Tighten access criteria to liquidity of last resort. In particular, overgenerous (that is, automatic, unlimited, and uncollateralized) central bank overdraft facilities should be phased out.

Reinforce prompt corrective regimes. Prompt correction can in part take the form of increasingly tight enforcement measures and restrictions on bank activities, to be applied automatically as the shortfall in capital ratio relative to the required level grows larger.

Avoid bank interventions that give rise to risks from co-administration. In other words, there should be a clear definition of the rights of shareholders. This is a problem with arrangements under which the supervisory authority assumes the administration (directly or via delegation) of an open bank that is still the property of its shareholders. Such arrangements implicitly invite shareholders to argue in lawsuits that the bank was ruined by the authorities.

Introduce efficient resolution techniques for a closed bank. In Argentina, to preserve asset value, assets of failed banks are immediately transferred to a trust administered by a sound bank, under a contract that provides incentives for maximum value recovery. To minimize contagion risk, as many deposits as possible are swiftly transferred (say, over a weekend) to other banks in the system, which receive, in compensation, participation in the asset trust.

Restrict the use of premium-based deposit insurance funds to closed-bank resolution. In some instances public agencies have purchased shares of (that is, injected capital into) a troubled open bank *after* its shareholders' equity was fully written off or substantially diluted. Ongoing reforms in the region seek to ensure that deposit insurance funds cannot be used to finance this sort of bank intervention/nationalization, from which governments have typically found it difficult to extricate themselves.

Source: de la Torre 2000; Burki and Perry 1998.

Figure 4.4
Increase in the market share of majority foreign-owned banks, selected countries, 1994 and 1999

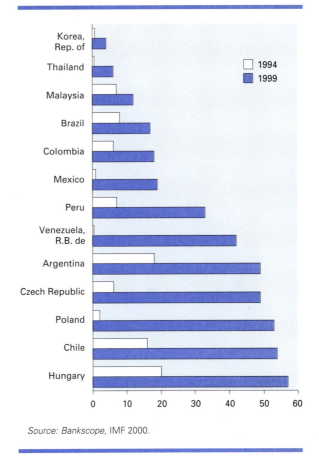

Source: Bankscope, IMF 2000.

Foreign banks tend to enter countries that have strong business ties with their home country.[49] While foreign banks tend to follow their clients abroad, there is also evidence that they are attracted to countries with large banking markets and high growth rates, which provide profitable opportunities.[50] This suggests that they seek out local profit opportunities and thus do not exclusively follow clients abroad. Even after accounting for the attractiveness of the destination market, however, some countries still have relatively little foreign bank presence. Much of the explanation lies in restrictive entry policies that limit competition from foreign sources.[51]

The steady increase in foreign bank assets in developing countries raises questions about the potential benefits, costs, and risks associated with international banking. Foreign banks may create competitive pressures that stimulate efficiency, innovation, and stronger supervision and regulation. Through these channels, liberalizing restrictions on foreign bank entry can im-

foreign entry has been through the acquisition of domestic banks in the host country. For example, since the mid-1990s Banco Santander Central Hispano (BSCH) and Banco Bilbao Vizcaya Argentaria (BBVA) have spent about $13 billion to purchase control of 30 major banks in Latin America. Those banks have $126 billion in assets—almost 10 percent of the region's banking assets, or 7.5 percent of regional GDP.[48]

prove the quality of financial services, boost economic growth, and reduce financial fragility. At the same time, foreign banks may facilitate the flows of international capital that suddenly withdraws from these markets for home-country reasons. Foreign-owned banks may overwhelm the capabilities of domestic regulators if their home countries also have weak supervisory and regulatory capacity.[52] There have also been concerns that the entry of foreign banks may be associated with less finance for the more disadvantaged segments of the economy, including smaller firms.

Recent evidence across many countries indicates that foreign bank presence is, in fact, associated with lower profitability and lower overhead expenses and interest margins for domestic banks. This suggests that foreign entry improves sector efficiency.[53] Moreover, evidence from Argentina indicates that foreign banks exerted competitive pressure on domestic banks, especially those focused on mortgage lending and on manufacturing.[54] As described in the previous section, restrictions on foreign entry are associated, on average, with lower loan portfolio quality and greater sector fragility.[55]

These efficiency improvements depend on the market that is entered and on the type of entrant. Empirical evidence indicates that foreign entrants are no more efficient than domestic ones in countries where banking sectors are well developed.[56] In countries with less-developed sectors, that result is reversed. Cross-country evidence indicates that reputable foreign entrants are more efficient than local competitors.[57] Country-level evidence from Argentina, Colombia, Greece, Hungary, Portugal, and Spain also indicates that foreign entry (typically from more industrial countries) has led to substantial gains in terms of efficiency.[58] The main conclusion is that the beneficial effects of foreign entry appear to be far more pronounced in developing countries, where local banks typically have high overhead costs and low profitability relative to entrants.[59] In developing countries, foreign banks' technological and efficiency advantages seem to be strong enough to overcome informational disadvantages they may have in lending or raising funds locally.

The arrival of reputable foreign banks is also generally associated with an improvement in prudential regulations. Foreign banks bring better accounting and information disclosure standards, since they adhere to their home country regulations. Furthermore, if local banks want to establish a reciprocal presence in industrial countries—to be able to match the range of services foreign banks are offering their local clients—they

must obtain licenses abroad. The need to satisfy the host countries that their home country regulation is adequate puts pressure on local regulators to upgrade their prudential regulations, as has happened in Mexico in the context of the North American Free Trade Agreement (NAFTA). Among the foreign entrants, some may also prove unsound, as illustrated by the failure of the Bank of Credit and Commerce International (BCCI), which was widely established in both developing and industrial countries. These considerations are another reason for strengthening prudential regulation and providing a better financial infrastructure.

There are also potential risks in foreign bank entry. One concern is that rapid foreign entry could erode the franchise values of domestic banks and therefore be destabilizing. This may require a transition period, to allow time for efficiency adjustments in the domestic sector and for improvements in prudential regulation and supervision. However, the available evidence indicates that foreign bank presence actually reduces the probability of systemic crisis in the banking sector.[60] In addition, there is evidence that during the Tequila Crisis private foreign banks in Argentina maintained higher loan growth rates than either the domestic private or the state-owned banks.[61]

Similarly, European banks have been very active in transition economies, and the expansion of Spanish banks into Latin America has led to policy concerns about increased foreign ownership in the banking industry.[62] So far, the benefits associated with entry appear to outweigh the risks associated with concentrated foreign ownership.

Another concern with foreign bank entry has been its potential impact on lending to small and medium-size enterprises (SMEs). If foreign banks dominate domestic banking systems, this might reduce the access of SMEs to finance, owing to information problems. But this problem is unlikely to be severe because foreign firms tend to enter by acquiring local banks and because competition from more efficient foreign banks may force local banks into new market niches, such as SME lending, where they have a comparative advantage.

The detailed evidence available from Hungary indicates that foreign banks are heavily involved in retail banking, in both deposit taking and consumer lending. There is also evidence that foreign competition has compelled some domestic banks to seek new market niches (box 4.9). In the Argentine experience, banks acquired by foreign banks did not at first emphasize con-

Box 4.9
The effects of foreign ownership of banks in Hungary

By allowing foreign banks to set up new operations and by privatizing its large commercial banks, involving strategic foreign investors, the Hungarian government has permitted foreign banks to penetrate more deeply and more quickly into its banking sector than has any other transition country government.

Within a relatively short period, the ownership structure of Hungarian banking has been completely overhauled. Despite some initial dislocation, service provision has slowly widened and improved. Notably, not all foreign banks have pursued the same objectives or clientele. Many are active in retail banking, in both deposit taking and lending to households.

At the end of 1999, banks in which foreign interests owned more than 50 percent of equity accounted for 56.6 percent of total banking assets, up from 19.8 percent in 1994. If the threshold level for foreign control is lowered to 40 percent of equity, the figure increases to 80.4 percent of total assets.

In 1990, under the communist system, Orszagos Takarekpenztar es Kereskedelmi Bank (OTP) held 98.4 percent of all loans to households and collected 93.2 percent of all primary deposits. By 1999 the reorganized OTP retained only 52.4 percent of household deposits and 55.7 percent of household credits. The combined share of deposits of the largest six banks—four of which are foreign owned—declined from 99.4 percent in 1990 to 84.6 percent in 1999. The share of household credit fell from 99.4 percent to 66.4 percent, which indi-

cates that the small and medium-size banks—most of which are foreign owned—made important inroads into retail banking. Both the domestic banks purchased by foreigners and the foreign greenfield operations made gains in retail banking. However, the greenfield banks did so earlier (see figure 4.3).

Banks have also actively sought specific market niches. For the most part, small banks use the household deposits that they collect to lend to other households, while larger banks use them to support other types of lending, such as commercial loans. With respect to intermediation, foreign greenfield banks return 23 percent of their deposits to the household sector in the form of loans, up from 9.9 percent in 1996. By contrast, private domestic banks return only 16 percent to the household sector, down from 18 percent in 1996.

Starting from a low level of checking accounts, Hungary "leapfrogged" that medium of payment and moved directly to electronic bank cards. Among transition countries in the region, Hungary had the second-highest number (after Slovenia) of Visa and Europay cards, at 358 per 1,000 inhabitants in 1999. The figures for the Czech Republic and Poland were 208 and 181, respectively. During this same period the number of ATMs increased by three and a half times, although about one-third of all ATMs are in Budapest.

Source: Bonin and Abel 2000.

---

sumer or mortgage and property lending. But they soon entered the mortgage business aggressively, driving down local banks' profit margins on this business.[63]

E-finance and alternative forms of entry

Developments in computing and communications technology are reshaping the way in which financial services are delivered worldwide. Technology is starting to allow consumers in developing countries to access some financial services on terms comparable to those available to consumers in advanced countries (box 4.10). For example, the growth of the Internet will make direct international financial transactions available even to small firms and individuals.[64] The speed of these developments and the extent to which they will displace the need for local presence of markets and financial intermediaries is unclear, but this issue is most pressing for the smallest developing countries.

Certain basic conditions are necessary before technological developments can provide widespread benefits. These include literacy (chapter 1) and electricity and telephone service (chapter 8). Also, some services that require face-to-face contact and established relationships between provider and user are crucial. But

while some services have to be provided locally, technology has the potential to facilitate the efficient entry of other service providers.

Policymakers in developing countries need to realize that electronic entry may rapidly erode the franchise values of domestic financial institutions and make it much harder to erect the kinds of barrier that are possible in the case of physical entry. Thus, it is important to develop effective exit policies so that weakened financial institutions can leave the market before they pose serious systemic risks. In addition, increased access to foreign financial services is likely to entail increased use of foreign currencies, which will accentuate the risks of exchange rate and interest rate volatility for countries that have their own currency.[65] The increased complexity of financial instruments being offered by the financial system and the ease with which fraudulent services can be offered over the Internet also increase the risks posed by criminal activities in financial markets. This underlines the need for greater prudential alertness.

How to enhance access to financial services

Whether they are based in New York or Nairobi, lenders need some assurance that they will be repaid. No mat-

Box 4.10
Technology and provision of financial services

Internet and wireless communications technologies are having a profound effect on financial services. Using credit-scoring and other data-mining techniques, for example, providers can create and tailor products over the Internet at very low cost. They can better stratify their customer base through analysis of Internet-collected data and allow consumers to build preference profiles online. This permits personalization of information and services. It also allows more personalized pricing of financial services and more effective identification of credit risks. At the same time, the Internet allows new financial service providers to compete more effectively for customers because it does not distinguish between traditional "bricks and mortar" providers of financial services and those without physical presence.

The lowering of scale economies has increased competition, particularly among financial services that can be easily unbundled and commoditized through automation. These include payment and brokerage services, mortgage loans, insurance, and even trade finance. Most of these services require limited capital outlays and no unique technology. Lower transaction costs can substantially increase competition among providers and cost savings for consumers. Commissions and fees fell from an average of $52.89 a trade in early 1996 to $15.67 in mid-1998. By mid-2000 some online brokerage services had reduced their commissions to zero.

Source: Claessens, Glaessner, and Klingebiel 2000.

ter how developed a country's financial system is, information problems about credit quality and the relatively high fixed costs of small-scale lending may limit access to financial services for poor people and for SMEs.

Where formal mechanisms are absent, microfinance institutions and informal group lending institutions such as rotating savings and credit associations (ROSCAs) are well known for their use of group lending and peer monitoring as reputational mechanisms to ensure payment and overcome information and enforcement problems (chapters 2 and 9). Their design features and potential benefits have been discussed in past *World Development Reports*.[66] In these institutions, reputation serves as a substitute for collateral.

But enforcement mechanisms that rely solely on reputation tend to limit the number of participants in market activities. And local groups often suffer from the same shocks, making insurance difficult. There are limits to the benefits that informal credit associations can

provide. To a lesser extent, the same limitations apply to microfinance programs. To expand the pool of investable resources, improve their allocation, and offer better opportunities for risk diversification, borrowers and firms typically need funds from a wider pool of providers.

This section provides examples of institutions that spur financial sector development by improving information flows or facilitating dispute resolution. Improving the collateral laws and establishing collateral registries, so that borrowers and lenders have clearly defined rights in the event of default, are effective ways of expanding access for those who currently do not have access to financial markets. Another way to improve access is to improve the availability of information on small borrowers. Credit registries, which collect information on payment histories, allow potential borrowers to use their good credit records to secure finance. Computerized credit-scoring models are already lowering the costs of collecting and analyzing such information. These vehicles for depersonalized credit mobilization point to concrete steps that governments can take to facilitate broader access to credit.

Traditional collateral law

A solution to the problem of access to credit, particularly for poorer people and for SMEs, is for a borrower to pledge assets that lenders find valuable as collateral. In the event of default, the lender seizes the collateral. While that concept is simple, establishing the types of permissible collateral, the priority of claimants, and workable enforcement and recovery mechanisms in the case of default can be very difficult.

First, countries may have several laws that cover secured transactions. As long as there is some method of assigning priority in laws, this may not be a problem. In developing countries, there is often no such method. Efficient enforcement of collateral law requires recognition that individual laws must work together within a broader framework. Difficulties arise in creating a security interest because laws may not anticipate many developments in terms of economic transactions, economic agents, or types of property. Laws may limit who can lend and what type of property can serve as collateral. They may limit the means for identifying the collateral by requiring a detailed description of each item of an inventory. Laws may also limit the use of future assets as collateral, such as claims on growing crops. All these factors may prevent private lenders from financing transactions because they cannot be sure that the security agreement they write is legally valid and enforceable in court.

A lender's willingness to accept collateral depends on enforcement: the prospects for seizing it and selling it quickly in the event of default and then applying the proceeds from the sale to the outstanding balance of the loan. When borrowers cannot use their assets as collateral for loans and cannot purchase goods on credit using those same goods as collateral, interest rates on loans tend to be higher to reflect the risk to lenders.

In many developing countries, where legal and regulatory constraints make it difficult to use movable property as collateral, high interest rates make capital equipment much more expensive for entrepreneurs relative to their counterparts in industrial countries. Many businesses postpone capital investment, which reduces productivity and keeps incomes low. Annual welfare losses caused by barriers to secured transactions have been estimated at 5 to 10 percent of GDP in Argentina and Bolivia.[67] Land is an obvious collateral asset (chapter 2). The benefits of expanding the range of permissible collateral options to include movable assets—such as automobiles, machinery, farm equipment, and livestock—are substantial. In the United States, for example, about half of all credit is secured by some kind of movable property. Roughly two-thirds of all bank loans is secured by either movable property or real estate, and nonbank institutions that lend against movable property, such as leasing and finance companies, do almost as much lending as banks.[68]

The key problem with movable property as collateral is that the lender faces a constant threat that it will disappear. Supporting institutions are necessary to manage this risk. For example, perfection—the establishment of the rank of priority of the claim against the collateral—is a crucial element of any secured transaction. Countries may differ as to how priority is determined for different instruments and transactions, but the issue is to set rules for defining priority. Fragmented legal frameworks (which lead to priority conflicts) still exist in many industrial countries, but in most Western European countries extensive jurisprudence or case law over the last 100 years has established priority rules among different claims. Similar processes relying on the judiciary may evolve in developing countries. One way in which developing country policymakers may simplify and speed up the process is by adopting a framework that establishes clear priority. In addition, for lenders to be able to assess the risk of a transaction, there need to be reliable and easily accessible registries of all security interests in collateralized assets.

Laws must be flexible enough to permit borrowers to use the assets that they have as collateral. In Argentina, Bolivia, El Salvador, Guatemala, Honduras, and Nicaragua the law calls for a specific description of any property that is pledged to secure credit.[69] Pledges against cattle must therefore identify the individual cows pledged—by the numbers tattooed on them, for example. In the event of default, this can cause serious problems, as the lender must ensure that the cattle designated in the pledge are the ones seized.

In industrial countries a binding pledge can be based on a security interest in, say, $200,000 worth of cattle. In the U.S. state of Kansas, for example, this more flexible method makes cattle the preferred collateral for bank loans, followed by machinery and real estate.[70] This is not only because such pledges are easy to verify but also because cattle that secure a loan in default in Kansas can be repossessed and sold, without judicial intervention, within one to five days. The appropriate legal framework and the threat of predictable court rulings can be enough to supplant real estate as the preferred form of collateral. The inherent liquidity of some types of movable property makes them ideal candidates for collateral.

The specifics of appropriate collateral systems across developing countries may vary, but this appears to be an area where policymakers can take concrete steps to expand access to credit. The first task is to establish what assets people, and the working poor in particular, actually own. Even the very poor often have movable property that could serve as collateral—such as equipment, tools, gold and silver jewelry, and inventories of goods to sell. The second step is to determine what legal framework would support their use as collateral. This could enable poor people to purchase equipment and tools on credit, using only those goods as collateral, or to use their existing stocks of goods (including inventories) as security for loans. The third step is to publish priority through public registries, so that lenders can establish their claims on pledged assets.

Registry frameworks for secured interests should require only notice that a security interest exists, rather than details of the entire contract. Notice filing systems should probably transfer to lenders the responsibility for the legality and validity of the security agreement, instead of giving such responsibilities to registry functionaries. Eliminating government legal review and government guarantee of the legal validity of security interests that are filed would also tend to simplify procedures. In addition, policymakers may eliminate tax and notary fees for filing and retrieving information, while providing for direct and full public access to the filing systems for reading and copying filed information.

Registries of secured interests can be publicly or privately operated. Both private and public suppliers, when exposed to competition, have incentives to improve quality, cut costs, and lower prices to increase the volume of business and the coverage of their registry. Determining the appropriate number of competing entities would appear to be better left to the market, provided there are no other public policy objectives that would be ignored by private providers. In private systems with many suppliers, lenders may have to search multiple collateral registries. But this concern may be less severe than having a monopoly provider with little incentive to provide accurate information.

Efforts to educate judges about the new collateral law and the priority of claims as reflected in the registry would result in more predictable rulings. That predictability, in turn, should imply less recourse to the courts, which should facilitate greater secured lending. In countries with weak judicial systems, it may make sense to rely on methods of private enforcement that shift out of the courts the bulk of the work of repossessing and selling collateral. A simple procedure could be added in the enforcement chapter of the secured transactions law whereby a creditor, under his own liability, may request a judge or other public official to order the seizure of collateral. Such a judge or official need not rule on the underlying debt. El Salvador, for example, has considered introducing this procedure. The United States and Canada use creditor-controlled repossession and sale of collateral, rather than judicially administered repossession and sale. Some Western European nations have emphasized judicial reform. This is a longer-term process, particularly in developing countries. Notaries in Spain have the power to seize property, for mortgages, without a court order and without the presence of court officials. In Jamaica a vendor's bailiff authorized by the court may be able to act on behalf of a particular vendor to repossess property that belongs to the vendor under the terms and conditions of a bill of sale or a hire-purchase agreement. In this case, because the bailiff has

permission from the court, court officials need not be present at the time the property is being seized.

Technology may make it easier to overcome other institutional weaknesses. For example, while many industrial countries took years to develop filing systems with clear rankings of priority of claims, developing countries could conceivably rely on simple databases and Internet-based systems, instead of manual confirmation and highly secure archival systems.[71]

Credit registries and credit reporting agencies

Credit access could further expand if potential borrowers could use reputation, as summarized in their payment histories, to secure funds from lenders that they do not personally know. For credit registries to function properly, at least two conditions must be met. First, some individual or group must recognize that there is potential value in collecting credit history information. Most often, it has been private firms that have found commercial benefit in providing information to lenders, although some public credit registries do exist.[72] Second, borrowers must recognize that it is in their interest to provide truthful information to creditors through the registry. All credit information–sharing devices necessitate the loss of a certain amount of privacy for potential borrowers.

An accurate registry can provide borrowers with strong incentives to honor their debt obligations because those that do not will damage their reputations and therefore curtail future access to credit. Credit registries use reputation to enhance enforcement in the same way as informal networks, but they have access to a wide variety of actual and potential business partners. In addition, by providing reliable information, registries can increase access to credit for underserved segments of society (box 4.11).

Many credit registries are run by credit-reporting agencies (CRAs), private third-party providers that make information available not just to members of an exclusive industry group but to any creditor willing to pay their subscription fee.[73] By equalizing access to information, CRAs enlarge the pool of creditors, enhance competition among them, and lower the prices of financial products. Moreover, agents are made more mobile, as registries reduce the cost of severing established lending relationships and seeking better opportunities. Indeed, this sort of information sharing is most valuable in large markets with high borrower mobility and

Box 4.11
Credit registries

Information sharing through credit registries is especially useful in large markets with high borrower mobility and heterogeneity, as in the case of the United States in the 19th century, when private credit registries took hold. Their rapid growth owes much to network externalities. As information on more and more debtors was amassed, the value of the registries to potential creditors grew, making it easier to transfer funds over ever-greater geographic and social distances.

While credit registries offer the greatest benefits in mobile, heterogeneous societies, there are potential benefits in almost all developing countries, especially those mired in a credit culture characterized by nonpayment. In addition, registries can benefit large segments of the population that have never enjoyed access to credit.

The credit-reporting agency system requires that business owners agree to scrutiny of past behavior, including personal spending habits. During the latter decades of the 19th century, Americans' initial suspicion gave way to wide acceptance. As the practice spread, the business press affirmed the agencies' usefulness, and courts further advanced acceptance by generally ruling in the agencies' favor. Although some Americans still see registries as an intrusion on their privacy, their development is partly responsible for the widespread access to credit that characterizes the U.S. market.

Source: Barron and Staten 2000; Olegario 2000, World Development Report 2002 background paper; Vose 1916.

heterogeneity.[74] Increases in the size of the community and open borders or increased competition, which are likely to bring new entrants to the business community, are likely to enhance demand for these registries.

One way to expand credit reporting and thus access to funds is through competition between private registries. Competition between companies expanded the scope of private registries in the 19th century United States.[75] Public institutions can also perform a role. Germany, for example, established the first public credit registry in 1934, followed by France in 1946, Italy and Spain in 1962, and Belgium in 1967. Since 1989, 12 of 56 nations surveyed reported that they had created a public registry; 9 of them were in Latin America.[76] But public registries tend to be tools for supervisors to measure the health of individual financial institutions, and they often provide less complete information on borrowers than private agencies. In many countries the public registry functions as a kind of "negative list" or

enforcement device, and data on defaults or late payments are erased once they have been paid. Also, many nations distribute only current data, such as data for the previous month, so that the public registry does not offer a complete history of a borrower's credit behavior. A study based on cross-country surveys concludes that, rather than being substitutes, public and private registries tend to be complementary parts of a nation's credit reporting system.[77]

There already has been substantial recent entry by private credit-reporting agencies into developing countries. In a recent survey of private credit registries, 25 of 50 respondents began operating their registries since 1989, with heavy entry in Latin America and Eastern Europe.[78] This suggests a role for governments as facilitators rather than as the actual administrators of registries.

As facilitators of registries, governments need to provide an environment where individuals and firms find it in their interest to provide truthful credit histories. Concrete steps include standardizing accounting procedures and improving tax administration to bolster the reliability of financial statements. One study found that survey respondents from credit reporting agencies in China and Kenya noted that many businesses do not follow accounting law in preparing financial statements and that many avoid taxes through secret bank accounts or by keeping multiple sets of books.[79] Respondents to the same survey from Russia and Mexico noted that many individuals and business owners are reluctant to provide truthful information about their financial situation because of fear of crime. Governments, therefore, must provide a general level of security for their citizens before credit registries can function well.

Policymakers also need to confront concerns over privacy. Distinctions between consumer and business credit are important. Less restricted flow of information is likely to be more important for business creditors, whose loans tend to be much larger, and for whom timeliness in reaching a lending decision is more critical. Because businesses are often both creditors and borrowers, they are more likely to understand the principles and risks involved and so are unlikely to require the same level of legal protection as consumers.[80] The courts need to enforce privacy laws in a timely and predictable manner, however a country's government decides to resolve privacy issues.

A number of related developments make it more likely that credit registry information can assist the working poor in developing countries. In Hungary, for example, all credit registry information has been computerized. This makes it easier for intermediaries to assess the creditworthiness of potential borrowers. Moreover, the foreign banks that are entering many developing countries may be more inclined to use this information. These foreign banks tend to have standard credit-scoring models for certain types of loans. Local banks will likely mimic these models within a short time.

The collection, processing, and use of borrowing history and other information relevant to household and small business lending is a rapidly growing activity in both the public and private sectors. Computer technology is greatly reducing unit costs in this area and improving the sophistication with which that data can be employed to give an assessment of creditworthiness. The poor can potentially benefit from these developments, but the fullest benefits will materialize only if basic preconditions such as literacy and access to the Internet are met. Without also improving the human capital of the poor, technological advances in provision of financial services will not be as empowering a force as they could be.

Conclusions

Financial development leads to growth and poverty alleviation. Policies are likely to be more effective if directed at improving the legal and regulatory environment to ensure efficient delivery of financial services, rather than at the structure of financial markets themselves. The importance of secure rights for investors and of the overall efficiency of contract enforcement mechanisms is key. Openness to trade, and to foreign entrants and competition, tends to contribute to the development of financial institutions regardless of a country's legal origin, colonial history, or political system.

Financial regulation today mostly focuses on improving the informational efficiency of financial markets. To be effective, these regulations need to be enforced. Enforcement becomes much easier if the regulation is incentive-compatible, that is, if it encourages and makes use of the monitoring and disciplining ability of market participants. In addition, an essential element of improving the quality and effectiveness of market discipline for financial institutions is ensuring the accuracy and availability of information on the operations of these institutions. Countries with poor information and human resources that face problems in monitoring and enforcing regulations such as capital standards may still benefit from additional buffers—such as liquidity requirements or prompt corrective action rules—that are easier to observe and enforce. Middle- and high-income countries may do better by complementing these standards, for example, through the use of subordinated—that is, uninsured—debt provided by market actors.

Mounting evidence on costs of public ownership highlights the need for bank privatization, especially in low-income countries where state ownership is high. But the evidence also indicates that it is important to complement bank privatization by institutional changes which strengthen the overall incentive environment and prepare the state banks for sale. Simple ownership change without institutions to foster the right incentives in new owners will not lead to a more efficient sector.

Instead it will lead to misallocation of resources and will endanger financial stability. Resource allocation affects poor people through negative effects on growth. Financial instability and crises also hurt poor people. In terms of foreign entry, existing evidence does not indicate that such entry, either de novo or through purchase of an existing domestic bank, has adverse consequences. In fact, such entrants bring competition, which improves efficiency and can also strengthen the demand for better institutions to support banking.

Information problems and the relatively high fixed costs of small-scale lending may limit access to financial services by the poor, and by small or micro enterprises. Improving the collateral laws and establishing collateral registries are effective ways of expanding access. Credit registries that collect information on payment histories can improve information flows on small borrowers and allow potential borrowers to use their good reputation to secure finance.

PART III

Government

MANY OF THE INSTITUTIONS THAT SUPPORT MARKETS ARE PRO-vided by the state. The ability of the state to provide these institutions—often referred to as governance—is therefore fundamental to vibrant and broad-based markets. Chapter 5 on *Political Institutions and Governance* discusses how political institutions shape governance around the world by setting limits on the ability of the state to exercise its power arbitrarily. This broad theme also runs through chapter 6 on *The Judicial System,* which examines the determinants of the efficiency of the judiciary and emphasizes the importance of judicial accountability and independence from political pressures. Chapter 7 on *Competition* stresses the central role of competitive pressures in creating well-functioning markets, the institutions that support or undermine competition, and the role of competition in spurring institutional change. Chapter 8 on *Regulation of Infrastructure* takes up the interplay between competition and regulation in ensuring that the market for infrastructure services operates fairly and is accessible to all.

CHAPTER 5

Political Institutions and Governance

In framing a government to be administered by men over men, the great difficulty lies in this: you must first enable the government to control the governed; and in the next place oblige it to control itself.

—James Madison, 1788

Many of the institutions that support markets are publicly provided. The ability of the state to provide these institutions is therefore an important determinant of how well individuals behave in markets and how well markets function. Successful provision of such institutions is often referred to as "good governance."[1] Good governance includes the creation, protection, and enforcement of property rights, without which the scope for market transactions is limited. It includes the provision of a regulatory regime that works with the market to promote competition. And it includes the provision of sound macroeconomic policies that create a stable environment for market activity. Good governance also means the absence of corruption, which can subvert the goals of policy and undermine the legitimacy of the public institutions that support markets.

Good governance matters for growth and poverty reduction. Many studies have documented strong associations between per capita incomes and measures of the strength of property rights and the absence of corruption. To a certain extent, this reflects the greater capacity of rich countries to provide good institutions. But recent findings also point to a strong effect running from better governance to better development outcomes.[2] There is evidence that excessive regulation undermines economic growth. There is also evidence that poor macroeconomic policy and restrictive trade regimes adversely affect a country's growth performance.[3] Through its powerful effects on overall economic growth, good governance is therefore central to the goal of poverty reduction. Moreover, several dimensions of poor governance—notably corruption and high inflation—impose costs that fall disproportionately on poor people.[4] Improvements in these dimensions of governance may be especially important for poor people.

Good governance requires the power to carry out policies and to develop institutions that may be unpopular among some—or even a majority—of the population. Public officials cannot enforce property rights without the ability to try, judge, and punish those who do not respect those rights. The state cannot provide costly public goods without the power to tax individuals and companies to raise public revenues. Public officials cannot promote competition without the power to enforce regulations against monopolistic abuses. They cannot provide a stable macroeconomic environment without the power to see the state's policies implemented.

There is a tension in the development of the modern state between ensuring that public officials have sufficient power to deliver good governance and ensuring that they are constrained from using this power arbitrarily in the interests of the privileged few.[5] When they are not constrained, their ability to provide the institutions that support markets—by increasing access to information, enhancing competition, and enforcing contracts—is impaired. This is particularly important in the case of the protection of property rights, where the formal establishment of such rights has little effect in the absence of a credible commitment by the state to respect and enforce them.

Box 5.1
Political institutions, property rights and fiscal outcomes in 17th century England

In England in the early 17th century, the Stuart monarchy, to finance its expenditures, increasingly resorted to "forced loans"—where the lender had no recourse if loans were not repaid. This practice was one of many highly visible signs that the regime had no commitment to protecting property rights. Other indications included outright confiscation of land and funds, forced public procurement at below-market prices, a willingness to remove judges who ruled against the Crown, and the sale of monopoly rights over various lucrative economic activities. This arbitrary exercise of sovereign power was interrupted during the civil war in the middle of the century, but the restoration of the monarchy was accompanied by the return of the same excesses.

The Glorious Revolution of 1688 ushered in a series of fundamental changes in political institutions that limited the arbitrary exercise of power by the sovereign. The revolution established the supremacy of parliament over the Crown and vested in parliament the exclusive right to raise taxes and audit the expenditures of the Crown. These steps were followed by the establishment of the Bank of England, which exercised important independent control over public finances. The result of these changes was a more equitable division of power between the executive, legislative, and judicial branches of government. These restraints on the arbitrary exercise of power greatly enhanced the state's ability to finance public expenditures by issuing debt.

The impact of these changes in political institutions and in the protection of property rights can be seen in the development of debt markets. In 1688 the Crown was able to place public debt equivalent to only 2 to 3 percent of GDP—and only of very short maturity and at very high interest rates. By 1697 the Crown was able to place and service debt equivalent to 40 percent of GDP, at lower interest rates and with longer maturities. The emergence of a functioning public debt market in turn benefited the development of the private capital markets that helped finance the Industrial Revolution that followed.

Source: North and Weingast 1989.

stitutions also influence the extent of *competition* in the political process and the extent to which this competition holds politicians accountable for their actions. For example, delegating responsibility to local governments can influence the incentives for competition between jurisdictions to provide improved public goods.

This chapter considers a wide variety of political institutions that, among other things, affect the behavior of public officials. In formal democracies, which constitute a growing share of the world's countries, political institutions include the electoral rules that lay out the procedures by which governments are elected and replaced. They also include the constitutional rules that determine the division of power between the executive and legislative branches of government—and the limits on the power of each. In all countries, political institutions and traditions delineate the division of power between central and local governments and the assignment of responsibilities to different agencies within the government. These institutions may be formal (such as electoral rules), or they may be informal (for example, the role of shared beliefs among members of the same political party in shaping behavior). There are also important interactions between political institutions. For example, the credibility of autonomous agencies will depend on the extent to which other political institutions limit the power of governments to revoke the agencies' independence in the future.

Institutions that limit the state's capacity for arbitrary action will improve its ability to provide institutions that support broad-based markets. But too often among the poorest countries in the world, the ability of the state to provide market-supporting institutions is hampered by the absence of effective restraints on public officials. This illustrates the broader theme that runs through this Report of complementarities among institutions: policymakers need to adjust institutional designs to take these complementarities into account. For example, in the absence of effective checks and balances in the political process, independent regulatory agencies will be independent in name only. When state capacity is weak, simpler and less discretionary regulation is less likely to be undermined by corruption. And when central government control is ineffective, the potential benefits of greater decentralization and competition among jurisdictions may not be realized.

No single set of political institutions can successfully support market institutions everywhere and at all levels of development; this points to the importance of inno-

Political institutions help determine limits on the arbitrary exercise of power by politicians and bureaucrats. They do so by delineating property rights between the state and the private sector and providing for their *enforcement.* A historical example of this can be found in the changes in political institutions in 17th century England, which placed limits on the power of the Crown to expropriate property and so contributed to the security of private property (box 5.1). Political in-

Figure 5.1
Variation in the quality of policies around the world

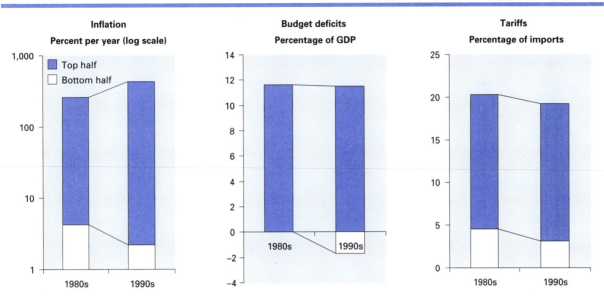

Note: The labels top half and bottom half refer to the averages of the top half and bottom half respectively in a sample of 85 industrial and developing countries for which all three variables are available for the 1980s and 1990s.
Source: World Bank data.

vation and experimentation in the design of the institutions of the state itself. This chapter also illustrates how open information sharing can improve governance and reduce corruption (see also chapter 10).

This chapter builds on past World Development Reports, especially *World Development Report 1997* on the role of the state. Part of the 1997 Report was devoted to the institutions that restrain arbitrary state action and corruption, and it stressed the importance of judicial independence, the formal separation of powers, and international institutions as a counterbalance to the power of the state. Since then, a large body of research has shed new light on these issues, and this chapter emphasizes what is new. This chapter is also selective in the topics it covers. The role of the state in protecting property rights and promoting the rule of law through the judicial system is taken up separately in the next chapter. The role of the state as a regulator to promote competition in markets is discussed in chapters 7 and 8.

This chapter addresses three dimensions of governance in detail. The first section explores the ways in which political institutions influence policy choices, focusing on fiscal, regulatory, and trade policies. This section emphasizes the types of institutions that limit the ability of the state to provide policies that favor special interests over the general interest. The second section discusses corruption. In light of the classic definition of corruption as the exercise of public power for private gain, the section emphasizes the types of institutions that limit the ability of public officials to act in their own self-interest in this way. The third section discusses how the institutions of taxation influence the incentives of the state to raise revenues and to provide the institutions that support markets.

Political institutions and policy choices

The quality of policies adopted by governments around the world varies tremendously. Figure 5.1 illustrates this variation in policy for several measures of policy outcomes—inflation, budget deficits, and tariffs—averaged over the 1980s and 1990s. Each panel shows the average value of the policy variable for the top half of a sample of 85 industrial and developing countries and the corresponding average for the bottom half of the sample. Average inflation in the best-performing half of the sample was 4 percent per year in the 1980s and 2 percent per year in the 1990s. Among the worst-performing countries, inflation averaged upward of 200 percent per year. The same is true for budget deficits, which were insignificantly small or in surplus in the

1990s among the best-performing countries but averaged over 10 percent of GDP among the worst-performing countries. The difference in tariffs between the top and bottom halves of the samples is around 15 percent.

If these differences in policy outcomes across countries matter so much for growth and poverty outcomes, why then do some countries end up with much worse policies and performance than others? This section focuses on one particular factor: the extent to which countries' political institutions are able to resolve the conflicts that inevitably arise when policies benefit some at the expense of others.

This section considers several such institutions, including the nature of the electoral system and the existence of checks and balances among different branches of government. These checks and balances can be constitutionally mandated, as in the formal division of powers between the legislative and executive branches of government or between the chambers of the legislature. They can also reflect the outcome of the electoral process, as seen in the election of a minority government that must seek support from coalition partners and is limited in its agenda by the need to make compromises with these partners. Other political institutions include the procedures by which budgets are determined and international agreements that help governments commit themselves to policies that may be unpopular at home.

This section discusses how political institutions that limit the ability of government to act arbitrarily do matter for policy outcomes. Examples from three areas—budget deficits, regulation of financial markets, and trade policy—are considered. The purpose of this discussion is not to lay out a blueprint for changes in political institutions in order to improve policy outcomes. Rather, its purpose is to illustrate how policy advice can be improved by taking political institutions into account.

Budget deficits

Budget deficits represent the difference between politically popular expenditure programs and politically unpopular taxation. Fiscal outcomes are therefore influenced by the extent to which governments are able to muster political support for necessary taxation and resist demands from interested constituencies for the expansion of spending programs that benefit them. Political institutions play an important role in this process. This section examines how cross-country differences in specific budget procedures, voting systems, and the tim-

ing of elections influence fiscal outcomes. While the overall message of this chapter emphasizes the importance of limits on state power, the discussion here illustrates some cases in which excessive limits can hinder the ability of governments to resolve conflicts over fiscal policy.

Budget processes and fiscal outcomes. Specific budget procedures can also affect the outcome of conflicts over fiscal policy. Two aspects of these procedures are noteworthy: whether governments choose to tie their hands using balanced budget rules, and whether the finance ministry has powers to resist demands from either the legislature or other branches of government for amendments to a proposed budget. To the extent that balanced budget rules—or, more generally, external constraints on finance—are effective, they can be a powerful motive for enforcing necessary compromises over fiscal policy. Similarly, when finance ministries have strong agenda-setting powers relative to the legislature or spending ministries, it is easier for central agencies to enforce fiscal discipline. Cross-country evidence from Latin America suggests that both these factors are important in determining fiscal outcomes. Countries with more hierarchical budgetary procedures favoring finance ministries tended to have better fiscal outcomes, controlling for a variety of other factors.[6] Similar evidence emerges from case studies of two Asian and three African countries. Success in instilling overall fiscal discipline was shown to be closely related to the strength of central agencies in the budget-setting process, the presence of hard budget constraints in the context of a medium-term budgeting framework, and institutions that held departments accountable for their spending.[7]

There is also some evidence from Latin American countries that balanced budget rules are associated with better fiscal outcomes.[8] But balanced budget rules alone are not enough. The design and enforcement of the rule matters as well. Evidence from the experience of individual states of the United States points to important differences in the effectiveness of different types of balanced budget rules.[9] While all U.S. states (with the exception of Vermont) have balanced budget rules, their stringency varies considerably. Some states only require the governor to submit a balanced budget to the legislature or allow the carryover of limited deficits from one year to the next. Other states strictly prohibit any deficits from being carried over by imposing end-of-year balanced budget requirements. Moreover, states differ in whether the balanced budget rule is enshrined in the state constitution or not and in whether the balanced budget rule is enforced by a state supreme court that is appointed by the executive.

These differences in institutional design have important consequences for the efficacy of balanced budget rules. Evidence suggests that more stringent rules are more effective in reducing deficits. Controlling for a variety of factors, states that switched from weak to stringent balanced budget rules were half as likely to run deficits as those that did not. In addition, constitutionally mandated balanced budget rules were much more likely to be effective than those that were legislatively imposed and so were more easily reversed. Balanced budget rules enforced by governor-appointed courts were less effective than those enforced by more independent courts.

The general lessons of this experience for developing countries is clear. Balanced budget rules can be effective, especially at the subnational level where there is little compelling rationale for countercyclical deficit spending. However, such rules are more likely to be effective if they are voluntarily adopted, if they impose hard constraints, if the rules themselves are difficult to reverse, and if they are effectively enforced by a credible third party such as a genuinely independent court or a higher level of government that has sufficient information to properly monitor subnational public finances.

Divided governments, electoral rules, and fiscal outcomes. The extent to which governments are required to share power in coalition governments is an important determinant of budgetary outcomes in OECD countries. When the power of government is checked by the need to make compromises with coalition partners, fiscal outcomes are often worse than when majority governments are in power. Figure 5.2 shows that the probability that a coalition government in an OECD country is able to sustain a fiscal adjustment (defined as four successive years of significantly lowered budget deficits) is less than half as large as the likelihood that a majority government accomplishes a fiscal adjustment.

The likelihood that countries are governed by divided governments is in turn influenced by the constitutional rules that determine how governments are selected. Coalition governments are more likely to occur under proportional electoral systems, where seats in the legislature are awarded in proportion to shares in the popular vote. A study of 60 industrial and developing

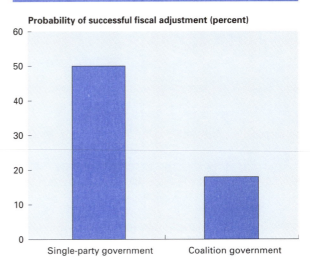

Figure 5.2
Divided governments have difficulty with fiscal adjustments

Probability of successful fiscal adjustment (percent)

Source: Alesina, Perotti, and Tavares 1998.

countries shows that, after accounting for a variety of socioeconomic factors, countries with systems of proportional election tended to have larger government expenditure and larger fiscal deficits as a share of GDP than countries with majoritarian systems. On average, fiscal deficits were 1.5 to 2 percentage points of GDP larger in countries with proportional systems.[10]

Electoral cycles in fiscal policy. Politicians motivated by the desire to remain in office have strong incentives to manipulate the fiscal process to improve their chances of reelection. This creates a tendency for fiscal performance to worsen in election years, leading to debt accumulation and macroeconomic instability. A recent study examined the effect of elections on fiscal performance in a sample of 123 industrial and developing countries. Controlling for a number of other factors, it found that fiscal deficits were on average 1 percent of GDP larger in election years and that this larger deficit persisted for several years after the election.[11] More striking is the difference between the magnitude of these electoral cycles in industrial and developing countries. Among developing countries, election year deficits were on average 2 percentage points of GDP higher. The same study found that these larger cycles in developing countries reflect the confluence of two institutional features of these countries. First, on average there are greater opportunities for incumbent pol-

Figure 5.3

Governments with fewer checks and balances than others are less likely to enforce banking regulations during crises

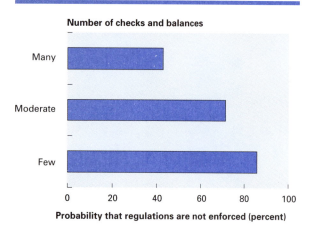

Number of checks and balances

Probability that regulations are not enforced (percent)

Note: This figure shows the probability that prudential regulations are not enforced, holding constant per capita income and the level of financial development.
Source: Keefer 2001.

iticians to extract rents from being in office, as measured by variables capturing the extent of corruption in the public sector. Second, the ability of politicians to successfully manipulate policy to influence voters was stronger when voters were poorly informed about the consequences of policy decisions. The study found that electoral cycles in fiscal policy were larger in countries where press freedoms were lower, providing evidence of the importance of open information sharing for institutional quality (chapter 10).

Financial market regulation

Banks can have strong incentives to undertake lending that is riskier than is socially optimal. Governments therefore provide prudential regulation in order to reduce banks' opportunities to engage in such lending (chapter 4). Governments can also intervene following financial crises to encourage the liquidation of insolvent banks. But the need for such regulation results in two types of conflict. First, bank owners are often politically influential and can seek to prevent politicians from approving or enforcing prudential regulations. Second, although governments may wish to commit in advance to not bail out insolvent financial institutions, after a crisis the political pressure to intervene in failed banks can be irresistible.

Many countries have established independent regulatory agencies charged with implementing financial

regulation in order to reduce these conflicts (chapter 4). However, despite their nominal independence, such regulatory agencies are often subject to political pressures. New research reveals an important possible countervailing force to these pressures—the existence of checks and balances in the political process. A recent study examined 40 banking crises occurring in a sample of 35 industrial and developing countries.[12] The study examined how the policy response to these crises depended on the extent of checks and balances in the political process, measured in terms of the number of bodies with potential veto power over policy, such as the presidency and the upper and lower chambers of the legislature. In 26 of the 40 crises, the government chose not to enforce prudential regulations. Even among countries with similar levels of income, the likelihood that regulations were not enforced was significantly higher in countries with fewer checks and balances (figure 5.3).

The example of bank crises illustrates a general difficulty that governments have in credibly committing to policies, and the potential of delegating decision-making authority to an independent agency to overcome this problem. This issue arises in many other contexts that are discussed later in this chapter, including the delegation of tax collection to an independent revenue agency or the delegation of some control over trade policy to an international organization. Given the large costs of high inflation for poor people, another important example is the problem of credibly committing to stable and noninflationary monetary policy and the role of delegating monetary policy to an independent central bank to achieve this credible commitment.

However, the empirical evidence on the effectiveness of central bank independence has been mixed. Especially among developing countries, there is little evidence that the statutory independence of the central bank makes a big difference for inflation outcomes. New research shows that when effective checks and balances limiting the ability of politicians to interfere in the decisions of a formally independent central bank are present, central bank independence can have greater payoffs in terms of improving monetary policy.[13]

International trading rules

Over the past decades countries around the world have made significant progress in reducing tariffs on international trade. Despite this progress substantial barriers to trade remain, ranging from high tariffs on certain goods in certain countries (notably industrial country barriers to agricultural imports from poor countries) to a variety of nontariff measures that serve to restrict trade and competition (see chapter 7).

The decision to liberalize trade is not simply a technocratic one but also reflects the balance of political power between the gainers and the losers from reform. Research on the politics of trade reform has been an active area, tracing back levels of protection to their more fundamental determinants. These include the incentives of those affected by trade policy changes to form lobby groups to influence policy, and the susceptibility of governments to the influence of these lobbies.[14] Cross-country and cross-industry studies of industrial and developing countries have found evidence that industries in decline, industries that are highly unionized, and industries that make substantial campaign contributions all tend to be rewarded with higher tariff protection.[15] A variety of political institutions influence the ability of those affected by trade policy to form coalitions to lobby governments. In a federal state such as Mexico, for example, trade policy legislation required broad regional support in the 1980s. As a result industries that were more geographically dispersed were more successful in obtaining tariff protection than those that were concentrated in particular regions.[16] More broadly, institutions that hold politicians accountable for their actions can help reduce special interest influence in trade policy.[17]

A particularly important institution that influences the domestic and international politics of trade policy is the World Trade Organization (WTO). The essence of the WTO is an agreement to subject bilateral negotiations over trade policy to a set of multilaterally agreed rules. These rules have evolved over time and have become increasingly complex. But they are based on two closely related basic principles: *reciprocity*, meaning that countries' reductions in tariffs are expected to be met by equivalent reductions in tariffs by other countries, and *nondiscrimination*, meaning that countries must offer the same tariffs to all members. Recent thinking on the role of the WTO reveals two important functions that this institution provides.[18]

The first function is helping countries commit to trade policy reforms that they might otherwise be tempted to reverse. For example, if formerly protected industries fail to make necessary efficiency-enhancing adjustments to free trade, then governments become vulnerable to political pressures to restore the trade barriers they had previously removed. Since WTO rules allow for costly retaliation by trading partners if tariff

Box 5.2
Packaging trade reforms

In the 1980s many developing countries turned their backs on import-substitution policies that protected domestic industries with high tariff barriers and began to liberalize trade. A lesson that emerged from this wave of trade reforms is the importance of "packaging" trade reforms to make them politically more palatable.

A widely cited study of trade liberalization episodes in developing countries identified 13 cases of particularly rapid trade reform in countries as diverse as Chile, Peru, and Turkey. In nearly half these cases, trade reforms were implemented during major macroeconomic crises as part of an overall stabilization package.

During such periods, political considerations driven by the distributional consequences of trade reform were overshadowed by a wider sense that "something needed to be done," providing the necessary political consensus for reforms. Once trade reforms had been given the opportunity to bear fruit, they created a new constituency for free trade that had not existed before. Chile's experience with trade liberalization in the 1980s is a leading example.

Source: Rodrik 1994.

cuts are reversed, governments can strengthen the credibility of their commitment to trade liberalization by subjecting themselves to the rules of this institution. Empirical evidence from the United States suggests that this credibility-enhancing role of the WTO is important.[19]

The second function that the WTO serves is to help create constituencies that provide political support for tariff reductions. In the case of unilateral tariff reductions, generating political support for trade liberalization is difficult since the efficiency gains from freer trade are widely dispersed, while the costs are highly concentrated among firms and workers in protected industries. The advantage of the WTO principle of reciprocity is that domestic tariff cuts that hurt particular protected industries can be "packaged" together with tariff cuts by trading partners, which benefit domestic producers in other industries. This means that the influence of the latter group can serve to counteract the influence of the former (box 5.2).

Corruption

It is now widely accepted that corruption has large costs for economic development. Across countries there is strong evidence that higher levels of corruption are associated with lower growth and lower levels of per capita income.[20] In the context of this Report, corruption can be thought of as a force that undermines well-function-

Box 5.3
Political connections and firm value in Indonesia

In Indonesia prior to 1998, many firms reputedly benefited from their close connections with the government in power at that time. A recent study examined 79 Indonesian firms with varying degrees of connectedness with the Suharto family and studied how their share prices responded to news about then-President Suharto's health. It found that the share prices of firms that relied more on connections with the Suharto family fell much more sharply than those of other firms in response to news that Suharto's health—and so his influence—were waning (see figure below). Based on this result, the study concluded that as much as one-quarter of the value of politically connected firms was attributable to their connections.

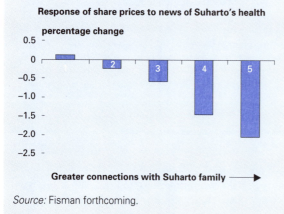

Response of share prices to news of Suharto's health

percentage change

Greater connections with Suharto family ⟶

Source: Fisman forthcoming.

ing markets in three ways: as a tax, as a barrier to entry, and by subverting the legitimacy of the state and its ability to provide institutions that support markets.

Corruption can be seen as a tax, which distorts the choice between activities and lowers the returns to public and private investments. But corruption is much worse than a tax because the revenues do not contribute to the public budget, to be spent on socially useful activities. Moreover, since corruption is illicit, there is much greater uncertainty over this form of "taxation" than conventional forms, rendering the corruption tax even more costly.[21] A study examining the impact of corruption on foreign direct investment found that an increase in corruption comparable to the difference between Singapore (which is widely perceived to have low corruption) and Mexico (which typically ranks around the middle of countries in the world in rankings of corruption perceptions) would have the same negative effect on foreign direct investment as a 50 percentage point increase in marginal tax rates on foreign invest-

ment income.[22] Another study, of manufacturing firms in Uganda, found that a 1 percent increase in bribes paid by a firm was associated with a reduction in firm growth of 3 percent, while a 1 percent increase in taxation reduced firm growth by only about 1 percent.[23] Survey evidence from transition economies suggests that firms would be willing to pay significantly higher formal taxes in exchange for eliminating corruption.[24]

Corruption also undermines the competitive forces that are central to well-functioning markets. A robustly competitive environment depends on the continuous entry of new firms (chapter 7). But when potential new firms must pay bribes at every turn in order to register and begin operations, many will decide simply not to enter, and competition will suffer. Evidence from transition economies indicates that this anticompetitive effect of corruption is important and that small firms and new entrants were significantly more likely to report corruption as an obstacle to business.[25] Corruption is also associated with lower public spending on health and education, which in turn limits opportunities for poor people to invest in their human capital and to participate in markets.[26] This problem is compounded by the fact that across countries, greater corruption is also associated with lower overall tax revenues.[27] At a deeper level, corruption undermines the legitimacy of the state itself and weakens the capacity of the state to provide institutions that support markets. A particularly pernicious form of corruption is "state capture," the ability of firms to subvert the entire political process to ensure that policies and regulations favorable to their business interests are implemented. This phenomenon has been studied most systematically in the transition economies of Eastern Europe and the former Soviet Union, but close and questionable links between businesses and governments are not unique to this region, nor are they unique to democratic systems.[28] A study of firms in Indonesia with close links to the Suharto regime concluded that one-quarter of the value of these firms was directly attributable to their political connections (box 5.3).

Given the high costs of corruption, research and policy advice have increasingly focused on identifying the root causes of corruption. *World Development Report 1997* emphasized three factors: a distorted policy environment, which creates greater opportunities for public officials to manipulate rules for their own benefit; a weak judiciary that is unable to provide a credible threat of punishment when official misconduct is discovered; and poor civil service management and low public sector pay. Subsequent research has highlighted additional factors contributing to corruption and has provided more evidence on the factors identified in *World Development Report 1997*. These are discussed below.

There is growing evidence that countries that are more *open to international trade* have lower corruption.[29] This may reflect a combination of factors. Greater openness induces more competition (chapters 1 and 7), which in turn lowers rents and lessens opportunities for corruption. Greater openness also improves information flows, which help expose official wrongdoing and also create constituencies in support of anti-corruption activities among trading partners abroad. In addition, countries that are naturally more disposed to trade because of favorable geographic characteristics will invest greater resources in developing institutions that make trade more attractive (see also chapter 1). Finally, there is some emerging evidence that as countries dismantle formal tariff barriers to trade, opportunities for corruption decrease.[30]

The evidence also shows that, controlling for the level of income, a more *complex regulatory environment* breeds corruption (chapters 1 and 7). Studies have found that countries with more elaborate procedures for registering new businesses have higher levels of corruption.[31] This in part reflects the fact that complex regulations increase opportunities for corruption. It may also reflect the fact that corrupt bureaucrats will favor the proliferation of rules and regulations that in turn create further opportunities for corruption.[32] In either case, the more complex the rules, the greater is the likelihood that officials will have discretion in how they are applied, creating opportunities for corruption (box 5.4).

Closely related to this are the effects of *inflation* on corruption. When inflation is high and variable, information about prices is difficult to obtain, creating greater opportunities for corruption in public procurement. Cross-country evidence shows that, controlling for a variety of other factors, corruption is significantly higher in countries where inflation is high and variable.

One area where the evidence is less clear-cut than the findings presented in *World Development Report 1997* is the issue of *public sector pay* and its effects on corruption. There is plenty of anecdotal evidence that the low wages available to civil servants in many developing countries drive them to take bribes in order to supplement their incomes. While at least one study has found systematic cross-country evidence of higher cor-

Box 5.4
Discretion and truck inspection in Gujarat, India

Inspectors responsible for enforcing restrictions on overloaded trucks in the Indian state of Gujarat were notoriously corrupt. They had considerable discretion over which trucks to stop for inspection. Moreover, since there was no system for reporting to the motor vehicle department the number of trucks found in violation of overloading rules, individual inspectors could negotiate a combination of reported fines and unreported bribes with individual truckers.

In 1998 a program to reduce corruption using information technology was implemented. Individual checkpoints—and their weigh-scales—were connected by computer to central offices, so that information on vehicle weights and collected fines was automatically reported to the motor vehicle department. In addition, inspectors' discretion over which trucks to stop was removed. The combination of these two measures to reduce discretion dramatically reduced opportunities for corruption.

Source: www1.worldbank.org/publicsector/egov/gujaratcs.htm.

ruption being associated with lower wages in a sample of 28 countries, other studies covering more countries fail to do so.[33] Many of these studies also do not distinguish between countries where petty corruption (which is more likely to be influenced by salaries) and grand corruption (which is less likely to be influenced by salaries) are important.[34]

Careful country-specific analysis is beginning to provide more nuanced evidence on the relative importance of wages and other factors for corruption. For example, a study of procurement contracts in public hospitals in Buenos Aires, Argentina, found that a 10 percent increase in the salary of procurement officers was associated with a 1.2 percent reduction in prices paid for hospital supplies.[35] However, this relationship between pay and performance was apparent only *after* a crackdown on corruption had been in effect for a period of six months. The crackdown itself also had significant effects on procurement prices, initially lowering them by an average of 18 percent—although this effect weakened over time. Interestingly, this particular crackdown achieved significant results without threats of penalties for wrongdoing. Instead, the staff of the health secretary simply collected data on the procurement prices of basic hospital supplies from each hospital and then circulated this information among all hospitals on a regular basis.

Political institutions that restrain politicians from arbitrary actions, and institutions that hold politicians accountable for their actions, can help reduce the opportunities and incentives for corruption. The rest of this section focuses on three such institutions that matter for corruption: the degree of decentralization, electoral rules, and press freedom and civil society. This is not an exhaustive list of political institutions that can affect corruption. Some countries have attempted political reforms as fundamental as redrafting the entire constitution, in part to reduce incentives for corruption (box 5.5). However, systematic evidence on the effects of these three institutions is beginning to emerge.

Decentralization and corruption

Many studies have considered the costs and benefits of decentralization. Advocates of the devolution of political power to lower levels of government point to the possibility of better tailoring of public services to local needs. However, there can also be costs, associated with weaker capacity to provide services on the part of governments at local levels. Similarly, decentralization can in principle either strengthen or weaken opportunities and incentives for corruption. To the extent that decisions on spending are devolved without commensurate responsibilities for revenue collection, public officials at lower levels may face looser budget constraints and hence have greater opportunities to engage in corrupt practices. Incomplete devolution of power to local levels may also result in a proliferation of regulations emanating from different levels of government, with a commensurate increase in opportunities for corruption. On the other hand, to the extent that citizens are more informed about the actions of their leaders at the local level, they may be better able to monitor and influence those in power and demand honest behavior. In addition, greater decentralization of power may encourage competition among jurisdictions to provide a corruption-free environment conducive to business.

A recent study of 55 industrial and developing countries shows that, on average, the greater the share of state and local governments in total public expenditures, the lower the perceptions of corruption.[36] But this result does not imply that decentralization will always reduce incentives for corruption in every country. For decentralization to be effective in meeting local needs, it must include a significant delegation of responsibility to local levels of government. With this responsibility come opportunities for corruption. The in-

centives of local government officials to take advantage of these opportunities in turn depend on the extent to which they are held accountable for their actions—by their constituents at the local level, as well as by higher levels of government.

Evidence from a recent study of the decentralization of health and education services in Uganda and the Philippines shows that these channels of accountability need not always work well.[37] Accountability to local electorates depends on the extent to which individuals are informed about local government actions. However, a survey showed that in the Philippines only 1 percent of respondents were able to name their municipal mayor or vice-mayor, while 41 percent of respondents were able to name the national-level vice-president. In addition, respondents indicated that local government officials were the main source of information about local government issues, leading to concerns about the independence of this information source.

Electoral rules and corruption

In democracies, elections serve as an important discipline on public officials. Citizens who are fed up with cronyism and corrupt politicians can express their dissatisfaction at the ballot box. However, the effectiveness of elections as a disciplining device depends on two factors. The first is the extent to which elections are free and fair. Without this minimum condition, elections cannot serve to discipline politicians and sanction them for corrupt practices. Second, provided that elections are in fact free and fair, there is evidence that the design of electoral rules themselves influence the accountability of individual politicians to their constituents.

Recent research has focused on two dimensions of electoral rules that matter for accountability. The first is the extent to which electoral systems reward or punish individual candidates relative to political parties. When legislatures are selected by proportional representation, with candidates chosen from party lists, voters can vote only against particular parties and not against individuals whom they perceive as corrupt. As a result individual politicians have less reason to fear that they will be punished at the ballot box for engaging in corrupt practices. The second is the extent to which electoral rules create barriers to entry for new political parties. When new parties find it difficult to gain representation in the legislature, it is more difficult for them to challenge corrupt incumbents. One factor determining the ease of entry for new political parties is the number of representatives per electoral district, since it is easier for smaller parties to win seats in districts with multiple representatives.

New empirical research suggests that both these factors are important predictors of corruption across countries. A recent study found that, controlling for a variety of other factors, countries where a greater fraction of legislators are selected from party lists, and where electoral districts have fewer representatives, tend to have more corruption.[38] Moreover, policymakers are aware of these considerations. Although constitutional changes are typically infrequent, when they do occur, there are cases where these considerations are explicitly taken into account. An example is the new Thai constitution (box 5.5).

Press freedom and civil society

Lack of information breeds corruption. When the actions of public officials are not subject to scrutiny by the general public, opportunities for official misconduct become more attractive. The availability of information can be a force for changing behavior in several dimensions. Without information on the prices that are supposed to be charged for public services—such as the provision of tax documents, or permit or registration fees—individuals cannot determine if they are being overcharged. Without information about the details of

regulations, individuals are vulnerable to bureaucratic harassment and demands for bribes. Without widespread information on the extent of public wrongdoing, the public disgust with corruption that is essential to implementing reforms is slow to form. Policymakers can take actions to provide information on public laws and regulations to those affected by them. Where those affected are not literate, special measures need to be taken to keep them informed of institutions that affect them.

The media can help provide information by vigorous investigation and reporting of allegations of public malfeasance. For the media to be effective in this role, they need to be free from political pressures that prevent investigation and reporting of scandals that would embarrass those in power. Across countries, there is a clear association between indicators of press freedom and absence of corruption. An important factor in this regard is media ownership. When the media are controlled by the state, they are more likely to be subject to political pressures (chapter 10).[39] The quality of media coverage is also likely to be important in determining the extent to which decentralization will lower corruption. When information concerning local government actions is scarce, it is less likely that decentralization will be effective in reducing corruption. In Uganda, for example, one study found that there was significantly less media coverage of local governments than of the national government.[40] At the same time, a study of voting patterns in 14 Indian states found evidence that state governments' performance while in office had a greater influence on their subsequent success in the polls than that of the central government, suggesting that voters were better able to monitor and reward local governments for good performance.[41]

Provision of information to civil society can also help in building institutions that reduce opportunities for corruption. Diagnostic surveys sponsored by the World Bank in several countries in recent years provide an example of this type of institution building. These diagnostic surveys gather information on perceptions of corruption in different public agencies and use this information as a basis for public discussion between government and civil society. One such survey, carried out in the municipality of Campo Elias in Venezuela, identified complex and poorly understood municipal procedures as facilitating corrupt practices (consistent with the cross-country evidence on regulatory complexity and corruption discussed above). In response, ad-

Figure 5.4
Tax collection around the world
Revenue effort improves with income and reliance on distortionary taxation falls

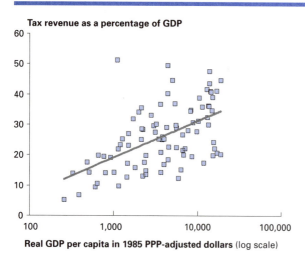

Tax revenue as a percentage of GDP

Real GDP per capita in 1985 PPP-adjusted dollars (log scale)

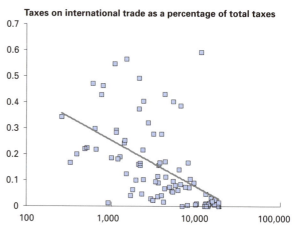

Taxes on international trade as a percentage of total taxes

Real GDP per capita in 1985 PPP-adjusted dollars (log scale)

Note: PPP stands for purchasing power parity.
Source: International Monetary Fund, Government Finance Statistics.

ministrative procedures were simplified, and several measures were enacted to improve public participation. While it is still too early to determine the long-term effects, immediate results were promising, with follow-up surveys indicating strong improvements in satisfaction with public services.[42]

Politics, institutions, and taxation

For the state to provide the institutions that support markets, it requires resources. Access to resources in turn depends on the effectiveness of the institutions of taxation. In too many countries around the world, especially poor countries, these institutions do not function adequately. This can readily be seen from the strong negative relationship between average tax revenue as a share of GDP and per capita income, as shown in the left-hand panel of figure 5.4. There is considerable room for debate about the appropriate size of public spending as a share of national income. But when tax collection is abysmally low—for example, dipping below 10 percent of GDP in Peru in the late 1980s—it is clear that the state does not have the resources necessary to build the institutions needed for markets to function effectively.

Weak tax collection institutions undermine well-functioning markets in several ways. When tax administration is weak, governments tend to focus their energies on easily collected taxes, which are often the most

distortionary. A prime example of this is the disproportionate reliance of poor countries on taxes on international trade (shown in the right-hand panel of figure 5.4). This is not uniquely a developing country problem. As recently as the early 20th century trade taxes accounted for half of public revenues in the United States, and before 1870 trade taxes accounted for over 90 percent of U.S. public revenues.[43] Nor is it any accident. International transactions are among the most visible and easiest to tax. But taxes on trade undermine competition by sheltering inefficient domestic producers (chapter 7). And by limiting openness, taxes on trade can also undermine institutional change.

Another consequence of weak tax administration is the disproportionate reliance on tax revenue from large firms, which are more visible and easier to tax (box 5.6). When these firms are also the most dynamic in the economy, the disincentive effects of taxation are particularly costly for smaller firms. High tax burdens, along with harassment by tax officials and unnecessarily high costs of compliance, can contribute to a firm's decision to exit the formal economy, with adverse consequences for competition and the functioning of markets. Weak tax administration may also increase the temptation for governments to rely on inflation taxes as a source of finance. Finally, low tax revenues can encourage governments to tax banks by forcing them to hold public debt at below-market interest rates, thus undermining the effectiveness of the financial system in supporting markets (chapter 4).

This section focuses on the interplay between politics and the institutions of taxation, using two examples: the experience with autonomous revenue agencies in Latin America, and the incentives for local governments created by intergovernmental tax-sharing arrangements.

Autonomous revenue agencies

The power to tax that is invested in the state is considerable, and so also are the temptations to use these powers to further political ends. Politicians can use tax policies to reward their friends and supporters with exemptions and other loopholes. They can also use the institutions of tax administration to persecute their enemies with repeated audits and harassment by tax inspectors. These actions undermine the effectiveness of tax administration by increasing the complexity of tax laws and encouraging the proliferation of exemptions, loopholes, and regulations. Arbitrary actions also contribute to perceptions of unfairness that feed taxpayer noncompliance.

Recognizing this temptation and its consequences, governments in industrial and developing countries—ranging from Canada and Japan to Mexico and Colombia—have delegated responsibility for tax collection to revenue agencies with varying degrees of autonomy from the rest of the public sector bureaucracy.[44] Two common ingredients of this particular institutional design are greater autonomy from the ministry of finance, especially over personnel decisions, and a budget that is linked to taxes actually collected. The former provides the opportunity to significantly strengthen the human capital of the agency to improve performance. The latter can in principle create incentives for greater revenue effort on the part of the agency. Moreover, to the extent that the establishment of an autonomous agency improves perceptions of the fairness and depoliticization of tax administration, taxpayers' incentives to comply with tax laws may also improve.[45]

However, the potential benefits of agency autonomy have not always been realized. The success of an independent revenue agency in improving tax compliance and tax collection depends to a great extent on the degree of political commitment to its autonomy. The experiences of Bolivia, Mexico, Peru, and Venezuela show that this commitment is not always sustained.[46]

Box 5.6
Business taxation in Uganda

Tax revenue in Uganda increased from less than 5 percent of GDP in 1986 to more than 11 percent of GDP in 1998. Uganda's experience in raising revenue collection is a cautionary tale about the adverse effects on businesses of sharp increases in revenue collection unsupported by effective tax administration and a widening of the tax base.

Large businesses in the formal sector represent a small share of the economy, but given their visibility they form a large portion of the effective tax base and are taxed more heavily than small firms. Prior to the 1997 tax reform, large firms in the manufacturing sector were subject to high marginal tax rates, combined with a variety of tax holidays that were granted on a fairly arbitrary basis. Firms faced marginal effective tax rates averaging 42.5 percent, if they did not qualify for tax holidays, or 22.3 percent, if they were successful in obtaining tax holidays. Small firms faced only a presumptive tax of 1 percent of their turnover, with an overall marginal effective tax rate of 8.9 percent. The overall high rates of taxation discouraged investment among large firms. As important, the arbitrary nature of the tax holidays contributed to perceptions of unfairness of the tax system, which in turn undermined incentives for compliance. This necessitated a very intrusive and inefficient rate of audits: nearly 70 percent of large firms were audited annually.

The 1997 tax reform abolished new tax holidays, with the result that unified marginal effective tax rates fell to 32.5 percent, and the distortions associated with existing holidays are gradually disappearing as they expire. However, much remains to be done to strengthen revenue administration. Survey evidence from 1997 indicates a very high level of dissatisfaction with the Uganda Revenue Authority. Respondents estimated that fully half of their competitors benefited from tax evasion, often by taking advantage of ad hoc tax holidays permitted by less-than-transparent tax regulations. Tellingly, firms that were successful in obtaining tax holidays were also much less likely to be audited. The proliferation of regulations facilitates arbitrary application of tax laws. Value added tax refunds were also identified as slow: 58 percent of firms that applied for the refunds received either no refund at all or only a partial refund.

Source: Chen and Reinikka 1999.

Nominally independent revenue agencies were established in these countries during times of fiscal crisis. In all four countries, noncommodity tax revenues as a share of GDP were very low—less than 10 percent of GDP when their respective autonomous revenue agencies were created. However, the extent of the actual autonomy of the tax collection agency varied considerably. In Bolivia and Mexico, where a tradition of using public agencies for patronage appointments was entrenched, only limited autonomy over personnel matters was granted to the revenue agencies. Only in Peru was the beginning of the operations of the revenue agency in 1991 accompanied by wholesale personnel reform. In Mexico and Venezuela the autonomy of the revenue agency was undermined by frequent changes in leadership, and in Bolivia the revenue agency survived only two years.

An important reason for the problems with these autonomous agencies was the intragovernmental conflicts that their establishment created. In all four cases, the revenue agencies were carved out of the ministry of finance, with a commensurate decline in the power and prestige of the latter. In the case of Mexico, 36,000 of the finance ministry's 39,000 employees were transferred to the revenue agency. At the same time, the ministries of finance remained to some extent accountable for the tax collection performance of the revenue agency. This combination of accountability without authority, as well as a desire to regain status, led to pressures to restore some of the powers of the revenue agencies to the ministry of finance, thus undoing the initial reforms. The lessons from this experience show that building autonomous revenue agencies requires much more than a simple declaration of autonomy. It requires a strong political commitment, which can be supported by fostering constituencies in the private sector that recognize that competent and fair tax collection is good for business.

Incentives and intergovernmental tax sharing

Numerous countries—often supported by the World Bank—have taken advantage of the opportunities offered by decentralization to transfer greater responsibility for public service delivery to lower levels of government, which can in principle tailor programs to local needs and tastes. But local governments require financial resources to provide these services. How these expenditures are financed can have important implications for the incentives to collect taxes and to build institutions that support markets.

To realize the full benefits of decentralization, local governments should ideally finance their expenditures with taxes under their control, with most of the cost borne by their local constituencies. In this way, local governments have the power to vary the level of local expenditures to reflect local preferences, and face strong incentives to collect taxes. Local citizens are also able to

see the direct link between the taxes they pay and the services they receive. This can be achieved by directly assigning taxes to local governments or by "piggybacking" schemes in which local governments levy taxes as a proportion of national taxes (as, for example, is the case with provincial income taxes in Canada).

However, this ideal is far from practical in most countries—and especially in many developing countries—for three reasons. First, the revenue raised by the taxes best assigned to local governments (such as property taxes) tends to be modest, resulting in large fiscal gaps for subnational governments. In India, for example, state government spending during the 1990s averaged 46 percent of total government spending, but state government–collected tax revenues represented less than half of state government revenues, with the balance made up by transfers from the central government.[47] Second, when local governments do receive some autonomy over taxation, they may choose not to set rates high enough or may not enforce collection vigorously enough, in the expectation that they will be bailed out of local budgetary shortfalls with grants from the central government. This effect contributed to weak municipal government finances in Hungary in the 1990s and prompted an innovative institutional response to instill fiscal discipline (box 5.7). Third, differences in the revenue-raising capacity of local governments may lead to unacceptable regional differences in public service provision.

In these situations, some form of revenue sharing between levels of government is necessary to supplement local revenues. Central-local transfers can take one of two broad forms: direct grants from higher to lower levels of government, and tax-sharing arrangements whereby tax revenues are collected by one level of government and are then divided according to a prespecified formula, with central control over rates and the sharing formula. Many countries employ both.

Direct grants are often discretionary and can be the subject of protracted annual negotiations between levels of government, undermining overall fiscal discipline. A potential advantage of tax-sharing arrangements is that they rely on prespecified formulas that can ensure greater predictability. In the case of India, for example, the Finance Commission sets tax revenue shares for five-year periods.[48] In Argentina the bulk of tax sharing occurs through a complex "co-participation" scheme. There have been changes in the revenue/tax-sharing arrangements over the past ten years, but they have generally left transfers quite stable. In fact, this stability makes transfers acceptable as collateral for provincial borrowing. The problem, however, is that the system is overly complex. For example, there is one main revenue-sharing pool plus several other tax-sharing pools. These factors affect the transparency of the system.

A difficulty with both methods of revenue sharing is that they can weaken governments' incentives to invest in tax collection capacity. If direct grants are based on actual revenue shortfalls, local governments have little reason to levy or collect local taxes, since the additional revenue will be offset by a reduction in grants from the center. In contrast, matching grants, which require local governments to commit their own resources to receive transfers, are less likely to have these perverse effects. Similarly, under tax-sharing systems, each level of government has weaker incentives to administer and enforce a shared tax because part of the revenues gained by improved administration must be shared with other levels of government. Each level of government has strong incentives to "free ride" on the others' tax collection efforts. This incentive problem can be mitigated when tax administration is efficient, technocratic, and free from political influences. But when the institutions of tax administration are weak and subject to political manipulation, tax sharing can succumb to these perverse incentives (box 5.8).

The incentive effects of revenue-sharing arrangements go much further than simply the effects on revenue collection discussed above. The design of revenue-sharing arrangements can also have important implications for how subnational levels of government use the economic policies at their disposal to foster market development. China and Russia's experience with intergovernmental fiscal relations illustrates the powerful effects of these incentives. In both China in the 1980s and Russia in the 1990s, substantial authority over local economic policies was delegated to subnational levels of government. Both countries also experienced declines in tax revenues relative to GDP, with a growing share of revenues and expenditures under the control of subnational levels of government.

Tax-sharing arrangements have had important incentive effects in both countries. In Russia a Law on Basic Principles of Taxation, specifying the assignment of taxes to different levels of government, was passed in 1991 but was not implemented consistently. In practice, the authority of different levels of government to levy taxes, and the rates at which revenues from shared

---

Box 5.7
Market discipline versus state discipline: municipal bankruptcy in Hungary

In 1996 Hungary adopted a law that established bankruptcy procedures for municipal governments. The objective of the law was to prevent municipalities from defaulting on their debt obligations by providing a clear set of rules to be followed in cases of financial distress. If a municipality falls behind in its debt service or other obligations, bankruptcy proceedings can be initiated either by creditors or by the municipality itself. The municipality then formulates an emergency budget covering mandated public services. It is prohibited from issuing new debt while it enters into negotiations with creditors. If all parties can reach a compromise debt workout agreement, it is implemented. If not, the case is turned over to the court system, which enjoys a constitutional guarantee of independence. The courts can then order liquidations of municipal assets to pay off creditors.

Since 1996 there have been nine cases of municipal bankruptcy, seven of which were resolved during 2000. Importantly, the central government has not provided financial assistance to any of the municipalities involved. This experience has served to strengthen the credibility of the central government's commitment not to bail out municipalities in financial distress. This in turn has helped to harden municipalities' budget constraints, as municipalities now face "market discipline" from their creditors, as well as "state discipline" in the form of monitoring and supervision by the central government. It is too soon to determine the ultimate effect of this institutional innovation. However, the fact that municipal debt service obligations are now well below centrally mandated ceilings is a promising sign.

Source: Wetzel and Papp 2001.

---

taxes were divided, were subject to continuous renegotiation, with the outcome reflecting shifting balances of political power.[49] Lower levels of governments that succeeded in raising local tax revenues often saw commensurate reductions in tax-sharing payments from higher levels. One study found that for some Russian cities, this reduction was almost exactly one for one.[50] The same study found that the extent to which local governments had control over incremental tax revenues mattered for local economic activity. The more that a city's incremental tax revenues were eroded by reduced transfers, the lower the rate of new business formation.

In China in the 1980s the central government set rates and defined the base for many taxes, but tax collection was delegated to provincial governments. Tax revenues were shared according to a "tax contracting"

Box 5.8
Tax sharing with weak tax administration: the case of Russia

The case of Russia in the 1990s provides a vivid illustration of the perverse incentives created by tax sharing when tax administration is weak. In the 1990s Russia experienced a sharp decline in tax revenues, with federal tax revenues collapsing from 18 percent of GDP in 1992 to 10 percent of GDP in 1997. A portion of this decline can be attributed to the overall poor performance of the Russian economy during this period and to declines in several key tax rates. Another factor was a decline in the effectiveness of tax administration, driven by competition between different levels of government. While in principle tax collection in Russia was a federal responsibility carried out by the State Tax Service, in practice local branches of this agency were heavily influenced by local governments. Local governments in turn tried to protect firms located in their jurisdictions from having to pay taxes to the federal government or simply lobbied for general tax relief for local firms, thus subverting tax administration. For example, firms would agree to pay their tax obligations "in kind" to local governments by providing goods or public services directly, so that cash payments that needed to be shared with higher levels of government were avoided. Another example was the vigorous and successful lobbying of the federal government for a reduction in the tax arrears of the truck manufacturer Kamaz undertaken by the president of Tatarstan, where Kamaz was located.

The federal government would also attempt to enforce collections at the expense of the local governments, again subverting tax administration. When the automobile manufacturer Avtovaz was threatened by bankruptcy proceedings by the federal government due to mounting tax arrears, it eventually came to an agreement to pay current taxes only to the federal government, with no mention of its delinquent obligations to the local government. More generally, all levels of government had weaker incentives to collect shared taxes precisely because a portion had to be shared with other levels.

The figure below illustrates more systematically the adverse consequences of this competition over tax revenues. While the effectiveness of tax collection in 1996 relative to 1995 (measured as the ratio of actual collections in the two years, adjusted for inflation and changes in rates) increased for almost all taxes, the increase was most pronounced for those taxes that were subject to the least revenue sharing. This case illustrates the importance of a competent and autonomous tax administration for limiting competition over tax revenues between levels of government that can subvert the entire process of tax collection. Wide-ranging reforms in the tax system since 1998 have reduced the complexity of the Russian tax system and have increased the transparency of revenue-sharing arrangements, representing important progress.

Shared taxes were less effectively collected in Russia

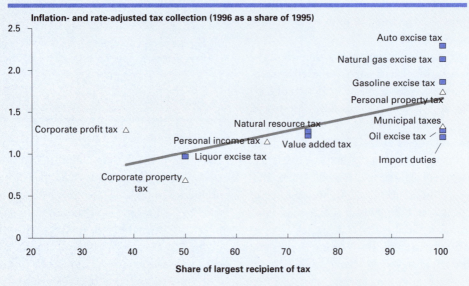

Note: Higher values on the vertical axis indicate improved tax collection effort.
Source: Treisman 1999.

system. Between 1985 and 1988 these contracts allowed provinces that ran deficits to retain a greater share of revenues, and provinces that ran surpluses a lower share. This weakened incentives to collect taxes, and revenue growth slowed in the richest provinces.

In response, between 1988 and 1993 the system was changed to give provincial governments greater claims over incremental tax revenues. For some provinces this amounted to an agreement to deliver a fixed sum to the center, with any additional revenues accruing to the province.[51] Throughout this period local governments also increasingly relied on "extrabudgetary revenues"—consisting of a range of locally collected fees and levies, as well as profits from state-owned enterprises under local government control—that were not subject to sharing with the center to finance local expenditures. This strengthened local governments' incentives to improve tax collection effort and to encourage local economic growth to expand the local tax base. A study found that during 1982 and 1991 the provincial budgetary revenues and expenditures were highly correlated (correlation coefficient 0.75); for extrabudgetary revenue and expenditure, the relationship was almost one for one.[52] The same study found that an increase in the marginal fiscal retention rate of 10 percent in a province was associated with a one percent increase in the growth rate of employment of nonstate enterprises in that province.

But even if tax-sharing arrangements create incentives for local governments to support market development, there are risks that local governments will do so in inefficient or anticompetitive ways. In China in the 1980s, for example, many provincial governments erected barriers to interprovincial trade to develop a wide range of manufacturing industries locally, rather than allow specialization in industries compatible with local comparative advantage.[53] Increased reliance on extrabudgetary funds reduced fiscal accountability and limited the central government's capacity for macroeconomic management. And differences in economic performance across provinces led to large differences in the level of provincial government expenditures per capita. In Russia one of the most dramatic manifestations of these risks was the high degree of tax competition between regions, which encouraged firms to shift accounting profits from one jurisdiction to the next in search of the most favorable tax treatment, all the while shrinking the overall tax base.[54]

In this environment, mechanisms of central government control are required to ensure healthy interjurisdictional competition. One important mechanism is the availability of information, since central governments need information on subnational governments' policy action to exert necessary control. This points to the importance of transparency in subnational government finances and policymaking. To this end China's fiscal reforms since the mid-1990s have emphasized increased accountability for extrabudgetary funds and a stronger central government share in revenues.

Another mechanism to limit local policymaking that conflicts with national interests are the incentives created by the political system for local government leaders. In many democracies, strong national political parties can use ties of party loyalty and party discipline to limit excesses in local policies. The absence of such strong national parties contributed to harmful interregional competition in Russia during the 1990s. As the Soviet Union disintegrated, there was a surge in regional political autonomy. Newly elected regional and local government officials no longer owed their allegiance to Moscow but rather to their local constituencies. This encouraged the pursuit of policies that benefited local interests at the expense of national interests. In China one mechanism of central government control over provincial policymaking was the center's influence over senior provincial-level appointments.[55] A study of these appointments found evidence that the exercise of this central control strengthened during the 1980s and 1990s, even as more and more economic powers were being delegated to lower levels of government.[56] One way in which this was done was to encourage rotations of senior officials from one province to another to prevent local officials from becoming too associated with local interests.

These experiences illustrate a broader principle relevant to other countries where economic power is shared between different levels of government: local government interests need not coincide with national interests. The design of intergovernmental relations needs to involve mechanisms of accountability to the center to ensure that the benefits of interjurisdictional competition are realized.

Conclusions

The ability of the state to provide those institutions that support growth and poverty reduction—often referred to as good governance—is essential to development. Countries that have failed in this respect have seen incomes stagnate and poverty persist. This chapter emphasizes the importance of political institutions in creating incentives for governments to provide good governance. Political institutions such as constitutional rules, the division of power among levels of government, independent agencies, mechanisms for citizens to monitor public behavior, and rules that inhibit corruption all succeed in restraining officials of the state from arbitrary action, and good governance will likely take root.

There is no blueprint for change in political institutions to support good governance. Political and social forces can push countries in diverse directions. But the nature of political institutions and the interaction of public officials with their constituencies dictate the type of policy advice most effective in a given country and affect the policies adopted. In designing particular government structures, it is critical to consider the incentives facing public officials in a particular country. Institutions can affect these incentives by helping to monitor the behavior of public officials. Institutions affect how responsive governments are to a broad spectrum of citizens in society, and how responsive they are to social and economic concerns. They do so by providing information, increasing competition, and clarifying and enforcing rights among different government agencies and between the state and the governed. This needs to be kept in mind when building particular structures. For example, the current popularity of policies such as greater decentralization, or greater formal autonomy for regulatory or revenue agencies, needs to

be tempered with the realization that the success of these innovations depends heavily on complementary political and social institutions. If governments lack the broader checks and balances that would keep them from intervening in independent agencies, these agencies will be independent in name only. If political institutions that align local government incentives with national interests are absent, and if local governments are no more accountable to their constituents than central governments, the benefits of decentralization may not be fully realized. Further, local capacity and general literacy levels may hinder the types of activities that can be effectively decentralized.

A degree of experimentation and competition can help identify effective political institutions both at the broader regional level and at local levels. Open information sharing, public debate, and information flows among regions and between public and private actors can facilitate this process. It can affect public officials' incentives and can also create pressures for change.

CHAPTER 6

The Judicial System

Fair trial, fair judgment . . .
Evidence which issued clear as day. . .
. . . [Q]uench your anger; let not indignation rain
Pestilence on our soil, corroding every seed
Till the whole land is sterile desert. . . .
. . . [C]alm this black and swelling wrath.

—Aeschylus, 458 B.C.

The *Gongyang Commentary* to the *Spring and Autumn Annals,* a fourth century B.C. text on law in China, illustrates a problem that all societies face. Analyzing a son's responsibility when the state has unjustly executed his father, the text concludes that without a public institution to settle disputes between private parties and between public and private parties, the only recourse open to those who seek justice is revenge. But revenge can spark an endless cycle of violence, as first one side and then the other retaliates. In many countries disputes over land and other assets have led to increased violence. The uprising led by Thomas Muentzer in 16th century Germany and the current debate in Zimbabwe are but two examples.

Adjudication of a dispute by a court of law offers an alternative, one where facts are carefully assayed and self-defense and other considerations that may excuse or explain the conduct are reviewed. In short, courts are a way to resolve disputes justly. Justice forms the basis of a lasting social order. The legal and judicial system must therefore provide a method for determining the truth and justice of the actions of private agents and of the state. Its primary responsibility is to ensure social peace.

Courts develop gradually, reflecting a society's own development. When society is a small, close-knit collection of kin, informal means of intervention suffice to resolve conflicts. But as economic activity becomes more complex and commerce expands, group ties weaken, and the demand for more formal means of intervention grows. This pattern is exemplified by the rapid growth of commercial litigation in modern China. In 1979 China embarked on a path of economic reform that spurred new enterprise creation, increased interprovincial trade, and allowed the entry of foreign investors. The expansion of business was followed by an increase in the number of cases filed in commercial courts. In 1979–82 the average number of commercial disputes filed in the courts was around 14,000 a year; by 1997, 1.5 million new cases were filed—more than a 100-fold increase.[1] At the same time, the number of commercial disputes arbitrated by community committees, the traditional mediation mechanism, hardly increased. As the number of entrepreneurs grew, the enforcement capacity of informal dispute resolution mechanisms weakened.

The simplest means for resolving disputes is mediation. Mediation has been used to settle disputes in both small and large cases and in both village and urban communities. Mediation provides a low-cost way to resolve disputes and is found in every society. But mediation has its limitations (box 6.1). There is nothing to compel the parties in a dispute to reach settlement; social norms may not provide a sufficient incentive.

A more formal method for exerting public control over disputants was employed in the ancient Near East, the Carolingian empire, and medieval France. A person who anticipated becoming the target of a self-help remedy initiated the process. This could be a debtor who feared that a creditor was about to seize his property to satisfy an obligation. The initiating party (the

Box 6.1
How mediation resolves disputes

Generally, a mediator has no enforcement powers. An elder or a community leader that both disputants respect may help them find common ground but need not have power to impose a solution. A pure negotiator presents each side's position to the other, while a mediator can suggest solutions of his or her own. In either case the only requirement is that the solution be acceptable to both parties.

Unlike judges, mediators need not sort out conflicting legal or factual claims. Nor do they usually prepare a written opinion showing how the settlement conforms to the law. They require no specialized training or expertise. Mediation does not require enforcement capacity, either. Compliance is ensured because the settlement rests on both parties' consent.

While a mediator is free to suggest any settlement the parties can agree upon, in all societies norms play a significant role in determining the type of solutions reached (chapter 9). Tacitus, the first-century Roman historian, reports that among German tribes a murderer could compensate for his crime by the payment of a certain number of cattle or sheep to the victim's family. Ethnographic studies of more contemporary tribal societies describe similar norms. Among the Nuer of Sudan, guidelines specify the compensation generally required to settle cases of homicide, bodily injury, theft, and other wrongs. While such norms reflect moral judgments, they serve a practical end as well. They reduce the cost of reaching a settlement by providing the mediator a point of reference in discussions with the two sides.

But even when underpinned by supportive social norms, mediation has its limitations. Even in a society such as the Chinese, where strong cultural preferences toward mediation prevail, less than two-thirds of cases filed with arbitration committees between 1979 and 1997 reached settlement. By 1997 six times more commercial disputes were handled through the formal commercial courts than through the arbitration committees. In Russia an enterprise survey conducted in mid-1997 revealed that less than 8 percent of managers who faced commercial disputes used private arbitration courts to resolve problems with their suppliers. In contrast, more than 92 percent of those managers used commercial courts to file grievances.

Source: Evans-Pritchard 1940; Hendley, Murrell, and Ryterman 2001; Pie 2001.

are visible in sanctions like these. Rather than urging or pressuring a party to accept a resolution, society is now imposing one.

These key elements—state-backed decisions, reached after an independent fact-finding and developed in harmony with prevailing social norms—are what distinguish courts from the various forms of mediation. Enforcement is entirely taken out of the hands of private individuals. This in itself can significantly reduce the potential for violence and improve the business climate.

But for courts to be effective, rulers must follow the law, too. The judicial system must also provide checks and balances on arbitrary state action. Forcing rulers to follow the law is a problem as old as government itself. Even when a ruler accepts the principle, there is the challenge of devising an institution that can determine when the government has violated the law and fix an appropriate sanction.

Once a court has been established, its efficiency is defined in terms of the speed, cost, and fairness with which judicial decisions are made and the access that aggrieved citizens have to the court. This chapter focuses on commercial dispute resolution. It presents evidence on the determinants of the efficiency of legal and judicial systems across countries today. It discusses elements of judicial reforms that are part of an overall reform of the government but also discusses elements of judicial reform that do not depend on comprehensive reform of the government or the legal system. This distinction is important. Different types of institutional reforms may be opposed by different interest groups—and this will vary between countries. But there are several areas in which countries can begin reform without fearing strong opposition.

A main finding is that the simplification of procedural elements is associated with greater judicial efficiency; both costs and delays are reduced. In many developing countries procedural complexity reduces judicial efficiency. This is particularly important given lower levels of administrative capacity and human capital, higher initial levels of corruption, and fewer complementary institutions. Complex procedures also facilitate corruption in the absence of transparency. Where supporting institutions, human capital, and resources exist, complexity has fewer costs for efficiency.

The experience with judicial reform over the last two decades highlights the importance of open information flows. The evidence suggests that reforms that introduce greater accountability of judges to the users of the

debtor, in this case) would request a declaration that under the circumstances, self-help was unjustified. If the court hearing the case agreed, the target of the expected attack was entitled to society's protection. If the court disagreed, it sanctioned the use of private force to secure redress. The seeds of a modern court system judicial system and to the general public have been more important in increasing efficiency than the simple increase in financial and human resources. In developing countries accountability can be enhanced through the provision of more information on judicial outcomes. In many cases strong civil society groups and the media, acting as outside monitors, have changed the behavior of judges and lawyers (chapter 10). Implementing judicial databases that make cases easy to track and hard to manipulate or misplace can enhance accountability and therefore the speed of adjudication. Individual calendars make explicit the link between a judge's case management record and his reputation. The provision of such statistics—even without any enforcement mechanism—has been found to reduce delay. Statistics are most effective when information on clearance rates and times to disposition for judges are individualized and when they are available to the media. Finally, partially delegating the mechanics of procedural reform to the judicial branch can speed the process of reform. Where procedures are transparent, allowing some degree of innovation and experimentation by judges can help increase judicial efficiency.

The provision of information, simplicity, and increased accountability affect not only cost and speed, but also fairness. The evidence shows that in judicial systems that rely excessively on written procedures, a shift toward oral hearings tends to make trials simpler, faster, and cheaper, without an appreciable loss in fairness, since the judge has direct contact with the evidence. Fairness, in the context of the judicial system, can be interpreted as the consistent application of the law regardless of the nature of the parties involved.[2] The *perceived* fairness of the rules or laws varies depending on each society's values and political and social structure. There are two main sources of unfairness. The first occurs when judicial decisions are not independent of political decisions, and when the courts cannot ensure that other branches of government will obey the law. Second, unfairness can also arise when powerful private parties influence court decisions.

Who benefits from the improvement in the quality of the judiciary in handling commercial disputes? The evidence suggests that well-developed formal mechanisms to enforce contracts make *everybody* better off (see box 6.2). For example, both debtors and creditors gain from efficient insolvency resolution.[3] The evidence also shows that greater judicial efficiency may be particularly important for smaller and unaffiliated entre-

Box 6.2
Who benefits from better courts?

During the early 1990s the collapse of formal enforcement mechanisms in Poland and Slovakia resulted in long delays in payments to farmers for delivering their products to upstream processing plants. In response, agricultural cooperatives attempted to build their own vertically integrated processing capacity. In turn, the processing plants introduced seeds and fertilizer and investment facilitation programs for farmers that delivered products to them. For example, the Polish dairy subsidiary of Land O'Lakes prefinanced feed for milk farmers and provided loans for milking equipment. While these private mechanisms in effect substituted for formal contract enforcement, they increased the cost of doing business. The development of judicial enforcement in the late 1990s in Poland and Slovakia resulted in the quick disappearance of these temporary private mechanisms.

Source: Gow and Swinnen 2001, p. 5.

preneurs and firms. Studies on commercial litigation in Italy, Romania, Russia, Slovakia, Ukraine, and Vietnam show that newly created private enterprises, which do not have established supplier and customer networks or significant market power, are most likely to resort to the use of commercial courts.[4] Older, especially state-owned, enterprises are often able to settle disputes out of court. Similarly, a study on firms in severe financial distress in Indonesia, the Republic of Korea, Malaysia, the Philippines, and Thailand finds that firms that are affiliated with business groups are half as likely to file for formal bankruptcy as unaffiliated businesses.[5] Instead, affiliated firms negotiate the rescheduling of debt payments with their creditors informally, relying more on reputational mechanisms and less on formal court procedures. This pattern is also illustrated in a recent study of the software industry in India.[6] The study shows that young firms are significantly more likely to have fixed-price contracts and to bear the overrun costs in complex contracts. This is not because of inferior product quality. Young firms often outperform established firms in the production of high-quality products. Rather, these findings suggest that the primary beneficiaries of well-functioning commercial courts are new, small firms, unaffiliated with either private business groups or the state, run by those who do not necessarily have established social connections.

This chapter begins with a comparison of legal systems around the world. It then assesses the recent re-

Box 6.3
Surveys on judicial performance

The most popular method for assessing judicial performance relies on surveys based on public perceptions of the weaknesses of the judicial system. Some surveys depend on in-house legal experts who summarize the relevant literature for each country but do not have first-hand knowledge of the judicial system, while others survey business executives.

However, people's perceptions are colored by their expectations. Coverage also depends on the availability of information, which is generally better in richer countries. Despite weaknesses with these surveys, they do convey some information. Richer countries have less corrupt judicial systems, which in turn helps their business community and supports economic growth. Other data show that the public's perception of corruption in the judiciary is very highly correlated with its perception of corruption in government.

Table 6.1
Inputs into the judicial system for selected countries, 1995
(per 100,000 population)

Country	Professional judges	Other judicial staff	Incoming cases in first-instance courts
Austria	21	117	29,294[a]
Brazil	2	n.a.	2,739
Ecuador	1	n.a.	10,467
England and Wales	5	4	4,718
France	10	41	2,242
Germany	27	69	2,655
Italy	12	60	1,227
Netherlands	10	n.a.	2,031
Panama	3	n.a.	1,656
Peru	1	n.a.	2,261
Portugal	12	70	3,719
Spain	9	83	1,898

a. Including summary cases.
Source: Contini 2000; Buscaglia and Dakolias 1996.

form experience of countries and concludes with a discussion of the determinants of judicial independence. Issues of civil service reform are not discussed here, but they were the topic of *World Development Report* 1997.

Comparison of legal and judicial systems

Legal and judicial systems vary substantially across countries in terms of their output. In Latin America the average duration of commercial cases is two years, and it is not uncommon for complex commercial cases to take more than five years. In Ecuador the average case takes almost eight years to reach a verdict. In contrast, it takes less than a year to reach a verdict in Colombia, France, Germany, Peru, Singapore, Ukraine, and the United States for similar cases.[7]

Reform of the legal and judicial system depends critically on a sound understanding of its existing structure and level of efficiency. Description of the key characteristics of the system and measurement of the speed and cost of judicial decisions are crucial. However, it is only in rare cases that governments have developed indicators to track the development of the judiciary. There is very little systematic evidence on the structure and performance of the judiciary and on the determinants of its performance. Recently, there have been some attempts to fill this gap (box 6.3). Legal scholars have focused their efforts on documenting the inputs into the judicial systems (number of judges, budget of the judiciary branch, number of administrative support staff),

access to justice, and the workload of judges (measured by the number of cases filed and resolved within a given period). The output these studies measure is the number of resolved cases. Examples include studies on eight European countries and a World Bank study on seven Latin American countries.[8] Table 6.1 reports some indicators compiled from these comparative studies.

There are significant problems in making meaningful comparisons between the ways that different judicial systems function. Difficulties are encountered even in defining the concept of a "judge." In one country a legal dispute might be dealt with by a professional judge in a formal courtroom, while in another country a similar dispute might be handled by a public official who is not a judge or a lawyer. In other cases the same dispute might be resolved by an unpaid volunteer lacking any legal qualifications.

The table shows large differences in the number of legal professionals, even across advanced European countries. In some countries lay judges staff labor tribunals and small claims courts. Austrian judges have the most support staff (117 per 100,000 inhabitants). Adjudication services are also organized differently across industrial countries. Ecuador and Peru have one judge per 100,000 people. This is an order of magnitude smaller than the number of judges in Western European countries. Not all countries with efficient judicial systems have many judges, however. Singapore and the United States have fewer than one judge per 100,000 people.

New evidence on two aspects of judicial efficiency: speed and cost

This Report uses a detailed survey of practicing lawyers to benchmark the relative efficiency of judicial systems and the access to civil justice in 109 countries (box 6.4 provides details of the methodology).[9] The survey focuses on the complexity of litigation, that is, on how difficult it is for a layperson to pursue a legal procedure in defense of his interests. Elements investigated include the various steps in the litigation process, the difficulty in notification procedures, the complexity of the complaint, and the possibility of suspension of enforcement because of appeal (box 6.5).

For the countries in which the procedures are complex, the adjudication process is perceived to be less efficient even after adjusting for the level of income (figure 6.1a). The data indicate that the complexity of litigation does not decrease uniformly as national income per capita declines (figure 6.1b). This shows that the developing countries with the fewest resources and weaker judicial capacity also have complex procedures. One explanation is that the judicial system in these countries is more prone to failure and that the complexity of litigation ensures the availability of checks and balances on the way to the final judicial decision. Alternatively, procedures may be put into place to limit access to the judicial system and favor more privileged individuals or firms. Some developing countries, however, have simpler procedures, and several countries have undertaken reforms of judicial processes. Among the industrial countries, while some may have more complex procedures, the superior enforcement capacity and presence of complementary institutions and higher levels of human capital counteract the negative effects of complexity (figure 6.1c). Complementary institutions include rules affecting judge's incentives, rules promoting greater transparency, rules affecting other litigants' incentives, and clearer substantive rules.

Another variable that distinguishes judicial systems is the type of judge that presides over a case. First, judges may preside over a general jurisdiction court or over a limited jurisdiction court. Limited jurisdiction courts include specialized courts, such as small claims courts or bankruptcy courts, and alternative dispute resolution mechanisms, such as arbitration committees and justices of the peace. Second, the judge or the mem-

Box 6.4
Comparing judicial efficiency

A survey developed for this Report analyzes particular aspects of judicial systems. It does so through detailed questions addressed to lawyers. The data systematically compare the pace of litigation by means of a standardized survey delivered to private law firms in 109 countries. The survey presents two hypothetical cases that represent typical situations of default of an everyday contract: (a) the eviction of a tenant; and (b) the collection of debt (a returned check or an invoice in countries where checks are not popular).

These two cases proxy for all types of commercial disputes that enter the courts. Two quite different cases are chosen in order to check whether the findings can be generalized to all civil litigation. The questions cover the step-by-step evolution of these cases before local courts in the country's largest city. Importantly, the survey studies both the structure of the judicial system—that is, where the plaintiff would seek redress in specific cases—and the efficiency with which judicial decisions are made.

The survey chooses cases in which the facts are undisputed by the parties but where the defendant still does not want to pay. The judge consistently rules in favor of the plaintiff. In this way the survey controls for fairness across countries, as judges follow the letter of the law. We assume that no postjudgment motions can be filed. Should any opposition to the complaint arise, the judge always decides in favor of the plaintiff. The data consist of the number of steps required in the judicial process, the time it takes to accomplish each step, and the cost to the plaintiff. The last provides a comparable measure of access to the judicial system, while all three address the issue of judicial efficiency. The questionnaire makes a distinction between what is required by law and what happens in practice.

The following are examples of questions asked: What is the most commonly used mechanism for collecting overdue debt in your country? Does this mechanism differ if the debt amount is small, equal to 5 percent of GNP per capita, or large, equal to 50 percent of GNP per capita? What types of court will this mechanism be applied through? Would the judgment in the debt collection case be an oral representation of the general conclusions, an oral argument on specific facts and applicable laws, or a written argument on specific facts and applicable laws?

Source: Lex Mundi, Harvard University, and World Bank. *World Development Report 2002* background project.

bers of the court may not be professional judges who have undergone professional training in the law. Further, their primary activity may not be to act as a judge or a member of the court. In contrast, a nonprofessional judge can be an arbitrator, an administrative officer, a merchant, or any other lay person who is authorized to hear and adjudicate the case.

Box 6.5
Index of the complexity of litigation

This index measures how complex judicial litigation of simple commercial disputes is, and therefore how difficult it is for a layperson to pursue a legal procedure by herself in defense of her interests. The index ranks from 0 to 1, where 1 means that litigation is very complex, while 0 means that it is not. The index is formed by adding five equally weighted variables:

Legal language or justification. This describes how much legal language or legal justification is required in different stages of the process.

Notification procedure. This describes the level of complexity involved in the process of notification of the complaint (service of process) and the notification of final judgment.

Legal representation. This describes whether for the case provided, the legal assistance of a licensed attorney would be required by law or by practice.

Complexity of complaint. This evaluates the level of complexity for preparing and presenting a complaint for the case.

Suspension of enforcement because of appeal. This describes whether the enforcement of final judgment would normally be suspended when the losing party files an appeal until the appeal is finally decided, or if judgment is generally enforceable.

Source: Lex Mundi, Harvard University, and World Bank. *World Development Report 2002* background project.

Figure 6.1
(a) Procedural complexity reduces efficiency

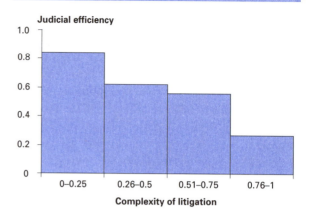

(b) Rich countries also have complex regulations, but . . .

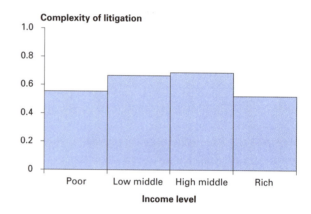

(c) . . . they have more efficient systems because of complementary institutions and capacity

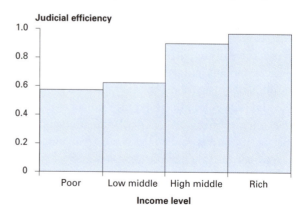

Note: Higher values indicate greater efficiency (figures 6.1a and 6.1c) or greater complexity (figure 6.1b).
Source: Lex Mundi, Harvard University and World Bank. *World Development Report 2002* background project.

Countries such as Australia, Belgium, Singapore, and the United States have fewer requirements for judges. At the other end of the spectrum, Ecuador, the Arab Republic of Egypt, Italy, Lebanon, and Morocco require simple debt collection cases to be heard by professional judges in general-jurisdiction courts. This increases the public finances necessary for litigation and greatly lengthens the duration of each trial.

A complementary measure is the type of legal assistance necessary for a lay person to bring a case to the court. As discussed below in the section on judicial reform, the need for professional legal representation greatly increases the cost of litigation, serving as an entry barrier to the court system for poor members of society. For the cases studied in this report, few countries make representation by a professional lawyer mandatory. Those that do are all middle- and low-income countries, such as Ecuador, Lebanon, Morocco, the Philippines, and Venezuela.

Countries differ significantly in terms of the duration of simple civil litigation related to commercial disputes. It takes less than three months to reach a judgment on small debt collection, equivalent to 5 percent of GNP per capita, in Denmark, Japan, New Zealand, Singapore, and the United States. In contrast, it takes more than two years to reach a judgment in Colombia, the Czech Republic, Kuwait, Malta, Mozambique, and the United Arab Emirates.

Enforcement of judgment differs significantly between countries. In the richest quartile of countries it takes on average 64 days to enforce a judgment on small debt collection once the judge has produced an opinion. The countries in the poorest quartile fare worse. On average, it takes 192 days—a long time, particularly for small businesses with little access to credit—to collect debts once a judgment is rendered.

There are also differences among countries at similar income levels. For example, countries differ in how long it takes to enforce a judgment. In the poorest quartile of countries the average duration from judgment to enforcement in debt collection cases is only 18 days in Ghana, but almost 450 days in Senegal. This diversity of enforcement efficiency again suggests that it is possible to undertake simple reforms of the judicial system in developing countries that can significantly enhance access for small firms and poorer entrepreneurs. This means that policymakers need not wait for overall reform of the judiciary but can work on improving certain aspects. While large-scale judicial reforms may face some political opposition, others may be more feasible in the short run. In some cases effective reform may mean building a new institution, such as a specialized court, rather than modifying old ones (see the discussion on judicial reforms below).

The survey underscores how countries vary greatly in the details of the law as well as the enforcement of the law. And these difficulties can affect efficiency. First, the speed with which the same case is adjudicated in different countries varies enormously. For example, it can take anywhere from 35 days (Singapore) to four years (Slovenia) to solve a commercial dispute that involves a returned check. Second, a large part of this difference can be explained by the procedural structure of the judicial system. This includes the prevalence of oral versus written procedures; the existence of specialized courts, including small claims courts; the possibility for appeal during or after the trial; and the allowed number of appeals. Third, some characteristics of the judicial system are much more likely to be associated with superior judicial performance. For example, the existence of oral procedures and continuous court cases

Box 6.6
Debt recovery in Tunisia

In Tunisia the recovery of overdue small debts is normally achieved by means of a special procedure called *injonction de payer* before a general-jurisdiction judge. Provided that the debt has been proven and established, the judge grants the injunction to pay. The debtor cannot oppose the order. Therefore, the civil lawsuit excludes the usual stages of service of process, opposition, hearing, and gathering of evidence. On average, the entire procedure from filing until payment takes less than a month.

This simplified procedure does not mandate legal representation. Legal costs are very low, approximately $54 when represented by a lawyer, and zero if the plaintiff represents herself. There are no court fees for the injunction, and the plaintiff only pays bailiff fees, of around $20, for the actual collection. In contrast, many countries at a similar level of economic development have a considerably lengthier and more costly process for small debt recovery. Recovering small debt in Venezuela, for example, involves a complicated process. The parties to the case and the adjudicators must go through 31 independent procedural actions from filing of the lawsuit to payment of the debt. The average duration of the process is about one year, and legal representation of parties is mandatory, as is the case in most other Latin American countries. Small debt recovery in Venezuela is also associated with markedly high legal costs. Average attorney fees are approximately $2,000, while court fees reach $2,500.

Source: Lex Mundi, Harvard University, and World Bank. *World Development Report 2002* background project.

(the court meets on continuous days until the case is resolved) explains much of the variation in the length of commercial dispute resolution (box 6.6).

The study also indicates that 90 percent of procedures for Costa Rica, Ecuador, Guatemala, Morocco, and Senegal, and 100 percent for Argentina, Honduras, Spain, and Venezuela, are written. Not surprisingly, the judicial process of collecting debt lasts on average 180 days in Honduras, 300 days in Argentina, and 432 days in Senegal. The predominance of written procedures is evident in some of the industrial countries as well. For example, in both Norway and Japan 80 percent of all judicial procedures in the debt recovery case studied require written documents. Yet the duration of cases is reasonably short: 90 and 60 days on average, respectively. This evidence suggests that complicated procedures are especially problematic in poorer countries, where they may facilitate corruption or be unsuitable given the existing levels of administrative capacity. Also, they frequently serve as barriers to entry for poor people.

Figure 6.2

Excessive written procedures limit access to justice

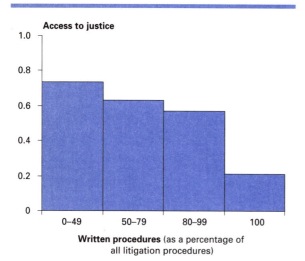

Written procedures (as a percentage of all litigation procedures)

Note: Equal number of countries in each category. Higher values indicate greater access. Access to justice is defined as the extent to which citizens are "equal under the law, have access to an independent, nondiscriminatory judiciary, and are respected by the security forces. Scale from 0 to 10. The higher the rating, the greater the degree of equality under the law" (Freedom House 2000).
Source: Access to justice: Freedom House 2000; written procedures: Lex Mundi, Harvard University, and World Bank, *World Development Report 2002* background project.

When building effective judicial institutions, policymakers aim to establish courts that decide cases cheaply, quickly, and fairly, while maximizing access. These variables are not independent of one another. However, the evidence indicates that tradeoffs among them exist only at the margin. For example, when judicial performance is very slow, improvements in speed can be made without compromising fairness. A recent study from Argentina suggests that policymakers are not always bound by such tradeoffs; it demonstrates that to be fair, the justice system need not be slow, but many policymakers use the existence of a tradeoff as an excuse for maintaining the status quo.[10]

Access to the judicial system, partly by the poorer members of society, can be limited by factors such as procedural complexity, whether legal representation is required, and high financial costs. For example, where most procedures are in written form rather than oral, access is limited (figure 6.2).

The types of cases a nation's courts tackle represent policy choices. The procedure for resolving a dispute must be proportionate to the value, importance, and complexity of the dispute. Low-value or simple disputes might be assigned to simpler and faster procedures consuming fewer court resources. For example, disputes over small amounts of money should be handled by small claims courts. The World Bank has been involved in establishing this system in the Dominican Republic, where it was discovered that more than 80 percent of commercial cases involved trivial amounts of money.

Policy choices should also be dictated by public preferences. For example, recent empirical work suggests that disputants value the chance to describe their version of the story to an impartial adjudicator; that is, oral procedures in front of a judge are perceived as particularly "fair." In fact, this "day in court" factor outweighs every other variable tested, including the actual outcome of the dispute.[11]

Judicial reform efforts

Attempts to improve judicial efficiency have varied widely across industrial and developing countries.[12] However, three key themes run through the successful initiatives to improve judicial efficiency.

■ *Increased accountability of judges.* For public sector employees, ensuring accountability is the mirror image of private sector contracting. The judge is contracted to provide efficient adjudication. However institutional features of the judicial system and the presence of complementary institutions (such as the media) affect the incentives of judges to provide such adjudication. The provision of information on judicial performance and monitoring play a key role in affecting judges' incentives and accountability. Accountability can also be increased through pressure from civil society.

■ *Simplification.* Simplification of legal procedures can lead to more efficient outcomes. Simplification may result from replacing written hearings by oral ones or by creating specialized courts. An excessive emphasis on procedure may undermine fairness, but so may excessive informality. As explained earlier, however, the evidence shows that judicial systems in developing countries which suffer from capacity constraints also suffer from an excess of formality and complexity of procedure.

■ *Increased resources.* In some countries the judiciary seriously lacks resources. In such cases, additional resources have been found to improve judicial efficiency. But in most cases, increased resources for the judiciary enhance efficiency only if they complement more fundamental reforms, such as eliminating all easily identifiable redundancies and inefficiencies in the judicial system. Recently, the Philippine Supreme Court asked for a large increase in public funding. However, a report by the Center for Public Resource Management, a Philippine NGO, has identified a large number of duplicative units and functions within the office of the clerk of court and the office of the court administrator. There are also 11 separate records divisions in the various offices of the Supreme Court. These units are not electronically or manually networked. Each maintains its own records processing, filing, and archiving functions. It is estimated that if these redundancies were eliminated from the judicial system, resources equivalent to 8 percent of its budget would be freed for other uses.[13]

Accountability

When judges are accountable for their actions, judicial systems can become more efficient, with judges providing faster and fairer solutions to cases. The incentives judges face affect judicial performance. Institutional design, in turn, affects judges' incentives. One of the primary factors affecting incentives is information on judicial performance, which allows the performance of judges to be monitored. A frequently used alternative is the imposition of legislated time limits on the resolution of particular types of cases. While legislated time limits have been a popular response to slow trials, the results to date have not been very encouraging. For example, in the United States time limits originally set by the Supreme Court have proved unenforceable. This is partly because it is difficult to monitor judicial effort. There is no objective way to tell whether a case drags on because it has legitimate difficulties or because a judge fails to do her job. As another example, judges in Argentina and Bolivia are given mandatory time limits to conduct and decide cases, but these are rarely enforced.

Systems where each judge works on the basis of an individual calendar have had some success. In such systems a single judge follows a case from beginning to end. This is in contrast to the master calendar, where the court can assign different parts of a case to different judges. The master calendar has some advantages; a case

can go on if a judge is sick or has a large workload, and judges can specialize in the procedural tasks that fall in their area of expertise. But there are drawbacks as well. No judge is fully familiar with the case, different judges can rule inconsistently in the same case, and—when a case takes a long time in a master-calendar jurisdiction—it is hard to know who is responsible. Some studies have found that the individual calendar is associated with reduced times to disposition, not only because the judge in charge is more familiar with her own cases, but also because judges feel more accountable.[14]

Generating accurate statistics reduces delay, since judges care about their reputation. Such an effect has been reported, for example, in Colombia and Guatemala.[15] The experience with delay reduction programs in the United States suggests that because problems on a case, such as excessive delay, can be uniquely traced to a judge, individual calendars make judges work harder and manage cases more effectively.[16] More broadly, reputational effects are a crucial determinant of whether delay in courts is severe. Reputational concerns are difficult to measure, however. Reforms such as reporting judicial statistics are effective because they provide a basis on which to assess judges' efficiency and therefore affect their reputation.

Apart from hard statistics, greater transparency in the conduct of judicial business, coupled with a judge's interest in her reputation and desire for prestige, improves judicial efficiency.[17] This has been documented in several industrial countries. When judges have open trials, lawyers, litigants, the media, and the general public observe their conduct. A review of the impact of televising judicial proceedings in New York state found that such scrutiny raises the efficiency of judges by one-third while at the same time increasing the quality of their judgments.[18]

Civil society groups can play an important role in helping to increase accountability in the judiciary. For example, in 1994 Argentina's Fundación para la Modernización del Estado and Instituto para el Desarrollo de Empresarios en la Argentina published a report on the need for greater transparency as part of a judicial reform proposal. Also in Argentina, Poder Ciudadano formed a commission with other civil society organizations to follow the work of the new Judiciary Council. This group requested public access to hearings of the council and issued reports on its functioning.

In the Philippines the Foundation of Judicial Excellence, the National Citizens Movement for Free Elections, and the Makati Business Club established the CourtWatch project in 1992. They sent two observers, usually law students, to courtrooms over an extended period of time. The observers rated judges after each visit, based on direct observation and surveys of lawyers and prosecutors involved in the case. The ratings included the judge's familiarity with the law, as well as the conduct of the proceedings, on such measures as promptness, efficiency, and courtesy. Soon after the program began, the media noticed that judges' behavior had changed and that the efficiency of the court had risen significantly.[19]

Simplification and structural reform

Simplification of procedures and enforcement has been found to improve judicial efficiency (as shown in figure 6.2). Three main types of simplification or structural reform are considered in this section: the creation of specialized courts, alternative dispute resolution mechanisms, and the simplification of legal procedures.

Specialized courts. The structure of adjudication can be changed by creating specialized courts. These courts may be specialized around the subject matter (such as bankruptcy and commercial courts) or around the size of the claim. Creating or extending small claims courts are among the most successful of all judicial reforms. There are many examples. In Brazil, for example, small claims courts have halved times to disposition and expanded access to justice.[20] In Hong Kong, China, it takes only four weeks from filing a case to its first hearing in the Small Claims Tribunal.

These courts are very popular in industrial countries too. Recently, the United Kingdom, which has had a history of success with small claims courts, increased the threshold on disputes that can be brought to these courts to £5,000. Small claims courts are also popular in Australia, Japan, and the United States.

Specialized courts with a particular subject-matter jurisdiction can also increase efficiency. Such courts have been set up for streamlined debt collection in several countries, including Germany, Japan, and the Netherlands. Labor tribunals in Ecuador have been associated with reduced times to disposition. Many of these specialized courts emphasize arbitration and conciliation, so some of the positive results for specialized courts may be the result of their emphasis on alternative dispute resolution methods.[21] Specialized courts also introduce simplified steps if they cut some of the general civil court procedures. For example, the re-

Box 6.7
The creation of a specialized commercial court in Tanzania

Tanzania's Commercial Court was established in 1999 as a specialized division of the country's High Court. It was launched at a time when the government of Tanzania had committed to embracing a market system and wanted to accelerate the process of building a legal and judicial system to support market reforms.

The Commercial Court has jurisdiction over cases involving amounts greater than Tsh10 million (about $12,500). It has a higher fee structure than the general division of the High Court. The filing fee is about 3 percent of the amount in dispute in the Commercial Court, while in the general division fees are capped at Tsh120,000 (about $150). The high fees discourage many litigants; these litigants use the High Court. Appeals of the Commercial Court's preliminary or interlocutory orders, a common source of delay in the Tanzanian system, are barred by rule until the case is finished.

The Commercial Court may keep filing fees until it has covered its annual operating budget. The general division must remit all fees collected to the Treasury. This means that the Commercial Court has a more stable and timely funding source. Cases filed with the court from September 1999 to November 2000 have an average value of about Tsh 52 million ($65,000). About half involve debt recovery, a quarter involve other contract disputes, and the rest involve tort, trademark, property, company law, insurance, or tax claims. Banks and financial institutions are the heaviest users of the Commercial Court. About 80 percent of cases that go to the court are settled out of court through mediation or settlement negotiations.

Source: Finnegan 2001.

cently established specialized commercial court in Tanzania cut the average time to disposition from 22 months to 3 months.[22] The creation of the Tanzanian commercial court was the result of the combined efforts of the government, private business, and international donors (box 6.7).

Alternative dispute resolution. In developing countries where judicial systems are ineffective, alternative dispute resolution (ADR) mechanisms can substitute for ineffective formal legal procedures. ADR mechanisms range from informal norm-based mediation to formal arbitration courts based on a simplified legal process. These systems may be run by communities or by the state. As formal systems develop, use of formal courts increases, so proportionately more disputes are resolved in these courts. Finally, as courts become very efficient and their judgments sufficiently predictable, the use of out-of-court settlements may increase relative to the number of court filings.

The experience on ADR mechanisms is generally positive. Many successful specialized courts and indigenous justice courts incorporate a strong element of arbitration and conciliation—including the Dutch *kort geding*, Ecuadorian labor mediation, justices of the peace in Peru, mediation centers in Latin America, Indian *lok adalats*, and the Russian *treteiskie* courts.[23]

The presence of alternative dispute resolution may reduce opportunities for corruption in developing economies. A judicial system in competition with other institutions is less able to extract rents from litigants. The poorest members of society and firms unaffiliated with large business groups are most likely to be affected adversely by inaccessible, corrupt, or inefficient courts. The experience with establishing a mediation facility in Bangladesh illustrates that transparent, swift, and accessible adjudication is possible with a relatively low budget (box 6.8). The evidence indicates that enforcement works best when all parties understand how the decisions are reached. The legitimacy of mediation depends in large part on incentives for agents to abide by the decisions of the forum. In most countries, this incentive is provided by societal norms, the prospect of repeat dealings, or the threat of court actions. As the Bangladeshi example shows, transparency in the mediation process is important.

The main criticism of alternative dispute resolution methods, voluntary or otherwise, is that such mechanisms generally work better when the courts are efficient. In other words, parties to a dispute have incentives to settle when they know what court judgments they will get; courts complement ADR systems. However this is clearly not the case in many developing countries, where ADR systems function as substitutes. But to function in this manner, they need to effectively represent the community for whom they adjudicate. The *lok adalats* in India, for example, are not very popular since they do not offer adequate compensation for victims, who face high costs in the courts to enforce their rights. These are more likely to be the poor people.

While few question the value of voluntary ADR mechanisms, mandatory systems have a mixed record and may have unintended consequences. This is partly due to the fact that litigants are bound by arbitration decisions. For example, they may go to the courts after mandatory arbitration. Voluntary arbitration systems may be set up by private parties or the government. In

Box 6.8
Alternative dispute resolution in Bangladesh

The Maduripur Legal Aid Association (MLAA), a Bangladeshi NGO, has set up a mediation structure in rural areas to deliver dispute settlement services for women. The local MLAA mediation committees meet twice a month to hear village disputes, free of charge. More than 5,000 disputes are mediated each year, of which two-thirds are resolved. The mediation program builds on the traditional *shalish* system of community dispute resolution and is not part of the court system. The MLAA staff is composed of only 120 people, since the mediation committees are made up of volunteers. The annual budget is small: only $80,000. The evidence suggests that a large majority of the settlements are respected because they are reached in full view of the community. Information on the process has helped strengthen legitimacy of the association. Approximately 60 percent of disputes involve family matters, 15 percent deal with property and land disputes, and the remainder mostly deal with disputes between neighbors. Plaintiffs prefer the mediation system since it is locally administered, free of charge, and relatively quick to render judgment; a decision is made within 45 days of the filing. In contrast, a court case will cost 250 taka in initial fees, and a minimum of 700 taka in lawyer's fees for a simple case. It will, on average, take three years to reach judgment.

Source: USAID 1998.

the United States, for example, the courts with the most intensive civil settlement efforts tend to have the slowest disposition times. Neither processing time nor judicial productivity is improved by extensive settlement programs.[24] Referring cases to mandatory arbitration has no major effect on time to disposition, lawyer work hours, or lawyer satisfaction and has an inconclusive effect on attorneys' views of fairness.[25] In some mediation programs—for instance in Japan and in some countries in Latin America—the mediator is also the judge. This situation may be procedurally unfair, as the judge may pressure the parties into a settlement. Parties will fear being frank before the same official who will pass judgment on them later.

Procedural law. Case studies also show that simplifying procedural law can increase judicial efficiency. A factor commonly associated with inefficiency in civil law countries is the predominance of written over oral procedures.[26] This is particularly important in Latin America.[27] A move toward oral procedures has produced positive results in Italy, Paraguay, and Uruguay.[28] In the Netherlands the *kort geding*—technically, the procedure for a preliminary injunction—has developed informally into a type of summary proceeding on matters of substantive law. A *kort geding* rarely requires more than one oral hearing. Each party presents its case and replies immediately. The president of the court indicates the parties' chances of success in a full action, and the oral hearing often ends in settlement. On average, *kort geding* cases take six weeks. Oral procedures are a dominant characteristic of small claims courts and specialized tribunals.

Simplification of procedures tends to have a positive impact on efficiency because greater procedural complexity reduces transparency and accountability, increasing corrupt officials' ability to obtain bribes. Procedural simplification tends to decrease time and costs and increase litigant satisfaction (for instance, the streamlined procedure of British small claims courts, or justices of the peace in Peru).[29] The efficiency of small claims courts seems to be driven by the simplicity of procedures. Indeed, English small claims courts are not a separate institution. County court procedures have merely been modified over the years to accommodate small claims.

The overall impact of procedural simplification depends on how burdensome the procedures were previously. Reforms in clogged systems may bring about a large increase in filings in the short run but in the long run will be associated with improved service, greater litigant satisfaction, and improvements in access.

Streamlining the system by which judicial procedure itself is determined can be beneficial. If every procedural change must go through the legislature, experimentation and innovation become difficult. Powers of the legislature to determine the organization and procedural rules of courts could be partially delegated to the judiciary; such a step has proved beneficial in Uruguay.[30] Or the legislature could partially delegate these powers to individual courts to encourage more flexibility, as has been done in the United Kingdom, where small claims judges have the ability to adopt any procedure they believe will be just and efficient. Many procedures have been adopted because they were believed to serve fairness, protect the accused, and improve access of the poor. But the judiciary itself needs checks and balances. Such authority is best devolved to judges when there are also measures established to enhance accountability.

Not every attempt at simplification is successful, however. Design needs to be adapted to country circumstances. Hence the need for some experimentation.

As Romania's experience shows, issues such as the limit on the amount of the claim to be settled in small claims courts or the relationship between small claims courts and other parts of the judicial system can be important in determining the impact of reforms.[31] In October 2000 the Romanian government passed a decree aimed at reducing the caseload burden of the commercial courts and shortening delays. However, the evidence suggests that certain features of the reforms have removed an element of competition within the court system that was provided by the ability to choose in some instances between the *Judecatorii,* the small claims court for firms, and the *Tribunale,* the general-jurisdiction court. Previously, choice among courts enabled firms to avoid costly delay.

Another constraint on the ability of procedural reform to deliver greater judicial efficiency is the law itself. When the substantive rules are unclear and other institutions are weak, there may be a limit as to how much judicial efficiency can be improved through procedural reform. For instance, when most land is untitled, land tenure is insecure because no one is sure how courts will rule on a contested claim. A land-titling program, as Peru's experience shows, may increase judicial efficiency.[32] In the Dominican Republic substantive changes in family and commercial law—reducing gender bias in custody cases, modernizing the commercial code, and implementing more effective sanctions against debtors—were necessary conditions for successful judicial reform.[33] Substantive simplicity may also be behind the efficiency gains associated with the small claims court studies.

Increased resources

Judicial officials and reformers have both cited the lack of resources and staff as the main factor constraining efficiency. However, the evidence on the effectiveness of increased resources is mixed. Data from the United States and from Latin American and Caribbean countries show no correlation between the overall level of resources and times to disposition.[34] Further, many efficiency-improving efforts include funding increases along with other initiatives, making it difficult to isolate the impact of increased resources relative to other factors. For example, in Paraguay the number of judges was increased at the same time as oral proceedings were introduced.[35]

The evidence indicates that funding increases help alleviate temporary backlogs in systems that have made a serious effort to work better but are of little use when inefficiencies are large. Crash programs to reduce backlogs through large infusions of resources have shown good results in the short term, but without deeper change, these results cannot be sustained. Introducing computer systems or other mechanization in the judiciary, often a major component of World Bank–sponsored reform efforts, has helped reduce delays and corruption in Latin America.[36] Resource increases are needed to introduce computer-based systems. Much of the reduction in corruption as a result of such a reform is probably due to the increased accountability in mechanized systems. Computerized case inventories are more accurate and easier to handle than the paper-based procedures they replace, and more than one person can have access to them, which makes them harder to manipulate.

Overall resource levels are often uncorrelated with judicial efficiency, but in cases of extreme underfunding, an infusion of resources can be effective. In Uganda, for example, backlogs were caused by shortages of stationery and were solved when another court donated paper. The Supreme Court of Cambodia has acknowledged that lack of funds has made it difficult to arrange travel for trial witnesses. The Supreme Court in Mongolia has abandoned circuit work due to lack of travel money.[37] Resources may also help judges improve management. A major inefficiency in many judicial systems is judges' responsibility for administrative work, such as signing paychecks and ordering office supplies. Centralizing administrative work in a single office, where the employees have administrative training, increased efficiency in Colombian and Peruvian courts and in the Guatemalan public ministry.

Fairness

Good governance requires impartial and fair legal institutions. This means guaranteeing the independence of judicial decisionmaking against political interference. A judiciary independent from both government intervention and influence by the parties in a dispute provides the single greatest institutional support for the rule of law. If the law or the courts are perceived as partisan or arbitrary in their application, the effectiveness of the judicial system in providing social order will be reduced. As discussed in previous sections, fairness also requires institutions that make judges accountable for their actions. Judicial independence needs to be coupled with a system of accountability in the judicial sys-

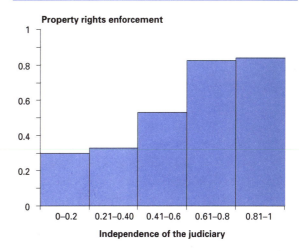

Figure 6.3

The independence of the judiciary enhances property rights

Property rights enforcement

Independence of the judiciary

Note: Higher values indicate better enforcement and more independence.
Source: La Porta and others, 2001, *World Development Report 2002* background paper.

tem. Civil society organizations and the media play a key role in monitoring judicial performance. The absence of checks on the judicial system can create arbitrariness.

Guarantees of judicial independence from the state

Judicial reform that aims to improve the quality and integrity of judicial decisions is best focused on creating politically independent, difficult-to-intimidate judges. Creating a system of checks and balances also improves fairness and integrity. For this, judicial independence needs to be coupled with a system of social accountability. The channels for such accountability can be the free media and civil society organizations or can be built into the judicial system itself. These are discussed above and in chapter 10.

A study commissioned for this Report collected data from the constitutions of 71 countries, examining three factors that guarantee judicial independence: the duration of appointment of supreme and administrative court judges; the extent to which administrative review of government acts is possible; and the role of legal precedent in determining how disputes are resolved.[38] The same study shows how judicial independence strengthens enforcement of property rights in countries (figure 6.3).

- *Duration of appointment.* When judges have life-long tenure, they are both less susceptible to direct political pressure and less likely to have been appointed by the politicians currently in office. Independence is particularly important when judges are adjudicating disputes between citizens and the state (for example, freedom of speech issues and contract disputes). Therefore, the study focuses on the tenure of two different sets of judges: those in the highest ordinary courts (the supreme courts), and those in administrative courts, which have jurisdiction over cases where the state or a government agency is a party to litigation. Countries in which judges are independent from the influence of the state also tend to be countries where the judiciary is free from interference by private parties. The tenure of judges matters in both cases. Peru is frequently rated as the country with the least judicial independence. Former President Fujimori kept more than half of judges on temporary appointments from 1992 to 2000.
- *Administrative review.* In some countries citizens can challenge administrative acts of the government only in administrative courts, which are part of the executive branch. In other countries, citizens can seek redress against administrative acts directly through ordinary courts, or they can request the supreme court to review decisions made by administrative courts. Arbitrary government actions, including those that limit the role of the judiciary, are less likely when the judiciary can review administrative acts.
- *The role of legal precedent.* In some countries the role of courts is merely to interpret laws. In other countries courts have "lawmaking" powers because jurisprudence is a source of law. Judges have greater independence when their decisions are a source of law. Indeed, many legal scholars consider that the existence of case law as a legitimate source of law is the clearest measure of judicial independence. In some countries case law exists de facto although not de jure. For example, the French Revolution stripped all legislative power (and power over administrative acts) from the judicial system. However, judges in many civil law countries such as France and Germany do pay attention to precedent.

In 53 out of the 71 countries in the sample, supreme court judges are appointed for life. This diverse group of countries includes, for example, Argentina and Ethiopia, Iran and Indonesia. Supreme court judges are appointed for terms of more than six years, but less than life, in nine countries, including Haiti, Japan, Mexico, Panama and Switzerland. Supreme court judges are appointed for less than six years in China, Cuba, Honduras, and Vietnam. The results for the tenure of administrative court judges follow a similar pattern.

The next indicator measures the independence of courts in ruling on the disputes between the government and its citizens. There are two aspects to this measure: which courts have the ultimate power over administrative disputes, and the tenure of judges in these courts. Administrative judges adjudicate many key disputes in this area. However, whereas in 17 countries, including France and Italy, the rulings of administrative judges are final, in 50 countries, including Bangladesh, Kenya, Mozambique, the United Kingdom, and the United States, these rulings can be appealed to judges in ordinary courts. A key implication of the ability to appeal administrative sentences in ordinary courts is that, as a result, the supreme court has ultimate jurisdiction over rulings of the administrative courts.

Supreme court control over administrative cases is possible in countries of any legal origin, but it tends to happen more in common law countries. Whereas the supreme court has ultimate control over administrative cases in 90 percent of the English legal origin countries, it has final authority only in 67 percent of the countries of French and German legal origin. But the ability of the supreme court to review sentences by administrative courts is a meaningful restraint on the power of the executive only when coupled with independent, tenured judges. Administrative review is conducted by judges with lifelong tenure and subject to supreme court review in 90 percent of English origin countries and 80 percent of Scandinavian countries, but only 37.5 percent of French origin countries and 16.7 percent of German origin countries.[39]

Jurisprudence is a source of law in all English origin countries. However, jurisprudence is also a source of law in all Scandinavian origin countries and in 80 percent of German origin countries, including Germany, Japan, Korea, and Switzerland. French origin countries occupy an intermediate position. Jurisprudence is a source of law in 36 percent of these cases, including in France and in many Latin American countries that modeled their constitutions after that of the United States. These differences in case law across legal origins are magnified by the tenure of supreme court judges, the judges who ultimately interpret the law. For example, not only do supreme court judges have law-making power in English and Scandinavian origin countries but they also have lifelong tenure.

The data indicate that independence of judges from the state can be built into any legal system. The main constraint is not the nature of the legal system, but rather political factors, which determine the degree of independence of the judicial system. Restraint of arbitrary state action and accountability of the state is a critical development that needs to accompany overall judicial system development. In many developing countries, judicial independence could be enhanced by giving judges lifelong tenure, by giving them lawmaking powers, and by allowing supreme court review over administrative cases.

There are several other ways to enhance judicial independence in addition to the three just listed. First, the budget of the judicial system can be set as a fixed percentage of the total government budget by law. In this way, it will not be possible to deny resources to the judiciary. In most courts, as the example of the Tanzania commercial court in box 6.7 illustrates, court fees can go toward the court budget. Only after this budget is replenished will money go toward the government budget. Second, transfers in judicial appointments can be made subject to the written approval of judges. This rule was instituted in France in 1976 and is necessary in countries like Kazakhstan, where the media recently reported cases of judges being reassigned after deciding cases against government agencies. Third, transparent criteria for career advancement are also likely to determine the degree of political independence. In most countries around the world, the executive or legislative branch decides on appointments to higher positions in the courts. This process creates opportunities for bargaining between politicians and judges in countries with high levels of corruption.

Intimidation by private actors

Intimidation by powerful private interests is as likely to result in arbitrary decisions as is intervention by the state. In Colombia, for example, powerful drug lords threaten the lives of judges and their families. In the 1990s alone more than 60 judges were assassinated. One solution to the problem is the creation of "faceless" judges or juries, who decide on cases without the public knowing their true identity. This method has been successfully tried in Colombia. But even this solution may be inadequate. In a corrupt society the identity of faceless judges can be revealed.

Another channel of influence is through bribes and corruption. In a number of countries judges' salaries are lower than those of other public servants and much lower than the salaries of private sector lawyers. This creates incentives to sell justice. While few countries can afford to pay judges $500,000 a year and more, as is the case in Singapore, numerous countries in the last decade have introduced a pay scale consistent with the salaries of other public officials. In Uruguay, for example, higher court judges receive salaries equivalent to those of cabinet ministers. While wage increases would not eliminate high-level corruption in the judiciary, they may eradicate small-scale bribery. Judges will have less need to supplement their income. To date, however, there has been little systematic evidence on this issue.

Conclusions

The judicial system plays an important role in the development of market economies. It does so in many ways: by resolving disputes between private parties, by resolving disputes between private and public parties, by providing a backdrop for the way that individuals and organizations behave outside the formal system, and by affecting the evolution of society and its norms while being affected by them. These changes bring law and order and promote the development of markets, economic growth, and poverty reduction. Judicial systems need to balance the need to provide swift and affordable—that is, accessible—resolution with fair resolution; these are the elements of judicial efficiency.

Judicial reform, like other institutional reforms, is often politically difficult. When considering institutional reform in this area, recognizing the complementarity among different institutional elements is key. Many elements affect judicial performance—for example, the institutional process for setting wages and promotions, procedural law, substantive law, the capacity of lawyers and judges, and the perceived relevance of the courts by people. Not all the elements that affect judicial performance are equally difficult politically. This is important: institutions work as systems. An improvement in one part can affect the efficiency of the whole system; that is, policymakers may complement various small reforms to improve efficiency while building momentum for larger reforms.

The success of judicial reforms depends on increasing the accountability of judges; that is, providing them with incentives to perform effectively, simplifying procedures, and targeting resource increases. One of the most important elements affecting judicial accountability is transparency, or the provision of information that makes it easy to monitor judicial performance and affect judges' reputations—for example, judicial databases that make cases easy to track and hard to manipulate or misplace.

Simplifying legal procedures tends to increase judicial efficiency. For example, for judicial systems that rely excessively on written procedures, a shift toward oral hearings tends to make trials simpler, faster, and cheaper, with little loss of accuracy. Reforms of this sort have improved efficiency and access in countries with diverse legal traditions. Small-claims courts and justices of the peace are widely popular because of their lay language and pared-down procedures. Simplification is particularly important in countries where complementary institutions are weak, and other types of reforms may be more difficult in the short run. Simplified procedures may also benefit the poorer members of society and increase their access to the judicial system. Alternative dispute resolution systems—based on social norms or on simplified legal procedures—can also enhance access of the disadvantaged to legal services. Partially delegating the "nuts and bolts" of procedural reform to the judicial branch can speed the process of innovation and experimentation.

Judicial reform that aims to improve the quality and integrity of judicial decisions is best focused on creating politically independent, difficult-to-intimidate judges. Creating a system of checks and balances also improves fairness and integrity. For this, judicial independence needs to be coupled with a system of social accountability. The channels for such accountability can be the free media and civil society organizations, or accountability can be built into the judicial system itself.

CHAPTER 7

Competition

Of all human powers operating on the affairs of mankind, none is greater than that of competition.

—Henry Clay, 1832

Competition has long been acknowledged as an important force bringing about economic development and growth. In the 18th century Adam Smith pointed out that China's lack of competition with the outside world limited its growth and development prospects at the time and allowed the persistence of the divide between the rich and the poor (box 7.1). The subsequent history of China—a weakened nation invaded and occupied by foreign powers, followed by the Communist Revolution brought on by inequality of wealth and incomes—seems to have illustrated Smith's prescience. The history of Western Europe provides many examples of institutional changes that promoted or restricted competition, or competition that promoted institutional change. In some instances governments initiated institutional changes. In Sweden in the 19th century, for instance, the government abolished the guilds, which supported an urban monopoly in some professions, to promote production in rural areas. In other instances institutional changes to promote competition occurred without government intervention. For example, in 19th century Germany professional guilds progressively lost their power because of competition from the emerging factory system.

Competition—domestic and international—provides incentives for institutional change around the world (chapter 1) by modifying the effect of existing institutions. Competition can also act as a substitute for other institutions. There is evidence that competition can substitute for an effective bankruptcy system because it exerts pressures on inefficient firms to go into liquidation.[1] There is evidence that competition can substitute for strong shareholder control in firms in raising productivity growth. Greater competition raises productivity growth in a firm with no dominant external shareholder, while competition has no positive impact on productivity performance in the presence of a dominant outside shareholder.[2] There is also evidence that competition can change the nature of labor market institutions (see the discussion below).

At the same time, there may be conflicts between promoting competition and promoting better corporate governance. For example, business groups established to solve information and enforcement problems might restrict entry into markets. Also, not all the institutional changes that arise from competition enhance the well-being of all members of society (chapters 4, 5, and 9).

The central element of competition in product markets is the freedom of traders to use their resources where they choose and to exchange them at a price they choose.[3] Product market competition increases efficiency (and productivity, and the growth of productivity in the economy) by providing incentives for managers to reduce costs, innovate, reduce slack, and improve the institutional arrangements in production.[4] Productivity growth, in turn, is one of the main sources of growth in countries.[5] In industrial countries productivity growth is generally the result of technological advances. In developing countries productivity growth has mostly been attained through technology spillovers from trade, foreign direct investment, licensing, and joint ventures.

Sometimes there may be a conflict between the static and dynamic effects of competition. Or firms may

Box 7.1
Adam Smith on competition, 1776

China seems to have been long stationary, and had probably long ago acquired that full complement of riches which is consistent with the nature of its laws and institutions. But this complement may be much inferior to what, with other laws and institutions, the nature of its soil, climate, and situation might admit of. A country which neglects or despises foreign commerce, and which admits the vessels of foreign nations into one or two of its ports only, cannot transact the same quantity of business that it might do with different laws and institutions. In a country, too, where though the rich or the owners of large capitals enjoy a good deal of security, the poor or the owners of small capitals enjoy scarce any . . . the quantity of stock employed in all the different branches of business transacted within it can never be equal to what the nature and extent of that business might admit. In every different branch, the oppression of the poor must establish the monopoly of the rich, who, by engrossing the whole trade to themselves, will be able to make very large profits.

—Adam Smith, *An Inquiry into the Nature and Causes of the Wealth of Nations,* 1776

not invest in innovations that require high initial investments. Institutions that protect intellectual property rights and reduce competition may be needed to resolve this problem.

A number of studies, concentrated on industrial countries, have found a positive relationship between competition and efficiency (measured by productivity levels), and between competition and the rate of productivity growth.[6] In the presence of competition, firms adjust operations to raise efficiency and thus maintain profitability, and less efficient firms exit the industry. The exit of these firms frees up resources, which can then be used by more efficient firms. Entry and exit has been shown to be an important source of industrywide productivity growth in semi-industrialized countries such as Chile (1979–85) and Morocco (1984–87).[7] In a study of Korea between 1990 and 1998, plant exit and entry accounted for as much as 45 percent of manufacturing productivity growth during cyclical upturns and 65 percent during downturns.[8]

Some studies have found that the benefits of competition do not depend on having large numbers of firms.[9] Studies show that technical efficiency falls with increased market concentration in industrial (Australia, Canada, Japan, the United Kingdom, and the United States) and developing (Korea) countries but that,

below a certain level of concentration, technical efficiency also falls.[10] A study of firms in transition economies finds that competition from one to three rivals is important in explaining innovation such as a firm's decision to launch new products.[11] Those firms with more than three competitors perform better than monopolists, but their advantage is only half as great as those facing one to three competitors.[12]

The preceding discussion suggests that to obtain the benefits of competition—greater efficiency and innovation in product markets—*some degree* of competition, but not always competition by a large number of firms, is needed. Moreover, it is not just market structure but also the threat of entry—either by firms or by products—that determines the degree of competition in domestic markets. It is difficult in practice to measure the extent of actual and potential competition in domestic markets (box 7.2). In developing countries with lim-

Box 7.2
Measuring competition

There are three main ways to measure competition. The first approach is to measure the extent to which production is concentrated among a small number of firms. This includes using indicators such as the four or five firm concentration ratios, the percentage of employment by the four largest firms, the Herfindahl index (sum of squares of market shares of firms), and the number of firms in the market.

The second approach is to look at the consequences of market structure rather than the market structure itself. This can be done by estimating the residual elasticity of demand for the firm's own product—the extent to which a price rise by the firm would lead customers to substitute away and buy from rival firms, or turn away from the product altogether.

The third approach is to look directly at the behavior of firms to infer the extent of competition the firms *perceive* they face. The price-cost margin is the most commonly used measure.

These three ways of measuring competition are consistent with one another and are complementary. The concentration measure is probably the easiest to use in developing countries, compared with the other two, which require extensive information. But focusing just on current market structure variables misses the importance of potential competitors—those that could enter the market and therefore act as a discipline on incumbent firms.

Note: The idea of contestability was originated in Willig (1980). See Baumol and others (1982).
Source: Carlin and Seabright 2000, *World Development Report 2002* background paper.

ited capacity and supporting institutions, the priority for policymakers should be to ensure both the *free entry and exit of firms* and *exposure to international competition*. This chapter looks at institutions that restrict or promote competition in markets. The institutions that enhance the provision of infrastructure services (laws and regulations and the agencies that enforce them) are also important for promoting competition. These institutions are discussed in chapter 8.

There are many potential barriers to competition. In developing countries the main institutional barriers to domestic competition are government regulations on exit and entry of firms.[13] Even in the tradable sector, international competition may not lead to domestic competition, partly because of institutional barriers to competition, such as government regulations in product and factor markets that deter firm entry, exit, and growth. Excessive and costly government regulations also facilitate corruption and lead to adverse distributional consequences by inducing workers and firms to escape into the informal market. Private institutions can also cause barriers to competition. For example, the monopolization of domestic distribution channels can mean that even when a good can be imported freely, there still may not be competition in the domestic market for that good.

Domestic institutions that promote competition include competition laws and competition authorities. In structure and mandate they differ significantly, even among industrial countries—that is, one size does not fit all. These were introduced by governments to tackle private barriers to product market competition, and to ensure that, in sectors characterized by natural monopolies, prices do not diverge too much from costs. Many developing countries suffer from human capital constraints. In resource-constrained countries governments may benefit from focusing on removing barriers to entry and exit in markets and opening the economy to international competition before turning their attention to building competition institutions, particularly for tradable sectors. But many developing countries already have competition laws and agencies. By focusing the agenda for these agencies, these institutions can be made more effective at promoting competition. The priority for competition authorities should usually be the cases that can harm competition, such as cartels and exclusive supply and distribution contracts.

International trade reform itself can be viewed as institutional reform, since it changes the rules of the game for those affected.[14] International trade promotes competition in markets. Openness to international trade also helps exert pressure on governments to reform those domestic product and factor market institutions that undermine the ability of firms to respond to competitive pressures from abroad. But the effect of this source of competition is mostly limited to tradable goods, such as manufactures. Some products, such as cement and infrastructure services, are by their nature not easily transportable. That is, transport costs are so high that sellers cannot make returns high enough to encourage trade. When infrastructure is poor, only consumers who live near the border can enjoy the benefits of price competition from freely traded products.

Governments worldwide need to build more effective institutions to address aspects of the international trade regime that can undermine competition. At the national level, this includes making further progress in liberalizing services as well as goods, and, for industrial countries, in providing access for developing country exports. At the international level, it includes reducing compliance and certification costs of trade-related product standards (such as food safety standards) and taking advantage of the flexibility allowed in the Agreement on Trade-Related Intellectual Property Rights (TRIPS) to allow developing countries to maximize benefits.

International standards do not always promote competition, and not all standards are appropriate for developing countries. Without attention to country circumstances, some standards, such as those for international property rights, can even have adverse distributional consequences. Moreover, complementary institutions or human capital to enforce these systems do not exist in many countries. In international forums human capital constraints can prevent developing country policymakers from engaging effectively in negotiations. These are areas that need attention if future development of international standards is to reflect developing country priorities and promote competition.

This chapter first discusses constraints on domestic competition—that is, government regulations on firm entry, and competition laws and agencies. It then discusses restrictions affecting international transactions: trade restrictions and intellectual property rights.

Domestic competition

This section focuses on the two main factors that determine the extent of competition in domestic markets.

The first, and the most important in developing countries, is government regulation of product and factor markets, which can inhibit firm exit, entry, and growth. The second is private or "natural" barriers to domestic product market competition. These include monopolies on domestic distribution or private barriers arising from localized markets, either because products are not transportable or because infrastructure is poor.

Regulations on entry and exit

Governments can inhibit firm entry either through direct restrictions on the establishment of new firms or through an excessive number of entry regulations. The poor functioning of factor markets can also inhibit firm entry. The failure to provide strong property rights for land can reduce firm entry (chapter 2). Poorly functioning credit markets that result in restricted access to credit for some groups—in particular, small and medium-size firms—can also deter firm entry into some activities, restricting firm growth and limiting the extent of competition in the product market (chapter 4).

Governments can also inhibit firm entry by raising exit costs. Firms are less likely to enter a market if exit costs are high or, in the extreme case, if exit is impossible.[15] Government institutions that raise the cost of exit include factor market regulations, such as labor legislation, that make it costly and sometimes even impossible for firms to lay off workers (box 7.3). Another example is restitution laws in transition countries, which inhibit land transactions and deter firm exit and hence firm entry (chapter 2). Unprofitable businesses may also keep operating when they receive budget subsidies or quasi-fiscal support such as soft loans or are permitted to fall behind in their taxes or other payments, in the process impeding entry and exit.

Removing or relaxing institutional barriers to product market competition promotes competition directly and exerts pressures on governments to remove rigidities in factor markets. Rigidities in land, labor, and capital markets can raise adjustment costs in the domestic economy, for example, causing higher unemployment, as firms are exposed to pressures of competition. It is not uncommon to find product and factor market restrictions coexisting.[16] It can also be argued that uncompetitive product markets allow the persistence of factor market restrictions. Box 7.4 presents an example

---

Box 7.3

Labor regulations and rigidities in the labor market: the example of India

Almost all countries have labor laws and regulations to protect workers. These fall into five categories:

- Establishment and protection of workers' rights, including the right to associate and organize, the right to bargain collectively, and the right to engage in industrial action
- Protection for vulnerable groups, including minimum working age requirements, equality of wages, and employment opportunities and special provisions for women
- Establishment of minimum compensation for work, including minimum wages, minimum nonwage benefits, and overtime pay
- Assurance of decent working conditions, including occupational health and safety provisions and maximum hours of work
- Provision of income security, including social security, job security, severance pay, and public works.

World Development Report 1995 provides a detailed analysis of labor legislation and its effects and shows that not all labor laws achieve their intended objectives. The Report suggests that labor laws in developing countries be simplified and focused on basic human rights and safety issues.

In developing countries excessively restrictive labor laws sometimes have the effect of benefiting a group of relatively well-off workers at the cost of limiting the employment of others (sometimes the majority) in the formal sector. In some countries labor laws have introduced significant rigidities into the labor market, with adverse consequences for production and growth.

An example is India, with 165 pieces of labor legislation (World Bank, 2000d; Zagha 1998). Indian labor laws provide for a wide scope for initiating industrial disputes, long procedures for settlement of industrial disputes, inflexible provisions on change in conditions of service, and provisions enabling government interventions in areas such as layoff, retrenchment, and closures. The proliferation of labor laws is made worse by definitional complexities, making their interpretation even more difficult. There are 11 different ways of defining "wages," and the meaning of "worker," "employee," and "employed person" changes depending on the piece of legislation.

Lack of clarity about the rights and obligations of employers and employees, litigiousness, and delays in settling disputes have consequently become key features in the application of India's labor laws. Most disputes take more than 1 year to settle, and 20 years is not infrequent. This legislative framework has impeded large-scale industrial restructuring, relocation, or exit—and hence entry into the formal sector—and even the relocation of labor within an enterprise and often even in the same city or town.

Box 7.4
Increased product market competition and increased labor market flexibility in India

Before India's wide-ranging economic liberalization program began in the early 1990s, the Indian production system was characterized by high rents created by industry licensing and protection from external competition. This system had enabled firms to pass on to consumers the cost of workers' privileges embedded in labor regulations and had eroded firms' incentives to minimize labor costs. Labor, through union activity, had captured part of the rents generated by the restrictions on competition.

With the liberalization of the economy, producers began to face competition in product markets, which restricted their ability to pass on to consumers the cost of workers' privileges. This made workers more conscious of the employment consequences of their demands. Firms became more adept at circumventing labor market regulations and at resisting union pressure, as reflected in the increase in lockouts (managers shutting down production to deny striking workers their wages). At the same time, incentives for union activity declined, as reflected in the decline in the number of strikes.

Product market competition raised the number of lockouts and reduced the number of strikes in India

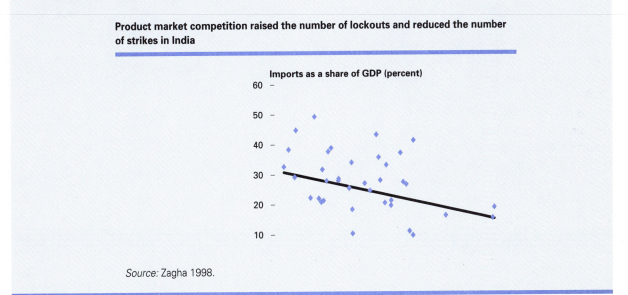

Source: Zagha 1998.

in which increased product market competition increased the flexibility of labor markets in India. Similar examples are found in industrial countries.[17]

Institutional barriers to firm entry erected by governments include restrictions on the establishment of new firms. For example, in Korea restrictions on the involvement of the *chaebol* in retail activity and an arduous bureaucratic store-opening evaluation process contributed to low productivity in the general merchandise retailing sector.[18] These regulations were established with the objectives of protecting small stores, discouraging consumption, and promoting more investment in the manufacturing sector. The regulations, however, led to the undesirable outcome that some profitable investments were prevented and others were distorted.

Governments can also raise the cost of entry through the procedures they mandate that firms undertake for starting up businesses.[19] Although some of these procedures—such as appropriate safety, health, and envi-

ronmental regulations—could be beneficial, others are not. Even beneficial regulations can inhibit firm entry if they are too numerous, too complex, or too costly, relative to the income level of the country.

A recent study covering 85 countries found that regulations may have unintended effects on business activities or outcomes.[20] For example, on average, neither pollution nor the number of accidental poisoning cases (as an example of work-related accidents) fell as the number of regulations imposed by governments across the world increased. This does not mean that socially beneficial regulations should be eliminated. Instead, it is the quality rather than the quantity of regulations that matters, along with their successful implementation.

The same study found that developing countries generally require more procedures to start a new business than industrial countries. But there are exceptions. Notably, France has the same number of procedures as Russia. Both countries require 16 procedures, compared with 20 in Bolivia. The countries with the fewest number of procedures or regulations are all industrial countries, with Canada and Australia having the least (two).

The procedures covered by the study fall into five categories: health and safety, environment, taxes, labor, and general screening. Screening—a set of general procedures whose purpose is often unclear—is typically the most onerous. Unsurprisingly, the larger the number of procedures required, the longer it takes to start a business and the greater the cost (relative to per capita income). For example, Mozambique and Bolivia, which are among those countries with the highest number of procedures, are also among the countries where it takes the most days to start a new business (174 and 82, respectively). It is also costly to start a business in these countries, with costs of 116 and 263 percent of GDP per capita, respectively (costs can rise to over 300 percent of GDP per capita in some countries). In comparison, in Canada, where there are two procedures, it takes only two days and costs only 1.4 percent of GDP per capita to start a new business.

Many of these procedures consist of obtaining approvals from several different offices and requiring formal notarizations at various steps, or of overly burdensome inspections for tax and other regulations. This implies that it is more costly for firms in developing countries than in industrial countries to start up new businesses. In those industrial countries where there are more procedures, the effect of more regulation is countered by the presence of a more accountable and transparent administration, and better information and enforcement. Entry regulations are also found to reduce competition in domestic markets, particularly in large countries, even when the country is open to international trade.[21]

The number of procedures is associated with larger unofficial economies and a higher level of corruption (figures 7.1 and 7.2). Many studies have shown that excessive product and labor market regulations induce firms to shift their activities into the informal market to bypass the high costs of doing business and employing labor in the formal sector.[22] Estimates of the size of the informal economy and of the proportion of workers employed in it show that both have been growing over the past decade in many transition and OECD countries. Rising state regulatory activities, labor market regulations, and an increasing burden of taxation and social security payments have driven this process.[23] These estimates also indicate that in general, the size of the

Figure 7.1

The size of the unofficial economy rises with the number of procedures required to start up new business

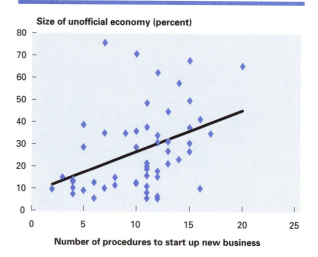

Size of unofficial economy (percent)

Number of procedures to start up new business

Source: Djankov and others forthcoming. *World Development Report 2002* background paper.

shadow economy as a percentage of GDP is larger in developing than in industrial countries.

The informal economy increases competition by providing services and small-scale manufacturing and by fostering dynamism and entrepreneurship and thus leads to greater efficiency. But the positive benefits of greater competition can be enhanced if the informal sector has access to the protection of the official judiciary system and to capital markets for finance and insurance.

A larger informal economy also has distributional consequences. Although employment in the informal sector is better than no employment at all, workers in the informal sector do not have access to the same benefits, such as social security and unemployment benefits, as do workers in the formal sector. Workers in the informal sector are predominantly poor (see chapter 9); this means that policies which prevent firm growth and formalization are biased against the more disadvantaged.

Competition laws and competition authorities

Some of the more prominent examples of private barriers to product market competition are monopolies, cartels, and vertical restraints (for example, contracts between producers and their distributors that prevent the distributors from carrying competitors' products). "Nat-

Figure 7.2
Corruption rises with the number of procedures required to start a new business

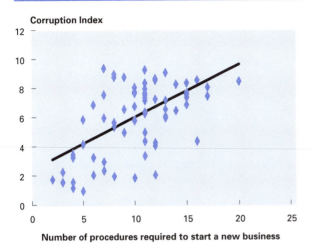

Source: Djankov and others forthcoming. *World Development Report 2002* background paper.

ural" entry barriers can arise from localized markets, infrastructure services, or natural monopolies. Governments can address private and natural barriers to product market competition using competition laws and competition authorities.

Building competition institutions. Canada and the United States were among the first countries to introduce competition law, in 1889 and 1890 respectively. Many European countries introduced competition laws in the 1950s, after World War II. Most developing and transition countries did not introduce competition laws until the 1990s. Around 90 countries have such laws in operation, with several more, including China, the Arab Republic of Egypt, and the Former Yugoslav Republic of Macedonia, drafting and debating competition laws. But the enforcement of competition laws in many developing countries—and in low-income countries in particular—is not very active. This is the result partly of the short tenure of these laws and partly of a lack of complementary institutions that would facilitate enforcement, such as courts or well-established information processing systems for the regulator.

Governments have introduced competition laws, and competition authorities to enforce them, because of concerns about the anticompetitive behavior of firms, in response to economic crises, or because of international pressures, which may or may not be crisis-induced. In the United States the Sherman Antitrust Act, for example, was introduced with a view to restraining the power of large business conglomerates operating in the country at that time. Sweden introduced an antimonopoly law in 1925 because of concerns about cartel abuses. Denmark, the Netherlands, and Norway gradually transformed their older laws controlling prices or regulating cartels into antitrust-type statutes, also in response to increasing cartelization in the late 1920s and early 1930s.

France, Indonesia, and Romania provide examples of countries that introduced competition laws in response to economic crises. The French government enacted its first modern antitrust measure, the Decree of 1953, in response to economic crisis—including inflationary problems following World War II and the Korean War, the need to attract foreign direct investment (FDI), and the perception that restrictive practices, especially in the distribution sector, were hindering economic recovery. More recently, economic crises in Indonesia and Romania led to the introduction of competition laws as part of overall economic stabilization and reform programs. In these two cases, international development and lending agencies, such as the World Bank, created pressures for adopting competition laws.

Japan, Germany, and most countries in Central and Eastern Europe are examples of countries that introduced competition laws because of international pressure. Japan and Germany enacted antitrust legislation following World War II, despite local objections. The Anti-monopoly Law of Japan and the De-cartelization and De-concentration Law of Germany were both enacted in 1947. They were significantly amended by later legislation, moving away from their U.S. origins to regimes considered more suitable to local conditions, particularly through a higher degree of tolerance for some types of cartel activities. Similarly, after the fall of the Berlin Wall in 1989, the countries of Central and Eastern Europe that aimed to join the European Union began enacting antitrust legislation, under some pressure from the European Commission. Most of these countries later amended their laws to make explicit matters that their advisers had originally taken for granted. In other words, the supporting legal framework for competition policy in these countries was missing, and there was a different understanding of the reach of the law. For example, the legal authority of an antitrust body to come to an agreement with a private party to settle a case had to be clarified. This was particularly the case where the private party had to go through a formal administrative or enforcement process within the competition authority or in the courts.

The European Union is a unique case. Its members have collective and national antitrust legislation, with the competition regime of the European Union incorporated into the national laws of individual member states. The primary focus of the European Union's competition regime—incorporated in articles of the Treaty of Rome and enforced by the European Commission—is economic integration among the member countries. Therefore the most serious prohibitions concern practices that would create or preserve fragmentation along national lines, such as country-specific vertical restraints and restrictions on the use of intellectual property.

Variations in competition laws and their enforcement. A survey of competition laws in 50 countries conducted for this report shows that different conceptions of competition exist across countries. This is reflected in two key elements of competition law: what constitutes dominance—the ability of a firm to unilaterally control price and output in the market—and how countries deal with cartels. Differences are also reflected in the way competition laws are enforced.

DOMINANCE. The survey reveals that 28 out of 50 countries have qualitative definitions of dominance, while the remaining 22 countries have a wide range of market shares as their benchmarks (table 7.1). Most OECD countries define dominance qualitatively. Several Latin American countries also define dominance qualitatively, but other developing countries tend to have quantitative benchmarks. Even though competitive processes in different industries differ, only one of the countries surveyed—Tanzania—has separate specifications for benchmarks of dominance for different sectors.

Given the importance of potential competition, as well as actual competition, and differences about what is needed to ensure competition based on industry characteristics, ideally a qualitative approach toward determining dominance is appropriate. But assessing dominance qualitatively is a difficult procedure, requiring sophisticated information and human resource capacity, both of which may be lacking in many developing countries. In these cases, quantitative benchmarks can provide important information. The priorities for developing countries in promoting competition should be liberalizing international trade and reducing government-erected entry and exit barriers in product markets. Building competition institutions is a lesser priority for many countries. But a large number of countries have already adopted competition laws and agencies. The issue in these countries is how to make these institutions more effective at enhancing competition in markets.

CARTELS. There are two main ways in which cartels can be treated in competition law. The first is to treat all cartels as illegal, meaning that practices such as price-fixing and other cartel-related behavior violate the law regardless of the market power of participants, their motives, or the purported business justifications. This stringent treatment of cartels is found in 13 of the 50 countries surveyed, including the United States. The second way is to use the rule-of-reason analysis, meaning that it is up to the competition authorities to prove the harmful economic effects of cartels. This less stringent way of treating cartels is found in most countries. European Union competition law has an automatic prohibition against anticompetitive practices and agreements. It is up to the competition authorities or national courts to prove that there has been an infringement and that the behavior (in the case of an agreement) does not qualify for an exemption.

ENFORCEMENT. Along with differences in competition law, differences in enforcement determine the ways in which countries treat competition.[24] The two dominant systems, which have been transplanted to many developing countries, are the U.S. and the European Union systems. The major difference between U.S. and European Commission cartel enforcement is in the levels and nature of enforcement. In the United States

Table 7.1
Benchmarks of product market dominance in competition laws around the world

Country group	Market share of the firm
Developing and transition countries	
East Asia	50–75 percent
Eastern Europe and Central Asia	30–40 percent
Africa	20–45 percent
Industrial countries	
United States	Two-thirds or more
European Union	40–50 percent

Source: Competition laws, national competition authorities. American Bar Association Antitrust Section. 2001. "Competition Laws Outside the U.S." Chicago.

Box 7.5
Differences between the United States and the EU on competition law and its enforcement

The differences in U.S. and EU competition laws and enforcement stem from their different objectives.

In the United States antitrust policy is primarily designed to protect consumer welfare and the production of a variety of products at reasonable prices. There is a modest element of fairness (the right of firms to be free of coercion) and hostility to vast concentrations of economic power. The underlying assumption of U.S. enforcement agencies and courts is that a robust competitive market is automatically efficient.

By contrast, in the EU, the dominant objective of competition policy is the economic integration of the member nations, which is closely linked to the principle of free movement of goods and services among member states. The EU also considers competitive opportunities for small and medium-size firms, raising the economic level of worse-off nations, and general notions of "fairness." Furthermore, EU member countries also consider that joint ventures, mergers, and other collaborations may be necessary to enhance technological development and therefore to allow European firms to compete effectively in global markets. However, there are strict guidelines for these.

In contrast with U.S. legislation, the EU's competition regime emphasizes equity objectives as well, such as employment and measures that encourage cooperation among small and medium-size enterprises.

Source: Graham and Richardson 1997.

Figure 7.3
Effectiveness of competition law increases with per capita income

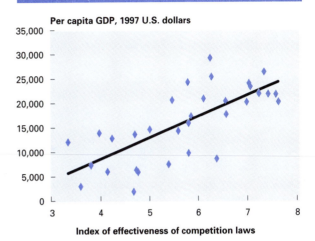

Source: For index of effectiveness of competition law, *World Competitiveness Yearbook* (2000); for per capita GDP, World Bank data.

price-fixing and other cartel behaviors are commonly treated with criminal sanctions, with potentially large fines and damages to injured parties. The U.S. Department of Justice devotes substantial staff in its head office and in regional offices in major cities to detecting and challenging cartels. The European Commission staff for cartel enforcement is much smaller, but they work together with staff in member states. There is no investigative staff, and as a result, cartels are normally investigated only following a complaint.[25]

In part, this weaker enforcement of cartels in the EU could be a legacy of the past. Before the 1957 Treaty of Rome, which codified European competition law, cartels were customary in Europe. The differences in the treatment of cartels between the United States and the EU also reflect the general differences in their objectives for competition policy (box 7.5). These differences are important for developing countries, which have modeled their institutions after those of the United States or the EU.

Building more effective competition institutions. The effectiveness of competition laws and competition authorities in promoting fair competition varies substantially around the world. Results from the survey conducted for this report indicate that the higher the per capita income of the country, the more effective is the competition law (figure 7.3). Also, the longer the competition authority has been in place, the more effective it tends to be, since learning by doing is important. The average tenure of competition authorities in industrial countries in the survey is 27 years, while that for developing countries is 10 years. On average, competition authorities in industrial countries are 40 percent more effective than competition authorities in developing countries, according to the *World Competitiveness Yearbook* (2000) index of effectiveness of competition law, which is based on surveys of top and middle management of firms in each country.[26] This is not surprising. As stressed throughout this report, institution building takes time and resources.

These two factors aside, there are many actions that governments can take to build more effective competition laws and authorities. Competition agencies need the statutory authority to force firms to supply necessary information. For example, the first competition law in Venezuela did not provide the competition agency with such authority, which seriously undermined the ability of the agency to perform its functions. Competition agencies need to have legal enforcement powers so that the agency can make decisions on competition cases without referring the simpler ones to the courts. This is true even in countries where courts work well because the competition authority has the technical expertise to make decisions. Where courts do not work, as in many developing countries, giving competition authorities the power of enforcement is even more crucial. For example, in Hungary in the early transition years, the court system was so slow that creative litigants began finding ways to bring their cases under the competition law rather than other laws so they could obtain a timelier ruling from the competition office. In India one of the least controversial proposals in the drafting of a replacement for the Monopolies and Trade Practices Acts is that new cases will be heard by a new, time-bound tribunal rather than going to the courts or waiting in queue behind old competition cases awaiting resolution. Competition authorities need to be accountable, and there needs to be checks and balances on these authorities. One possibility is to allow appeals to higher courts, particularly for the larger cases.

Governments need to ensure the independence of the competition authority. One suggestion is that the head of the authority be appointed by a committee or the parliament rather than by the president or the prime minister. Another suggestion is that the competition authority should be independent of a government ministry and should have its own budget. Independence of competition authorities from government ministries may be more important in developing than industrial countries, where there are more checks and balances in the political systems and where greater transparency protects the independence of competition authorities. Of the countries surveyed, 63 per cent of industrial countries have competition authorities independent of any ministry, compared with 59 percent in developing countries.

Competition authorities need adequate budgets and staff to perform their functions. On average, competition authorities in industrial countries have 75 percent more staff (relative to the size of the economy) than developing countries. For example, the competition authorities in Colombia and Peru have fewer than six professionals dealing with antitrust.[27]

The competition agency and the private sector should have the authority to lodge suits. For instance, in Tunisia only the ministry can initiate cases. If the government is the only agent with this authority, the effectiveness of the competition law in promoting competition can be undermined. Decisions by competition authorities should be publicly available. Public availability of competition decisions has a deterrent effect on potential future violations of the competition law, which should help promote the effectiveness of the law and, by providing checks and balances, could also help ensure the fairness of the proceedings. One of the most important factors underlying the effectiveness of competition laws—as for any institutions—is recognition of the importance of the law and a willingness to enforce it by both the government and civil society at large.

In light of the human resource constraints in developing countries, those nations that already have competition authorities may want to focus their efforts on issues such as cartels and exclusive supply or distribution contracts. Other issues—such as price discrimination, predatory pricing (pricing below cost to drive out competitors), or complex vertical restraint cases (such as tie-ins, where a product can be purchased from a supplier only if related products are purchased from the same supplier)—are more complicated and less critical. Moreover, they tax the capacities of competition authorities even in industrial countries.

International competition

Exposure to international markets plays a central role in promoting competition in domestic markets. Imports directly introduce international competition pressures to domestic markets. This pressure is also introduced indirectly, through exports, since domestic firms have to compete in the global marketplace.

There is a sizable body of empirical work based on microeconomic data (firm or plant-level) that provides evidence that trade liberalization increases competition and, consequently, efficiency and productivity growth.[28] Case studies show that even in a large industrial country such as the United States, international competition raises productivity. One study compares productivity in Germany, Japan, and the United States and finds that international competition has a greater impact than regional or local competition in raising productivity because international competition exposes countries to the most efficient production techniques.[29] A recent cross-country empirical study also found that openness promotes competitive domestic markets, measured by estimates of average economywide price-cost margins (figure 7.4).[30] Moreover, this empirical work finds that the impact of openness on markups is smaller in large coun-

Figure 7.4
Openness reduces price-cost margins

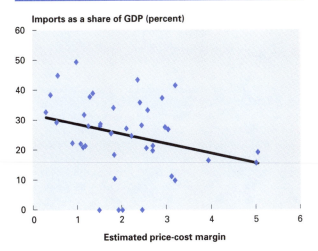

Imports as a share of GDP (percent)

Estimated price-cost margin

Note: Four observations with extreme values were not included in the graph.
Source: Hoekman and others 2001. *World Development Report 2002* background paper.

tries. There is also cross-country evidence that openness promotes economic growth through technology-embodied imports and because the larger potential market raises the returns to innovation.[31] The evidence shows that economic growth reduces poverty, which suggests that openness, on average, reduces poverty.[32]

International trade is particularly useful in promoting competitive markets in developing countries, where there are information difficulties, inadequate contract enforcement, and human capital constraints. These circumstances imply that it would be easier to use an instrument to promote competition that depends strictly on rules, such as international trade, compared with an instrument like competition law, which requires investigations and adjudication.

International trade also creates pressures for governments to address institutional barriers to competition in the domestic product and factor markets because these barriers undermine the domestic economy's ability to respond to foreign competition. India provides a good example of the role of international trade in liberalizing domestic regulations on entry (box 7.6). In Latin America trade reform was accompanied by labor market reforms to facilitate adjustment to global integration.[33]

While trade liberalization confers the benefits of enhanced competition and growth, trade reforms, like any reforms, can have adverse distributional consequences.[34]

Box 7.6
Open trade and institutional change: product markets in India

Before the 1990s India had one of the most highly protected economies in the world, supported by an extremely restrictive industrial licensing regime that regulated firm entry and exit. Beginning in the early 1990s India undertook a wide-ranging reform program that included substantial liberalization of trade. Restrictions of various kinds have remained in the economy. One of the most severe examples has been the garment industry. The garment industry was covered by the Small-Scale Industry Act, which restricts production to small-scale firms in more than 1,000 products. In the garment sector, besides restricting garment production to small-scale firms, it capped foreign direct investment in the industry at 24 percent of total equity.

In 2000, because of its membership in the World Trade Organization (and in anticipation of the elimination of quotas set by industrial countries on garment imports under the Multi-Fiber Agreement), India took a major step in liberalizing the garment sector. It removed garments from the list of industries covered by the Small-Scale Industry Act and removed restrictions on foreign direct investment. The objective of this policy change—which allows investment to expand the scale of production—is to enable the Indian garment industry to become more competitive in the world market.

Source: Kathuria, Martin, and Bhardwaj 2000.

In particular, some segments of the population may be temporarily thrown into unemployment or poverty. Flexible product and labor markets reduce adjustment costs (see discussion above). Other measures to address these adjustment costs include safety nets, as discussed in *World Development Report 2000/2001.*

The merits of international competition are now widely accepted among policymakers. Accordingly, governments worldwide significantly reduced tariff and nontariff barriers on goods in the 1980s and the 1990s, although significant scope exists for further reduction in tariff and nontariff barriers in many countries (box 7.7). The World Trade Organization (WTO) and its predecessor, the General Agreement on Tariffs and Trade (GATT), have helped secure gains in unilateral trade liberalization through multilateral negotiations. (*World Development Report 1999/2000* includes a detailed discussion of the role of the WTO.)

In addition to further reductions in tariff and nontariff barriers in both industrial and developing countries, governments need to build more effective institutions to

Box 7.7
Benefits of liberalization of industrial country markets for agriculture and textiles

The benefits of trade liberalization for developing countries would be significantly enhanced if industrial countries also reduced their tariff and nontariff barriers, especially on agriculture and textiles. Uruguay Round agreements in these areas have yet to yield benefits for developing countries. The replacement of quotas by tariffs on agricultural products by industrial countries, in accordance with the Agreement on Agriculture, only minimally reduced the protection of agriculture (and in some cases increased protections). Because of the complexities of the agreement, industrial country support to agriculture rose from 31 percent of gross farm receipts in 1997 to 40 percent in 1999, without violating the Uruguay Round agreement. Industrial countries have until 2005 to liberalize trade under the Agreement on Textiles and Clothing. Much of the liberalization to date in these areas has been on products that were not under restraint to begin with (Finger and Nogues 2000).

Further improvements in access to industrial country markets for exports can substantially increase welfare in developing countries. World Bank estimates indicate that benefits to developing countries from abolishing their own protection amount to around $65 billion a year. If, in addition, industrial countries also abolished protectionist measures, including the Multi-Fiber Agreement quotas, developing countries would gain an added $43 billion a year—$12 billion from removing barriers to agricultural exports and $31 billion a year from the abolition of tariffs on manufactures, one-third of which would come from removing barriers on the sensitive textile and clothing sectors.

Recently, industrial countries, including European Union members, Canada, and the United States, have announced several initiatives to liberalize market access for the least-developed countries. While this marks progress in liberalizing market access for developing countries, free access needs to be extended to all products by the EU, the United States, Japan, and Canada (the QUAD countries) if developing countries are to gain material benefits. For instance, the World Bank estimates that the United States' Africa initiative would increase Africa's exports by only 0.1 percent. The increase would double to 0.2 percent if the United States extended duty-free access to all products. African exports would increase by as much as 5 percent (or $2 billion) if all the other QUAD countries extended duty-free access to all products.

Even after the elimination of the MFA quotas, developing countries will still face significant tariffs on their textile and clothing exports because of some remaining tariff peaks (tariffs of 15 percent and higher), that are obscured by the low average most favored nation (MFN) tariffs of industrial countries. World Bank estimates suggest that granting developing countries free access to U.S. markets would increase total developing country exports by around 5 percent. Tariff peaks also occur in Canada and Japan, affecting 10 and 3 percent of total developing country exports, respectively.

Source: Hoekman, Ng, and Olarreaga 2001; Ianchovichina, Mattoo, and Olarreaga 2001.

---

deal with forces that can undermine competition. For example, there are troubling signs that progress in trade liberalization in developing countries is being rolled back through the increasing use of antidumping measures.[35] Other examples include the use of product standards, limited liberalization of services such as financial services and telecommunications, intellectual property rights, and private international cartels. Aside from their important effect on trade and competition, these issues are selected for discussion in this report because they help clearly illustrate the key factors about institution building highlighted in chapter 1.

Product standards

Standards can improve information flows and facilitate production and exchange. International standards have the potential to facilitate trade beyond what bilateral standards may achieve. But in practice, countries may also use standards to block trade. For example, mandatory regulations may discriminate against foreign suppliers or exclude both domestic and foreign entrants from a market. Technical regulations may also be

stronger than is necessary for achieving a particular level of social protection, thus imposing excess costs on consumers and eroding the benefits of liberalized trade.

Product standards have increasingly been used as a technical barrier to trade in recent years.[36] This issue was explored in detail in a recent World Bank report.[37] This section focuses on the purpose of product standards and what can be done to reduce or eliminate their potential negative effects on international trade.

The term *product standards* refers to the characteristics that goods should possess. Process standards refers to the conditions under which products are manufactured, packaged, or refined. Labeling requirements deal with the provision of information about product characteristics or conditions of production. Standards can be voluntary, such as those in the International Organization for Standardization (ISO) 9000 series on quality. Or they can be mandatory, such as domestic regulations that affect imports through technical requirements, testing, certification, and labeling.

Implementing standards is costly. Costs include the one-time expense of product redesign, building an administrative system, and the continuing cost of monitoring compliance. Firms must decide whether to establish an expensive platform design, which can be easily modified to accommodate particular markets, or to design a product initially solely for the home market, with modifications for export. Compliance costs can provide an advantage to large multinational firms, which can afford expensive platform design.

Conformity assessment—the verification that regulations are met—can also be an expensive procedure. Governments in importing countries may refuse to recognize tests performed by exporting firms or their public authorities and may not accept conformity declarations. Conformity assessment is vulnerable to bureaucratic and nontransparent rulemaking and is highly susceptible to capture by domestic companies seeking protection. Moreover, the uncertainty in complying with such procedures can reduce the willingness of firms to compete in markets.

Governments could endorse the wider use of "suppliers' declaration of conformity" to regulatory requirements, with a systematic review of products currently subject to mandatory government testing and certification that can be moved to declaration of conformity status. Products accorded this status would require only that suppliers *declare* that they meet certain standards, and importing countries would have to accept such declarations. A multilateral "Global Conformity Agreement" could then be developed, based on this list, for negotiation and agreement at the WTO. It is critical that developing countries participate in this agreement and that the distributional impacts of these standards across countries be explicitly considered. As an enforcement mechanism, postmarket surveillance systems by governments of importing countries could ensure that the standards are actually being met.

In agriculture the lack of progress toward harmonized, internationally accepted standards has the potential to undermine the gains made by removing traditional barriers because countries are erecting new barriers through the unilateral introduction of standards for traded agricultural products. In such a situation the creation of international standards for these products could enhance the welfare of developing countries, but only if developing countries participate in the setting of standards as equal partners.

Trade and investment in services

The benefits of liberalization of trade in goods are often limited by the lack of competition in services. This is particularly true of those services that are basic inputs or components of the economic infrastructure, including financial services, telecommunications, transport, and business services. The increasing share of services in production and employment in both industrial and developing countries underscores the importance of liberalizing services. Many of the fastest-growing sectors are services—telecommunications, health, and finance—and foreign direct investment in services currently makes up more than half of annual global FDI flows.

The WTO's General Agreement on Trade in Services (GATS) has not produced significant liberalization. Current levels of protection in services are as high as, if not higher than, those applied to goods 10 or 15 years ago. In many instances the available information on the level of protection suggests that ad valorem tariff equivalents range from 50 to 100 percent.[38] In general, barriers in transport, financial, and telecom services are higher than in business and distribution services. Barriers are higher in developing countries than in industrial countries.

Liberalization of services can significantly enhance the gains from liberalization of merchandise trade (box 7.8). For instance, if trade is liberalized but exclusive distribution remains in place, this in effect transfers the rents previously captured as tariff revenues by the government to the private interests that control the distribution of imports.

Most industries use services as inputs to production.[39] A study of the telecommunications sector in Egypt shows that adopting a more competitive regula-

Box 7.8
Lack of competition in services restricts gains from merchandise trade liberalization

In Egypt the lack of competition in services that facilitate trade reduces the gains from the liberalization of merchandise trade. Only Egyptian nationals are allowed to engage in the business of importing, which clearly reduces competition in distribution and competition in domestic markets. Also, the lack of competition in the provision of port services in Egypt, which are provided by public companies, has resulted in handling and storage fees 30 percent higher than in neighboring countries, which have broadly similar quality of services (Hoekman and Messerlin 1999). There is also no competition in maritime shipping in Egypt, which is monopolized by a state-owned firm. According to a 1994 survey, the cost of shipment and handling in Egypt of a standard container was 20 to 30 percent higher than in the nearby countries of Jordan, Syria, and Turkey (Hoekman and Konan 1999).

tory regime would generate a net welfare gain of around $800 million (1.2 percent of GDP).[40] A similar study of Tunisia shows that liberalization of services would raise both GDP and welfare by about 7 percent.[41] It is interesting to note that in Tunisia's case the gains from having foreign service providers establish local operations would far exceed those from cross-border supply of services from suppliers remaining abroad.

Liberalization of services should aim to establish a more uniform system of intervention and greater competition in markets. Priority in liberalization should be given to "backbone" sectors such as transport, telecommunications, and financial services, as well as to clusters of interdependent services vital to economic development and participation in the world economy, such as transport and express courier services. The primary objective should be to ensure that potential entrants are free to enter service markets and that policies do not discriminate against foreign, as opposed to domestic, entrants.

Intellectual property rights

Intellectual property rights (IPRs) include patents, trademarks, copyrights, geographic indications, undisclosed information (such as trade secrets), industrial designs, and layout designs of integrated circuits, and plant variety protection (see also chapter 2 for a discussion of IPRs).[42] By granting an exclusive right to control the commercial use of inventions, IPRs restrict product market competition so as to create incentives for innovation.

IPRs have gained prominence in global economic policymaking over the last 15 years, most notably because of the 1994 Agreement on Trade-Related Aspects of Intellectual Property Rights, which harmonizes minimum standards of IPRs in WTO member countries. Industrial countries were obliged to comply with TRIPS provisions by January 1, 1996. Developing countries were obliged to comply by January 1, 2000, while least-developed countries have until January 1, 2006, to meet TRIPS requirements.

All WTO members have made a commitment to implement TRIPS, and there is a broad consensus that some form of intellectual property safeguards is needed to protect innovation. But the empirical evidence on the potential benefits of IPRs is weaker than might be expected. Research in industrial countries does not provide strong evidence that IPRs are necessary to stimulate R&D or innovation in most sectors. One frequently quoted survey of 100 U.S. firms reported that patents seem to be very important to R&D investment decisions mainly in the pharmaceutical and chemicals industries.[43] Other studies report that first mover advantages are more important in high technology industries and that competitive markets are a greater stimulus to innovation than patents.[44]

Proponents of IPRs argue that stronger IPRs benefit developing countries by promoting technology transfer through foreign direct investment, trade, licensing, and vertical integration of multinational firms. But the empirical support for these potential benefits is mixed. Various studies document positive associations between foreign direct investment and IPRs, but others are unable to identify a relationship.[45] The empirical evidence provides somewhat stronger support for the argument that IPRs promote technology transfer through trade flows. Some studies find that imports of IPR-sensitive goods in large developing economies increase with the strength of IPRs.[46]

IPRs are generally more beneficial to industrial countries than to developing countries. Developing countries are net importers of technology, while, in general, industrial countries are the producers of technology. Industrial countries therefore reap the static benefits of higher prices resulting from the market power provided by IPRs, at the expense of developing countries. It has been estimated that the United States stands to gain $5.7 billion in net transfers from TRIPS, while Germany, Sweden, and Switzerland are also expected to receive substantial net inward transfers. In contrast, developing countries are expected to experience net outward transfers, amounting to $430 million for India, $434 million for Korea, $481 million for Mexico, and $1.7 billion for Brazil.[47]

Although ensuring a core level of IPR protection may increase developing country access to foreign technologies by safeguarding returns for foreign technology producers, excessively strong IPRs can inhibit the diffusion of knowledge. In developing countries, knowledge is built more through access, imitation, and diffusion of foreign technologies rather than only local research. Legitimate ways to transfer technology under some IPR systems such as reverse engineering or "inventing around" patents are restricted under strong IPRs. The importance of adopting appropriate IPR policies that allow access to technologies can be seen for some East Asian countries in their early stages of development (box 7.9). This principle is generally followed worldwide, with countries adopting more flexible IPRs at lower levels of per capita income. Figure 7.5 shows that patent strength rises with per capita income.

Box 7.9
Weak IPR systems promoted access to technology and growth in East Asia

The experiences of some East Asian countries suggest that having IPR systems that maximize access to and diffusion of technologies is appropriate in the early stages of industrialization. In Malaysia and Korea, growth in industrial sectors took place under weak IPR regimes, and in later periods governments emphasized incentives for innovation in IPRs as sophisticated local technology sectors developed. Japan introduced patents in the early 20th century after reviewing IPR systems in Europe and the United States. The Japanese system adapted other patent regimes to suit local needs. Emphasis was placed on securing access to foreign technologies, incremental technology development, and diffusion of innovation, through features such as strong antitrust guidelines for technology licensing and a central licensing office as a countervailing influence on foreign bargaining power pressuring for change in its IPR system.

Figure 7.5
Patent strength rises with per capita income

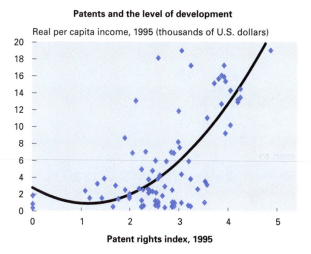

Patents and the level of development

Real per capita income, 1995 (thousands of U.S. dollars)

Patent rights index, 1995

Note: The index of patent rights is based on the strength of patent laws and includes whether the laws have provisions for enforcement (for example, whether the government can impound the goods while investigating whether the law has been violated).
Source: For index of patent rights, Park, Vijaya, and Wagh (2001); for per capita income, World Bank data.

IPR systems may be less effective in poorer countries because these will have less administrative, human, and financial capacity to implement IPRs as well as fewer complementary institutions. In particular, it is more difficult for developing countries to combat the potential anticompetitive abuse of IPRs than for industrial countries, because the former generally have weaker regulatory capacity, competition laws, and enforcement agencies. In many industrial countries intellectual property is subject to general competition law, IPR statutory provisions, or other regulations and guidelines. In some countries, such as Canada, IPRs and their enforcement are central to competition law. Attention to the link between IPRs and competition policy has been on the rise in industrial countries. For example, the EU and the United States have released further guidelines for applying competition policy to IPRs in recent years.

In developing countries competition laws and policies in general do not address monopoly abuse of IPRs. A survey of competition laws in developing countries found that only 5 out of 33 countries ban IPR agreements that restrict competition, compared with 9 out of 21 industrial countries. A lack of capacity to enforce competition laws also constrains the ability to control restrictive practices. Unless developing countries rapidly establish adequate competition frameworks and regulatory institutions that also address monopoly abuse of IPRs, it is possible that increasing IPR protection could result in welfare losses from monopoly behavior.

But there are also some potential gains to developing countries from stronger IPR protection. For example, if adaptation of imported technology to local needs requires a significant amount of investment, local firms will be willing to undertake the investment if they can be assured that their intellectual property rights are protected. IPR systems may also benefit developing countries by protecting indigenous property rights and traditional knowledge. Developing countries hold approximately 90 percent of world biological resources, which are particularly important in the development of new pharmaceuticals. Mechanisms for sharing the proceeds from commercializing genetic resources can be written into the IPR law, as for Costa Rica. Alternatively, institutions can be built to protect the collective intellectual property rights for traditional knowledge held by cultural groups, as is proposed in Venezuela.

How to maximize developing country benefits from TRIPS. Developing countries have made a commitment to implement TRIPS. To maximize their net gains, these countries need to take advantage of the flexibility built into TRIPS. There are several areas of flexibility within TRIPS that provide the potential for developing countries to maximize benefits by promoting access to technology and preventing anticompetitive abuses while maintaining incentives to innovate, tackle piracy, and still meet TRIPS minimum standards.

SCOPE AND EXCLUSION. Developing countries can narrow the scope of what falls under IPRs in the following areas in conformity with TRIPS. First, developing countries can adopt a narrow interpretation of what constitutes an invention and hence what needs to be patented. For example, Argentina, Brazil, and China have elected not to extend patent protection to software. Second, developing countries can take advantage of the TRIPS article that allows limitations and exceptions to copyright. For example, some countries permit unauthorized use for social purposes such as education and scientific research. Third, developing countries can avoid patenting life forms (see also chapter 2) and can apply special provisions under TRIPS to exempt public goods from IPR protection. Finally, developing countries can expand IPR scope to protect genetic resources, traditional knowledge and folklore, as is promoted by the World Intellectual Property Organization.

COMPULSORY LICENSING. Countries can use compulsory licensing, allowed by TRIPS under some circumstances, to control anticompetitive behavior that results from IPRs or in national emergencies, such as public health crises. The license, issued by national authorities, authorizes the use of IPR-protected subject matter without the consent of the rights holder, with compensation to the latter to be determined by the government. Every OECD country has legal provisions for compulsory licensing under some conditions, and many developing countries, including Argentina, Chile, China, Poland, and South Africa, have already introduced such provisions. The United States has granted thousands of licenses under antitrust decrees.

PARALLEL IMPORTS. Parallel imports refers to IPR-protected products imported into a country after being released legitimately in another country. Parallel imports therefore allow international competition in IPR-protected goods. Proponents of parallel imports argue that free trade in IPR-protected goods ensures competition in product markets, reduces prices, and enhances consumer access to new technologies. But trade in IPR-protected products may restrict access to new technologies for developing countries. Under a system with parallel imports and uniform protection of IPRs, prices are set to maximize global profit. This means that technology producers will set prices using aggregate demand, rather than individual country demand. As a result countries with small markets and elastic demand—typ-

ically the case of developing countries—could be priced out of the market.

TRIPS neither endorses nor prohibits parallel imports. In the absence of comprehensive empirical analysis on the impact of parallel imports, a policy of regional exhaustion with respect to parallel imports is one possibility that may create value. Under such a policy, parallel trade is permitted among a group of nations—but not beyond that group. Since the structure of demand is likely to be similar within a region, parallel trade limited to regions can simultaneously encourage competition in IPR-protected product markets and avoid the negative effects of countries being priced out of the market. The EU provides an example of how parallel imports under a policy of regional exhaustion has helped prevent price discrimination and encourage competition among the member countries.

PRICE REGULATION. Some countries regulate price levels and price increases—as is allowed under TRIPS—to ensure that IPRs do not restrict consumer access through excessively high prices, particularly in pharmaceutical products. But price regulations do not always work. When prices are regulated on a "cost-plus" basis, foreign pharmaceutical firms simply inflate the import price to their local subsidiary, as was found to be the case in India. Even when price regulations do work, as they do in various European countries, they may lead to less competition from generic producers of pharmaceuticals, less R&D spending, and lower productivity of drug production.

COMPETITION LAW. Countries can use competition laws to combat the potential anticompetitive abuse of IPRs. They can do so by introducing IPR provisions into their competition laws and strengthening their competition authorities.

Complementary actions

The impact of IPRs depends on the broader institutional and policy environment. IPRs are more likely to create wealth if they are complemented by open trading rules. There is some empirical evidence that IPRs can promote growth in open economies. More liberal trading rules also reduce the risk of monopoly abuse of IPRs by domestic firms. Human capital development is also important. IPRs are more likely to increase technology transfer and encourage domestic innovation in countries with higher levels of human capital. Another factor is the promotion of national innovation systems. Integration of IPR rules with complementary policies, to foster innovation such as public sector research involvement where appropriate (chapter 2), can stimulate growth by increasing the commercialization of inventions.[48]

Under TRIPS Article 67, industrial country members are obligated to provide technical and financial support for implementing the agreement. Only limited assistance has been provided so far to fulfill this commitment: mostly training and technical assistance in drafting IPR laws. The World Intellectual Property Organization (WIPO) has supplied much of the technical assistance to date. Going forward, more technical support that is geared toward helping developing countries take advantage of the flexibility allowed in the TRIPS agreement is needed. Concrete financial assistance targets and grants of patents to developing countries (especially for emergency human development needs such as HIV/AIDS treatment) are some of the proposals made for better implementation of Article 67. Others include increased technology transfer assistance and fiscal incentives, such as guaranteed purchase of new drugs for developing countries.

Another factor that will affect TRIPS implementation is bilateral agreements on IPRs. Since bilateral agreements usually provide for stronger IPRs than TRIPS—which mandates only minimum standards—these agreements may impede the ability of developing countries to implement the flexibility permitted in TRIPs. For example, in 1998 the United States had signed bilateral agreements on IPRs with 21 countries and had included many IPR provisions in science and technology agreements and bilateral investment treaties.[49] In general, the validity of international agreements and standards loses force if bilateral agreements proliferate, superseding the international agreement. The political and economic balance of power does not usually tip in favor of poorer developing countries in negotiating cross-border agreements, and this imbalance is probably accentuated when they enter bilateral agreements.

Conclusions

Competition in markets promotes equal opportunity. With free entry, smaller entrepreneurs and those who lack social or network connections, often the poorer members of society, have a better chance at undertaking productive activities. With more international competition and trade, and greater access to industrial country markets and technology, poor countries have a better chance at developing their markets. Competition is an important force in promoting institutional change as well as economic development and growth. Competition can create demand for more effective institutions, and it can sometimes also substitute for complicated regulation—a very important benefit, given the often limited capacities of developing country governments. Sometimes, however, the degree of competition may need to be limited in markets in order to encourage innovation—particularly in those areas where technology developers are unable to gain sufficient profits to cover costs in the absence of such protection.

The priority for countries in promoting competition in product markets is trade liberalization—and removal of entry and exit barriers for firms. For example, increases in market openness in industrial countries can help provide impetus to developing country markets and institutions. International standards in trade can help promote trade. They can also help limit potential inefficiencies and distributional effects created by a proliferation of bilateral agreements between nations. The distributional impact of standards across countries, and within countries, as well as their efficiency impacts, depends on which standards are chosen. The costs to developing countries need to be considered in international spheres when standards are established. Developing countries need to be empowered to play a stronger role in the development of standards, and to implement provisions in current standards that would benefit them. For example, the TRIPS agreement allows for some flexibility in IPR systems, and technical assistance to take advantage of such flexibility is important.

In many developing countries, barriers to competition in domestic markets arise from public policy: onerous regulations on potential new entrants or exit barriers can deter entry. Such regulations often discriminate against poor or small entrepreneurs, who are least able to pay the higher costs associated with them as well as the costs of corruption, which is facilitated by overregulation of business activity. Competition laws and competition authorities who enforce these laws, diverse across countries, are also important. While many developing countries have recently adopted competition laws and established competition agencies, the scarcity of human capital implies that such authorities may do well to focus their attention on a smaller set of issues: an important concern in many countries would be addressing exclusive supply or distribution contracts.

CHAPTER 8

Regulation of Infrastructure

No one can argue that a monopolist is impelled by "an invisible hand" to serve the public interest.

—R. H. Tawney, 1921

Infrastructure sectors, because of scale economies and demand externalities, have traditionally been thought of as the exception to the rule that competition improves the provision of goods and services. In many countries government provision of infrastructure services was considered the only way to avoid both the monopolistic abuses of infrastructure operations and the vagaries of the market, given its importance for the general population. This led, first, to the regulation of private infrastructure providers and then, in many countries, to the nationalization of infrastructure enterprises.

In practice, publicly provided infrastructure services have often delivered poor quality and inadequate coverage. Governments in many countries have begun to allow private provision of infrastructure services, both to enhance efficiency and to ease the strain on public finances. Changes in technology have created the conditions for competition in some areas once considered "natural monopolies," particularly the energy and telecommunications sectors. This has spurred increasing private provision. Private provision has been less prominent in the water sector, where technological progress has been less pronounced and political barriers to reform can be strong.

Overall, private sector provision of infrastructure rose tremendously during the 1990s in all sectors in all regions (table 8.1). Countries in Latin America and the Caribbean, which were in the vanguard of infrastructure reform, attracted almost half of the investment commitments in infrastructure projects with private participation during the 1990s. Regional differences were also the result of disparities in market size and investor perceptions of risk.

But the increase in private provision during the 1990s, although large by historical standards, has been smaller than might be possible. By 1999 total private investment in infrastructure provision in the developing world had fallen significantly from its peak in 1997, although there were signs of some recovery in 2000. To encourage private investment, two factors need attention: political and regulatory reform, particularly in pricing, and efforts to enhance the credibility in the government's new regulatory framework.[1] Policies that allow for full cost recovery and that ensure the investor a reasonable rate of return without government contributions are the preferred alternative for expanding private investment. Often, governments have failed to adopt such policies or to implement them through credible regulatory arrangements, deterring private investment.

Sometimes, even such pricing policies have not been sufficient to ensure that coverage goals are met. When this happens, governments may complement user fees with subsidies. Experience indicates that subsidies, when needed, should be transparent and carefully designed to serve poor people. When budget constraints limit the scope for financing subsidies, governments may need to reconsider their coverage goals.[2]

On average, private provision has relaxed capital constraints, enhanced efficiency, and increased investments.[3] A recent survey of studies on privatization in the past 30 years showed that out of 24 studies on the relative performance of public and private enterprises in infrastructure, half found significantly superior performance by private or privatized enterprises, seven

Table 8.1

Investment in infrastructure projects with private participation in developing countries by sector and region, 1990–99

(billions of U.S. dollars)

	1990	1991	1992	1993	1994	1995	1996	1997	1998	1999	Total
Sector											
Telecommunications	6.7	13.3	8.1	11.0	19.6	24.0	29.9	42.8	54.3	39.2	249.0
Energy	1.6	1.2	12.1	14.6	17.0	24.1	33.7	47.9	25.7	14.9	192.8
Transport	8.0	3.1	4.2	7.7	8.2	10.1	16.5	22.4	17.6	8.4	106.1
Water and sanitation	—	0.1	1.9	7.5	0.7	1.7	2.2	8.9	2.6	5.9	31.4
Region											
East Asia and Pacific	2.6	4.1	8.9	16.2	17.7	23.4	33.4	38.8	9.5	14.1	168.6
Europe and Central Asia	0.1	0.3	1.3	1.5	3.9	8.6	11.6	15.1	11.5	8.7	62.5
Latin America and the Caribbean	13.2	12.6	15.8	18.5	18.9	19.4	28.8	51.1	71.0	36.3	285.6
Middle East and North Africa	0.0	—	0.0	3.4	0.3	0.1	0.4	5.3	3.5	2.4	15.3
South Asia	0.3	0.8	0.1	1.3	4.0	7.6	6.1	7.1	2.3	4.0	33.5
Sub-Saharan Africa	0.1	—	0.1	0.0	0.7	0.8	2.1	4.5	2.4	2.9	13.6
Total	16.3	17.8	26.1	40.9	45.5	59.9	82.3	121.9	100.2	68.5	579.3

Note: 0.0 means zero or less than half the unit shown. Data may not sum to totals because of rounding.
Source: World Bank, PPI Project database.

found the differences small or ambiguous, and only five concluded that public enterprises had performed at a level superior to private enterprises.[4]

Among the reasons for private sector successes have been more careful preparation and preliminary analysis of sectors and the establishment of appropriate and transparent regulatory structures. Emerging evidence on the design of concession arrangements for private participation in infrastructure (box 8.1) provides some lessons for policymakers. For example, governments have enhanced competition in infrastructure services by making structural changes before privatization. In developing countries where the capacity for enforcing regulations is particularly weak, there is a strong argument for introducing competition as much as possible in those infrastructure sectors where it can substitute for regulation. Competition, by changing incentives of agents, has added benefits in weak institutional environments; it reduces dependence on regulation (such as price reviews) to achieve desired outcomes. Governments have also ensured greater coverage of poor people by, for example, incorporating coverage targets in the initial contract design or by allowing flexibility in prices and quality.

The regulation of private providers is complicated when there is the possibility of competition in some branches of infrastructure provision while natural monopoly conditions persist in other branches. Under such circumstances policymakers must decide whether the operators of the monopoly enterprise will be permitted to participate in the related competitive sector as well. Inexperienced regulatory agencies, particularly in poor countries, will face challenges in dealing with possible discrimination in access. Institutional design needs to account for this. There are typically two alternatives: *vertical separation* could be imposed, or the sector could *remain integrated.* In the second case, reliance on intersectoral or source competition could reduce the need for regulations.

Building effective regulatory structures in developing countries requires accounting for the quality and existence of supporting institutions and capacity. Sometimes this translates into fewer, simpler, or more cost effective regulations, or into economizing on structure. Because of differences in the capacity of complementary institutions, standards of regulation imposed in industrial countries may not be appropriate for poorer ones, and particularly for poorer regions, which are often served by smaller or informal providers. Distributional concerns can be met with flexibility in price-quality standards, the establishment of investment and access targets, encouragement of the informal sector, or direct subsidies.

Costs of infrastructure provision can be reduced by innovative approaches that involve community participation. Greater information flows between the users

Box 8.1
Private provision: recent evidence from concession arrangements

Concessions (or franchises) are one way to introduce private provision in infrastructure—and to stimulate competition *for* the market. Concessions grant a private company the right to use assets, to operate a defined infrastructure service, and to receive revenues from it, usually following a competitive bidding process. The competitive bidding mechanism for concession contracts should eliminate monopoly rents and hence reduce the regulatory burden. In Côte d'Ivoire, for example, the World Bank supported concessions in the water sector. The winning bidder, SODECI, now provides water throughout the country at rates comparable to state companies in neighboring countries, but at excellent quality and with very high repayment rates from private consumers.

But a recent study on concession contracts in Latin America indicates that they can produce mixed results, for reasons that are applicable to privatization in general. (Concessions are the dominant mode of private entry in the region.) Many of the problems are attributable to initial contract design and regulations. The study finds that of more than 1,000 concessions awarded since the late 1980s, over 60 percent appear to have been renegotiated within three years—over 80 percent of these in the water and transport sectors (Guasch 2000). The concession holder has initiated the overwhelming majority of renegotiations. The degree of renegotiation is higher than is warranted by changes in economic conditions. One reason may be that investors submit low bids to secure the contract because they expect that after the contract is awarded, they can renegotiate for better terms on a bilateral basis, without competition. This means that the most efficient provider may not win the contract.

Contract renegotiation initiated by governments can reflect lack of commitment to the protection of investors. There are some ways to guard against this. First, in developing countries with well-established and effective judicial court systems, such as Jamaica, the government may sign a concession or franchise contract with the provider that may be enforced by the courts (Spiller and Sampson 1996). Second, governments can gradually establish a reputation for nonexpropriation by structuring a concession or franchise agreement so that it calls for a gradual sinking of investments over time. The investor sinks more resources after observing government behavior. This is how Hungary structured its national telecommunications concession (Armstrong and Vickers 1996). Or the government may seek to attract domestic private investors so that future expropriation would be at the expense of locals as well as foreigners, making expropriation more politically costly and thus less likely. A variation on this strategy is to use the existence of an international lending program as a commitment device, or "hostage": the investor knows that bad behavior by the government in this sector may be punished by international lenders in a variety of other sectors (Armstrong and Vickers 1996; Levy 1998; Ordover, Pittman, and Clyde 1994).

Before concession negotiations and privatization, a careful study should focus on the objectives of the liberalization and privatization program, taking into account the experience of other countries. This was done for the Peruvian toll road sector, for example. It is also important to undertake price reform while the enterprise is still in public hands. Prices have to be increased to cover costs (or be headed in that direction), or investors will lack confidence that they will be allowed to earn a profit on their in-

vestments. This problem affected privatization of the electricity sector throughout Central and Eastern Europe and elsewhere (Stern and Davis 1998). A system of transparent cross-subsidies or lifeline services designed to benefit all citizens, including the poorest, should be agreed upon at the start.

Any vertical unbundling—for example, separating electricity generation from transmission and distribution—should be done before privatization to avoid creating strong opposition to restructuring later on. Even if a sector is not to be unbundled at the point of privatization, the necessary separation in cost accounting should be done in preparation for any future restructuring or access issues. Several Latin American toll road projects have caused severe regulatory problems because the policymakers did not establish a mechanism for the transmission of information to regulators at the time the concessions were granted (Estache, Romero, and Strong 2000).

A critical component of a privatization strategy is an independent regulatory body. This is supported by the finding from Latin America that if a regulatory body existed at the award of the concession, the probability of renegotiation was 28 percent; if it did not, the probability was 62 percent (Estache, Romero, and Strong 2000). Although the effectiveness and independence of any regulatory authority vary between countries, the preexistence of a regulatory agency has helped, on average. Hungary tried—and failed—to open up its gas sector to private investment without having a regulatory structure in place.

Regulators need information to regulate. To obtain information, they need their rights to information to be in the contract. An important complement to such contract design is to ensure that firms use good regulatory accounting and that regulators have the capacity to analyze such data.

The presence of an independent regulatory agency mitigates the risks of political interference in the privatization process and hence provides more comfort to investors. Moreover, an independent regulatory body provides a focal point for negotiation of the concession contract and technical expertise to deter unwarranted contract negotiations. And, a regulatory agency generally has specific knowledge that reduces uncertainty and better predicts the path of technology and demand. The study on Latin America found that the presence of a regulatory agency facilitates a careful review of the contract itself and of the qualifications of the bidders before the contract is awarded.

The study also found that a rate-of-return type of regulation (which ensures the investor a guaranteed rate of return by adjusting prices according to costs) was less likely to lead to renegotiation of contracts than a price-cap type of regulation (which limits the price a firm is able to charge). A firm that is regulated by a price cap bears all the risks associated with cost change and is subject to significant regulatory discretion. In Latin America the probability of renegotiation is 9 percent with a rate-of-return price regime and 56 percent with a price-cap regime (Estache, Romero, and Strong 2000).

Finally, using a single one-time payment as the principal award criterion, rather than the lowest tariff to be charged or the lowest annual subsidy to be provided, seems to reduce the likelihood of renegotiation, since the latter criteria are operationally more conducive to future dispute and subsequent adjustment. The one-time payment locks the investor in and strengthens his commitment (Guasch 2000).

and providers of services can also produce institutional designs that serve communities better.

Competition between firms and benchmarking across jurisdictions can improve service provision and help reduce the burden on regulators. For example, competition in a sector may reduce the need for frequent price reviews.

Establishing credible regulatory systems is one of the most important factors affecting private investment in infrastructure. However, countries' success in building such systems depends as much on political issues (chapter 5) as on technical factors and human capacity. Relevant political issues range from lack of independence of the regulator to weak systems of checks and balances for the regulatory agency. Transparency for both the regulator and the regulated is also key. For example, accounting standards increase transparency for the regulated. Open disclosure of the rules of the game enhances transparency for the regulator.

This chapter reviews how competition may reduce the regulatory burden on the state; the form that regulatory institutions should take; and how institutional design may affect access by poor people. It does not discuss all the important issues in the design of regulation, but it does cover areas where recent evidence has shed some light or those that were not covered extensively in *World Development Report 1994*. Governance issues within *public* infrastructure firms are not discussed here except in certain cases, such as the design of subsidies for poor people.

Competition in infrastructure sectors

There are different ways to introduce competition *in* the market (as opposed to *for* the market) in infrastructure sectors. This section addresses this issue.

Competition and regulation

As noted in *World Development Report 1994*, services such as electricity generation and long-distance telecommunications can be provided competitively. Some services still subject to economies of scale may face competition from other services using separate technologies.

Under either scenario, competition may substitute for regulation in protecting the economy from monopoly abuses. This is all the more important in developing countries, where the capacity for enforcing regulations is generally weak. First of all, regulation is not a simple task and can lend itself to arbitrary government action. This is more likely to happen in countries where

governance is weak and where there are insufficient checks and balances to curb abuse of power by a particular branch of government. Regulation imposes costs on both the enterprises being regulated and the government doing the regulating.[5] Sometimes government inefficiency and corruption within state firms may be replaced by corruption in the regulatory agency. Moreover, government authorities in developing countries are frequently unable to gain adequate access to the information needed for effective regulation.[6] They may also be unfamiliar with the concept of an independent regulator and have difficulties enforcing regulatory orders. In other words, competition can avoid many of the incentive, information, and enforcement problems created by regulatory regimes and, where it is effective, can substitute for regulation.

Another form of competition that could help reduce the burden on regulators is yardstick competition. Regulators can assess the performance of an infrastructure service provider—for example, in terms of prices and coverage—by comparing it with one in another locality (such as in a neighboring country) and can adjust regulation accordingly. Although this is not competition in the market, it can have similar effects on incentives for infrastructure providers.

Competition among "monopolists" can reduce the need for sectoral regulation in sectors such as petroleum and electricity distribution.

- The long-distance transmission of petroleum by pipeline between two points may well be a natural monopoly. Producers at a particular location, however, may not require regulatory protection if they have alternative customers to a particular pipeline—for example, local buyers, or shipment by water, or a pipeline from the same producing location that serves different destinations. Similarly, customers at a particular point on a pipeline that is an origin-destination monopoly may not require regulatory protection if they have alternative sources of petroleum—for example, local producers, or shipment by water, or a pipeline to the same destination that comes from a different origin.[7] Similar conditions hold for some natural gas pipelines. For example, pipelines from two different gas-producing areas in Argentina, Gas Atacama (a joint venture of Chile's Endesa and the U.S. firm CMS Energy) and Norandino (Belgium's Tractebel), are just beginning to compete to bring natural gas across the Andes Mountains to northern Chile.[8]

■ Similarly, even if the long-distance transmission of electricity between the generation facility and the consuming enterprise or municipality is a natural monopoly, generators at a particular location may not require regulatory protection if they are served by different long-distance transmission lines serving different sets of customers. Customers at a particular location may not require regulatory protection if they are served by different long-distance transmission lines carrying power from different generators. Municipal and large industrial users are currently enjoying such competition from different generation facilities in Argentina, Brazil, Chile, and Peru.[9]

Other examples include competition provided to the railroad sector by truck and barge operators and competition among different energy sectors such as oil and gas. A more recent development is competition between telecommunications networks and cable television providers in communications services. Moreover, both these natural monopolies face competition from wireless communications technologies.

Sometimes competition may create new regulatory problems or may simply displace old ones. In many of the cases where competition is recognized as an effective way of organizing the provision of service, that service is part of a larger infrastructure sector where some natural monopoly elements may remain. If electricity generation is considered a potentially competitive sector, electricity long-distance transmission and local distribution are less clearly so. If long-distance telecommunications is considered a potentially competitive sector, local wireline telecommunications are less clearly so.

Many of the most important issues involving risks, contracts, incentives, and knowledge have involved sectors where "unbundling" is possible—that is, where *some of the* services formerly provided by vertically integrated monopolies are being opened up to competition but other services remain monopoly provided. In these broader sectors, therefore, competition and regulation are *complements* rather than *substitutes.*

The next section focuses on an issue that is currently very important in developing countries. Vertical separation can provide more opportunities for competition in developing countries.

Vertical integration or separation

In virtually every infrastructure sector there is some service that can now be provided competitively, while there remains some service that is likely to remain a monopoly "bottleneck" in the production chain.[10] This raises the question whether the traditional vertically integrated model of the infrastructure enterprise should be maintained when it might be possible to introduce competition. One problem of undertaking cost-benefit analysis in this area is that it is not possible to measure the dynamic benefits of competition, while the costs of restructuring and evidence of scale economies may be known.

It seems likely that in particular infrastructure sectors there are economies of scope to the coordinated provision of all services, for example, generation of electricity with long-distance electricity transmission and local electricity distribution. But where there remains a monopoly bottleneck to which all competitive suppliers require access, there is an incentive for the monopoly provider to discriminate in favor of its own integrated subsidiaries over their competitors (for example, in access prices or access quality). There are three main institutional options to consider:

■ Option A, in which the owner of the monopoly bottleneck enterprise continues to operate in the "competitive" sector in competition with other providers in that sector (that is, an integrated firm subject to competition in the nonbottleneck market)
■ Option B, in which the owner of the monopoly bottleneck enterprise operates as a monopolist in the (otherwise) competitive sector as well (that is, an integrated monopolist)
■ Option C, in which the owner of the monopoly bottleneck enterprise is not permitted to operate in the competitive sector but, rather, provides connecting service to the competitive firms operating there (that is, vertical separation with competition).

In practice, intermediate forms of vertical separation may be used (this is a subset of option A) because they facilitate detecting discrimination. For example, accounting separation between different units, or restructuring the units into separate corporate entities with common ownership, could help detect discrimination.

The option most appropriate for a particular sector in a particular country depends on four main issues (table 8.2). First is the *extent of economies of scope between the provision of different services within the sector.* It appears that the extent of economies of scope may not be that large, based on the fact that, in the infrastructure sectors in most industrial countries, at least

Table 8.2
Strategy for vertical separation or integration

		Vertical integration with competition in non-bottleneck market (Option A)	Integrated monopolist (no competition) (Option B)	Vertical separation (with competition) (Option C)
Economies of scope	Large	✓	✓	
	Small			✓
Detection of discrimination	Easy[a]	✓		
	Difficult		✓	✓
Consequences of discrimination	Little effect on competition	✓		
	Bad for competition		✓	✓
Likelihood of competition in nonbottleneck market	Significant competition	✓		✓
	Little competition		✓	

a. Requires separation of the accounts of the different units of the vertically integrated producer.

some vertical transactions take place between enterprises rather than within enterprises. For example, under certain circumstances integrated electricity providers buy some power from independent generators, and integrated railroads allow some other train operators to operate on their tracks.

Second is the *ease of detecting discrimination by the integrated owner of the bottleneck in favor of its subsidiary*. Difficulty in enforcing interconnection quality even in the United States was one reason for the breakup of the integrated telecom supplier AT&T in the early 1980s.[11] Independent electricity generators have argued that there are so many dimensions of quality of access to long-distance transmission lines that it is virtually impossible for a regulator to prevent favoritism.[12] In contrast, the use of neutral railroad schedulers (dispatchers) in both the United States and the Czech Republic seems in some cases to have been successful in preventing discrimination against nonintegrated train operators.[13] In the absence of separate accounts between units of the integrated producer, discrimination can be difficult to detect.

Third is the *consequences of undetected discrimination for competition*. Financial data for the United States suggest that the long-distance transmission costs of electricity are less than 5 percent of the total delivered cost to end users, while track and structure costs make up nearly 20 percent of the total delivered cost of railroad service.[14] This suggests that a competing train opera-

tor, facing discriminatory access to the track, may be at a greater potential disadvantage than a competing electricity generator facing discriminatory access to the long-distance transmission grid. The possibility of discriminatory access is even more acute in the case of water and sewerage, where the fixed network costs in a developing country may be as much as 75 percent of the total cost of the delivered product.[15]

Fourth is the *likelihood that there would be sufficient competition in the nonbottleneck market which would significantly improve efficiency or access for users*.[16] Where there are strong economies of scale in the competitive sector, as in water and rail, for example, this sector may attract at best only a very small number of entrants, making large gains from competition unlikely. This is likely to be more of a problem the smaller or poorer the country—since demand levels will support fewer suppliers with given scale economies. This limitation can be addressed where international trade of the service is feasible.

Both information availability and contract enforcement are important for combining competition and regulation in an infrastructure sector. The owner of an integrated bottleneck asset may be required by the terms of its privatization or concession contract to supply nondiscriminatory access to the bottleneck asset to all who want to use it. But someone must enforce this contract, and whoever enforces it may require a great deal of complex information. In both these areas, developing countries are at a disadvantage. This suggests that it will often be more beneficial in a developing country to impose vertical separation on an infrastructure sector as competition is being created (option C) or continue to keep it an integrated monopolist (option B), rather than have it remain as an integrated firm subject to competition in the upstream market (option A). These questions have attracted policymaker attention in the developing Internet services sector (box 8.2).

In countries where regulators tend to be experienced and skilled, the relevant question may be simply, given that competitive access is desired, is vertical integration or vertical separation likely to provide the better outcome? In the context of the information and contract enforcement problems in the developing world, however, the more relevant questions may be: Are the benefits of competition likely to be achieved, and do they exceed the costs of implementation? Are the price and quality delivered to the final consumer really likely to be significantly improved by the first or third option compared with the much simpler to implement second option? Five infrastructure sectors are considered in turn.

Telecommunications. As wireless technology continues to progress, it is less clear than in the past that even the local service is a natural monopoly.[17] Nondiscriminatory access appears increasingly to be a possibility, especially in those conditions where competing providers of long-distance and other auxiliary services have a presence in the local market as well. This was a feature of Morocco's successful telecommunications reform in 1999, which was supported by the World Bank. In Chile competition in local service provision has come mainly from long-distance carriers entering into the provision of local service.[18] In Guatemala the (integrated) incumbent monopolist has also been required to provide interconnection to new market entrants.[19] Throughout the transition world individuals and businesses have avoided the traditional endless waiting periods for installation of fixed line service by signing up for wireless service.[20] Thus this appears to be a sector where *competition can often coexist with vertical integration,* that is, option A.

Water. The fixed costs of the network are so high in the water sector that competition in supplying water may not offer much benefit in the way of increased efficiencies, so the regulated, integrated monopoly model (option B) may work best in this sector. It appears that no country has actually instituted competition in the supply of water to the system, although Chile has stud-

Box 8.2

Vertical integration and discrimination in the provision of Internet services

Internet "content" (information, music, and graphics) is carried over long distances by Internet "backbone" providers and then delivered to users by Internet service providers (ISPs), such as America Online (AOL) and Mindspring, which in turn must (at least under current technological circumstances) use the wires of local telecommunications or cable television providers to reach final users. An important consideration for regulators and competition enforcers has been the degree to which vertical integration among enterprises operating at these various levels may be harmful.

For example, when AOL recently agreed to merge with Time Warner, a major content and cable television provider, U.S. antitrust enforcers were concerned that AOL might discriminate in favor of its own content and against the content of suppliers competing with Time Warner. The antitrust enforcers and the merging companies eventually agreed that AOL would provide access to its network on the same terms as were applied to all content providers. At the same time, the Federal Communications Commission, the U.S. telecommunications regulator, was concerned that the cable operations of the integrated company would discriminate against rival, nonintegrated ISPs, and it insisted on a similar settlement agreement designed to prevent discrimination. Both settlement agreements will arguably require ongoing regulatory vigilance to ensure compliance, although both are designed to be incentive-compatible and hence, to a degree, self-enforcing.

In another example, the Lithuanian Competition Council has been concerned about possible discriminatory behavior vis-à-vis independent ISPs by the local telecommunications provider, Telecom, since it has its own integrated ISP. The council has already fined Telecom for installing "filters" on its lines that reduce the speed of data transmission by the independents, although this case has been appealed to the courts.

Source: United States Department of Justice, available at www.usdoj.gov; United States Federal Communications Commission, available at www.fcc.gov.

ied the option.[21] It may be argued that this is a sector in which it is easiest to detect and prevent discrimination against nonintegrated suppliers, so, especially if the quality of different suppliers can be adequately monitored and as regulatory capabilities develop, *vertical integration can coexist with competition in supply* (option A).

Oil and natural gas. Like the water sector, oil pipelines and natural gas pipelines have expensive networks, so the relative cost savings from competitive product supplies may be smaller than in other sectors, but with relative ease of detection and prevention of discrimination. Where discrimination can be detected and prevented—and this will not be the case in every country—vertical integration may be consistent with a competitive supply market (option A). Where discrimination cannot be prevented, the benefits of competition are not great enough compared with the costs of regulation and the harm from discrimination to justify option A, nor are they great enough compared with the costs of vertical separation to justify option C; in this case an integrated monopoly operating in both markets—that is, option B—is probably the best outcome available. *Source competition among integrated monopolists may be a possibility* in these sectors in larger countries. As noted above, pipelines from two different gas-producing areas in Argentina are beginning to compete to supply natural gas to customers in Chile.

Railroads. One model of rail reform, favored by the European Union, entails separation of ownership and control of infrastructure ("tracks") from operations ("trains"), with the ultimate goal of having multiple private train operators compete with each other for the business of shippers over a common track system. The experience of the United Kingdom—one of the few countries that have tried to implement this model of reform fully—has not been encouraging. It raises the question whether *vertical integration without competition at the train level* (option B) *may be the best of imperfect choices* in this sector.

In medium-size and large countries, option B may allow for competition between vertically integrated firms through services offered to different destinations, or from different origins, to particular customers (that is, "parallel" or "source" competition).[22] This is the model that was eventually chosen by reforming governments in both Brazil and Mexico and that has been the arrangement for some time in Canada and the United States. Competition from other types of carriers such as trucks is also a probability.

Smaller countries with sophisticated regulators may find that discrimination is easy enough to detect that some entry may be allowed—for example, entry of large shippers that may already own their own railcars, or entry of foreign train operators from neighboring countries. The European Union (EU), for example, has enacted regulations requiring its member countries to allow train operators from other EU member countries to use the tracks of national integrated firms. In the Czech Republic, for example, the vertically integrated

rail company must permit other train operators on its tracks.

Power. In the power sector, it is difficult to detect and prevent discrimination against nonintegrated electricity generators even in industrial countries with experienced regulators, and the problems facing new regulators charged with monitoring the behavior of entrenched, powerful incumbent monopolists are that much more formidable.[23] Nevertheless, except in the smallest of economies (where economies of scale even with the most modern generation technology may rule out the presence of more than one or two generation enterprises), the benefits of competition in generation are potentially so massive that *vertical disintegration may be the best outcome* (option C).[24]

A recent study shows that vertical disintegration in the power sector is the most widely followed approach for countries (Malaysia and many EU countries being the exceptions).[25] It concludes that vertical disintegration—breaking up integrated power companies into separate generating, transmission, and distribution entities—can introduce competition into power generation. Results indicate that introducing competition can be positive.

In Argentina, for example, the switch to a private competitive system quickly resolved urgent problems of power shortages. In contrast, some recent experiences have illustrated how political considerations and incomplete reform can dilute the benefits of competition in the power sector. While vertical disintegration of power companies obviates the need to regulate generation operations (as these are subject to competition), power distribution and transmission operations remain monopolies and need to be regulated. As a caveat, there is some evidence that even vertical disintegration may not significantly improve efficiency unless some type of end-user competition is also introduced.

Structure of the regulatory system

By now it is well accepted that a country should have *independent* regulatory bodies following *transparent* procedures (chapters 5 and 10), subject to oversight by a *strong and independent judiciary* (chapter 6). In practice, each of these requirements is difficult to establish. Further, without checks and balances, bureaucratic inefficiencies may be replaced by private corruption. Moreover, human capital is scarce in many developing countries (chapter 1). All these factors call for modification of institutional design. This section addresses some other attributes that are necessary for a regulatory body to function effectively in developing countries, taking into account in particular the informational and capacity constraints in these countries.

Courts versus regulatory tribunals

Regulatory agencies may play more than one role. They may design rules, monitor compliance with rules, and enforce compliance with rules. While many regulatory agencies may do the first two well, they may still need courts for enforcement. Even in cases where the regulator has strong enforcement powers, courts are important for hearing appeals after a regulatory decision. In most developing countries the courts are overburdened, and judges may lack strong technical skills. For these reasons it would be advisable to build regulatory systems that lower their burdens. The regulator needs to be given strong enforcement authority in the first instance. Since courts are weaker in developing countries, many international investors rely on international arbitration.

One question is whether courts relying on competition laws provide sufficient oversight for service providers. The experience of New Zealand demonstrates the importance of a regulatory body that monitors compliance with the laws. As part of its broad program of deregulation in the 1990s, New Zealand eliminated sector-specific regulation and sought to rely on the competition authority, enforcing the competition law through the court system, to prevent monopoly abuses in the telecommunications and electricity sectors. Policymakers found, however, that in the absence of sector-specific regulation, proceedings were lengthy and the outcomes unsatisfying. Courts at three levels took five years to try to determine the appropriate price for a new entrant to pay to have access to the incumbent's local network. At the end there was still no general principle or direction for the companies to follow.[26] Recent reports by the Ministerial Inquiry into Telecommunications and the Ministerial Inquiry into the Electricity Industry have concluded that, at least at the current stage of technological development of these sectors, specialized regulatory tribunals will be an important part of an effective regulatory regime.

Scope of regulators

A second set of questions concerns the scope of action for particular local regulatory agencies. Should such bodies operate at the national level, or should local regulatory bodies control local infrastructure enterprises? Should there be a different regulatory body for each principal infrastructure sector or for a particular function?

Local versus national regulation. There are some arguments made in favor of localized regulation of infrastructure enterprises: (a) the better knowledge of local conditions of a local regulator; (b) the more direct political accountability under which a local regulator is likely to work, with the resulting greater involvement of the affected population in regulatory decisionmaking (as urged in *World Development Report 1994*); (c) the more effective monitoring of the regulated enterprise that proximity is likely to provide; and (d) the frequent difficulties faced by national- or federal-level regulators in coordinating with local governments, especially in matters as politically sensitive as access to infrastructure.

These factors, however, are opposed by others in favor of centralization of regulation at the national level: (a) the technical sophistication required of regulators, at least in some sectors, leading to economies of scale in regulation; (b) the shortage of local experts; (c) the presence of external effects (such as the network demand effects mentioned above, but not limited to those) among users at different locations in a single country, which may require both a single set of rules and a single agency; and (d) the increased likelihood of industry "capture" of an agency, the more limited is the agency's jurisdictional scope. (Some would argue in favor of centralization on the basis of a perceived lesser likelihood of corruption, but the evidence here is mixed; see chapter 5.)

The arguments in favor of local regulatory agencies are probably weaker, and the first three in favor of national regulation are stronger, the smaller a country is. For small developing countries, national regulatory agencies may be preferable. Technologically less complex sectors such as water provision and highway repair are an exception. In both of these sectors the local population has been especially important in directing the provision of services (again, see *World Development Report 1994*). Even in these sectors there are often centralized bodies and rules that take care of broad interconnection and pricing issues and externality-generating activities (such as watershed management), activities that may benefit from specialized expertise (such as overseeing the bidding process for highway construction). More decentralized actors such as municipal governments and NGOs may be responsible for monitoring performance, setting local standards, dealing with customer complaints, and in general ensuring accountability to the local citizenry.[27]

With larger countries, it may be preferable to decentralize regulatory functions. In some cases, even though regulatory rules may be set at the national level, monitoring compliance with rules may be done at the local level, for example, by NGOs or communities. Arguments in favor of decentralization are affected by political factors. Central governments in larger countries have sometimes lacked the power to impose regulation (including demands for the basic information required for regulation) on local or regional enterprises without the agreement of the local or regional governments. However, there are still areas where it does not make sense to decentralize responsibility—such as in long-distance telecommunications regulation and interstate power and gas transmission—since much of the service is *between* areas.

There are two striking examples from the toll road sector in Brazil. First, on the toll road between Rio de Janeiro and Teresopolis, the mayor of a small town along the route has refused to cooperate in preventing illegal access by nonpaying drivers. Second, in the state of Parana the governor forced the concessionaire to charge only half the toll level agreed upon in the contract between the concessionaire and the central government.[28] Large developing countries such as Argentina, Brazil, India, and Russia have devolved regulatory power (sometimes completely, but often only partially) to local or regional governments in the face of these difficulties of national-level regulation and policy enforcement.

Yet a third form of regulatory structure that has emerged is supranational regulatory organizations such as those established among the smallest and poorest countries in Africa. Such supranational structures have been established for apparently the same reasons that in other countries have led to centralization: the complexity of regulation, economies of scale in regulation, and the shortage of qualified personnel to staff regulatory agencies. Another factor in this case may be the increased bargaining power of a multinational regulator, compared with a regulatory body in a small country, vis-à-vis large multinational investors.[29] The Organisation for Eastern Caribbean States has recently created a regional regulator for telecommunications and is considering the possible extension of this arrangement to other infrastructure sectors. Similarly, in 1995 the countries of the Southern African Development Community formed the Southern African Power Pool to coordinate national-level power production and regulation.

While these are compelling arguments for and against centralization of regulatory structure, in practice the design of effective regulatory structures depends on political realities. For example, France, which has a very centralized political system, has mostly adopted a centralized structure (except for water and local transportation, which are largely controlled by municipalities). By contrast, in the United States, the states, being large and autonomous, have large regulatory powers. Since it is generally politically costly to remove those in power, regulatory structures have shown a strong inertia over time.

This provides an important lesson for transition and developing countries: their political structures will also determine the types of regulatory institutions that can be implemented. Reforms or regulatory designs are likely to be extremely difficult to implement without recognition of these obstacles and without efforts to overcome them. Sometimes the establishment of a new institution rather than modification of the old authority can deliver benefits. Such seems to have been the case in the privatization of the Moroccan telecommunications industry.

Sectoral specialization. Factors that are important for the choice between local and national regulators are also important for the consideration of sectoral specialization of regulatory bodies and have led to similar answers. Arguments in favor of having a specialized agency for each broad sector (transportation, energy, telecommunications, and so on) are that different sectors have different characteristics, so there are economies of specialization and no particular economies of aggregation; that more agencies diversify the risk of institutional failure; and that more agencies allow for more policy experimentation.

Conversely, there are without question some issues that cut across sectoral lines and that would benefit from a coherent policy framework. Sectoral lines are not always very clear and are probably becoming less so (as in the case, noted above, of telephony and cable television). Further, as in the localization/centralization debate, many developing countries face a shortage of qualified personnel to staff multiple regulatory agencies, and an agency with broader jurisdiction probably has a lower likelihood of "capture" by industry (or by sectoral ministries).

Again, many of these arguments are principally related to country size and capacity. Smaller developing countries such as Costa Rica, Jamaica, and Panama have responded to the scarcity of regulatory experts by creating multisectoral regulatory bodies (although regulatory rules are obviously specialized to the sector)—a practice followed at the state level in Australia, Brazil, Canada, and the United States. Hungary has followed the example of the United Kingdom in combining its electricity and gas regulators.[30] At the same time, following from the economic arguments above, some larger developing countries—such as Argentina, Brazil, and Russia—have created different regulators for different sectors.

Functional specialization. In some countries different agencies have responsibility for different functions; for example, an agency may do economic regulation of, say, the water sector but may not have responsibility for the sector's technical and environmental regulation. In the United Kingdom, for example, the Office of Water Regulation has responsibility for controlling end-user prices and ensuring the viability of suppliers, while the Drinking Water Inspectorate oversees the quality of tap water and the Environment Agency is responsible for maintaining the quality of rivers, canals, and groundwater. Along these lines, it is possible to have similar divisions of responsibility regarding, say, the economic and the technical, environmental, and safety aspects of electricity generation and transmission. But there are costs to the creation of multiple agencies, and likely economies of coordination.[31] Where there is a clear need to rely on detailed knowledge of local conditions and to have the endorsement of local political forces, there may be an argument for different levels of regulation for economic versus technical regulation. For a developing country with scarce human capital, functional specialization is more difficult.

One strategy that has been attempted to "stretch" the limited supply of qualified personnel for regulatory agencies is to contract out some aspects of regulation, such as the design of pricing schemes or the monitoring of compliance, to private firms. Chile contracts out the technical monitoring of water standards, and Angola and the Philippines have considered doing the same.[32] The telecommunications regulator in Argentina has hired private consultants to assist in rate rebalancing between both commercial and business customers and long-distance and local rates.[33] There seems to be wide scope for expansion in this area.

Competition authority versus infrastructure regulator. One question frequently raised is whether a competition law enforcement agency can be relied upon to act as a day-to-day economic regulator. Every country in Central and Eastern Europe and the former Soviet Union that has set up competition authorities has done so before creating sectoral regulators, relying—at least initially—on the competition authorities to use the abuse-of-dominance provisions of the competition statutes to prevent monopolistic abuses.[34] Subsequently, they have complemented the economywide competition authorities with infrastructure regulators. With the increasing introduction of competition into utilities, however, the interface between competition authorities and regulators is gaining increasing attention.

Competition authorities in developing countries as diverse as Venezuela and Poland have shown that they can, like their North American and Western European counterparts, act as effective "competition advocates" in the regulatory arena without assuming the regulatory portfolio themselves. In other countries, as diverse as Australia, Bolivia, and Russia, the competition authority has at least overall coordination and management authority over the regulatory bodies—though in all three of these cases some of the details remain to be worked out.

Designing infrastructure regulation to deliver services to poor people

The quality and coverage of infrastructure services such as electricity, water, telecommunications, and transport have a major impact on living standards. Many of the world's poor today continue to lack access to many basic infrastructure services.

The findings of a recent study on the impact of infrastructure reforms on poor people in Latin America may provide lessons for policymakers elsewhere on how to design such reforms to take into account distributional and welfare effects.[35] The two main findings of the study are as follows.

First, private sector provision has had mixed effects on tariffs and hence mixed effects on the poor. Tariffs have fallen in cases where competition and effective regulation have cut costs. For instance, in Chile liberalization of the long-distance telecommunications market in 1994 reduced call prices by more than 50 percent. Prices fell by a similar magnitude in the mobile telephony industry when the number of mobile phone

Table 8.3

Access to electricity, water, sanitation, and telephone services in 22 Latin American countries, 1986–96
(percentage of households)

	Weighted				Unweighted			
	Water	Sanitation	Telephone	Electricity	Water	Sanitation	Telephone	Electricity
1986	75.99	66.99	5.46	82.19	68.34	73.63	4.58	72.16
1989	80.85	79.85	6.13	85.37	69.88	77.21	5.23	76.26
1992	81.33	79.84	7.44	87.72	70.16	77.50	6.54	80.19
1995		79.65	9.41	89.37	73.19	79.67	8.54	81.76
1996			10.30	90.10			9.42	80.91

Note: Weighted—equal weights assigned to all countries; unweighted—represents population-based access rates.
Source: Estache and others 2000a, p.16.

companies rose from two to four in 1998. In Argentina wholesale prices of electricity fell by 50 percent in the five-year period after privatization due to intense competition in the generation sector with the entry of 21 new generators. Residential customers enjoyed a 40 percent drop in tariffs in the five years after privatization (1992–97). In contrast, there are also examples where tariffs have risen because of the need to ensure the financial viability of service providers.

Second, the reforms have brought about increased provision of infrastructure services by the private sector. This improves access in general and can perhaps also increase access for poor people, since they have been particularly lacking access in the past. Table 8.3 shows the increase in access to electricity, water, and telephone services in 22 Latin American countries over the 1986–96 period.

The policy challenge for governments seeking to improve access to infrastructure services on the part of the poorest citizens is to square the circle of providing incentives for service to the poor while keeping the rates charged to the poor affordable, taking into account their willingness and ability to pay. This is illustrated in the case of the water concession in the Tucumán Province, Argentina (box 8.3).[36] Although the causes of the failure of this water concession are many and complex, earlier attention to social and distributive issues could have increased its chances of success, or an explicit subsidy program could have helped ease the situation.

There are five main ways in which regulatory policy can promote distributional objectives: (a) setting investment targets; (b) being flexible with respect to price-quality combinations in regulatory decisions;

(c) allowing liberal entry of informal infrastructure providers; (d) involving communities in the regulatory process; and (e) subsidies.

Setting investment targets

Some governments have tried to promote access to infrastructure services by including investment targets at the time of privatization or award of concession contracts. Bolivia adopted such an approach in La Paz and El Alto, where enterprises bidding for the water supply concession in 1997 had to say how many connections they would make in return for a specified tariff. The winner, Aguas del Illimani, committed to achieving 100 percent water coverage by December 2001.[37] Similarly, in Monteria, Colombia, specific water and sewerage expansion targets were set.[38]

The way a contract or company is tendered in the privatization process and the variable chosen to award the contract will determine the distribution of benefits among all stakeholders. If poor households are connected to the service, then they tend to benefit more if tariffs are chosen as the competitive variable. If they are not connected, then choosing investment commitments as the tendering variable has a higher potential for benefiting the poor.

Flexibility in price/quality combination

In awarding concession contracts, if quality standards are set too high (using industrial country standards, for example), the service may be too expensive for poorer households and poorer countries. This means that there should be some flexibility in the contract to allow for the company, the regulator, and future users to agree to

Box 8.3
Water concession in Tucumán, Argentina

In 1995 the concession for water and sanitation services for Tucumán Province, Argentina, was awarded to Compania de Aguas del Aconquija (CAA) for a period of 30 years. To fund the required investment program, the concessionaire bid a tariff increase of 68 percent. The tariff increase was to be immediate and to affect all consumer groups equally in a population with a significant share of urban and rural poor.

The tariff increase proved very unpopular and was considered unjust by low-consumption users. The situation deteriorated with a series of episodes of turbid water. The result was a nonpayment campaign by consumers, which provoked a financial crisis for the concessionaire. Provincial elections brought to power a new administration that was much more hostile to the concession program. At first the authorities and the concessionaire began renegotiating the contract. One initiative was to introduce a special tariff for low-income users and a system of rising block tariffs for regular customers. The negotiations did not prosper, however, and the case ended in international arbitration.

Source: Estache, Gómez-Lobo, and Leipziger 2000.

a different price-quality combination when it is necessary (as in specific geographic areas).[39] Insisting on high quality and safety standards for all providers will only prevent small, local enterprises from providing "imperfect" but essential services to the poor. Regulators could tighten quality and safety standards for such providers over time as incomes improve.

The principles of such a multitiered regulatory structure, in which different regulatory treatment is provided for different technologies or dimensions, have already been employed by regulators under other circumstances. For instance, in the telecommunications sector just about every country imposes different regulatory requirements on cell phones and fixed-wire operators, with the latter presumed to have greater market power and hence greater need for more intensive regulatory scrutiny. Also, many countries (Bolivia, for example) establish different regulatory requirements for the "interconnected system" (that is, those parts of the national grid) and "isolated systems," with the former requiring closer regulation for many reasons, including the need to ensure system reliability.

Providers could also be allowed to offer a menu of services and to charge a corresponding menu of tariffs. Users could make their own choice; this type of flexi-

bility would benefit low-income users. This also reduces the informational requirements for the regulator in determining best quality or service standards. Aguas del Illimani in Bolivia, for example, offers a choice between the regular connection fee for the water service or a lower fee if households supply their own labor for connection activities. In Brazil jointly owned sewers have been introduced in shantytowns as a form of lower-quality, affordable sewerage system.[40]

Regulating outputs or outcomes rather than inputs or processes can provide incentives to providers (formal or informal) to search for and apply lower-cost ways of achieving the required result. For example, the private water concessionaire in La Paz and El Alto, Bolivia, was able to keep access costs down because regulations specified outputs (type of service and service quality) rather than inputs (material standards and construction techniques).[41]

Liberalizing entry

New and innovative approaches may be needed to enhance services to poor users. Such approaches include, for example, community participation in the construction and operation of networks, which may reduce their costs. An example is the water sector in Argentina, where the population in some neighborhoods provides the labor needed to work on the connections or on maintenance. Similar programs were implemented in the early 1990s in Mexico for road maintenance. Regulators need to be open to experimentation in institutional design.

In many parts of the developing world, small-scale private vendors or networks have sprung up in response to the needs of poor users who do not have access to formal providers. For example, in Paraguay about 300 to 400 private firms and individuals—called *aguateros*—supply piped water to households not served by municipal water companies. The *aguateros* range from very small operations supplying a local neighborhood to larger companies with as many as 800 connections.[42] Similar service is provided by men driving 15-ton tanker trucks carrying water around the narrow streets of the shantytowns surrounding the *maquiladoras* on the Mexican side of the Mexico-U.S. border.[43] In Yemen small enterprises provide power services to rural towns and villages that are beyond the reach of the formal utility. Suppliers range from individual households that generate for their own use and sell power to a small number of neighbors to larger operators with diesel generators supplying up to 200 households.[44] In Senegal small private enterprises rent telephone lines from the national operator (privatized in 1998) and run telecenters for local households.[45]

Liberalizing entry for informal providers is a policy priority particularly in the lowest-income areas of low-income countries, where infrastructure networks are underdeveloped or nonexistent and potential formal providers are nowhere in evidence. Regulators could limit such liberal entry to areas or customers not served by the incumbent provider. It seems very unlikely that entry in the service of such customers would pose a threat to the viability of the overall network. Enterprises providing services through the national network should enjoy significant cost advantages over small-scale rivals (who are often providing an imperfect substitute in any case) and should be able to win over the customers if and as the network expands.

Consultations with the community

To address the needs of the poorest citizens in countries, regulators need to engage a larger and more diverse group of stakeholders. Public education thus becomes an important part of this special regulatory agenda. In particular, regulators need to:

- Understand the needs and priorities of the poorest, including those who are not customers of traditional utilities
- Understand the needs and perspective (including costs) of a larger and more diverse group of actual and prospective service providers, ranging from small-scale or informal entrepreneurs to more traditional utilities
- Engage municipalities, NGOs, and other groups with an interest in representing and advancing the needs of the poorest.

In this context, exclusive reliance on formal regulatory hearings will not be enough. Greater efforts to engage stakeholders will ensure that decisions are well informed and help bolster the legitimacy of the regulatory system. Some promising experiments along these lines are being undertaken in many developing countries. These include:

- Visiting communities and engaging them in a dialogue on needs and priorities or establishing specialist consultative or advisory bodies to provide the regula-

tor with reliable access to a range of views. Regulators in Jamaica reach out to communities through local churches, and regulators in Bolivia hold town hall meetings across the country. In Brazil concessions in the power sector each include a special committee that comprises representatives of local government as well as different categories of users, including slum dwellers, farmers, and businesses.
- Developing information strategies aimed at educating citizens about the regulatory system. Regulators in Peru make extensive use of radio commercials, while regulators in Jamaica use "talk-back" radio shows.
- Delegating to municipal governments or NGOs particular roles in monitoring service provision and managing more intensive consultations with their constituencies. In Brazil there is a national system of consumer protection that delegates to subnational governments certain responsibilities for dealing with consumer issues within their jurisdictions.[46]

Subsidies

This section discusses how infrastructure services can be made affordable for the poor. The method used to subsidize poor people needs to be settled along with other decisions on industry structure, the standards applied to the service provided, and pricing and quality regulation. Clear definition of objectives and careful targeting of intended beneficiaries can help reduce the costs of subsidy. Competition can also do so. For example, rights (and obligations) to provide subsidized services may be allocated through competitive auctions to the bidder demanding the lowest subsidy, as is done for rural electrification and rural telephony in Chile and for passenger railways in Argentina. This section addresses five issues with respect to the provision of subsidies: (a) targeting the recipients; (b) the good or service being subsidized; (c) the source of funding; (d) the delivery mechanism; and (e) subsidy costs.

Targeting the subsidy. There are two broad approaches to targeting subsidies in infrastructure: according to the consumption level of the household (lifeline) or according to socioeconomic or other characteristics (means-testing).

There are two ways the *lifeline* approach can operate. The first is the rising block tariff structure, whereby a low rate is charged for an initial lifeline block of consumption and progressively higher rates for successive blocks thereafter. The second is a subsidy whose amount depends negatively on consumption, under the assumption that the poor tend to consume less than the rich. In Honduras the unit charge is reduced for customers with total consumption below 300 kilowatt-hours (kWh) per month, and the amount of the reduction has a block structure.

Both approaches are easy to implement and have low administrative costs, but the results have been mixed. In Latin America they have been found to do poorly in terms of targeting because consumption is only weakly correlated with income and, therefore, poverty.[47] In contrast, transition countries that use the lifeline approach manage to reach two-thirds of the poor for electricity and water.[48] Since there can be problems with targeting lifeline tariffs for the poor (even the nonpoor receive subsidies), policymakers need to decide whether they wish to err on the side of exclusion or inclusion.

Under the *means-testing* approach, the eligibility of households is based on observable characteristics of the household or its dwelling, under the assumption that these characteristics are correlated with income and, therefore, with poverty. The individual targeted subsidy

Box 8.4
Targeting subsidies: Chile's approach

Chile replaced its cross-subsidy system with a comprehensive subsidy scheme for low-income households, assisting them with the purchase of a variety of public services. The program is financed by the central government but administered through the municipalities. Subsidies are paid to the public service operator, rather than to the household, on the basis of each subsidized user served.

In the case of water, the subsidy covers 40 to 85 percent of the charges for the first 20 cubic meters of consumption. The goal of the scheme is to ensure that water and sanitation services do not take up more than 5 percent of household income. There are multiple criteria for eligibility, including region, average cost of water, household income and wealth, and family size. Eligibility is reassessed every three years. Households failing to pay their share of the bill have their subsidy suspended. Initially, the burden of proving entitlement to the subsidies was placed on the households. Low participation rates prompted the government to ask the water companies to collaborate in identifying needy customers by examining tariff payment records. It is now believed that all eligible households in urban areas (about 20 percent of the population) are covered by the scheme.

Source: Brook and others 2001, *World Development Report 2002* background paper.

scheme implemented in the Chilean water sector—where households are selected on the basis of a socioeconomic interview before they are declared eligible for subsidized water tariffs—appears to be one of the most effective schemes developed so far (box 8.4). In Colombia all utility tariffs are differentiated according to the characteristics of the property and its surrounding neighborhood. On the downside, means-tested subsidies can have the undesirable consequence of affecting incentives, especially with respect to labor market participation. This is sometimes labeled the "poverty trap" problem in the welfare system.

Variations on the means-tested approach described above that have been used by countries include ones that determine eligibility according to some other categorical variables or geographic zones. For instance, in Argentina subsidies are provided to specific groups (such as pensioners and students), while in Colombia consumers are taxed or subsidized in their utility bills according to a national socioeconomic classification system based on neighborhood characteristics. Operators of toll roads in some developing countries have been required by the original contract to provide free or reduced-charge access to vehicles that are likely to be driven or occupied by poorer citizens, such as farm equipment, small trucks carrying farm products, and commuter buses.[49] In both cases, however, there are large exclusion and inclusion errors, and both these approaches are found to be inferior to the standard means-tested one.

Aside from the above approaches, the government could also reach the poorest by providing the basic minimum of service to customers, such as a single public phone or water tap in a village not yet served. Yet another approach to providing lifeline services that is typical of the telephony sector is to have a telephone to receive incoming calls, with a capability to make a fixed number of outgoing calls (or a total fixed number of minutes of such calls), as well as the capability to make calls to emergency services, collect (reverse charge) calls, and calls to toll-free numbers.[50]

Consumption or connection subsidies? Subsidies can be in the form of a consumption or a connection subsidy. In principle, the subsidy should be directed to those goods or services with the highest difference between the willingness to pay and costs. In countries where capital market failures have a stronger impact on connections (as in many developing countries), subsidies for connections or network expansion should be favored over consumption subsidies because in these countries it is almost impossible for consumers to borrow to pay for the connection, even if they were willing to do so.

Delivery mechanism. Direct subsidies may be transferred to the targeted beneficiary, either in cash form or as a tax deduction, or as a voucher tied to expenditure on the specified service. Cash payments and tax deductions may be efficient means of meeting distributional objectives but may raise concerns over the subsidy being expended on matters other than intended. Voucher schemes address this concern but can involve large administrative costs. Another means is for the subsidy to be channeled through the service provider, which will require the consumer to demonstrate her eligibility and may be conditional on paying the unsubsidized portion of the bill. This is the approach adopted in Chile.

Source of funding. The use of subsidies raises the question of the source of funding for such subsidies, which can come from general tax revenues for governments, cross-subsidies, or a common fund to which all companies contribute. Which type of funding is more convenient depends in part on the efficiency, equity, and administrative costs associated with the distortions created by the general tax system. When the tax-financed subsidies are too costly to enforce and tax reform is not a realistic option, it may be more efficient to raise funds from the utility industry, especially if done through the fixed-charge part of utility tariffs—that is, the second and third options.

General tax revenues are typically the source of subsidy funding in the case of urban transport and "negative concessions," such as those awarded for toll roads. The issue with this source of funding is that in most developing countries the tax system is usually quite inefficient and is unable to raise resources at a low enough cost to enable sufficient funding of a welfare system.

Cross-subsidies raise funding by charging certain customers a higher price than the cost of service. This has been quite standard for public utilities in Latin America and is likely to continue to be common for private utilities when governments cannot make credible commitments to finance subsidies. The drawback of this scheme is that it could inefficiently discourage use or encourage inefficient regulatory evasion or bypass.

Traditional cross-subsidies require monopolistic market structures, without which those paying the higher prices would defect to other suppliers and so undermine the basis for the cross-subsidy. Some countries have introduced cross-subsidy schemes that are more compatible with competitive markets. For instance, in the telecommunications sector in Australia and the United States cross-subsidies are funded from levies on the naturally monopolistic components of the system—the interconnection—rather than on consumption.[51]

In a variation of the cross-subsidies scheme, all companies are required to make a contribution to a *common fund* according to a rule (for example, proportional to the number of customers that each company serves or proportional to each company's revenues). Companies still charge customers a price-cost markup to pay for this contribution. But they are free to decide which prices to charge which customer. The drawback here is that this allows for less transparent subsidies.

Conclusions

Infrastructure services are critical to the operation and efficiency of a modern economy. Improvements in infrastructure services can help promote competition in other markets, and there is evidence that infrastructure has a positive impact on growth and poverty reduction. As highlighted in *World Development Report 2000/2001*, access to infrastructure is a key concern for poor people.

Inefficiencies with public sector provision of infrastructure services and fiscal constraints led governments around the world to shift to private sector provision of infrastructure services beginning in the late 1980s. The consequent increase in private provision has expanded the provision of infrastructure services through improvements in efficiency and increases in investments. But recent experiences also shed light on institutional factors that, if improved, could increase the benefits from private provision. This chapter addresses the challenges faced by governments in regulating private infrastructure providers in order to meet both efficiency and distributional goals.

An important factor affecting service provision is the nature and extent of competition in infrastructure markets. To the extent possible, policymakers need to encourage competition in the provision of infrastructure services. Competition can help reduce the regulators' burden of monitoring prices and quality. Key factors affecting the quality of infrastructure provision are initial contract design at the time of privatization and the presence of a strong regulatory agency. Governments that have paid the most attention to detail at the time of privatization have been better able to expand service provision, particularly to poor people. Failure to set up strong regulatory agencies can result in bureaucratic inefficiencies and public corruption being replaced by corruption in the private sector or an excessive transfer of rents to private parties. Small poor countries could benefit from coordinating the regulation of infrastructure providers at a regional level. Attention to preprivatization restructuring of the sector and postprivatization monitoring, for example, through better accounting systems (chapter 3), is important. Information flows among those who are regulated, the regulators, and the customers are essential to effective service provision.

Policymakers can also expand coverage goals by encouraging new, low-technology, informal providers, and by modifying regulations to enable their operation. Regulators can benefit from flexibility in institutional design—that is, in price-quality combinations. Innovative approaches by communities—and information sharing between communities and regulators—can help improve coverage. Distributional objectives can also be met with investment targets. In cases where subsidies are needed, they need to be transparent. Targeting is a concern, and while no system is perfect, country experience suggests that some workable solutions exist.

PART IV

Society

SOCIETAL FORCES SHAPE THE EFFECTIVENESS, GROWTH, AND LEGIT-imacy of market institutions, which in turn affect the rules and values of societal actors. The chapters in this part of the Report explore the range of interactions between society and market institutions. Chapter 9 on *Norms and Networks* discusses how the informal institutions used by societal groups influence transactions in the market. Finally, Chapter 10 on the *Media* looks at the institution that, in reflecting and disseminating the views of members of society, can improve the working of markets by greatly reducing the costs of information flows.

CHAPTER 9

Norms and Networks

In civilized society [man] stands at all times in need of the cooperation and assistance of great multitudes. In almost every other race of animals each individual, when it is grown up to maturity, is entirely independent, and in its natural state has occasion for the assistance of no other living creature. But man has almost constant occasion for the help of his brethren.

—Adam Smith, 1776

Immigrants in California raise credit through rotating credit associations rather than from banks. Small traders in Mexico use informal mechanisms rather than courts to resolve disputes. Bankers in Japan seal deals with a handshake rather than a legal contract.[1] All three groups rely on institutional arrangements far removed from the formal constructs of governments and modern organizations. In all societies systems based on social norms or networks—alternatively referred to as informal institutions and sometimes as "culture"—are a central means of facilitating market transactions.[2] Such norm-based institutions are especially critical for the poor, who often lack formal alternatives.

Transactions that rely on informal institutions are regulated by a set of expectations about other people's behavior. These expectations derive from a common understanding of the rules of the game and the penalties for deviation and are based on shared beliefs and shared identities of network members. Such norm-based behavior is not always confined to small groups but is also evident on a broader scale. One example is tax compliance, when individuals in society tend to act more honestly if they sense that other people's behavior is similar and when there is a social penalty for deviation.[3]

Individuals, when deciding to comply, either with taxes or with a contractual obligation, have three reasons to do so. First, because of an *individual* or "internalized" norm, such as honesty, which may be founded in a shared belief system, such as a religion or in a sense of obligation to one's peers. Second, because deviant action will be not be socially tolerated by others and this lack of acceptance will result in some form of *social* sanction. Third, because of an *economic* sanction associated with the deviation, such as a fine, imprisonment, or denial of future business, often with added social stigma attached to the economic punishment. Formal institutions focus on the third incentive and thus can be ineffective if this economic sanction is weak.

Norm-based institutions can supplement or supplant laws and formal rules. They may substitute for formal institutions where the latter do not exist or are not accessible or where they fail to facilitate business transactions. In these cases informal institutions allow those sharing norms or culture to behave predictably, lowering the risks in a transaction (chapter 1).[4] Corrupt environments, for example, are often the result of ineffective formal institutions that coexist with weak social deterrence, sometimes called a "culture of corruption" (chapter 5).[5] In such situations incentives for corruption rise as peers also become corrupt, leading to a vicious cycle of socially undesirable behavior.

For geographically isolated and poor market participants, formal institutions are not easily accessible. These groups are more likely to use informal mechanisms to improve information flows and enforce contractual arrangements. For much of the world's poor, informal institutions play a primary role in making business easier.[6]

But informal mechanisms are used not only by those in poorer environments. Social networks grounded in class, caste, tribe, and neighborhoods—as well as school background and membership in clubs—can be as important for cementing deals in corporate towers as in rural markets. Work is habitually helped by the use of conventions, personal relationships, and shortcuts that complement codified rules in large corporations as well as small firms.[7] In these markets informal institutions tend to *complement* formal ones.

For policymakers, building new formal institutions that complement existing informal institutions is a challenge. When inadequate attention has been paid to norms and culture, formal institutions have not delivered desired outcomes. But many successful institutional arrangements have flourished precisely because of their ability to harness, or adapt to, prevailing norms.

An important issue is that new laws or organizations can make some market participants worse off than they were under norm-based institutions. In extreme cases new institutions may not bring many benefits while destroying old norms that have benefited market activities. Thus, in some situations, replacing informal institutions with formal institutions may not be the preferred policy (as is the case with community-based land tenure in some regions, discussed in chapter 2). That is even more likely if, as in many poorer countries, the preconditions for effective and efficient formal institutions are not met.

Connecting communities through trade can bring about a demand for formal institutions to complement norm-based institutions. Norm-based institutions become less effective as the number of trading partners grows and they become more socioculturally diverse. Moreover, because informal institutions often function by restricting access to new members, they can be inaccessible for many market participants and may hinder competition in markets. Widespread income growth and poverty reduction require formal institutions that can serve as bridges between separate groups. These can help support more complex transactions and widen the set of opportunities and agents that can benefit from various market transactions.

Experimenting with innovative elements that recognize the presence and effect of norms creates more effective formal institutions. Policies that allow parallel operation of informal and formal institutions increase options for market participants. Examples are courts that operate in parallel with informal enforcement

mechanisms, formal rural credit schemes that explicitly use elements of local norms of solidarity, and institutions such as affirmative action that try to reduce discrimination.

This chapter draws on established research and new analysis in the social sciences as well as studies of the development experience to elucidate the role of informal institutions and their interactions with formal institutions. Finally, it provides insights for policymakers building new institutions by addressing three questions: How do informal institutions aid market transactions? Why do informal institutions facilitate transactions for some and not for others? And how can the interaction of informal and formal institutions be used to ensure a dynamically supportive market environment?

Informal institutions in markets: their utility and shortcomings

This section first illustrates when and where norms lower transaction costs in markets and facilitate activity. It then discusses examples of situations where norms, though aiding transactions, can be exclusionary or less efficient than formal institutions. This includes cases where norms restrict entry and so reduce competition.

When norms and networks help market-based activity

Informal institutions develop to spread risk and to raise relative returns from market transactions. They do this by improving information flows, defining property rights and contracts, and managing competition.

Informal institutions for sharing information within groups. Well-established informal mechanisms for *information-sharing* have been used all over the world. Armenian traders in the 17th and 18th centuries, and Chinese immigrant trading communities until today, shared valuable trading information among themselves to ease transactions. Less sophisticated devices are used by members of small business and trading groups all over the world, from street vendors in Peru, to mutual aid groups in Benin, to wealthier members of clubs and business associations. In each case, an informal network communicates information about business opportunities, barriers, and potential partners to fellow group members.

The information networks in these groups can lower the riskiness of transactions, as members gain information about the quality of partners and the business environment. In developing countries formal alternatives—

credit-rating agencies or chambers of commerce, for example—do not exist or do not serve the small trader. Without informal knowledge channels, the costs of conducting business would be prohibitive. Informal networks lower these costs and enable smaller businesses to enter the market. Over time, groups coalesce to lower the costs of coordination.[8]

This type of informal information exchange is based on trust. Close familial bonds and friendships permit information sharing. Things are different when groups are larger. Trust among kinfolk and strongly bound ethnic groups is built through multiple or repeated interactions, which allow each group member to assess the other for reliability in adhering to contracts. Ghanaian fishmongers in Accra, for example, share business information even among competitors. This sharing of information is helped by multiple bonds: the women live in the same neighborhood and sell in the same market, they share a common ethnicity, and their husbands (the fishermen) are business partners as well.[9]

Different types of information may be exchanged within networks. Agents may have *specific information* about their counterparts, gained through previous interactions. In the absence of specific information, their only recourse is *generic information*, such as shared value systems (stemming from shared ethnicity, say, or common socioeconomic circles) or indirect "symbolic" denoters of quality or honesty (such as whether male or female, white or black, or the same or different ethnicity).[10]

The groups that have access to information may be formed in many different ways. For example, in markets in Africa, women market traders form close-knit groupings that offer mutual support, with even direct competitors selling for a member if she is sick. Their bond exists even though they may be of different tribal affiliations because their group is bound together by their common gender.[11] A second binding element is their repeated interactions that build up *specific* knowledge about one another. This helps cement the trust, letting the group know who among them can be relied on to use the information. Specific knowledge thus also helps determine the boundaries of the group sharing the information.

Informal institutions for dispute resolution or contract enforcement within groups. Some informal institutions also define property rights and enforce contracts. In modern-day rural Indonesia, for example, an informal system inhibits participants in business or credit transactions from defaulting on fellow members of the commu-

Table 9.1
Types of informal sanctions in contract-enforcement mechanisms

Level	Short-run sanctions	Longer-term sanctions
Individual	Personal (for example, guilt) Retaliation by partner in transaction Sanctioned punishment by an outside mediator	Reputation loss and resulting exclusion from future transactions of the kind where cheating occurred.
Community	Direct sanction from community	Exclusion from other social transactions

nity. One of the key instruments is the knowledge that a reputation for untrustworthiness would exclude people from future transactions.[12] Informal contract enforcement mechanisms are *self-enforcing*—the costs of deviating are high even in the absence of formal contract enforcement mechanisms.[13] Such incentive structures may be devised in a variety of ways—some at an individual level, some at a community level, and some involving the informal use of outside mediators or enforcers. Broadly speaking these incentive mechanisms can be divided into six groups, summarized in table 9.1.[14]

In a world where information—about the other party in a transaction and about the transaction itself—is imperfect, there needs to be a way for the aggrieved parties to resolve their differences amicably. In developed markets participants can use formal institutions such as the justice system and the police. But the use of formal mechanisms for dispute resolution may be uncommon in many communities, where official dispensation of justice may be regarded as too costly or inefficient. It may also be unavailable, if, for example, the courts are too far away. In industrial countries efficient court systems also offer an incentive to develop privately negotiated solutions to disputes, whether through formal channels, such as trade associations, or informal (chapter 6). Studies of the United States, for example, have found that private solutions to dispute resolution predominate. In richer countries, formal institutions complement informal ones; informal rules can be very effective as they have formal laws as the backup. In developing countries market participants use informal mechanisms as substitutes.

In some instances, use of formal mechanisms is minimal. Among a sample of Malagasy traders, for example, a study found that a vast majority never used formal mechanisms at all.[15] In other situations informal enforcement mechanisms may explicitly reinforce formal ones. This, for example, is the case for the Grameen Bank in Bangladesh. Repayment rates are kept relatively high for small business loans to women not just through formal credit histories, but also through explicit social mechanisms. Group members are urged to select one another with an eye to as much homogeneity as possible. Then, loan eligibility of each member in a group is made subject to the credit history of the other members of the group, creating a strong element of peer pressure.[16]

The short-run mechanisms in table 9.1 have their direct counterparts in the formal sphere as well. There, the punitive act comes from the state, usually a fine, imprisonment, or both, imposed by a court of law. Mediation is also a common, and often effective, alternative to a drawn-out judicial process (chapter 6). For informal contracts, loss of reputation is especially important if the partner in the transaction is one of few in the particular line of business. This may be a village moneylender, or the sole supplier of inputs for a farmer in a remote area, or a community member. In more competitive markets, where business partners outside the group are available, informal mechanisms become less effective. They are also less useful during economic or political upheavals and similar situations, where the composition of communities is volatile.

Such multidimensional and long-term punishment structures are effective so long as the individual needs to remain part of the community. But their utility diminishes when the relevant group involved in transactions is large and is spread across different communities or regions, as when lower transport costs or changes in policies increase the range of trading partners.

When norm-based institutions may not be enough

Reliance on informal institutions alone is not enough for the growth of inclusive markets. Some groups may be excluded from the use of such institutions. Also, such institutions may limit the scale of operation, or they may have multiple objectives. In some cases the problems of, for instance, no access or multiple objectives are common to poorly designed formal institutions as well. But because policymakers have more dis-

cretion over the reform of formal institutions, these shortcomings can be more easily remedied.

Limits on entry and exclusion from informal institutions. A persistent problem in many poorly designed formal institutions, as discussed throughout this Report, is that they may not be available to all interested parties. Informal institutions, by their very nature, suffer from this problem as well. Information flows about business opportunities may be available only to members of a group, with outsiders excluded because of linguistic or cultural barriers (box 9.1). Also, because information is usually shared during the process of intracommunity *social* occasions, even among today's ethnic business communities, it may be difficult for outsiders to gain access.

Sociocultural barriers to using informal mechanisms can be costly in multicultural or multiethnic societies. In parts of Africa there are often scores—and sometimes hundreds—of societies that were institutionally autonomous until recently.[17] One example is The Gambia. Within its more than 4,000 square miles, main ethnic communities include groups such as the Madinko, Fula, Wolof, Jola, and Serahuli, each with endogamous profession-based "castes" among them. Other significant examples are the Mauritanian Moorish and Lebanese trading communities.[18] In such situations formal institutions may be the only way to lower the costs of doing business for all concerned. Similar conditions, among them barriers to using cultural traditions that build trust, exist for minority groups. A case in point is the Korean minority in Japan, which is excluded from the bonding *iemoto* groups that help build trust and ease transactions even in today's Japan.[19] The same is true for those indigenous people in many countries throughout the world who live culturally separate existences from the mainstream.

Issues of access can be important even for those who benefit from norm-based practices in some transactions. Reliance on their own networks alone can mean that other possible businesses and potentially high-yielding projects, governed by different institutional arrangements, are unavailable. The situation in box 9.2 illustrates how reliance on networks alone implies that more efficient producers may be denied access to credit.

Therefore, the very mechanisms that promote lower transaction costs for participants can discriminate against those denied access to the networks. In such cases there is a clear need for good formal institutions.

Box 9.1
Exclusion in trading in African history

An interesting example of exclusion because of lack of access to informal institutions comes from the cattle trade in Nigeria in the 18th and 19th centuries. The Hausa cattle traders who operated there shared a common set of values, based on Islam and the Hausa language, which generated trust in partners. When French traders tried to enter the market, they ran into barriers. Much of the problem arose because the French could not enter into credible contracts in credit transactions with the Hausa, because there was little trust among the transactors. The French were not part of the social sanction mechanisms used by the Hausa. Without formal institutions for dispute resolution, these contracts between the Hausa and the French could not be enforced.

Source: Austin 1993.

Box 9.2
Tiripur in Tamil Nadu (India): insiders and outsiders in the use of informal institutions

Since 1985 Tiripur has become a hotbed of economic activity in the production of knitted garments. By the 1990s, with high growth rates of exports, Tiripur was a world leader in the knitted garment industry. The success of this industry is striking. This is particularly so as the production of knitted garments is capital-intensive, and the state banking monopoly had been ineffective at targeting capital funds to efficient entrepreneurs, especially at the levels necessary to sustain Tiripur's high growth rates.

What is behind this story of development? The needed capital was raised within the Gounder community, a caste relegated to land-based activities, relying on community and family networks. Those with capital in the Gounder community transfer it to others in the community through long-established informal credit institutions and rotating savings and credit associations. These networks were viewed as more reliable in transmitting information and enforcing contracts than the banking and legal systems that offered weak protection of creditor rights. The intense competition in the garment industry ensured that good money would not follow bad and that firms would pay attention to the needs of customers.

But there is more to this story. Outsiders (non-Gounders) have entered the industry. These participants do not have access to community funds. Yet outsiders, starting with around one-third as much capital as the Gounders, have outperformed them, developing larger-scale and better-integrated production capacity and making up more of the complicated export business.

Thus, the Gounders' networks have stimulated trade, but for those not part of the network, many opportunities for using better ideas remain unexploited because they do not have access to the same network of funding sources. Public institutions, such as collateral law (and enforcement), would allow stronger creditor protection and promote lending by formal institutions such as banks, allowing entrants not part of the network to better participate in the market.

Source: Banerjee, Besley, and Guinnane 1994.

Otherwise, without shared heritage or even geographic proximity, many people can be excluded from the benefits of market-led growth in incomes. Even those in networks may not be able to engage in profitable business opportunities with outsiders.

Over time, a natural result of excluding people from higher-return economic activity is a widening in disparities of income and wealth and perhaps an increase in social unrest, crime, and violence. This is illustrated by historical examples, where small elite groups or colonizers used their own "clubs" and other informal networks to do business more efficiently than others in the economy, differences that have persisted. It is also true in today's world, where economic outcomes differ between ethnic groups that have strong norm-based business practices and those that do not.

Moreover, informal contract enforcement may rely on third-party mediators, such as the Mafia in Sicily, which historically developed to fill the void left by non-functioning formal institutions.[20] Similar phenomena are observed today in other parts of the world. The danger, as is obvious from the examples, is that the informal institutions that arise when formal alternatives do not exist may bring with them significant negative externalities. These can range from a worsening of the business climate (and thus the discouragement of legitimate and honest businesses) to the simultaneous operation of unrelated criminal activity. To avoid this outcome, effective formal institutions are needed.

Informal institutions and scale diseconomies. As the scale and breadth of transactions increase, there are two other problems with informal institutions: *coordination failures* and the possibility of *exit from institutional structures.*

In situations where there is asymmetric information, coordination failures arise from the inability to trust business partners to keep to bargains that may improve outcomes for both parties. For instance, as there are more ethnic groups in a given economy, each with its own set of customs and norms for doing business, the complexity of the coordination problem also mushrooms. As group size grows, information processing and enforcement *within* the group also become difficult. Again, a shared set of formal institutions may be the solution.

With more alternative trading opportunities outside the community, the number and diversity of potential trading partners grow, and the relative benefit from staying in the network declines. In this situation, a trader may find it less costly to violate a community norm because any sanctions (such as loss of shared information) that can be imposed by the group are less effective. With increased competition and other trading partners, the trader may find it feasible to exit the community and exist comfortably without dealing again with those the trader has cheated.

Norm-based mutual insurance networks are an example. Small communities use these to protect members from individual economic shocks by sharing excess resources such as food, labor, and land (where land is abundant). Such systems are extremely valuable as a means of protecting every member of the community against misfortune. But as communities grow larger, commitments become more difficult to coordinate and deviations harder to punish. Moreover, a feature of mutual insurance mechanisms is that they come with a built-in set of incentives that may inhibit the community from encouraging economic experimentation, entrepreneurship, and processes where individuals compete among themselves. This is usually because of concern that excessive riches will allow the individual to "opt out" of the mutual insurance systems essential for the community's survival.[21] In more complex economies, therefore, such mutual insurance systems have been formalized under often more efficient systems of explicit taxes and transfers.

Multiple objectives of informal institutions. Well-functioning formal institutions are designed to solve a focused economic problem in the most efficient way possible. But norm-based practices almost always have *multiple objectives*. Take the example of a credit transaction. Institutions that address, among other things, two key elements of uncertainty—the borrower's ability to repay the loan and his propensity to default—mitigate the riskiness of the deal. Different formal institutions would act separately to mitigate the two risks; for example, a formal record of the borrower's credit history decides his creditworthiness, while the lender has recourse to specialized courts of law to enforce the formal loan contract.

In contrast, credit transactions within the community are carried out through an institution—the community network—built to facilitate an array of economic activity. This includes information about a person's creditworthiness and possible social sanctions on default. But it also incorporates mutual insurance schemes where a borrower, at a different time, may lend to today's lender or help him with information or connections in a totally different business matter. So a bad credit history may be discounted, or the punishment for default may not be as strong, as when impersonal formal institutions operate.

One problem is that poorer borrowers may not feel obliged to repay richer lenders and instead may see default as part of an implicit mechanism to equalize wealth among the kin or community.[22] In a survey of 58 firms in Ghana, no credit sales were made to kin because the potential creditors worried that they would not be able to compel relatives to pay.[23]

Such concerns, reinforced by cultural values about egalitarianism and fairness, can also hinder the process of development, although they serve a social purpose. A study in Cameroon, for example, found that village development committees in the north worked inefficiently because of concerns that no single person should benefit from the development work more than others.[24] In a village in the Republic of Congo another study found that fishermen who got new technology because of a fishery development project gave up using the new nets because fellow community members were not able to share in the improved incomes.[25]

As policymakers set up formal and more specialized institutions, however, the equity-enhancing roles of the informal institutions they displace often cannot be recreated. In these cases the policy choice is made more difficult because the creation of a more efficient formal institution can undermine long established risk-mitigating or redistributive functions played by norm-based structures.

Building and adapting formal institutions

Formal institutions are either superfluous or counterproductive when transactions take place within small communities and in larger communities with a shared set of effective informal institutions. But as economies develop, formerly distant communities become more integrated. Changes in individual behavior and government policies create new rules of the game that affect, directly and indirectly, even the most isolated communities. These growing forces of urbanization and globalization undermine the long-standing rules traditionally used by communities (box 9.3).[26] With greater competition and more trading opportunities, the exit of individuals from communities and their idiosyncratic norm-based institutions weakens the effectiveness of these traditional mechanisms. In such cases market activity stimulates a demand for formal institutions, supplanting community norms or networks. The stories of the medieval Genovese traders and the 19th century Thai rice farmers in chapter 1 illustrate how trade and openness helped the historical building of formal institutions.

Where there is a strong and widespread demand for formal institutions, policymakers looking to build institutions that will improve the market environment have a relatively simple job. But in many situations the demand for new and modern institutions may not be evident. In these cases the first step is to diagnose how well existing informal institutions support transactions. The second step, when formal institutions already exist, is to decide whether these are effective in reaching their stated goals, and if not, to decide whether to dismantle or reform them.

Open discussion and debate with the relevant users of institutions in the economy can help identify how well existing norm-based institutions are addressing their needs. This debate should include the costs of building or changing formal institutions, which may be significant. It may be the case that informal institutions are operating adequately in helping the existing level of market transactions (as they do for property rights in land in parts of Africa).

Conversely, existing informal institutions may be inappropriate for two distinct groups:

- Those that want to expand their activity beyond the community and trade with those outside their neighborhood, kinship group, or country
- Those ill served by existing socioeconomic norms, either because the norms exclude certain groups (such as the poor, isolated groups, and minorities) or because use of the norms is bundled with features that these groups find objectionable (such as xenophobia, exclusion, or even overly zealous egalitarianism).

Box 9.3
The influence of formal institutions on norms: colonial Uganda

In colonial Uganda, on what were called Mailo lands, chiefs had traditional feudal rights under a community system of reciprocal obligation in which they acted as trustees on behalf of the people of the tribe or clan. When the colonial government turned this informal institution into Western-style proprietary tenure, this gave the chiefs personal property rights over the land—and community members cultivating the land became legal tenants. This, according to some historians, led some of these new landlords to exact exorbitant rents and evict those in the tribe who were unable to pay. Thus, the situation caused by the introduction of the new formal institutions had to be addressed, eventually, by new formal laws fixing rents and limiting evictions—laws that would not have been needed under the set of traditional norms of community obligations and reciprocity.

Source: Firth 1963.

When there needs to be a shared norm to help transactions across diverse communities, the solutions can be straightforward. In many parts of the developing world, the language of the colonists and occupiers—English in India and Uganda, Spanish in Latin America, Russian in Eastern Europe and Central Asia—served as a common language among disparate cultures. Today, English has emerged as the language of the Internet, offering a common platform for those using it to communicate and exchange information.

But where there are discriminatory practices, the relevant societal norms may have to be explicitly supplanted rather than amended. Most societies prohibit such practices—or formally institute affirmative action—in order to promote equity and access. Sometimes economic pressures such as a tightening labor market may overcome deeply rooted discriminatory practices. Women, for example, have gained access to high-productivity work in countries enjoying swift growth.[27] Still, removing discriminatory practices on a more permanent basis may call for the building of explicit formal institutions such as antidiscrimination laws.[28] For example, affirmative action programs in India, while not always promoting the greatest efficiency of labor use, have met an important objective—providing to members of the scheduled castes and tribes opportunities, including political representation and government jobs, that might not otherwise be available to them. Thus,

Box 9.4
Islamic banking: informal and formal approaches

The *Qur'an* explicitly forbids usury, or *riba*. As a result, various Islamic communities have tried to develop ways to conduct credit transactions while refraining from charging interest. In rural areas of The Gambia, for instance, transactions are kept as short as possible—most for no longer than seven months—so that interest on the loan does not add up to large "usurious" amounts. So, credit sales of large farm machines are usually impossible.

Although countries from Malaysia to Iran have tried to institute forms of Islamic banking, one of the most ambitious attempts to adopt a widespread system of formal Islamic finance is taking place in Pakistan. The government, by order of the Supreme Court in December 1999, was given until mid-2001 to announce measures for "Islamizing" the financial system in the country, though more time may be needed. This transition is a laboratory for the introduction of a whole set of formal institutions that need to be consistent with the socioreligious norms prevalent in much of Pakistani society. Initial efforts have been varied. One bank has introduced a deposit plan that does not ensure fixed interest but shares the bank's losses and profits with the depositor. Other practices include rotating saving-investment associations among businessmen. Leasing and hire-purchase arrangements, where the monthly payment by the lessee is seen as a fee rather than interest, are an additional option. As more such systems are introduced, the one that eventually emerges as the dominant way of dispensing norm-consistent credit is likely to be decided through competition among the alternative institutional arrangements.

Source: Bokhari 2000; Shipton 1994.

Box 9.5
Education among the Orma in Kenya: adapting well-established norms

Formal education was controversial among the Orma herders in Kenya when it was first introduced in the 1950s and remained so when primary education became compulsory in the 1970s. The reason was that it conflicted with long-standing norms and practices of the community, where male children were crucial to herding. Many elders were strongly opposed to the practice, believing that it would jeopardize their livelihood. The Kenyan government, rather than imposing compulsory education, used the chief to gradually exercise persuasive pressure on the households he knew could afford to send their children to school. This gradual process allowed the demonstration of the beneficial effects of education, while preventing the hardening of opposition against it from the elders. By the late 1980s enrollments had increased greatly, and opposition to formal education had become muted.

Source: Ensminger 1994.

these laws potentially offer minority groups both voice and participation in the building and reform of market institutions.

Integrating informal and formal institutions

Building bridges between existing formal and informal institutions is an effective means of enhancing the success of formal institutions.[29] One way is to use the contract enforcement and information-transfer mechanisms that exist in tightly knit communities. The development of credit mechanisms in various parts of the world offers good examples. Credit cooperatives in 19th century Germany were effective intermediaries between banks and farmers, supplementing the formal contractual arrangements with the banks with informal mechanisms of information gathering and enforcement among each cooperative's members.[30] Intervillage collectors of agricultural products provided similar bridg-

ing functions in rural Indonesia in the 1980s. These intermediaries raised capital in the formal credit market and then made loans to smaller collectors, relying on informal mechanisms to create and enforce the credit contracts.[31] In the 1990s successive rural credit projects in Albania, supported by the World Bank, made use of community norms that emphasized reputation within the village to encourage repayment.

Instituting product standards is another way to build bridges between informal systems and formal ones. Historical examples include regional craft associations in late imperial China, which set product standards and inspected product quality, to serve as a bridge to formal sector buyers. Today, similar standard setting is seen among Indian handicraft producers in Gujarat, where an NGO (SEWA) has helped the villagers devise a quality-rating system to ensure that products are of sufficient quality to be marketed outside the immediate locality. (Chapters 2 and 7 contain broader discussions of product standards.)

On a larger scale, some efforts are being made to align formal institutions with prevailing norms. In formerly colonial countries, for example, colonial institutions have been redesigned to make them consistent with local practices; a prime case is the spread of formal Islamic banks in Asia and Africa (box 9.4).

One thing to keep in mind is that many formal institutions that try to supplant or even coexist with informal institutions may not be valued by the user at first, meaning that it will take time for them to succeed. Socioeconomic norms develop through social learning and imitation and are slow to change (much slower than formal institutions, which can be altered by some combination of market demand, political will, and administrative capacity). It may be desirable to introduce formal alternatives gradually with some experimentation to identify the most effective institutional form (box 9.5 gives an example from Kenya).

Conclusions

Market activities are supported by a complex blend of informal and formal institutions. In many poor regions of the world, and particularly for many poor people, informal institutions such as community networks are the only ones that are relevant, because access to formal institutions is relatively scarce. Moreover, in many situations, even if governments could establish formal institutions, the costs of doing so, relative to the benefits, may be high. Informal institutions can be superior to formal alternatives, either because they are more efficient at achieving the objective or because they embody features that formal institutions are unable to provide. But in other cases, informal institutions may prevent further market development, as when closed networks restrict the scale and breadth of possible transactions. In developing markets, informal institutions tend to substitute for the lack of formal systems, whereas in developed markets informal and formal institutions tend to complement each other.

While informal institutions provide people with a way to access and benefit from market opportunities and to manage market risks, they may also exclude potential entrants and partners. Formal institutions are important because they can deal with a larger group of participants and because, if well designed, they can serve to include more people rather than exclude them.

Imposing a formal legal system on an environment where informal contract enforcement has been the norm can either raise the transaction costs of dispute resolution considerably (formal legal procedures are often costly) or weaken the implicit contracts that governed relations until that time (without significantly strengthening the effectiveness of alternatives). Such considerations need to be kept in mind when examining the development of formal systems. When formal institutions replace one of the functions provided by informal ones (such as efficiency in a particular transaction) but not others (such as risk sharing), policymakers need to be aware of the effect of their choices not just on economic outcomes, but also on political and social effects; they can then either modify the pace of change or design complementary institutions. Take, for example, any policy that serves to weaken community ties, such as those that support out-migration or the breaking up of communities in order to resettle them to otherwise better areas. These actions could weaken the informal enforcement mechanisms for contracts, and alternative formal institutions for contract enforcement may be needed.

Finally, the greater use of formal institutions requires the removal of overly onerous regulatory barriers that help foster informal economic activity (chapters 1 and 7). A second, and critical, set of policies relates to literacy and education—without which sophisticated formal institutions may be unusable.

CHAPTER 10

The Media

One of the objects of a newspaper is to understand the popular feeling and give expression to it; another is to arouse among the people certain desirable sentiments; the third is fearlessly to expose popular defects.

—Mahatma Gandhi

The first records of written news stretch back more than two thousand years to the Han dynasty in China and to Julius Caesar's reign in ancient Rome. Daily handwritten news sheets, circulated by the government, presented news on trials, military campaigns, and political developments. After the invention of a printing press using movable type in the mid-15th century, international commerce became the main impetus for newspapers in Europe. Newspapers with international commercial news and advertising appeared in Germany in 1609 and spread rapidly throughout Europe.[1] (Because of tight government regulation of information, domestic political news became a feature in newspapers only in the middle of the 19th century.)

The press also became an impetus for commerce. Newspapers gave accounts of commercial voyages and the risks and opportunities of new trading routes. Advertising stimulated the demand for products. Frequent features of financial reports, insolvency proceedings, and trials of merchants and manufacturers helped merchants choose their business partners. All this information expanded trade links beyond tightly knit trading associations and communities, stimulating competition among traders and manufacturers from different nations.

Today, with higher literacy rates, lower printing costs, and new broadcast technologies (and the Internet), the media are even more important in informing traders, consumers, and investors. The vernacular media, particularly radio, carry information and encourage commerce in geographically isolated markets. In Indonesia, for example, local-language radio broadcasts of agricultural prices helped develop vegetable markets for poorly educated farmers.[2] At the other end of the spectrum, the growing global and foreign media report on international economic issues, moving currency markets and international trade. The media also provide information on political markets, exposing corrupt and unethical politicians (box 10.1) and giving people a platform to voice diverse opinions on governance and reform (chapters 5 and 6).

Because of their reach, the media can inform poor and marginalized people, giving them voice as well. Radio broadcasts reaching poor areas where illiteracy is high are particularly effective in this. And because of the media's ability to provide information otherwise unavailable, they can supplement traditional school education (box 10.2). In Nicaragua, for example, an innovative radio program to teach mathematics to primary school students improved test scores, especially for children in rural areas with less access to quality schools.[3] Publicizing information through the media has also made public services more responsive to the poor. In Brazil, for example, school lunches in one state cost eight times as much as those in another state. With media publicity, prices were equalized at the cheaper rate in two weeks.

The media can also improve public health efforts, as demonstrated by successful AIDS education campaigns in Thailand and Uganda. Empirical studies show that women's access to the media is associated with better health and fertility outcomes, even after accounting for different income and education.[4] The media are also involved with civic education as well—

Box 10.1
The media's role in reducing corruption in Peru

Even in a country with regulatory and informal controls on the press, the media can expose corruption and increase pressure for better governance. In September 2000 a local television station broadcast a video that showed the national security chief bribing an opposition member of Congress in return for voting for the incumbent government. The story spread rapidly in other publications, compounded by reports that the security chief was smuggling arms to Colombian guerrillas. The revelations led to his dismissal and in November 2000 to the resignation of the president. Following these events, the newly elected president announced his intentions to fight corruption.

This shows how the media can change the incentives for corruption for public officials. By providing information to the public, the media increase transparency of government action. The *risk of exposure* of corruption is therefore higher with effective media. The media also help build the public consensus required to fight corruption—creating the public disapproval that presses corrupt agents to resign—raising the *penalties for corruption*.

Box 10.2
Improving education through the media in Panama

The commercial Panamanian daily *La Prensa* designed a six-week educational supplement to its Sunday edition in May–July 2000, targeted to children in first and second grades. Since textbooks were seldom updated in Panama, *La Prensa* editors felt that students lacked basic information on their country. Providing a course in the history, geography, and politics of Panama, the supplements could be fitted together in a special album provided by the newspaper to interested readers by mail. The contents included new information previously unavailable to students, such as an updated political map of Panama. Many schools added the supplements to their curriculum, and the newspaper donated copies to 140 primary schools.

The cost of the album and the six supplements was $3 (free to subscribers). Circulation increased from 35,000 copies to 42,500 in the weeks that the supplements came out, and added advertising more than offset the extra print costs.

Source: La Prensa: www.prensa.com

a study in Botswana showed that media programs about the government, its procedures, and civil rights substantially increased people's knowledge about ways for them to participate in government processes.[5]

And the media can affect politics and culture, supporting institutional change and market development. Open information flows can promote institutional reform by affecting people's incentives and by sharing ideas and knowledge. New information can change people and culture—and create demand for new institutions. Information on how other institutions work can stimulate public debate and facilitate collective action. And greater access to all media, including the foreign and the vernacular, can provide a voice for social groups to press for changes in institutions and norms of behavior.

To achieve these outcomes—improving governance and supporting markets—the media need to be independent, accountable, and able to provide relevant information and reflect diverse social views. Too often, however, the media do not have these qualities. Concentrated ownership, restricted competition, financial dependence, and onerous regulations on press freedom distort the provision of information and can reduce independence. Poor access to information and the low capacity of journalists also reduce the quality of information. Finally, lack of competition, as well as poverty and low levels of literacy, human capital, and technology, can limit the reach of the media.

But the media also need checks and balances. And competition in the industry, as well as some kinds of regulation, keep the media in check.

The main factors that make the media effective in producing better social, economic, and political outcomes—independence (including accountability), quality, and reach—are discussed here. First, effective media are independent. Higher levels of perceived media freedom or independence are associated with lower levels of perceived corruption, regardless of differences in a country's level of income, and with better responses from public actors.[6] Second, effective media provide high-quality reporting, defined as the capacity to provide information demanded by diverse market agents in society. Competition among media firms, open access to public and private information, and journalistic capacity are key elements affecting quality. And third, effective media have a broad reach in society. Literacy, access to communications technologies, and the removal of entry barriers all expand the media's reach.

Complementary institutions can strengthen the role of the media. For example, while information provision can affect behavior through reputational penalties, it may not be sufficient to change outcomes. An effective judiciary and independent regulatory agencies can strengthen the media's effect on outcomes.

Independence

Ownership is a principal determinant of independence

What determines independence? Ownership is a central factor because it is the owners who control information flows and thus influence economic, political, and social outcomes. That is why control of media enterprises is likely to be concentrated in the hands of a few individuals or politicians.[7]

Some analysts have argued for state ownership of the media, asserting that information is a public good. Once supplied to some customers, it is costly to keep it away from others who have not paid for it. So the commercial media tend to provide less information than is desirable because they cannot extract a private return. In addition, the provision and dissemination of information are subject to strong increasing returns. The fixed costs of gathering information and establishing distribution facilities are significant, but once these costs are incurred, the marginal costs of making information available are relatively low. For these reasons, many countries have made a case for organizing the media industry as a government-owned monopoly.

Another argument for public ownership is consumer protection. In the extreme form, private ownership is seen to corrupt the media industry by serving a narrow interest group in society. More moderate is the view that state ownership of some parts of the media is justified because the public needs to be exposed to educational and cultural information, or public values, that privately owned firms might not provide. For example, one of the objectives of publicly owned television in many European countries is to ensure broadcasts of locally produced content in local languages.

Critics of these views counter that government control of the media could distort and manipulate information in the incumbent government's favor, undermining markets and precluding voters and consumers from making informed decisions. They believe this to be less likely with private media enterprises, which might also be more responsive to consumer demand for better-quality information.

Ownership structures around the world. A project for this Report gathered new evidence on the ownership structures of the largest five newspapers and five television stations in each of 97 countries (box 10.3).[8] It found state ownership to be pervasive (figure 10.1). On average, the state controls about 30 percent of the top five newspapers and 60 percent of the top five television stations in these countries. The state also owns a huge share—72 percent—of the largest radio stations. Moreover, private ownership is mostly in family hands

---

Box 10.3

Measuring media independence through data on media ownership

As with many institutional indicators, the data on media independence are based on analysts' assessments. Several indexes have been constructed, the most comprehensive by Freedom House in its annual survey of press freedom, which appraises media laws, repression of journalists, and economic and political influences on the media.

The data provide valuable indicators of media freedom, but they also have drawbacks. They are fundamentally subjective, with construction difficult to verify and with scores open to debate on why, for instance, a country gets a "3" rather than a "2" on some criterion. As with data on governance, they indicate the extremes of media freedom, but they do not permit more precise conclusions about smaller differences between countries. And with their measurement criteria based on general factors, they offer little information on the specific policies that determine media freedom.

Because there was so little information on media ownership—an important determinant of media independence—a special study for this Report examined who controls the media in 97 countries. Ownership structures were recorded for the top five television and the top five daily newspaper enterprises, measured by share of viewing and share of circulation, respectively, as well as for the top radio station, measured by peak audience. Only enterprises that provided local news content were included. The ultimate controllers of these firms were identified by tracing the shareholders with the largest controlling interest, held through direct ownership stakes or through holding companies and intermediaries. Each media outlet was classified according to whether the controlling owner was the state, an individual or family, employees, a political party, or a widely held corporation (where no single owner controls more than a 20 percent interest). The study also constructed a quantitative index of journalist harassment for each of the 97 countries based on reports by the Committee to Protect Journalists and by Reporters sans Frontières. Although the media ownership data do not measure all the factors that affect media independence, particularly media regulations and financing, they do measure one of the most important factors affecting the media.

Source: Djankov, McLiesh, and others 2001, *World Development Report 2002* background paper.

Figure 10.1
Who owns the media?

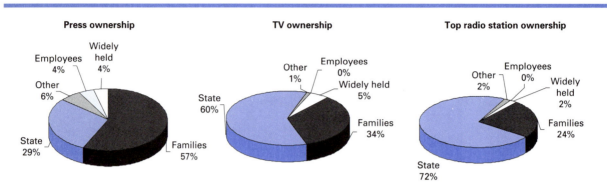

Note: Average ownership of top five daily newspaper and top five television enterprises in 97 countries.
Source: Djankov, McLiesh, and others 2001, *World Development Report 2002* background paper.

rather than in widely dispersed shareholdings. Some privately held media are also closely related to the state, through business, family, and personal associations. So, the influence of state control is even greater. State ownership also varies significantly by region. On average governments in African and Middle Eastern countries are more likely to own media outlets, but media outlets in North and South America are owned almost exclusively by families. Although most countries in the sample permit foreign ownership of the media, only 10 percent of the top five newspapers and 14 percent of the top five television stations are controlled by foreigners.

Why is state ownership much more prevalent in television than in the press? Perhaps because television has higher fixed costs and greater economies of scale. And perhaps because governments believe that commercial media organizations are unwilling to invest in markets with small audiences—such as services for minorities, remote and rural markets, or educational programs. But the evidence does not support this. The percentage of state-owned firms is still high even when ownership is weighted by market share of the audience. If the state-owned media serve mainly minority markets, their market share should be low. Besides, governments could require privately owned broadcasters to serve rural markets and provide cultural or educational content by regulation rather than by ownership.

A second argument is that state ownership of television is higher because of limited availability of broadcasting frequencies—that it may be more efficient for the state to control television stations directly than to regulate the allocation of frequencies and monitor com-

pliance. This argument has been disputed on the grounds that a simple system of property rights is enough to overcome problems of signal intervention.[9] New cable and satellite broadband spectrum technologies make the argument even less relevant.

Monopolies mean worse outcomes. The evidence indicates that monopoly control over information or high levels of state ownership reduce the effectiveness of the media in providing checks and balances on public sector behavior. Analysis of the 97 countries in the same study established that media in countries with high levels of state ownership are much less free, measured by the media freedom indexes; they also transmit much less information to people in economic and political markets. In addition, state ownership of the media is found to be negatively correlated with economic, political, and social outcomes. Generally speaking, this translates into more corruption, inferior economic governance, less-developed financial markets, fewer political rights for citizens, and poorer social outcomes in education and health (figure 10.2).

For all regions of the world, these associations between ownership and outcomes hold even after accounting for different levels of income, general state ownership in the economy, and a measure of political freedoms. This is important because poorer countries—and those with high state ownership in the economy and more autocratic governments—were more likely to have high state ownership of the media.

Privatization can help reduce monopolies. The negative consequences of state control of information through ownership highlighted by the experience in

Figure 10.2
State media ownership and low competition are associated with poor outcomes

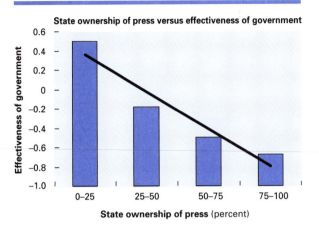

State ownership of press versus effectiveness of government

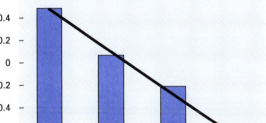

State ownership versus quality of regulation

Note: The figure reports data on state ownership of the top five newspapers, adjusted by share of circulation.
Source: Djankov, McLiesh, and others 2001, *World Development Report 2002* background paper.

liberalization and knowledge transfers from foreign owners with experience in journalism—has generated dramatic increases in the coverage of economic and financial news as well.[12] But private ownership can also restrict media freedom. For example, private owners associated with the state or political parties—or protecting their business interests—can control information flows. In Ukraine, for example, privately owned television stations with links to the state provided more favorable coverage of the incumbent party during elections than did more independent privately owned television stations (box 10.4). In some Latin American countries, privatization led to increased market concentration and reduced competition among the private media (discussed in the following section). In short, monopolies or concentrated ownership of the media industry that provide control over information to any individuals or organizations, public or private, will reduce the effectiveness of

several countries underscores the importance of media ownership in pressing for better governance. In Mexico, for example, the privatization of broadcasting in 1989 substantially increased the coverage of government corruption scandals and other stories previously unreported by the state station. This greater coverage contributed to a 20 percent increase in the private station's market share, forcing the government-owned station to cover these issues as well.[10] Similarly, a new, privately owned television station in Ghana in 1997 reported more information on government activities and evaluated government performance more openly.[11]

The privatization of state-owned media in transition countries, for example—supported by broader market

Box 10.4
Media ownership influences content: Ukraine

Election monitors recorded significant biases in media coverage along the lines of ownership structures in the 1999 Ukrainian presidential elections. Although all major television stations devoted more time to the incumbent than to the six opposition candidates, the state-owned television station was the most unbalanced in coverage and biased in content—this despite legal requirements for the state-owned media to provide balanced and neutral coverage. The percentage of coverage devoted to the incumbent and the percentage of positive coverage of the incumbent were directly and positively related to the degree of state involvement in the station ownership (box table).

Channel	Ultimate owner	Percentage	
		Coverage of incumbent	Positive coverage of incumbent
UTI	State	51	75
Inter	Family (deputy speaker of parliament)	48.5	73
1+1	Family (+ state non-voting 49% share)	34	50
STB	Family	23	40

Note: The shareholdings of Inter are approximately equally distributed—33, 33, and 34 percent—among three individuals, with the deputy speaker holding one of the 33 percent stakes.
Source: European Institute for the Media 2000.

the media in improving economic, political, and social outcomes.

Independent state media organizations. To reduce state control of media ownership, countries have established independent state media organizations—new institutional structures that provide checks and balances. The aim is to provide public interest programs that the private sector would not offer, without the drawbacks of political interference. For example, the British Broadcasting Corporation (BBC) is state owned, and its board of governors, appointed by government officials, is accountable to the government. But its charter establishes it as an independent corporation. Explicitly guaranteed in the charter and accompanying agreement is freedom from government interference in the content and timing of its broadcasts and in the management of its internal affairs. And funding is provided almost entirely by government-regulated license fees, not directly from the government budget.

Other countries have experimented with more extended arrangements to ensure autonomy from the state. Austrian state television, besides having the same safeguards for independence as the BBC, has various stakeholder groups represented on its board of directors, with only one-third of the appointees from the federal government.[13]

Some developing countries, such as Ethiopia in the mid-1990s, have implemented similar models to grant autonomy to state-owned television. And Benin established an oversight committee of state and nonstate appointees to protect the government-owned newspaper from interference.

Then, in stark contrast, there is Myanmar. The largest television station is controlled directly by the Ministry of Information and Culture, and the second-largest by the military—with full powers to manage content and appoint and remove staff. Similarly, in Turkmenistan the state maintains direct control over the press, with the president officially the head of the major newspapers.

A problem with autonomous state media organizations is that their independence can be eroded.[14] In 1981 the Zimbabwe government established the independent Mass Media Trust to manage Zimpapers, the only national newspaper chain. The trust emerged as an innovative solution, combining public ownership with politically independent management. Yet in June 1985 and again in September 2000 the government dismissed the entire board in retaliation for unfavorable

media coverage, and it now regularly intervenes in content decisions.

Developing countries are not the only ones to have government interference in ostensibly independent state media. But in developing countries, with their less-developed systems of checks and balances, maintaining independence can be more difficult. Experience shows that without the political commitment and supporting institutions to maintain autonomy, ensuring independent content is unlikely.

Media regulations

Throughout the world, government regulations—ranging from constitutional freedom of expression provisions to tax and business laws—affect media enterprises. Many of them aim to balance freedom of speech and protection of the public interest. Three such regulations are reviewed here: licensing, content laws, and defamation and insult laws.

Licensing. Licensing media enterprises can be a way to control content. For television some form of licensing broadcasters is needed to define property rights for the limited broadcasting frequencies. Yet many governments extend licensing systems beyond what is required for technical reasons, including imposing restrictions on the content of broadcasts. Some restrictions are explicit, as with licenses that prohibit the broadcast of local news, as in Zimbabwe. Others are implicit, as when licenses might not be renewed unless broadcasting content is perceived as favorable to the government.

Nor is there a technical reason for licensing newspapers, unlike the case for licensing television and radio broadcasting, so its primary purpose is to allow governments to influence information flows. In some countries newspapers have to renew their licenses annually. And editors of newspapers that publish views critical of government have been pressed to resign before licenses are renewed. To avoid suspension under such conditions, the media censors itself.

Removing newspaper licensing restrictions can thus do much to enhance competition and improve information coverage. In Korea the government replaced the newspaper licensing requirements with a more liberal set in 1987, simply requiring publishers to inform it of their plans to publish newspapers. As a result, the number of daily newspapers grew from 6 to 17 in Seoul alone, and dozens more were launched in other parts of the country. Newspapers also became more diverse, with opposition, progovernment, business, sports, and church papers competing with one another.[15]

Licensing of journalists can also influence media content. Proponents argue that it serves the public interest by encouraging responsibility and standards in reporting. Opponents counter that licenses allow regulators to prevent the employment of journalists who might cover the government unfavorably. International courts have supported the latter argument. In 1985, in a landmark case concerning an uncertified journalist in Costa Rica, the Inter-American Court of Human Rights found that licensing journalists contravened the American Convention on Human Rights. Yet more than a third of Latin American countries regulate journalists through licensing or accreditation procedures.[16]

Content laws. Censorship is another direct way for governments to distort the provision of information, often through legal requirements for prepublication or prebroadcast reviews by government agencies. Often the restrictions are defended on the grounds of protecting cultural interests. And it is possible to have content regulations that reflect cultural preferences while still allowing diverse opinions. In the Netherlands a 1998 act requires that public service programming be at least 25 percent news, at least 20 percent culture, and at least 5 percent education. Italy requires that 50 percent of broadcasting be of European origin.[17] But these days the control of information published on the Internet is posing basic challenges for regulators of content (box 10.5).

Defamation and insult laws. Restrictive defamation laws can repress investigative journalism.[18] They are necessary to protect the reputations of individuals and ensure the accuracy of reported news. But they also justify harassing journalists in many countries, leading to self-censorship.[19]

There are three key issues in striking a balance between protecting people from defamation and encouraging investigative journalism. The first is whether libel is considered a criminal rather than a civil offense. When libel is a criminal offense, journalists lean toward self-censorship.

A second issue is whether truth is a defense in a defamation suit. In Germany and the United States truth is a defense, and the plaintiff bears the burden of proof that allegations were untrue, giving journalists considerable freedom in reporting. In Turkey, by contrast, truth is not a defense for libel, unless the accused is a government official and the alleged libel relates to the performance of duties. If the defendant does not

Box 10.5
Controlling news on the Internet

The Internet has generated an unprecedented increase in the availability of news and information and thus presents a significant challenge to governments that want to control information. In the Federal Republic of Yugoslavia, for example, the radio station B92 began broadcasting over the Internet when the government tried to close it down, reaching a greater audience than before. In Malaysia Internet sites provide information on domestic and foreign news stories not reported by the mainstream press.

A study of 107 countries by the Committee to Protect Journalists indicated that 17 countries place significant controls on the Internet. Two types of restrictions are imposed. Some countries—such as the Democratic People's Republic of Korea, Iraq, Myanmar, and Syria—restrict access to the Internet under criminal law. A milder solution is to establish government Internet service monopolies, restricting citizens from viewing some Internet sites and monitoring information from abroad.

Source: Committee to Protect Journalists 2000; Robertson 2000.

prove truth in such cases, the sentence is increased by half. That creates strong incentives for journalists to limit their investigations.[20]

A third issue is whether the law provides protection for libelous statements about matters of public interest. If it does, journalists can better investigate arbitrary government behavior and predatory business practices. India and Korea are examples of countries where defamation can be defended on the basis of truth if the statements are in the public interest. Requirements to show that defamatory statements are knowingly or recklessly false, and made with malicious intent, also favor the freedom of journalists.

Particularly restrictive are insult laws, protecting select groups such as royalty, politicians, and government officials from criticism. Usually, insult laws make it a criminal offense to injure the "honor and dignity" or reputation of these selected individuals and institutions, regardless of truth. A study of 87 countries found such laws to be surprisingly prevalent, particularly in developing nations.[21] In most industrial countries insult laws are rarely, if ever, invoked. Yet in many developing countries, they are the primary means of harassing journalists. In the Arab Republic of Egypt 99 journalists and writers were prosecuted under insult laws in the 12 months following their introduction in May 1995. Such laws, at their best, are an anachronism—and at their worst, a severe restriction on media independence. That is why some governments, such as those of Argentina and Ghana, have taken steps to abolish them.

Financing and other economic pressures

Economic pressures can also interfere with the independent provision of information. When government owns the printing presses or restricts the import and distribution of newsprint, it can influence content. Preferential subsidies and advertising are another way to influence media content. In Cameroon the government refused to advertise in the privately owned press after some critical coverage. And in Uganda in July 1993 the government banned its departments from advertising in the one privately owned daily newspaper; since state advertising accounted for 70 percent of its advertising revenues, this had a significant negative impact.

Such heavy state support provides incentives for favorable coverage of the incumbent government and reduces the watchdog role of the media. To prevent biased reporting, the Mexican government recently stopped subsidizing the press. Some European governments, such as Germany's, prohibit by law direct subsidies of media organizations to prevent the state from jeopardizing independence.[22] But several countries in Western Europe provide direct subsidies to media outlets. France subsidizes radio stations if their profit from advertising and sponsorship is less than 20 percent of revenue. Since the criteria for allocating these subsidies is not directly linked to media content, it is argued that such state support does not compromise media independence.[23]

Advertising revenues from concentrated private sources can also influence content. In a recent survey of journalists, editors, and news executives in the United States, more than one-third responded that news is not reported if it might hurt advertising revenues and thus harm the financial position of media firms. Advertising from diverse sources is likely to reduce bias in content. In Russia the Press Development Institute, with support from the World Bank, trains newspaper managers to build independent sources of finance through advertising and paid subscriptions—and thus to reduce reliance on state support and improve editorial independence.

Quality

The media do more to support integrated and inclusive markets when they have the capacity to provide high-quality information demanded by diverse market agents, reflecting a diversity of opinion. Three factors that affect the quality of the media are discussed here: competition among outlets, access to public and private information sources, and human capacities.

Competition

Competition among media outlets promotes the supply of alternative views to voters and consumers—and helps prevent one firm from distorting too heavily the information it supplies. It is argued that competition from state media stimulates private media to provide more educational and culturally diverse content.[24] Competition between media outlets is closely related to ownership issues. One potential downside of public-private competition is that governments can give advantages to the media firms that they own.

In practical terms, the issue of monopoly pertains solely to state ownership, since no country has private newspaper or television monopolies. The global incidence of state monopolies of newspapers and television is surprisingly high. In this Report's survey of 97 countries, 21 countries (all of them developing) have government monopolies of daily newspapers, and 43 countries (40 of them developing) have state monopolies of television stations with local news.[25]

Evidence supports the argument that competition in the media is crucial (see figure 10.2). In countries with media monopolies, political, economic, and social outcomes are worse than in those where the media are competitive, in part because the former are less effective in improving institutional quality (governance). The data also show that dominance of state media, even if some private media exist, can affect the relationship between information flows and outcomes. For example, 75 percent state ownership of the media still leads to outcomes comparable to those when there is 100 percent state ownership. For newspapers, state ownership, on average, is detrimental whether there is a state monopoly or not. But the only countries with significant state ownership in newspapers are those in which there may be other reasons for weak institutional quality as well. For television, monopolies appear to account for most of the associations between state ownership and poor outcomes.

Competition among privately owned media firms is also critical for effective media. When there is little competition, information flows reflect only the views of a private elite or the government and private firms can collude in distorting information flows. Rivalry among firms in the media industry ensures a broader range of social and political views and greater incentives for demand-driven reporting. With such information, voters, consumers, and investors are less likely to be exposed to abuse in economic and political markets, and minority views—including those of the poor—are more likely to be represented.

These arguments have gained prominence because of increasing media market concentration over the last decade, especially in Europe, spurred by new technologies and national deregulation.[26] Across countries the concentration of media firms is high. In the same survey of 97 countries conducted for this report, the top five daily newspapers account for two-thirds of circulation, and the top five television firms for nine-tenths of total viewing, on average.

Many countries try to encourage competition in the media by regulating market concentration. In most of Europe the state limits the share of audience and circulation that media outlets (and their owners) can control. In Germany broadcasters are limited to 30 percent of the national audience, and in the United Kingdom, to 15 percent. How these laws work in practice depends greatly on the details of the law. In Italy media firms are limited to 25 percent of the national communications market, but because of the difficulty in defining this cutoff, the law has never been applied.[27]

Access to public information

Access to public information is essential for the media to investigate issues effectively and transmit news to the public. And because better information flows can improve resource allocation, they may be able to mitigate global financial volatility and crises; as a result, more attention now goes to building institutions that guarantee access to information. To understand and anticipate market movements, investors require timely and accurate information on company financial indicators and macroeconomic data. Similarly, information on asset ownership, government contracts, and public agency expenditures helps the public monitor government officials. Information on price and product standards helps consumers select products. Records of health inspections, school performance, and environmental data help citizens make informed social choices. Data on politicians' voting records enable more informed choice of candidates. The media can transmit most of this information—if they have access to it.

A recent study in Southeast Asia revealed that few countries are close to providing open access to data of interest to the media and citizens.[28] It looked at the availability of 40 public records, including economic, education, and health indicators, as well as information on government and court proceedings, financial disclosures of firms and officials, and government budgets and contracts. The Philippines ranked highest. At the other end of the spectrum was Myanmar, where even such basic macroeconomic data as GNP and inflation are not always available. Ill-defined procedures for access to information and inadequate information infrastructure were identified as common problems across countries.

Legal frameworks to support access to information vary tremendously. The United Kingdom has a tradition of protecting information, captured in law by the Official Secrets Act, which provides broad powers for government to classify and restrict access. Until 1989 even the type of biscuits served to the prime minister was an official secret. Many countries that adopted aspects of the British legal system have official secrets acts. Some, such as Fiji, have taken steps to introduce a more liberal approach to information access. Others, such as Kenya, Malaysia, and Singapore, retain their official secrets laws.

Other countries use laws to guarantee, rather than limit, access to information. In many cases governments incorporate freedom of information provisions into constitutions, into other government directives, or into media laws. Another solution growing in popularity is the freedom of information (FOI) law, imposing disclosure obligations on government departments, courts, regulatory agencies, the military, and private organizations that carry out statutory functions. FOI laws also enable access to certain information on request, such as personal information held by the government. Since FOI laws tend to be more detailed and operational then constitutional provisions, they can provide strong guarantees for the media of access to information. In Nepal, for example, even with the right to information enshrined in the constitution, access remains difficult because is no FOI law or other mechanism to support it.

Beginning with Sweden in 1766, 44 industrial and developing countries have adopted FOI laws. Two-thirds were passed in the last 10 years, including those in many transition countries, where information access had been severely restricted.[29] Many more countries, such as Fiji, India, and Nepal, are considering FOI acts to improve information flows.

Experience shows that FOI laws can have limitations, for the freedom of information must be balanced with privacy and the legitimate need to retain information for national security. But some FOI legislation is constrained severely by broadly defined exemptions and loopholes that extend beyond these public interest concerns. For example, the FOI law proposed in the United Kingdom in 1999 enabled the government to withhold information if disclosure would lead to prosecution of the authority concerned. Clearly this would check the ability of journalists to investigate corruption charges. The code on access to information in Hong Kong, China, is considered ineffective because it permits departments to withhold information in 16 categories.

Another limitation of FOI laws is that their success in guaranteeing access to information depends on the capacity of the government to collect, process, store, and manage information. The ongoing costs can be significant—estimated at $286 million annually in the United States. And without an adequate information infrastructure, the cost, time, and complexity of obtaining information may be prohibitive. This lack of capacity has proved to be a barrier to FOI laws, especially in developing countries. An added element of capacity is the ability to produce timely statistics. Information on such statistics as public finances and the balance of payments needs to be reliable and timely if it is to improve the functioning of markets.

As Thailand shows, the laws may also take time to implement because of lack of understanding (box 10.6). But building capacity in communications management can help to overcome the obstacles. In Romania efforts to increase government capacity to manage and communicate information significantly improved the media's ability to report on economic reforms and secure public support for them.[30]

Even with FOI acts, journalists may lack the training to cover such issues as privatization, economic reforms, and environmental issues. Several countries are addressing this by training reporters in business journalism and investigative journalism. A World Bank evaluation in Uganda and Tanzania found that such training raised the quality of newspaper reporting on corruption issues.[31]

Broadening the media's reach

Access to the media, and being able to provide a diversity of views through the media, holds enormous potential for supporting integrated and inclusive markets. But the reach of newspapers, television, and radio varies tremendously, with wealth a clear determinant of media penetration. On average, residents of industrial coun-

Box 10.6
Improving access to information in Thailand

Triggered in part by the Asian financial crisis, in 1997 the Thai government passed the Official Information Act. With a few exceptions regarding the monarchy and national security, the act guarantees people's rights to gain access to all information held by the government. Government agencies are required to publish official information in the *Government Gazette,* make other standard documents such as agency plans and manuals available to the public, and provide other information upon individual request. These initiatives depart radically from previous policies and attitudes toward transparency. But there have been some difficulties in implementation—including political interference and a lack of understanding among officials and journalists about how to use the act.

Despite the problems, the act has received widespread praise as a significant step toward improving information flows. Requests for access to government information are growing. The act has even helped spark further efforts to improve transparency. In October 2000 the Bank of Thailand established an office to provide the public with access to financial and economic information. The government is now focusing on implementing the act more effectively through public awareness campaigns and training journalists and officials in applying it.

Source: Chongkittavorn 2001.

tries are more than 25 times more likely to receive a daily newspaper than residents in African countries, as measured by newspaper circulation (figure 10.3). But in many African countries, according to the World Association of Newspapers, the average newspaper copy is read by as many as a dozen people. Literacy also plays a role, but even after accounting for it, large disparities in newspaper circulation remain. Both GNP per capita and literacy are lower in Ecuador than in the former Yugoslav Republic of Macedonia, but newspaper circulation is more than three times greater in Ecuador.

Television viewers do not have to be literate, but they do need costly equipment, technology, and electricity. Radio broadcasting is cheaper, does not require electricity mains, and can be transmitted to remote areas to people who do not know how to read. Not surprisingly, radio receiver penetration is higher than other media penetration in all regions, and radio is the primary medium for reaching citizens in many developing countries. The difference between the reach of radio and the reach of other media is far greater in developing than in industrial countries.

Figure 10.3
Media penetration rates by region and by OECD compared with non-OECD countries

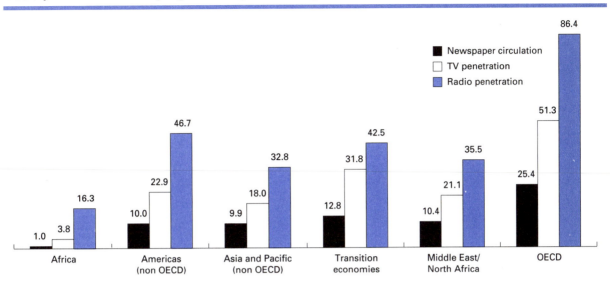

Note: Newspaper circulation = daily newspapers circulated per 100 people; TV penetration = television sets per 100 people; radio penetration = radios per 100 people.
Source: World Development Indicators 2000.

Even in countries with low penetration rates, the media can affect behavior and improve outcomes. In Kenya, despite the low newspaper penetration rate of 9 per 1,000 people, the local press instigated a corruption investigation that led to the health minister's resignation (chapter 1).

Higher media penetration promotes greater responsiveness of public and private agents. This is best demonstrated by comparisons of media access within countries, since such comparisons adjust to a large extent for different political and economic systems in different countries. A study in India compared state government allocations of relief spending and public food distribution during natural disasters, such as floods and droughts. Adjusting for the size of shocks, distribution of relief was greater in states with higher newspaper circulation. The greater local presence of media allowed citizens to develop a collective voice, and the effect was greater for newspapers in local languages than for those in English or Hindi.[32]

Access to foreign media can also create demand for institutional change. Foreign or global media enable access to information on issues not reported by local media—as evidenced by countless examples of citizens first receiving news of domestic political crises through the foreign media. They also provide a yardstick for local media—and for the performance of governments.

Three main strategies have proved successful in increasing access to the media. The first is to remove barriers to entry for new media enterprises. This includes eliminating restrictive licensing and registration requirements, or introducing competition when there are monopolies—factors closely related to media independence (see above).

Second, private participants and donors have been innovative in their efforts to expand the reach of the media, especially in poor and remote areas. In Nigeria and the Democratic Republic of Congo, newspaper vendors charge one price for buying a newspaper, but customers can pay a fraction of this price to read the newspaper at the stand. And international donors have supported telecenters, which provide public access to a range of media and communications facilities in remote areas.

Community and nonprofit efforts have been instrumental in increasing media penetration in poorer countries, as demonstrated by the distribution of newspapers in Nepal (box 10.7). Nonprofit foundations have significantly increased access to community radio in de-

Box 10.7
Increasing access to the media: wall newspapers in Nepal

Since the publication of the first Nepalese newspaper in 1901, access to the press has been constrained by poverty, low literacy, and inadequate transport. Daily newspaper circulation averages only 11 copies per 1,000 people, and residents of rural areas are particularly unlikely to receive information from the media. In 1984 a group of media professionals established the nonprofit Nepal Press Institute to help expand the media industry. The institute provides training and capacity-building services for journalists and media organizations.

One of its most successful projects is the wall newspaper *Gaon Ghar,* started in 1987 as an experiment to increase information flows in rural areas. The newspapers are printed in large fonts and pasted on walls in public places so that many people can read the paper simultaneously. The content is development oriented, with features on public health, environment, water and sanitation, and gender. Extremely popular, *Gaon Ghar* is now distributed in villages in all 75 Nepali districts, inspiring similar projects in Bangladesh, India, and Pakistan.

Source: Nepal Press Institute 2000.

veloping countries, through wind-up radios and satellite technology. These services have proved especially important in delivering leading-edge information on health, education, environment, and microenterprises. They have also provided a channel for residents of remote communities to voice their concerns and share information with other communities.

Third, a broader development policy framework can enhance access to the media. Increasing literacy rates expands the demand for newspapers. Establishing or strengthening journalist schools expands the supply of the media. Developing the technological infrastructure for the media—installing telephone and cable systems for the Internet to distribution of radio receivers—also increases access. In Korea, for example, government distribution of radio sets as a part of a literacy program significantly increased access to the media and stimulated rapid growth in community radio stations in the 1960s. And competition among media organizations can increase access by broadening supply.

Institutions to complement the media

The media can be more effective if complementary institutions reinforce their independence and quality—and act on the information provided. But the independence to freely publish information must also be balanced with systems to ensure responsibility and accountability of the media. Some types of government regulation are needed (see above). Self-regulation is another supporting institution for the effective functioning of the media.

Self-regulatory bodies are well established in some industrial countries, but they are only beginning to emerge in developing countries. Guyana, Tanzania, and Trinidad and Tobago are all building self-regulatory press councils, which establish codes for honesty, fairness, respect for privacy, and general standards of taste. The councils use these codes to guide their decisions on complaints.

In many cases the press councils replace traditional court processes. In Australia the complainants are required to sign a declaration that they will not take their complaint to court if they are dissatisfied with the council's decision. What determines the success of councils? Ethical guidelines have to balance press freedom and responsibility. The application of standards has to be consistent. And media firms have to comply with their decisions.[33] Civil society organizations for media freedom and responsibility can reinforce the work of councils.

Effective judicial systems and other mechanisms that penalize undesirable behavior can complement the media's role in improving governance (see chapter 6). In the Philippines the media's exposure of toxic waste dumped by foreign military forces led to a congressional investigation, then to an official government investigation, and eventually to government enforcement of orders to discontinue the dumping. By contrast, media coverage of corrupt activities in Ukraine did little to instigate further investigations or remove the allegedly corrupt officials from power.[34] So even with the best of investigative journalism, the ability of the media to effect change is diminished severely if court systems or enforcement agencies are inadequate.

Media also have more impact when political parties, democratic elections, and civil society organizations hold governments accountable. Greater media penetration encourages greater government responsiveness. The reach of newspapers, television, and radio is particularly important when citizens can make political choices based on information they receive. Governments are more responsive when they are held accountable to informed citizens.

Conclusions

The media can play an important role in development by affecting the incentives of market participants—

businesses, individuals, or politicians—and by influencing the demand for institutional change. Information flows through the media can affect people's ideas, monitor people's actions, and thereby create constituencies for change and institutional reform. Across both developing and industrial countries, newspapers, broadcasts, and new media such as the Internet have promoted competition in economic and political markets, and helped create incentives for public and private agents to become more accountable. And the media can empower people, including the poor, by giving them a platform for voicing diverse opinions, participating in governance, and engaging in markets.

To achieve these outcomes, the media need to be independent, to reach people, and to be of high quality—that is, the media must have the capacity to reflect diverse views but also the ability to report on various subjects and be accountable. Control of the media by any single or concentrated interest group can hinder their ability to improve governance, be a force for change, and hold people to account. Very often, private

and public parties seek control of the media in order to influence their content. In many countries, policymakers have attempted to control media content through sole or concentrated ownership. Privatization and relaxation of controls on the media (such as by allowing new private entrants) can, in many cases, enable the media to support markets better. Though there are no private monopolies in the media industry, in some countries a limited number of private interests have substantial control over the industry. Regulations on concentration would help in this regard. Encouraging competition in the industry keeps the media in check and promotes diversity of views. Other, and complementary, avenues for reform are eliminating restrictive media regulations and financing arrangements, ensuring open access to information, and building journalistic capacity. Widespread access to media and complementary institutions—such as an effective judiciary and regulatory agencies—further strengthens the media's role in supporting market development and providing people with access to market opportunities.

Bibliographic Note

This Report draws on a wide range of World Bank documents and on numerous outside sources. The following authors prepared background papers for this Report: István Ábel, Cecile Aubert, Arup Banerji, Erik Berglöf, Lisa Bernstein, Timothy Besley, John P. Bonin, Juan Carlos Botero, Penelope Brook, Wendy Carlin, Nazmul Chaudhury, Klaus Deininger, Simeon Djankov, Cristian Pop-Eleches, David Finnegan, Heywood Fleisig, Tim Hanstad, Bernard Hoekman, Karen Hudes, Timothy Irwin, Roumeen Islam, Sanjay Jain, Hiau Looi Kee, Yoram Keinan, Leora Klapper, Jan Kleinheisterkamp, Jean-Jacques Laffont, Rafael La Porta, Zvi Lerman, Margaret Levenstein, Florencio Lopez-de-Silanes, Keith Maskus, Caralee McLiesh, Claudio Montenegro, Tatiana Nenova, Marcelo Olarreaga, Rowena Olegario, Katharina Pistor, Roy Prosterman, Raghuram G. Rajan, Howard Rosenthal, Brian Schwarzwalder, Paul Seabright, Andrei Shleifer, Warrick Smith, Charles Soludo, Valerie Suslow, Nicola Tynan, Ernst-Ludwig von Thadden, Alexander Volokh, Mark West, and Luigi Zingales.

Background papers for the World Development Report are available online at http://www.worldbank.org/wdr. The views expressed in these papers are not necessarily those of the World Bank or of this Report.

Many persons, both inside and outside the World Bank, provided advice and guidance to the team. Valuable comments and contributions were provided by: Alberto Agbonyitor, Sadiq Ahmed, Zafar Ahmed, Emmanuel Akpa, Harold Alderman, Myrna Alexander, Nagavalli Annamalai, Lystra Antoine, Ismail Arslan, Ian Bannon, Kaushik Basu, Abhijit Banerjee, Luca Barbone, Maria Benito-Spinetto, Tim Besley, Deepak Bhattasali, Vinay Bhargava, Dominique Bichara, Milan Brahmbhatt, Lilia Burunciuc, Gerard Byam, Derek Byerlee, Robert Calderisi, Anthony Cholst, Paul Collier, Nancy Cooke, Csaba Csaki, Maria Dakolias, Klaus Deininger, Shanta Devarajan, Christian Delvoie, William Easterly, David Ellerman, Peter Fallon, Gershon Feder, J. Michael Finger, Alan Gelb, Hafez Ghanem, Daniele Giovannuci, Ian Goldin, Roger Grawe, Avner Greif, Christopher Hall, Peter Harrold, Ronald Hood, Ingrid Ivins, Steven Jaffee, Cally Jordan, Satu Kahkonen, Mats Karlsson, Phil Keefer, Ali Khadr, Homi Kharas, Mylene Kherallah, Michael Klein, Steve Knack, Anjali Kumar, Victoria Kwakwa, Peter Kyle, Patrick Labaste, Jean-Jacques Laffont, Donald Larson, Robert Liebenthal, Nora Lustig, Cheryl Martin, Ricardo Martin, Keith Maskus, Bonaventure Mbida-Essama, John McIntire, Oey Astra Meesook, Richard Messick, Nicholas Minot, Paul Mitchell, Peter Moll, Celesin Monga, Paul Moreno-Lopez, Ijaz Nabi, Mustapha Kamel Nabli, John Nash, Vikram Nehru, Benno Ndulo, Mark Nelson, Peter Nicholas, Lucas Ojiambo, Nwanze Okidegbe, Fayez Omar, Guillermo Perry, Guy Pfeffermann, Robert Picciotto, Vijayendra Rao, Martin Ravallion, Thomas Reardon, Dirk Reinermann, Ritva Reinikka, Elliot Riordan, Richard Rogers, Antoinette Sayeh, Julian Schweitzer, Marcelo Selowsky, Mary Sheehan, Andrei Shleifer, Iain Shuker, Warrick Smith, Charles Soludo, John Staatz, Roger Sullivan, Frederick Thomas Temple, Vinod Thomas, Elaine Tinsley, M. Willem van Eeghen, Tara Vishwanath, Erich Vogt, Michael Woolcock, Joachim von Amsberg, Andrew Vorkink, Eliza Winters, Paolo Zacchia, and Roberto Zagha.

The team wishes to thank individuals who participated in the following events during the planning and drafting stages of this Report: **Berlin Workshop on the**

Institutional Foundations of a Market Economy (held February 23–25, 2000 in Berlin, Germany): Masahiko Aoki, Christopher Mark Armstrong, Bhuban Bajra Bajracharya, Pranab Bardhan, Jean-Christophe Bas, Robert H. Bates, Andreas Beckermann, Erik Berglöf, Timothy J. Besley, Hans-Gert Braun, Heinz Bühler, Paul Collier, Dieter Duwendag, Thomas Elhaut, Julian Franks, Thomas F. Hellman, Martin Hellwig, Michael Hofmann, Simon Johnson, Daniel Kaufmann, Ioannis Kessides, Gudrun Kochendörfer-Lucius, Jean-Jacques Laffont, Rolf J. Langhammer, Colin P. Mayer, Claus Offe, Christoph G. Paulus, Katharina Pistor, Jean Philippe Platteau, Boris Pleskovic, Rudolf Richter, Jozef M. Ritzen, Hans-Bernd Schaefer, Wolfgang Schmitt, Kenneth Sokoloff, Joseph E. Stiglitz, Thierry Verdier, Robert Wade, Ralf Wegener, Jennifer Widner, William Witherell, Thomas Wollenzien, Luigi G. Zingales, and Michaela Zintl; *Summer Research Workshop* (held July 17–19, 2000 in Washington, D.C.): Jean-Paul Azam, Timothy J. Besley, Gerard Caprio, Nicholas R. Crafts, David Dollar, William Easterly, Marcel Fafchamps, Alan Gelb, Cheryl Gray, Jose Luis Guasch, John Haltiwanger, Daniel Kaufmann, Tarun Khanna, Homi Kharas, Jan Kleinheisterkamp, Jean-Jacques Laffont, Janet T. Landa, Rafael La Porta, Ross Levine, Florencio Lopez-de-Silanes, Keith E. Maskus, Ugo Mattei, John McMillan, Curtis J. Milhaupt, Paul Miranti, Pradeep Mitra, Roger Noll, Rowena Olegario, Santos Pastor, Guy Pfeffermann, Richard H. Pildes, Boris Pleskovic, Jozef M. Ritzen, Jean-Laurent Rosenthal, Jennifer Prah Ruger, Friedrich Schneider, Nemat Shafik, Andrei Shleifer, Timothy Sinclair, Warrick Smith, Kenneth Sokoloff, Charles Soludo, Pablo Spiller, Nicholas Stern, Joseph Stiglitz, Richard Sylla, Shang-Jin Wei, and Jennifer Widner; *Consultative Meeting on the Role of the Media in Development* (held April 12, 2001 in Washington, D.C.): Mahfuz Anam, Stuart Auerbach, Ana Elisa Luna Barros, Kenneth Best, David Black, Robin Burgess, Tim Carrington, M.G. Chandrasekhar, Luckson Chipare, Kavi Chongkittavorn, Diana Daniels, Sunil Dasgupta, Araceli De Leon-Herlihy, Stephen Fidler, Kristen Guida, Gary Hansen, Chris Haws, Nancy Hedin, Gracia Hillman, Craig Hobbs, Ann Hudock, Mats Karlsson, Hisham Kassem, Aristides Kattopo, Daniel Kaufmann, Tim Kenny, Reinhard Keune, Tatiana Khaborova, Mark Koenig, Ronald Koven, Dale Lautenbach, Georges Leclere, Jesus Meza Lueza, Rod Macdonell, Sokol Mici, Tahir Mirza, Gumisai Mutume, Rebeccah Nelems, Jenny Ng, Pippa Norris, Alfred Ogbamey, Dapo Olorunyomi, Manuel Orozco, Anil Padmanabhan, Rob Paul, Sharmini Peries, Guy Pfeffermann, Reuben Phiri, Nikolina Sajn, Danny Schechter, Petko Shishkov, Andrei Shleifer, Frank Smyth, Rick Stapenhurst, Nicholas Stern, Leonard Sussman, Guennadi Tchernov, Fissehaye Tesfaindrias, Rich Thomas, Ricardo Trotti, K. Viswanath, Frank Vogl, Erich Vogt, Ruth Walden, Ting Wang, Matthew White, and Ivan Zassoursky; *Consultative Meeting on Judicial Systems* (held May 18, 2001 in Washington, D.C.): Elizabeth Adu, Nagavalli Annamalai, Ferid Belhaj, Sandra Bloemenkamp, Juan Botero, Chas Cadwell, Maria Dakolias, Alfredo Dammert, David Finnegan, Xavier Forneris, Bohdan Futey, Heike Gramckow, Cheryl Gray, Linn Hammergren, Irina Kichigina, Bert Kritzer, Alfredo Larrea-Falcony, Gail M. Lecce, Florencio Lopez-de-Silanes, Waleed Malik, Richard Messick, Peter Messitte, Isabelle Mouysset, Peter Murrell, Joe Onek, Brian Ostrom, Friedrich Peloschek, Randi Ryterman, Andrei Shleifer, Nan Shuker, Visu Sinnadurai, Stefka Slavova, Loren Smith, Donna Stienstra, Melissa Thomas, Ko-Yung Tung, Donna Valdez, Russ Wheeler, and Steven Williams.

In addition to these events, the team held consultative videoconferences with audiences in Bangladesh, Brazil, Egypt, Japan, Mexico, Morocco, South Africa, and Thailand. They wish to thank the following individuals: *in Bangladesh:* Abu Abdullah, Abu Ahmed, Fakhrul Ahsan, Debapriya Bhattacharya, Abul Bayes, Tawfiq-e-Elahi Chowdhury, Shamsul Haque, Yussuf Abdullah Harun, Akmal Husain, Khushi Kabir, Zakir Ahmed Khan, Akbar Ali Khan, J.A. Maas, Sattar Mandal, Wahiuddin Mahmud, John Moore, Hossain Zilllur Rahman, Latifur Rahman, Masihur Rahman, Rokia A. Rahman, Syed Abdus Samad, Phiphit Suphaphiphat, and Irene Wilson; *in Brazil:* Murillo de Aragão, Reginaldo Oscar de Castro, David Fleischer, Paulo Springer de Freitas, Amaro Luiz de Oliveira Gomes, Katherine Hennings, Roberto Shoj Ogasavara, Adriano Pereira Rubin Silva, Sergei Soares, and Silvia Valadares; *in Egypt:* Moataz El-Alfy Rashed, Hanaa Kheir El Din, Reda El Edel, Nagui El Fayoumi, Nadir El Fregany, Hussein El Gammal, Laila El-Khawaga, Alia El Mahdy, Faika El-Rifaei, Hala El Said, Ganat El Samalouty, Nabil El Shamy, Amin El Sharkawy, Nermine El Sheimy, Mahmoud Aboul Eyoun, Ahmed Ezz, Mahmoud Abdel Fadil, Samiha Fawzi, Laila Gad, Ahmed Galal, Nemat Genena, Amina Ghaniem, Heba Handoussa, Aziza Helmy, Tarek Kamel, Sara Louza, Ibrahim Moharam, Mahmoud Mohieldin, Heba Nassar, Osman Osman, Mohamed Ragab, Hoda Rashad, Darren Schemmer, Kamel Ahmed Sed-Ahmed, and Magda Tantawy; *in Japan:* Koji Fujimoto, Yukiko Fukagawa, Tetsuya Fukunaga, Yujiro Hayami, Kaoru Hayashi, Kenichi Ishida, Shigeru Ishikawa, Masahiro Kawai, Fukunari Kimura, Naonobu Minato, Morio Miyazaki, Megumi Muto, Takakyuki Nakaya, Naoya Ochi, Tosió Ogata, Kenichi Ohno, Kan Sato, Hiroko Shimizu, Toyomitsu Tamao, Ippei Yamazawa, and Toru Yanagihara; *in Mexico:* Ismael Díaz Aguilera, Santiago Levy Algazi, Everardo Elizondo Almaguer, Jonathan Davis Arzarc, Salvador Kalifa Assad, Enrique Dávila Capalleja, Fernando Clavijo, Roberto del Cueto, Rafael del Villar, Carlos Elizondo-Mayer, Jorge Nicolín Fischer, Mauricio González Gómez, José Gabriel Martínez González, Manuel Sánchez González, Gerardo Jacobs, Adriaan Ten Kate, Luis Landa, Lorenza Martínez, Jorge Mier, Pedro Noyola, Ricardo Ochoa, Arturo Fernández Pérez, Dionisio Pérez-Jácome, Cecilia Ramos, Federico Reyes-Heróles, Luis Rubio, Julio Santaella, Moises Schwartz, Jaime Serra, Manuel Suárez-Mier, Lucy Tacher, Francisco Barrios Terrazas, Guillermo Prieto Treviño, Fernando Sánchez Ugarte, Angel Villalobos, Ariel Yepes, and Alejandro Werner; *in Morocco:* Abdelaziz Al Mechatt, Mouatassim Belghazi, Driss Benhima, Azzeddine Benmoussa, Mohamed Brahimi, Idriss Chater, Hassan Chami, Omar Derraji, Sean Doyle, Abdessadeq El Glaoui, Ahmed Ghazali, Najib Guédira, Nezha Hayat, Said Ibrahimi, Abdelhakim Kammou, Karim Mansouri, Abderrahmane Saaidi, Mostafa Terrab, and Abdellah Zouhir; *in South Africa:* Andre Donaldson, Jonathan Katzenellenbogen, Daniel Kekana, Richard Gerber, Mathew Glasser, Mervin Gumede, Chris Heymans, Dumisani Hlophe, Tom Lebert, Lot Mlati, Charles Nevhutanda, Charles Okeahalam, Randy Randal, and Mphanama Tshivangavho; *in Thailand:* Supoj Arewas, Peter Brimble, Pichart Gesaruang, Ejaz Ghani, Somchai Jitsuchon, Suwanee Khamman, Prasit Kovilaikol, Angkanee Luangpenthong, Somnuk Phimolsathian, Priyanut Piboolsravut, Poldej Pinprathep, Nipon Poapongsakorn, Isra Sarntisart, Orapin Sopchokchai, Suthirat Vanasrisawasd, and Porametee Vimolsiri.

We also worked with attorneys of Lex Mundi associated firms.

Despite efforts to compile a comprehensive list, some who contributed may have been inadvertently omitted. The team apologizes for any oversights and reiterates its gratitude to all who contributed to this Report.

Endnotes

Chapter 1

1. North 1994; Coase 1937, 1959; Williamson 1985.

2. Scholars have differed in the definitions of institutions. The most widely used one is "Institutions . . . consist of formal rules, informal constraints—norms of behavior, conventions, and self-imposed codes of conduct—and their enforcement characteristics (North 1991). Nabli and Nugent (1989) apply the principles of the New Institutional Economics literature to developing countries, in particular looking at the case of Tunisia. In their definition they discuss how institutions may vary in their organizational nature; that is, the extent to which organizations and institutions coincide. Many of the institutions in this Report have activities distinct from supporting markets as well, for example, the judiciary.

3. The term "effective" in this Report means effectiveness relative to desired goals.

4. Informal institutions may also be designed to serve more than one purpose: specifically, they often aim to distribute risks and gains, as well as to enable production or exchange. For example, a study of eight African countries that analyzes the methods African firms use to gain information about, and enforce contracts with, manufacturing firms, finds that breaches of contract are not necessarily punished by a rupture of the business relationship. A failure to pay that results from circumstances beyond the control of the trading partner results in renegotiations and continued dealings. In other words, the system is flexible, and both parties share risk. The manner of the sharing may not be determined precisely ex ante, but norms do affect the outcome. In formal systems, contracts between borrowers and lenders are often written so that the defaulter has to pay regardless of the source of risk (though contracts may also specify the types of risks each party to the transaction bears).

5. Organizations, of course, engage in productive activity as well. The Report considers the market-supporting functions of organizations.

6. *World Development Report 1998/1999: Knowledge for Development* discusses the importance of information-sharing institutions.

7. High information and enforcement costs can stymie individual or collective action and result in missed opportunities to increase welfare gains. For example, development of common property or preservation of the environment can fail to materialize owing to information and enforcement costs and because people cannot agree to balance the degree of competition versus cooperation in their economic activities.

8. Acemoglu, Johnson, and Robinson 2000.

9. Rodrik 1999.

10. Country case studies also suggest that countries that adapted the transplanted law to local conditions—or had a population already familiar with the basic legal principles of the transplanted law—have a higher probability of constructing an effective legal framework. For example, French law was transplanted to Ecuador between 1831 and 1881. But

because the people of Ecuador had a poor understanding of the law, it was not adapted or developed. In France itself, where legal institutions were widely used and understood, there has been continuing institutional development.

11. Djankov and others forthcoming.

12. World Bank 2000a, 2000b.

13. World Bank 2000a.

14. Trujillo and Nombela 2000.

15. Baker and Tremolet 2000c.

16. Rodrik (2000) considers how democratic institutions allow good ideas to percolate up and encourage debate over priorities.

17. Scholars, including North and Weingast (1989), have written about the importance of trade in general in promoting institutional change.

18. Feder and Feeny 1991.

19. Islam and Montenegro 2001.

20. Rajan and Zingales 2001, *World Development Report 2002* background paper.

21. Besley and Burgess 2000.

22. Caldwell cited in Olson (2000), foreword.

23. Noll forthcoming.

24. North 1993.

25. Andre and Platteau 1998.

26. Israel 1987.

27. Aubert and Laffont 2000, *World Development Report 2002* background paper.

28. Beck, Levine, and Loayza 2000; Rajan and Zingales 2001. *World Development Report 2002* background paper.

29. Rajan and Zingales 2001, *World Development Report 2002* background paper.

30. Svensson 1998.

31. Easterly 2000; Alesina and others 1999.

32. Eagerman and Sokoloff (1994); Sokoloff (2000).

33. Informal social transfers have two advantages over more arm's length (public) social assistance. First, it is likely that families or communities are better able than the government to get information about who among them is suffering from poverty. If the onset of poverty is sudden, they are also arguably better able to respond quickly to meet the need. Second, in many cases, families or communities may also be better at enforcing the implicit contract on assistance—recognizing when the recipient is no longer in distress and breaking off assistance (Morduch 1999).

34. Rajan and Zingales 2001, *World Development Report 2002* background paper.

35. Pistor 1999.

36. Pistor 1999.

Chapter 2

1. Between 1965 and 1988, productivity growth in agriculture was clearly associated with declines in the share of agriculture in output as well as faster overall growth. The decline in share of agriculture, as well as the growth of output, was highest in East Asian countries, followed by Latin America, South Asia, and Sub-Saharan Africa (Turnham 1993).

2. This issue is addressed in many countries by traveling judges—but the time lag between visits of such judges may

prove to be too expensive as well for a farmer whose production is strictly time-bound.

3. Powelson 1998.

4. As historical examples have shown, the effect of increased productivity on lower poverty would result not just through the direct effect of increased incomes to farmers but also indirectly as the higher rural incomes translate into higher demand for local products and thus raise incomes of local artisans, traders, and service providers. Finally, increased productivity of agricultural labor would mean that families would not need as many members to cultivate the land, allowing children to invest more in education and letting others search for higher-productivity jobs.

5. Commodity price and trade issues were discussed in World Bank 2000h, and some issues pertaining to labor markets in agriculture were dealt with in World Bank 1995a. A recent discussion of the institutional aspects of water is in Saleth and Dinar (1999). Irrigation issues have also been recently addressed in Hillel (1987), and, for Eastern Europe, Branscheid (1998).

6. Prosterman and others 2001; Lerman 2000.

7. Soludo 2001, *World Development Report 2002 (WDR 2002)* background paper.

8. See, for instance, Prosterman and others (2001) and Carter and Yao (1999) and the references therein.

9. See de Soto 2000.

10. *WDR 2000/2001* points out that incorporating the views of various stakeholders can improve the quality and sustainability of land reforms.

11. Also see Alston, Libecap, and Schneider (1995, 1996) for other cases for the Amazon frontier.

12. World Bank 1999d.

13. Platteau 1992.

14. Soludo 2001, *WDR 2002* background paper.

15. Bruce, Migot-Adholla, and Atherton, 1994

16. See Carter, Wiebe, and Blarel 1994; Migot-Adholla, Place, and Olucoch-Kosura 1994; and Pinckney and Kimuyu 1994

17. Alston, Libecap, and Schneider 1995, 1996.

18. Siamwalla and others 1990; Feder and others 1986; World Bank 1999d.

19. Pender and Kerr 1994.

20. Carter, Fletschner, and Olinto 1996.

21. Ensminger 1997.

22. See, for instance, a similar discussion for the transition countries in Dale and Baldwin (2000).

23. Deininger 2001, *WDR 2002* background paper.

24. Deininger 2001, *WDR 2002* background paper.

25. Deininger 2001, *WDR 2002* background paper.

26. Deininger forthcoming.

27. Gabriel Kirkpatrick, "Rural Credit in North Carolina," available at <http://www.cuna.org/data/cu/research/irc/archive 4_1.html.>

28. In many countries, however, informal finance is still used across income classes, despite access to formal institutions. This was found to be the case, for example, in a study of microfinance in Cameroon in the early 1990s (Heidhues 1994).

29. These motives and mechanisms for credit, savings, and insurance services are likely to be inextricably linked. For exam-

ple, in the absence of formal insurance markets, the precautionary motive for saving may be especially important. Alternatively, the credit market may serve an insurance purpose by smoothing consumption. A study of northern Nigerian villages, for instance, found that credit contracts were dependent on the nature and number of shocks received by the borrowers; in effect the contracts bundled credit with insurance (Udry 1990). Thus, in this chapter credit refers also to these more general services, except where it is clear from the context that the chapter is referring specifically to savings or to insurance.

30. Adams 1995.

31. Besley, Jain, and Tsangarides 2001, *WDR 2002* background paper, and Ijere 1986 (cited in Adegbite 1997), respectively.

32. Besley, Jain, and Tsangarides 2001, *WDR 2002* background paper.

33. The study of villagers in southern India found that as farm size grew, banks became more important to farmers than private credit sources—village moneylenders, pawnbrokers, chit funds, and friends and relatives (Chinnappa 1977). The survey of farmers in Sindh and Punjab provinces, Pakistan, in the 1990s revealed that landlords, the richest households in the survey, borrowed from formal institutional lenders and from traders, while poor share tenants and fixed-rent tenants borrowed exclusively from informal lenders such as traders, landlords, and shopkeepers (Mansuri 1998).

34. Siamwalla and others 1990.

35. North (1991) argues that the development of long-distance trade spurred the development of mechanisms for contract enforcement. In turn, contract enforcement, by lowering the transaction costs associated with trade, increased its profitability and spurred its growth.

36. For a discussion, see Meyer and Nagarajan (2000) and Swaminathan (1991). Bell, Srinivasan, and Udry (1997) describe a similar situation for Punjab. There is an interesting parallel here with the postbellum southern United States, as agrarian relations changed with the creation of a new class of sharecroppers whose input needs were financed by trader-merchants (Ransom and Sutch 1977). For Pakistan, see Mansuri (1998). For the Philippines, see Floro and Ray (1997) and Fuentes (1998).

37. In northern Sudan the merchant-lender extended credit as an advance in money or kind against the next crop, an ancient system called *shayl*. The oldest form of *shayl* was an advance of grain or seed, valued at a price substantially above the estimated price at the next harvest. The borrower had to settle the loan by returning at harvest time enough grain to make up the money equivalent of the loan. If a good crop followed a bad crop, with a resulting drop in market prices, the lender could get back as much as five to six times the volume of goods he loaned out (Wilmington 1955).

38. Siamwalla and others 1990.

39. Causing social embarrassment to the defaulter can also work. Fleisig and la Pena (1996), cited in Yaron and Piprek (1997), give an example from Costa Rica, where *Canarios* (Canaries), dressed in yellow bird suits, followed nonpayers to publicly humiliate them.

40. In both shared-risk finance organizations, such as rotating savings and credit associations (ROSCAs) and accumulated savings and credit associations (ASCRAs), and group-based lending programs (where the creditworthiness of the group as a whole is affected by individual default), monitoring of repayment by peers is a key to success (chapter 9).

41. The Bank for Agriculture and Agricultural Cooperatives in Thailand, on the other hand, assesses a penalty of 3 percent a year on arrears (Yaron and Piprek 1997).

42. The Microfinance Practical Guide, available at <http://fpsicd01.worldbank.org/root/public/990124_1.613/deb/fipsi/web/guide.htm.>

43. Yunus 1994.

44. Jain and Mansuri 2000.

45. Schreiner 2000, pp. 22–23.

46. *MicroBanking Bulletin*, various issues, The Microfinance Program, The Economics Institute, Boulder, Colo.

47. Farrington 2000.

48. Waterfield 1999.

49. GTZ 1997.

50. Meyer and Nagarajan (2000) examined rural finance in Asian countries; Yaron and Piprek (1997) was not limited to Asia.

51. For example, the BAAC experimented with loans to cooperatives, groups, and individuals, with differing collateral requirements and loan terms. Grameen has tried other income-generation projects, such as for-profit spin-offs to provide Internet service (Morduch 1999).

52. Webster and Fidler 1996.

53. It is also instructive to note that the most widely cited Latin American success story, BancoSol of Bolivia, operates primarily in urban areas.

54. Morduch (1999, p. 1587), conversely, cites studies suggesting that repayment rates in village banking schemes in Costa Rica and rural Bangladesh are higher in remote communities, because there are fewer alternatives available to defaulting borrowers. The lack of available alternatives might also explain the observed high rates of repayment in programs, such as Grameen, that lend predominantly to women (Morduch 1999, pp. 1583–84).

55. A recent exception, SafeSave in Bangladesh, has emphasized savings.

56. Seibel 2000.

57. Barnett and Coble 1999; Hazell 1992.

58. Moseley and Krishnamurthy 1995.

59. For a theoretical discussion of reciprocal insurance, see Coate and Ravallion (1993). Grimard (1997) finds evidence of risk-sharing across ethnic networks in Côte d'Ivoire. Overall, tests of informal risk-sharing within villages find some qualified support, although perfect risk-sharing does not appear to be occurring. For a discussion, see the survey by Morduch (1995).

60. Udry 1990.

61. It is important to recognize that the same social cohesiveness that enables information transmission may also rule out certain enforcement mechanisms (see chapter 9).

62. Between 1973 and 1994 small farmers increased average incomes by 90 percent, and average income increases for the landless were 125 percent. Calorie and protein intakes rose

58–81 percent and 103–115 percent, respectively (Rosenzwieg 1998).

63. The crops are wheat, corn, and rice (Pardey and Beintema 2001).

64. *World Development Indicators 2001.*

65. Alston and others 2000. Social returns tend to exceed private returns on investment.

66. Fuglie and others 1996.

67. Gautam 2000.

68. By a multiple of six in Latin America, three in Asia, and more than two in Africa between 1959 and 1980 (Feder, Willett, and Zijp 1999).

69. Swanson, Farner, and Bahal 1990. The expenditure on extension services varies significantly between developing and industrial countries. Per farmer expenditure averages $2–$3 in developing countries, compared with $65 in high-income countries, although on average developing countries allocate higher proportions of their agricultural budgets to extension (Feder, Willett, and Zijp 1999).

70. Alston and others 2000.

71. Evenson (1997) summarizes these studies.

72. Gautam 2000.

73. Purcell and Anderson 1997.

74. Feder, Willett, and Zijp 1999.

75. Participation of farmers in the design and implementation of extension in economies from France to Taiwan, China, has improved accountability, integration of extension with complementary services, and cost-effectiveness. More extensive use of mass media has been shown to be a cost-effective method of increasing awareness of new technologies (Feder, Willett, and Zijp 1999).

76. World Bank 2000a.

77. World Bank 2000a.

78. Feder, Willett, and Zijp 1999.

79. Following the near collapse of the government livestock-marketing system in 1973, farmers compensated by building a member-based association to distribute veterinary drugs. This role was later expanded to include extension services and education programs (Umali-Deininger 1997).

80. As happened in Chile in the 1970s (Umali-Deininger 1997).

81. Dinar and Keynan 1998.

82. Feder, Willett, and Zijp 1999.

83. Gisselquist and Grether 2000.

84. Tripp and Byerlee 2000.

85. Unless otherwise stated, all dollar amounts are U.S. dollars.

86. Gisselquist and Grether 2000; Cortes 1997.

87. Significant variation also occurs among developing counties. In some Latin American countries, where large commercial farms produce export crops, the private sector accounts for up to 40 percent of R&D expenditures (Alston, Pardey, and Roseboom 1998; Pardey and Beintema 2001).

88. UNDP 1999.

89. Pray and Umali-Deininger 1998.

90. Public support for private research is also provided through various incentive systems, ranging from cash subsidies and interest rate concessions to more common tax incentives for private sector R&D. The value of R&D tax incentives is uncertain. Evidence from some empirical studies suggests that R&D incentives are cost-ineffective. In a 1995 study the Australian Government Industry Commission documented that for every $1 of forgone tax revenue, only between $0.60 and $1 in research expenditure was generated. Furthermore, it was noted that between 83 and 90 percent of the research conducted would have taken place without the tax incentive. In Canada, however, tax incentives stimulated significantly higher investment in R&D: $1.80 of research expenditure was generated by every $1 of tax credit (Pray and Umali-Deininger 1998).

91. Richer 2000.

92. The effect on access is dependent on the extent to which users can share in rents from new technologies, as well as the effective functioning of information, credit, and commodities markets to enable access to new technologies (Lele, Lesser, and Horstkotte-Wesseler 1999).

93. Two other TRIPS provisions refer directly to plants. First, TRIPS enables countries to exclude from patent protection plants and animals other than microorganisms and biological processes for the production of plants and animals. Second, products may be excluded from patents to "protect *ordre public* or morality, including to protect human, animal or plant life or health or to avoid serious prejudice to the environment." Most developing countries will have to strengthen their intellectual property systems substantially to meet TRIPS requirements. In 1988, 53 countries explicitly excluded plant varieties from patent protection (WIPO 1990).

94. Qaim 1999.

95. Byerlee and Alex 1998.

96. Pardey and Beintema 2001.

97. Mudahar, Jolly, and Srivastava 1998.

98. Tripp and Byerlee 2000.

99. Purcell and Anderson 1997; Rukuni, Blackie, and Eicher 1998.

100. Rozelle, Pray, and Huang 1997.

101. World Bank 2000a.

102. Purcell and Anderson 1997.

103. World Bank 2000a.

104. World Bank 1998.

105. World Bank 1998.

106. Byerlee and Maredia 1999.

107. Pardey and others 1996.

108. This section relies mainly on Byerlee (2000).

109. Rockey 2000.

110. Echeverria 1998.

111. In theory, whether private long-term negotiated contracts could replace public research institutes will depend to a large extent on the principal/agent problems in monitoring long-term contracts.

112. Alston, Pardey, and Roseboom 1998.

Chapter 3

1. Wurgler 2000.

2. Nugent and Nabli 1992.

3. Rajan and Zingales 1998.

4. Klapper 2001. "Worldscope," the main international database of publicly listed companies, has data for 59 countries

as of December 2000. Of those, 14 countries report fewer than 10 publicly listed companies.

5. Demirgüç-Kunt and Maksimovic 2001.

6. Demirgüç-Kunt and Maksimovic 2001.

7. Miranti 2000.

8. La Porta, Lopez-de-Silanes, and Shleifer 1999.

9. La Porta, Lopez-de-Silanes, and Shleifer 1999.

10. Claessens, Djankov, and Lang 2000.

11. La Porta and others 1999.

12. Megginson, Nash, Netter, and Poulsen forthcoming.

13. Megginson and Boutchkova 2000.

14. Claessens, Djankov, and Klingbiel 2000.

15. Djankov and Murrell forthcoming.

16. Definition from Leff (1978).

17. Khanna and Rivkin 2000.

18. Claessens, Djankov, and Lang (2000, p. 108).

19. Performance was measured by the market value of assets within the firm relative to their replacement cost (Tobin's Q). Khanna and Palepu 2000a.

20. Claessens Djankov, and Lang 2000.

21. Morck, Strangeland, and Yeung 2000.

22. For a survey of countries that have adopted compulsory membership, see Djankov and others (2000). In the paper, the authors reports mandatory membership in business associations in only 13 out of 75 countries.

23. See Schneider 1997a, 1997b.

24. Doner and Schneider 2000a, 2000b; Johnson and others 2000; Nadvi 1999a.

25. See Doner and Schneider (2000b) for a more detailed discussion.

26. For a more general discussion on the "information sharing" and "cooperation" role played by these organizations, see Johnson and others (2000).

27. The more effective associations surveyed appear to have adopted a mediation system characterized by transparency in the decision process, voting weighted by size, flexibility in adjusting the system to changes in membership, and opportunities for extensive deliberations.

28. Kumar, Rajan, and Zingales 2000.

29. Pistor, Raiser, and Gelfer 2000.

30. Bebchuk 1999; Claessens, Djankov, and Lang 2000; La Porta and others 1999.

31. Grossman and Hart 1980.

32. This work builds on previous work such as Knack and Keefer 1995 and has been extended by other authors such as Pistor, Raiser, and Gelfer 2000 to include additional countries and expanded indices.

33. Nenova 2001a.

34. Lambert-Mogiliansky, Sonin, and Zhuravskaya 2000.

35. Foley 2000.

36. Berkowitz and White 2000.

37. Hart 2000.

38. Foley 2000.

39. La Porta and others 1998.

40. Chaudhuri 2000.

41. Hart and others 1997.

42. Gilson 2000.

43. See Bhagat and Black (1999) and Weisbach and Hermalin (2000).

44. Wurgler 2000.

45. LaPorta and others 1999

46. Khanna and Palepu 2000b.

47. IMF 2000 (p. 73).

Chapter 4

1. Hicks (1969); Bagehot (1873); Schumpeter (1934).

2. These results hold after controlling for possible endogeneity. For cross-country studies, see King and Levine (1993a, 1993b) and Levine and Zervos (1998). For industry-level studies, see Rajan and Zingales (1998) and Wurgler (2000). For firm-level studies, see Demirgüç-Kunt and Maksimovic (1998, 1999). For pooled cross-country, time-series studies, see Beck, Levine, and Loayza (2000) and Rousseau and Wachtel (2000).

3. Li, Squire, and Zhou 1997.

4. Dollar and Kraay 2000.

5. Sylla 2000.

6. Neal 1990.

7. Easterly, Islam, and Stiglitz 2001; Denizer, Iyigun, and Owen 2000.

8. There is evidence that financial development insulates output growth from terms of trade shocks, but it actually seems to magnify the impact of inflationary shocks on output volatility in low- and middle-income countries. See Beck, Lundberg, and Majnoni 2000.

9. Levine 1997; Merton and Bodie 1995.

10. World Bank 2001a.

11. Gurley and Shaw (1955, 1960); Goldsmith 1969.

12. The data set cited in Box 4.2 also includes nonbank financial institutions—insurance companies, finance companies, pooled investment schemes (mutual funds), savings banks, and private pension funds—and develops indicators using these. For brevity, here we limit our discussion to banks vs. markets, since development of nonbank intermediaries closely mirrors the development markets.

13. Mayer 1988.

14. For example, Vogel 1994; Porter 1992.

15. Gerschenkron 1962.

16. Rajan and Zingales 1999.

17. Stiglitz 1985; Boot, Greenbaum, and Thakor 1993.

18. Bhide 1993.

19. Demirgüç-Kunt and Levine forthcoming 2001. In other words, in regression equations, while overall financial development indicators are found to have significant effects, financial structure indicators almost never enter significantly.

20. For case studies see Chui, Titman, and Wei 2000 (Indonesia); Denizer, Gultekin, and Gultekin 2000 (Turkey); Chang 2000 (Korea); and Gallego and Loayza 2000 (Chile).

21. Beck, Demirgüç-Kunt, and Levine 2000b.

22. Kane 1989; Demirgüç-Kunt and Detragiache 1998, 2000.

23. Stiglitz 1972.

24. Barth, Caprio, and Levine 2000.

25. Barth, Caprio, and Levine 2000.

26. Routledge 1998.

27. World Bank 2001a.

28. Caprio and Honohan, 1999.

29. Caprio and Honohan 1999.

30. Figure 4.2 and the correlation result are taken from World Bank 2001a.

31. Barth, Caprio, and Levine (2000) find that state ownership is negatively associated with bank efficiency and financial development, controlling for real GDP per capita and general (that is, nonfinancial) measures of institutional development. Using data from the 10 largest commercial and development banks in each of 92 countries, La Porta, Lopez-de-Silanes, and Shleifer (forthcoming) demonstrate that greater state ownership in 1970 is associated with less financial development, lower growth, and lower productivity, all measured in 1995, and that these effects are larger at lower levels of income, with less financial sector development, and with weaker property rights protection. These results provide support for a causal link between state ownership and poor banking performance.

32. Comparisons between industrial and developing countries come from La Porta, Lopez-de-Silanes, and Shleifer (forthcoming). Barth, Caprio, and Levine (2000) provide econometric evidence that higher state ownership does not reduce the probability of systemic banking crisis. La Porta, Lopez-de-Silanes, and Shleifer (forthcoming) show that greater state ownership is actually associated with various measures of financial instability. Using a logit model, Caprio and Martinez-Peria (2000) show that greater state ownership at the start of the 1980–97 period was associated with a greater probability of a banking crisis and higher fiscal costs of crisis (though their cost data cover far fewer countries). This casts doubt on the notion that state ownership is a stabilizing force relative to private ownership.

33. It also makes it easier to appropriate surplus from finance through direct financial sector taxation.

34. Clarke and Cull 1999a, 1999b; World Bank 2001a. In Hungary, where public banks were sold to foreign shareholders, there was substantial postprivatization growth in retail banking, both in deposit taking and in consumer lending. There is also evidence that foreign competition has compelled some domestic banks to seek new market niches, which also has had implications for the distribution of credit. The Hungarian evidence is presented in detail in the section on foreign bank entry, below.

35. See Barth, Caprio, and Levine (2000) and La Porta, Lopez-de-Silanes, and Shleifer (forthcoming). La Porta, Lopez de Silanes, and Shleifer (forthcoming) also find that, at relatively high per capita income levels, the negative effects of state ownership diminish and become insignificant. This is largely attributable to European countries like Germany, France, and Italy that had high levels of state ownership. Because those countries also enjoyed high levels of general institutional development, it is unlikely that their results can be duplicated in developing countries. Note also that the results do *not* indicate that state banks outperformed private ones in very high income countries, but rather that they were no worse in a statistical sense.

36. The description of the bank privatization experiences in the Czech Republic, Hungary, and Poland is taken from Bonin and Wachtel (1999).

37. Barth, Caprio, and Levine 2001, forthcoming.

38. Tello 1984.

39. World Bank 1999a.

40. See Berger, Demsetz, and Strahan (1999); Boyd and Graham (1991, 1998); and Demirgüç-Kunt and Levine (2000) for reviews of the literature on concentration.

41. Shaffer 1993.

42. Demirgüç-Kunt and Levine 2000.

43. Demirgüç-Kunt and Huizinga 1999.

44. Barth, Caprio, and Levine 2001, forthcoming. Their measure of entry restrictions is based on how many of the following are required to obtain a banking license: draft by-laws; intended organizational chart; first three-year financial projections; financial information on shareholders; information on background/experience of future directors; information on background/experience of future managers; sources of funds to be used to capitalize the new bank; and intended differentiation of the new bank from other banks.

45. Barth, Caprio, and Levine 2001, forthcoming. Their index of restrictions on foreign entry is based on survey responses from regulators on two questions: Are any limitations placed on the ownership of domestic banks by foreign banks?; Are any limitations placed on the ability of foreign banks to enter the domestic banking industry?

46. Claessens and Klingebiel 2000b.

47. Claessens and Klingebiel 2000b.

48. IMF 2000.

49. Home–host country business ties are typically measured by bilateral trade between the two nations or by flows of foreign direct investment from the banks' home country to the host country. See, for example, Goldberg and Saunders (1981); Grosse and Goldberg (1991); and Hultman and McGee (1989).

50. Results on large banking markets and fewer entry restrictions come from Goldberg and Grosse (1994), who studied the location choice of foreign banks within the United States. Focarelli and Pozzolo (2000) provide cross-country evidence that foreign banks enter where expected profits are larger, owing to higher expected economic growth, and where the prospect of reducing local banks' inefficiency is high.

51. Miller and Parkhe 1998; Focarelli and Pozzolo 2000.

52. Domestic authorities might find it easier to supervise a foreign bank if it entered the market as a wholly-owned subsidiary of the parent bank rather than as a branch. Subsidiaries typically are permitted to engage in a broader range of financial services; however, they must lend based on their own capitalization. Conversely, branches typically are restricted to deposit-taking and lending activities, but they can draw upon the parent's capital base. In developing countries, bank supervisors would likely find it difficult to monitor the parent's capital base and thus would be reliant on supervisors in the bank's home country.

53. Claessens, Demirgüç-Kunt, and Huizinga 2001.

54. As Clarke and others (2000) show, through 1997, overhead costs, profitability, and interest margins were affected least in the domestic banks focused on consumer lending, an area where foreign banks had yet to make a large impact.

55. Barth, Caprio, and Levine 2000.

56. In the United States, foreign banks tend to be less efficient than domestic ones. See DeYoung and Nolle (1996) and Hasan and Hunter (1996). Demirgüç-Kunt and Huizinga (1999) provide cross-country evidence that foreign banks are less efficient than domestic ones in industrial economies. Some stud-

ies, however, particularly those that did not use the United States. as host nation, find that foreign banks have about the same efficiency as domestic ones. See, for example, Vander Vennet (1996) on foreign bank entry in the countries of the European Community.

57. Demirgüç-Kunt and Huizinga 1999.

58. On Argentina, see Clarke and others (2000); on Colombia, Barajas, Salazar, and Steiner (2000); on Hungary, Kiraly and others (2000). Greece and Portugal, Honohan (2000). All these papers can be found in Claessens and Jansen (2000).

59. Demirgüç-Kunt and Huizinga 1999; Claessens, Demirgüç-Kunt, and Huizinga 2000.

60. Demirgüç-Kunt, Levine, and Min 1998.

61. Goldberg, Dages, and Kinney 2000.

62. Peek and Rosengren (2000) show that Japanese banks cut back their U.S. activities as a result of the Japanese recession.

63. Clarke and others 2000.

64. World Bank 2001a.

65. World Bank 2001a.

66. See, for example, World Bank 2001d, p. 75.

67. Fleisig 1996; Bogetic and Fleisig 1997.

68. Fleisig 1996.

69. Fleisig and de la Pena 2001.

70. Bogetic and Fleisig 1997.

71. However, technological advance can overly complicate the specification of land property rights. As noted by DeSoto 1990, establishing clear title is a legal issue, not a technical one, which needs to be resolved with expensive land mapping and cadastral projects. Peru's boundary conflicts are increasingly resolved under a parallel titling system (see chapter 2), which seeks agreement on the natural boundaries among all neighbors. This agreement is then appended to the title registration.

72. Miller (2000) cautions against expecting public credit registries to substitute fully for private ones because their objectives differ. Olegario (2000) notes, for example, that unlike private credit registries, public ones do not collect information on trade credit.

73. Olegario 2000, p. 8.

74. Causation runs in both directions. The need for registries is greatest in heterogeneous, mobile societies, while their existence further facilitates that mobility.

75. Olegario 2000.

76. Miller 2000.

77. Miller 2000.

78. Miller 2000.

79. Olegario 2000.

80. National Association of Credit Managers (U.S.), newsletter, available at (www.nacm.org; Olegario 2000).

Chapter 5

1. There are many different definitions of governance. The following definition appears in "Governance: The World Bank's Experience." "Good governance is epitomized by predictable, open and enlightened policy making; a bureaucracy imbued with a professional ethos; an executive arm of government accountable for its actions; a strong civil society participating in public affairs; and all behaving under the rule of law" (World Bank, 1994a).

2. On property rights and growth, see Knack and Keefer (1995). On corruption and growth, see Mauro (1995). Recent papers that seek to unravel the causal effects of governance on per capita incomes include Acemoglu, Johnston, and Robinson (2000), Hall and Jones (1999) and Kaufmann, Kraay, and Zoido-Lobatón (1999).

3. See Bruno and Easterly (1998) and Barro (1997) on inflation and growth and Easterly and Rebelo (1993) on budget deficits and growth. See Frankel and Romer (1999) on the evidence on openness and growth; Dollar and Kraay (2000) for a discussion of the links between trade policy and growth; and Srinivasan and Bhagwati (1999) for a review of the methodological issues.

4. See Easterly and Fischer (2000), Tanzi and Davoodi (1998), and Dollar and Kraay (2000) for evidence on the distributional effects of inflation and corruption.

5. See, for example, Olson (2000) and North and Weingast (1989).

6. See Alesina and others (1999) and Stein, Talvi and Grisanti (1999). These authors also emphasize the importance of having a meaningful budget process that is enforced over the course of the fiscal year. See also Eichengreen, Hausmann, and von Hagen (1999) for a proposal for specific reforms to fiscal institutions in Latin America to help ensure fiscal discipline.

7. Campos and Pradhan 1996.

8. Alesina and others 1999.

9. Bohn and Inman 1996. There is also evidence from U.S. states that rules that seek to ensure fiscal discipline by placing constitutional limits on spending lead to lower public sector borrowing costs, while those that limit taxation lead to higher borrowing costs (Poterba and Reuben 1999). A recent survey of the empirical evidence on the effects of budget rules on fiscal outcomes focusing on the evidence from U.S. states can be found in Poterba (1997).

10. Persson and Tabellini 2000.

11. Shi and Svensson 2000.

12. Keefer 2001.

13. Keefer and Stasavage 2000.

14. The leading theoretical model in this area is developed in Grossman and Helpman (1994). Goldberg and Maggi (1999) and Gawande and Bandyopadhyay (2000) provide empirical evidence in support of the specific predictions of the model, relating patterns of protection to the political strength of protected sectors.

15. Lee and Swagel 1997; Goldberg and Maggi 1999.

16. Grether, de Melo, and Olarreaga (forthcoming).

17. Mansfield and Busch (1995) provide evidence that the incidence of nontariff barriers is higher in countries with larger numbers of parliamentary constituencies. Mansfield and others (2000) provide evidence that, controlling for the geographical determinants of trade, pairs of countries that are democracies are significantly more likely to trade with each other. Banerji and Ghanem (1997) find that, controlling for a variety of other factors, distortions in international trade tend to be higher in more autocratic countries where accountability is lower.

18. An extensive discussion and formal theoretical models of these functions can be found in Bagwell and Staiger (1999, 2000). These authors also note a third function of more theo-

retical interest: that the WTO can help in correcting the market failures that arise when domestic trade policies have adverse effects on welfare in other countries, along the lines of competitive tariff setting in a model of optimal tariffs. Hoekman and Kostecki (1999) provide a detailed description of the institutional structure of the GATT/WTO.

19. Staiger and Tabellini (1999) show that under the 1974–79 Tokyo Round GATT negotiations, exemptions to agreed-upon across-the-board tariff cuts were more likely to occur in sectors that would require the most adjustment in the face of greater import competition. This is the opposite of what one would expect if governments have difficulty in committing to trade liberalization.

20. Mauro 1995; Kaufmann, Kraay, and Zoido-Lobatón 1999.

21. Shleifer and Vishny 1993.

22. Wei 2000a, 2000b, 2000c.

23. Fisman and Svensson 2000.

24. World Bank 2000a.

25. Tanzi and Davoodi 2001.

26. Mauro 1997; Gupta, Davoodi, and Tiongson 2001.

27. Friedman and others 2000.

28. See Hellman, Jones, and Kaufmann (2000), World Bank (2000a), and EBRD (2000).

29. Wei 2000c; Treisman 2000; Ades and di Tella 1999. Knack and Azfar (2000) criticize the Wei (2000c) findings on the grounds that there are a number of small open countries that are not included in many cross-country measures of corruption where corruption is high, and the inclusion of these countries into the sample undoes the Wei results. However, Islam and Montenegro (2001) find evidence of a relationship between openness and corruption in a sample that is larger than Wei (2000c) but slightly smaller than Knack and Azfar (2000).

30. Gatti (2001) provides evidence that the dispersion of tariffs across products is positively related to corruption in the small sample of countries for which tariff dispersion data are available. Islam and Montenegro (2001) provide evidence from a large sample of industrial and developing countries.that higher average tariffs are associated with higher corruption, after controlling for a variety of factors.

31. Djankov and others (forthcoming).

32. See also Kaufmann and Wei (1999) and Svensson (1999) for more systematic evidence.

33. Van Rijckeghem and Weder (1997) find evidence of a negative effect of wages on perceptions of corruption. However, Rauch and Evans (2000), Tresiman (2000), and Swamy and others (2001) do not.

34. See World Bank (2000a) for a detailed discussion of differing policy options for countries with differing degrees of petty and grand corruption.

35. Di Tella and Shargrodsky 2000.

36. Fisman and Gatti (forthcoming) find that a greater share of subnational government spending in total spending is significantly associated with lower perceptions of corruption. They also show that the earlier Treisman (2000) finding that federal states appear to have higher corruption is driven by that paper's omission of population as an explanatory variable. Populous countries are more likely to be federal states, and in the sample

of countries studied by both authors, populous countries also tend to be perceived to be more corrupt.

37. Azfar, Kahkonen, and Meagher 2001.

38. Persson, Tabellini, and Trebbi 2000. Rose-Ackerman (2001) provides a detailed theoretical discussion of how differences in the structure of democratic institutions may influence the incentives for politicians to engage in corrupt practices.

39. Djankov, McLiesh, Nenova, and Shleifer 2001.

40. Azfar, Kahkonen, and Meagher 2001.

41. Khemani 2001

42. A summary of the Campo Elias project can be found in Gonzalez de Asis (2000).

43. Baack and Ray 2000.

44. Das-Gupta and Mookherjee (1998) cite 15 countries that have established autonomous revenue agencies.

45. Andreoni and others (1998) review the limited experimental evidence on the effects of perceived "fairness" on tax compliance. Taliercio (2000a) provides evidence of the partial association between perceptions of the fairness of the tax administration and perceptions of the extent to which the revenue agency is perceived as autonomous, using firm-level survey data from four Latin American countries.

46. This discussion is based on Taliercio (2000b, 2001).

47. IMF Government Finance Statistics, various issues. Figures on state government shares in total government expenditure refer to budgetary central government accounts.

48. Hemming, Mates, and Potter 1997.

49. Shleifer and Treisman 2000.

50. Zhuravskaya 2000.

51. Other provinces were able to keep revenue growth in excess of a pre-set target. See Ma (1997) for details. Wong (1997) provides details on sub-provincial arrangements.

52. Jin, Qian, and Weingast 1991.

53. Young (2000) provides a detailed study of this pattern of local protection in China and its consequences for distorted industrial development.

54. Shleifer and Treisman (2000, chapter 6).

55. This point is also developed in Blanchard and Shleifer (2000).

56. Huang 1996a, 2001. See also Huang (1996b) for a much more detailed study of this phenomenon and a discussion of its implications for inflation control in China.

Chapter 6

1. Pie 2001, p. 4.

2. Grote 1999. Before the 1930s the dominant view of European legal scholars, for example, was that it was not the content of the law but procedural regularity that mattered for fairness. The enforcement of anti-Semitic laws by the courts of the Third Reich in Germany changed this view.

3. Foley 2000.

4. Guiso, Sapienza, and Zingales (2000) on Italy; Hendley and others (1997) on Russia; Johnson, McMillan, and Woodruff (2000) on Romania and Slovakia; McMillan and Woodruff (1999a, 1999b) on Vietnam.

5. Claessens, Djankov, and Klapper 2001.

6. Banerjee and Duflo 2000.

7. Dakolias 1996.

8. Contini 2000; Buscaglia and Dakolias 1996, respectively.

9. Lex Mundi, Harvard University, and the World Bank 2001.

10. Garavano and others 2000.

11. Tyler, Huo, and Lind 1999.

12. The discussion in this section draws upon Botero and others (2001).

13. Center for Public Resource Management 2000.

14. Church 1978; Neubauer and others 1981; Dakolias 1996.

15. Dakolias and Said 1999; Hendrix 2000.

16. Neubauer and others 1981.

17. Posner 1995.

18. New York State Committee 1997.

19. Hudes 2001.

20. See Bermudes (1999, p. 347), who argues that the introduction of small claims courts in Brazil in 1995 "succeeded in bringing justice closer to the Brazilian people [by allowing them to] litigate at a very low cost, in an informal manner, and see immediate results for their judicial initiative."

21. Hendrix 2000.

22. Some claim that the introduction of specialized courts may create boundary problems, as wasteful litigation can arise whether a case belongs in a specialized court or the regular courts. This feature, however, is of secondary importance and does not obviate the positive impact of such courts in recent reform efforts.

23. Blankenburg 1999; Dakolias 1996; Brandt 1995; Hendrix 2000; Hendley, Murrell, and Ryterman 2000, 2001, respectively.

24. Church 1978.

25. Kakalik 1997.

26. Varano 1997.

27. Véscovi 1996.

28. Dakolias 1996, Tarigo 1995, and Véscovi 1996; Weill 1961; and Varano 1997, respectively.

29. For the United Kingdom, see Baldwin (1997). For Peru, see Brandt (1995).

30. Tarigo 1995.

31. Murrell 2001.

32. De Soto 2000.

33. Varela and Mayani 2000.

34. Buscaglia and Ulen 1997. But see Buscaglia and Dakolias (1996), where "resources allocated for court personnel" emerged as an important factor, and Church (1978).

35. Dakolias 1996.

36. Buscaglia and Ulen 1997.

37. Malcolm 2000.

38. La Porta, Lopez-de-Silanes, and Shleifer 2001.

39. La Porta, Lopez-de-Silanes, and Shleifer 2001.

Chapter 7

1. Nickell 1997. For a theoretical treatment, see Aghion and others (1999).

2. Nickell 1997.

3. This is taken from Stigler (1987).

4. A theoretical treatment of how competition can raise productive or technical efficiency by raising managerial effort can be found in Vickers (1995) and Nickell (1996). Theoretical treatment of the relationship between competition and innovation was pioneered by Schumpeter in *Capitalism, Socialism, and Democracy* in 1942; see Scherer (1992). Theoretical developments since Schumpeter were summarized in Scherer (1992) for the 1950s to the 1980s and in Van Cayseele (1998) for the period after the late 1970s.

5. Easterly and Levine 2000. Easterly and Levine suggest, based on stylized facts of economic growth around the world, that factor accumulation does not account for cross-country differences in the level or growth rate of GDP per capita. Rather, it is total factor productivity (TFP)—the residual in growth accounting—that accounts for a substantial amount of these differences. TFP has been variously modeled, depending on the theory, as changes in technology, or externalities (including spillovers), or changes in the sector composition of production, or adoption of lower-cost production methods.

6. Baily and Gersbach 1995; Djankov and Murrell forthcoming; Geroski 1990; Nickell 1996, 1997; Porter 1990; Porter and Sakakibara forthcoming.

7. Tybout 1996.

8. Hahn 2000.

9. Various theories have been posited to explain this nonmonotonic relationship between competition and managerial effort. For instance, Torii (1992) posited that when the number of firms in the market is relatively small, the efficiency level increases as the number of firms increases; this is due mainly to competition forcing firms to produce more efficiently. However, when the number of firms is relatively large, the opposite is true: the efficiency level decreases as the number of firms increases. This is due to indivisible replacement investment (or lumpy assets), which means that as the replacement costs of investments go up, firms are more reluctant to replace plants, and technical efficiency decreases. A theory posited by Schmidt (1996a) suggested that as the number of competitors increases to three or more, it becomes less likely that one or more of them will become a monopolist, with the consequence that efforts to raise efficiency go down as the gain from such efforts to reduce costs goes down.

10. Caves 1992.

11. The enterprise survey was conducted in 1999 jointly by the World Bank and the EBRD and covered approximately 125 firms in each of 20 transition countries, except for Poland and Ukraine (over 200 firms) and Russia (over 500 firms). The sample is dominated by small and medium-size enterprises. The econometric study was done by Carlin and others (1999). The provisional findings of the study and the survey have been published in EBRD (1999).

12. Bresnahan and Reiss 1991.

13. Soft budget constraints and preferential treatment of state-owned firms are other major constraints on competition in developing countries.

14. As pointed out in Rodrik (2000).

15. The concept of "exit barriers as entry barriers" has been formalized by Caves and Porter (1976) and Eaton and Lipsey (1981), among others.

16. A statistical correlation of 0.73 was found between restrictive regulatory environments in the product market and re-

strictive employment protection policies in OECD countries; see OECD (2000b).

17. See Stewart (1990) for a study on the United Kingdom and Duca (1998) for a study on the United States.

18. Baily and others 1998.

19. De Soto (1990) did pioneering work in this area.

20. Djankov and others 2000.

21. Hoekman and others (2001), based on entry regulation data from Djankov and others (2000).

22. See Schneider and Enste (2000) for a review of the literature on this issue. Johnson, Kaufmann, and Zoido-Lobaton (1998) find evidence that general economic regulations raise the size of the informal economy for 49 countries in Latin America, the OECD, and the former Soviet Union. Loayza (1997) finds evidence that labor market restrictions raise the size of the informal economy for 14 Latin American countries.

23. Schneider and Enste 2000.

24. The discussion in this paragraph is taken from Graham and Richardson (1997).

25. Graham and Richardson 1997, p. 342.

26. This index is based on the responses of 3,678 executives to the survey question on the degree to which "competition laws prevent unfair competition in your country."

27. Guash and Rajapatirana (1998, p. 19).

28. See, for instance, Dixit (1988); Harrison (1994, 1996); Krishna and Mitra (1998); Roberts and Tybout (1996); Tybout, de Melo, and Corbo (1991); and Tybout and Westbrook (1995).

29. Baily and Gersbach 1995.

30. Hoekman and others 2001.

31. For empirical evidence see, for instance, Edwards (1997); Frankel and Romer (1999); Harrison and Hanson (1999); and Sachs and Warner (1995).

32. See for example, Dollar and Kraay (2000) and Ravallion (2000).

33. World Bank 2000e.

34. World Bank (2000e) also discusses the benefits and other effects of trade liberalization, such as "agglomerations"—the concentration of business activities in a few locations—which can raise productivity.

35. Antidumping is allowed by GATT to be used unilaterally by countries for temporary import protection. GATT/WTO rules allow the imposition of antidumping duties when there is both dumping (when the export price of a good is below the exporter's home market price, or below the export price in a third market, or below the cost of production in the exporting country) and material injury (such as output reductions leading to job losses).

36. The discussion in this section is drawn largely from Wilson (2001).

37. For a detailed treatment of this issue, see World Bank (2000h).

38. Hoekman and Messerlin 1999.

39. The benefits of liberalization of services are also discussed in World Bank (2000h).

40. World Bank (2000c). Welfare here is measured as the sum of net efficiency gains to consumers from lower prices; gains from removing the resource waste that is derived from reg-

ulations; and gains from having services provided by efficient foreign firms rather than higher-cost domestic firms.

41. Konan and Maskus 1999.

42. The majority of IPR research focuses on patents, as does this section.

43. Mansfield 1986.

44. Braga and others 2000, UNDP 1999.

45. World Bank (1999h) has a detailed discussion of the empirical evidence.

46. Maskus and Penubarti (1995) and Smith (2000).

47. Maskus 2000.

48. Maskus 2000.

49. Compiled from U.S. Trade Representative list of trade agreements, 1998.

Chapter 8

1. Although some institutions offer insurance or a guarantee for these types of risk, the cost of the guarantee may be so high as to dissuade investment.

2. This situation might arise, for example, in countries where poverty levels are very high and user prices cannot be structured so as to make services accessible to many, or where political risks are very high and insurance against these risks is either unavailable or too expensive.

3. One interpretation is that the most important factor here is the placement of both residual control rights and residual cash flow rights in the hands of private shareholders (Boycko, Shleifer, and Vishny 1992, 1993; Sappington and Stiglitz 1987; Shapiro and Willig 1990). Another is that privatization is a way for the government to credibly deny itself the private information concerning enterprise costs that would be necessary for easy intervention and subsidization (Schmidt 1996b; Shirley and Walsh 2000).

4. Shirley and Walsh 2000.

5. Bradburd 1992.

6. Noll (1999, p. 31) notes also that "regulatory agencies are likely to exhibit significant economies of scale. . . . Thus, the cost of regulation is higher in relation to the welfare at stake in the regulatory process in a small developing country."

7. U.S. Department of Justice 1986; Untiet 1987.

8. "International Energy Outlook 1999—Natural Gas," U.S. Department of Energy, Energy Information Administration; Quirno, "Latin America in the Pipeline," Worldlink, March 17, 2000.

9. Briceno 2001.

10. Noll (1999) argues that the development of cellular and wireless technologies has rendered local telephony, long considered the natural monopoly bottleneck of the telephony sector, no longer subject to natural monopoly cost conditions.

11. Brennan 1987, 1995.

12. U.S. Federal Energy Regulatory Commission 1999.

13. OECD 2001.

14. Pittman 1999. Newbery (1994) believes that long-distance transmission costs in the United Kingdom may be closer to 10 percent of total costs.

15. Klein and Irwin 1996.

16. According to Kessides and Willig (2001, p. 5), "Separation is likely to be a particularly attractive option when

market size would permit many entities to function in the final products market and to provide both active and potential competition to each other."

17. Spiller and Cardilli (1997, p. 128) conclude: "Once the right to interconnect is assured, local telecommunications do not constitute a natural monopoly as classically defined."

18. Spiller and Cardilli 1997; Wellenius 1997.

19. Spiller and Cardilli 1997.

20. Armstrong and Vickers 1996; EBRD 1996.

21. Klein and Irwin 1996.

22. Garcia de Alba 2000; Pittman 2000.

23. Stern and Davis (1998, p. 453) note that concerns such as these "must be greater in countries with little regulatory experience—including the CEE [Central and Eastern European] economies. Clearly, collecting, monitoring and enforcing the conditions of the [EU electricity liberalization] Directive on powerful, integrated incumbent utilities is unlikely to be a straightforward or undemanding task."

24. See *World Development Report 1994* for a discussion on the possibility of vertical separation for different infrastructure sectors.

25. Guasch 2000, chap. 11.

26. Kerf and Garadin 2000, pp. 27–77.

27. Brook and others 2001.

28. Estache, Romero, and Strong 2000, p. 21.

29. Aubert and Laffont 2000.

30. Newbery 2000.

31. For example, it is common for infrastructure enterprises to fall back on technical, environmental, or safety factors when arguing for changes in economic regulations.

32. For Chile, see Kerf 2000; for Angola and the Philippines, see Brook 1997.

33. Estache 1997.

34. Ordover, Pittman, and Clyde 1994.

35. Since the Latin America region has been at the forefront of infrastructure reforms, it is also the only region for which a relatively systematic analysis of the impact of such reforms is available.

36. Estache, Gómez-Lobo, and Leipziger 2000.

37. Komives and Brook Cowen 1999, cited in Brook and others 2001.

38. Estache, Gómez-Lobo, and Leipziger 2000.

39. Baker and Tremolet (2000c) suggest that governments either allow lower-quality service provision by alternative suppliers or, where feasible, permit the main supplier to offer a menu of service categories differentiated by quality and price. Brook and others (2001, p. 19) argue that "minimal standards tied to essential health and safety concerns may be appropriate in areas not served by traditional utilities, with progressively higher standards applied to more affluent customers with access to network services."

40. Baker and Tremolet 2000a.

41. Komives and Brook Cowen 1999, cited in Brook and others 2001.

42. Solo and Snell 1998, cited in Brook and others 2001.

43. Thompson 2001.

44. Ehrhardt and Burdon 1999, cited in Brook and others 2001.

45. Baker and Tremolet 2000b, cited in Brook and others 2001.

46. Brooke and others 2001.

47. Estache, Foster, and Wodon 2000, p. 39.

48. Lovei and others 2000.

49. Estache, Romero, and Strong 2000, pp. 29, 39.

50. Armstrong and Rees 2000.

51. Brook and others 2001.

Chapter 9

1. Light 1972; Acheson 1994; Fukuyama 1995, respectively.

2. Fehr and Gächter (2000, p. 166) define a social norm as "(1) a behavioral regularity; that is (2) based on a socially shared belief of how one ought to behave; which triggers 3) the enforcement of the prescribed behavior by informal social sanctions."

3. See, for example, Alm, Jackson, and McKee (1993); Alm, McClelland, and William Schulze (1999); and Erard and Feinstein 1994.

4. This discussion is similar in spirit to that in Manski (2000), which distinguishes among endogenous, contextual, and correlated interactions between an individual and the group.

5. See, for example, Levin and Satarov (2000).

6. This point is partially captured by the increased literature on *social capital*, discussed, for example in the *World Development Report 2000/2001*, chapter 7.

7. The importance of these networks becomes most obvious when "work-to-rule" practices are observed as a form of worker protest.

8. For a theoretical model, see Prescott and Townsend (1999).

9. Fafchamps 1996. Fukuyama (1995) examines the issue of trust in an economywide context.

10. Moore 1999.

11. Chamlee-Wright (1998) argues that West African women have a distinct culture separate from the men, which serves as the trust mechanism. Burger, Collier, and Gunning (1996) find that male- and female-headed households in Kenya adopt innovations only from households headed by the same sex.

12. Hayami and Kawagoe 1993

13. Greif (1994, 1997b) defines informal enforcement as self-enforcing when it is known that the interacting individuals will take the actions that they were expected to assume, despite the lack of formal contract enforcement mechanisms.

14. Greif (1997b) discusses enforcement by a "first party" (individual), "second party" (business partner), and "third party" (outside mediator or state).

15. Fafchamps and Minten 2000.

16. Isa 1995.

17. Ensminger 1994.

18. Shipton 1994.

19. Fukuyama 1995.

20. Gambetta 1993.

21. Platteau 2000.

22. Platteau 2000.

23. Fafchamps 1996.

24. Drijver and Van Zorge 1995, cited in Platteau 2000.

25. Melard, Platteau, and Wotongoka 1998, cited in Platteau 2000.

26. Another example is the waning influence of caste in determining economic groupings and transactions in urban India. It is also less relevant in the upper economic strata of society than in the poorer groups—particularly because those in the upper strata have greater access to formal institutions and the formation of community and relationship across caste lines. It has been argued that this is especially so in larger Indian cities, where residential groupings correspond more to occupation and incomes, and not to caste (Beteille 1997).

27. For instance, when the U.S. labor market tightened during World War II, the Philadelphia rapid transit system tried to hire blacks. It was, prevented from doing so, however, by a successful strike by the white transit workers (Arrow 1998).

28. Darity and Mason 1998.

29. In the absence of such bridging mechanisms, ethnic diversity may be correlated with undesirable outcomes; for example, a study of sub-Saharan Africa found that high ethnic fragmentation explained a significant part of most of the factors that slow economic growth (Easterly and Levine 1997).

30. Banerjee, Besley, and Guinnane 1994.

31. Hayami and Kawagoe 1993.

Chapter 10

1. Newspapers appeared in Switzerland (1610), the Netherlands (1616), England (1621), France (1631), Italy (1636), and Poland (1661).

2. Shepherd and Schalke 1995.

3. Galda and Searle 1980.

4. Chaudhury and Hammer 2001; Thomas, Strauss, and Henriques 1991.

5. Byram, Kaute, and Matenge 1980.

6. Djankov, McLiesh, and others 2001; Stapenhurst 2000.

7. Demsetz and Lehn 1985.

8. Djankov, McLiesh, and others 2001.

9. Coase 1959.

10. This is according to the private station's management.

11. Stapenhurst 2000.

12. Nelson 1999a.

13. Nine members of the 29-member board are appointed by the federal government, 6 members are appointed by political parties, each of the 9 federal states appoints a member, the Council of Viewers and Listeners appoints 6 members, and the employees appoint 5 representatives.

14. The autonomy of privately owned media can also be eroded through, for example, restrictive media regulations or financing arrangements. This is discussed in the following sections.

15. Heo, Uhm, and Chang 2000; Webster 1992.

16. Inter-American Press Association Press Laws Database: www.sipiapa.org

17. Harcourt and Verhulst 1998.

18. Walden 2000.

19. Conversely, an effective libel system can reduce harassment by encouraging resolution of disputes through the courts rather than through intimidation and crime.

20. Article 19, International Center against Censorship 1993; Walden 2000.

21. Walden 2000.

22. Harcourt and Verhulst 1998.

23. Commissioner of the Council of Baltic Sea States Survey of Media, May 2000.

24. McKinsey & Company 1999.

25. State monopolies are defined as cases where the market share of state-controlled media exceeds 75 percent.

26. Harcourt 1998.

27. Harcourt and Verhulst 1998.

28. Philippine Center for Investigative Journalists and South East Asian Press Alliance, in Chongkittavorn 2001.

29. Calculated from Banisar 2000.

30. World Bank 2001b.

31. Stapenhurst 2000.

32. Besley and Burgess 2000.

33. Article 19, International Center against Censorship 1993.

34. Nelson 1999b.

Background Papers

Armstrong, Mark, and Ray Rees. "Pricing Policies in the Infrastructure Sectors."

Aubert, Cecile, and Jean-Jacques Laffont. "Multiregulation in Developing Countries."

Banerji, Arup. "Which Countries Can Afford Poverty-Eliminating Transfers? A Notional Framework for Policymakers."

Bernstein, Lisa. "The Potential Role of Private Legal Systems in the Revival of the of Trade in Transition Economies."

Besley, Timothy J, Sanjay Jain, and Charalambos Tsangarides. "Household Participation in Formal and Informal Institutions in Rural Credit Markets in Developing Countries."

Bonin, John, and István Abel. "Retail Banking in Hungary: A Foreign Affair?"

Botero, Juan, Florencio Lopez-de-Silanes, Rafael La Porta, Andrei Shleifer, and Aleksandr Volokh. "Judicial Reform."

Briceno Garmendia, Cecilia. "General Behavior of Electricity End-User Prices."

Brook, Penelope, Warrick Smith, Nicola Tynan, and Timothy Irwin. "Improving Access to Infrastructure Services by Low-Income Households: Institutional and Policy Responses."

Carlin, Wendy, and Paul Seabright. "The Importance of Competition in Developing Countries for Productivity and Innovation."

Chaudhury, Nazmul, and Arup Banerji. "Agricultural Marketing Institutions."

Deininger, Klaus. "Land Policy and Its Impact on Competition and Functioning of Factor Markets: Conceptual Issues and Empirical Evidence."

Demirgüc-Kunt, Asli and Vojislav Maksimovic. "Firms as Financial Intermediaries: Evidence from Trade Credit Data."

Djankov, Simeon, Rafael La Porta, Florencio Lopez-de-Silanes, and Andrei Shleifer. "Regulation of Entry."

Djankov, Simeon, Caralee McLiesh, Tatiana Nenova, and Andrei Shleifer. "Who Owns the Media?"

Finnegan, David. "The Creation and Operation of the Tanzania's Commercial Court."

Fleisig, Heywood, and Nuria de la Pena. "Design of Collateral Law and Institutions: Their Impact on Credit Allocation and Growth in Developing Economies."

Guasch, Jorge Luis, Anastassia V. Kartacheva, and Lucia Quesada. "Concessions Contracts Renegotiations in Latin America and Caribbean Region: An Economic Analysis and Empirical Evidence."

Hegarty, John. "World Development Report 2002 Background Note on Accounting Reforms."

Hoekman, Bernard, Hiau Looi Kee, and Marcelo Olarreaga. "Markups, Entry Regulation and Trade: Does Country Size Matter?"

Hudes, Karen. "Holding Courts Accountable."

Islam, Roumeen, and Claudio E. Montenegro. "The Determinants of the Quality of Institutions: A Study in a Cross Section of Countries."

Keinan, Yoram. "The Evolution of Secured Transactions."

Kessides, Ioannis, and Robert Willig. 2001. "Network Access Pricing Rules for Developing and Transition Economies."

Klapper, Leora. "Bankruptcy around the World: Explanations of its Relative Use."

La Porta, Rafael, Florencio Lopez-de-Silanes, and Andrei Shleifer. "Guarantees of Freedom."

Lerman, Zvi. "Comparative Institutional Evolution: Rural Land Reform in the ECA Region."

Levenstein, Margaret, and Valerie Suslow. "Private International Cartels and Their Effect on Developing Countries."

Lex Mundi, Harvard University, and The World Bank. "Judicial Project."

McLiesh, Caralee. "Technology and Innovation in Agriculture."

McLiesh, Caralee, and Keith Maskus. "Competition, Innovation and Intellectual Property Rights in Developing Countries: A Review."

Messick, Richard E. "The Origins and Development of Courts."

Olegario, Rowena. "Credit-Reporting Agencies: Their Historical Roots, Current Status, and Role in Market Development."

Pistor, Katharina, Yoram Keinan, Jan Kleinheisterkam, and Mark West. "The Evolution of Corporate Law."

Pittman, Russell. "Vertical Restructuring of the Infrastructure Sectors of Transition Economies."

Prosterman, Roy, Brian Schwarzwalder, and Tim Hanstad. "Reforming China's Rural Land System."

Rajan, Raghuram G., and Luigi Zingales. "The Great Reversals: The Politics of Financial Development in the 20th Century."

Soludo, Charles. "Comparative Institutional Development: Lessons from Rural Land Markets in Africa."

Wilson, John S. "Standards, Regulation, and Trade: Recommendations for Reforms from a Development Perspective."

References

The word *processed* describes informally reproduced works that may not be commonly available through libraries.

Ablo, Emmanuel, and Ritva Reinikka. 1998. "Do Budgets Really Matter?: Evidence for Public Spending on Education and Health in Uganda." Policy Research Working Paper No. 1926. World Bank, Washington, D.C.

Acemoglu, Daron, Simon Johnson, and James A. Robinson. 2000. "The Colonial Origins of Comparative Development: An Empirical Investigation." National Bureau of Economic Research, Working Paper No. 7771. Cambridge, Massachusetts. Available on-line at http://www.nber.org/papers/w7771.

Acheson, James. 1994. "Transactions Cost and Business Strategies in a Mexican Indian Pueblo." in James M. Acheson (ed.) *Anthropology and Institutional Economics*. Lanham, Maryland: University Press of America.

Adams, Dale W. 1995. "From Agricultural Credit to Rural Finance." *Quarterly Journal of International Agriculture* 34(2): 109–120.

Adegbite, Mudasiru Aderemi. 1997. "The Credit Delivery Methods in the Rural Areas of the Nigerian Economy and Implications for Labour Productivity and Human Welfare (1970–1995)." Paper presented at the Tenth World Productivity Congress, World Confederation of Productivity Science, School of Industrial Engineering, Universidad Del Mar. Santiago de, Chile.

Ades, Alberto, and Rafael di Tella. 1999. "Rents, Competition, and Corruption." *American Economic Review* 89(4): 982–993.

Aghion, Philippe, Mathias Dewatripont, and Patrick Rey. 1999. "Competition, Financial Discipline and Growth." *Review of Economic Studies* 66(4):825–852.

Alesina, Alberto, Reza Baqir, and William Easterly. 1999. "Public Goods and Ethnic Divisions." *Quarterly Journal of Economics* 114(4):1243–84.

Alesina, Alberto, Roberto Perotti, and José Tavares. 1998. "The Political Economy of Fiscal Adjustments." *Brookings Papers on Economic Activity* 1:197–266.

Alesina, Alberto, Ricardo Hausmann, Rudolf Hommes, and Ernesto Stein. 1999. "Budget Institutions and Fiscal Performance in Latin America." *Journal of Development Economics* 59(2):253–73.

Alm, James, Betty R. Jackson, and Michael McKee. 1993. "Fiscal Exchange, Collective Decision Institutions, and Tax Compliance." *Journal of Economic Behavior and Organization* 22: 285–303.

Alm, James, Gary McClelland, and William Schulze. 1999. "Changing the Social Norm of Tax Compliance by Voting." *Kyklos* 52(2):141–171.

Alston, Julian, Philip Pardey, and Johannes Roseboom. 1998. "Financing Agricultural Research: International Investment Patterns and Policy Perspectives." *World Development* 26(6):1057–71.

Alston, Julian, Connie Chan-Kang, Michele C. Marra, Philip G. Pardey, and T. J. Wyatt. 2000. *A Meta-Analysis of Rates of Return to Agricultural R&D*. IFPRI Research Report 113. International Food Policy Research Institute. Washington, D.C.

Alston, Lee, Gary Libecap, and Robert Schneider. 1995. "Property Rights and The Preconditions For Markets: The Case of the Amazon Frontier." *Journal of Institutional and Theoretical Economics* 151(1):89–111.

———. 1996. "The Determinants And Impact of Property Rights: Land Titles on the Brazilian Frontier." *Journal of Law, Economics and Organization* 12(1):25–61.

Anderson, M., and M. W. Rosenberg. 1990. "Ontario's Underserviced Area Program Revisited: An Indirect Analysis." *Social Science and Medicine* 30(1):35–44.

Andre, Catherine, and Jean-Paul Platteau. 1998. "Land Relations under Unbearable Stress: Rwanda Caught in the Malthusian Trap." *Journal of Economic Behavior and Organization* 34(1): 1–47.

Andreoni, James, Brian Erard, and Jonathan Feinstein. 1998. "Tax Compliance." *Journal of Economic Literature* 36(2): 818–860.

Armstrong, Mark, and John Vickers. 1996. "Regulatory Reform in Telecommunications in Central and Eastern Europe." *Economics of Transition* 4:295–318.

Arrow, Kenneth. 1998. "What Has Economics to Say About Racial Discrimination?" *Journal of Economic Perspectives* 12(2):91–100.

Article 19, International Centre against Censorship. 1993. *Press Law and Practice: A Comparative Study of Press Freedom in European and other Democracies,* Report published by Article 19 for the United Nations Educational, Scientific, and Cultural Organization, London.

Austin, Gareth. 1993. "Indigenous Credit Institutions in West Africa, 1750–1960." in Austin Gareth and Kaoru Sugihara (eds.) *Indigenous Credit Institutions in West Africa*, New York: St. Martin's Press.

Austin, Gareth, and Kaoru Sugihara, eds. 1993. *Local Suppliers of Credit in the Third World*, 1750–1960. New York: St. Martin's Press.

Azfar, Omar, Satu Kahkonen, and Patrick Meagher. 2001. "Conditions for Effective Decentralized Governance: A Synthesis of Research Findings." University of Maryland. Processed.

Baack, B. D., and E. J. Ray. 1983. "The Political Economy of Tariff Policy: A Case Study of the United States." *Explorations in Economic History* 20:73–93.

Bagehot, Walter. 1873. *Lombard Street*. Homewood, IL: Richard D. Irwin, (1873) 1962 Edition.

Bagwell, Kyle, and Robert W. Staiger. 1999. "An Economic Theory of GATT." *American Economic Review* 89(1): 215–248.

———. 2000. "GATT-Think." National Bureau of Economic Research Working Paper No. 8005. Cambridge, Massachusetts.

Baily, Martin Neil, and Hans Gersbach. 1995. "Efficiency in Manufacturing and the Need for Global Competition." *Brookings Papers on Economic Activity* Microeconomics 1995: 307–47.

Baily, Martin Neil, Eric Zitzewitz, Barry Bosworth, and Larry E. Westphal. 1998. "Extending the East Asia Miracle: Microeconomic Evidence from Korea." *Brookings Papers on Economic Activity.* Microeconomics 1998: 249–73.

Baker, W., and S. Tremolet. 2000a. "Micro Infrastructure: Regulators Must Take Small Operators Seriously." World Bank Private Sector Note 220, October 2000. World Bank, Washington, D.C. Available on-line at: www.worldbank.org/html/fpd/notes.

———. 2000b. "Regulation of Quality of Infrastructure Services in Developing Countries." Paper presented at conference, "Infrastructure for Development: Private Solutions and the Poor," PPIAF, DFID, and World Bank, London.

———. 2000c. "Utility Reform: Regulating Quality Standards to Improve Access for the Poor." World Bank Private Sector Note 219 October 2000. World Bank, Washington, D.C. Available on-line at: www.worldbank.org/html/fpd/notes.

Baldwin, John. 1997. "Monitoring the Rise of the Small Claims Limit: Litigants' Experiences of Different Forms of Adjudication." Lord Chancellor's Department, Research Secretariat. London, United Kingdom.

Banerjee, Abhijit, Timothy Besley, and Timothy Guinnane. 1994. "Thy Neighbor's Keeper: The Design of a Credit Cooperative with Theory and a Test." *Quarterly Journal of Economics* 109(2): 491–515.

Banerjee, Abhijit, and Esther Duflo. 2000. "Reputation Effects and the Limits to Contracting: A Study of the Indian Software Industry." *Quarterly Journal of Economics* 115(3): 989–1019.

Banerji, Arup. 1995. "Workers in the 'Informal Sector' in Developing Countries." World Development Report 1995/6 Background Paper. World Bank, Washington, D.C.

———. 2001. "Which Countries Can Afford Poverty-Eliminating Transfers? A Notional Framework for Policymakers." World Development Report 2002 Background Paper, World Bank, Washington, DC.

Banerji, Arup, and Hafez Ghanem. 1997. "Does the Type of Political Regime Matter for Trade and Labour Market Policies?." *World Bank Economic Review* 11(1):171–194.

Banisar, David. 2000. "Freedom of Information around the World." Privacy International. Available on-line at http://www.privacyinternational.org/issues/foia/foia-survey.html.

Barajas, Adolfo, Natalia Salazar, and Roberto Steiner. 2000. "Foreign Investment in Colombia's Financial Sector," in S. Claessens and M. Jansen (eds.) *The Internationalization of Financial Services: Issues and Lessons for Developing Countries.* Boston, MA: Kluwer Academic Press.

Barnett, Barry J., and Keith H. Coble. 1999. "Understanding Uneven Agricultural Liberalization in Madagascar." *Journal of Modern African Studies* 32:449–76.

Barro, Robert. 1997. *Determinants of Economic Growth: A Cross-Country Empirical Study.* Cambridge: MIT Press.

Barron, John M., and Michael Staten. 2000. "The Value of Comprehensive Credit Reports: Lessons from the U.S. Experience." World Bank. Processed.

Barth, James, Gerard Caprio, and Ross Levine. 2000. "Prudential Regulation and Supervision: What Works and What Doesn't." World Bank. Processed.

———. Forthcoming. "Banking Systems Around the Globe: Do Regulation and Ownership Affect Performance and Stability?"

Forthcoming in Mishkin, Frederic (ed.) *Prudential Regulation and Supervision: What Works and What Doesn't.* National Bureau of Economic Research, Cambridge, Massachusetts.

Beaumol, William J., John C. Panzar, and Robert D. Willig, with contributions by Elizabeth E. Bailey, Dietrich Fischer and Herman C. Quirmbach. 1982. *Contestable Markets and the Theory of Industry Structure.* New York: Harcourt Brace Jovanovich.

Bebchuk, Lucian. 1999. "A Rent-Protection Theory of Corporate Ownership and Control" National Bureau of Economic Research Working Paper No. 7203. Cambridge, Massachusetts.

Beck, Thorsten; Asli Demirgüç-Kunt, and Ross Levine. 2000a. "A New Database on Financial Development and Structure." *World Bank Economic Review* 14(3):597–605.

———. 2000b. "Law, Politics, and Finance." World Bank. Processed.

Beck, Thorsten; Ross Levine, and Norman Loayza. 2000. "Finance and the Sources of Growth." *Journal of Financial Economics* 58(1–2):261–300.

Beck, Thorsten, Mattias Lundberg, and Giovanni Majnoni. 2000. "Financial Development and Economic Volatility: Does Finance Dampen or Magnify Shocks?" World Bank. Processed.

Bell, Clive, T. N. Srinivasan, and Christopher Udry. 1997. "Rationing, Spillover, and Interlinking in Credit Markets: The Case of Rural Punjab." *Oxford Economic Papers* 49:557–585.

Berger, Allen N., Rebecca S. Demsetz, and Philip E. Strahan. 1999. "The Consolidation of the Financial Services Industry: Causes, Consequences, and Implications for the Future." *Journal of Banking and Finance* 23(2–4):135–94.

Berkowitz, Jeremy, and Michelle White. 2000. "Bankruptcy and Small Firms' Access to Credit." Department of Economics, University of Michigan, Ann Arbor, Michigan. Processed.

Bermudes, Sergio. 1999. "Administration of Civil Justice in Brazil." in Adrian A.S. Zuckerman *Civil Justice in Crisis: Comparative Perspectives of Civil Procedure.*

Bernstein, Lisa. 1999. "The Questionable Empirical Basis of Article 2's Incorporation Strategy: A Preliminary Study." *The University of Chicago Law Review* 66(3): 710–780.

———. 2000. "The Potential Role of Private Legal Systems in the Revival of Trade in Transition Economies." The University of Chicago. Processed.

Besley, Timothy, and Robin Burgess. 2000. "The Political Economy of Government Responsiveness: Theory and Evidence from India." Working Paper, Department of Economics, London School of Economics, November.

Beteille, Andre. 1997. "Caste in Contemporary India," in Chris J. Fuller (ed.) *Caste Today.* Delhi: Oxford University Press.

Bhagat, Sanjai, and Bernard Black. 1999. "The Uncertain Relationship Between Board Composition and Firm Performance." *Business Law* Vol. 54:921–963.

Bhide, Amar. 1993. "The Hidden Costs of Stock Market Liquidity." *Journal of Financial Economics* 34(1):1–51.

Bigsten, Arne, Paul Collier, Stefab Dercon, Bernard Gauthier, A. Isaksson, Abena Oduro, Remco Oostendorp, Cathy Pattillo, Måns Söderbom, M. Sylvain, Francis Teal, and Albert

Zeufack. 2000. "Contract Flexibility and Dispute Resolution in African Manufacturing." *The Journal of Development Studies* 36(4): 1–37.

Blanchard, Olivier, and Andrei Shleifer. 2000. "Federalism with and Without Political Centralization: China versus Russia." National Bureau of Economic Research Working Paper No. 7616. Cambridge, Massachussets.

Blankenburg, Erhard. 1999. "Civil Justice: Access, Cost, and Expedition. The Netherlands." in Adrian A.S. Zuckerman, *Civil Justice in Crisis: Comparative Perspectives of Civil Procedure*, 442, 1999.

Bogetic, Zeljko, and Heywood Fleisig. 1997. "Collateral, Access to Credit, and Investment in Bulgaria." In Jones, Derek C., and Jeffrey Miller (eds.) *The Bulgarian Economy: Lessons from Reform During Early Transition.* Aldershot, UK; Brookfield, VT, and Sydney: Ashgate.

Bohn, Henning, and Robert P. Inman. 1996. "Balanced Budget Rules and Public Deficits: Evidence from the U.S. States." *Carnegie Rochester Conference Series on Public Policy* 45:13–76.

Bokhari, Farhan. 2000. "Islam's Interest and Principles." *Financial Times*, August 31.

Bonin, John, and István Abel. 2000. "Retail Banking in Hungary: A Foreign Affair?" World Development Report 2002 Background Paper.

Bonin, John, and Paul Wachtel. 1999. "Lessons from Bank Privatization in Central Europe." In Harvey Rosenblum (ed.) *Proceedings of the World Bank/Dallas Federal Reserve Conference on Bank Privatization.* Dallas, TX: Dallas Federal Reserve.

Boot, Arnoud W.A., Stuart J. Greenbaum, and Anjan V Thakor. 1993. "Reputation and Discretion in Financial Contracting." *American Economic Review* 83:1165–83.

Boycko, Maxim, Andrei Shleifer, and Robert W. Vishny. 1992. "Property Rights, Soft Budget Constraints, and Privatization." Harvard University and University of Chicago. Processed.

———. 1993. "Privatizing Russia." *Brookings Papers on Economic Activity: Microeconomics* (0)2:139–181.

Boyd, John H., and Stanley L. Graham. 1991. "Investigating the Banking Consolidation Trend," *Federal Reserve Bank of Minneapolis Quarterly Review*, 15(2), 3–15.

———. 1998. "Consolidation in U.S. Banking." In Yakov Amihud and Geoffrey Miller (eds.) *Bank Mergers and Acquisitions*, Norwell, MA: Kluwer Academic.

Bradburd, Ralph. 1992. "Privatization of Natural Monopoly Public Enterprises: The Regulation Issue," Policy Research Working Paper WPS 864. World Bank, Washington, D.C.

Braga, Carlos Alberto Primo, Carsten Fink, and Claudia Paz Sepulveda. 2000. "Intellectual Property Rights and Economic Development." World Bank Discussion Paper No. 412. World Bank, Washington, D.C.

Brandt, Hans-Jürgen. 1995. "The Justice of the Peace as an Alternative: Experiences with Conciliation in Peru." in Judicial Reform in Latin America and the Caribbean: Proceedings of a World Bank Conference 92. (Malcom Rowat, Waleed H. Malik, and Maria Dakolias eds., August).

Branscheid, Volker 1998: "Irrigation Development in Eastern Europe and the Former Soviet Union." ECSRE Rural Development and Environment Sector Working Paper No. 3, The World Bank, Washington, D.C.

Brennan, Timothy J. 1987. "Regulated Firms in Unregulated Markets: Understanding the Divestiture in U.S. v. AT&T." *Antitrust Bulletin* 32, 749–793.

———. 1995. "Is the Theory Behind U.S. v. AT&T Applicable Today?" *Antitrust Bulletin* 455–482.

Bresnahan, Timothy F., and Peter C. Reiss. 1991. "Entry and Competition in Concentrated Markets." *Journal of Political Economy* 99(5):977–1009.

Brook, Penelope J. 1997. "Getting the Private Sector Involved in Water—What to Do in the Poorest of Countries?" World Bank Public Policy for the Private Sector, Viewpoint Note No. 102, January. World Bank, Washington, D.C.

Bruce, John W. and Shem E. Migot-Adholla, eds. 1994. *Searching for Land Tenure Security in Africa.* Dubuque, Iowa: Kendall Hunt.

Bruce, John W., Shem E. Migot-Adholla, and Joan Atherton. 1994. "The Findings and Their Policy Implications: Institutional Adaptation or Replacement?" in John W. Bruce and Shem E. Migot-Adholla (eds.) *Searching for Land Tenure Security in Africa*, Dubuque, Iowa: Kendall Hunt.

Bruno, Michael, and William Easterly. 1998. "Inflation Crises and Long-Run Growth." *Journal of Monetary Economics* 41: 3–26.

Burger, K., P. Collier, and J. W. Gunning. 1996. "Social Learning: An Application To Kenyan Agriculture." Free University, Amsterdam, cited in Collier and Gunning (1999): 18n. Processed.

Buscaglia, Edgardo, and Maria Dakolias. 1996. "Judicial Reform in Latin American Courts: The Experience in Argentina and Ecuador." World Bank Technical Paper No. 350. World Bank, Washington, D.C.

Buscaglia, Edgardo, and Thomas Ulen. 1997. "A Quantitative Assessment of the Efficiency of the Judicial Sector in Latin America." *International Review of Law and Economics* 17(2): 275–91.

Byerlee, Derek. 2000. "Competitive Funding of Agricultural Research in the World Bank: Lessons and Challenges." Conference Paper. Competitive Grants in the New Millennium. Conference organized by EMBRAPA, The Inter-American Development Bank, and The World Bank. Brasilia, Brazil. May 16–18, 2000. Available on-line at: www.worldbank.org/akis.

Byerlee, Derek, and Gary E. Alex. 1998. "Strenghening National Agricultural Research Systems: Policy Issues and Good Practice." Environmentally and Socially Sustainable Development: Rural Development Series. World Bank, Washington, DC.

Byerlee, Derek, and M. Maredia. 1999. "Measures of Technical Efficiency of National and International Wheat Research Systems." in Maredia, M., and D. Byerlee (eds.) *The Global Wheat System: Prospects for Enhancing Efficiency in the Presence of Spillovers.* International Maize and Wheat Improvement Center (CIMMYT) Research Report no.5.

Byerlee, Derek, and G. Traxler. 2001. "The Role of Technology Spillovers and Economies of Size in the Efficient Design of Agricultural Research Systems." in Alston, J., P. Pardey and M. Taylor (eds.) *Agricultural Science Policy: Changing Global Agendas,* International Food Policy Research Institute (IFPRI), Johns Hopkins University Press.

Byram, M., C. Kaute, and K. Matenge. 1980. "Botswana takes Participatory Approach to Mass Media Education Campaign." Development Communication Report, No 32.

Calomiris, Charles. 1996. "Building an Incentive-Compatible Safety-Net: Special Problems for Developing Countries," Columbia University, Processed.

Calomiris, Charles, and Andrew Powell. 2000. "Can Emerging Market Bank Regulators Establish Credible Discipline? The Case of Argentina," World Bank, Processed.

Campos, Ed, and Sanjay Pradhan. 1996. "Budgetary Institutions and Expenditure Outcomes." Policy Research Department Working Paper No. 1646. World Bank, Washington, D.C.

Caprio, Gerard, and P. Honohan. 1999. "Restoring Banking Stability: Beyond Supervised Capital Requirements." *Journal of Economic Perspectives* 13(4): 43–64.

Caprio, Gerard, and Maria Soledad Martinez-Peria. 2000. "Avoiding Disaster: Policies to Reduce the Risk of Banking Crises." World Bank. Processed.

Carlin, Wendy, Steven Fries, Mark Schaffer, and Paul Seabright. 1999. "Competition and Enterprise Performance in Transition Economies: Evidence from a Cross-country Survey." Processed.

Carter, Michael, and Yang Yao 1999: "Specialization without regret: Transfer rights, productivity and investment in an industrializing economy," World Bank Policy Research Working Paper No. 2202, The World Bank, Washington, D.C.

Carter, Michael, Diana Fletschner, and Pedro Olinto (1996): "Does land titling activate a productivity-promoting land market? Econometric evidence from rural Paraguay," U. of Wisconsin, Madison, Wisconsin. Processed.

Carter, Michael, Keith Wiebe, and Benoit Blarel. 1994. "Tenure Security for Whom? Differential Effects of Land Policy in Kenya." in Bruce and Migot-Adholla (eds.) *Searching for Land Tenure Security in Africa.* Dubuque, Iowa: Kendall Hunt.

Caves, Richard E., and associates. 1992. *Industrial Efficiency in Six Nations.* Massachusetts: MIT Press.

Caves, Richard E., and M. R. Porter. 1976. "Barrier to Exit" in R. Masson and P. Qualls (eds.) *Essays in Industrial Organization in Honor of Joe Bain.* Cambridge, MA: Ballinger.

Center for Public Resource Management. 2000. "Formulation of Administrative Reforms," Supreme Court–World Bank Judicial Reform Project, Jakarta, July.

CGIAR (Consultative Group on International Agricultural Research). 2001. "South Africa: CGIAR Partnership Results in New Maize Varieties with 30 to 50 Percent Higher Yields." Washington, D.C. Processed. Available at www.cgiar.org.

Chamlee-Wright, Emily. 1998. "Indigenous African Institutions and Economic Development." In James A. Dorn, Steve H. Hanke, and Alan A. Walters (eds.) *The Revolution in Development Economics.* Washington, D.C.: Cato Institute.

Chang, Chun. 2000. "The Informational Requirement on Financial Systems at Different Stages of Economic Development: The Case of South Korea." World Bank, Washington, D.C. Processed.

Chaudhuri, Sudip. 2000. "Insolvency Procedure and Corporate Restructuring." Indian Institute of Management, Calcutta, India. Processed.

Chaudhury, Nazmul, and Jeffrey Hammer. 2001. "The Role of Informational Pathways and Intra-Household Decision Making in Affecting Fertility, Child Mortality and Nutrition Outcomes: Evidence from Egypt." Processed.

Chen, Duanjie, and Ritva Reinikka. 1999. "Business Taxation in a Low-Revenue Economy. A Study on Uganda in Comparison with Neighboring Countries." Africa Regional Working Paper Series No. 3. World Bank, Washington, D.C.

Chinnappa, B. N. 1977. "Adoption of the New Agricultural Technology in North Arcot Division." Farmer, B.H. (ed.) *Green Revolution? Technology and Change in Rice-Growing Areas of South Asia,* Macmillan, 1977.

Chongkittavorn, Kavi. 2001. "Media and Access to Information in Thailand." Conference Paper. *The Role of the Media in Development,* April 12 2001. World Bank, Washington D.C.

Chui, Andy; Sheridan Titman, and John Wei. 2000. "Corporate Groups, Financial Liberalization and Growth: The Case of Indonesia," World Bank, Washington, D.C. Processed.

Church, Thomas, Jr. 1978. Justice Delayed: The Pace of Litigation in Urban Trial Courts. VA: NCSC.

Claessens, Stijn and Marion Jansen (eds.). 2000. The Internationalization of Financial Services: Issues and Lessons for Developing Countries, Boston, MA: Kluwer Academic Press.

Claessens, Stijn, and Daniela Klingebiel. 2000a. "Alternative Frameworks for the Provision of Financial Services: Economic Analysis and Country Experiences." Processed.

Claessens, Stijn, Asli Demirgüç-Kunt, and Harry Huizinga, 2001. "How Does Foreign Entry Affect the Domestic Banking Market?" *Journal of Banking and Finance* 25(5): 891–911.

Claessens, Stijn, Simeon Djankov, and Leora Klapper. 2001. "Resolution of Financial Distress: Evidence from East Asia." World Bank, Washington, D.C. Processed.

Claessens, Stijn, Simeon Djankov, and Daniela Klingebiel. 2000. "Stock Markets in Transition Economies." World Bank Financial Sector Discussion Paper No. 5, World Bank, Washington, DC.

Claessens, Stijn, Simeon Djankov, and Larry H. P. Lang. 2000. "The Separation of Ownership and Control in East Asian Corporations," *Journal of Financial Economics* 58(2):81–112.

Claessens, Stijn, Thomas Glaessner, and Daniela Klingebiel, 2000. "Electronic Finance: Reshaping the Financial Landscape around the World." Financial Sector Discussion Paper No. 4, World Bank. Washington, D.C.

———. 2000b. "Competition and Scope of Activities in Financial Services," World Bank. Processed.

Clarke, George R. G., and Robert Cull, 1999a. "Why Privatize? The Case of Argentina's Public Provincial Banks." *World Development* 27(5):867–888.

———. 1999b. "Provincial Bank Privatization in Argentina: The Why, the How and the So What." Policy Research Working Paper No. 2159, World Bank, Washington, D.C.

———. Forthcoming. "Political and Economic Determinants of the Likelihood of Privatizing Argentine Public Banks" *Journal of Law and Economics.*

Clarke, George, Robert Cull, Laura D'Amato, and Andrea Molinari. 2000. "On the Kindness of Strangers? The Impact of Foreign Entry on Domestic Banks in Argentina," in S. Claessens and M. Jansen, (eds.) *The Internationalization of Financial Services: Issues and Lessons for Developing Countries.* Boston, MA. Kluwer Academic Press.

Coase, Ronald H. 1937. "The Nature of the Firm." *Economica,* Vol. 4, pp. 386–405.

———. 1959. "The Federal Communications Commission." *Journal of Law and Economics* 2: 1–40.

———. 1960. "The Problem of Social Cost." *Journal of Law and Economics,* 3, pp. 1–44.

Coate, S., and M. Ravallion. 1993. "Reciprocity Without Commitment: Characterisation and Performance of Informal Insurance Arrangements." *Journal of Development Economics* 40:1–24.

Collier, Paul and J.W. Gunning. 1999. "The Microeconomics of African Growth, 1950–2000." Thematic Paper for the AERC Collaborative Research Project on "Explaining African Economic Growth, 1950–2000." Processed.

Committee to Protect Journalists. 2000. *Attacks on the Press in 1999: A Worldwide Survey by the Committee to Protect Journalists.* Available online at http://www.cpj.org.

Contini, Francesco. 2000. "European Database on Judicial Systems," European Research Network on Judicial Systems, processed.

Cortes, J. 1997. "Reform, Regulations and Recent Developments in the Seed System in Peru." in David Gisselquist and Jitendra Srivastava (eds.). *Easing Barriers to Movement of Plant Varieties for Agricultural Development.* Discussion Paper No. 367. World Bank, Washington, D.C.

Cox, Donald and Emmanuel Jimenez. 1995. "Private Transfers and the Effectiveness of Public Income Redistribution in the Philippines." In Dominique Van de Walle and Kimberly Nead (eds.) *Public Spending and the Poor.* Baltimore: John Hopkins University Press.

Cull, Robert, Lemma Senbet, and Marco Sorge. 2000. "Deposit Insurance and Financial Development." World Bank. Processed.

Dakolias, Maria. 1996. "The Judicial Sector in Latin America and the Caribbean: Elements of Reform." World Bank Technical Paper No. 319. World Bank, Washington, D.C.

Dakolias, Maria, and Javier Said. 1999. "Judicial Reform: A Process of Change through Pilot Courts." World Bank Report No. 20176. World Bank, Washington, D.C.

Dale, P., and R. Baldwin. 2000. "Emerging Land Markets in Central and Eastern Europe." in Csaba Csaki and Zvi Lerman (eds.) *Europe and Central Asia Environmentally and*

Socially Sustainable Development Series. 81–109. Technical Paper No. 465.

Darity, William, and Patrick Mason. 1998. "Evidence of Discrimination in Employment: Codes of Color, Codes of Gender." *Journal of Economic Perspectives* 12(2):63–90.

Das-Gupta, Arindam, and Dilip Mookherjee. 1998. Incentives and Institutional Reform in Tax Enforcement: an Analysis of Developing Country Experience. Delhi: Oxford University Press.

De Soto, Hernando. 1990. *The Other Path.* New York: Harper and Row.

———. 2000. *The Mystery of Capital. Why Capitalism Triumphs in the West and Fails Everywhere Else.* New York: Basic Books.

Deininger, Klaus. 2001. "Land Policy and Its Impact on Competition and Functioning of Factor Markets: Conceptual Issues and Empirical Evidence." World Development Report 2002 Background Paper. World Bank, Washington, D.C.

Deininger, Klaus (ed.). Forthcoming. "Land Policy and Administration: Lessons Learned and New Challenges for the Bank's Development Agenda Land Policy and Administration Thematic Group." Rural Development, The World Bank, Washington DC.

Demirgüç-Kunt, Asli, and Enrica Detragiache. 1998. "The Determinants of Banking Crises in Developing and Developed Countries." *International Monetary Fund Staff Papers* 45(1): 81–109.

———. 2000. "Does Deposit Insurance Increase Banking System Stability?" World Bank. Processed.

Demirgüç-Kunt, Asli, and Harry Huizinga. 1999. "Determinants of Commercial Bank Interest Margins and Profitability: Some International Evidence." *World Bank Economic Review.* 13(2):379–408.

———. 2000. "Market Discipline and Financial Safety Net Design." World Bank. Processed.

Demirgüç-Kunt, Asli, and Ross Levine. 2000. "Bank Concentration: Cross-Country Evidence." World Bank. Processed.

———. Forthcoming 2001. *Financial Structures and Economic Development.* Cambridge, Massachusetts: MIT Press.

Demirgüç-Kunt, Asli, and Vojislav Maksimovic. 1998. "Law, Finance, and Firm Growth," *Journal of Finance* (6):2107–2137.

———. 1999. "Institutions, Financial Markets and Firm Debt Maturity." *Journal of Financial Economics* 54:295–336.

Demirgüç-Kunt, Asli, and Tolga Sobaci. 2000. "Deposit Insurance around the World: A Data Base." World Bank. Processed.

Demirgüç-Kunt, Asli, Ross Levine, and Hong G. Min. 1998. "Opening to Foreign Banks: Issues of Stability, Efficiency and Growth." In Proceedings of the Bank of Korea Conference on the Implications of Globalization of World Financial Markets, December 1998.

Demsetz, Harold, and Kenneth Lehn. 1985. "The Structure of Corporate Ownership: Causes and Consequences." *The Journal of Political Economy* 93(6):1155–1177.

Denizer, Cevdet. 2000. "Foreign Entry in Turkey's Banking Sector, 1980/1997." In Claessens, S. and M. Jansen (eds.) *The Internationalization of Financial Services: Issues and*

Lessons for Developing Countries. Boston, MA: Kluwer Academic Press.

Denizer, Cevdet; Bulent Gultekin and Mustafa Gultekin. 2000. "Distorted Incentives and Financial Structure in Turkey." World Bank, Washington, D.C. Processed.

Denizer, Cevdet, Murat Iyigun, and Ann Owen. 2000. "Finance and Macroeconomic Volatility" Board of Governors of the Federal Reserve System, International Finance Discussion Paper No 670, June 2000.

Desai, Bhupat M., and John W. Mellor. 1993. "Institutional Finance for Agricultural Development." Food Policy Review 1. International Food Policy Research Institute, Washington, D.C.

DeYoung, Robert, and Daniel E. Nolle. 1996. "Foreign-owned banks in the United States: Earning Market Share of Buying it?" *Journal of Money, Credit, and Banking* 28(4):622–36.

Di Tella, Rafael, and Ernesto Shargrodsky. 2000. "The Role of Wages and Auditing during a Crackdown on Corruption in the City of Buenos Aires." Harvard Business School. Processed.

Dillinger, William, and Steven B. Webb. 1999. "Fiscal Management in Federal Democracies: Argentina and Brazil." Policy Research Working Paper No. 2121. World Bank, Washington, D.C.

Dinar, A., and G. Keynan. 1998. "The Cost and Performance of Paid Agricultural Extension Services." Policy Research Working Paper No. 1931. World Bank, Washington, D.C.

Dixit, Avinash. 1988. "Optimal Trade and Industrial Policies for U.S. Automobile Industry." In David B. Audretsch, *Industrial Policy and Competitive Advantage, Industry and Country Studies.* Elgar Reference Collection. International Library of Critical Writings in Economics, vol. 84. Cheltenham, U.K. and Northampton, Mass.: Elgar; distributed by American International Distribution Corporation, Williston, Vt.

Djankov, Simeon, and Peter Murrell. Forthcoming. "Enterprise Restructuring in Transition: A Quantitative Survey," *Journal of Economic Literature.*

Djankov, Simeon, and Tatiana Nenova. Forthcoming."Why Did Privatization Fail in Kazakhstan?" in The Determinants of Non-extractive Growth, Kazakhstan Country Report.

Djankov, Simeon, Rafael La Porta, Florencio Lopez-de-Silanes, and Andrei Shleifer. Forthcoming. "Regulation of Entry." *Quarterly Journal of Economics.*

Djankov, Simeon, Rafael La Porta, Florencio Lopez-de-Silanes, and Andrei Shleifer. 2001b. "The Structure of Regulation of Labor Markets: Analytical Framework, Historical Background, Indices, and Preliminary Conclusions," Harvard University, Cambridge, MA. Processed.

Dollar, David, and Aart Kraay. 2000. "Growth is Good for the Poor." *International Monetary Fund Semnar Series* (International) 2000-35:1–44.

Doner, R., and B.R. Schneider. 2000a. "The New Institutional Economics, Business Associations and Development." Geneva: ILO/International Institute for Labor Studies, DP/110/2000.

———. 2000b. "Business Associations and Economic Development: Why Some Associations Contribute More than Others." *Business and Politics* 2(3), 2000.

Drijver, C. A., and Y. J. J. Van Zorge. 1995. "With a Little Help From Our Friends." in Van Den Breemer, C. A. Drijver and L. B. Venema (eds.) *Local Resource Management in Africa.* Wiley and Sons, New York: 147–60.

Duca, John V. 1998. How Increased Product Market Competition May be Reshaping America's Labor Markets. *Federal Reserve Bank of Dallas Economic Review* 0(0):2–16.

Easterly, William. 2000. "The Middle Class Consensus and Economic Development." Development Research Group, Working Paper No. 2346, World Bank, Washington, D.C.

Easterly, William, and Stanley Fischer. 2000. "Inflation and the Poor." Policy Research Department Working Paper No. 2335. World Bank, Washington, D.C.

Easterly, William, and Ross Levine. 1997. "Africa's Growth Tragedy: Policies and Ethnic Divisions." *Quarterly Journal of Economics* 112(4):1203–50.

———. 2000. "It's Not Factor Accumulation: Stylized Facts and Growth Models." World Bank, Washington, D.C. Processed.

Easterly, William, and Sergio Rebelo. 1993. "Fiscal Policy and Economic Growth: An Empirical Investigation." *Journal of Monetary Economics* 32(3):417–58.

Easterly, William, Roumeen Islam, and Joseph E. Stiglitz. 2001. "Shaken and Stirred: Explaining Growth Volatility." In Boris Pleskovic and Joseph Stiglitz (eds.) *Annual Bank Conference on Development Economics*, World Bank, Washington, D.C.

Eaton B. C., and R. G. Lipsey. 1981. "Capital, Commitment and Entry Equilibrium." *Bell Journal of Economics* 12(2): 593–604.

Echeverria, R. 1998. "Agricultural Research Policy Issues in Latin America." *World Development* 26(6):1103–12.

Edwards, Sebastian. 1997. "Openness, Productivity and Growth: What Do We Really Know?" *Economic Journal* 108(447):383–98.

Ehehardt, D., and R. Burdon. 1999. "Free Entry in Infrastructure." Policy Research Working Paper No. 2093. World Bank, Washington, D.C.

Eichengreen, Barry, Ricardo Hausmann, and Jurgen von Hagen. 1999. "Reforming Budgetary Institutions in Latin America: The Case for a National Fiscal Council." *Open Economies Review* 10(4): 415–442.

Engerman, Stanley L., and Kenneth L Sokoloff. 1994. "Factor Endowments, Institutions, and Differential Paths of Growth among New World Economies: A View from Economic Historians of the United States." National Bureau of Economic Research Working Paper H0066. Cambridge, Mass.

Ensminger, Jean. 1994. "Transaction Costs Through Time: The Case of the Orma Pastoralists in East Africa." in James M. Acheson (ed.) *Anthropology and Institutional Economics.* Lanham, Maryland: University Press of America.

———. 1997. "Changing Property Rights: Reconciling Formal and Informal Rights to Land in Africa." in Drobak, John N. and John Nye (eds.) *The Frontiers of the New Institutional Economics.* San Diego, London and Toronto: Harcourt Brace.

Erard, Brian, and Jonathan S. Feinstein. 1994. "The Role of Moral Sentiments and Audit Perceptions in Tax Compliance." *Public Finance/Finances Publiques* 49:70–89.

Estache, Antonio. 1997, "Designing Regulatory Institutions for Infrastructure—Lessons from Argentina," Private Sector Note 114, The World Bank, May 1997.

Estache, Antonio, Vivien Foster, and Quentin Wodon. 2000a. "Infrastructure Reform and the Poor: Learning from Latin America's Experience." LAC Regional Studies Program, World Bank Institute, Studies in Development. World Bank, Washington, D.C.

Estache, Antonio, Andrea Goldstein, and Russell Pittman. 2000b. "Privatization and Regulatory Reform in Brazil: The Case of Freight Railways." US Department of Justice, Antitrust Division, Economic Analysis Group Discussion Paper 00-5, September. Washington, D.C.

Estache, Antonio, Andres Gómez-Lobo, and Danny Leipziger. 2000c. "Utility Privatization and the Needs of the Poor in Latin America. Have We Learned Enough to Get it Right?" London, UK: Infrasucture for Development.

Estache, Antonio, Manuel Romero, and John Strong. 2000d. "The Long and Winding Path to Private Financing and Regulation of Toll Roads." World Bank, Washington, D.C. Processed.

European Bank for Reconstruction and Development. 1996. *Transition Report 1996: Infrastructure and Savings.* London: EBRD.

———. 1999. *Transition Report 1999: Ten Years of Transition.* London: EBRD.

———. 2000. *Transition Report 2000: Employment, Skills and Transition.* London: EBRD.

European Institute for the Media. 2000. *Monitoring the Media Coverage of the Presidential Elections in Ukraine.* Final Report. February 2000. European Institute for the Media and European Commission. Dusseldorf.

Evans-Pritchard, Edward E. 1940. *The Nuer: A Description of the Modes of Livelihood and Political Institutions of a Nilotic People.* Oxford: Clarendon Press.

Evenson, R. 1997. "The Economic Contributions of Agricultural Extension to Agricultural and Rural Development." in Improving Agricultural Extension, a Reference Manual, Food and Agriculture Organization of the United Nations, Rome, 1997.

———. Forthcoming. "Economic Impact Studies of Agricultural Research and Extension." in *Handbook of Agricultural Economics,* Food and Agriculture Organization of the United Nations, Rome, 1997.

Fafchamps, Marcel. 1996. "The Enforcement of Commercial Contracts in Ghana." *World Development* 24(3):427–448.

Fafchamps, Marcel, and Bart Minten. 1999. "Property Rights in a Flea-Market Economy." Paper presented at WDR summer workshop. World Bank, Washington, D.C. Processed.

Fafchamps, Marcel, Christopher Udry, and Katherine Czukas. 1998. "Drought and Saving in West Africa: Are livestock a Buffer Stock?" *Journal of Development Economics* 55:273– 305.

Farrington, T. 2000. "Efficiency in Microfinance Institutions." MicroBanking Bulletin February 2000.

Feder, Gershon, and David Feeney. 1991. "Land Tenure and Property Rights: Theory and Implications for Developing Policy." World Bank Economic Review 5(1):135–53.

Feder, G., Onchan, T., Chalamwong, Y., and Hangladoran, C.; 1986. *Land Policies and Farm Productivity in Thailand;* Baltimore, Md.: Johns Hopkins.

Feder, G., A. Willett, and W. Zijp. 1999. "Agricultural Extension: Generic Challenges and Some Ingredients for Solutions." Policy Research Working Paper No. 2129. World Bank, Washington, D.C.

Fehr, Ernst, and Simon Gächter. 2000. "Fairness and Retaliation: The Economics of Reciprocity." *Journal of Economic Perspectives* 14(3):159–181.

Finger, J. Michael, and Julio J. Nogues. 2000. "The Unbalanced Uruguay Round Outcome: The New Areas in Future WTO Negotiations." Processed.

Firth, Raymond. 1963. *Elements of Social Organization.* Boston: Beacon Press.

Fisman, Raymond. Forthcoming. "It's Not What You Know. Estimating the Value of Political Connections." *American Economic Review.*

Fisman, Raymond, and Roberta Gatti. Forthcoming. "Decentralization and Corruption: Evidence Across Countries." *Journal of Public Economics.*

Fisman, Raymond, and Jakob Svensson. 2000. "Are Corruption and Taxation Really Harmful to Growth? Firm-Level Evidence." World Bank and Columbia University. Processed.

Fleisig, Heywood. 1996. "Secured Transactions: The Power of Collateral." *Finance and Development* 33(2): 44–46.

Floro, M.S., and D. Ray. 1997. "Vertical Links Between Formal and Informal Financial Institutions." *Review of Development Economics* 1(1):34–56.

Focarelli, Dario, and Alberto Franco Pozzolo. 2000. "The Determinants of Cross-Border Bank Shareholdings: An Analysis with Bank-Level Data from OECD Countries." Bank of Italy, Research Department. Processed.

Foley, Fritz. 2000. "Going Bust in Bangkok: Lessons from Bankruptcy Law Reform in Thailand." Harvard Business School. Processed.

Frankel, Jeffrey A., and David Romer. 1999. "Does Trade Cause Growth?" *American Economic Review* 89:379–399.

Franks, Julian, and Oren Sussmann. 2000. "Financial Innovations and Corporate Insolvency." Paper presented at the WDR Berlin Workshop, February 2000.

Freedom House. 2000. *Freedom in the World.* Available on-line at www.freedomhouse.org.

Friedman, Eric, Simon Johnson, Daniel Kaufmann, and Pablo Zoido-Lobatón. 2000. "Dodging the Grabbing Hand: The Determinants of Unofficial Activity in 69 Countries." *Journal of Public Economics* 76:459–493.

Fuentes, G. 1998. "Middlemen and Agents in The Procurement of Paddy: Institutional Arrangements from the Rural Philippines." *Journal of Asian Economics* 9(2):307–331.

Fuglie, K., N. Ballenger, K. Day, C. Koltz, M. Ollinger, J. Reilly, U. Vasavada, and J. Yee. 1996. *Agricultural Research and Development: Public and Private Investments under Alternative Markets and Institutions.* Agricultural Economic Report No. 735. Economic Research Service. United States Department of Agriculture. Washington D.C.

Fukuyama, Francis. 1995. *Trust: The Social Virtues and the Creation of Prosperity.* New York: Free Press.

Fundacao Palmares. 2000. "Quilombos no Brasil." *Revista Palmares* No. 5.

Galda, K., and Searle, B. 1980. The Nicaragua Radio Mathematics Project: Introduction. California: Stanford University, Institute for Mathematical Studies in Social Studies.

Gallego, Francisco, and Norman Loayza. 2000. "Financial Structure in Chile: Macroeconomic Developments and Microeconomic Effects." World Bank, Washington, D.C. Processed.

Gambetta, Diego. 1993. *The Sicilian Mafia: The Business of Private Protection*. Cambridge, Massachusetts and London: Harvard University Press.

Garavano, Germán C., Natalia Calcagno, Milena Ricci, and Liliana Raminger. 2000. "Indicadores de Desempeño Judicial." in *Poder Judicial*, Mendoza, Boletín del Centro de Capacitación e Investigaciones Judiciales "Dr. Manuel A. Saez," República Argentina.

Garcia de Alba, Francisco. 2000. Presentation at OECD Workshop on Railroad Restructuring. Moscow, December.

Gatti, Roberta. 2001. "Corruption and Trade Tariffs, or a Case for Uniform Tariffs." Policy Research Department Working Paper No. 2216. World Bank, Washingon, D.C.

Gautam, M. 2000. "Agricultural Extension: The Kenya Experience." Operations Evaluation Department Report. World Bank, Washington, D.C.

Gawande, Kishore, and Ursee Bandyopadhyay. 2000. "Is Protection for Sale? Evidence on the Grossman-Helpman Theory of Endogenous Protection." *Review of Economics and Statistics* 82(1):139–152.

Geroski, P.A. 1990. "Innovation, Technological Opportunity, and Market Structure." *Oxford Economic Papers* 42(3): 586–602.

Gerschenkron, Alexander. 1962. Economic Backwardness in Historical Perspective, A Book of Essays. Cambridge, MA: Harvard University Press.

Gilson, Ronald. 2000. "Transparency, Corporate Governance and Capital Markets." Paper presented at the Latin American Corporate Governance Roundtable, April, 2000.

Gisselquist, Ddavid, and Jean-Marie Grether. 2000. "An Argument for Deregulating the Transfer of Agricultural Technologies to Developing Countries." *World Bank Economic Review* 14(1): 111–127.

Githongo, John. 1997. "Civil Society, Democratization and the Media in Kenia." *Development* 40(4):41–45.

Goldberg, Lawrence G., and Robert Grosse. 1994. "Location Choice of Foreign Banks in the United States." *Journal of Economics and Business* 46(5):367–379.

Goldberg, Lawrence G., and Anthony Saunders. 1981. "The Determinants of Foreign Banking Activity in the United States." *Journal of Banking and Finance* 5: 17–32.

Goldberg, Linda, B. Gerard Dages, and Daniel Kinney. 2000. "Foreign and Domestic Bank Participation in Emerging Markets: Lessons from Mexico and Argentina." Federal Reserve Bank of New York. Processed.

Goldberg, Pinelopi Koujianou, and Giovanni Maggi. 1999. "Protection for Sale: An Empirical Investigation." *American Economic Review* 89(5):1135–1155.

Goldsmith, Raymond. 1969. *Financial Structure and Development*. New Haven, CT: Yale University Press.

Gonzalez De Asis, Maria. 2000. "Reducing Corruption: Lessons from Venezuela." World Bank PREM Note No. 39. World Bank, Washington, D.C.

Goodheart, Charles. 1998. *Financial Regulation: Why, How, and Where Now?* London: Routledge.

Gow, Hamish, and Johan Swinnen. 2001. "Private Enforcement Capital and Contract Enforcement in Transition Economies." Policy Research Group, Katholieke Universiteit Leuven, Belgium. Processed.

Graham, Edward M., and J. David Richardson. 1997. *Global Competition Policy*. Institute for International Economics. Washington, D.C.

Gray, Cheryl, Sabine Schlorke, and Miklos Szanyi. 1996. "Hungary's Bankruptcy Experience, 1992–1993." *World Bank Economic Review* 10(3): 425–50.

Greif, Avner. 1994. "Cultural Beliefs and the Organization of Society: A Historical and Theoretical Reflection on Collectivist and Individualistic Societies." *Journal of Political Economy* 102(5):912–50.

———. 1997a. "On the Social Foundations and Historical Development of Institutions the Facilitate Impersonal Exchange: From the Community Responsibility System to Individual Legal Responsibility In Pre-Modern Europe." Stanford University, Economics Department Working Paper, 12 June 1997.

———. 1997b. "Contracting, Enforcement and Efficiency: Economics Beyond the Law," Proceedings of the Annual World Bank Conference on Development Economics. 1996. World Bank, Washington D.C: 239–265.

Grether, Jean-Marie, Jaime de Melo, and Marcelo Olarreaga. Forthcoming. "Who Determines Mexican Trade Policy?" *Journal of Development Economics.*

Grimard, Franque. 1997. "Household Consumption Smoothing Through Ethnic Ties: Evidence from Côte d'Ivoire." *Journal of Development Economics* 31:38–61.

Grosse, Robert, and Lawrence G. Goldberg. 1991. "Foreign Bank Activity in the United States: An Analysis by Country of Origin." *Journal of Banking and Finance* 15(6): 1092–1112.

Grossman, Gene, and Elhanan Helpman. 1994. "Protection for Sale." *American Economic Review* 84(4):833–850.

Grossman, S. J., and O. D. Hart. 1980. "Takeover Bids, the Free-Rider Problem, and the Theory of the Corporation." *Bell Journal of Economics* 11:42–62.

Grote, Rainer. 1999. "Rule of Law, Rechtsstaat and 'Etat de Droit.'" in Christian Starck (ed.) *Constitutionalism, Universalism and Democracy—A Comparative Analysis.* Baden-Baden: Nomos Verlagsgesellschaft.

GTZ. 1997. *Comparative Analysis of Savings Mobilization Strategies (Overview of the four case studies).* Financial Systems Development and Banking Services, Deutsche Gesellschaft für Technische Zusammenarbeit (GTZ—German Technical Cooperation). Eschborn, Germany.

Guasch, Jorge Luis. 2000. "Concessions: Bust or Boom? An Empirical Analysis of Ten Years of Experience in Concessions in Latin America and Caribbean." World Bank., Washington, D.C. Processed.

Guasch, Luis, and Sarath Rajapatirana. 1998. "Antidumping and Competition Policies in Latin American and the

Caribbean: Total Stranger or Soul Mates?." World Bank Policy Research Working Paper No. 1958. The World Bank, Washington DC.

Guasch, Luis, and Pablo Spiller. 2001. "Managing the Regulatory Process: Design, Concepts, Issues, and the Latin America and Caribbean Story." World Bank: WBI Learning Resource Series.

Guiso, Luigi, Paola Sapienza, and Luigi Zingales. 2000. "The Role of Social Capital in Financial Development," Working Paper No. 7563, National Bureau of Economic Research. Cambridge, Mass.

Gupta, Sanjeev, Hamid Davoodi, and Erwin Tiongson. 2001. "Corruption and the Provision of Health Care and Education Services." in Arvind Jain (ed.) The Political Economy of Corruption, Routledge.

Gurley, John G., and Edwards S. Shaw. 1955. "Financial Aspects of Economic Development." American Economic Review 45:515–38.

———. 1960. Money in a Theory of Finance. Washington, D.C.: Brookings Institution.

Hahn, Chin-Hee. 2000. "Entry, Exit, and Aggregate Productivity Growth: Micro Evidence on Korean Manufacturing." Organisation for Economic Co-operation and Development Economic Department (OECD) Working Paper No. 272. Paris.

Hall, Robert E., and Charles I Jones. 1999. "Why Do Some Countries Produce So Much More Output Per Worker Than Others?." The Quarterly Journal of Economics 114(1): 83–116.

Hamilton, Walton H. 1932. "Institutions." reprinted in Edwin R.A. Seligman and Alvin Johnson (eds.) 1963. Encyclopaedia of the Social Sciences 7:84–89.

Harcourt, Alison. 1998. "EU Media Ownership Regulation: Conflict over the Definition of Alternatives." Journal of Common Market Studies 36(3): 369–389.

Harcourt, Alison, and Stefaan Verhulst, 1998. "Support for Regulation and Transparency of Media Ownership and Concentration—Russia: Study of European Approaches to Media Ownership." Programme in Comparative Media Law and Policy, University of Oxford. Processed. Available online at http://www.medialaw.ru/e_pages/laws/ero_union/e-conc.htm.

Harrison, Ann. 1994. "Productivity, Imperfect Competition and Trade Reform: Theory and Evidence." Journal of International Economics (Netherlands) 36:56–73.

———. 1996. "Determinants and Effects of Foreign Direct Investment in Côte D'Ivoire, Morocco, and Venezuela." In Mark Roberts and Jim Tybout (eds.), Industrial Evolution in Developing Countries, World Bank, Oxford University Press.

Harrison, Ann, and Gordon Hanson. 1999. "Who Gains From Trade Reform? Some Remaining Puzzles?" National Bureau of Economic Research Working Paper No. 6915. Cambridge, Massachusetts.

Harrison, P. 1987. The Greening of Africa. London: Paladin Grafton Books.

———. 1990. "Sustainable Growth in African Agriculture." In World Bank, The Long-Term Perspective Study of Sub-Saharan Africa: vol. 2, Economic and Sectoral Policy Issues. World Bank, Washington, D.C.

Hart, Oliver. 2000. "Different Approaches to Bankruptcy." National Bureau of Economic Research Working Paper No. 7921. Cambridge, Massachusetts.

Hart, Oliver, Rafael La Porta, Florencio Lopez-de-Silanes, and John Moore. 1997. "A New Bankruptcy Procedure with Multiple Auctions." European Economic Review 41(3–5): 461–73.

Hasan, Iftekhar, and William Curt Hunter. 1996. "Efficiency of Japanese Multinational Banks in the United States." In Andrew H. Chen (ed.), Research in Finance, Volume 14, Greenwich, Conn.: JAI Press. 157–173.

Hayami, Yujiro, and Toshihiko Kawagoe. 1993. The Agrarian Origins of Commerce and Industry. New York: St. Martin's Press.

Hazell, Peter B.R. 1992. "The Appropriate Role of Agricultural Insurance in Developing Countries." Journal of International Development 4:567–81.

Heidhues, F. 1994. "Consumption Credit in Rural Financial Market Development." in F.J.A. Bouman and O. Hospes (eds.) Financial Landscapes Reconstructed, Westview Press: Boulder, Colorado, 1994.

Hellman, Joel S., Geraint Jones, and Daniel Kaufmann. 2000. "Seize the State, Seize the Day: An Empirical Analysis of State Capture and Corruption in Transition." Paper Prepared for the Annual Bank Conference on Development Economics. World Bank, Washington, D.C.

Hendley, Kathryn, Barry Ickes, Peter Murrell, and Randi Ryterman. 1997. "Observations on the Use of Law by Russian Enterprises." Post-Soviet Affairs 13(1):19–41.

Hendley, Kathryn, Peter Murrell, and Randi. Ryterman. 2000. "Law, Relationships and Private Enforcement: Transactional Strategies of Russian Enterprises." Europe-Asia Studies 52(4): 627–656.

———. 2001. "Law Works in Russia: The Role of Law in Inter-Enterprise Arrears," in Peter Murrell (ed.) Assessing the Value of Law in Transition Economies. Ann Arbor: University of Michigan Press.

Hendrix, Steven E. 2000. "Guatemalan "Justice Centers": The Centerpiece for Advancing Transparency, Efficiency, Due Process, and Access to Justice." American University International Law Review 15:813.

Heo, Chul, Ki-Yul Uhm, and Jeong-Heon Chang. 2000. "South Korea," in Shelton A. Gunaratne (ed.) Handbook of the Media in Asia, New Delhi: Sage Publications.

Hicks, John, 1969. A Theory of Economic History. Oxford: Clarendon Press.

Hillel, Daniel 1987: "The Efficient Use of Water in Irrigation: Principles and Practices for Improving Irrigation in Arid and Semiarid Regions," World Bank, Technical Paper No. 64.

Hoekman, Bernard (ed.). 2001. Developing Countries and the Next Round of WTO Negotiations. In press. London: Oxford University Press.

Hoekman, Bernard, Hiau Looi Kee, and Marcelo Olarreaga. 2001. "Markups, Entry Regulation and Trade: Does Country Size Matter?" World Development Report 2002 Background Paper. World Bank., Washington, D.C.

Hoekman, Bernard, and Denise Eby Konan. 1999. "Deep Integration, Nondiscrimination and Euro-Mediterranean Free Trade." World Bank, Washington, D.C. Processed.

Hoekman, Bernard, and Michel Kostecki. 1999. *The Political Economy of the World Trading System: From GATT to WTO.* Oxford: Oxford University Press.

Hoekman, Bernard, and Patrick A. Messerlin. 1999. "Liberalizing Trade in Services: Reciprocal Negotiations and Regulatory Reform." World Bank, Washington, D.C. Processed.

Hoekman, Bernard., F. Ng and M. Olarreaga. 2001. "Eliminating Excessive Tariffs on Exports of Least Developed Countries." World Bank Policy Research Working Paper No. 2604. World Bank, Washington DC. Available on-line at: www.worldbank.org/trade

Hemming, Richard, Neven Mates, and Barry Potter. 1997. "India." In Teresa Ter-Minassian (ed.) *Fiscal Federalism in Theory and Practice.* Washingon, D.C.: International Monetary Fund.

Hendley, Kathryn, Peter Murrell, and Randi Ryterman. 2001. "Law Works in Russia: The Role of Law in Inter-Enterprise Arrears," in Peter Murrell (ed.) *Assessing the Value of Law in Transition Economies,* University of Michigan Press, Ann Arbor, Michigan, 2001.

Honohan, Patrick. 2000. "Consequences for Greece and Portugal of the Opening-up of the European Banking Market." In Claessens, S. and M. Jansen (eds.) *The Internationalization of Financial Services: Issues and Lessons for Developing Countries.* Boston, MA: Kluwer Academic Press.

Huang, Yasheng. 1996a. "Central-Local Relations in China During the Reform Era: The Economic and Institutional Dimensions." *World Development* 24(4):655–672.

———. 1996b. *Inflation and Investment Controls in China.* Cambridge: Cambridge University Press.

———. 2001. "Political Institutions and Fiscal Reforms in China." *Problems of Post-Communism* 48, no. 1.

Hultman, Charles W., and Randolph McGee. 1989. "Factors Affecting the Foreign Banking Presence in the United States." *Journal of Banking and Finance* 13(3):383–96.

Ianchovichina, E., A. Mattoo, and M. Olarreaga. 2001. "Unrestricted Market Access for Sub-Saharan Africa: How Much Is It Worth and Who Pays?." World Bank Policy Research Working Paper No. 2595. World Bank, Washington DC. Available on-line at: www.worldbank.org/trade.

International Energy Agency. 1999. "Looking at Energy Subsidies: Getting the Prices Right—World Energy Outlook," Insights, Paris.

International Institute for Management Development (IMD). 2000. *The World Competitiveness Yearbook.* Geneva.

International Monetary Fund. 2000. *International Capital Markets: Developments, Prospects, and Key Policy Issues,* Washington DC: IMF Publication Services.

Isa, M. Masud. 1995. "Designing an Effective Financial System for the Poor: The Experience of the Grameen Bank." in Asian Productivity Organization: Strategies for Developing the Informal Sector: 36–72.

Israel, Arturo. 1987. *Institutional Development: Incentives to Performance.* World Bank. Baltimore: Johns Hopkins University Press.

Jain, Sanjay, and Ghazala Mansuri. 2000. "A Little at a Time: the Use of Regularly Scheduled Repayments in Microfinance Programs." George Washington University. Processed.

Jin, Hehui, Yingyi Qian, and Barry R. Weingast. 2001. "Regional Decentralization and Fiscal Incentives: Federalism, Chinese Style." Processed.

Johnson, Simon, Daniel Kaufmann, and Pablo Zoido-Lobaton. 1998. "Regulatory Discretion and the Unofficial Economy." *American Economic Review* 88(2):387–92.

Johnson, Simon, Rafael La Porta, Florencio Lopez-de Silanes, and Andrei Shleifer. 2000. "Tunneling." *American Economic Review* 90(2):22–27.

Johnson, Simon, John McMillan, and Christopher Woodruff. 2000. "Courts and Relational Contracts." Sloan School of Management, Massachusetts Institute of Technology, Cambridge, Mass. Available on-line at: http://web.mit.edu/sjohnson/www/research.htm. Processed.

Kakalik, James S. 1997. "Just, Speedy, and Inexpensive? An Evaluation of Judicial Case Management Under the Civil Justice Reform Act." 49 ALA. L. REV. 1.

Kane, Edward J. 1989. *The S&L Insurance Mess: How Did it Happen?.* Washington: Urban Institute Press.

———. 2000. "Adjusting Financial Safety Nets to Country Circumstances." World Bank. Processed.

Kathuria, Sanjay, Will Martin, and Anjali Bhardwaj. 2000. "Implications for MFA Abolition for South Asian Countries." World Bank, Washington, D.C. Available on-line at: http://www1.worldbank.org/wbiep/trade/services/KATHURIA-MARTIN.pdf.

Kaufmann, Daniel, and Shang-jin Wei. 1999. "Does Grease Money Speed Up the Wheels of Commerce?" Policy Research Department Working Paper No. 2254. World Bank, Washington, D.C.

Kaufmann, Daniel, Aart Kraay, and Pablo Zoido-Lobaton. 1999. "Governance Matters." Policy Research Working Paper No. 2196. World Bank, Washington, D.C.

Kawagoe, Toshihiko. 1998. "Technical and Institutional Innovations in Rice Marketing in Japan." in Yujiro Hayami (ed.) *Toward the Rural-Based Development of Commerce and Industry.* Education Development Institute Learning Resources Series. World Bank, Washington, D.C.

Keefer, Philip. 2001. "When Do Special Interests Run Rampant? Disentangling the Role of Elections, Incomplete Information, and Checks and Balances in Banking Crises." World Bank, Washington, D.C. Processed.

Keefer, Philip, and David Stasavage. 2000. "Bureaucratic Delegation and Political Institutions: When Are Independent Central Banks Irrelevant?." Policy Research Department Working Paper No. 2356. World Bank, Washington, D.C.

Kerf, Michel. 2000. "Do State Holding Companies Facilitate Private Participation in the Water Sector? Evidence from Côte d'Ivoire, The Gambia, Guinea, and Senegal." Policy Research Working Paper 2513. World Bank, Washington, D.C.

Kerf, Michel, and Damien Garadin. 2000. "Post Liberalization Challenges in Telecommunications: Balancing Antitrust and Sector-Specific Regulation. Tentative Lessons from the Experiences of the United States, New Zealand, Chile, and Australia." *Journal of World Competition* 23:27–77.

Khanna, Tarun, and Krishna Palepu. 2000a. "Is Group Membership Profitable in Emerging Markets? An Analysis of Diversified Indian Business Groups," *Journal of Finance* 40(2):867–91.

———. 2000b. "Emerging Market Business Groups, Foreign Investors and Corporate Governance," in Randall Morck (ed.) *Concentrated Corporate Ownership.* Chicago: University of Chicago Press.

Khanna, Tarun and Jan Rivkin. 2001. "Estimating the Performance Effects of Business Groups in Emerging Markets." *Strategic Management Journal* Vol. 22:45–74.

Khemani, Stuti. 2001. "Decentralization and Accountability: Are Voters More Vigilant in Local than in National Elections?" Policy Research Department Working Paper No. 2557. World Bank, Washington, D.C.

King, Robert G., and Ross Levine. 1993a. "Finance and Growth: Schumpeter Might Be Right." *Quarterly Journal of Economics* 108:717–38.

———. 1993b. "Finance, Entrepreneurship, and Growth: Theory and Evidence." *Journal of Monetary Economics* 32: 513–42.

Király Júlia, Bea Májer, László Mátyás, Béla Öcsi, András Sugár, and Éva Várhegyi. 2000. "Experience with Internationalization of Financial Sector Providers: Case Study: Hungary." In S. Claessens and M. Jansen (eds.) *The Internationalization of Financial Services.* London: Kluwer Law International.

Klein, Michael, and Timothy Irwin. 1996. "Regulating Water Companies," World Bank, Private Sector and Infrastructure Network, Viewpoint Note No. 77, May. World Bank, Washington, D.C.

Knack, Stephen, and Omar Azfar. 2000. "Are Larger Countries Really More Corrupt? Sample Selection, Country Size and the Quality of Governance." World Bank Policy Research Working Paper No. 2470, World Bank, Washington D.C.

Knack, Stephen, and Philip Keefer. 1995. "Institutions and Economic Performance: Cross-country Test Using Alternative Institutional Methods." *Economics and Politics* 7(3): 207–227.

Kochar, Anjini. 1997. "An empirical investigation of rationing constraints in rural credit markets in India." *Journal of Development Economics* 53:339–371.

Komives, K., and P. Brook Cowen. 1999. "Expanding Water and Sanitation Services to Low Income Households: The Case of the La Paz-El Alto Concession." World Bank, Private Sector and Infrastructure Network, Viewpoint Note No. 178. World Bank, Washington, D.C.

Konan, Denise Eby, and Keith E. Maskus. 1999. "Service Liberalization in WTO 2000: A Computable General Equilibrium Model of Tunisia." World Bank, Washington, D.C. Processed.

Krishna, Pravin, and Devashish Mitra. 1998. "Trade Liberalization, Market Discipline and Productivity Growth: New Evidence from India." *Journal of Development Economics* 56(2):447–62.

Kumar, Krishna, Raghuram Rajan, and Luigi Zingales. 2000. "What Determines Firm Size?." University of Chicago. Processed.

La Porta, Rafael, Florencio Lopez-de-Silanes, and Andrei Shleifer. 1999. "Corporate Ownership Around the World." *Journal of Finance* 54(2):471–517.

———. Forthcoming. "Government Ownership of Banks." *Journal of Finance.*

La Porta, Rafael, Florencio Lopez-de-Silanes, Andrei Shleifer, and Robert W. Vishny. 1998. "Law and Finance," *Journal of Political Economy* 106(6):1113–1155.

———. 1999. "The Quality of Government." *Journal of Law, Economics, and Organization* 15(1):222–279.

Lambert-Mogiliansky, Ariane, Constantin Sonin, and Ekaterina Zhuravskaya. 2000. "Capture of Bankruptcy: Theory and Evidence from Russia." Discussion Paper No. 2488. Center for Economic and Policy Research, London.

Levin, Mark, and Georgy Satarov. 2000. "Corruption and institutions in Russia." *European Journal of Political Economy,* 16(1):113–32, March 2000.

Lee, Jong-Wha, and Phillip Swagel. 1997. "Trade Barriers and Trade Flows across Countries and Industries." *Review of Economics and Statistics* 79(3):372–382.

Leff, Nathaniel. 1978. "Industrial Organization and Entrepreneurship in the Developing Countries: The Economic Groups." *Economic Development and Cultural Change* 26(4): 661–675.

Lele, U., W. Lesser, and G. Horstkotte-Wesseler. 1999. "Intellectual Property Rights in Agriculture: The World Bank's Role in Assisting Borrower and Member Countries." Environmentally and Socially Sustainable Development Series, Rural Development. World Bank, Washington D.C.

Levine, Ross. 1997. "Financial Development and Economic Growth: Views and Agenda." *Journal of Economic Literature* 35(2):688–726.

———. 2000. "Bank-Based or Market-Based Financial Systems: Which Is Better?" University of Minnesota. Processed.

Levine, Ross, and Sara Zervos. 1998. "Stock Markets, Banks, and Economic Growth." *American Economic Review* 88(3): 537–558.

Levy, Brian. 1998. "Between Law and Politics-Private Infrastructure in Africa." World Bank, Washington, D.C. Processed.

Li, Hongyi, Lyn Squire and Heng-fu Zou. 1997. "Explaining International and Intertemporal Variations in Income Inequality." *Economic Journal,* 108 (January) 1–18.

Light, Ivan H. 1972. Ethnic Enterprise in America: *Business and Welfare among Chinese, Japanese and Blacks.* Berkeley, California: University of California Press.

Loayza, Norman V. 1997. "The Economics of the Informal Sector: A Simple Model and Some Empirical Evidence from Latin America." Policy Research Working Paper No. 1727. World Bank, Washington, D.C.

Lovei, L., E. Gurenko, M. Haney, P. O'Keefe, and M. Shkaranta. 2000. "Scorecard for Subsidies: How Utility Subsidies Perform in Transition Economies." Public Policy for the Private Sector, Note No. 218. World Bank, Washington, D.C.

Ma, Jun. 1997. *Intergovernmental Relations and Economic Management in China.* New York: Saint Martin's Press.

Macaulay, S. 1992. "Non-Contractual Relations in Business: A Preliminary Study." in Granovetter, M. and R. Swedburg (eds.) *The Sociology of Economic Life*. Boulder, Colorado: Westview Press.

Malcolm, David. 2000. "Judicial Reform in the 21st Century in the Asia Pacific Region." Office of the Chief Justice of Western Australia, Perth, Australia. Processed.

Mansfield, Edwin. 1986. "Patents and Innovation: An Empirical Study." In Edwin Mansfield (ed.) *Innovation, Technology and the Economy: Selected Essays of Edwin Mansfield*, Vol. 2. Economists of the Twentieth Century series. Aldershot, U.K.: Elgar; distributed in the U.S. by Ashgate, Brookfield, Vt.

Mansfield, Edward D., and Marc L. Busch. 1995. "The Political Economy of Nontariff Barriers: A Cross-national Analysis." *International Organization* 49(4):723–49.

Mansfield, Edward D., Helen V. Milner, and B. Peter Rosendorf. 2000. "Free to Trade: Democracies, Autocracies, and International Trade." *American Political Science Review* 94(2):302–21.

Manski, Charles F. 2000. "Economic Analysis of Social Interactions." *Journal of Economic Perspectives* 14(3):115–136.

Mansuri, Ghazala. 1998. "Credit Layering in Rural Financial Markets." Ph.D. thesis, Boston University.

Maskus, K. 2000. "Intellectual Property Rights in the Global Economy." Institute for International Economics, Washington, D.C.

Maskus, Keith E., and Mohan Penubarti. 1995. "How Trade Related are Intellectual Property Rights?" *Journal of International Economics* 39(3–4):227–48.

Mauro, Paolo. 1995. "Corruption and Economic Growth." *Quarterly Journal of Economics* 110(3):682–712.

———. 1997. "The Effects of Corruption on Growth, Investment, and Government Expenditure: A Cross-Country Analysis." in Kimberly Ann Elliott (ed.) *Corruption and the Global Economy*. Institute for International Economics, Washington, D.C.

Mayer, Colin. 1988. "New Issues in Corporate Finance." *European Economic Review* 32(5):1167–88.

McKinsey and Company. 1999. Public Service Broadcasters around the World. A McKinsey Report for the BBC, January 1999.

McMillan, John, and Christopher Woodruff. 1999a. "Dispute Prevention without Courts in Vietnam." *Journal of Law Economics and Organization* 15(3):637–658.

———. 1999b. "Interfirm Relationships and Informal Credit in Vietnam." *Quarterly Journal of Economics* 114(6): 1285–1320.

Megginson, William L., and Maria Boutchkova. 2000. "The Impact of Privatization on Capital Market Development and Individual Share Ownership." Paper presented at the ABN-AMRO International Conference on Initial Public Offerings, July 3–4, 2000, Universiteit van Amsterdam, The Netherlands. Available on-line at: http://www.fee.uva.nl/conferences/ipo2000/papers/Megginson-Boutchkova.pdf.

Megginson, William L., Robert C. Nash, Jeffrey M. Netter, and Annette B. Poulsen. Forthcoming. "The choice of private versus public capital markets: Evidence from Privatization." *Journal of Financial Economics*.

Melard, C., J-P Platteau, and H. Wotongoka. 1998. *Etude des Incidences Socio-Economiques de L'introduction de la Technique de Peche au Filet Maillant au Lac Kivu*. Belgium: FUCID, University of Namur. Cited in Platteau 2000.

Merton, Robert C., and Bodie, Zvi. 1995. "A Conceptual Framework for Analyzing the Financial Environment." In Crane, Dwight B. and others (eds.) *The Global Financial System: A Functional Perspective*. Boston, MA: Harvard Business School Press.

Meyer, R. L., and G. Nagarajan. 2000. *Rural Financial Markets in Asia: Policies, Paradigms, and Performance*, Oxford University Press, for the Asian Development Bank.

Migot-Adholla, Shem E., George Benneh, Frank Place and Steven Atsu. 1994a. "Security of Tenure and Land Productivity in Kenya." in Bruce and Migot-Adholla (1994). *Searching for Land Tenure Security in Africa*. Dubuque, Iowa: Kendall Hunt: 97–118.

Migot-Adholla, Shem E., Frank Place and W. Olucoch-Kosura. 1994b. "Security of tenure and land Productivity in Kenya," in Bruce and Migot-Adholla (1994) *Searching for Land Tenure Security in Africa*. Dubuque, Iowa: Kendall Hunt: 119–140.

Miller, Margaret. 2000. "Credit Reporting Systems Around the Globe: The State of the Art in Public and Private Credit Registries." World Bank. Processed.

Miller, Stewart R., and Arvind Parkhe, 1998. "Patterns in the Expansion of U.S. Banks' Foreign Operations." *Journal of International Business Studies* 29(2):359–390.

Miranti, Paul J., Jr. 2000. "U.S. Financial Reporting Standardization." Paper presented at the World Development Report Summer Research Workshop, Washington DC, July 17–19, 2000. Processed.

Moore, Mick. 1999. "Truth, Trust and Market Transactions: What Do We Know?" *Journal of Development Studies* 36(1): 74–88.

Morck, Randall K., David A. Strangeland, and Bernard Yeung. 2000. "Inherited Wealth, Corporate Control and Economic Growth: The Canadian Disease." In Randall K. Morck (ed.) *Concentrated Corporate Ownership*, University of Chicago Press.

Morduch, Jonathan. 1995. "Income Smoothing and Consumption Smoothing." *Journal of Economic Perspectives* 9(3): 103–114.

———. 1999. "Between the State and the Market: Can Informal Insurance Patch the Safety Net?" *World Bank Research Observer* 14(2):187–207.

Moseley, Paul, and R. Krishnamurthy 1995. "Can Crop Insurance Work? The case of India." *Journal of Development Studies* 31(3):428–50.

Mudahar, M., R. Jolly, and J. P. Srivastava. 1998. "Transforming Agricultural Research Systems in Transition Economies." Discussion Paper No. 396. World Bank, Washington, D.C.

Murrell, Peter. 2001. "Institutional Reform Shunning Empirical Analysis: Demand and Supply in Romanian Commercial Courts," Department of Economics, University of Maryland, College Park, Maryland. Processed.

Nabli, Mustapha K., and Jeffrey B. Nugent eds. 1989. *The New Institutional Economics and Development: Theory and Applications to Tunisia*, Amsterdam: North Holland.

Nadvi, Khalid. 1999a. "Collective Efficiency and Collective Failure." *World Development.* 27(9):1605–1626.

———. 1999b. "Facing the new competition: Business associations in developing country industrial clusters." Geneva: International Labor Organization/International Institute for Labor Studies." No. 103.

Neal, Larry. 1990. *The Rise of Financial Capitalism: International Capital Markets in the Age of Reason.* Cambridge: Cambridge University Press.

Nelson, Mark. 1999a. "After the Fall: Business Reporting in Eastern Europe." *Media Studies Journal,* 13(3):150–157.

———. 1999b. "Anticorruption in Transition: the Role of the Media." World Bank Institute. Processed.

Nenova, Tatiana. 2001a. "The Value of Corporate Votes and Control Benefits: A Cross-Country Analysis." Ph.D. Thesis, Harvard University, Cambridge, Mass.

———. 2001b. "Changes in Corporate Law in Brazil and the Value of ontrol." Ph.D. Thesis, Harvard University, Cambridge, MA.

Nepal Press Institute. 2000. Available on-line at http://www.pressasia.org/PFA/members/index.html.

Neubauer, David W., Marcia Lipetz, Mary Luskin, and John Ryan. 1981. "Managing the Pace of Justice: An Evaluation of LEAA's Court Delay-Reduction Programs." Washington, D.C.: National Institute of Justice, U.S. Department of Justice.

New York State Committee to Review Audio-Visual Coverage of Court Proceedings. 1997. *An Open Courtroom: Cameras in New York Courts.* New York: Fordham University Press.

Newbery, David. 1994. "Restructuring and Privatizing Electric Utilities in Eastern Europe." *Economics of Transition* 2(1994), 291–316.

Newbery, David. 2000. "Romania: Oil and Gas Reform," in Ioannis Kessides (ed.) *"Romania: Regulatory and Structural Assessment in the Network Utilities."* Washington, D.C.: World Bank.

Nickell, Stephen J. 1996. "Competition and Corporate Performance." *Journal of Political Economy* 104(4):724–46.

———. 1997. "What Makes Firms Perform Well?." *European Economic Review* 41(3–5):783–96.

Noll, Roger. 1999a. "Telecommunications Reform in Developing Countries." in Anne O. Krueger, ed., *Economic Policy Reform: The Second Stage.* University of Chicago Press.

———. 1999b. "Notes of Privatizing Infrastructure Industries." Paper presented at WDR summer workshop. World Bank, Washington, D.C. Processed.

North, Douglass C. 1991. "Institutions." *Journal of Economic Perspectives* 5(1):97–112.

———. 1993. "Competition and Values in the Rise of the West." *Swiss Review of World Affairs* 11:23–24.

———. 1994. "Integrating Institutional Change and Technical Change in Economic History: A Transaction Cost Approach." *Journal of Institutional and Theoretical Economics* 150(4) 609–24.

North, Douglass C., and Barry Weingast. 1989. "Constitutions and Commitment: The Evolution of Institutions Governing Public Choice in Seventeenth-Century England." *Journal of Economic History* 49(4):803–832.

Nugent, Jeffrey B., and Mustapha K. Nabli, 1992. "Development of Financial Markets and the Size Distribution of Manufacturing Establishments: International Comparaisons." *World Development* 20(10):1489–1499.

Odoki, Benjamin J. 1994. "Reducing Delay in the Administration of Justice: The Case of Uganda." 5 CRIM. L.F. 57.

Olson, Mancur. 2000. "Power and Prosperity: Outgrowing Communist and Capitalist Dictatorships." New York: Basic Books.

Ordover, Janusz A., Russell W. Pittman, and Paul Clyde. 1994. "Competition Policy for Natural Monopolies in a Developing Market Economy." *Economics of Transition* 2:317–343.

OECD (Organisation for Economic Co-operation and Development). 1999a. "OECD Principles of Corporate Governance." Paris.

———. 1999b. "Regulatory Reform in Japan." Paris.

———. 2000a. "Regulatory Reform in Korea." Paris.

———. 2000b. "Summary Indicators of Product Market Regulation with an Extension to Employment Protection Legislation." Economics Department Working Papers No. 226 by Giuseppe Nicolette, Stefano Scarpetta, and Olivier Boylaud. Paris.

———. 2001. "Czech Republic Regulatory Reform Country Review". Paris, February. Processed.

Pardey, Philip G., and Nienke M. Beintema. 2001. "Science for Development in a New Century: Reorienting Agricultural Research Policies for the Long Run." Background paper for UNDP Human Development Report 2001 *Channeling Technology for Human Development.* United Nations Development Program. New York.

Pardey, Philip G., Julian M. Alston, Jason E. Christian, and Shenggen Fan. 1996. "Hidden Harvest: U.S. Benefits from International Research Aid." International Food Policy Research Institute, Washington, D.C. Available on-line at: http://www.ifpri.org/

Park, Walter, Ramya Vjaya, and Smita Wagh. 2001. "Determinants of Patent Rights, a Cross-National Study: An Update." Department of Economics, American University, Washington, D.C. Processed.

Peek, Joe, and Eric S. Rosengren, 2000. "Collateral Damage: Effects of the Japanese Bank Crisis on Real Activity in the United States." *American Economic Review* 90(1): 30–45.

Pender, J. L., and J. M. Kerr. 1994. "The Effect of Transferable Land Rights on Credit, Investment and Land Use: Evidence from South India." Brigham Young University, Provo, Utah. Processed.

Perez-Casas, Carmen, D. Berman, P. Chirac, T. Kasper, B. Pecoul, I. De Vincenzi, and T. Von Schoen-Angerer. 2000. "HIV/AIDS Medicines Pricing Report. Setting Objectives: Is There a Political Will?." Medicins Sans Frontieres. Published on-line at http://www.msf.org/advocacy/accessmed/reports/2000/07/aidspricing.

Persson, Torsten, and Guido Tabellini. 2000. "Political Institutions and Policy Outcomes: What Are the Stylized Facts?" Institute for International Economic Studies at the University of Stockholm. Processed.

Persson, Torsten, Guido Tabellini, and Francesco Trebbi. 2000. "Electoral Rules and Corruption." Institute for International Economic Studies at the University of Stockholm. Processed.

Pew Research Center. 2000. "Journalists Avoiding the News. Self Censorship: How Often and Why." Available online at http://www.people-press.org/jour00rpt.htm.

Pie, Minxin. 2001. "Does Legal Reform Protect Economic Transactions? Commercial Disputes in China," in Peter Murrell (ed.) *Assessing the Value of Law in Transition Economies.* Ann Arbor: University of Michigan Press.

Pinckney, T. C., and P. K. Kimuyu. 1994. "Land Tenure Reform in East Africa: Good, Bad or Unimportant?" *Journal of African Economies* 3(1):1–28.

Pistor, Katharina. 1999. "Law as a Determinant for Equity Market Development: The Experience of Transition Economies." University of Maryland, Institutional Reform and the Informal Sector (IRIS), Working Paper.

Pistor, Katharina, Yoram Keinan, Jan Kleinheisterkam, and Mark West. 2000. "The Evolution of Corporate Law." World Development Report 2002 Background Paper, World Bank, Washington, D.C.

Pistor, Katharina, Martin Raiser, and Stanislaw Gelfer. 2000. "Law and Finance in Transition Economies." *Economics of Transition* 8(2):325–368.

Pittman, Russell. 1999. "Competition, Regulation, and Deregulation." Romanian Academy of Sciences. Processed.

———. 2000. Presentation at OECD Workshop on Railroad Restructuring, Moscow, December.

———. 2001. "Vertical Restructuring of the Infrastructure Sectors of Transition Economies." World Development Report 2002 Background Paper. World Bank, Washington, D.C.

Place, Frank, and Peter Hazell. 1993. "Productivity Effects of Indigenous Land Tenure Systems in Sub-Saharan Africa." *American Journal of Agricultural Economics* 75(1):10–19.

Platteau, Jean-Philippe. 1992. "Land Reform and Structural Adjustment in Sub-Saharan Africa: Controversies and Guidelines." FAO Economic and Social Development Paper No. 107. Food and Agricultural Organization, Rome.

———. 2000. *Institutions, Social Norms and Economic Development.* Amsterdam: Harwood Academic Publishers.

Porter, Michael E. 1990. *The Competitive Advantage of Nations.* New York: Free Press.

———. 1992. "Capital Choices: Changing the Way America Invests in Industry." *Journal of Applied Corporate Finance* 5(2):4–16.

Porter, Michael E., and Mariko Sakakibara. Forthcoming. "Competing at Home to Win Abroad: Evidence from Japanese Industry." *Review of Economics and Statistics.*

Posner, Richard. 1995. "What Do Judges Maximize?" Chapter 3 in *Overcoming Law.* Cambridge: Harvard University Press.

Poterba, James. 1997. "Do Budget Rules Work?" in Alan Auerbach (ed.) *Fiscal Policy: Lessons from Empirical Research,* Cambridge: MIT Press.

Poterba, James, and Kim Reuben. 1999. "State Fiscal Institutions and the U.S. Municipal Bond market." in James Poterba and Jurgen von Hagen (eds.) *Fiscal Institutions and Fiscal Performance.* University of Chicago Press.

Powelson, John P. 1998. "The State and the Peasant: Agricultural Policy on Trial." In James A. Dorn, Steve H. Hanke, and Alan A. Walters (eds*.) The Revolution in Development Economics.* Washington, D.C.: Cato Institute.

Pray, C., and D. Umali-Deininger. 1998. "The Private Sector in Agricultural Research Systems: Will It Fill the Gap?" *World Development* 26(6):1127–48.

Prescott, Edward S., and Robert M. Townsend. 1999. "The Boundaries and Connectedness of Collective Organizations." University of Chicago. Processed.

Purcell, D., and J. Anderson. 1997. "Agricultural Extension and Research: Achievements and Problems in National Systems." Operations Evaluation Study. World Bank, Washington, D.C.

Qaim, M. 1999. "The Economic Effects of Genetically Modified Orphan Commodities: Projections for Sweetpotato in Kenya." ISAAA (International Service for the Acquisition of Agri-biotech Applications) Brief Series No. 13. Ithaca, New York.

Quirno, Pablo. 2001. "Latin America in the Pipeline." Worldlink. March/April 2000. Available on-line at www.worldlink.co.uk.

Rahman, Zubaidur. 1998. "The Role of Accounting Disclosure in the East Asian Financial Crisis: Lessons Learned." Division on Investment, Technology and Enterprise Development, Enterprise Development Strategies, Finance and Accounting Section, Geneva: UNCTAD (United Nations Conference on Trade and Development).

Rajan, Raghuram G., and Luigi Zingales. 1998. "Financial Dependence and Growth." *American Economic Review* 88(3): 559–586.

———. "Financial Systems, Industrial Structure, and Growth." University of Chicago. Available on line at: http://gsblgz.uchicago.edu/PSpapers/finsys.pdf.

Ransom, Roger L., and Richard Sutch. 1977. *One Kind of Freedom: The Economic Consequences of Emancipation.* New York: Cambridge University Press.

Rauch, James, and Peter Evans. 2000. "Bureaucratic Structure and Bureaucratic Performance in Less-Developed Countries." *Journal of Public Economics* 75(1):49–71.

Ravallion, Martin. 2000. "Growth, Inequality and Poverty: Looking Beyond Averages." World Bank, Washington, D.C. Processed.

Recanatini, F., and R. Ryterman. 2000. "Disorganization or Self-Organization?." Policy Research Working Paper Series, World Bank, Washington, D.C.

Richer, D. 2000. "Intellectual Property Protection: Who Needs It?" in Persley, G. and M. Lantin (eds.) *Agricultural Biotechnology and the Poor: Proceedings of an International Conference.* October 21–22 1999. Consultative Group on International Agricultural Research. Washington, D.C.

Roberts, Mark J., and James R. Tybout (eds). 1996. *Industrial Evolution in Developing Countries.* New York: Oxford University Press.

Robertson, Geoffrey. 2000. "How Does the Media Support the Reform Process." Conference paper, Seminar on Legal and Judicial Development. June 5–7, 2000. World Bank, Washington, D.C.

Rockey, Sally. 2000. "Competitive Grants for U.S. Agricultural Research: The Long and Hard Road to Success." Conference Paper. Competitive Grants in the New Millennium. Conference organized by EMBRAPA, the Inter-American Development Bank, and the World Bank. Brasilia, Brazil. May 16–18, 2000.

Rodrik, Dani. 1994. "The Rush to Free Trade in the Developing World: Why So Late? Why Now? Will it Last?" in Haggard, Stephan, and Steven Webb (eds.) *Voting for Reform: Democracy, Political Liberalization, and Economic Adjustment.* Oxford University Press.

———. 1999. "Institutions for High-Quality Growth: What They Are and How to Acquire Them." Paper prepared for the International Monetary Fund Conference on Second-Generation Reforms, Washington, D.C., November 8–9, 1999.

———. 2000. "Trade Policy Reform as Institutional Reform." In Hoekman (ed.) *Developing Countries and the Next Round of WTO Negotiations.* In press. London: Oxford University Press.

Rohter, Larry. 2001. "Brazil's Former Slave Havens Slowly Pressing for Rights." *New York Times,* January 23: A4.

Rose-Ackerman, Susan. 2001. "Political Corruption and Democratic Structure." In Arvind Jain, (ed.) *The Political Economy of Corruption.* London: Routledge.

Rosenzweig, Mark R., and Kenneth I. Wolpin. 1993. "Credit Market Constraints, Consumption Smoothing, and the Accumulation of Durable Production Assets in Low-Income Countries: Investments in Bullocks In India." *Journal of Political Economy* 101(2):223–44.

Rousseau, Peter L. and Richard Sylla, 1999. "Emerging Financial Markets and Early U.S. Growth." National Bureau of Economic Research Working Paper No. 7448. Cambridge, Mass.

Rousseau, Peter L., and Paul Wachtel. 2000. "Equity Markets and Growth: Cross-Country Evidence on Timing and Outcomes, 1980–1995." *Journal of Banking and Finance* 24(12): 1933–57.

Rozelle, Scott, Carl Pray, and Jikun Huang. 1997. "Agricultural Research Policy in China: Testing the Limits of Commercialization-led Reform." *Comparative Economic Studies* 39(2):37–71.

Rosenzweig, Mark. 1998. "Social Learning and Economic Growth." World Development Report 1998/1999 commissioned paper. World Bank, Washington, D.C.

Rukuni, M., J. Blackie, and C. Eicher. 1998. "Crafting Smallholder-Driven Agricultural Research Systems in Southern Africa." *World Development* 26(6): 1073–88.

Sachs, Jeffrey D., and Andrew Warner. 1995. "Economic Reform and the Process of Global Integration." *Brookings Papers on Economic Activity* 1:1–95.

Saleth, R. Maria, and Ariel Dinar. 1999. "Water Challenge and Institutional Response (a Cross-Country Perspective)." Policy Research Working Paper No. 2045. World Bank, Washington, D.C.

Sappington, David E. M., and Joseph E. Stiglitz. 1987. "Privatization, Information and Incentives." *Journal of Policy Analysis and Management* 6:567–582.

Shepherd, Andrew. 1997. *Market Information Services—Theory and Practice.* FAO, Rome.

Shepherd, Andrew, and Alexander Schalke. 1995. "The Indonesian Horticultural Market Information Service." AGSM Occasional Paper No.8. FAO, Rome. Quoted in Shepherd, Andrew. 1997. *Market Information Services—Theory and Practice.* FAO, Rome.

Scherer, F.M. 1992. "Schumpeter and Plausible Capitalism." *Journal of Economic Literature* 30(3):1416–33.

Schmidt, Klaus M. 1996a. "Managerial Incentives and Product Market Competition." Center for Economic Policy Research Discussion Paper Series No. 1382, London.

———. 1996b. "The Costs and Benefits of Privatization: An Incomplete Contracts Approach." *Journal of Law, Economics, and Organization* 12(1):1–24.

Schneider, Ben Ross. 1997a. "Big Business and the Politics of Economic Reform: Confidence and Concertation in Brazil and Mexico." In Sylvia Maxfield and Ben Ross Schneider (eds.) *Business and the State in Developing Countries.* Ithaca: Cornell University Press.

———. 1997b. "Organized Business Politics in Democratic Brazil." *Journal of Interamerican Studies and World Affairs* 39(4):95–127.

Schneider, Friedrich, and Dominik H. Enste. 2000. "Shadow Economies: Size, Causes, and Consequences." *Journal of Economic Literature* 38(1):77–114.

Schreiner, Mark. 2000. "Microfinance in Rural Argentina." Washington University, St. Louis. Processed.

Schultz, Theodore W. (1980): "Nobel lecture: The Economics of Being Poor," *Journal of Political Economy* 88(4): 640–51.

Schumpeter, Joseph A. 1934. *Theorie der Wirtschaftlichen Entwicklung* (The Theory of Economic Development). Leipzig: Dunker & Humblot, 1912; translated by Redvers Opie. Cambridge, Mass: Harvard University Press.

Schwartz, Gerd, and Claire Liuksila. 1997. "Argentina." In Teresa Ter-Minassian (ed.) *Fiscal Federalism in Theory and Practice.* Washington, D.C.: International Monetary Fund.

Seibel, Hans Dieter. 2000. "Agricultural Development Banks: Close Them or Reform Them?" *Finance and Development* 37(2):45–48.

Shaffer, Sherrill. 1993. "Test of Competition in Canadian Banking." *Journal of Money, Credit, and Banking* 25(1): 49–61.

Shapiro, Carl, and Robert D. Willig. 1990. "Economic Rationales for the Scope of Privatization," in E. Saleiman and J. Waterbury (eds.) *The Political Economy of Public Sector Reform and Privatization.* Boulder: Westview Press.

Shi, Min, and Jakob Svensson. 2000. "Conditional Political Business Cycles: Theory and Evidence." Harvard University and Insitute for International Economic Studies, Stockholm University. Processed.

Shipton, Parker. 1994. "Time and Money in the Western Sahel." in James M. Acheson (ed.) *Anthropology and Institutional Economics*. Lanham, Maryland: University Press of America: 283–327.

Shirley, Mary, and Patrick Walsh. 2000. "Public versus Private Ownership: The Current State of the Debate." World Bank, Policy Research Working Paper 2420. Washington, D.C.

Shleifer, Andrei, and Daniel Treisman. 2000. *Without a Map: Political Tactics and Economic Reform in Russia*. Cambridge: MIT Press.

Shleifer, Andrei, and Robert W. Vishny. 1988. "Value Maximization and the Acquisition Process," *Journal of Economic Perspectives* 2: 7–20.

———. 1993. "Corruption." *Quarterly Journal of Economics* 108(3):599–617.

———. 1997. "A Survey of Corporate Governance." *Journal of Finance* 52:737–783.

Siamwalla, Ammar, Chirmsak Pinthong, Nipon Poapongsakorn, Ploenpit Satsanguan, Prayong Nettayarak, Wanrak Mingmaneenakin, and Yuavares Tubpun. 1990. "The Thai Rural Credit System: Public Subsidies, Private Information, and Segmented Markets," *World Bank Economic Review* 4(3):271–295.

Slater, Joanna. 2000. "Riches among the Poor." *Far Eastern Economic Review* 163(43):52–56.

Smith, Pamela J. 1999. "Are Weak Patent Rights a Barrier to U.S. Exports?" *Journal of International Economics* 48(1): 151–177.

Smith, Warrick. 2000. "Regulating Utilities: Thinking about Location Questions." Paper prepared for the World Bank Summer Workshop on Market Institutions, July. World Bank, Washington, D.C.

Sokoloff, Kenneth L. 2000. "Institutions, Factor Endowments, and Paths of Development in the New World." *Journal of Economic Perspectives*, 14(3):217–232.

Solo, T., and S. Snell. 1998. "Water and Sanitation Services for the Urban Poor," United Nations Development Programme—World Bank. Processed.

Spiller, Pablo, and Carlo G. Cardilli. 1997. "The Frontier of Telecommunications Deregulation: Small Countries Leading the Pack." *Journal of Economic Perspectives* 11:127–138.

Spiller, Pablo, and C. Sampson. 1996. "Telecommunications Regulation in Jamaica." In Brian Levy and Pablo Spiller (eds.) *Regulation, Institutions, and Commitment: Comparative Studies of Telecommunications*. Cambridge University Press.

Srinivasan, T. N., and Jagdish Bhagwati. 1999. "Outward Orientation and Development: Are the Revisionists Right?" Economic Growth Center Discussion Paper No. 804, Yale University.

Staiger, Robert, and Guido Tabellini. 1999. "Do GATT Rules Help Governments Make Domestic Commitments?" *Economics and Politics* 11(2):109–144.

Stapenhurst, Frederick. 2000. "The Media's Role in Curbing Corruption." World Bank Institute Departmental Working Paper. World Bank, Washington D.C. Available on-line at http://www.worldbank.org/wbi/governance/wp.htm#corruption.

Stein, Ernesto, Ernesto Talvi, and Alejandro Grisanti. 1999. "Institutional Arrangements and Fiscal Performance: The Latin American Experience." in James Poterba and Jurgen von Hagen (eds.) *Fiscal Institutions and Fiscal Performance*. University of Chicago Press.

Stern, Jon, and Junior R. Davis. 1998. "Economic Reform of the Electricity Industries of Central and Eastern Europe." *Economics of Transition* 6:427–460.

Stewart, Mark B. 1990. "Union Wage Differentials, Product Market Influences and the Division of Rents." *Economic Journal* 100(403):1122–37.

Stigler, G. J. 1987. "Competition." In J. Easwell, M. Milgate, and P. Newman (eds.) "The New Palgrave." London: MacMillan.

Stiglitz, Joseph E. 1972. "Some Aspects of the Pure Theory of Corporate Finance: Bankruptcies and Takeovers." *Bell Journal of Economics* 3(3):458–82.

———. 1985. "Credit Markets and the Control of Capital." *Journal of Money, Credit and Banking* 17(2):133–52.

Svensson, Jakob 1998. "Investment, Property Rights and Political Instability: Theory and Evidence." *European Economic Review* 42(7):1317–1341.

———. 1999. "Who Must Pay Bribes and How Much? Evidence from a Cross-Section of Firms." Policy Research Department Working Paper No. 2486. World Bank, Washington, D.C.

Swaminathan, M. 1991. "Segmentation, Collateral Undervaluation, and the Rate of Interest in Agrarian Credit Markets: Some Evidence from Two Villages in South India." *Cambridge Journal of Economics* 15(2):161–78.

Swamy, Anand, Stephen Knack, Young Lee, and Omar Azfar. 2001. "Gender and Corruption." *Journal of Development Economics* 64:25–55.

Swanson, B., B. J. Farner, and R. Bahal. 1990. "The Current Status of Agricultural Extension Worldwide," in FAO *Report of the Global Consultation on Agricultural Extension,* Food and Agriculture Organization of the United Nations. Rome.

Sylla, Richard. 2000. "Financial Systems and Economic Modernization: A New Historical Perspective" New York University. Processed.

Taliercio, Robert. 2000a. "Administrative Reform as Credible Commitment: The Link Between Revenue Authority Autonomy and Performance in Latin America." Manuscript. Harvard University.

———. 2000b. "The Political Incentives for and against Administrative Reform: The Establishment of Semi-Autonomous Revenue Authorities in Latin America." World Bank, Washington, D.C. Processed.

———. 2001. "Administrative Reform as Credible Commitment: The Link between Revenue Authority Autonomy and Performance in Latin America." Manuscript. World Bank, Washington, D.C.

Tanzi, Vito, and Hamid Davoodi. 1998. "Does Corruption Affect Income Inequality and Poverty?" International Monetary Fund Working Paper No. 98/76. Washington, D.C.

———. 2001. "Corruption, Growth and Public Finances." in Arvind Jain (ed.) *The Political Economy of Corruption.* London: Routledge.

Tarigo, Enrique. 1995. "Legal Reform in Uruguay: General Code of Procedure." in Judicial Reform in Latin America and the Caribbean: Proceedings of a World Bank Conference 48. (Malcom Rowat, Waleed H. Malik, & Maria Dakolias eds., August).

Taylor, Michael, and Alex Fleming. 1999. "Integrated Financial Supervision: Lessons of Northern European Experience," World Bank, Washington, D.C. Processed.

Tello, Carlos. 1984. *La Nacionalización de la Banca en México.* Siglo Veintiuno Editores.

Tendler, Judith, and Sara, Freedheim. 1994. "Trust in a Rent Seeking World: Health and Government Transformed in Northeastern Brazil." *World Development* 22(2):1771–91.

The Probe Team. 1994. *Public Report on Basic Education in India.* New Delhi: Oxford University Press.

Thomas, Duncan, John Strauss, and Maria-Helena Henriques, 1991, "How Does Mother's Education Affect Child Height?" *Journal of Human Resources* 26(2):183–211.

Thompson, Ginger. 2001. "Chasing Mexico's Dream into Squalor." *New York Times,* February 11.

Torii, Akio. 1992. "Technical Efficiency in Japanese Industries." In Caves, Richard, and Associates, *Industrial Efficiency in Six Nations.* Cambridge: MIT Press.

Treisman, Daniel. 1999. "Russia's Tax Crisis: Explaining Falling Revenues in a Transitional Economy." *Economics and Politics* 11(2):145–169.

———. 2000. "The Causes of Corruption: A Cross-National Study." *Journal of Public Economics* 76(3):399–457.

Tripp, R., and D. Byerlee. 2000. "Public Plant Breeding in an Era of Privatisation." *Natural Resource Perspectives* No. 57. Overseas Development Institute.

Trujillo, Lourdes, and Gustavo Nombela. 2000. "Multiservice Infraestructure." Private Sector and Infrastructure Network, Viewpoint No. 222, October. Available on-line at: www.worldbank.org/html/fpd/notes.

Tuck, Laura, and Kathy Lindert. 1996. "From Universal Food Subsidies to a Self-Targeted Program: A Case Study in Tunisian Reform." World Bank Discussion Paper No. 351. Washington, D.C.

Turnham, David. 1993. *Employment and Development: A New Review of Evidence.* Paris: Organisation for Economic Co-operation and Development.

Tybout, James R. 1996. "Heterogeneity and Productivity Growth: Assessing the Evidence." In Roberts and Tybout (eds.) *Industrial Evolution in Developing Countries.* New York: Oxford University Press.

Tybout, James R., and M. Daniel Westbrook. 1995. "Trade Liberalization and Dimensions of Efficiency Change in Mexican Manufacturing Industries." *Journal of International Economics* 39:1–2.

Tybout, James, Jaime de Melo, and Vittorio Corbo. 1991. "The Effects of Trade Reforms on Scale and Technical Efficiency: New Evidence from Chile." *Journal of International Economics* 31:3–4.

Tyler, Tom R., Yuen Huo, and E. Allan Lind. 1999. *The Two Psychologies of Conflict Resolution: Differing Antecedents of Pre-Experience Choices and Post-Experience Evaluations,* 2(2) Group Processes and Intergroup Relations 99.

Udry, Christopher. 1990. "Credit Markets in Northern Nigeria: Credit as Insurance in Rural Economy." *World Bank Economic Review* 4(3):251–69.

U.S. Department of Justice. 1986. *Oil Pipeline Deregulation.* Washington, D.C.

U.S. Federal Regulatory Commission. 1999. "Notice of Proposed Rulemaking: Regional Transmission Organizations," Docket No. RM99-2000, May 13, 1999.

Umali-Deininger, D. 1997. "Public and Private Agricultural Extension: Partners or Rivals." *World Bank Research Observer* 12(2):203–24.

United Nations Development Programme. 1999. *Human Development Report 1999.*

———. 2000. *Human Development Report 2000.*

Untiet, Charles. 1987. "The Economics of Oil Pipeline Deregulation: A Review and Extension of the DOJ Report." U.S. Department of Justice, Antitrust Division, Economic Analysis Group Discussion Paper 87-3, May. Washington, D.C.

USAID (U.S. Agency for International Development). 1998. "Alternative Dispute Resolution: Practitioner's Guide." Washington, D.C. Processed.

Uwanno, Borwonsornsak. 2000. "Depoliticizing Key Institutions for Combatting Corruption: Case Study of the New Thai Constitution." Processed.

Van Cayseele, P.J.G. 1998. "Market Structure and Innovation: A Survey of the Last Twenty Years." *De Economist* 146(3): 391–417.

Van de Walle, Dominique, and Kimbery Nead, eds. 1995. *Public Spending and the Poor: Theory and Evidence.* Baltimore: Johns Hopkins Press.

Vander Vennet, Rudi. 1996. "The Effect of Mergers and Acquisitions on the Efficiency and Profitability of EC Credit Institutions." *Journal of Banking and Finance* 20: 1531–1558.

VanRijckeghem, Caroline, and Beatrice Weder. 1997. "Corruption and the Rate of Temptation. Do Low Wages in the Civil Service Cause Corruption?" International Monetary Fund Working Paper No. 97/73. Washington, D.C.

Varano, Vincenzo. 1997. "Civil Procedure Reform in Italy." *American Journal of Comparative Law* 45:657.

Varela, David, and Veena Mayani. 2000. "The Dominican Republic: A First Statistical Review of the Justice Sector." World Bank Working Paper. Washington, D.C.

Véscovi, Enrique. 1996. "Nuevas Tendencias y Realidades del Proceso Civil. El Código Procesal Civil Modelo para Iberoamérica. La Experiencia Uruguaya del Proceso Oral. El Código Judicial Uniforme de la Nueva Union Europea." in August M. Morello (ed.) *La Prueba.* Buenos Aires: Libreria, Editora Platense.

Vickers, John. 1995. "Concepts of Competition." *Oxford Economic Papers* No. 47. Oxford University Press.

Vissi, Ferenc. 1992. "The Peculiarities of Regulating the Monopolies in the Economies in Transition in General, and in Hungary in Particular." Presentation at World Bank Conference on Treatment of Natural Monopolies in Eastern Europe, Vienna. World Bank.

Vogel, Ezra. 1994. *Japan as Number One in Asia.* American Assembly, Columbia University, series. New York and London: Norton.

Vose, Edward. 1916. Seventy-Five Years of the Mercantile Agency: R.G. Dun & Co., 1841–1916. New York: R.G. Dun and Co.

Walden, Ruth. 2000. "Insult Laws: An Insult to Press Freedom." World Press Freedom Committee, Reston, Virginia.

Waterfield, C. 1999. "Paperless Loan Processing Technology." *MicroBanking Bulletin* July 1999.

Webster, David. 1992. "Building Free and Independent Media." Freedom Paper No. 1. United States Information Agency, Washington D.C.

Webster, Leila, and Peter Fidler. 1996. The Informal Sector and Microfinance Institutions in West Africa." World Bank: Washington, D.C.

Wei, Shang-jin. 2000a. "How Taxing Is Corruption on International Investors?" *Review of Economics and Statistics* 82(1): 1–11.

Wei, Shang-jin. 2000b. "Local Corruption and Global Capital Flows." *Brookings Papers on Economic Activity* 2:303–351.

———. 2000c. "Natural Openness and Good Government." National Bureau of Economic Research Working Paper No. 7765. Cambridge, Massachusetss.

Weill, Herman. 1961. *Frederick the Great and Samuel von Cocceji: A Study in the Reform of the Prussian Judicial System.* Madison: University of Wisconsin.

Weisbach, Michael, and Benjamin Hermalin. 2000. "Boards of Directors as an Endogenously Determined Institution: A Survey of the Economic Literature." Berkeley. Processed.

Wellenius, Bjorn. 1997. "Extending Telecommunications Service to Rural Areas: The Chilean Experience." World Bank, Public Policy for the Private Sector, Viewpoint Note No. 105, February. Washington, D.C.

Wetzel, Deborah, and Anita Papp. 2001. "Strengthening Hard Budget Constraints in Hungary", in Jonathan Rodden, Gunnar Eskeland, and Jennie Litvack (eds.) *Fiscal Decentralization and the Challenge of Hard Budget Constraints.* Washington: World Bank.

Williamson, Oliver E. 1985. "Reflections on the New Institutional Economics." *Zeitschrift fur die gesamte Staatswissenschaft* 141(1):187–95.

Willig, R. D. 1980. "What Can Markets Control?" in R. Sherman (ed.), *Perspectives on Postal Service Issues*, Washington, D.C.: American Enterprise Institute.

Wilmington, Martin W. 1955. "Aspects of Moneylending in Northern Sudan." *Middle East Journal* 9:139–46 (The Middle East Institute, Washington, D.C.).

Wong, Christine P. W. 1997. *Financing Local Government in the People's Republic of China.* Oxford University Press.

World Bank. 1974. "Land Reform." Development Series. World Bank: Washington, D.C.

———. 1989a. "Argentina Agricultural Sector Review, Volume II: Technical Annex." Report No. 7733-AR. Country Department I, Latin America and the Caribbean Region, Washington D.C.

———. 1989b. *World Development Report 1989, Financial Markets and Development.* New York: Oxford University Press.

———. 1992. Malaysia: Fiscal Reform for Stable Growth. Washington, D.C.

———. 1994a. "Governance: The World Bank's Experience." Washington, D.C.

———. 1994b. Indonesia: Health, Man Power Report. 1994. Washington, D.C.

———. 1994c. "Public Expenditures for Poverty Alleviation in Northeast Brazil: Promoting Growth and Improving Services." Washington, D.C.

———. 1995a. *World Development Report 1995: Workers in an Integrating World.* World Bank, Washington, DC.

———. 1995b. "Preshipment Inspection Services." World Bank Discussion Paper No. 278. Washington, D.C.

———. 1996. Rural Energy and Development: Improving Energy Supplies for Two Billion People. Washington, DC: World Bank. Chapter 9

———. 1997. *World Development Report 1997: The State in a Changing World.* New York: Oxford University Press.

———. 1998. "Reforming Agricultural Research Organizations: Creating Autonomous Bodies and Managing Change." Agricultural Knowledge and Information Systems (AKIS) Good Practice Note No. 01/99. World Bank, Washington D.C.

———. 1999a. "Initiating Memorandum: Bank Restructuring Facility Loan to Mexico." Finance, Private Sector, and Infrastructure, Country Management Unit 1, Latin America and the Caribbean Regional Office, Washington DC.

———. 1999b. "Moldova: Poverty Assessment. A World Bank Country Study." Washington, DC.

———. 1999c. *World Development Report 1998/1999: Knowledge for Development.* New York: Oxford University Press.

———. 1999d. *Land Administration and Rural Development: Two Cases from Thailand.* OED/World Bank; Report 184. Washington, D.C.

———. 2000a. "Decentralizing Agricultural Extension: Lessons and Good Practice," Agricultural Knowledge and Information Systems (AKIS) Good Practice Note August 2000. Washington D.C. Available on-line at: www.worldbank.org/akis.

———. 2000b. "Anticorruption in Transition: A Contribution to the Policy Debate." Washington, D.C.

———. 2000c. "Implementation Completion Report on a Loan to the Republic of Mauritius for a Technical Assistance to Enhance Competitiveness Project." March 30. Washington, D.C.

———. 2000d. *India: Reducing Poverty, Accelerating Development.* Washington, D.C.

———. 2000e. *Securing Our Future in a Global Economy.* Washington, D.C.

———. 2000f. *World Development Report 1999/2000: Entering the 21st Century.* New York: Oxford University Press.

———. 2000g. *Can Africa Claim the 21st Century?* Washington, D.C.

———. 2000h. *Global Economic Prospects and the Developing Countries 2000.* Washington, D.C.

———. 2001a. *Finance for Growth: Policy Choices in a Volatile World.* Policy Research Report. New York: Oxford University Press.

———. 2001b. "Capacity Building for Economic Communication." Internal Report. Communications Department. Romania Country Office. World Bank, Bucharest.

———. 2001c. "Sri Lanka Poverty Assessment." In process.

———. 2001d. *World Development Report 2000/2001: Attacking Poverty.* New York: Oxford University Press.

———. 2001f. *Public Expenditure Review: Zambia.* Washington, DC.

World Competitiveness Yearbook. 2000. Available on-line at http://www.imd.ch/wcy/.

WIPO (World Intellectual Property Organization). 1990. "Exclusions from Patent Protection." HL/CM/INF/1 Rev., May.

Wurgler, Jeffrey. 2000. "Financial Markets and the Allocation of Capital," *Journal of Financial Economics* 58(1–2):187–214.

Yaron, Jacob, and Benjamin Piprek. 1997. "Rural Finance: Issues, Designs and Best Practices." Environmentally and Socially Sustainable Development Studies and Monograph Series 14. World Bank, Washington, D.C.

Young, Alwyn. 2000. "The Razor's Edge: Distortions and Incremental Reform in the People's Republic of China." *Quarterly Journal of Economics* 115(4):1091–1136.

Yunus, Muhammad. 1994. *Credit Is a Human Right.* Dhaka: Grameen Bank.

———. 1997. *Banker to the Poor: Micro-Lending and the Battle Against World Poverty.* New York. Public Affairs.

Zagha, Roberto. 1998. "Labor and India's Economic Reforms." *Policy Reform* Vol. 2.

Zhuravskaya, Ekaterina V. 2000. "Incentives to Provide Local Public Goods: Fiscal Federalism, Russian Style." *Journal of Public Economics* 76:337–368.

Selected World Development Indicators

Introduction to Selected World Development Indicators

In this year's edition, development data are presented in a reduced set of tables. The *World Development Indicators 2001* (WDI) covers the full range of development data produced by the World Bank. The four main tables included here retain the layout of earlier editions of the Selected World Development Indicators, presenting comparative socioeconomic data for more than 130 economies for the most recent year for which data are available and, for some indicators, for an earlier year. An additional table presents basic indicators for 75 economies with sparse data or with populations of less than 1.5 million.

The indicators presented here are a selection from more than 800 included in *World Development Indicators 2001*. Published annually, *World Development Indicators* reflects a comprehensive view of the development process. Its opening chapter reports on the record of and the prospects for social and economic progress in developing countries, measured against seven international development goals. The other five main sections recognize the contribution of a wide range of factors: human capital development, environmental sustainability, macroeconomic performance, private sector development, and the global links that influence the external environment for development. *World Development Indicators* is complemented by a separately published CD-ROM database that gives access to over 1,000 data tables and 800 time-series indicators for 224 economies and regions.

Data sources and methodology

Socioeconomic and environmental data presented here are drawn from several sources: primary data collection by the World Bank, member country statistical publications, research institutes, and international organizations such as the United Nations and its specialized agencies, the International Monetary Fund (IMF), and the OECD. Although international standards of coverage, definition, and classification apply to most statistics reported by countries and international agencies, there are inevitably differences in timeliness and reliability arising from differences in the capabilities and resources devoted to basic data collection and compilation. For some topics, competing sources of data require review by World Bank staff to ensure that the most reliable data available are presented. In some instances, where available data are deemed too weak to provide reliable measures of levels and trends or do not adequately adhere to international standards, the data are not shown.

The data presented are generally consistent with those in *World Development Indicators 2001*. However, data have been revised and updated wherever new information has become available. Differences may also reflect revisions to historical series and changes in methodology. Thus data of different vintages may be published in different editions of World Bank publications. Readers are advised not to compile data series from different publications or different editions of the same publication. Consistent time-series data are available on *World Development Indicators 2001* CD-ROM.

All dollar figures are in current U.S. dollars unless otherwise stated. The various methods used to convert from national currency figures are described in the *Technical notes*.

Because the World Bank's primary business is providing lending and policy advice to its low- and middle-income members, the issues covered in these tables focus mainly on these economies. Where available, information on the high-income economies is also provided for comparison. Readers may wish to refer to national statistical publications and publications of the Organisation for Economic Cooperation and Development (OECD) and the European Union for more information on the high-income economies.

Changes in the System of National Accounts

For the first time, this edition of the Selected World Development Indicators uses terminology in line with the 1993 System of National Accounts (SNA). For example, in the 1993 SNA *gross national income* replaces *gross national product*. See the technical notes for tables 1 and 3.

Most countries continue to compile their national accounts according to the 1986 SNA, but more and more are adopting the 1993 SNA. A few low-income countries still use concepts from older SNA guidelines, including valuations such as factor cost, in describing major economic aggregates.

Classification of economies and summary measures

The summary measures at the bottom of each table include economies classified by income per capita and by region. GNI per capita is used to determine the following income classifications: low-income, $755 or less in 2000; middle-income, $756 to $9,265; and high-income, $9,266 and above. A further division at GNI per capita $2,995 is made between lower-middle-income and upper-middle-income economies. See the table on classification of economies at the end of this volume for a list of economies in each group (including those with populations of less than 1.5 million).

Summary measures are either totals (indicated by **t** if the aggregates include estimates for missing data and nonreporting countries, or by an **s** for simple sums of the data available), weighted averages (**w**), or median values (**m**) calculated for groups of economies. Data for the countries excluded from the main tables (those presented in Table 1a) have been included in the summary measures, where data are available, or by assuming that they follow the trend of reporting countries. This gives a more consistent aggregated measure by standardizing country coverage for each period shown. Where missing information accounts for a third or more of the overall estimate, however, the group measure is reported as not available. The section on *Statistical methods* in the *Technical notes* provides further information on aggregation methods. Weights used to construct the aggregates are listed in the technical notes for each table.

From time to time an economy's classification is revised because of changes in the above cutoff values or in the economy's measured level of GNI per capita. When such changes occur, aggregates based on those classifications are recalculated for the past period so that a consistent time series is maintained.

Terminology and country coverage

The term *country* does not imply political independence but may refer to any territory for which authorities report separate social or economic statistics. Data are shown for economies as they were constituted in 1999, and historical data are revised to reflect current political arrangements. Throughout the tables, exceptions are noted.

Technical notes

Because data quality and intercountry comparisons are often problematic, readers are encouraged to consult the *Technical notes*, the table on Classification of Economies by Income and Region, and the footnotes to the tables. For more extensive documentation see *World Development Indicators 2001*.

Readers may find more information on the WDI 2001, and orders can be made online, by phone, or fax as follows:

For more information and to order online: http://www.worldbank.org/data/wdi2001/index.htm.

To order by phone or fax: 1-800-645-7247 or 703-661-1580; Fax 703-661-1501.

To order by mail: The World Bank, P.O. Box 960, Herndon, VA 20172-0960, U.S.A.

Table 1.   Key indicators of development

	Population			Gross national income (GNI)[a]		PPP gross national income (GNI)[b]		Gross domestic product	Life expectancy	Under-5 mortality rate	Adult illiteracy rate	Carbon dioxide emissions
	Millions 2000	Avg. annual % growth 1990–2000	density people per sq. km 2000	Billions of dollars 2000	per capita dollars 2000	Billions of dollars 2000	per capita dollars 2000	per capita % growth 1999–2000	at birth Years 1999	Per 1,000 1999	% of people 15 and above 1999	Millions of tons 1997
Albania	3	0.4	124	..	..[c]	12	3,550	5.9	72	..	16	1.7
Algeria	30	1.9	13	48.3	1,590	153[d]	5,040[d]	1.1	71	39	33	98.7
Angola	13	3.2	10	3.1	240	16[d]	1,230[d]	−0.8	47	208	..	5.3
Argentina	37	1.3	14	275.5	7,440	448	12,090	−1.7	74	22	3	140.6
Armenia	4	0.8	136	2.0	520	10	2,570	5.5	74	18	2	2.9
Australia	19	1.2	2	394.1	20,530	487	25,370	3.0	79	5	..	319.6
Austria	8	0.5	98	204.2	25,220	213	26,310	3.5	78	5	..	62.6
Azerbaijan	8	1.2	93	4.9	610	22	2,760	10.4	71	21	..	32.0
Bangladesh	130	1.6	997	49.9	380	213	1,650	3.8	61	89	59	24.6
Belarus	10	−0.2	48	30.0	2,990	76	7,550	6.3	68	14	1	62.3
Belgium	10	0.3	312	252.5	24,630	282	27,500	3.5	78	6	..	106.5
Benin	6	2.8	57	2.4	380	6	970	2.2	53	145	61	1.0
Bolivia	8	2.4	8	8.3	1,000	20	2,380	0.2	62	83	15	11.3
Botswana	2	2.3	3	5.3	3,300	12	7,190	2.5	39	95	24	3.4
Brazil	170	1.4	20	606.8	3,570	1,245	7,320	3.2	67	40	15	307.2
Bulgaria	8	−0.7	74	12.4	1,510	45	5,530	5.5	71	17	2	50.3
Burkina Faso	11	2.4	41	2.6	230	12[d]	1,020[d]	3.1	45	210	77	1.0
Burundi	7	2.2	265	0.7	110	4[d]	580[d]	−1.6	42	176	53	0.2
Cambodia	12	2.7	68	3.1	260	17	1,410	1.7	54	143	61	0.5
Cameroon	15	2.7	32	8.6	570	24	1,570	1.5	51	154	25	2.7
Canada	31	1.0	3	647.1	21,050	840	27,330	4.0	79	6	..	496.6
Central African Republic	4	2.0	6	1.1	290	4[d]	1,210[d]	2.4	44	151	55	0.2
Chad	8	2.9	6	1.5	200	7[d]	860[d]	−2.1	49	189	59	0.1
Chile	15	1.5	20	69.9	4,600	139	9,110	4.0	76	12	4	60.1
China	1,261	1.1	135	1,064.5	840	4,966	3,940	7.3	70	37	17	3,593.5
Hong Kong, China	7	1.8	..	176.4	25,950	174	25,660	9.3	80	5	7	23.8
Colombia	42	1.9	41	88.0	2,080	249	5,890	1.0	70	28	9	71.9
Congo, Dem. Rep.	51	3.2	23	5.0	100	33	682	..	46	161	40	2.3
Congo, Rep.	3	2.8	9	1.8	630	2	590	4.8	48	144	21	0.3
Costa Rica	4	2.0	71	14.4	3,960	30	8,250	0.0	77	14	5	5.4
Côte d'Ivoire	16	3.0	50	10.5	660	24	1,520	−4.5	46	180	54	13.3
Croatia	4	−0.7	80	20.1	4,510	35	7,780	3.8	73	9	2	20.1
Czech Republic	10	−0.1	133	50.6	4,920	140	13,610	3.2	75	5	..	125.2
Denmark	5	0.4	126	171.0	32,020	145	27,120	2.5	76	6	..	57.7
Dominican Republic	9	1.9	177	18.0	2,100	49	5,720	6.5	71	47	17	14.0
Ecuador	13	2.1	46	15.3	1,210	37	2,920	0.4	69	35	9	21.7
Egypt, Arab Rep.	64	2.0	64	95.2	1,490	235	3,690	3.2	67	54	45	118.3
El Salvador	6	2.1	303	12.5	1,990	28	4,390	0.0	70	36	22	5.9
Eritrea	4	2.7	41	0.7	170	4	950	−11.4	50	105	47	..
Estonia	1	−0.9	34	4.9	3,410	13	9,050	7.0	71	12	..	19.1
Ethiopia	64	2.3	64	6.7	100	42	660	2.2	42	166	63	3.8
Finland	5	0.4	17	129.0	24,900	127	24,610	5.4	77	5	..	56.6
France	59	0.4	107	1,429.4[e]	23,670[e]	1,440	24,470	2.9	79	5	..	349.8
Georgia	5	0.0	78	3.2	590	13	2,470	1.8	73	20	..	4.5
Germany	82	0.3	235	2,057.6	25,050	2,054	25,010	2.9	77	5	..	851.5
Ghana	19	2.6	84	6.8	350	37[d]	1,940[d]	1.8	58	109	30	4.8
Greece	11	0.4	82	126.2	11,960	179	16,940	3.8	78	7	3	87.2
Guatemala	11	2.6	105	19.2	1,690	43	3,770	0.6	65	52	32	8.3
Guinea	7	2.5	30	3.3	450	14	1,930	−0.5	46	167	..	1.1
Haiti	8	2.1	289	4.0	510	12[d]	1,500[d]	−0.8	53	118	51	1.4
Honduras	6	2.8	58	5.5	850	16	2,390	2.1	70	46	26	4.6
Hungary	10	−0.3	109	47.5	4,740	121	12,060	5.7	71	10	1	59.6
India	1,016	1.8	342	471.2	460	2,432	2,390	3.9	63	90	44	1,065.4
Indonesia	210	1.7	116	119.9	570	598	2,840	3.1	66	52	14	251.5
Iran, Islamic Rep.	64	1.6	39	104.6	1,630	378	5,900	3.2	71	33	24	296.9
Ireland	4	0.8	55	87.1	22,960	97	25,470	9.8	76	7	..	37.3
Israel	6	2.9	302	99.6	16,310	120	19,320	3.5	78	8	4	60.4
Italy	58	0.2	196	1,154.3	20,010	1,348	23,370	2.8	78	6	2	424.7
Jamaica	3	0.9	242	6.4	2,440	9	3,500	0.0	75	24	14	11.0
Japan	127	0.3	337	4,337.3	34,210	3,354	26,460	1.7	81	4	..	1,204.2
Jordan	5	4.3	55	8.2	1,680	20	4,040	0.8	71	31	11	15.7
Kazakhstan	15	−0.9	6	17.6	1,190	82	5,490	10.1	65	28	..	123.0
Kenya	30	2.4	53	10.7	360	30	1,010	−2.4	48	118	19	7.2
Korea, Rep.	47	1.0	479	421.1	8,910	820	17,340	7.8	73	9	2	457.4
Kuwait	2	−0.7	111	..	..[f]	..	..	..	77	13	18	51.0
Kyrgyz Republic	5	1.2	26	1.3	270	13	2,590	3.6	67	38	..	6.8
Lao PDR	5	2.6	23	1.5	290	8[d]	1,530[d]	3.3	54	143	53	0.4
Latvia	2	−1.0	39	6.9	2,860	17	6,960	7.2	70	18	0[g]	8.3
Lebanon	4	1.7	423	16.2	3,750	20	4,530	−0.8	70	32	14	17.7
Lesotho	2	2.2	71	1.2	540	5[d]	2,490[d]	−0.1	45	141	17	..
Lithuania	4	−0.1	57	10.7	2,900	26	6,960	3.3	72	12	1	15.1
Macedonia, FYR	2	0.7	80	3.5	1,710	10	4,960	4.6	73	17	..	10.9
Madagascar	16	2.9	27	4.0	260	13	830	1.6	54	149	34	1.2
Malawi	11	2.6	117	1.9	170	7	600	−0.7	39	227	41	0.8
Malaysia	23	2.5	71	78.5	3,380	195	8,360	6.0	72	10	13	137.2

Note: For data comparability and coverage, see the technical notes. Figures in italics are for years other than those specified.

| | Population | | | Gross national income (GNI)[a] | | PPP gross national income (GNI)[b] | | Gross domestic product | Life expectancy | Under-5 mortality | Adult illiteracy | Carbon dioxide |
	Millions 2000	Avg. annual % growth 1990–2000	density people per sq. km 2000	Billions of dollars 2000	per capita dollars 2000	Billions of dollars 2000	per capita dollars 2000	per capita % growth 1999–2000	at birth Years 1999	rate Per 1,000 1999	rate % of people 15 and above 1999	emissions Millions of tons 1997
Mali	11	2.5	9	2.6	240	9	790	2.1	43	223	60	0.5
Mauritania	3	2.8	3	1.0	370	4	1,650	2.4	54	142	58	3.0
Mexico	98	1.6	51	498.0	5,080	864	8,810	5.4	72	36	9	379.7
Moldova	4	−0.2	129	1.4	400	10	2,240	2.3	67	22	1	10.4
Mongolia	2	1.3	2	0.9	390	4	1,660	−0.3	67	73	38	7.8
Morocco	29	1.8	64	33.8	1,180	98	3,410	−0.8	67	62	52	35.9
Mozambique	18	2.2	22	3.7	210	14[d]	820[d]	2.0	43	203	57	1.2
Myanmar	46	1.2	69	..	..[h]	..	..	..	60	120	16	8.8
Namibia	2	2.5	2	3.6	2,050	11[d]	6,440[d]	1.6	50	108	19	..
Nepal	24	2.4	167	5.3	220	33	1,360	3.1	58	109	60	2.2
Netherlands	16	0.6	469	400.3	25,140	417	26,170	3.8	78	5	..	163.6
New Zealand	4	1.1	14	50.1	13,080	72	18,780	3.1	77	6	..	31.6
Nicaragua	5	2.8	42	2.1	420	11[d]	2,100[d]	1.7	69	43	32	3.2
Niger	11	3.4	9	2.0	180	8[d]	760[d]	−0.3	46	252	85	1.1
Nigeria	127	2.8	139	32.8	260	101	790	0.4	47	151	37	83.7
Norway	4	0.6	15	151.2	33,650	134	29,760	2.4	78	4	..	68.5
Pakistan	138	2.5	179	64.6	470	270	1,960	3.4	63	126	55	98.2
Panama	3	1.7	38	9.3	3,260	16[d]	5,700[d]	1.0	74	25	8	8.0
Papua New Guinea	5	2.2	11	3.7	760	11[d]	2,280[d]	−1.8	58	77	36	2.5
Paraguay	5	2.6	14	8.0	1,450	24[d]	4,460[d]	−1.5	70	27	7	4.1
Peru	26	1.7	20	53.9	2,100	121	4,720	1.9	69	48	10	30.1
Philippines	76	2.2	253	78.7	1,040	319	4,220	2.1	69	41	5	81.7
Poland	39	0.1	127	162.2	4,200	349	9,030	4.1	73	10	0[g]	357.0
Portugal	10	0.1	109	110.7	11,060	169	16,880	3.0	75	6	8	53.8
Romania	22	−0.3	97	37.4	1,670	143	6,380	1.7	69	24	2	111.3
Russian Federation	146	−0.2	9	241.1	1,660	1,168	8,030	8.8	66	20	1	1,444.5
Rwanda	9	2.0	345	2.0	230	8	930	2.8	40	203	34	0.5
Saudi Arabia	21	2.7	10	139.4	6,900	223	11,050	..	72	25	24	273.7
Senegal	10	2.6	49	4.7	500	14	1,480	2.3	52	124	64	3.5
Sierra Leone	5	2.3	70	0.6	130	2	460	1.3	37	283	..	0.5
Singapore	4	2.8	6,587	99.4	24,740	100	24,970	8.1	78	4	8	81.9
Slovak Republic	5	0.2	112	20.0	3,700	59	11,000	2.1	73	10	..	38.1
Slovenia	2	−0.1	99	20.0	10,070	35	17,390	4.7	75	6	0[g]	15.5
South Africa	43	2.0	35	129.2	3,020	393[d]	9,180[d]	1.4	48	76	15	321.5
Spain	39	0.2	79	590.1	14,960	757	19,180	4.0	78	6	2	257.7
Sri Lanka	19	1.3	300	16.6	870	67	3,470	4.2	73	19	9	8.1
Sweden	9	0.4	22	237.5	26,780	211	23,770	3.9	79	4	..	48.6
Switzerland	7	0.7	182	273.7	38,120	218	30,350	2.7	80	5	..	42.6
Syrian Arab Republic	16	2.8	88	16.0	990	52	3,230	−1.1	69	30	26	49.9
Tajikistan	6	1.8	45	1.1	170	7	1,060	6.6	69	34	1	5.6
Tanzania	34	2.8	38	9.3[i]	280[i]	18[i]	530[i]	2.7	45	152	25	2.9
Thailand	61	0.9	119	121.8	2,010	385	6,330	3.5	69	33	5	226.8
Togo	5	2.8	86	1.4	300	7	1,450	1.6	49	143	44	1.0
Tunisia	10	1.6	62	20.1	2,090	58	6,090	3.4	73	30	30	18.8
Turkey	65	1.5	85	201.5	3,090	459	7,030	5.7	69	45	15	216.0
Turkmenistan	5	2.8	10	4.0	840	20	4,040	16.1	66	45	..	31.0
Uganda	22	3.0	111	6.8	310	27[d]	1,230[d]	2.2	42	162	34	1.2
Ukraine	50	−0.5	86	34.7	700	184	3,710	6.7	67	17	0[g]	370.5
United Kingdom	60	0.4	247	1,463.5	24,500	1,407	23,550	2.6	77	6	..	527.1
United States	282	1.2	31	9,645.6	34,260	9,646	34,260	4.0	77	8	..	5,467.1
Uruguay	3	0.7	19	20.3	6,090	30	8,880	−1.8	74	17	2	5.7
Uzbekistan	25	1.8	60	15.2	610	59	2,380	2.9	70	29	12	104.8
Venezuela, RB	24	2.1	27	104.1	4,310	139	5,750	1.2	73	23	8	191.2
Vietnam	79	1.7	241	30.7	390	159	2,030	5.4	69	42	7	45.5
Yemen, Rep.	18	3.9	33	6.7	380	14	780	3.7	56	97	55	16.7
Yugoslavia, Fed. Rep.	11	0.1	..	..	..[c]	..	..	..	72	16	..	50.2
Zambia	10	2.6	14	3.0	300	8	750	1.3	38	187	23	2.6
Zimbabwe	12	2.2	31	5.8	480	31	2,590	−6.7	40	118	12	18.8
World	**6,054 s**	**1.4 w**	**47 w**	**31,171.0 t**	**5,150 w**	**44,506 t**	**7,350 w**	**2.9 w**	**66 w**	**78 w**	**.. w**	**23,868.2 s**
Low income	2,459	2.0	76	1,029.6	420	4,892	1,990	3.1	59	116	39	2,496.5
Middle income	2,693	1.2	40	5,307.7	1,970	15,229	5,650	4.8	69	38	15	10,034.3
Lower middle income	2,046	1.1	47	2,322.0	1,140	9,374	4,580	5.5	69	40	16	6,767.5
Upper middle income	647	1.4	28	2,986.0	4,620	5,930	9,170	3.9	69	35	11	3,266.7
Low & middle income	5,152	1.6	52	6,335.6	1,230	20,056	3,890	4.2	64	85	25	12,530.8
East Asia & Pacific	1,853	1.2	116	1,963.9	1,060	7,631	4,120	6.5	69	44	15	5,075.6
Europe & Central Asia	475	0.2	20	955.9	2,010	3,145	6,620	6.3	69	26	3	3,285.6
Latin America & Carib.	516	1.6	26	1,895.3	3,680	3,627	7,030	2.3	70	38	12	1,355.4
Middle East & N. Africa	296	2.2	27	602.0	2,040	1,527	5,170	..	68	54	36	1,111.8
South Asia	1,355	1.9	283	616.9	460	3,060	2,260	3.8	63	99	46	1,200.5
Sub-Saharan Africa	659	2.6	28	313.0	480	1,030	1,560	0.5	47	159	39	501.8
High income	903	0.7	29	24,828.8	27,510	24,781	27,450	3.2	78	6	..	11,337.4

a. Preliminary World Bank estimates calculated using the World Bank Atlas method. b. Purchasing power parity; see the Technical Notes. c. Estimated to be lower middle income ($756 to $2,995); d. The estimate is based on regression; others are extrapolated from the latest International Comparison Programme benchmark estimates. e. GNI and GNI per capita estimates include the French Overseas departments of French Guiana, Guadeloupe, Martinique, and Réunion. f. Estimated to be high income ($9,266 or more). g. Less then 0.5. h. Estimated to be low income ($755 or less). i. Data refer to mainland Tanzania only.

Table 2.   Poverty and income distribution

Economy	National poverty lines Survey year	Population below the poverty line (%) Rural	Urban	National	International poverty line Survey year	Population below $1 day %	Poverty gap at $1 day %	Population below $2 a day %	Poverty gap at $2 day %	Survey year	Gini index	Percentage share of income or consumption Lowest 10%	Highest 10%
Albania		..	..	..		..	..	..	..		..	..	..
Algeria	1995	30.3	14.7	22.6	1995	<2	<0.5	15.1	3.6	1995 a,b	35.3	2.8	26.8
Angola		..	..	..		..	..	..	..		..	..	..
Argentina	1993	..	..	17.6		..	..	..	..		..	..	..
Armenia		..	..	..	1996	7.8	1.7	34.0	11.3	1996 a,b	44.4	2.3	35.2
Australia		..	..	..		..	..	..	..	1994 c,d	35.2	2.0	25.4
Austria		..	..	..		..	..	..	..	1987 c,d	23.1	4.4	19.3
Azerbaijan	1995	..	..	68.1	1995	<2	<0.5	9.6	2.3	1995 c,d	36.0	2.8	27.8
Bangladesh	1995–96	39.8	14.3	35.6	1996	29.1	5.9	77.8	31.8	1995–96 a,b	33.6	3.9	28.6
Belarus	1995	..	..	22.5	1998	<2	<0.5	<2	0.1	1998 a,b	21.7	5.1	20.0
Belgium		..	..	..		..	..	..	..	1992 c,d	25.0	3.7	20.2
Benin	1995	..	..	33.0		..	..	..	..		..	..	..
Bolivia	1995	79.1	..	..	1997	29.4	15.2	51.4	27.8	1997 c,d	58.9	0.5	45.7
Botswana		..	..	..	1985–86	33.3	12.5	61.4	30.7		..	..	..
Brazil	1998	51.4	13.7	22.0	1997	9.0	2.1	25.4	9.8	1997 c,d	59.1	1.0	46.7
Bulgaria		..	..	..	1997	<2	<0.5	21.9	4.2	1997 c,d	26.4	4.5	22.8
Burkina Faso		..	..	..	1994	61.2	25.5	85.8	50.9	1994 a,b	48.2	2.2	39.5
Burundi	1990	..	..	36.2		..	..	..	..	1992 a,b	33.3	3.4	26.6
Cambodia	1997	40.1	21.1	36.1		..	..	..	..	1997 a,b	40.4	2.9	33.8
Cameroon	1984	32.4	44.4	40.0		..	..	..	..		..	..	..
Canada		..	..	..		..	..	..	..	1994 c,d	31.5	2.8	23.8
Central African Republic		..	..	..	1993	66.6	38.1	84.0	58.4	1993 a,b	61.3	0.7	47.7
Chad	1995–96	67.0	63.0	64.0		..	..	..	..		..	..	..
Chile	1994	..	..	20.5	1996	<2	<0.5	18.4	4.8	1996 c,d	57.5	1.4	46.9
China	1998	4.6	<2	4.6	1998	18.5	4.2	53.7	21.0	1998 c,d	40.3	2.4	30.4
Hong Kong, China		..	..	..		..	..	..	..		..	..	..
Colombia	1992	31.2	8.0	17.7	1996	11.0	3.2	28.7	11.6	1996 c,d	57.1	1.1	46.1
Congo, Dem. Rep.		..	..	..		..	..	..	..		..	..	..
Congo, Rep.		..	..	..		..	..	..	..		..	..	..
Costa Rica		..	..	..	1997	6.9	2.0	23.3	8.5	1997 c,d	45.9	1.7	34.6
Côte d'Ivoire		..	..	..	1995	12.3	2.4	49.4	16.8	1995 a,b	36.7	3.1	28.8
Croatia		..	..	..	1998	<2	<0.5	<2	<0.5	1998 a,b	29.0	3.7	23.3
Czech Republic		..	..	..	1996	<2	<0.5	<2	<0.5	1996 c,d	25.4	4.3	22.4
Denmark		..	..	..		..	..	..	..	1992 c,d	24.7	3.6	20.5
Dominican Republic	1992	29.8	10.9	20.6	1996	3.2	0.7	16.0	5.0	1998 c,d	47.4	2.1	37.9
Ecuador	1994	47.0	25.0	35.0	1995	20.2	5.8	52.3	21.2	1995 a,b	43.7	2.2	33.8
Egypt, Arab Rep.	1995–96	23.3	22.5	22.9	1995	3.1	0.3	52.7	13.9	1995 a,b	28.9	4.4	25.0
El Salvador	1992	55.7	43.1	48.3	1997	26.0	9.7	54.0	25.3	1997 c,d	50.8	1.4	39.3
Eritrea		..	..	..		..	..	..	..		..	..	..
Estonia	1995	14.7	6.8	8.9	1998	<2	<0.5	5.2	0.8	1998 c,d	37.6	3.0	29.8
Ethiopia		..	..	..	1995	31.3	8.0	76.4	32.9	1995 a,b	40.0	3.0	33.7
Finland		..	..	..		..	..	..	..	1991 c,d	25.6	4.2	21.6
France		..	..	..		..	..	..	..	1995 c,d	32.7	2.8	25.1
Georgia	1997	9.9	12.1	11.1	1996	<2	<0.5	<2	<0.5	1996 c,d	37.1	2.3	27.9
Germany		..	..	..		..	..	..	..	1994 c,d	30.0	3.3	23.7
Ghana	1992	34.3	26.7	31.4	1998	38.8	3.4	74.6	16.1	1998 a,b	39.6	2.4	29.5
Greece		..	..	..		..	..	..	..	1993 c,d	32.7	3.0	25.3
Guatemala	1989	71.9	33.7	57.9	1998	10.0	2.2	33.8	11.8	1998 c,d	55.8	1.6	46.0
Guinea	1994	..	..	40.0		..	..	..	..	1994 a,b	40.3	2.6	32.0
Haiti	1995	66.0	..	..		..	..	..	..		..	..	..
Honduras	1993	51.0	57.0	53.0	1996	40.5	17.5	68.8	36.9	1997 c,d	59.0	0.4	44.3
Hungary	1993	..	..	8.6	1998	<2	<0.5	7.3	1.7	1998 a,b	24.4	4.1	20.5
India	1994	36.7	30.5	35.0	1997	44.2	12.0	86.2	41.4	1997 a,b	37.8	3.5	33.5
Indonesia	1999	..	..	27.1	1999	7.7	1.0	55.3	16.5	1999 a,b	31.7	4.0	26.7
Iran, Islamic Rep.		..	..	..		..	..	..	..		..	..	..
Ireland		..	..	..		..	..	..	..	1987 c,d	35.9	2.5	27.4
Israel		..	..	..		..	..	..	..	1992 c,d	35.5	2.8	26.9
Italy		..	..	..		..	..	..	..	1995 c,d	27.3	3.5	21.8
Jamaica	1992	..	..	34.2	1996	3.2	0.7	25.2	6.9	1996 a,b	36.4	2.9	28.9
Japan		..	..	..		..	..	..	..	1993 c,d	24.9	4.8	21.7
Jordan	1997	..	..	11.7	1997	<2	<0.5	7.4	1.4	1997 a,b	36.4	3.3	29.8
Kazakhstan	1996	39.0	30.0	34.6	1996	1.5	0.3	15.3	3.9	1996 a,b	35.4	2.7	26.3
Kenya	1992	46.4	29.3	42.0	1994	26.5	9.0	62.3	27.5	1994 a,b	44.5	1.8	34.9
Korea, Rep.		..	..	..	1993	<2	<0.5	<2	<0.5	1993 a,b	31.6	2.9	24.3
Kuwait		..	..	..		..	..	..	..		..	..	..
Kyrgyz Republic	1997	64.5	28.5	51.0		..	..	..	..	1997 c,d	40.5	2.7	31.7
Lao PDR	1993	53.0	24.0	46.1	1997	26.3	6.3	73.2	29.6	1997 a,b	37.0	3.2	30.6
Latvia		..	..	..	1998	<2	<0.5	8.3	2.0	1998 c,d	32.4	2.9	25.9
Lebanon		..	..	..		..	..	..	..		..	..	..
Lesotho	1993	53.9	27.8	49.2	1993	43.1	20.3	65.7	38.1	1986–87 a,b	56.0	0.9	43.4
Lithuania		..	..	..	1996	<2	<0.5	7.8	2.0	1996 a,b	32.4	3.1	25.6
Macedonia, FYR		..	..	..		..	..	..	..		..	..	..
Madagascar	1993–94	77.0	47.0	70.0	1997	63.4	26.9	89.0	53.2	1997 a,b	46.0	2.2	37.3
Malawi	1990–91	..	..	54.0		..	..	..	..		..	..	..
Malaysia	1989	..	..	15.5		..	..	..	..	1997 c,d	49.2	1.7	38.4

Note: For data comparability and coverage, see the technical notes. Figures in italics are for years other than those specified.

Economy	National poverty lines				International poverty line					Percentage share of income or consumption	
	Survey year	Population below the poverty line (%)			Survey year	Population below $1 day %	Poverty gap at $1 day %	Population below $2 a day %	Poverty gap at $2 day %	Survey year	Gini index	Lowest 10%	Highest 10%
		Rural	Urban	National									
Mali		..	..	..	1994	72.8	37.4	90.6	60.5	1994 a,b	50.5	1.8	40.4
Mauritania	1989–90	..	..	57.0	1995	28.6	9.1	68.7	29.6	1995 a,b	37.3	2.5	28.4
Mexico	1988	..	..	10.1	1996	12.2	3.5	34.8	13.2	1996 c,d	51.9	1.6	41.1
Moldova	1997	26.7	..	23.3	1997	11.3	3.0	38.4	14.0	1997 c,d	40.6	2.2	30.7
Mongolia	1995	33.1	38.5	36.3	1995	13.9	3.1	50.0	17.5	1995 a,b	33.2	2.9	24.5
Morocco	1998–99	27.2	12.0	19.0	1990–91	<2	<0.5	7.5	1.3	1998–99 a,b	39.5	2.6	30.9
Mozambique		..	..	..	1996	37.9	12.0	78.4	36.8	1996–97 a,b	39.6	2.5	31.7
Myanmar		..	..	..		..	..	..	..		..	..	..
Namibia		..	..	..	1993	34.9	14.0	55.8	30.4		..	..	..
Nepal	1995–96	44.0	23.0	42.0	1995	37.7	9.7	82.5	37.5	1995–96 a,b	36.7	3.2	29.8
Netherlands		..	..	..		..	..	..	..	1994 c,d	32.6	2.8	25.1
New Zealand		..	..	..		..	..	..	..		..	..	..
Nicaragua	1993	76.1	31.9	50.3		..	..	..	..	1998 a,b	60.3	0.7	48.8
Niger	1989–93	66.0	52.0	63.0	1995	61.4	33.9	85.3	54.8	1995 a,b	50.5	0.8	35.4
Nigeria	1992–93	36.4	30.4	34.1	1997	70.2	34.9	90.8	59.0	1996–97 a,b	50.6	1.6	40.8
Norway		..	..	..		..	..	..	..	1995 c,d	25.8	4.1	21.8
Pakistan	1991	36.9	28.0	34.0	1996	31.0	6.2	84.7	35.0	1996–97 a,b	31.2	4.1	27.6
Panama	1997	64.9	15.3	37.3	1997	10.3	3.2	25.1	10.2	1997 a,b	48.5	1.2	35.7
Papua New Guinea		..	..	..		..	..	..	..	1996 a,b	50.9	1.7	40.5
Paraguay	1991	28.5	19.7	21.8	1998	19.5	9.8	49.3	26.3	1998 c,d	57.7	0.5	43.8
Peru	1997	64.7	40.4	49.0	1996	15.5	5.4	41.4	17.1	1996 c,d	46.2	1.6	35.4
Philippines	1997	50.7	21.5	36.8		..	..	..	..	1997 a,b	46.2	2.3	36.6
Poland	1993	..	..	23.8	1998	<2	<0.5	<2	<0.5	1998 a,b	31.6	3.2	24.7
Portugal		..	..	..	1994	<2	<0.5	<2	<0.5	1994–95 c,d	35.6	3.1	28.4
Romania	1994	27.9	20.4	21.5	1994	2.8	0.8	27.5	6.9	1994 c,d	28.2	3.7	22.7
Russian Federation	1994	..	..	30.9	1998	7.1	1.4	25.1	8.7	1998 a,b	48.7	1.7	38.7
Rwanda	1993	..	..	51.2	1983–85	35.7	7.7	84.6	36.7	1983–85 a,b	28.9	4.2	24.2
Saudi Arabia		..	..	..		..	..	..	..		..	..	..
Senegal		..	..	..	1995	26.3	7.0	67.8	28.2	1995 a,b	41.3	2.6	33.5
Sierra Leone	1989	76.0	53.0	68.0	1989	57.0	39.5	74.5	51.8	1989 a,b	62.9	0.5	43.6
Singapore		..	..	..		..	..	..	..		..	..	..
Slovak Republic		..	..	..	1992	<2	<0.5	<2	<0.5	1992 c,d	19.5	5.1	18.2
Slovenia		..	..	..	1998	<2	<0.5	<2	<0.5	1998 c,d	28.4	3.9	23.0
South Africa		..	..	..	1993	11.5	1.8	35.8	13.4	1993–94 a,b	59.3	1.1	45.9
Spain		..	..	..		..	..	..	..	1990 c,d	32.5	2.8	25.2
Sri Lanka	1995–96	27.0	15.0	25.0	1995	6.6	1.0	45.4	13.5	1995 a,b	34.4	3.5	28.0
Sweden		..	..	..		..	..	..	..	1992 c,d	25.0	3.7	20.1
Switzerland		..	..	..		..	..	..	..	1992 c,d	33.1	2.6	25.2
Syrian Arab Republic		..	..	..		..	..	..	..		..	..	..
Tajikistan		..	..	..		..	..	..	..		..	..	..
Tanzania	1991	..	..	51.1	1993	19.9	4.8	59.7	23.0	1993 a,b	38.2	2.8	30.1
Thailand	1992	15.5	10.2	13.1	1998	<2	<0.5	28.2	7.1	1998 a,b	41.4	2.8	32.4
Togo	1987–89	..	..	32.3		..	..	..	..		..	..	..
Tunisia	1990	21.6	8.9	14.1	1995	<2	<0.5	10.0	2.3	1995 a,b	41.7	2.3	31.8
Turkey		..	..	..	1994	2.4	0.5	18.0	5.0	1994 a,b	41.5	2.3	32.3
Turkmenistan		..	..	..	1993	20.9	5.7	59.0	23.3	1998 a,b	40.8	2.6	31.7
Uganda	1999–2000	10.3	39.1	35.2		..	..	..	..	1996 a,b	37.4	3.0	29.8
Ukraine	1995	..	..	31.7	1999	2.9	0.6	31.0	8.0	1999 a,b	29.0	3.7	23.2
United Kingdom		..	..	..		..	..	..	..	1991 c,d	36.1	2.6	27.3
United States		..	..	..		..	..	..	..	1997 c,d	40.8	1.8	30.5
Uruguay		..	..	..	1989	<2	<0.5	6.6	1.9	1989 c,d	42.3	2.1	32.7
Uzbekistan		..	..	..	1993	3.3	0.5	26.5	7.3	1993 c,d	33.3	3.1	25.2
Venezuela, RB	1989	..	..	31.3	1997	18.7	6.5	44.6	19.0	1997 a,b	48.8	1.6	37.6
Vietnam	1993	57.2	25.9	50.9		..	..	..	..	1998 a,b	36.1	3.6	29.9
Yemen, Rep.	1992	19.2	18.6	19.1	1998	15.7	4.5	45.2	15.0	1998 a,b	33.4	3.0	25.9
Yugoslavia, Fed. Rep.		..	..	..		..	..	..	..		..	..	..
Zambia	1993	..	..	86.0	1998	63.7	32.7	87.4	55.4	1998 a,b	52.6	1.1	41.0
Zimbabwe	1990–91	31.0	10.0	25.5	1990–91	36.0	9.6	64.2	29.4	1990–91 a,b	56.8	1.8	46.9

a. Refers to expenditure shares by percentiles of population. b. Ranked by per capita expenditure. c. Refers to income shares by percentiles of population. d. Ranked by per capita income.

Table 3. Economic activity

	Gross domestic product		Agricultural productivity Agr. Value added per agricultural worker 1995 dollars		Value added as % of GDP			Household final cons. expenditure % of GDP	General gov't final cons. expenditure % of GDP	Gross capital formation % of GDP	External balance of goods and services % of GDP	GDP implicit deflator Avg. annual % growth
	Millions of dollars 2000	Avg. annual % growth 1990–2000	1987–89	1997–99	Agricultural 2000	Industry 2000	Services 2000	2000	2000	2000	2000	1990–2000
Albania	3,704	3.7	1,124	1,934	55	28	17	90	10	19	−19	39.0
Algeria	53,817	2.1	1,909	1,876	10	69	21	46	8	26	19	17.9
Angola	8,738	1.3	243	126	6	70	24	36	32	24	8	740.2
Argentina	285,473	4.3	7,167	9,951	5	28	68	71	14	16	−1	5.2
Armenia	1,914	−1.9	..	5,180	29	33	39	99	11	19	−29	212.5
Australia	394,023	4.1	22,932	31,432	3	25	72	60	18	25	−3	1.4
Austria	190,957	2.0	20,356	28,410	2	29	69	56	20	24	0	2.1
Azerbaijan	4,904	−5.3	..	..	21	43	36	77	11	46	−34	194.2
Bangladesh	47,864	4.8	247	292	26	25	49	78	4	23	−5	4.1
Belarus	35,940	−1.9	..	3,744	13	42	45	59	20	24	−3	354.6
Belgium	231,016	2.0	28,767	48,529	1	25	73	54	21	21	4	2.0
Benin	2,262	4.7	377	558	37	14	49	82	11	19	−13	8.7
Bolivia	8,469	4.1	..	1,054	18	34	48	74	16	18	−8	8.6
Botswana	5,285	4.7	708	681	4	44	52	58	28	20	−6	9.7
Brazil	587,553	2.9	2,918	4,300	9	32	59	64	16	23	−2	207.5
Bulgaria	12,052	−2.1	3,251	6,007	14	24	62	72	14	19	−5	103.0
Burkina Faso	2,406	4.1	147	162	31	28	40	77	14	28	−18	5.5
Burundi	689	−2.6	185	140	51	18	31	93	13	9	−15	12.3
Cambodia	3,207	4.6	386	406	51	15	35	86	9	15	−10	25.0
Cameroon	8,687	1.7	882	1,072	44	19	38	71	10	19	−1	5.0
Canada	689,549	2.9	23,026	34,922	..	..	..	58	19	20	3	1.4
Central African Republic	959	2.1	383	460	55	20	25	81	12	14	−7	4.5
Chad	1,408	2.2	171	220	36	15	49	95	8	10	−13	7.1
Chile	70,710	6.8	4,533	5,491	8	34	57	65	11	22	1	7.3
China	1,079,954	10.3	222	316	16	49	34	49	11	38	2	7.1
Hong Kong, China	163,261	4.0	..	..	0	15	85	58	10	27	5	4.1
Colombia	82,849	3.0	3,698	3,454	15	29	56	70	9	20	1	19.0
Congo, Dem. Rep.	5,584	−5.1	247	252	..	..	..	..	..	..	..	1,423.1
Congo, Rep.	2,689	−0.2	475	498	10	49	41	60	11	22	7	9.2
Costa Rica	15,751	5.4	3,568	4,973	11	37	53	76	5	17	2	17.1
Côte d'Ivoire	9,319	3.5	902	1,104	28	29	43	65	11	19	6	7.3
Croatia	19,030	0.6	..	7,123	9	32	59	57	27	23	−7	86.2
Czech Republic	49,510	0.8	..	5,091	4	43	53	53	20	28	−2	11.3
Denmark	160,780	2.4	27,379	52,809	2	21	76	50	26	20	4	2.1
Dominican Republic	19,894	6.1	1,937	2,710	11	32	58	79	8	24	−10	9.4
Ecuador	13,607	1.8	1,432	1,789	11	25	64	62	9	17	12	37.1
Egypt, Arab Rep.	98,333	4.6	953	1,222	17	33	50	72	10	24	−7	8.2
El Salvador	13,217	4.7	1,606	1,690	10	30	61	85	11	16	−13	7.4
Eritrea	600	3.8	..	..	17	29	54	78	65	39	−82	9.4
Estonia	4,969	−0.5	..	3,646	6	28	66	58	21	26	−5	53.1
Ethiopia	6,304	4.6	..	144	52	11	37	81	16	18	−15	7.0
Finland	119,823	2.8	21,944	36,384	3	28	68	51	21	20	8	1.9
France	1,286,252	1.7	29,079	50,171	3	23	74	55	24	19	3	1.5
Georgia	3,048	5.6	..	1,952	36	13	52	89	10	18	−17	11.6
Germany	1,870,136	1.5	..	28,924	1	28	71	58	19	22	1	1.7
Ghana	5,419	4.3	547	552	35	8	56	75	10	31	−16	27.0
Greece	111,955	2.4	10,605	12,711	7	20	72	69	15	23	−7	8.8
Guatemala	19,041	4.1	1,901	2,099	23	20	57	86	6	16	−8	10.4
Guinea	3,120	4.3	253	285	24	38	38	77	6	22	−5	5.2
Haiti	3,826	−0.6	510	394	30	20	50	100	7	11	−18	20.6
Honduras	5,932	3.2	824	1,008	18	32	51	66	13	35	−14	18.8
Hungary	45,716	1.5	4,968	4,860	6	34	61	63	10	29	−2	19.3
India	479,404	6.0	324	395	27	27	46	68	11	25	−4	8.2
Indonesia	153,255	4.2	656	740	17	47	36	67	7	18	8	15.5
Iran, Islamic Rep.	98,990	3.6	2,773	3,679	20	37	43	66	17	17	1	26.2
Ireland	94,388	7.3	..	..	..	..	..	49	14	23	14	3.6
Israel	110,332	5.1	..	..	..	..	..	59	29	19	−7	10.0
Italy	1,068,518	1.5	13,460	23,906	3	26	71	60	18	20	2	3.8
Jamaica	6,892	0.2	947	1,229	7	28	65	60	18	31	−10	24.5
Japan	4,677,099	1.3	21,914	30,620	2	36	62	61	10	26	2	0.1
Jordan	8,340	5.0	1,712	1,434	3	26	72	72	24	22	−19	3.2
Kazakhstan	18,264	−4.6	..	1,414	9	30	60	68	17	14	0	206.3
Kenya	10,410	2.1	262	226	23	16	60	81	16	12	−9	14.0
Korea, Rep.	457,219	5.7	6,581	12,252	5	44	51	56	10	31	3	5.0
Kuwait	29,674	..	..	..	..	..	..	50	27	13	10	..
Kyrgyz Republic	1,304	−4.1	..	3,430	38	27	36	78	19	18	−15	110.2
Lao PDR	1,709	6.5	446	558	53	22	25	81	5	25	−12	27.0
Latvia	7,138	−3.4	..	2,523	4	26	71	68	18	25	−10	49.2
Lebanon	16,584	5.9	..	26,946	12	21	67	95	14	21	−30	17.6
Lesotho	913	4.2	550	544	18	38	44	122	13	47	−82	10.2
Lithuania	11,232	−3.1	..	3,192	9	32	59	65	22	23	−10	75.2
Macedonia, FYR	3,295	−0.3	..	2,141	12	35	53	74	19	21	−14	77.1
Madagascar	4,020	2.0	194	184	30	14	56	87	8	13	−8	19.1
Malawi	1,692	3.8	91	138	40	19	41	84	12	18	−14	33.7
Malaysia	89,321	7.0	5,495	6,578	12	40	48	54	7	26	12	3.9

Note: For data comparability and coverage, see the technical notes. Figures in italics are for years other than those specified.

| | Gross domestic product | | Agricultural productivity Agr. Value added per agricultural worker 1995 dollars | | Value added as % of GDP | | | Household final cons. expenditure % of GDP | General gov't. final cons. expenditure % of GDP | Gross capital formation % of GDP | External balance of goods and services % of GDP | GDP implicit deflator Avg. annual % growth |
	Millions of dollars 2000	Avg. annual % growth 1990–2000	1987–89	1997–99	Agricultural 2000	Industry 2000	Services 2000	2000	2000	2000	2000	1990–2000
Mali	2,345	3.8	240	280	45	17	38	79	15	21	–15	7.2
Mauritania	935	4.2	392	469	25	29	46	78	15	18	–11	5.9
Mexico	574,512	3.1	1,518	1,758	4	28	67	71	7	23	–2	18.9
Moldova	1,285	–9.7	. .	1,277	25	22	53	74	19	22	–15	120.2
Mongolia	975	1.0	1,031	1,193	32	30	39	63	18	26	–5	57.7
Morocco	33,364	2.2	1,704	1,651	13	33	54	64	17	25	–6	3.0
Mozambique	3,812	6.4	119	132	33	25	41	82	11	33	–26	32.5
Myanmar	. .	. .	. .	. .	60	9	31	90	. .[a]	11	–1	26.1
Namibia	3,479	4.1	981	1,417	11	28	61	54	29	24	–7	9.5
Nepal	5,450	4.8	181	189	39	20	41	77	9	21	–8	8.3
Netherlands	364,948	2.9	31,328	51,594	3	24	74	50	23	22	5	1.9
New Zealand	49,983	3.0	22,073	27,083	. .	. .	. .	65	15	19	1	1.4
Nicaragua	2,397	3.5	1,313	1,919	33	23	44	87	16	38	–41	33.2
Niger	1,861	2.6	204	205	41	17	42	81	15	10	–6	6.0
Nigeria	41,248	2.4	470	641	39	33	28	56	14	22	9	29.1
Norway	149,349	3.6	20,164	32,848	2	31	67	48	21	24	6	2.4
Pakistan	61,673	3.7	497	626	26	23	50	78	10	15	–4	10.1
Panama	9,911	4.1	2,235	2,580	7	17	76	61	15	30	–6	2.0
Papua New Guinea	4,011	4.0	662	808	26	44	30	66	13	18	3	7.9
Paraguay	7,680	2.2	3,090	3,512	29	26	45	81	8	23	–12	12.7
Peru	53,882	4.7	1,323	1,569	8	38	55	71	8	22	–2	26.8
Philippines	75,186	3.2	1,322	1,342	17	30	53	67	15	20	–2	8.4
Poland	158,839	4.6	. .	1,583	3	32	65	80	4	27	–11	22.8
Portugal	103,871	2.6	5,140	7,621	4	27	69	64	19	25	–9	5.3
Romania	36,692	–0.7	1,896	3,228	15	30	55	71	14	19	–4	98.0
Russian Federation	251,092	–4.8	. .	2,282	7	38	56	53	14	14	20	162.0
Rwanda	1,762	–0.2	302	234	46	20	34	89	13	14	–16	14.5
Saudi Arabia	139,383	1.6	6,191	10,930	7	48	45	39	30	19	12	1.2
Senegal	4,372	3.6	343	307	18	26	56	76	11	19	–6	4.6
Sierra Leone	654	–4.5	433	379	43	27	30	94	15	8	–16	29.3
Singapore	92,252	7.8	25,165	51,241	0	34	66	40	10	31	18	1.3
Slovak Republic	19,123	2.1	. .	3,491	4	32	64	54	19	32	–5	10.6
Slovenia	18,174	2.7	. .	30,136	4	38	58	56	21	28	–4	20.4
South Africa	125,887	2.0	3,471	3,910	3	31	66	64	18	15	3	9.6
Spain	555,004	2.4	. .	21,687	4	28	69	59	17	24	–1	3.9
Sri Lanka	16,402	5.3	683	746	21	27	52	71	9	27	–7	9.2
Sweden	227,369	1.8	24,506	34,285	. .	. .	. .	51	27	17	6	2.1
Switzerland	240,323	0.7	. .	. .	. .	. .	. .	61	14	21	4	1.4
Syrian Arab Republic	16,485	5.6	. .	. .	. .	. .	. .	72	12	16	–1	6.1
Tajikistan	987	–1.7	. .	296	19	25	57	. .	. .	. .	. .	115.1
Tanzania[b]	9,316	3.1	. .	188	45	15	40	86	12	17	–15	21.7
Thailand	121,927	4.2	754	916	10	40	49	58	12	22	8	4.2
Togo	1,281	2.6	435	543	41	21	38	85	11	13	–10	7.0
Tunisia	19,462	4.7	2,132	3,047	12	28	59	61	14	28	–3	4.4
Turkey	199,902	3.7	1,823	1,850	16	25	59	69	14	24	–7	76.3
Turkmenistan	4,404	–4.8	. .	1,116	27	45	28	62	12	46	–20	407.5
Uganda	6,248	7.1	287	350	44	18	38	85	10	16	–12	12.4
Ukraine	32,171	–9.4	. .	1,383	13	40	47	63	18	20	–1	271.3
United Kingdom	1,413,432	2.5	27,636	34,730	1	25	74	66	18	18	–2	2.9
United States	9,882,842	3.4	. .	. .	. .	. .	. .	67	14	20	–2	2.1
Uruguay	20,195	3.3	6,505	8,679	6	29	65	71	14	17	–2	31.3
Uzbekistan	13,517	–0.5	. .	997	33	24	43	72	9	18	1	246.6
Venezuela, RB	120,484	1.6	4,489	5,125	5	47	47	68	8	14	11	45.5
Vietnam	31,344	7.9	173	236	25	34	40	70	7	25	–2	15.3
Yemen, Rep.	8,667	3.5	. .	355	17	40	42	71	17	19	–7	24.9
Yugoslavia, Fed. Rep.	. .	. .	. .	. .	. .	. .	. .	. .	. .	. .	. .	. .
Zambia	2,911	0.5	161	212	24	25	51	91	10	18	–19	51.4
Zimbabwe	7,350	2.4	287	369	11	14	75	72	23	2	3	25.8
World	**31,336,893 t**	**2.6 w**	**. . w**	**. . w**	**5 w**	**31 w**	**63 w**	**62 w**	**15 w**	**23 w**	**. . w**	
Low income	1,078,946	3.4	304	. .	23	33	44	69	11	21	0	
Middle income	5,490,802	3.6	. .	. .	11	36	54	62	12	25	1	
Lower middle income	2,358,673	3.6	. .	. .	15	43	42	56	12	27	5	
Upper middle income	3,138,826	3.6	. .	. .	8	31	61	65	13	23	–1	
Low & middle income	6,567,734	3.6	. .	. .	13	35	52	63	12	24	1	
East Asia & Pacific	2,059,259	7.2	. .	. .	15	46	38	55	10	31	4	
Europe & Central Asia	960,670	–1.6	. .	2,220	10	33	57	63	13	19	6	
Latin America & Carib.	1,995,118	3.3	. .	. .	8	31	61	67	13	21	–2	
Middle East & N. Africa	591,584	3.0	. .	. .	14	38	48	57	19	21	2	
South Asia	620,253	5.6	306	. .	27	26	47	70	11	23	–4	
Sub-Saharan Africa	322,212	2.4	369	380	15	28	57	65	17	16	2	
High income	24,772,147	2.4	. .	. .	. .	. .	. .	62	16	22	1	

a. Data on general government final consumption expenditure figures are not available separately; they are included in household final consumption expenditure. b. Data cover mainland Tanzania only.

Table 4. Trade, aid, and finance

| | Merchandise trade | | Manufactured exports | High technology exports | Current account balance | Net private capital flows | Foreign direct investment | Official development assistance[a] | External debt | | Domestic credit provided by banking sector |
| | exports | imports | % of total merchandise exports | % of manufactured exports | | | | | Total | Present value | |
	Millions of dollars 2000	Millions of dollars 2000	1999	1999	Millions of dollars 1999	Millions of dollars 1999	Millions of dollars 1999	Dollars per capita 1999	Millions of dollars 1999	% of GNI 1999	% of GDP 2000
Albania	260	975	*68*	*1*	−155	37	41	142	975	18	48.2
Algeria	19,550	9,200	3	4	..	−1,486	7	3	28,015	64	*50.3*
Angola	8,200	3,400	..	..	−249	2,373	2,471	31	10,871	344	−14.2
Argentina	26,251	25,508	32	8	−12,312	32,296	23,929	2	147,880	56	34.4
Armenia	290	850	63	2	−307	122	122	55	932	36	11.5
Australia	63,872	71,344	29	11	−23,070	..	6,363	..	..	..	90.8
Austria	64,907	68,813	83	13	−5,747	..	2,834	..	..	..	..
Azerbaijan	1,750	1,390	10	..	−1,106	596	510	20	1,036	17	10.3
Bangladesh	5,700	8,480	*91*	*0*	−394	198	179	9	17,534	23	34.8
Belarus	7,575	8,960	75	4	−257	394	225	2	1,136	4	19.2
Belgium	184,130[b]	171,178[b]	79[b]	8	11,685	..	117,211[b]	..	..	..	..
Benin	350	650	*3*	*0*	−158	31	31	34	1,686	40[c]	8.4
Bolivia	1,210	1,760	41	..	−556	1,016	1,016	70	6,157	37[c]	63.2
Botswana	2,250	2,380	..	..	517	36	37	38	462	8	−71.9
Brazil	55,086	58,585	54	13	−25,073	22,793	32,659	1	244,673	48	51.6
Bulgaria	4,760	6,540	*61*	*4*	−685	1,112	806	32	9,872	78	18.2
Burkina Faso	230	700	..	..	−312	10	10	36	1,518	25[c]	15.4
Burundi	55	140	..	..	−27	0	0	11	1,131	96	34.4
Cambodia	590	700	..	..	−66	122	126	24	2,262	61	7.3
Cameroon	2,050	1,203	..	..	−396	−13	40	30	9,443	76	16.7
Canada	277,233	249,118	67	15	−2,273	..	25,129	..	..	..	89.0
Central African Republic	210	120	..	..	−42	13	13	33	913	54	11.5
Chad	200	350	..	..	−161	14	15	25	1,142	43	12.1
Chile	18,158	18,101	17	*4*	−80	11,851	9,221	5	37,762	55	74.7
China	249,212	225,097	88	17	15,667	40,632	38,753	2	154,223	14	132.7
Hong Kong, China	202,440[d]	214,200	95[d]	21	10,541	..	..	.1	..	..	140.9
Colombia	13,345	11,675	31	8	−61	3,635	1,109	7	34,538	40	35.8
Congo, Dem. Rep.	580	400	..	..	*−583*	1	1	3	11,906	*244*	..
Congo, Rep.	2,400	930	..	..	*−252*	5	5	49	5,031	301	10.4
Costa Rica	5,874	6,373	68	..	−649	924	669	−3	4,182	30	30.5
Côte d'Ivoire	3,780	3,150	..	..	38	74	350	29	13,170	117[c]	25.8
Croatia	4,390	7,911	76	8	−1,522	2,392	1,408	11	9,443	47	45.7
Czech Republic	28,980	32,245	88	9	−1,032	4,837	5,093	31	22,582	43	58.7
Denmark	49,215	44,567	66	20	2,964	..	11,730	..	..	..	*57.4*
Dominican Republic	5,700	9,700	*8*	*0*	−429	1,404	1,338	23	4,771	28	38.0
Ecuador	4,872	3,417	9	6	955	944	690	12	14,506	76	0.0
Egypt, Arab Rep.	4,700	13,600	37	0	−1,708	1,558	1,065	25	30,404	27	100.6
El Salvador	2,933	4,888	50	7	−242	360	231	30	4,014	31	42.3
Eritrea	..	..	..	..	−282	0	0	37	254	19	..
Estonia	3,160	4,265	69	13	−295	569	305	57	2,879	55	40.0
Ethiopia	450	1,100	..	..	−709	78	90	10	5,551	55	63.3
Finland	45,511	33,702	85	24	7,588	..	4,649	..	..	..	*55.8*
France	298,127	305,444	81	23	36,579	..	38,828	..	..	..	..
Georgia	320	645	..	..	−220	86	82	44	1,652	45	21.6
Germany	551,566	500,060	84	17	−19,313	..	52,232	..	..	..	*145.2*
Ghana	1,400	2,400	20	14	−766	−16	17	32	6,928	66[c]	38.7
Greece	10,609	28,254	50	10	*−4,860*	..	984	..	..	..	102.4
Guatemala	2,630	4,750	34	9	−1,026	98	155	26	4,660	24	16.9
Guinea	940	1,200	*20*	*0*	−138	63	63	33	3,518	72	8.7
Haiti	170	1,130	*84*	*4*	−38	30	30	34	1,190	17	30.9
Honduras	1,450	2,865	32	3	−211	251	230	129	5,333	63	31.5
Hungary	28,090	32,080	85	23	−2,101	4,961	1,950	25	29,042	60	*52.1*
India	42,358	49,830	76	6	−3,699	1,813	2,169	1	94,393	16	48.2
Indonesia	62,016	33,547	54	10	5,785	−8,416	−2,745	11	150,096	114	66.2
Iran, Islamic Rep.	30,170	14,900	8	1	*−1,897*	−1,385	85	3	10,357	9	49.3
Ireland	77,102	50,202	85	47	595	..	19,091	..	..	..	*93.8*
Israel	31,338	38,130	93	19	−1,881	..	2,363	148	..	..	86.6
Italy	234,613	233,277	89	8	6,304	..	6,783	..	..	..	*92.0*
Jamaica	1,350	3,170	*70*	*0*	−256	425	524	−9	3,913	61	*46.8*
Japan	479,328	379,514	94	27	106,865	..	12,308	..	..	..	143.9
Jordan	1,960	4,580	*56*	*2*	390	112	158	91	8,947	104	84.8
Kazakhstan	9,140	5,100	25	8	−171	1,477	1,587	11	5,764	38	14.5
Kenya	1,650	3,200	23	4	11	−51	14	10	6,562	49	48.0
Korea, Rep.	172,620	160,493	91	32	24,477	6,409	9,333	−1	129,784	31	104.1
Kuwait	22,700	7,640	20	1	5,062	..	72	4	..	..	*110.3*
Kyrgyz Republic	505	565	20	6	−185	−16	36	55	1,699	105	12.6
Lao PDR	300	560	..	..	90	79	79	58	2,527	100	10.7
Latvia	1,865	3,210	57	4	−647	303	348	40	2,657	37	24.2
Lebanon	714	6,228	..	..	−5,626	1,771	250	45	8,441	51	182.3
Lesotho	180	720	..	..	−221	168	163	15	686	41	4.0
Lithuania	3,860	5,385	67	12	−1,194	1,148	487	35	3,584	33	14.5
Macedonia, FYR	1,365	2,220	*72*	*2*	−109	51	30	135	1,433	37	15.7
Madagascar	260	660	50	3	*−289*	52	58	24	4,409	80	15.2
Malawi	410	610	..	..	..	60	60	41	2,751	76[c]	7.2
Malaysia	98,237	82,210	80	59	12,606	3,247	1,553	6	45,939	64	143.9
*Taiwan, China	148,370	140,010	95	40	5,861	..	..	..	..	..	..

Note: For data comparability and coverage, see the technical notes. Figures in italics are for years other than those specified.

	Merchandise trade		Manufactured exports	High technology exports	Current account balance	Net private capital flows	Foreign direct investment	Official development assistance[a]	External debt		Domestic credit provided by banking sector
	exports	imports	% of total merchandise exports	% of manufactured exports	balance	flows	investment	assistance[a]	Total	Present value	by banking sector
	Millions of dollars 2000	Millions of dollars 2000	exports 1999	exports 1999	Millions of dollars 1999	Millions of dollars 1999	Millions of dollars 1999	Dollars per capita 1999	Millions of dollars 1999	% of GNI 1999	% of GDP 2000
Mali	510	690	1	7	−178	19	19	33	3,183	57c	14.7
Mauritania	400	340	..	..	140	0	2	84	2,528	169	0.3
Mexico	166,415	182,635	85	21	−14,166	26,780	11,786	0	166,960	37	26.1
Moldova	470	780	27	4	−34	12	34	24	943	73	25.3
Mongolia	400	440	..	..	−52	28	30	92	891	59	6.7
Morocco	7,210	10,630	49	0	−167	−118	3	24	19,060	51	93.4
Mozambique	235	890	..	..	−429	374	384	7	6,959	28c	11.2
Myanmar	1,310	2,450	..	..	−232	203	216	2	5,999	..	26.8
Namibia	1,350	1,470	..	..	204	..	114	104	..	..	48.0
Nepal	795	1,590	69	..	−168	−8	4	15	2,970	32	43.5
Netherlands	211,731	196,980	70	33	17,576	..	43,189	..	..	..	118.1
New Zealand	13,347	14,065	33	15	−3,596	..	1,410	..	..	..	..
Nicaragua	625	1,792	9	6	−587	382	300	137	6,986	278c	3.4
Niger	320	450	2	5	−174	−8	15	18	1,621	55c	8.9
Nigeria	20,100	12,910	1	13	506	860	1,005	1	29,358	90	12.4
Norway	58,058	33,758	27	17	5,961	..	7,900	..	..	..	60.4
Pakistan	9,132	11,060	84	0	−2,187	53	530	5	34,269	43	49.0
Panama	800	3,406	17	1	−1,376	620	22	5	6,837	78	110.6
Papua New Guinea	2,050	1,150	9	..	120	499	297	46	2,695	77	27.0
Paraguay	852	2,252	15	3	−235	109	72	14	2,514	31	27.5
Peru	6,982	8,790	21	5	−1,822	3,140	1,969	18	32,284	63	26.2
Philippines	40,000	34,600	41	59	7,910	4,915	573	9	52,022	64	62.9
Poland	31,590	49,290	77	3	−12,487	10,452	7,270	25	54,268	33	37.6
Portugal	23,267	37,911	87	5	−9,629	..	1,127	..	..	..	103.9
Romania	10,365	13,055	78	4	−1,297	714	1,041	17	9,367	26	13.6
Russian Federation	105,200	44,200	25	16	20,960	3,780	3,309	12	173,940	72	23.9
Rwanda	58	215	..	..	−2	2	2	45	1,292	36	12.9
Saudi Arabia	84,060	32,800	13	0	412	..	−782	1	..	..	85.7
Senegal	1,020	1,570	57	13	−308	54	60	58	3,705	53	25.1
Sierra Leone	12	150	..	..	..	1	1	15	1,249	136	53.0
Singapore	137,953	134,675	86	61	21,254	..	6,984	0	..	..	89.6
Slovak Republic	11,870	12,785	82	5	−1,155	281	354	59	9,150	44	60.2
Slovenia	8,770	10,150	90	4	−782	..	181	16	..	..	47.0
South Africa	29,985e	29,695e	55c	8	−553	4,533	1,376	13	24,158	19	76.6
Spain	113,747	153,516	78	8	−13,761	..	15,541	..	..	..	108.9
Sri Lanka	5,410	7,205	75	3	−493	109	177	13	9,472	46	37.8
Sweden	86,715	72,646	83	22	5,982	..	59,386	..	..	..	79.3
Switzerland	80,537	82,543	92	22	29,119	..	9,944	..	..	..	178.8
Syrian Arab Republic	4,400	3,800	7	..	201	87	91	15	22,369	138	30.4
Tajikistan	785	710	..	..	67	10	24	20	889	66	..
Tanzania	658	1,540	16	6	−635	171	183	30	7,967	53	11.7
Thailand	68,920	62,040	74	32	12,428	2,471	6,213	17	96,335	79	122.0
Togo	320	490	18	1	−127	30	30	16	1,500	82	22.6
Tunisia	5,970	8,740	80	3	−443	739	350	26	11,872	59	73.2
Turkey	27,324	53,983	78	4	−1,364	8,667	783	0	101,796	52	1.8
Turkmenistan	2,700	1,400	..	..	−571	−54	80	4	2,015	52	30.5
Uganda	380	1,650	3	11	−746	221	222	27	4,077	27c	12.1
Ukraine	14,550	14,000	..	..	1,658	371	496	10	14,136	43	23.1
United Kingdom	280,061	331,661	83	30	−15,981	..	84,476	..	..	..	136.1
United States	782,429	1,258,027	83	35	−331,481	..	275,535	..	..	..	161.3
Uruguay	2,375	3,542	38	2	−605	65	229	7	7,447	37	54.3
Uzbekistan	3,010	2,810	..	..	−14	658	113	5	4,573	25	..
Venezuela, RB	32,800	16,250	12	3	3,689	3,130	3,187	2	35,852	37	14.4
Vietnam	14,308	15,200	..	..	−64	828	1,609	18	23,260	76	35.0
Yemen, Rep.	4,200	2,200	1	..	769	−150	−150	27	4,610	58	5.3
Yugoslavia, Fed. Rep.	1,727	3,698	..	..	..	0	0	60f	12,949g	..	..
Zambia	780	800	..	..	..	151	163	63	5,853	175	78.1
Zimbabwe	1,600	1,700	27	2	..	70	59	21	4,566	77	48.6
World	6,350,105 t	6,550,720 t	79 w	21 w	.. s		912,520 s	10 w	.. s		126.9 w
Low income	217,569	200,257	51	6		2,255	9,750	9	570,711		43.3
Middle income	1,529,860	1,417,789	66	21		217,184	175,640	9	1,989,925h		69.4
Lower middle income	656,925	570,941	58	19		73,441	64,842	9	873,475		91.4
Upper middle income	872,934	846,841	72	23		143,743	110,798	6	1,116,450h		52.6
Low & middle income	1,747,436	1,618,121	64	20		219,440	185,390	10	2,560,636h		65.1
East Asia & Pacific	711,806	621,336	81	31		51,062	56,041	5	674,693		116.2
Europe & Central Asia	306,731i	311,632i	56i	10		43,164	26,534	23	486,059		23.6
Latin America & Carib.	357,646	381,551	48	14		111,315	90,335	12	812,763		37.6
Middle East & N. Africa	214,254	137,948	17	1		1,277	1,461	18	206,163		78.5
South Asia	63,736	79,157	79	4		2,172	3,070	3	164,600		46.9
Sub-Saharan Africa	93,246	86,396	39	9		10,449	7,949	20	216,359		42.6
High income	4,602,927	4,932,665	82	22		..	727,130	..	2	..	147.4

a. Regional aggregates include data for economies that are not specified elsewhere. World and income group totals include aid not allocated by country or region.
b. Includes Luxembourg. c. Data are from debt sustainability analysis undertaken as part of the Heavily Indebted Poor Countries (HIPC) initiative. d. Includes re-exports.
e. Data on total exports and imports refer to South Africa only. Data on export commodity shares refer to the South African Customs Union (Botswana, Lesotho, Namibia, South Africa, and Swaziland). f. Aid to the states of the former Socialist Federal Republic of Yugoslavia that is not otherwise specified is included in regional and income group aggregates. g. Data are estimates and reflect borrowings by the former Socialist Federal Republic of Yugoslavia that are not yet allocated to the successor republics. h. Includes data for Gibraltar not included in other tables. i. Data include the intratrade of the Baltic states and the Commonwealth of Independent States.

Table 1a.   Key indicators for other economies

	Population			Gross national income (GNI)[a]		PPP gross national income (GNI)[b]		Gross domestic product	Life expectancy at birth	Under-5 mortality rate	Adult illiteracy rate	Carbon dioxide emissions
	Thousands 2000	Avg. annual % growth 1990–2000	density people per sq. km 2000	Millions of dollars 2000	per capita dollars 2000	Millions of dollars 2000	per capita dollars 2000	per capita % growth 1999–2000	Years 1999	Per 1,000 1999	% of people 15 and above 1999	Thousands of tons 1997
Afghanistan	26,550	4.1	41	..	..[c]	..	..	..	46	220	64	1,153
American Samoa	65	..	325	..	..[d]	..	..	..	..	..	..	282
Andorra	67	..	149	..	..[e]	..	..	..	..	..	..	..
Antigua and Barbuda	68	0.6	155	625	9,190	653	9,610	0.8	75	20	..	337
Aruba	101	..	532	1,657[f]	16,900[f]	..	..	..	..	..	..	1,872
Bahamas, The	302	1.7	30	4,533	15,010	4,981	16,490	3.1	73	21	4	1,740
Bahrain	690	3.2	1,000	4,909	7,640	7,798	12,130	..	73	12	13	14,932
Barbados	268	0.4	623	2,487	9,280	3,958	14,770	2.0	76	18	..	984
Belize	255	3.0	11	751	2,940	1,313	5,140	4.6	72	37	7	388
Bermuda	63	..	1,260	..	..[e]	..	..	..	..	..	..	462
Bhutan	805	2.9	17	441	550	1,088[g]	1,350[g]	3.9	61	..	..	472
Bosnia and Herzegovina	3,923	−1.3	77	4,930	1,260	..	..	8.4	73	18	..	4,537
Brunei	328	2.4	62	7,754	24,630	7,974[g]	25,320[g]	..	76	11	9	5,454
Cape Verde	441	2.6	109	587	1,330	2,063[g]	4,680[g]	1.9	69	50	26	121
Cayman Islands	35	..	135	..	..[e]	..	..	..	..	..	..	282
Channel Islands	149	0.4	481	..	..[e]	..	..	..	79	..	..	..
Comoros	558	2.6	250	213	380	834[g]	1,490[g]	−3.6	61	86	41	66
Cuba	11,234	0.6	102	..	..[h]	..	..	..	76	8	3	25,967
Cyprus	766	1.2	83	9,086	11,950	14,511[g]	19,080[g]	..	78	9	3	5,954
Djibouti	660	2.4	28	556	840	..	..	0.4	47	177	37	366
Dominica	73	0.1	97	238	3,260	381	5,210	1.0	76	18	..	81
Equatorial Guinea	454	2.5	16	516	1,170	2,166	4,770	18.3	51	170	18	612
Faeroe Islands	45	..	32	..	..[e]	..	..	..	..	..	..	634
Fiji	810	1.0	44	1,480	1,830	3,645	4,500	−9.0	73	22	7	797
French Polynesia	234	1.7	64	4,064	17,370	5,501[g]	23,510[g]	2.6	73	13	..	561
Gabon	1,237	2.5	5	3,928	3,180	6,719	5,430	−0.4	53	133	..	3,430
Gambia, The	1,286	3.3	129	422	330	2,109[g]	1,640[g]	2.4	53	110	64	216
Greenland	56	..	0	..	..[e]	..	..	..	..	..	..	520
Grenada	98	0.5	288	345	3,520	640	6,540	4.1	72	18	..	183
Guam	155	1.4	281	..	..[e]	..	..	..	78	10	..	4,078
Guinea–Bissau	1,207	2.2	43	221	180	843[g]	700[g]	6.7	44	214	62	231
Guyana	863	0.8	4	667	770	3,016[g]	3,490[g]	1.7	64	76	2	1,022
Iceland	281	1.0	3	8,736	31,090	8,084	28,770	2.3	79	5	..	2,140
Iraq	23,264	2.5	53	..	..[h]	..	..	..	59	128	45	92,339
Isle of Man	75	..	131	..	..[d]	..	..	..	..	..	..	..
Kiribati	91	2.3	124	86	950	..	..	−4.2	61	72	..	22
Korea, Dem. Rep.	23,620	1.4	196	..	..[c]	..	..	..	60	93	..	260,532
Liberia	3,130	2.5	32	..	..[c]	..	..	..	47	188	47	339
Libya	5,540	2.3	3	..	..[d]	..	..	..	71	28	21	43,462
Liechtenstein	32	..	200	..	..[e]	..	..	..	..	..	..	..
Luxembourg	438	1.4	169	19,420	44,340	19,892	45,410	6.6	77	5	..	8,241
Macao, China	442	1.8	..	6,161	14,200	7,350[g]	16,940[g]	..	78	..	..	1,473
Maldives	276	2.6	920	403	1,460	1,348[g]	4,880[c]	5.0	68	35	4	304
Malta	382	0.8	1,194	3,566	9,410	5,963[g]	15,730[g]	..	77	7	8	1,759
Marshall Islands	52	..	287	102	1,970	..	..	−1.4	..	..	..	..
Mauritius	1,186	1.2	584	4,512	3,800	11,795	9,940	7.5	71	23	16	1,704
Mayotte	145	..	388	..	..[d]	..	..	..	..	..	..	..
Micronesia, Fed. Sts.	118	2.1	168	250	2,110	..	..	1.2	68	33	..	..
Monaco	32	..	16,410	..	..[e]	..	..	..	..	..	..	..
Netherlands Antilles	217	1.4	271	..	..[e]	..	..	..	76	16	4	6,760
New Caledonia	213	2.4	12	3,203	15,060	4,654	21,880	0.3	73	12	..	1,801
Northern Mariana Islands	72	..	151	..	..[e]	..	..	..	..	..	..	..
Oman	2,395	3.9	11	15,607[f]	6,720[f]	..	..	..	73	24	30	18,418
Palau	19	..	41	..	..[d]	..	..	..	..	..	..	238
Puerto Rico	3,920	1.0	442	..	..[d]	..	..	..	76	..	7	17,054
Qatar	585	1.9	53	..	..[e]	..	..	..	75	22	19	38,264
Samoa	169	0.6	60	246	1,460	861[g]	5,090[g]	6.6	69	..	20	132
San Marino	27	..	450	..	..[e]	..	..	..	..	..	..	..
São Tomé and Principe	149	2.6	155	43	290	..	..	0.8	65	66	..	77
Seychelles	81	1.5	181	593	7,310	..	..	−0.3	72	15	..	198
Solomon Islands	442	3.2	16	278	630	765[g]	1,730[g]	−16.5	71	26	..	161
Somalia	9,711	2.2	15	..	..[c]	..	..	..	48	203	..	30
St. Kitts and Nevis	41	−0.2	114	273	6,660	456	11,120	3.5	71	..	..	103
St. Lucia	156	1.5	256	634	4,070	853	5,470	−1.2	72	19	..	198
St. Vincent and the Grenadines	115	0.7	295	309	2,690	584[g]	5,080[g]	−0.1	73	19	..	132
Sudan	29,677	2.1	12	9,596	320	..	..	..	56	109	43	3,809
Suriname	415	0.3	3	558	1,350	1,467[g]	3,550[g]	..	70	34	..	2,135
Swaziland	1,045	3.1	61	1,350	1,290	4,882[g]	4,670[g]	0.6	46	113	21	399
Tonga	100	0.4	139	166	1,660	..	..	5.5	71	24	..	121
Trinidad and Tobago	1,301	0.7	254	6,477	4,980	10,844	8,340	4.9	73	20	6	22,291
United Arab Emirates	2,905	4.5	35	49,205	18,060	52,924[g]	19,430[g]	..	75	9	25	82,488
Vanuatu	200	3.0	16	228	1,140	587	2,940	−1.3	65	44	..	62
Virgin Islands (U.S.)	121	1.5	356	..	..[e]	..	..	..	77	12	..	11,553
West Bank and Gaza	2,945	3.9	..	4,745	1,610	..	..	−9.6	72	..	..	..

a. Preliminary World Bank estimates calculated using the World Bank Atlas method. b. Purchasing power parity; see the Technical Notes c. Estimated to be low income ($755 or less). d. Estimated to be upper middle income ($2,996 to $9,265). e. Estimated to be high income ($9,266 or more). f. Refers to GDP and GDP per capita.

Classification of economies by region and income, 2001

East Asia and the Pacific		Latin America and the Caribbean		South Asia		High income OECD
American Samoa	UMC	Antigua and Barbuda	UMC	Afghanistan	LIC	Australia
Cambodia	LIC	Argentina	UMC	Bangladesh	LIC	Austria
China	LMC	Belize	LMC	Bhutan	LIC	Belgium
Fiji	LMC	Bolivia	LMC	India	LIC	Canada
Indonesia	LIC	Brazil	UMC	Maldives	LMC	Denmark
Kiribati	LMC	Chile	UMC	Nepal	LIC	Finland
Korea, Dem. Rep.	LIC	Colombia	LMC	Pakistan	LIC	France
Korea, Rep.	UMC	Costa Rica	UMC	Sri Lanka	LMC	Germany
Lao PDR	LIC	Cuba	LMC			Greece
Malaysia	UMC	Dominica	UMC	**Sub-Saharan Africa**		Iceland
Marshall Islands	LMC	Dominican Republic	LMC	Angola	LIC	Ireland
Micronesia, Fed. Sts.	LMC	Ecuador	LMC	Benin	LIC	Italy
Mongolia	LIC	El Salvador	LMC	Botswana	UMC	Japan
Myanmar	LIC	Grenada	UMC	Burkina Faso	LIC	Luxembourg
Palau	UMC	Guatemala	LMC	Burundi	LIC	Netherlands
Papua New Guinea	LMC	Guyana	LMC	Cameroon	LIC	New Zealand
Philippines	LMC	Haiti	LIC	Cape Verde	LMC	Norway
Samoa	LMC	Honduras	LMC	Central African Republic	LIC	Portugal
Solomon Islands	LIC	Jamaica	LMC	Chad	LIC	Spain
Thailand	LMC	Mexico	UMC	Comoros	LIC	Sweden
Tonga	LMC	Nicaragua	LIC	Congo, Dem. Rep.	LIC	Switzerland
Vanuatu	LMC	Panama	UMC	Congo, Rep.	LIC	United Kingdom
Vietnam	LIC	Paraguay	LMC	Côte d'Ivoire	LIC	United States
		Peru	LMC	Equatorial Guinea	LMC	
Europe and Central Asia		Puerto Rico	UMC	Eritrea	LIC	**Other high income**
Albania	LMC	St. Kitts and Nevis	UMC	Ethiopia	LIC	Andorra
Armenia	LIC	St. Lucia	UMC	Gabon	UMC	Aruba
Azerbaijan	LIC	St. Vincent and the		Gambia, The	LIC	Bahamas, The
Belarus	LMC	Grenadines	LMC	Ghana	LIC	Barbados
Bosnia and Herzegovina	LMC	Suriname	LMC	Guinea	LIC	Bermuda
Bulgaria	LMC	Trinidad and Tobago	UMC	Guinea-Bissau	LIC	Brunei
Croatia	UMC	Uruguay	UMC	Kenya	LIC	Cayman Islands
Czech Republic	UMC	Venezuela, RB	UMC	Lesotho	LIC	Channel Islands
Estonia	UMC			Liberia	LIC	Cyprus
Georgia	LIC	**Middle East and North Africa**		Madagascar	LIC	Faeroe Islands
Hungary	UMC	Algeria	LMC	Malawi	LIC	French Polynesia
Isle of Man	UMC	Bahrain	UMC	Mali	LIC	Greenland
Kazakhstan	LMC	Djibouti	LMC	Mauritania	LIC	Guam
Kyrgyz Republic	LIC	Egypt, Arab Rep.	LMC	Mauritius	UMC	Hong Kong, China
Latvia	LMC	Iran, Islamic Rep.	LMC	Mayotte	UMC	Israel
Lithuania	LMC	Iraq	LMC	Mozambique	LIC	Kuwait
Macedonia, FYR	LMC	Jordan	LMC	Namibia	LMC	Liechtenstein
Moldova	LIC	Lebanon	UMC	Niger	LIC	Macao, China
Poland	UMC	Libya	UMC	Nigeria	LIC	Malta
Romania	LMC	Morocco	LMC	Rwanda	LIC	Monaco
Russian Federation	LMC	Oman	UMC	São Tomé and Principe	LIC	Netherlands Antilles
Slovak Republic	UMC	Saudi Arabia	UMC	Senegal	LIC	New Caledonia
Tajikistan	LIC	Syrian Arab Republic	LMC	Seychelles	UMC	Northern Mariana Islands
Turkey	UMC	Tunisia	LMC	Sierra Leone	LIC	Qatar
Turkmenistan	LMC	West Bank and Gaza	LMC	Somalia	LIC	San Marino
Ukraine	LIC	Yemen, Rep.	LIC	South Africa	UMC	Singapore
Uzbekistan	LIC			Sudan	LIC	Slovenia
Yugoslavia, Fed. Rep.	LMC			Swaziland	LMC	Taiwan, China
				Tanzania	LIC	United Arab Emirates
				Togo	LIC	Virgin Islands (U.S.)
				Uganda	LIC	
				Zambia	LIC	
				Zimbabwe	LIC	

This table classifies all World Bank member economies, and all other economies with populations of more than 30,000. Economies are divided among income groups according to 2000 GNI per capita, calculated using the World Bank Atlas method. The groups are: low income (LIC), $755 or less; lower middle income (LMC), $756–2,995; upper middle income (UMC), $2,996–9,265; and high income, $9,266 or more.

Source: World Bank data.

Technical Notes

These technical notes discuss the sources and methods used to compile the indicators included in this edition of Selected World Development Indicators. The notes follow the order in which the indicators appear in the tables. For the first time the Selected World Development Indicators uses terminology in line with the 1993 System of National Accounts (SNA). For example, in the 1993 SNA *gross national income* replaces *gross national product*. See the technical notes for tables 1 and 3 for other examples.

Sources

The data published in the Selected World Development Indicators are taken from *World Development Indicators 2001.* Where possible, however, revisions reported since the closing date of that edition have been incorporated. In addition, newly released estimates of population and gross national income (GNI) per capita for 2000 are included in table 1.

The World Bank draws on a variety of sources for the statistics published in the *World Development Indicators.* Data on external debt are reported directly to the World Bank by developing member countries through the Debtor Reporting System. Other data are drawn mainly from the United Nations and its specialized agencies, from the International Monetary Fund (IMF), and from country reports to the World Bank. Bank staff estimates are also used to improve currency or consistency. For most countries, national accounts estimates are obtained from member governments through World Bank economic missions. In some instances these are adjusted by staff to ensure conformity with international definitions and concepts. Most social data from national sources are drawn from regular administrative files, special surveys, or periodic censuses.

For more detailed notes about the data, please refer to the World Bank's *World Development Indicators 2001.*

Data consistency and reliability

Considerable effort has been made to standardize the data, but full comparability cannot be assured, and care must be taken in interpreting the indicators. Many factors affect data availability, comparability, and reliability: statistical systems in many developing economies are still weak; statistical methods, coverage, practices, and definitions differ widely; and cross-country and intertemporal comparisons involve complex technical and conceptual problems that cannot be unequivocally resolved. For these reasons, although the data are drawn from the sources thought to be most authoritative, they should be construed only as indicating trends and characterizing major differences among economies rather than offering precise quantitative measures of those differences. Also, national statistical agencies tend to revise their historical data, particularly for recent years. Thus, data of different vintages may be published in different editions of World Bank publications. Readers are advised not to compile such data from different editions. Consistent time series are available from the *World Development Indicators 2001* CD-ROM.

Ratios and growth rates

For ease of reference, the tables usually show ratios and rates of growth rather than the simple underlying values. Values in their original form are available from the *World Development Indicators 2001* CD-ROM. Unless otherwise noted, growth rates are computed using the least-squares regression method (see *Statistical methods* below). Because this method takes into account all available observations during a period, the resulting growth rates reflect general trends that are not unduly influenced by exceptional values. To exclude the effects of inflation, constant price economic indicators are used in calculating growth rates. Data in italics are for a year or period other than that specified in the column heading—up to two years before or after for economic indicators and up to three years for social indicators, because the latter tend to be collected less regularly and change less dramatically over short periods.

Constant price series

An economy's growth is measured by the increase in value added produced by the individuals and enterprises operating in that economy. Thus, measuring real growth requires estimates of GDP and its components valued in constant prices. The World Bank collects constant price national accounts series in national currencies and recorded in the country's original base year. To obtain comparable series of constant price data, it rescales GDP and value added by in-

243

dustrial origin to a common reference year, currently 1995. This process gives rise to a discrepancy between the rescaled GDP and the sum of the rescaled components. Because allocating the discrepancy would give rise to distortions in the growth rate, it is left unallocated.

Summary measures

The summary measures for regions and income groups, presented at the end of most tables, are calculated by simple addition when they are expressed in levels. Aggregate growth rates and ratios are usually computed as weighted averages. The summary measures for social indicators are weighted by population or subgroups of population, except for infant mortality, which is weighted by the number of births. See the notes on specific indicators for more information.

For summary measures that cover many years, calculations are based on a uniform group of economies so that the composition of the aggregate does not change over time. Group measures are compiled only if the data available for a given year account for at least two-thirds of the full group, as defined for the 1995 benchmark year. As long as this criterion is met, economies for which data are missing are assumed to behave like those that provide estimates. Readers should keep in mind that the summary measures are estimates of representative aggregates for each topic and that nothing meaningful can be deduced about behavior at the country level by working back from group indicators. In addition, the estimation process may result in discrepancies between subgroup and overall totals.

Table 1. Key indicators of development

Population is based on the de facto definition, which counts all residents, regardless of legal status or citizenship, except for refugees not permanently settled in the country of asylum, who are generally considered part of the population of the country of origin.

Average annual population growth rate is the exponential rate of change for the period (see the section on statistical methods below).

Population density is midyear population divided by land area. Land area is a country's total area excluding areas under inland bodies of water and coastal waterways. Density is calculated using the most recently available data on land area.

Gross national income (GNI—formerly gross national product or GNP), the broadest measure of national income, measures total value added from domestic and foreign sources claimed by residents. GNI comprises gross domestic product (GDP) plus net receipts of primary income from foreign sources. Data are converted from national currency to current U.S. dollars using the World Bank Atlas method. This involves using a three-year average of exchange rates to smooth the effects of transitory exchange rate fluctuations. (See the section on statistical methods below for further discussion of the Atlas method.)

GNI per capita is GNI divided by midyear population. It is converted into current U.S. dollars by the Atlas method. The World Bank uses GNI per capita in U.S dollars to clas-

sify economies for analytical purposes and to determine borrowing eligibility.

PPP Gross national income, which is GNI converted into international dollars using purchasing power parity (PPP) conversion factors, is included because nominal exchange rates do not always reflect international differences in relative prices. At the PPP rate, one international dollar has the same purchasing power over domestic GNI that the U.S. dollar has over U.S. GNI. PPP rates allow a standard comparison of real price levels between countries, just as conventional price indexes allow comparison of real values over time. The PPP conversion factors used here are derived from the most recent round of price surveys conducted by the International Comparison Programme, a joint project of the World Bank and the regional economic commissions of the United Nations. This round of surveys, completed in 1996 and covering 118 countries, is based on a 1993 reference year. Estimates for countries not included in the survey are derived from statistical models using available data.

PPP GNI per capita is PPP GNI divided by midyear population.

Gross domestic product (GDP) per capita growth is based on GDP measured in constant prices. Growth in GDP is considered a broad measure of the growth of an economy. GDP in constant prices can be estimated by measuring the total quantity of goods and services produced in a period, valuing them at an agreed set of base year prices, and subtracting the cost of intermediate inputs, also in constant prices. See the section on statistical methods for details of the least-squares growth rate.

Life expectancy at birth is the number of years a newborn infant would live if patterns of mortality prevailing at its birth were to stay the same throughout its life.

Under-5 mortality rate is the probability that a child born in the indicated year will die before reaching age 5, if the child is subject to current age specific mortality rates. The probability is expressed as a rate per 1,000.

Age specific mortality data such as infant and child mortality rates, along with life expectancy at birth, are probably the best general indicators of a community's current health status and are often cited as overall measures of a population's welfare or quality of life. The main sources of mortality data are vital registration systems and direct or indirect estimates based on sample surveys or censuses. Because civil registers with relatively complete vital registration systems are fairly uncommon in developing countries, estimates must be obtained from sample surveys or derived by applying indirect estimation techniques to registration, census, or survey data. Indirect estimates rely on estimated actuarial ("life") tables, which may be inappropriate for the population concerned. Because life expectancy at birth is constructed using infant mortality data and model life tables, similar reliability issues may arise for this indicator. Life expectancy at birth and age specific mortality rates are generally estimates based on the most recently available census or survey; see the Primary data documentation table in *World Development Indicators 2001*.

Adult illiteracy rate is the percentage of persons aged 15 and above who cannot, with understanding, read and write a short, simple statement about their everyday life. Measuring literacy using such a definition requires census or sample survey measurements under controlled conditions. In practice, many countries estimate the number of illiterate adults from self-reported data or from estimates of school completion rates. Because of these differences in method, comparisons across countries—and even over time within countries—should be made with caution.

Carbon dioxide emissions (CO_2) measures those emissions stemming from the burning of fossil fuels and the manufacture of cement. These include carbon dioxide produced during consumption of solid, liquid, and gas fuels and from gas flaring.

The Carbon Dioxide Information Analysis Center (CDIAC), sponsored by the U.S. Department of Energy, calculates annual anthropogenic emissions of CO_2. These calculations are derived from data on fossil fuel consumption, based on the World Energy Data Set maintained by the UNSD, and from data on world cement manufacturing, based on the Cement Manufacturing Data Set maintained by the U.S. Bureau of Mines. Each year the CDIAC recalculates the entire time series from 1950 to the present, incorporating its most recent findings and the latest corrections to its database. Estimates exclude fuels supplied to ships and aircraft engaged in international transportation because of the difficulty of apportioning these fuels among the countries benefiting from that transport.

Table 2. Poverty and income distribution

Survey year is the year in which the underlying data were collected.

Rural population below the national poverty line is the percentage of the rural population living below the rural poverty line determined by national authorities. **Urban population below the national poverty line** is the percentage of the urban population living below the urban poverty line determined by national authorities. **Total population below the national poverty line** is the percentage of the total population living below the national poverty line. National estimates are based on population weighted subgroup estimates from household surveys.

Population below \$1 PPP a day and **\$2 PPP a day** are the percentages of the population living on less than \$1.08 a day and \$2.15 a day at 1993 international prices (equivalent to \$1 and \$2 in 1985 prices adjusted for purchasing power parity). Poverty rates are comparable across countries, but as a result of revisions in PPP exchange rates, they cannot be compared with poverty rates reported in previous editions for individual countries.

Poverty gap at \$1 PPP a day and **Poverty gap at \$2 PPP a day** is the mean shortfall below the poverty line (counting the non-poor as having zero shortfall), expressed as a percentage of the poverty line. This measure reflects the depth of poverty as well as its incidence.

International comparisons of poverty data entail both conceptual and practical problems. Different countries have different definitions of poverty, and consistent comparisons between countries can be difficult. Local poverty lines tend to have higher purchasing power in rich countries, where more generous standards are used than in poor countries. Is it reasonable to treat two people with the same standard of living—in terms of their command over commodities—differently because one happens to live in a better-off country? Can we hold the real value of the poverty line constant across countries, just as we do when making comparisons over time?

Poverty measures based on an international poverty line attempt to do this. The \$1 a day standard, measured in 1985 international prices and adjusted to local currency using purchasing power parities (PPPs), was chosen for the World Bank's *World Development Report 1990: Poverty* because it is typical of the poverty lines in low-income countries. PPP exchange rates, such as those from the Penn World Tables or the World Bank, are used because they take into account the local prices of goods and services not traded internationally. But PPP rates were designed not for making international poverty comparisons but for comparing aggregates from national accounts. As a result, there is no certainty that an international poverty line measures the same degree of need or deprivation across countries.

Past editions of the *World Development Indicators* and the Selected World Development Indicators used PPPs from the Penn World Tables. Because the Penn World Tables updated to 1993 are not yet available, this year's edition (like last year's) uses 1993 consumption PPP estimates produced by the World Bank. The international poverty line, set at \$1 a day in 1985 PPP terms, has been recalculated in 1993 PPP terms at about \$1.08 a day. Any revisions in the PPP of a country to incorporate better price indexes can produce dramatically different poverty lines in local currency.

Problems also exist in comparing poverty measures within countries. For example, the cost of living is typically higher in urban than in rural areas. (Food staples, for example, tend to be more expensive in urban areas.) So the urban monetary poverty line should be higher than the rural poverty line. But it is not always clear that the difference between urban and rural poverty lines found in practice properly reflects the difference in the cost of living. In some countries the urban poverty line in common use has a higher real value—meaning that it allows the purchase of more commodities for consumption—than does the rural poverty line. Sometimes the difference has been so large as to imply that the incidence of poverty is greater in urban than in rural areas, even though the reverse is found when adjustments are made only for differences in the cost of living. As with international comparisons, when the real value of the poverty line varies, it is not clear how meaningful such urban-rural comparisons are.

The problems of making poverty comparisons do not end there. More issues arise in measuring household living standards. The choice between income and consumption as a welfare indicator is one issue. Income is generally more difficult to measure accurately, and consumption accords better with the idea of the standard of living than does income, which can vary over time even if the standard of living does not. But consumption data are not always available, and when they are not there is little choice but to use income. There are still other problems. Household survey questionnaires can differ widely, for example, in the number of distinct categories of consumer goods they identify. Survey quality varies, and even similar surveys may not be strictly comparable.

Comparisons across countries at different levels of development also pose a potential problem, because of differences in the relative importance of consumption of nonmarket goods. The local market value of all consumption in kind (including consumption from own production, particularly important in underdeveloped rural economies) should be included in the measure of total consumption expenditure. Similarly, the imputed profit from production of nonmarket goods should be included in income. This is not always done, though such omissions were a far bigger problem in surveys before the 1980s. Most survey data now include valuations for consumption or income from own production. Nonetheless, valuation methods vary. For example, some surveys use the price in the nearest market, while others use the average farm gate selling price.

Whenever possible, consumption has been used as the welfare indicator for deciding who is poor. When only household income was available, average income has been adjusted to accord with either a survey-based estimate of mean consumption (when available) or an estimate based on consumption data from national accounts. This procedure adjusts only the mean, however; nothing can be done to correct for the difference in Lorenz (income distribution) curves between consumption and income.

Empirical Lorenz curves are weighted by household size, so they are based on percentiles of population, not households. In all cases the measures of poverty have been calculated from primary data sources (tabulations or household data) rather than existing estimates. Estimation from tabulations requires an interpolation method; the method chosen was Lorenz curves with flexible functional forms, which have proved reliable in past work.

Gini index measures the extent to which the distribution of income (or, in some cases, consumption expenditure) among individuals or households within an economy deviates from a perfectly equal distribution. A Lorenz curve plots the cumulative percentages of total income received against the cumulative number of recipients, starting with the poorest individual or household. The Gini index measures the area between the Lorenz curve and a hypothetical line of absolute equality, expressed as a percentage of the maximum area under the line. Thus a Gini index of zero represents perfect equality, while an index of 100 implies perfect inequality.

Percentage share of income or consumption is the share that accrues to subgroups of population indicated by deciles or quintiles.

Inequality in the distribution of income is reflected in the percentage shares of either income or consumption accruing to segments of the population ranked by income or consumption levels. The segments ranked lowest by personal income receive the smallest share of total income. The Gini

index provides a convenient summary measure of the degree of inequality.

Data on personal or household income or consumption come from nationally representative household surveys. The data in the table refer to different years between 1985 and 1999. Footnotes to the survey year indicate whether the rankings are based on per capita income or consumption. Each distribution is based on percentiles of population—rather than of households—with households ranked by income or expenditure per person.

Where the original data from the household survey were available, they have been used to directly calculate the income (or consumption) shares by quintile. Otherwise, shares have been estimated from the best available grouped data.

The distribution indicators have been adjusted for household size, providing a more consistent measure of per capita income or consumption. No adjustment has been made for spatial differences in cost of living within countries, because the data needed for such calculations are generally unavailable. For further details on the estimation method for low- and middle-income economies see Ravallion and Chen (1996).

Because the underlying household surveys differ in method and in the type of data collected, the distribution indicators are not strictly comparable across countries. These problems are diminishing as survey methods improve and become more standardized, but achieving strict comparability is still impossible.

Two sources of noncomparability should be noted. First, the surveys can differ in many respects, including whether they use income or consumption expenditure as the living standard indicator. The distribution of income is typically more unequal than the distribution of consumption. In addition, the definitions of income used usually differ among surveys. Consumption is usually a better welfare indicator, particularly in developing countries. Second, households differ in size (number of members) and in the extent of income sharing among members. And individuals differ in age and consumption needs. Differences among countries in these respects may bias comparisons of distribution.

World Bank staff have made an effort to ensure that the data are as comparable as possible. Whenever possible, consumption has been used rather than income. The income distribution and Gini indexes for high-income countries are calculated directly from the Luxembourg Income Study database using an estimation method consistent with that applied for developing countries.

Table 3. Economic activity

Gross domestic product is gross value added, at purchasers' prices, by all resident producers in the economy plus any taxes and minus any subsidies not included in the value of the products. It is calculated without deducting for depreciation of fabricated assets or for depletion or degradation of natural resources. Value added is the net output of a sector after adding up all outputs and subtracting intermediate inputs. The industrial origin of value added is determined by the International Standard Industrial Classification (ISIC) revision 3. The World Bank conventionally uses the U.S.

dollar and applies the average official exchange rate reported by the International Monetary Fund for the year shown. An alternative conversion factor is applied if the official exchange rate is judged to diverge by an exceptionally large margin from the rate effectively applied to transactions in foreign currencies and traded products.

Gross domestic product average annual growth rate is calculated from constant price GDP data in local currency.

Agricultural productivity refers to the ratio of agricultural value added, measured in constant 1995 U.S. dollars, to the number of workers in agriculture.

Value added is the net output of an industry after adding up all out-puts and subtracting intermediate inputs. The industrial origin of value added is determined by the International Standard Industrial Classification (ISIC) revision 3.

Agriculture value added corresponds to ISIC divisions 1–5 and includes forestry and fishing.

Industry value added comprises mining, manufacturing, construction, electricity, water, and gas (ISIC divisions 10–45).

Services value added correspond to ISIC divisions 50–99.

Household final consumption expenditure (private consumption in previous editions) is the market value of all goods and services, including durable products (such as cars, washing machines, and home computers), purchased by households. It excludes purchases of dwellings but includes imputed rent for owner-occupied dwellings. It also includes payments and fees to governments to obtain permits and licenses. Here, household consumption expenditure includes the expenditures of nonprofit institutions serving households, even when reported separately by the country. In practice, household consumption expenditure may include any statistical discrepancy in the use of resources relative to the supply of resources.

General government final consumption expenditure (general government consumption in previous editions) includes all government current expenditures for purchases of goods and services (including compensation of employees). It also includes most expenditures on national defense and security, but excludes government military expenditures that are part of government capital formation.

Gross capital formation (gross domestic investment in previous editions) consists of outlays on additions to the fixed assets of the economy plus net changes in the level of inventories. Fixed assets include land improvements (fences, ditches, drains, and so on); plant, machinery, and equipment purchases; and the construction of buildings, roads, railways, and the like, including commercial and industrial buildings, offices, schools, hospitals, and private dwellings. Inventories are stocks of goods held by firms to meet temporary or unexpected fluctuations in production or sales, and "work in progress." According to the 1993 SNA net acquisitions of valuables are also considered capital formation.

External balance of goods and services is exports of goods and services less imports of goods and services. Trade in goods and services comprise all transactions between residents of a country and the rest of the world involving a change in ownership of general merchandise, goods sent for processing and repairs, non-monetary gold, and services.

The **GDP implicit deflator** reflects changes in prices for all final demand categories, such as government consumption, capital formation, and international trade, as well as the main component, private final consumption. It is derived as the ratio of current to constant price GDP. The GDP deflator may also be calculated explicitly as a Paasche price index in which the weights are the current period quantities of output.

National accounts indicators for most developing countries are collected from national statistical organizations and central banks by visiting and resident World Bank missions. Data for high-income economies come from the Organization for Economic Co-operation and Development data files.

Table 4. Trade, aid, and finance

Merchandise exports show the f.o.b. value of goods provided to the rest of the world valued in U.S. dollars.

Merchandise imports show the c.i.f. value of goods (the cost of the goods including insurance and freight) purchased from the rest of the world valued in U.S. dollars. Data on merchandise trade come from the World Trade Organization (WTO) in its annual report.

Manufactured exports comprise the commodities in Standard Industrial Trade Classification (SITC) sections 5 (chemicals), 6 (basic manufactures), 7 (machinery and transport equipment), and 8 (miscellaneous manufactured goods), excluding division 68.

High technology exports are products with high R&D intensity. They include high-technology products such as in aerospace, computers, pharmaceuticals, scientific instruments, and electrical machinery.

Current account balance is the sum of net exports of goods and services, net income, and net current transfers.

Net private capital flows consist of private debt and nondebt flows. Private debt flows include commercial bank lending, bonds, and other private credits; nondebt private flows are foreign direct investment and portfolio equity investment.

Foreign direct investment is net inflows of investment to acquire a lasting management interest (10 percent or more of voting stock) in an enterprise operating in an economy other than that of the investor. It is the sum of equity capital, re-investment of earnings, other long-term capital, and short-term capital, as shown in the balance of payments. Data on the current account balance, private capital flows, and foreign direct investment are drawn from the IMF's *Balance of Payments Statistics Yearbook* and *International Financial Statistics*.

Official development assistance or official aid cover net concessional flows to developing countries, transition economies of Eastern Europe and the former Soviet Union and to certain advanced developing countries and territories as determined by the Development Assistance Committee (DAC) of the OECD. The flows are from members of the DAC, multilateral development agencies, and certain Arab countries. Data on aid are compiled by DAC and published in its annual statistical report, *Geographical Distribution of*

Financial Flows to Aid Recipients, and in the DAC chairman's annual report, *Development Co-operation*.

Total external debt is debt owed to nonresidents repayable in foreign currency, goods, or services. It is the sum of public, publicly guaranteed, and private non-guaranteed long-term debt, use of IMF credit, and short-term debt. Short-term debt includes all debt having an original maturity of one year or less and interest in arrears on long-term debt.

Present value of debt is the sum of short-term external debt plus the discounted sum of total debt service payments due on public, publicly guaranteed, and private nonguaranteed long-term external debt over the life of existing loans.

The main sources of external debt information are reports to the World Bank through its Debtor Reporting System from member countries that have received World Bank loans. Additional information has been drawn from the files of the World Bank and the IMF. Summary tables of the external debt of developing countries are published annually in the World Bank's *Global Development Finance*.

Domestic credit provided by banking sector includes all credit to various sectors on a gross basis, with the exception of credit to the central government, which is net. The banking sector includes monetary authorities, deposit money banks, and other banking institutions for which data are available (including institutions that do not accept transferable deposits but do incur such liabilities as time and savings deposits). Examples of other banking institutions include savings and mortgage loan institutions and building and loan associations. Data are from the IMF's *International Finance Statistics*.

Statistical methods

This section describes the calculation of the least-squares growth rate, the exponential (endpoint) growth rate, and the World Bank's Atlas methodology for calculating the conversion factor used to estimate GNI and GNI per capita in U.S. dollars.

Least-squares growth rate

Least-squares growth rates are used wherever there is a sufficiently long time series to permit a reliable calculation. No growth rate is calculated if more than half the observations in a period are missing.

The least-squares growth rate, r, is estimated by fitting a linear regression trendline to the logarithmic annual values of the variable in the relevant period. The regression equation takes the form

$$\ln X_t = a + bt,$$

which is equivalent to the logarithmic transformation of the compound growth equation,

$$X_t = X_o (1 + r)^t.$$

In this equation, X is the variable, t is time, and $a = \log X_o$ and $b = \ln (1 + r)$ are the parameters to be estimated. If b^*

is the least-squares estimate of b, the average annual growth rate, r, is obtained as $[\exp(b^*)-1]$ and is multiplied by 100 to express it as a percentage.

The calculated growth rate is an average rate that is representative of the available observations over the entire period. It does not necessarily match the actual growth rate between any two periods.

Exponential growth rate

The growth rate between two points in time for certain demographic data, notably labor force and population, is calculated from the equation

$$r = \ln (p_n /p_1)/n,$$

where p_n and p_1 are the last and first observations in the period, n is the number of years in the period, and ln is the natural logarithm operator. This growth rate is based on a model of continuous, exponential growth between two points in time. It does not take into account the intermediate values of the series. Note also that the exponential growth rate does not correspond to the annual rate of change measured at a one-year interval which is given by $(p_n - p_{n-1})/p_{n-1}$.

The Gini index

The Gini index measures the extent to which the distribution of income (or, in some cases, consumption expenditure) among individuals or households within an economy deviates from a perfectly equal distribution. A Lorenz curve plots the cumulative percentages of total income received against the cumulative number of recipients, starting with the poorest individual or household. The Gini index measures the area between the Lorenz curve and a hypothetical line of absolute equality, expressed as a percentage of the maximum area under the line. Thus a Gini index of zero represents perfect equality, and an index of 100 percent implies perfect inequality.

World Bank Atlas method

In calculating GNI and GNI per capita in U.S. dollars for certain operational purposes, the World Bank uses a synthetic exchange rate commonly called the Atlas conversion factor. The purpose of the Atlas conversion factor is to reduce the impact of exchange rate fluctuations in the cross-country comparison of national incomes.

The Atlas conversion factor for any year is the average of a country's effective exchange rate with the G-5 countries (or alternative conversion factor) for that year and those for the two preceding years, after adjusting for differences in rates of inflation between the country and the G-5 countries. A country's effective exchange rate is an average of its exchange rates with a selection of other countries, usually weighted by the country's trade with those countries. The G-5 (Group of Five) countries are France, Germany, Japan, the United Kingdom, and the United States. A country's inflation rate is measured by its GNI deflator. The inflation rate for the G-5 countries is measured by changes in the SDR deflator. (Special drawing rights, or SDRs, are the International Monetary Fund's (IMF) unit of account.) The SDR deflator is calculated as a weighted average of the G-5 countries' GDP deflators in SDR terms. The weights are determined by the amount of each currency included in one SDR unit. Weights vary over time because the currency composition of the SDR and the relative exchange rates for each currency both change. The SDR deflator is calculated in SDR terms first and then converted to U.S. dollars using the SDR-to-dollar Atlas conversion factor.

This three-year averaging smooths annual fluctuations in prices and exchange rates for each country. The Atlas conversion factor is then applied to a country's GNI. The resulting GNI in U.S. dollars is divided by the country's midyear population for the latest of the three years to derive its GNI per capita. When official exchange rates are deemed to be unreliable or unrepresentative during a period, an alternative estimate of the exchange rate is used in the Atlas formula (see below).

The following formulas describe the computation of the Atlas conversion factor for year t:

$$e_t^* = \frac{1}{3}\left[e_{t-2}\left(\frac{p_t}{p_{t-2}}\ \frac{p_t^{S\$}}{p_{t-2}^{S\$}} \right) + e_{t-1}\left(\frac{p_t}{p_{t-1}}\ \frac{p_t^{S\$}}{p_{t-1}^{S\$}} \right) + e_t \right]$$

and for calculating GNP per capita in U.S. dollars for year t:

$$Y_t^{\$} = (Y_t / N_t)/e_t^*$$

where e_t^* is the Atlas conversion factor (national currency to the U.S. dollar) for year t, e_t is the average annual exchange rate (national currency to the U.S. dollar) for year t, p_t is the GNI deflator for year t, $p_t^{S\$}$ is the SDR deflator in U.S. dollar terms for year t, $Y_t^{\$}$ is the Atlas GNI in U.S. dollars in year t, Y_t is current GNI (local currency) for year t, and N_t is the midyear population for year t.

Alternative conversion factors

The World Bank systematically assesses the appropriateness of official exchange rates as conversion factors. An alternative conversion factor is used when the official exchange rate is judged to diverge by an exceptionally large margin from the rate effectively applied to domestic transactions of foreign currencies and traded products. This is the case for only a small number of countries (see the *Primary data documentation* table in *World Development Indicators 2001*). Alternative conversion factors are used in the Atlas method and elsewhere in the Selected World Development Indicators as single-year conversion factors.

DISTRIBUTORS OF WORLD BANK GROUP PUBLICATIONS

Prices and credit terms vary from country to country. Please consult your local distributor or bookseller before placing an order.

DISTRIBUTORS

ARGENTINA
World Publications SA
Av. Cordoba 1877
1120 Buenos Aires
Tel: (54 11) 4815 8156
Fax: (54 11) 4815 8156
E-mail:
wpbooks@infovia.com.ar
URL: www.wpbooks.com.ar

AUSTRALIA, PAPUA NEW GUINEA, FIJI, SOLOMON ISLANDS, VANUATU, AND SAMOA
D.A. Information Services
648 Whitehorse Road
Mitcham 3132
Victoria, Australia
Tel: (61 3) 9210 7777
Fax: (61 3) 9210 7788
E-mail:
service@dadirect.com.au
URL: www.dadirect.com.au

AUSTRIA
Gerold and Co.
Weihburggasse 26
A-1010 Wien
Tel: (43 1) 512 47310
Fax: (43 1) 512 473129
E-mail: buch@gerold.telecom.at

BANGLADESH
Micro Industries Development
Assistance Society (MIDAS)
House 5, Road 16
Dhanmondi R/Area
Dhaka 1209
Tel: (880 2) 326427
Fax: (880 2) 8111188
E-mail: midas@raspit.com

BELGIUM
Jean de Lannoy
Av. du Roi 202
1060 Brussels
Tel: (32 2) 538 5169
Fax: (32 2) 538 0841
E-mail:
jean.de.lannoy@infoboard.be
URL: www.jean-de-lannoy.be

BOSNIA AND HERZEGOVINA
Book Trading Company
"Sahinpasic"
Marsala Tita 29/II
71000 Sarajevo
Tel: (387 33) 21 05 20
Fax: (387 33) 66 88 56
E-mail:
tajib@btcsahinpasic.com
URL: www.btcsahinpasic.com

BRAZIL
Publicacoes Tecnicas
Internacionais Ltda.
Rua Peixoto Gomide, 209
Bela Vista
01409-901 Sao Paulo, SP
Tel: (55 11) 259 6644
Fax: (55 11) 258 6990
E-mail: webmaster@pti.com.br
URL: www.pti.com.br

CANADA
Renouf Publishing Co. Ltd.
5369 Canotek Road
Ottawa, Ontario K1J 9J3
Tel: (613) 745-2665
Fax: (613) 745-7660
E-mail: order.dept@renouf-books.com
URL: www.renoufbooks.com

CHILE
Alfaomega Grupo Editor
Dr. Manuel Borgoño 21
Providencia
Santiago
Tel: (56 2) 235 7107
Fax: (56 2) 235 5786
E-mail: galileo@terra.cl

CHINA
Chinese Corporation for
Promotion and Humanities
Building No.7, 1-502
No. 81 Wu Ke Son Lu
Haidian District 100039
Beijing China
Tel:(86 10)682 15048
Fax:(86 10)682 15048
E-mail:ccphibcd@yahoo.com

China Book Import Centre
P.O. Box 2825
Beijing

China Financial & Economic
Publishing House
Room No. 916, Xinzhi Massion
No. Jia 28, Fucheng Road,
Haidan District
Beijing 100038
China
Tel: (86 10) 8819 0915
Fax: (86 10) 8819 0916

COLOMBIA
Infoenlace Ltda./An IHS Group
Company
Calle 72 No. 13-23 - Piso 3
Edificio Nueva Granada
Santafé de Bogotá, D.C.
Tel: (57 1) 600 9480/1/2
Fax: (57 1) 248 0808, 217 6435
E-mail:
infoenlace@andinet.com

COTE D'IVOIRE
Centre d'Edition et de Diffusion
Africaines (CEDA)
04 B.P. 541
Abidjan 04
Tel: (225) 24 6510
Fax: (225) 25 0567
E-mail: info@ceda-ci.com
URL: www.ceda-ci.com

CYPRUS
Center for Applied Research
6, Diogenes Street, Engomi
P.O. Box 2006
Nicosia
Tel: (357 2) 59 0730
Fax: (357 2) 66 2051
E-mail: ttzitzim@sting.cycol-lege.ac.cy

CZECH REPUBLIC
UVIS, odd. publikaci
Havelkova 22
130 00 Prague 3
Tel: (42 2) 2271 5738
Fax: (42 2) 2272 0734
E-mail: posta@uvis.cz
URL: : www.uvis.cz

DENMARK
Samfundslitteratur
Solbjerg Plads 3
DK-2000 Frederiksberg
Tel: (45 38) 153870
Fax: (45 38) 153856
E-mail: ck@sl.cbs.dk
URL: www.sl.cbs.dk

ECUADOR
Libri Mundi - Libreria
Internacional
Juan Leon Mera 851
P.O. Box 17-01-3029
Quito
Tel: (593 2) 521 606
Fax: (593 2) 504 209
E-mail:
librimu1@librimundi.com.ec

CODEU
Ruiz de Castilla 763, Edif.
Expocolor
Primer piso, Of. #2
Quito
Tel: (593 2) 507-383
Fax: (593 2) 507-383
E-mail: codeu@impsat.net.ec

EGYPT, ARAB REPUBLIC OF
Al Ahram Distribution Agency
Al Galaa Street
Cairo
Tel: (20 2) 578 60 83
Fax: (20 2) 575 93 88

MERIC (Middle East Readers
Information Center)
2 Bahrat Aly St.
Building "D" 1st Floor, Apt. 24
Cairo
Tel: (20 2) 341 3824
Fax: (20 2) 341 9355
E-mail: order@meric-co.com
URL: www.meobserver.com.eg

For publications in French only:
Middle East Observer
41, Sherif Street
11111 Cairo
Tel: (20 2) 392 6919
Fax: (20 2) 393 9732
E-mail:
inquiry@meobserver.com
URL: www.meobserver.com

FINLAND
Akateeminen Kirjakauppa
PL 128 (Keskuskatu 1)
FIN-00101 Helsinki
Tel: (358 9) 121 4385
Fax: (358 9) 121 4450
E-mail: sps@akateeminen.com
URL: www.akateeminen.com

FRANCE
Editions Eska; DJB/Offilib
12, rue du Quatre-Septembre
75002 Paris
Tel: (33 1) 42 86 56 00
Fax: (33 1) 42 60 45 35
E-mail: offilib@offilib.fr
URL: www.offilib.fr

GERMANY
UNO-VERLAG
Am Hofgarten 10
D-53113 Bonn
Tel: (49 228) 949 020
Fax: (49 228) 949 0222
E-mail: unoverlag@aol.com
URL: www.uno-verlag.de

GHANA
Epp Books Services
Post Office Box 44
TUC
Accra
Tel: (233 21) 778 843
Fax: (233 21) 779 099
E-mail:
epp@africaonline.com.gh

GREECE
Papasotiriou S.A.,
International Technical
Bookstore
35, Stournara Str.
106 82 Athens
Tel: (30 1) 364 1826
Fax: (30 1) 364 8254
E-mail: pap4@ioa.forthnet.gr
URL: www.papasotiriou.gr

HAITI
Culture Diffusion
76, Ave John Brown (Lalue)
Port-au-Prince
Tel: (509) 511 8090
Fax: (509) 223 4858

HUNGARY
Euro Info Service
Szt. Istvan krt. 12. II emelet 1/A
H-1137 Budapest
Tel: (36 1) 329 2487; 329 2170
Fax: (36 1) 349 2053
E-mail: euroinfo@euroinfo.hu
URL: www.euroinfo.hu

INDIA
Allied Publishers Ltd.
751 Mount Road
Madras 600 002
Tel: (91 44) 852 3938
Fax: (91 44) 852 0649
E-mail: aplchn@vsnl.com

JAPAN
Eastern Book Service (EBS)
3-13 Hongo 3-chome,
Bunkyo-ku
Tokyo 113
Tel: (81 3) 3818 0861
Fax: (81 3) 3818 0864
E-mail: orders@svt-ebs.co.jp
URL: www.svt-ebs.co.jp

Bookwell
Head Office: 2/72,
Nirankari Colony
Delhi - 110009
Tel: (91 11) 725 1283
Sales Office: 24/4800,
Ansari Road, Darya Ganj
New Delhi-110002
Tel: (91 11) 326 8786, 325 7264
Fax: (91 11) 328 1315
E-mail: bkwell@nde.vsnl.net.in

INDONESIA
Pt. Indira Limited
Jalan Borobudur 20
PO Box 181
Jakarta 10320
Tel: (62 21) 390 4290
Fax: (62 21) 390 4289

PF Book
J1. dr. Setia Budhi No. 274
Bandung 40143
Tel: (62 22) 2011 149
Fax: (62 22) 2012 840
E-mail: pfbook@bandung.was-antara.net.id

IRAN
Ketab Sara Co. Publishers
P.O. Box 15745-733
Tehran 15117
Tel: (98 21) 871 6104
Fax: (98 21) 871 2479
E-mail: ketab-sara@neda.net.ir

Kowkab Publishers
P.O. BOX 19575-511
Tehran
Tel: (98 21) 258 3723
Fax: (98 21) 258 3723
E-mail: info@kowkabpublish-ers.com

ISRAEL
Yozmot Literature Ltd.
P.O. Box 56055
3 Yohanan Hasandlar St.
Tel Aviv 61560
Tel: (972 3) 5285 397
Fax: (972 3) 5285 397

ITALY
Licosa Libreria Commissionaria
Sansoni S.P.A.
Via Duca di Calabria 1/1
50125 Firenze
Tel: (39 55) 648 31
Fax: (39 55) 641 257
E-mail: licosa@ftbcc.it
URL: www.ftbcc.it/licosa

JAMAICA
Ian Randle Publishers Ltd
11 Cunningham Avenue
Kingston 6
Tel: (876) 978-0739, 978-0745
Fax: (876) 978-1156
E-mail: irpl@colis.com

KENYA
Legacy Books
Loita House
P.O. Box 68077
Nairobi
Tel: (254 2) 330 853
Fax: (254 2) 330 854
E-mail: legacy@form-net.com

Africa Book Service (E.A.) Ltd.
Quaran House, Mfangano Street
P.O. Box 45245
Nairobi
Tel: (254 2) 223 641
Fax: (254 2) 330 272

KOREA, REPUBLIC OF
Eulyoo Publishing Co., Ltd.
46-1, Susong-Dong
Jongro-Gu
Seoul
Tel: (82 2) 734 3515
Fax: (82 2) 732 9154
E-mail: eulyoo@chollian.net
Dayang Intelligence Co.
954-22, Banghae-Dong,
Socho-ku
Seoul
Tel: (82 2) 582 3588
Fax: (82 2) 521 8827
E-mail: dybook@kornet.net
Web site: www.dayang.co.kr

LEBANON
Librairie du Liban
P.O. Box 11-9232
Beirut
Tel: (961 9) 217 944
Fax: (961 9) 217 434
E-mail: hsageh@cyberia.net.lb
URL: www.librairie-du-liban.com.lb

MALAYSIA
University of Malaya
Cooperative Bookshop, Limited
P.O. Box 1127, Jalan Pantai
Baru
59700 Kuala Lumpur
Tel: (60 3) 756 5000
Fax: (60 3) 755 4424
E-mail: umkoop@tm.net.my

MEXICO
INFOTEC
Av. San Fernando No. 37
Col. Toriello Guerra
14050 Mexico D.F.
Tel: (52 5) 624 2800
Fax: (52 5) 624 2822
E-mail: infotec@rtn.net.mx
URL: www.rtn.net.mx

Mundi-Prensa Mexico,
S.A. de C.V.
c/Rio Panuco, 141 - Colonia
Cuauhtemoc
06500 Mexico DF
Tel: (52 5) 533 56 58
Fax: (52 5) 514 67 99
E-mail: 1015245.2361@com-puserve.com

MOROCCO
Librarie Internationale
70, Rue T'ssoule
P.O. Box 302
Rabat (Souissi) MA 10001
Tel: (212 7) 75 01 83
Fax: (212 7) 75 86 61

NEPAL
Everest Media International
Services (P.) Ltd.
GPO Box 5443
Kathmandu
Tel: (977 1) 416 026
Fax: (977 1) 250 176
E-mail: emispltd@wlink.com.np

NETHERLANDS
De Lindeboom/Internationale
Publikaties b.v.
M.A. de Ruyterstraat 20A
7482 BZ Haaksbergen
Tel: (31 53) 574 0004
Fax: (31 53) 572 9296
E-mail:
books@delindeboom.com
URL: www.delindeboom.com

NEW ZEALAND
Oasis Official
P.O. Box 3627
Wellington
Tel: (64 4) 4991551
Fax: (64 4) 499 1972
E-mail: oasis@clear.net.nz
URL: www.oasisbooks.co.nz

NIGERIA
University Press Plc
Three Crowns Building Jericho
Private Mail Bag 5095
Ibadan
Tel: (234 22) 411356
Fax: (234 22) 412056
E-mail: unipress@skannet.com

PAKISTAN
Mirza Book Agency
65, Shahrah-e-Quaid-e-Azam
Lahore 54000
Tel: (92 42) 7353601
Fax: (92 42) 576 3714
E-mail: merchant@brain.net.pk

Oxford University Press
5 Bangalore Town,
Sharae Faisal
P.O. Box 13033
Karachi 75350
Tel: (92 21) 446307; 449032;
440532
Fax: (92 21) 4547640;449032
E-mail: mallr@oup.net.pk
URL: www.oup.com.pk

Pak Book Corporation
Aziz Chambers 21
Queen's Road
Lahore
Tel: (92 42) 636 3222; 636
0885
Fax: (92 42) 636 2328
E-mail: pbc@brain.net.pk

PERU
Editorial Desarrollo SA
Apartado 3824
Ica 242, OF. 106
Lima 1
Tel: (51 14) 285 380
Fax: (51 14) 286 628

PHILIPPINES
International Booksource
Center, Inc.
1127-A Antipolo St.
Barangay, Venezuela
Makati City
Tel: (63 2) 896 6501
Fax: (63 2) 896 6497

POLAND
International Publishing Service
Ul. Piekna 31/37
00 677 Warsaw
Tel: (48 2) 628 6089
Fax: (48 2) 621 7255
E-mail: books@ips.com.pl
URL: www.ips.com.pl

PORTUGAL
Livraria Portugal
Apartado 2681
Rua Do Carmo 70-74
1200 Lisbon
Tel: (351 1) 347 4992
Fax: (351 1) 347 0264

ROMANIA
Compani De Librarii Bucuresti
s.a.
Str. Lipscani nr. 26, sector 3
Bucharest
Tel: (40 1) 313 9645
Fax: (40 1) 312 4000

RUSSIAN FEDERATION
Izdatelstvo << Ves Mir >>
Moscow 101831
Tel: (7 95) 917 8749
Fax: (7 95) 917 9259
E-mail: vesmirorder@vesmir.ru
URL: www.vesmirbooks.ru

SENEGAL
Librairie Clairafrique
2, Rue El Hadj Mbaye Gueye
Place de l'Independance
B.P. 2005
Dakar
Tel: (221) 822 21 69
Fax: (221) 821 84 09

**SINGAPORE; TAIWAN,
CHINA, MYANMAR;
BRUNEI**
Hemisphere Publishing
Services
240 Macpherson Road #08-01
Pines Industrial Building
Singapore 348574
Tel: (65) 741 5166
Fax: (65) 742 9356
E-mail:
info@hemisphere.com.sg

SLOVAK REPUBLIC
Slovart G.T.G. Ltd.
Krupinská 4
P.O. Box 152
852 99 Bratislava 5
Tel: (42 7) 839 471; 472; 473
Fax: (42 7) 839 485
E-mail: gtg@internet.sk

SLOVENIA
Gospodarski vestnik Publishing
Group
Dunajska cesta 5
1000 Ljubljana
Tel: (386 61) 133 83 47
Fax: (386 61) 133 80 30
E-mail: repansekj@gvestnik.si
URL:
www.gvestnik.si/EUROPA/index
.htm

TAIWAN, CHINA
Tycoon Information, Inc.
Ms. Eileen Chen
5 Floor, No. 500
Chang-Chun Road
Taipei 105, Taiwan
Tel: (866 2) 8712 8886
Fax: (886 2) 8712 4747; 8712
4777
E-mail: eiutpe@ms21.hinet.net

**SOUTH AFRICA,
BOTSWANA**
Oxford University Press
Southern Africa
P.O. Box 12119
N1 City 7463
Cape Town, South Africa
Tel: (27 21) 595 4400
Fax: (27 21) 595 4430
E-mail: oxford@oup.co.za

SPAIN
Mundi-Prensa Libros, s.a.
Castello 37
28001 Madrid
Tel: (34 91) 436 37 00
Fax: (34 91) 575 39 98
E-mail:
libreria@mundiprensa.es
URL: www.mundiprensa.es

Mundi-Prensa Barcelona
Consell de Cent No. 391
08009 Barcelona
Tel: (34 3) 488 3492
Fax: (34 3) 487 7659
E-mail: barcelona@mundipren-
sa.es

**SRI LANKA,
THE MALDIVES**
Lake House Bookshop
P.O. Box 244
100, Sir Chittampalam Gardiner
Mawatha
Colombo 2, Sri Lanka
Tel: (94 1) 32 104
Fax: (94 1) 432 104
E-mail: LHL@sri.lanka.net

SWEDEN
Akademibokhandeln
Mäster Samuelsgatan 32
103 94 Stockholm
Tel: (46 8) 613 6100
Fax: (46 8) 222 543
URL: www.akademibokhan-
deln.se

SWITZERLAND
Librairie Payot S.A.
Service Institutionnel
Côtes-de-Montbenon 30
1002 Lausanne
Tel: (41 21) 341 3229
Fax: (41 21) 341 3235
E-mail: institutionnel@payot-
libraire.ch

ADECO Van Diermen Editions
Techniques
Ch. de Lacuez 41
CH-1807 Blonay
Tel: (41 21) 943 2673
Fax: (41 21) 943 3605

**TANZANIA
TEPUSA**
The Network of Technical
Publications in Africa
P.O. Box 22638
Dar es Salaam
Tel: (255 51) 114 876
Fax: (255 51) 112 434
E-mail: tepusa@intafrica.com

THAILAND
Centrac International Ltd.
ATTN: Central Books
Distribution Co., Ltd.
Sinnrat Bldg. 13th Floor
3388/42-45 Rama 4 Rd.
Klong-Teoy
Bangkok 10110
Tel: (66 2) 367-5030-41 X178
URL: www.mundiprensa.es
Fax: (66 2) 3675049

**TRINIDAD & TOBAGO AND
THE CARIBBEAN**
Systematics Studies Ltd.
St. Augustine Shopping Center
Eastern Main Road
St. Augustine
Tel: (868) 645 8466
Fax: (868) 645 8467
E-mail: tobe@trinidad.net

UGANDA
Gustro Limited
P.O. Box 9997
Madhvani Building
Plot 16/4, Jinja Road
Kampala
Tel: (256 41) 251467
Fax: (256 41) 251468
E-mail: gus@swiftuganda.com

UKRAINE
LIBRA Publishing House
Ms. Sophia Ghemborovskaya
53/80 Saksahanskoho Str.
252033, Kiev 33
Tel: (7 44) 227 62 77
Fax: (7 44) 227 62 77

UNITED KINGDOM
HCN
P.O. Box 3, Omega Park
Alton
Hampshire GU34 2 PG
Tel: (44 1420) 86 848
Fax: 44 1420) 89 889
E-mail: wbank@microinfo.co.uk
URL: www.microinfo.co.uk

The Stationery Office
51 Nine Elms Lane
London SW8 5DR
Tel: (44 20) 7 873 8372
Fax: (44 20) 7 873 8242
E-mail: chris.allen@theso.co.uk
URL: www.the-stationery-
office.co.uk/ai/

VENEZUELA, R.B. de
Tecni-Ciencia Libros, S.A.
Sr. Luis Fernando Ramirez,
Director
Centro Cuidad Comercial
Tamanaco
Nivel C-2
Caracas
Tel: (58 2) 959 5547
Fax: (58 2) 959 5636
E-mail: lfrg001@ibm.net

VIETNAM
FAHASA (The Book Distribution
Co. of Hochiminh City)
246 Le Thanh Ton Street
District 1
Hochiminh City
Tel: (84 8) 829 7638, 822 5446
Fax: (84 8) 822 5795
E-mail: fahasa-sg@hcm.vnn.vn
URL: www.tlnet.com.vn/fahasa

ZAMBIA
University Bookshop, University
of Zambia
Great East Road Campus
P.O. Box 32379
Lusaka
Tel: (260 1) 252576
Fax: (260 1) 253952
E-mail:
hunene@admin.unza.zm

ZIMBABWE
Rolden Trading and Prestige
Books
13 Belgrave House
21 Aberdeen Road
Avondale
Harare
Tel: (263 4) 335 105
Fax: (263 4) 335 105
E-mail:
mccs@africaonline.co.zw

BOOKSELLERS

CHINA
China National Publications
Import
& Export Corporation
16 Gongti East Road
Post Code 100020
Beijing

HUNGARY
Foundation for Market Economy
112 Pf 249
1519 Budapest
Tel: (36 1) 204 2951; 2948
Fax: (36 1) 204 2953
E-mail: ipargazd@hungary.net

JORDAN
Global Development Forum
(GDF)
P.O. Box 941488
Amman 11194
Tel: (962 6) 465 6124
Fax: (962 6) 465 6123
E-mail: gdf@index.com.jo

KOREA, REPUBLIC OF
Sejong Books, Inc.
81-4 Neung-dong
Kwangjin-ku
Seoul 143-180
Tel: (82 2) 498 0300
Fax: (82 2) 3409 0321
E-mail: danielchoi@sejong-
books.com
URL: http:
www.sejongbooks.com

MALAYSIA
MDC Publishers Printers SDN
BHD
MDC Building
2718, Jalan Permata Empat
Taman Permata, Ulu Kelang
53300 Kuala Lumpur
Tel: (60 3) 4108 6600
Fax: (60 3) 4108 1506
E-mail: mdcpp@mdcpp.com.my
URL: www.mdcpp.com.my

NEPAL
Bazaar International
228 Sanchaya Kosh Building
GPO Box 2480, Tridevi Marg
Kathmandu
Tel: (977 1) 255 125
Fax: (977 1) 229 437
E-mail: bazaar@mos.com.np

NIGERIA
Mosuro Booksellers
5 Oluware Obasa Street (Near
Awolowo Ave.)
P.O. Box 30201
Ibadan
Tel: (234 2) 810-2560
Fax: (234 2) 810-2042
E-mail:
Kmosuro@linkserve.com.ng

POLAND
A.B.E. Marketing
Ul. Grzybowska 37A
00-855 Warsaw
Tel: (48 22) 654 06 75
Fax: (48 22) 682 22 33; 682 17
24
E-mail: abe@ikp.atm.com.pl

THAILAND
Chulalongkorn University Book
Center
Phyathai Road
Bangkok 10330
Tel: (66 2) 235 5400
Fax: (66 2) 255 4441

Book Link Co. Ltd.
118/4 Ekamai Soi 28
Vadhana
Bangkok 10110
Tel: (662) 711 4392
Fax: (662) 711 4103
E-mail: bbatpt@au.ac.th

TURKEY
Dünya Infotel A.S.
"Globus" Dünya Basinevi
100, Yil Mahallesi
34440 Bagcilar-Istanbul
Tel: (90 212) 629 08 08
Fax: (90 212) 629 46 89; 629
46 27
E-mail: dunya@dunya-
gazete.com.tr
URL: http: www.dunya.com

URUGUAY
Librería Técnica Uruguaya
Colonia 1543, Piso 7, Of. 702
Casilla de Correo 1518
Montevideo 11000, Uruguay
Tel: (598 2) 490072
Fax: (598 2) 41 34 48
E-mail: ltu@cs.com.uy

VIETNAM
Vietnam Development
Information Center
Ground Floor
63 Ly Thai To Street
Hanoi
Tel: (84 4) 934 6845
E-mail: ctran@worldbank.org
URL: www.vdic.org.vn